MENTAL RETARDATION AND DEVELOPMENTAL DISABILITIES

MENTAL RETARDATION AND DEVELOPMENTAL DISABILITIES

Second Edition

Edited by

Phillip J. McLaughlin and Paul Wehman

pro·ed

8700 Shoal Creek Boulevard
Austin, Texas 78757-6897

pro·ed

© 1996, 1992 by PRO-ED, Inc.
8700 Shoal Creek Boulevard
Austin, Texas 78757-6897

Library of Congress Cataloging-in-Publication Data

Mental retardation and developmental disabilities / Phillip J.
  McLaughlin & Paul Wehman, eds. — 2nd ed.
       p.   cm.
  Includes bibliographical references and index.
  ISBN 0-89079-643-2 (hardcover : alk. paper)
    1. Developmentally disabled—Services for.   2. Developmental
  disabilities.   I. McLaughlin Phillip J.   II. Wehman, Paul.
HV1570.M45   1996
362.1'968—dc20   95-38189
                                                            CIP

This book is designed in Caslon.

Production Manager: Alan Grimes
Production Coordinator: Karen Swain
Managing Editor: Tracy Sergo
Art Director: Thomas Barkley
Reprints Buyer: Alicia Woods
Editor: Cynthia Woerner Halm
Editorial Assistant: Claudette Landry
Editorial Assistant: Martin Wilson

Printed in the United States of America

2   3   4   5   6   7   8   9   10   00   99   98   97

Contents

Preface

It is a pleasure to present a significantly expanded and updated second edition of this book on developmental disabilities. We have endeavored to expand the information into the area of mental retardation as well as across an array of different developmental disabilities. The book has also been rearranged in order to reflect much more of a life-span-perspective approach. It includes three major sections. First, in Section 1, Life-Span Perspective, the chapters that are presented relate to key aspects of service delivery, early intervention, school issues, transition from secondary school to adulthood, and working with older Americans with disabilities. Each of these chapters is important because they set the foundation for the book, but, more important, they move us away from a singular focus on individual disability categories and more into the generic community service delivery issues that are important to all people.

Section 2, Developmental Disabilities, includes chapters on mild mental retardation, severe mental retardation, cerebral palsy, seizure disorders, behavior disorders, autism, self-injurious behavior, multiple sensory impairment, and learning disabilities and attention-deficit/hyperactivity disorders. In this section we have added information on attention-deficit/hyperactivity disorder and seizure disorders. Furthermore, we have recognized the changes that are now in place with the current American Association of Mental Retardation definition of mental retardation (1992).

In the third section, Service and Program Issues, information is presented on service and program issues that are critical to people with mental retardation and developmental disabilities. These chapters include information on case management, community-based vocational training, supported employment, supported living, and social security. We have found from our review of the mental retardation and developmental disability literature that very few books cover this information to the depth that is necessary to help those who are working in schools and other community service programs.

The purpose of this book is straightforward: to provide a basic, introductory reference text for students and professionals beginning their careers in or expanding their careers to include developmental disabilities. As we noted previously, many publications are devoted to specialized topics, which usually do not provide the "big picture" of services. In this book we not only present best practices but also try to show a comprehensive view of different disabilities and the range of services necessary to work with people who have such disabilities. The new and updated material will appeal to a wide range of people working in many disciplines within the field of developmental disabilities.

To achieve this goal, we have assembled a number of experts in developmental disabilities. Some of the authors are academicians, and some are practitioners who work daily with people with developmental disabilities. Each chapter utilizes a case study approach. A brief overview of each chapter follows.

In the first chapter, Pamela Wolfe, John Kregel, and Paul Wehman have developed an excellent chapter that outlines the challenges for service providers in the community. They provide an extensive discussion of community services and ways to access these services, with a more consumer-oriented focus to service delivery than was presented in the first edition.

The chapter by Rebecca Anderson Weissman and David Littman on early intervention offers practical tools for working with young children and their families. Information is organized around a service delivery cycle. The components of this cycle include assessment, program design, delivery, and evaluation, with the evaluation serving as the start point for the subsequent trip through the cycle. Individualized family service plan components are addressed. Assessment and intervention checklists are included.

In the chapter on special education, Kathryn Blake, Paul Sale, and Lisa Ehrhart consider how best to deliver instruction to youngsters with developmental disabilities. First, they discuss special education and related services as they are defined in the Education for All Handicapped Children Act of 1975. Then, they describe components of instructional programs and how they are used with the targeted youngsters. Finally, information is presented about how work is organized within special education law. Throughout, the authors emphasize the importance of coordination among services as well as the need to apply the principle of normalization as frequently as possible when working with children with developmental disabilities.

Chapter 4 is a new chapter on transition from school to adulthood by Katherine Inge, Paul Wehman, Tom Clees, and Stacy Dymond. They have developed a basic framework for understanding the transition process with the emphasis on individualized planning for each student.

Also, Michael Malone and Nancy Kropf, in Chapter 5, Growing Older, discuss the fact that individuals with lifelong disabilities are living longer than ever before. As a result, the individuals, their families, and service providers are facing a host of situations that challenge each of them to respond in an enlightened manner. The mission of service providers is to help the elderly individual with developmental disabilities create a meaningful set of life resources that enables him or her to enjoy a high quality of life.

In the sixth chapter, Mild Mental Retardation, John Langone provides an overview of the major cognitive, learning, and affective characteristics exhibited by individuals with developmental disabilities as well as an updated look at the current definition of mental retardation. Topics such as self-care, language development, learning and cognition, mobility, and self-direction are developed along practical lines that provide readers with suggestions for implementing program options in these areas. In addition, sections on transition from school to work and on independent living skills include preferred strategies for developing activities to assist learners with mild to moderate cognitive deficits in becoming productive members of society.

In Chapter 7, Severe Mental Retardation, William Sharpton and Michael West illustrate competencies developed by individuals with severe retardation and their abilities to learn and perform complex tasks in a variety of integrated settings. The key to success in this area has been the manner in which service providers train and support persons with disabilities and the commitment of service providers to achieving meaningful outcomes and community integration and participation. A framework for services for this population is presented, involving training, adaptation, and support of tasks and activities.

Katherine Inge's chapter, Cerebral Palsy, provides a solid foundation on cerebral palsy and implications for diagnosis and treatment. The problems in identifying good community services are also discussed.

In another new chapter, Elizabeth Perry-Varner discusses seizure disorders. This important topic was unfortunately omitted in the first edition. As a consumer with a seizure disorder, Perry-Varner is uniquely suited to write on this topic.

In Chapter 10, Behavioral Disabilities, Elaine Clark describes areas of dysfunction that are typically seen in individuals with emotional and behavior disturbances. Although some areas of daily living remain relatively intact, others are devastated. As Clark points out, learning deficits that are related to emotional problems contribute heavily to the general dysfunction, especially the capacity for independent living and economic self-sufficiency. Clark analyzes frequently used interventions and provides suggestions for best practices for intervention. Important resources for parents, teachers, and professionals are recommended.

In Ronald Eaves's chapter on autism, the reader is provided with four important components of dealing with individuals with autism. First, a brief history is presented to explain the many competing terms that have been applied to the person with autism. Second, the problem of differential diagnosis is addressed. A functional description of autistic characteristics is presented in the third component. Finally, the majority of the chapter details treatments for the more common behaviors displayed by individuals with autism, that is, self-injurious behavior, aggression, and aberrant speech and language development.

In Chapter 12, the treatment of self-injury is discussed in depth by David Pitonyak. This is a specialized area but one in which tremendous abuses have taken place over the years against persons with developmental disabilities. Pitonyak discusses nonaversive interventions and in this updated edition provides new information on a series of guidelines for intervention.

JoAnn Marchant's chapter on deaf-blind disabling conditions details strategies for teaching students with dual sensory disabilities. It also presents an historic perspective of how services have been provided for these students. Case studies are cited and concrete suggestions are offered for classroom teachers, parents, and caregivers.

William Bender follows with an excellent chapter on learning disabilities. He emphasizes how service delivery for this population—ranging from assessment to instruction—has changed radically within the last two decades. Despite this constant change, similarities among children with learning disabilities can be identified, including academic problems that are not attributable to identifiable disabling conditions; difficulties in social–emotional–behavioral functioning; difficulties in expressive language, particularly pragmatic use of language; and poor attention and memory skills. Despite these difficulties, the prognosis for most children and adolescents with learning disabilities is positive. Bender has expanded his chapter in this edition to also include individuals with attention-deficit/hyperactivity disorders.

In Chapter 15 on case management, Susan Neal and Beth Gilson discuss case management. Everything about these services continues to be questioned, reviewed, and revised, as its impor-

tance is documented in legislation, research, literature, and programming. This chapter, based on a set of values as a framework for responsive case management, addresses what case management has been, is now, and can be. Topics in case management that are addressed include components of service coordination, role of the supervisor, in-service and preservice training needs, and quality assurance. Examples of interventions with consumers and their families provide the reader with a practical approach to enhancing case management services.

In Chapter 16, Katherine Inge, Stacy Dymond, and Paul Wehman present a discussion of how community-based instruction can impact program effectiveness. Within the past decade especially, this has become a recognized form of excellent instructional practice.

Supported employment is the topic of the chapter by Paul Wehman and Wendy Parent. The impact of supported employment is discussed, and several case studies portray supported employment implementation. Major new information is presented in the important area of natural supports with many new ideas given.

Tom Clees, in the chapter on supported living and collaborative transition, discusses the degree to which people with disabilities obtain and maintain independence from restrictive settings, including institutions, nursing homes, group homes, workshops, and other segregated settings. The current continuum-of-services model restricts individuals with disabilities by allocating the vast majority of fiscal, direct, and related service supports to segregated living arrangements and places of employment. Clees describes alternatives to current service models, most notably supported living models, and provides procedures for identifying and teaching relevant independent living skills. In addition, the importance of collaboration and advocacy within and between schools, agencies, and postschool support programs is discussed. Finally, a collaborative model for assisting individuals with disabilities to make transitions to and maintain independent living status within integrated community settings is offered.

Susan O'Mara and John Kregel tackle one of the toughest areas in the field today: Social Security. The complicated regulations and their far-ranging implications are discussed.

This book is comprehensive in scope. Although it is impossible to cover all topics in the area of developmental disabilities, we believe that this book will be an excellent core reference for providers in most of the helping disciplines. Extensive use of case studies brings the information to life. We believe this is a greatly improved and more comprehensive book on the program issues associated with mental retardation and developmental disabilities.

Life-Span Perspective

Service Delivery

Pamela Wolfe, John Kregel, and Paul Wehman

LEARNING GOALS

Upon completion of this chapter the reader will be able to

■ describe the differences between consumer empowerment and normalization philosophies;

■ describe briefly the educational and community integration needs of people with developmental disabilities;

■ list and discuss five major challenges for service providers in working with families;

■ discuss what outcome-based transition planning is for youth with developmental disabilities; and

■ list and discuss three major competency areas for training of professionals.

For the past 20 years, the concept of normalization has been the philosophical and ideological cornerstone of human service programs for persons with developmental and other severe disabilities. Beginning with Nirje's (1969) conceptualization of the normalization principle as making available to individuals with disabilities "patterns and conditions of everyday life which are as close as possible to the norms and patterns of the mainstream of society" (p. 181), normalization represented a sharp philosophical shift away from segregated services for people with disabilities. Wolfensberger (1972) expanded the concept to include not only the outcomes or goals of human service programs but also the means (strategies, techniques, technologies, etc.) used to achieve these goals. Wolfensberger (1972) further refined the term to remove the notion that individuals with disabilities should somehow be "shaped" through appearance and experiences to fit the statistical norm of their community.

Rather, normalization focuses on enabling individuals to lead lives that are *valued* by other members of their community. Hence, some professionals are now using the term *social valorization* in place of *normalization*.

During the 1970s and 1980s, normalization quickly became accepted as the guiding philosophy of the majority of human service programs. The administrators of sheltered workshops, community residential programs, and even large state institutions adopted mission statements for their agencies that featured strong commitments to normalization as the primary purpose for their services. Major components of the concept were imbedded into numerous federal laws.

Normalization has had a tremendous positive impact on the lives of millions of individuals. It did much to eliminate the deprivation from purposeful activities, overcrowding, lack of individualization, and isolation from other people and ordinary places, all of which plagued earlier human service programs. Normalization should be viewed as directly responsible for, or significantly contributing to, the increase in community residential alternatives, the development of community-based employment programs, the rise in the self-advocacy movement (e.g., Longhurst, 1994), and the trend toward inclusive, integrated educational opportunities.

The 1990s, however, will see the end of normalization as the philosophical basis underlying human services. In its place, *consumer empowerment* is becoming the driving force behind the development, implementation, and evaluation of human service programs. This trend is not meant to imply that the importance placed on the concept of normalization was misplaced or to detract from the immense positive effect the adoption of the normalization philosophy had on the lives of individuals with disabilities. However, at least three key factors have combined to lead to the emergence of consumer empowerment as the focal point of human service programs in the 1990s.

1. Recent changes in public policies affecting individuals with disabilities are based on the assumption that discrimination is the greatest obstacle confronting persons with disabilities as they attempt to live independent and productive lives.

Many have expressed the view that the accepting, supporting community described in the normalization literature as providing a mutually supportive network of relationships exists in far too few areas of the United States. On the contrary, many individuals with disabilities are quick to cite instances of discrimination in employment, housing, transportation, and health care. Furthermore, the nature and structure of our human service programs often contribute to the maintenance of commonly held prejudices. Continuing efforts to physically isolate individuals with disabilities from other members of the community prevent the development of mutually supportive relationships. Similarly, an over-reliance on "technologies" that can be properly provided only by specially trained professionals

has made individuals with disabilities seem unapproachable by many community members. The intent of a major new civil rights law, the Americans with Disabilities Act of 1990 (ADA; Wehman, 1992) is to eliminate all forms of discrimination toward individuals with disabilities in all public and private entities. Given the current size and unresponsiveness of most human service systems, increased self-advocacy on the part of consumers will be required if the law is to have its intended effect.

2. The universal acceptance of the normalization concept has led to misunderstandings, misapplication, and outright corruption of the principle.

When nearly all human service programs, even those of poor quality and design, subscribe to the philosophical principle of normalization, the usefulness of the concept as a guiding principle is substantially diminished. A few examples of the types of questionable or outrageous practices implemented under the pretext of normalization are listed here:

• People have been told when to get up and when to go to sleep in the name of normalization. Other people have been told what to eat and what to wear; still others have been told what type of job they would like to have and what types of recreational pursuits they should enjoy, all in the name of normalization.

• When an individual becomes separated from his or her job as a result of being denied the basic supports he or she needed to maintain employment, this separation is rationalized as being tolerable—it's normal to lose a job.

• People have been denied the opportunity to watch television in the name of normalization; others have been forced to watch certain television programs in the name of normalization.

• Children have been transported in a yellow school bus from their institutional wards across the institution's grounds to a freestanding school building a quarter of a mile away because it is normal for children to ride the school bus.

- The death of an individual due to a lack of supervision and concern was rationalized as the "dignity of risk."
- A woman was denied her request for a different and shorter haircut because it is normal for women to have longer hair.
- Hundreds of thousands of individuals have been "dumped" into nursing facilities across the nation in the belief that a nursing facility is a more normal place than an institution for an adult with disabilities to live.

These offensive misinterpretations of the normalization principle combine to reduce the strength and clarity of its concept. Recent policies and regulations have concentrated less on concepts such as normal or culturally valued and instead have focused significant attention on issues such as consumer-directed, consumer-responsive, and individual autonomy.

3. Individuals with disabilities, their families, and their friends have come to understand that the activity of the past two decades has created a far-reaching, paternalistic human services bureaucracy.
Wolfensberger (1991), looking back over the past two decades, described the creation of a human service industry that is so large that it can fulfill its mission only if a large number of individuals are considered dependent and "in need of" human services. The bureaucracy changes the basic needs of individuals with disabilities (e.g., housing, employment, friendship) into programs, interventions, and therapies that can be properly supplied only by members of the bureaucracy. In other words, normalization, for all the positive effects and program improvements it has generated, too frequently is reduced to one individual, usually a professional or service provider (usually a person without a disability) who decides what is normal or valuable for another individual (the person with a disability). Recently, consumers have attempted to establish control over the design and delivery of the supports and services necessary for them to achieve their specific goals.

DEFINING CONSUMER EMPOWERMENT

Many terms have been used to describe the concept of consumer empowerment. *Self-determination, self-direction, consumer decision making, choice, autonomy,* and *self-advocacy* have all been used to describe individuals' exerting of power over their own lives. These terms all have much in common. They all emphasize the individuals' making choices that direct their daily lives, exerting control over the decisions that affect their lifestyle, and asserting their rights and pursuing opportunities. In the following section, we describe self-determination, control, and self-advocacy, all of which are key components of consumer empowerment, to illustrate the many ways this concept can be applied to supported employment.

Self-Determination

Self-determination refers to an individual's ability to express preferences and desires, to make decisions, and to initiate actions based on those decisions (Mithaug, 1992). In essence, self-determination simply refers to *choice*. It emphasizes the person's setting goals for oneself and then actively engaging in activities designed to achieve these goals.

The emphasis on self-determination for persons with disabilities can be traced to the independent-living and self-advocacy movements that emerged in the 1960s (Ward, 1993). Persons with various disabling conditions began to organize in order to assert their own rights of citizenship; express their needs and concerns regarding services designed to assist them; advocate for social and political change; and demand access to the neighborhoods, jobs, schools, and other community-based amenities and activities enjoyed by persons without disabilities. As the self-advocacy movement gained adherents and political legitimacy, disability legislation followed suit, culminating with the passage of the Americans with Disabilities Act of 1990

(P.L. 101-336), a broad-based civil rights bill for citizens with disabilities, and the Rehabilitation Act Amendments (1992). Yet, as Ward (1993) noted, self-determination for persons with disabilities goes far beyond advocating and legislating for personal freedoms and choices. It also requires that persons with disabilities be empowered by educational systems, adult service providers, and society at large to realize those freedoms and to make choices meaningful.

How do people learn to become self-determined? Most learn to develop and pursue goals as children and adolescents, as they are given greater responsibilities and freedom of choice by their parents and teachers. Yet, as we discuss later, research on children and youth with disabilities indicates that they have fewer opportunities to make choices, express preferences, develop personal goals, and gain independence than do their peers (Guess & Siegel-Causey, 1985; Kishi, Teelucksingh, Zollers, Park-Lee, & Meyer, 1988; Martin, Marshall, & Maxson, 1993). Parents and teachers often neglect to give children with disabilities the opportunity to participate in decision making, to take risks, to suffer consequences, to learn from both positive and negative experiences, in short, to develop a sense of self-direction (White et al., 1982). The terms *learned helplessness* and *programmed dependence* have often been used to describe an all-too-frequent result: Children with disabilities fail to learn to control events within their immediate environments and instead are passively and willingly dominated by other persons or circumstances within those environments. Mithaug (1992) has perhaps written the most eloquently on this topic, particularly in describing the key role of (a) competence, (b) intelligence, and (c) persistence in helping to shape self-determination. Many individuals with disabilities, however, develop a self-image of powerlessness, alienation, and futility that can follow them into postsecondary education and training or adult activities and that, undoubtedly, is a contributing factor for high dropout rates in high school and college, high levels of unemployment and underemployment, and economic dependence (Allard,

Dodd, & Peralez, 1987; Babbit & Burbach, 1990; Edgerton & Bercovica, 1976; Goldberg, 1989; Mithaug, Martin, Agran, & Rusch, 1988).

Control

The concept of control expands and extends the principles of self-determination. Control focuses on the extent to which individuals are independent and self-sufficient. Recently, federal legislators have for the first time begun to recognize the importance of consumers' control over their lives. The Developmental Disabilities Assistance and Bill of Rights Act of 1990 (P.L. 100-146) defines independence as "the extent to which persons with developmental disabilities exert *choice and control* [italics added] over their own lives." Control, as the concept is used here, refers to an individual's ability to access the resources necessary to freely act on his or her choices and decisions. Whereas self-determination emphasizes goal setting and actions designed to achieve these goals, control focuses on the extent to which these decisions are made free from excessive external control. In supported employment services, control issues focus on the individual's ability to direct his or her own career. Supported employment service providers who practice the concepts presented here would focus on the following areas.

Individuality and personal responsibility are highly valued in American society. However, citizens with disabilities historically have had limited opportunities to learn and use decision-making skills, to develop individuality and autonomy, and to assume responsibility for their own lives (Lovett, 1991; Williams, 1991). This failure to promote individuality and autonomy begins early in the person's life and can continue throughout the lifespan. Students with disabilities are often excluded from educational planning or have their choices and preferences in educational programming ignored (Guess & Siegel-Causey, 1985; Houghton, Bronicki, & Guess, 1987; Knowlton, Turnbull, Backus, & Turnbull, 1988). Moreover, students with disabilities tend to perceive themselves as having little control in educational situations and to have a low sense of self-efficacy, much less so than do nondisabled students (Gresham, Evans, & Elliot, 1988; Taylor, Adelman, Nelson, Smith, & Phares, 1989). Lack of choice and lack of control have also been identified as problems within the adult service system, such as vocational and residential programs (Dattilo & Rusch, 1985; Guess, Benson, & Siegel-Causey, 1985; Ward, 1993; West & Parent, 1992).

In recent years, choice making and self-directed behavior have been recognized as an expression of dignity and autonomy for persons with disabilities and have become a focus of educational and habilitative programs (Guess et al., 1985; Shevin & Klein, 1984). A growing number of parents, professionals, and individuals with disabilities themselves are convinced that students and adults with even very severe and multiple disabilities can and should be taught to express preferences, make choices, and exert greater control over the major and minor decisions that affect their lives and have demonstrated methods for enabling these behaviors (Reid & Parsons, 1990, 1991; Wacker, Wiggins, Fowler, & Berg, 1988; Williams, 1991). This conviction has been translated into educational theories and practices for those students. For example, Shevin and Klein (1984) described procedures for developing a choice-making curriculum and incorporating choice throughout the student's school day.

Self-Advocacy

Self-advocacy refers to an individual's ability to assert and protect his or her rights (Longhurst, 1994). It may occur when an individual acts alone to promote his or her self-interest or when the individual is participating in a group. Self-advocacy has at least two dimensions. The first applies to basic legal rights and benefits available under federal and state laws and regulations. For example, when applying for employment, has the individual been treated in accordance with the provisions of the ADA and all other pertinent legislation?

The second dimension focuses on participation. This dimension goes beyond simple legal rights and focuses on the individual's ability to cause change within programs and systems.

IMPLICATIONS FOR HUMAN SERVICE PROGRAMS

A human service program designed according to the principle of consumer empowerment would be very different from most programs existing today. For example, with this approach unemployment among individuals with disabilities is viewed as the direct result of the employment discrimination they experience while pursuing their careers. Unemployment is also viewed as being caused by an absence of necessary supports (assistive technology, personal assistant services, job coaching) in local communities. The mission of such an agency might be stated as follows:

> The mission of this agency is to provide the support and services necessary to enable individuals to meet their self-chosen career goals. The agency works with individuals to assist them in making choices and career decisions. The agency is committed to assisting the individual in whatever way is necessary and for as long as is necessary.

The characteristics of human service programs based on the consumer empowerment principle are compared to those of more traditional human services approaches in Figure 1.1. Rather than focusing on diagnostic labels, functional deficits, perceived lack of motivation on the part of the individual, or a suspected lack of enthusiasm on the part of the individual's family, a consumer empowerment approach is far more likely to focus on uninformed employers or unresponsive components of the service system as sources of employment problems.

Consider the following four descriptions of people with developmental disabilities. Ask

Issues	Traditional Human Services Approach	Consumer Empowerment Approach
What is the problem?	Individual's lack of job skills or lack of motivation	Discrimination Lack of supports
Where is the problem?	In the individual or in his or her family	In the environment (employers, service system, etc.)
What is the solution?	Evaluate, prescribe, prepare for special services	Obtain supports only as needed to facilitate career movement
Who is in charge?	Professionals in the service system	Individual with help from support providers

Figure 1.1.   Comparison of a traditional approach and a consumer empowerment approach.

yourself how empowerment and self-determination could help them in their desire for work:

- Jim has been diagnosed as having autism from birth, with an IQ between 32 and 45, depending on the test. When frustrated, he becomes very agitated and rocks rapidly, sometimes shrieking loudly. Modulating his voice has been a problem, and he cannot stay on task very long. The special education director and teacher are very negative, but his parents are hopeful. Does Jim have an employment outlook?

- Doug, aged 19, has severe cerebral palsy. He wears a head pointer and can use a computer keyboard. He has been in the cerebral palsy center all of his life. Doug cannot move his arms or legs independently and has significant spasticity in the upper trunk. He is in an electric wheelchair, which he can partially operate. Does Doug have an employment outlook?

- Larry, aged 30, has a measured IQ of 27, periodically head rocks in a self-stimulative manner, and is totally nonverbal. He can walk and has most self-care skills but acts socially immature at times. He cannot read, write, count, or use public transportation. Local vocational rehabilitation services and the sheltered workshops cannot service

him. Does Larry have an employment outlook?

- Marie is 19 years old and is considered autistic. Videotaped observations during classroom activity indicate 65 body rocks per minute, periodic hand biting, and shrieking. Marie throws things when she becomes upset, and her parents are concerned about how long they can keep her at home. Her IQ is 24, and she is marginally verbal. Does Marie have an employment outlook?

A human service program focused on consumer empowerment would also differ from traditional programs in the types of services provided to participants. As Figure 1.1 shows, traditional and nontraditional approaches to human services differ significantly. In traditional programs, individuals requesting services are first diagnosed and evaluated. Then, a package of special services is prescribed from the array of available services. Individuals who need extra assistance or require services not currently available face a difficult choice—either to accept services not designed to meet their needs or not to receive any assistance whatsoever.

As becomes evident in the next section, a philosophy that embraces consumer empowerment has significant ramifications for the way services are delivered to people with disabilities.

CONSUMER EMPOWERMENT AND PROGRAM DESIGN

Individuals with even the most severe disabilities are now believed to be able to live, work, and recreate successfully in integrated community settings, as evidenced in employment (Black & Meyer, 1992; Levy, Jessop, Rimmerman, & Levy, 1992; Mank, 1994; Moon, Inge, Wehman, Brooke, & Barcus, 1990; Wehman & Kregel, 1990, 1995; Yan, Mank, Sandow, Rhodes, & Olson, 1993), in residential settings (Amado, Lakin, & Menke, 1990; Hayden & Abery, 1994; Larson & Lakin, 1989), and in recreational activities (Hamre-Nietupski et al., 1992; Kiernan & Moon, 1993; Moon, 1994; Schleien & Meyer, 1995). The concept of the least restrictive placement and environment is being replaced increasingly by a support service model in which consumers have greater control over their choice of supports and services. The support service model contrasts with a readiness model in which individuals with developmental disabilities "wait" to participate until needed prerequisite skills are in place. The support service model suggests that all individuals, regardless of the severity of their disability, be placed with necessary supports instituted to allow full participation (Gardner 1990; Schalock et al., 1994). Professionals are challenged to provide the training and support necessary to sustain success in the environment.

Consider, for example, the dramatic shift in the way the American Association on Mental Retardation (AAMR, 1992) now defines mental retardation: "Mental retardation refers to substantial limitations in present functioning. It is characterized by significantly subaverage intellectual functioning, existing concurrently with related limitations in two or more of the following applicable adaptive skill areas: communication,

self-care, home living, social skills, community use, self-direction, health and safety, functional academics, leisure and work. Mental retardation manifests before age 18" (p. 5).

The AAMR 1992 definition changes the classification system of the 1983 definition (mild, moderate, severe, and profound) and supports the expectation of individual potential and growth (Schalock et al., 1994). It supports the reality that not all persons with mental retardation will have the same limitations. The new system changes the old terminology to more supportive and encouraging descriptions. The diagnosis might reflect a person with mental retardation who needs limited support in social skills or in self-direction. One's potential for growth and self-fulfillment is nurtured by the provision of services and support provided.

In the AAMR (1992) definition manual, the following assumptions are considered essential:

- Valid assessment considers cultural and linguistic diversity as well as differences in communication and behavioral factors.

- The existence of limitations in adaptive skills occurs within the context of community environments typical of the individual's age peers and is indexed to the person's individualized need for supports.

- Specific adaptive limitations often coexist with strengths in other adaptive skills or other personal capabilities.

- With appropriate supports over a sustained period, the life functioning of a person with mental retardation will generally improve. (p. 5)

(In Chapter 6, Langone provides additional information on this definition and how it applies to services.)

Ideologic changes, such as those reflected in the AAMR definition, occurring in the field of special education and rehabilitative services have been mirrored by legislative mandates. Change is evident in research and demonstration, in formalized definitions, and in created venues for funding. Table 1.1 provides an overview of major legislation affecting service provision for individuals with developmental disabilities. Legislative changes have occurred in virtually every area of service provision ranging from education to residential and vocational services. Further, major legislation passed in recent years by Congress such as the Americans with Disabilities Act of 1990 has provided basic and far-reaching legislative protection and advocacy for increased civil rights for individuals with disabilities (Wehman, 1993).

WHO ARE PERSONS WITH DEVELOPMENTAL DISABILITIES?

Those professionals working with individuals with developmental disabilities know well that definitions and labels rarely provide a comprehensive picture of the needs and strengths of the individuals with whom they work. Those working in the fields of education and the helping professions have long struggled with issues of labeling, the stigma that may accompany labels, and the inevitable ability of such labels to generate necessary funds. The Developmental Disabilities Assistance and Bill of Rights Act of 1990 addresses functional rather than categorical issues in the definition of developmental disabilities. The major components of the definition of developmental disabilities are listed in Table 1.2. An individual categorized as developmentally disabled can be both mentally and physically impaired, with disabilities originating before the age of 22. Typical categories include epilepsy, cerebral palsy, mental retardation, and autism. According to the definition included in the Developmental Disabilities Act, individuals who are developmentally disabled show deficits in three of seven life activities: self-care, language, learning, mobility, self-direction, capacity for independent living, and economic self-sufficiency. The act defines disability in terms of what an individual is and is not able to do rather than in

terms of a clinical diagnosis (Summers, 1986; Tarjan, 1989). The move away from an emphasis on cause and effect to an emphasis on adaptive life activities highlights areas where human service professionals may be asked to provide assistance. Consider the contrast in utility of the following two descriptions in pinpointing service provision needs:

- Lisa is an 8-year-old girl who is mentally handicapped because of trisomy 21 and has a recorded IQ of 45 on the Wechsler intelligence scales.

- Lisa is an 8-year-old girl who is developmentally disabled and who experiences significant difficulties in self-care, learning, and capacity for independent living.

Although service providers must always individualize, the second definition brings professionals much closer to knowing how they can assist Lisa.

A further examination of the definition of developmental disabilities reveals that an individual must show deficits in three life areas and must manifest the disability before age 22. An individual who has suffered a severe head injury at age 19 would probably be considered developmentally disabled because the sustained injury would probably limit life activities such as language, learning, capacity for independent living, and economic self-sufficiency. Conversely, an individual who was born with a congenital hearing loss might not be considered developmentally disabled if he or she experienced only a deficit in language (Summers, 1986).

In some instances, an individual with a learning disability may be considered developmentally disabled if the individual is viewed as having a significant functional deficit in three or more areas such as language, self-direction, and economic self-sufficiency. However, many individuals with learning disabilities are able to function successfully within their homes, schools, and communities and would not be viewed as having a developmental disability. Similarly, many individuals with behavior disorders would meet the criteria of the federal definition because they may

Table 1.1. Major Legislation Affecting Individuals with Developmental Disabilities

Date	Legislation	Provision
1970	The Developmental Disabilities Services and Facilities Construction Act (P.L. 91-517)	First introduced the concept of "developmental disabilities"
1971	Title XIX of the Social Security Act (P.L. 92-223)	Required ICFs/MR to provide "active treatment"
1975	Education for All Handicapped Children Act (P.L. 94-142)	Guaranteed a free and appropriate education to all children
1978	Rehabilitation, Comprehensive Services, and Developmental Disabilities Amendment (P.L. 95-602)	Revised the definition of developmental disabilities to emphasize "functionality"
1984	Developmental Disabilities Act Amendment (P.L. 98-527)	Included employment-related activities as a priority
1990	Developmental Disabilities Assistance and Bill of Rights Act	Reauthorized the DD Act for 3 years and emphasized the empowerment of individuals with disabilities
		Placed particular emphasis on protection and advocacy
1990	Education of the Handicapped Act Amendments (P.L. 101-476)	Reauthorized parts of the EHA
		Changed the name of the law to Individuals with Disabilities Education Act (IDEA) to reflect people before disability
		Expanded the definition of disability to include children with autism and traumatic brain injury
		Increased emphasis on transition planning
		Provided support for projects for students with serious emotional disturbances
1990	Americans with Disabilities Act (ADA)	Offered important civil rights for individuals with disabilities
		Extended rights to access in employment settings, public transportation, and public establishments
1992	Rehabilitation Act Amendments (P.L. 102-569)	Supported the service systems through which employers can find assistance and expertise in identifying and completing the reasonable and appropriate job accommodations called for in the ADA
		Established a basis in the adult service system for accomplishing the transition preparation, planning, and implementation activities in the IDEA
		Put the abilities and choices of people with a disability first and challenged the services system and the greater community to support their efforts to work, live, and participate in the community

Table 1.2. Federal Definition of Developmental Disabilities

The term "developmental disability" means a severe, chronic disability of a person 5 years of age or older which

— is attributable to a mental or physical impairment or combination of mental and physical impairments;

— is manifested before the person attains age twenty-two;

— is likely to continue indefinitely;

— results in substantial functional limitations in three or more of the following areas of major life activity:
  • self-care
  • receptive and expressive language
  • learning
  • mobility
  • self-direction
  • capacity for independent living
  • economic self-sufficiency

— reflects the person's need for a combination and sequence of special interdisciplinary, or generic care, treatment, or other services which are of lifelong or extended duration and are individually planned and coordinated except that such term, when applied to infants and young children means individuals from birth to age 5, inclusive, who have substantial developmental delay or specific congenital or acquired conditions with a high probability of resulting in a developmental disability if services are not provided.

Note. From the Developmental Disabilities Assistance and Bill of Rights Act of 1990, Title 42, U.S.C. 6000-6083. *U.S. Statutes at Large, 104*, 1191–1204.

possess deficits in several areas and require consistent and coordinated services to be successful in their communities. However, individuals with adult onset of mental illness or persons who do not have significant deficits in several areas would not be considered developmentally disabled.

Although the definition itself may not provide an easy answer as to who is developmentally disabled, it does place an important emphasis on functionality and draws attention to the need for diverse and extended services.

MEETING THE NEEDS OF PEOPLE WITH DEVELOPMENTAL DISABILITIES

As they are depicted by the Developmental Disabilities Assistance and Bill of Rights Act of 1990, the needs of individuals with disabilities may be unique, varied, and extensive. Over the course of a lifetime, an individual may have educational, independent-living, economic self-sufficiency, and psychosocial needs.

Education

Perhaps nowhere has service provision for individuals with developmental disabilities been more comprehensive than in the educational setting. The Education for All Handicapped Children Act (P.L. 94-142) set forth the right not only to a free and appropriate education but also to any services deemed necessary to meet the needs of students with disabilities. The number of children receiving special education services has grown every year since 1976 with an increase of 3.7% in the years from 1992 to 1993 (Council for Exceptional Children, 1994; Wehman, 1995). The Education of the Handicapped Act of 1975 was amended in 1990 to expand the definition of disability specifically to include children with autism and traumatic brain injury. The name of the law was also amended to Individuals with Disabilities Education Act (IDEA; P.L. 101-476) to emphasize the concept of person before that of disability.

The education of students with developmental disabilities has taken on a new and comprehensive meaning. Debate over the issues of educability of students, particularly those with severe disabilities, has been raging for some time (Bailey, 1981; Kauffman & Krouse, 1981), and the issues continue to be evident in court cases (e.g., *Timothy v. Rochester, N.H. School District,* 1989). Under IDEA, the term *education* encompasses training in areas such as self-help, vocational training, and community living in addition to more traditional academic content. For example, a student with severe disabilities may spend a large part of his or her educational day in the community. A community-based outing such as a trip to a fast-food restaurant can provide the student with opportunities to increase his or her competency in skills such as money and word recognition and in social situations. Similarly, a student who is blind may spend an equal amount of time in the community acquiring mobility skills and increasing opportunities for independence. The definition of developmental disabilities itself and current best practices together stress the need for functional, age-appropriate skills that will generalize to environments beyond the school doors.

Independent Living

The deinstitutionalization movement dramatically decreased the number of individuals residing in institutions and placed many individuals with disabilities into community residential settings (Hayden & Abery, 1994). Amado and colleagues (1990) reported that in 1967, 85% of the developmentally disabled population lived in institutions but that this number had decreased to approximately 34% by 1988. For many individuals, institutional living has given way to residence in smaller, more normalized settings in the community. Amado et al. estimated that 23.9% of individuals with severe mental retardation and 17.8% of individuals with profound retardation live in facilities with six or fewer residents. Residential options now include foster family care, semiindependent and supported living, state and nonstate group residences, state and nonstate institutions, and nursing homes. Figure 1.2 provides the percentage of individuals with developmental disabilities in each residential option. Whereas institutional living continues to be a way of life for some, research has provided evidence that even those with the most severe disabilities can successfully live in the community if they are given adequate support (Amado et al., 1990).

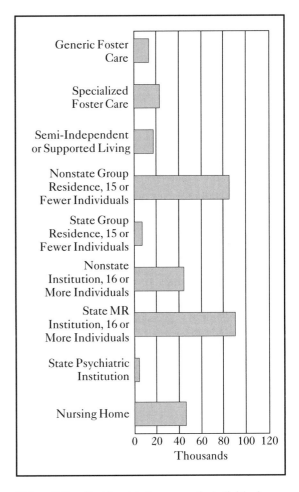

Figure 1.2. Residential placements for individuals with developmental disabilities during 1988. *Note:* From *Chartbook on Services for People with Developmental Disabilities* (p. 9) by A. N. Amado, K. C. Lakin, & J. M. Menke, 1990, Minneapolis: University of Minnesota, Institute on Community Integration. Reproduced with permission.

Economic Self-Sufficiency

The right to work is an important concept in our society; individuals who work are afforded greater opportunities for increased revenue and greater respect from others. Approximately 250,000 students with disabilities exit school programs each year (Wehman, 1992). Once they are beyond the school doors, however, many individuals with disabilities find a startling lack of services. Individuals with disabilities are notoriously underrepresented in the workforce (Peraino, 1992), with unemployment rates ranging from 58% (Wehman, Kregel, & Seyfarth, 1985b) to 88% (Wehman, Kregel, & Seyfarth, 1985a). Vocational options for individuals with developmental disabilities traditionally have consisted of day or activity centers. Available vocational options are expanding, however, and now include competitive or supported competitive employment. (See Chapter 17 for more information on supported employment.) Supported employment is characterized by permanent, ongoing, or intermittent support; at least minimum wage; and opportunities for community integration (Wehman, Sale, & Parent, 1992). The growth of supported employment has been marked (West & Parent, 1992). Wehman (1990a), in a national analysis of supported employment, found an increase in supported employment participation of 226% from 1986 to 1988. Categories of disability represented in supported employment included mental retardation (70.5%), mental illness (16.7%), cerebral palsy (1.8%), sensory impairment (2.5%), and other (8.5%) (Wehman, 1990a). Although individuals with severe and profound mental retardation have been successful in supported employment, they compose a relatively small portion of the population with disabilities who are placed (Kregel, Wehman, & Banks, 1989; Thompson, Powers, & Houchard, 1992; Wehman, 1990a).

These data have been further expanded in an additional study conducted by Revell et al. (1994). They found that over the past decade there has been steady growth nationally in the use of supported employment, with increasing numbers of consumers with severe disabilities obtaining competitive work for the first time. Representatives of 42 state/territorial systems responded to a national survey, which was conducted to assess the impact of supported employment, and reported that a total of 74,960 individuals participated in supported employment in 1991. Persons with the primary disability classification of mental retardation accounted for 62.8% of all supported employment participants; 30.4% of these individuals with mental retardation were in the *moderate* mental retardation classification, and 8.7% in the

severe or *profound* classification. The individual placement model (79.7%) was the dominant supported employment option utilized. A weighted mean hourly wage of $4.45 and a mean weekly wage of $111.44 were reported. The total of Vocational Rehabilitation (VR) funds was $74,860,404 with a non-VR funds reported at $160,164,388. Despite a severe economic recession in many parts of the United States in recent years, the supported employment program initiative continues to grow. Revell, Wehman, Kregel, West, and Rayfield (1994) concluded that the major areas of further effort in supported employment are (a) more diversity in funding base, (b) conversion from segregated to integrated programs, (c) participation by people with more severe disabilities, and (d) sustaining and expanding the rate of growth so more people can participate.

The primary impetus behind supported employment has been the placement of individuals with disabilities typically unable to be placed in community vocational settings. Such an emphasis on individuals with more severe disabilities has translated into service needs that may be extensive and long term. Cost–benefit analyses illustrate that even with extensive support and long-term assistance, supported employment is more cost effective than other, alternative day or activity programs (Conley, Rusch, McCaughrin, & Tines, 1989; Kregel, 1992). More important, however, the benefits of increased opportunities for economic self-sufficiency and integration cannot be overlooked. Exemplary supported employment programs emphasize work for at least minimum wages, which thereby enhance opportunities for community integration and self-respect. Although the often intangible rewards attained from competitive placements cannot always be factored into an equation, they certainly affect the sum.

Psychosocial Needs

All individuals have unique and varied needs. These needs typically do not fall neatly into service provision realms but are complex, interrelated, and subject to change over time. To fully serve individuals with developmental disabilities, professionals must be aware of the psychosocial needs of their clients. The illusive construct of "quality of life" must be considered. Although it is difficult to quantify, quality of life can be based on personal observations of an individual's needs, preferences, and aspirations (Halpern, 1993). Quality of life includes tangible and intangible rewards and benefits such as self-esteem, wages, and friendships (Steere, Wood, Pancsofar, & Butterworth, 1990). For example, although securing and maintaining employment is a desired outcome for many individuals with developmental disabilities, it is not the only desired outcome. Professionals must view their clients in a holistic manner and examine aspects such as opportunities for integration, formation of friendships, and enhanced feelings of self-worth. As we noted previously, choice and consumer empowerment must factor heavily into service planning and delivery for individuals with developmental disabilities; its inclusion represents advocacy for individuals with disabilities and the best chance for successful programming.

ISSUES FOR SERVICE PROVIDERS

Following are some major issues facing professionals working with individuals with developmental disabilities. Central issues emerging in the service profession field are outlined, and challenges to professionals are suggested.

Transdisciplinary Planning and Implementation

The terminology used to denote group planning and implementation of services has included "interdisciplinary," "multidisciplinary," and "transdisciplinary" models or approaches. Although their meanings vary slightly, each stresses the need for input from many disciplines in service delivery. The need for an interdisciplinary approach to service provision is apparent in the passage of IDEA (P.L. 101-476) and is supported by the Developmental Disabilities Assistance and Bill of Rights Act of 1990. With the diverse needs of individuals with disabilities, many different disciplines must converge for the provision of optimal services. Although professionals are cognizant of the need for coordination among their disciplines, actual service provision is often fragmented and uncoordinated. According to Giangreco (1990), related service professionals (occupational therapists, physical therapists, and communication specialists) believe that whereas recommendations should be shared, the final authority of their discipline should be retained. With such territorial attitudes, programming efforts can all too easily fall to the wayside.

The need for an interdisciplinary approach is most marked in service provision for individuals with the more severe disabilities. As the severity of the disability increases, so does the number of disciplines involved in providing services (Downing & Bailey, 1990). Obviously individuals in need of the most extensive services cannot be faced with rhetoric such as "It's not my area." Szymanski, Hanley-Maxwell, and Parker (1990) have suggested the need for a transdisciplinary model for coordinating the efforts of service providers. Central to the model is the sharing of information and skills by professionals, with service delivery carried out by one or two facilitators (Orelove, 1994). The transdisciplinary approach suggests use of an indirect model of services and utilization of role release. The indirect model of services centers on professionals who work as consultants with other disciplines and requires role release, or flexible role performance, and facilitative communication. Whatever the terminology, the imperative is the same: cooperation and communication between service professionals.

Challenges for Service Providers

- Understand that professional roles must be flexible and will change over time.

- Work to foster communication among professional disciplines through active listening, brainstorming, and the open sharing of ideas.

- Keep egos in check; remember that you work for the client first.

- Learn from others—Do not feel that adhering to others' ideas in any way diminishes your professional status; it only enhances it.

- Recognize that different disciplines may have different beliefs and professional jargon (Orelove & Sobsey, 1994).

- Value all ideas, even if they are different from your own.

Ecologic Approach to Planning and Service

Individuals interact with their environment in a complex way. Service planning and provision must incorporate a "systems approach" in meeting the needs of individuals with developmental disabilities (Powers, 1988). A systems approach takes into account the characteristics and constraints of each level of a system (e.g., individuals, groups, societies) and the interrelationships between each system (Powers, 1988). The approach notes that a change in one aspect of the system may affect in some manner other parts of the system to create an imbalance that may cause stress. If a change in the system is to be implemented successfully, many aspects must be examined. For example, an educational program instituted in the school setting may have profound effects on the family of the student for whom the program was designed. Similarly, an individual's participating in supported employment may effect change in the family and in the community. Professionals must understand how service provision may affect all the individuals who are participating in environments with the individual with a disability.

The ecologic approach to service provision, like the systems approach, stresses the need to examine the many elements that compose an individ-

ual's life. Steps in an ecologic assessment typically include identification of domain areas (such as self-help, leisure, or community living), identification of current and future environments, division of relevant environments into subenvironments, inventory of the subenvironments for needed skills, and examination of the activities to isolate required skills (Falvey, 1989). For example, an ecologic approach for a teacher of a secondary student with severe disabilities would require that the teacher find out about possible future environments for his or her student. Possible future environments for a secondary student might include vocational programs such as supported employment placement, residential options such as group homes or supervised apartments, and possible recreational pursuits. The teacher could gather information by using a published ecologic inventory that aids in the identification of domain areas and prioritization of goals, or the teacher could informally interview professionals in potential future environments to pinpoint potential areas of need. Imagine the consternation of a parent whose child is denied acceptance in a group home due to inadequate self-care skills after 12 years of schooling in the special education system. By looking ahead and utilizing an ecologic approach, the teacher, families, and future service providers can project needs and begin working on necessary skills. Absence of an ecologic approach may result in lack of training necessary for success in future environments and perhaps in an overlap in training efforts.

Challenges for Service Providers

- Assess current levels of functioning and skills exhibited by the client.

- Assess levels of functioning needed in possible future environments.

- Utilize discrepancy analyses to assess strengths and weaknesses and to gain a socially valid perspective of skills and behaviors of the general population.

- Be aware of the many environments in which your client/student may participate. Understand that needs and behaviors will change in different environments.

- Be aware that needs and skills will change continuously over time and so will service needs.

- Understand that many individuals are involved in a person's life and that each will affect service provision in a unique way.

- Examine both the strengths and weaknesses of your client. Utilize strengths to offset possible weaknesses.

- Understand how change can affect an individual and his or her environment and be sensitive to his or her needs.

- Be prepared to meet resistance when instituting some changes.

Family Involvement in Service Provision

The Education for All Handicapped Children Act (P.L. 94-142) brought family involvement into the educational process by mandating parental participation. Recent legislation has also emphasized the importance of family support and input in service provision (e.g., Amended Developmental Disabilities Act of 1990 and the Amended Education for Handicapped Children Act of 1990). Parents have been given the rights of informed consent, due process, and involvement in the educational planning of their child's curriculum.

The amount and type of participation undertaken by parents and families obviously will vary. Professionals must encourage participation at whatever level parents feel most comfortable. The complex nature of interactions and of their effect on the family has been explored in both the family systems approach (Turnbull & Turnbull, 1990) and the social support approach (Dunst, Trivette, & Deal, 1988). Both approaches require an examination of the complex nature of the family and emphasize that family input must be valued and respected.

Challenges for Service Providers

- Understand the maxim "no one is an island" and be cognizant of how the family may affect service provision.

- Work toward understanding the "family system approach" (Turnbull & Turnbull, 1990).

- Understand the value of family input to service provision.

- Understand that needs change over time and that professionals must meet these changing needs.

- Be aware that family values may differ from those of service providers but must be respected and valued.

- Understand that families have different coping styles and may react to professional input and ideas differently.

- Work toward empowering parents with the means to institute change beyond professional intervention.

- Be aware of the impact your service suggestions (or demands) may place on the family.

- Be an advocate for the rights of the parents and family to institute change in the child's life.

Transition from School to Work and Independent Living

The term *transition* conjures up many different meanings. Because transition typically denotes change or movement, individuals with developmental disabilities undoubtedly experience many different transitions during their lifetime. Transition can include movement from one educational setting to another or from one stage in life to another. (See Chapter 4 for more detail about transition from school to adulthood.)

During times of transition, assistance from service providers is critical. Voids of service at times of change can translate into unsuccessful or poor transition or simply into no transition at all. The

Amended Education of the Handicapped Act (1990) emphasized the need for transition planning by mandating increased grant revenue and the specification of vocational or educational goals as part of a student's individual education plan (see Wehman, 1995, for a curriculum that provides teachers with over 40 sample Individual Transition Plans). A transition plan must be developed, if determined appropriate, by the child's age of 16, or in some cases, by the age of 14.

Transition planning should focus on vocational, residential, and social-interpersonal domains (Morgan, Moore, McSweyn, & Salzberg, 1992). Table 1.3 outlines the types of services needed by students with disabilities leaving the school sys-tem. As the data in Table 1.3 illustrates, many potential needs must be met. Wehman (1990b, 1992, 1995) has suggested that transition is based heavily on the community and its characteristics and cannot be successfully implemented by schools or vocational rehabilitation agencies alone.

Successful transition includes plans (Wehman, 1995) for the sending and receiving programs to share information on eligibility requirements, entrance and exit criteria, program goals and objectives, follow-up and feedback procedures, and personnel responsible for promoting transition (Sileo, Rude, & Luchner, 1988). Further, all transition planning and execution must be concerned with many different quality outcomes. Quality-of-life issues should figure prominently in any transition planning. Steere and coworkers (1990) outlined a process that may aid in the attainment of quality-of-life outcomes. The process helps guide the selection of employment placements. Table 1.4 outlines the major steps in the process. Although it is specific to employment outcomes, the model can be applied to other transition areas such as independent living.

The reality of transition for individuals with developmental disabilities often means long waiting lists for vocational and residential services and gaps in eligibility for services in movement from one service provision to another. Hayden and De-Paepe (1994) have written perhaps the best overall summary of how the waiting-list dilemma is adversely affecting people with disabilities in this country. For example, they indicate that as of 1991, 60,876 people with disabilities were waiting for residential services. Also, eligibility for special education does not necessarily ensure eligibility for vocational rehabilitation services (Szymanski, King, Parker, & Jenkins, 1989); hence, many individuals may "graduate" into inadequate or wholly absent service provision.

Table 1.3.   Anticipated Services Needed by Children with Disabilities Aged 14 and Older, Exiting the Educational System During the 1990–1991 School Year

Area	%
Counseling/Guidance	11.5
Transportation	3.5
Technological Aids	1.3
Interpreter Services	.5
Reader Services	.5
Physical/Mental Restoration	2.0
Family Services	3.7
Independent Living	3.6
Maintenance	3.4
Residential Services	1.8
Vocational Training Services	14.9
Transitional Employment Services	9.2
Vocational Placement	11.5
Postemployment	4.6
Evaluation of Vocational Rehabilitation Services	11.8

Note. From *Fifteenth Annual Report to Congress on the Implementation of the Individuals with Disabilities Act* by U.S. Department of Education, 1993, Washington, DC: Department of Education, Office of Special Education and Rehabilitative Services.

Challenges for Service Providers

- Understand that transition will be ongoing and will occur many times in an individual's life.

- Be aware that successful transition requires the cooperation of many different service agencies.

Table 1.4. Outcome-Based Transition Planning for Individuals with Developmental Disabilities

---

1. *Orientation.* Establishment of transition planning team and appointment of a team leader: The team should include individuals who represent all the environments of the student or consumer. Members should be oriented to the intent and purpose of the meeting.

2. *Development of a Personal Profile.* Development of a "biographical sketch" outlining the student's or client's characteristics (likes and dislikes) and achievements: The profile's purpose is to help team members identify appropriate employment matches with the individual's desired outcomes.

3. *Identification of Employment Outcomes.* Brainstorming session generating a list of potential quality-of-life outcomes: The list should contain hoped-for and dreamed-for outcomes in order of priority.

4. *Measurement System.* Outline of "standards of acceptance": Each outcome is further defined, and ideal and minimum standards are delineated. An outcome of increased community participation might include an ideal standard of one outing per day to a minimum standard of one outing per week.

5. *Compatibility Process.* Integration of outcomes and objectives with employment possibilities: Team members look for a match or degree of compatibility between available jobs and the consumer's abilities. Challenges to placement are outlined and potential solutions are generated through brainstorming. Potential solutions are ranked according to their feasibility, and "action plans" are drawn up. Action plans specify activities, personnel, timelines, and follow-up activities necessary to ensure that activities are successfully completed.

6. *Evaluation.* Team members continue to meet to monitor completion of team activities.

Note. Adapted from "Outcome-Based School-to-Work Transition Planning for Students with Severe Disabilities" by D. E. Steere, R. Wood, E. L. Pancsofar, and J. Butterworth, 1990, *Career Development for Exceptional Individuals, 13,* pp. 57–70.

- Be aware that a multidisciplinary, transdisciplinary, or team approach provides the most optimal transition services.

- Be aware that transition requires preplanning and projection of needed services from one service system to another.

- Understand the value of and need for quality communication between and among service delivery disciplines.

- Understand the roles and responsibilities of other professionals and how to work with other agencies.

- Have empathy for clients and consumers undergoing transition. Change is often difficult and may require time to adjust.

- Understand that transition may result in new and unique service needs for clients. Service providers must remain flexible and attuned to new needs.

- Focus on outcomes in transition that include aspects of quality of life.

Training of Professional Staff

Rapid changes in the field of developmental disabilities have resulted in many new roles for service providers. Changing roles mean that service providers must stay abreast of changes and translate these new changes into satisfactory services for the consumers they serve. Throughout their professional career, professionals working with individuals with developmental disabilities may be called upon to play the role of communicator, facilitator, teacher, evaluator, negotiator, business person, advocate, or counselor (Garner & Orelove, 1994). Some roles may be formally defined; others are only informally defined. The service delivery system for individuals with developmental disabilities is currently experiencing a shortage of qualified staff, as many as 27,000 special education professionals (Council for Exceptional Children, 1994; U.S. Department of Education, 1993). Several professions related to vocational rehabilitation can expect rapid expansion because of increased need in community programs (Karan & Berger-Knight, 1986). Further, preservice training is often discipline specific and may not adequately prepare professionals working with individuals with developmental disabilities (Szymanski, Linkowski, Leahy, Diamond, & Thoreson,

1993). Special education may not prepare professionals to work with adults with developmental disabilities or to work effectively with the rehabilitation system. Equally true is the fact that vocational rehabilitation counselors may not be trained in systematic instructional techniques (Kregel & Sale, 1988; Wehman, Sale, & Parent, 1992). Table 1.5 outlines competency areas important in supported employment training but which apply equally to many service areas for professionals involved in work with individuals with developmental disabilities.

Table 1.5.   Competency Areas for Professionals Working with Individuals with Developmental Disabilities

---

1. *Philosophical, Legal, and Policy Issues.* Critical issues surrounding services for individuals with developmental disabilities, such as legislation and litigation, eligibility requirements, definitions, and related services provided by state and local agencies.

2. *Program Development.* Options and programs for individuals with developmental disabilities, assessment of client needs, and coordination of efforts among professional disciplines.

3. *Program Implementation.* Implementation of a service program.

4. *Program Management.* Understanding of legal issues, regulations, processes, and the allocation of personnel, equipment, and resources.

5. *Program Evaluation.* Evaluation of client progress and overall program effectiveness.

6. *Systematic Instruction.* Understanding of use of instructional techniques and use of prompts and reinforcers.

7. *Transition Planning.* Identification and analysis of skills needed in current and future environments of clients.

Note. Adapted from "Preservice Personnel Preparation of Supported Employment Professionals" by J. Kregel and P. Sale, 1988, in *Vocational Rehabilitation and Supported Employment* (pp. 129–143) by P. Wehman and M. S. Moon (Eds.), Baltimore: Brookes.

Challenges for Service Providers

- Understand the need for flexibility of professional roles and responsibilities.

- Understand that as needs arise, roles and responsibilities of service providers change and are redefined.

- Learn to communicate to facilitate professional and personal growth.

- Create a balance between advocacy for individuals with developmental disabilities and the inherent role of employee of a service system (Karan & Berger-Knight, 1986).

- Work toward continued professionalism in the field by action and advocacy.

- Translate new changes in the field into current best practice for clients.

Utilization of the Community as a Training Site

Trends toward greater community integration of individuals with developmental disabilities mean that service providers must learn to use the community as a training site (Inge & Wehman, 1993). Use of the community can lead to greater generalization of skills to other environments (McDonnell, Hardman, Hightower, Keifer-O'Donnell, & Drew, 1993; Vandercook, 1991) and can provide opportunities for integration with nondisabled peers (Apter, 1992; Moon et al., 1990; Vandercook, 1991).

Although the individual can make great gains while training in the community, more than skill acquisition must be considered when that training occurs in public. Training occurring in the community must be concerned with how training is undertaken. Activities that are age inappropriate or in any way demeaning may negatively affect how individuals with disabilities are perceived (Billingsley & Kelley, 1994; Wolfe, 1994). Professionals must work to foster community integration and remain sensitive to activities and behaviors occurring in the community. Brawner-Jones (1993) provided six excellent insights into the necessary reforms that must occur for community inclusion to occur for those with the most severe developmental disabilities:

• Support for adults with profound disabilities in the community must shift to natural supports whenever possible. Public services must augment, not supplant, those efforts of persons who are informally supporting a person's lifestyle choices (Froland, Pancoast, Chaptman, & Kimboko, 1981; Smull & Bellamy, 1991).

• People providing support, both professionals and persons providing natural supports, must receive training to effectively provide needed services. Training should include training of preservice personnel as well as ongoing training of those who continue to support people in the community. Research has shown that personnel training results in improved attitudes, increased appropriate interactions between support personnel and persons being supported, and job satisfaction.

• Inadequacy of salaries and staffing patterns must be addressed. Pay for direct care staff in residential settings tends to be very low, often little more than minimum wage; however, the demands from people providing supports for adults with profound disabilities can be great. Much of the imbalance between performance demands and compensation is attributed to the high turnover in personnel that occurs in residential support systems. Improvement of this situation will require legislative action to appropriate more funding for support adults in community living options.

• Another requirement for change is the use of limited resources in creative ways, such as lowering administrative costs and transferring savings to direct care support personnel, identifying mixes of direct wages and fringe benefits that allow employees to select from a menu of possible fringes, modifying scheduling of support personnel around level of demand for support, and increasing use of natural supports to reduce demand on paid support staff.

• Training and support must be provided in a manner that engenders respect, both for people with disabilities and for persons providing support. Respect is essential for adults with profound disabilities to be successfully included in the community. Equitable relationships cannot develop without respect between the people in the relationship. Therefore, only persons who have respect for the needs and contributions of adults with profound disabilities should be providing support.

• Persons providing support must be assured that they are valued. This display of respect must come from management of agencies, family members, and the persons receiving support.

Challenges for Service Providers

• Know your community and its needs and values.

• Understand other disciplines such as marketing, business, and personnel management and the impact these can have on your profession.

• Understand the impact of actions and training occurring in the community. How individuals with developmental disabilities are treated will influence attitudes toward and expectations for such individuals.

• Advocate and educate others to the benefits of increased integration.

Funding

A central issue in service provision for individuals with developmental disabilities is funding. During the 1980s, the amount of public funding for individuals with mental retardation and related conditions increased considerably, reaching approximately $12 billion in 1988 (excluding funding for education and certain entitlement). Well over 100 federal programs provided funds for individuals with developmental disabilities as did state, local, and private sources (Amado et al., 1990). Whereas coordination between special education and vocational programs was stimulated by the 1984 Office of Special Education and Rehabilitation Services (OSERS) Transitional Initiative, use of different definitions for individuals with disabilities has often translated into inconsistent service delivery. The rehabilitation system is not an entitlement service like the educational system and may have an order of selection for clientele served (Szymanski et al., 1989). Differences in definition can result in ineligibility for individuals previously classified as disabled. Szymanski et al. noted that eligibility for vocational rehabilitation services can be difficult for individuals with mild disabilities because their disability may not directly affect employment and may render them ineligible for services. It is equally true that because vocational rehabilitation programs require that individuals be expected to receive reasonable benefits from services, individuals with severe disabilities who have an unfavorable prognosis may be denied services. Funding for disability categories may also be discrepant. Kregel, Shafer, Wehman, and West (1989) found that individuals with mental retardation could secure necessary funding for supported employment but that funding was not equally available for other disability categories such as cerebral palsy, brain injury, physical disabilities, and sensory impairments.

One of the most critical issues in funding provisions for individuals with developmental disabilities is lack of long-term funding. Long-term funding for rehabilitative services is often unstable, a characteristic thereby creating funding lapses and inconsistencies. Lack of long-term funding may translate into inadequate services for individuals with developmental disabilities (Wehman & Kregel, 1995). Lack of long-term funding may mean that although a client is initially provided a needed service, the service may be discontinued when funding expires. The needs of the client do not usually end when funding ends. The issue of funding is further complicated by the inclusion of individuals with the most severe disabilities. Kregel and Wehman (1989) recommended that differentiated funding levels be established and

that programs be reimbursed on the basis of the intensity and complexity of training and support needs. As more and more individuals with more severe disabilities take part in sevice delivery systems, the intensity of services may need to be factored into funding strategies and funding incentives provided to agencies taking on more severe cases (Moon et al., 1990).

Challenges for Service Providers

- Be knowledgeable about federal laws and how they may affect your clients.

- Be aware of model programs and utilize information and ideas to implement state-of-the-art practices.

- Utilize grant award opportunities for innovation.

- Lobby Congress for legislative change.

Changing Attitudes and Advocacy

Attitudes impact integrally on service provision, funding, the way individuals with disabilities are treated, and belief in what can be accomplished. Service providers need to continue to champion the rights of individuals with disabilities to exercise choice, to work, and to access the services necessary to attain their full potential (Wehman, 1992). Individuals with disabilities in the community and in integrated work settings must be the norm rather than the exception. Individuals with disabilities working in appropriate settings and demonstrating competence will further the development of more positive attitudes (Wolfe, 1994). Although contact alone cannot be assumed to induce positive attitudes (Roper, 1990), situations promoting the similarities between individuals with disabilities and their nondisabled peers may serve to enhance such attitudes (Hamre-Nietupski, Hendrickson, Neitupski, & Sasso, 1993; Haring & Breen, 1992; Giangreco, Dennis, Cloninger, Edelman, & Schattman, 1993). Finally, service providers must place increased emphasis on accountability and quality of programming. As always, service providers must be accountable to those they seek to serve and must be able to validate socially the services they provide by continually asking if the services they provide are necessary and sufficient for the maximum functioning of their clients.

Challenges for Service Providers

- Work toward increased services for individuals with developmental disabilities.

- Strive for services that truly meet the needs of your clients rather than simply supplying readily available services.

- Demonstrate accountability in programming and service provision.

- Assess techniques for training, methods, and skills for measures of social validity.

IMPLICATIONS FOR FUTURE SERVICE DELIVERY PLANNING AND RESEARCH

- Rob is a 2-year-old boy who has been totally blind since birth. Rob is entering the educational system for the first time.

- Susan is a 12-year-old girl who experienced severe traumatic brain injury during an auto accident. Prior to the accident, Susan was in a regular sixth-grade class. Now she has trouble walking independently, can no longer attend to many self-care needs, and has trouble with memory loss. Susan's family is having a difficult time adjusting to the changes in their lives since the accident.

- Melody is an 18-year-old girl who is severely mentally disabled. Melody has deficits in many life areas although she fiercely desires a "real job."

- Glenn is a 46-year-old man with chronic mental illness. Glenn is living independently but still needs supervision in areas such as money management, time management, cooking, cleaning, and hygiene. Glenn loves living in the community and has recently expressed a desire to learn golf and tennis in order to "get in shape."

Service provision for individuals with developmental disabilities has substantially changed in breadth and intensity. Advances in the educational field have meant that all students with disabilities, regardless of the severity of the disability, can be educated in the least restrictive environment. Residential placements have moved from large institutional settings to a range of options including small, community-based settings. Vocational placements have similarly expanded to include a range of placements, many of which occur in the community. All of these changes have and will continue to have an impact on the services available to individuals like Rob, Susan, Melody, and Glenn. Where once Glenn might have resided in an institution, he may now successfully live in a group home or a supervised apartment. Likewise, Melody may leave the school system and be placed in a supported job in the community where she can earn competitive wages. The changes are, without a doubt, exciting. They offer chances for independence, increased self-esteem, and friendships for individuals with developmental disabilities. The changes also offer service providers in every realm of service provision new challenges. Future challenges facing professionals include the following:

- *The need to coordinate efforts among many different disciplines:* The educational, rehabilitation, and residential systems must come together to provide more successful transitions for students like Melody in their move into the adult world. This coordination of effort will create new roles and will redefine existing ones. The coordination of efforts represents the best chances of successful programming for individuals requiring diverse service needs.

• *Provision of services that examine client outcomes:* Service providers will be challenged to focus on multiple student and client outcomes. No longer will simple placement in the community be enough. Individuals like Glenn will need to express their values and dreams to service providers who can help translate them into a realistic, yet satisfying, match in vocational and residential placements. Glenn may want to work in the community and receive benefits and wages that allow him to participate in his favored leisure pursuits. Professionals working with individuals like Glenn will need to work toward a satisfactory match between services and client needs.

• *Inclusion in services of individuals with the most severe disabilities:* Professionals will need to work toward the continued inclusion of individuals with the most severe disabilities into the delivery system. A burgeoning in the assistive technology field will mean that many more adaptations can be made to accommodate individuals with disabilities. With assistance and support, individuals like Melody can be successfully employed in competitive worksites.

• *Comprehensive training for professional staff:* The new and changing roles of professionals will require better training of professional staff. Training will need to focus on coordination of efforts between professionals and on strategies that foster communication and cooperation. Professionals working with new students like Rob just entering the school system will need to know characteristics of disabilities, systematic instructional techniques, and ways of accessing community facilities outside the school.

• *Development of comprehensive and coordinated funding sources:* Although all the individuals just described would probably be eligible for special education services, individuals like Melody and Glenn, who are outside of or who are leaving the school system, might not be able to receive needed services. Melody, who is severely disabled, may be judged a poor candidate for employment and may be denied vocational rehabili-

tation services. Because of inconsistencies of long-term funding sources, Glenn may initially receive some services but then be denied further service when funding expires. Long-term and coordinated funding for services must be established to ensure that all individuals receive necessary services.

• *The need for continued research in the field of developmental disabilities:* Research in the area of developmental disabilities must continue and should include a focus on more advanced technology to foster independence, examination of attitudes and how to enhance favorable attitude change, methods of fostering choice-making skills, and longitudinal data on outcomes in all facets of life of individuals who are developmentally disabled. Research represents forward movement in the field.

FINAL THOUGHTS

The challenges outlined throughout the chapter should not serve to daunt professionals working with individuals with disabilities but rather should serve as a means of generating an introspective look at services offered and areas where improvement can be made. Challenge does not denote insurmountable odds but offers a means with which to reach a goal. Individuals like Rob, Susan, Melody, and Glenn count on service providers undertaking the professional challenges facing them.

REFERENCES

Allard, W. G., Dodd, J. M., & Peralez, E. (1987). Keeping LD students in college. *Academic Therapy, 22,* 359–365.

Alper, S., & Ryndak, D. L. (1992). Educating students with severe handicaps in regular classes. *Elementary School Journal, 92*(3), 373–388.

Amado, A. N., Lakin, K. C., & Menke, J. M. (1990). *Chartbook on services for people with developmental disabilities.* Minneapolis: University of Minnesota, Institute on Community Integration.

American Association on Mental Retardation. (1992). *News and Notes, 5*(1), 1–8.

Americans with Disabilities Act, 42 U.S.C. § 12101 *et seq.* (1990).

Apter, D. (1992). A successful competitive/supported employment program for people with severe visual disabilities. *Journal of Vocational Rehabilitation, 2*(1), 21–27.

Babbit, C. E., & Burbach, H. J. (1990). Note on the perceived occupational future of physically disabled college students. *Journal of Employment Counseling, 27*(3), 98–100.

Bailey, J. S. (1981). Wanted: A rational search for the limiting conditions of habilitation in the retarded. *Analysis and Intervention in Developmental Disabilities, 1,* 45–52.

Billingsley, F. F., & Kelley, B. (1994). An examination of the acceptability of instructional practices for students with severe disabilities in general education settings. *Journal of the Association for Persons with Severe Handicaps, 19*(2), 75–83.

Black, J. W., & Meyer, L. H. (1992). But . . . is it really work? Social validity of employment training for persons with very severe disabilities. *American Journal on Mental Retardation, 96*(5), 463–474.

Brawner-Jones, N. (1993). Support needs and strategies for adults with profound disabilities. In L. Sternberg (Ed.), *Individuals with profound disabilities* (pp. 412–444). Austin, TX: PRO-ED.

Conley, R., Rusch, F. R., McCaughrin, W. B., & Tines, J. (1989). Benefits and costs of supported employment: An analysis of the Illinois Supported Employment Project [Special issue: Supported employment]. *Journal of Applied Behavior Analysis, 22*(4), 441–447.

Council for Exceptional Children. (1994). *Today, 1*(7).

Dattilo, J., & Rusch, F. R. (1985). Effects of choice on leisure participation for persons with severe handicaps. *Journal of the Association for Persons with Severe Handicaps, 10,* 194–199.

Developmental Disabilities Assistance and Bill of Rights Act of 1990, Title 42, U.S.C. 6000–6083. *U.S. Statutes at Large, 104,* 1191–1204.

Downing, J., & Bailey, B. R. (1990). Sharing the responsibility: Using a transdisciplinary team approach to enhance the learning of students with severe disabilities. *Journal of Educational and Psychological Consultation, 1*(3), 259–278.

Dunst, C. J., Trivette, C. M., & Deal, A. (1988). *Enabling and empowering families.* Cambridge, MA: Brookline Books.

Edgerton, R. B., & Bercovica, S. M. (1976). The cloak of competence: Years later. *American Journal of Mental Deficiency, 80,* 485–497.

Falvey, M. A. (1989). *Community-based curriculum: Instructional strategies for students with severe handicaps.* Baltimore: Brookes.

Froland, F., Pancoast, K., Chaptman, R., & Kimboko, S. (1981). *Helping networks and human services.* Beverly Hills, CA: Sage.

Gardner, J. F. (1990). Introduction: A decade of change. In J. F. Gardner & M. S. Chapman (Eds.), *Program issues in developmental disabilities. A guide to effective habilitation and active treatment* (pp. 13–18). Baltimore: Brookes.

Garner, H., & Orelove, F. (1994). *Teamwork in human services.* New York: Elsevier.

Giangreco, M. F. (1990). Making related service decisions for students with severe disabilities: Roles, criteria, and authority. *Journal of the Association for Persons with Severe Handicaps, 15,* 22–31.

Giangreco, M., Dennis, R., Cloninger, C., Edelman, S., & Schattman, R. (1993). "I've counted Jon": Transformational experiences of teachers educating students with disabilities. *Exceptional Children, 59*(4), 359–372.

Goldberg, R. T. (1989). A comparative study of vocational development of able bodied and disabled persons. *International Journal of Rehabilitation Research, 12*(1), 3–15.

Gresham, F. M., Evans, S., & Elliot, S. N. (1988). Self-efficacy differences among mildly handicapped, gifted, and non-handicapped students. *Journal of Special Education, 22,* 231–241.

Guess, D., Benson, H. A., & Seigel-Causey, E. (1985). Concepts and issues related to choice-making with autonomy among persons with severe disabilities. *Journal of the Association for Persons with Severe Handicaps, 10,* 79–86.

Guess, D., & Siegel-Causey, E. (1985). Behavioral control and education of severely handicapped students: Who's doing what to whom and why? In D. Bricker & J. Filler (Eds.), *Severe mental retardation: From theory to practice* (pp. 241–255). Reston, VA: Council for Exceptional Children.

Halpern, A. (1993). Quality of life as a conceptual framework for evaluating transition outcomes. *Exceptional Children, 59*(6), 486–498.

Hamre-Nietupski, S., Hendrickson, J., Nietupski, J., & Sasso, G. (1993). Perceptions of teachers of students with moderate, severe, or profound disabilities on facilitating friendships with nondisabled peers. *Education and Training in Mental Retardation, 28*(2), 111–127.

Hamre-Nietupski, S., Krajewski, L., Riehle, R., Sensor, K., Nietupski, J., Moravec, J., McDonald, J., & Cantine-Stull, P. (1992). Enhancing integration during the summer: Combined educational and community recreation options for students with severe disabilities. *Education and Training in Mental Retardation, 27*(1), 68–74.

Haring, T. G., & Breen, C. G. (1992). A peer-mediated social network intervention to enhance the social integration of persons with moderate and severe disabilities. *Journal of Applied Behavior Analysis, 25*(2), 319–333.

Hayden, M., & Abery, B. (Eds.). (1994). *Challenges for a service system in transition.* Baltimore: Brookes.

Hayden, M., & DePaepe, P. (1994). Waiting for community services: The impact on persons with mental retardation and developmental disabilities. In M. Hayden & B. Abery (Eds.), *Challenges for a service system in transition* (pp. 173–206). Baltimore: Brookes.

Houghton, J., Bronicki, G. J., & Guess, D. (1987). Opportunities to express preferences and make choices among students with severe disabilities in classroom settings. *Journal of the Association for Persons with Severe Handicaps, 12,* 18–27.

Individuals with Disabilities Education Act of 1990, 20 U.S.C. § 1400 *et seq.*

Inge, K., & Wehman, P. (Eds.). (1993). *Vocational Options Project* [Monograph]. Richmond: Virginia Commonwealth University, Rehabilitation Research and Training Center on Supported Employment.

Karan, O. C., & Berger-Knight, C. (1986). Training and staff development issues in developmental disabilities. *Remedial and Special Education 7*(6), 40–45.

Kauffman, J. M., & Krouse, J. (1981). The cult of educability: Searching for the substance of things hoped for; the evidence of things not seen. *Analysis and Intervention in Developmental Disabilities, 1,* 53–60.

Kiernan, W., & Moon, S. (1993). *Project REC: Integrated social and leisure recreation services for students with severe disabilities.*

Final report. Boston: Children's Hospital, Training and Research Institute for People with Disabilities.

Kishi, G., Teelucksingh, B., Zollers, N., Park-Lee, S., & Meyer, L. (1988). Daily decision-making in community residences: A social comparison of adults with and without mental retardation. *American Journal on Mental Retardation, 92,* 430–435.

Knowlton, H. E., Turnbull, A. P., Backus, I., & Turnbull, H. R. (1988). Letting go: Consent and the "yes, but . . ." problem in transition. In B. L. Ludlow, A. P. Turnbull, & R. Luckasson (Eds.), *Transition to adult life for people with mental retardation* (pp. 45–66). Baltimore: Brookes.

Kregel, J. (1992). The subtle and salient points of program evaluation: An illustration from supported employment. *Journal of Vocational Rehabilitation, 2*(2), 53–61.

Kregel, J., & Sale, P. (1988). Preservice personnel preparation of supported employment professionals. In P. Wehman & M. S. Moon (Eds.), *Vocational rehabilitation and supported employment* (pp. 129–143). Baltimore: Brookes.

Kregel, J., Shafer, M. S., Wehman, P., & West, M. (1989). Policy development and public expenditures in supported employment: Current strategies to promote statewide systems change. *Journal of the Association for Persons with Severe Disabilities, 14,* 283–292.

Kregel, J., & Wehman, P. (1989). Supported employment: Promises deferred for persons with severe disabilities. *Journal of the Association for Persons with Severe Handicaps, 14,* 293–303.

Kregel, J., Wehman, P., & Banks, P. D. (1989). The effects of consumer characteristics and type of employment model on individual outcomes in supported employment. *Journal of Applied Behavioral Analysis, 22,* 407–415.

Larson, S. A., & Lakin, K. C. (1989). Deinstitutionalization of persons with mental retardation: Behavioral outcomes. *Journal of the Association for Persons with Severe Handicaps, 14,* 324–332.

Levy, J., Jessop, D. J., Rimmerman, A., & Levy, P. H. (1992). Attitudes of Fortune 500 corporate executives toward the employability of persons with severe disabilities: A national survey. *Mental Retardation, 30*(2), 67–75.

Longhurst, N. (1994). *The self-advocacy movement by people with developmental disabilities.* Washington, DC: American Association on Mental Retardation.

Lovett, H. (1991). Empowerment and choices. In L. H. Meyer, C. A. Peck, & L. Brown (Eds.), *Critical issues in the lives of people with severe disabilities* (pp. 625–626). Baltimore: Brookes.

Mank, D. (1994). The underachievement of supported employment: A call for reinvestment. *Journal of Disability Policy Studies, 5*(2), 1–24.

Martin, J. E., Marshall, L. H., & Maxson, L. L. (1993). Transition policy: Infusing self-determination and self-advocacy into transition programs. *Career Development for Exceptional Individuals, 16,* 53–61.

McDonnell, J., Hardman, M. L., Hightower, J., Keifer-O'Donnell, R., & Drew, C. (1993). Impact of community-based instruction on the development of adaptive behavior of secondary-level students with mental retardation. *American Journal on Mental Retardation, 97*(5), 575–584.

Mithaug, D. (1992). *Self-determined kids.* New York: Lexington Press.

Mithaug, D. E., Martin, J. E., Agran, M., & Rusch, F. R. (1988). *Why special education graduates fail.* Colorado Springs, CO: Ascent.

Moon, M. S. (1994). *Making school and community recreation fun for everyone.* Baltimore: Brookes.

Moon, M. S., Inge, K. J., Wehman, P., Brooke, V., & Barcus, J. M. (1990). *Helping persons with severe mental retardation get and keep employment.* Baltimore: Brookes.

Morgan, R. L., Moore, S. C., McSweyn, C., & Salzberg, C. L. (1992). Transition from school to work: Views of secondary special educators. *Education and Training in Mental Retardation, 27*(4), 315–323.

Nirje, B. (1969). The normalization principle and its human management implications. In R. B. Kugel & W. W. Wolfensberger (Eds.), *Changing patterns in residential services for the mentally retarded* (pp. 179–188). Washington, DC: U.S. Government Printing Office.

Orelove, F. (1994). Transdisciplinary staffing. In H. Garner & F. Orelove (Eds.), *Teamwork in human services* (pp. 212–224). Boston: Butterworth.

Orelove, F., & Sobsey, D. (1994). *Educating students with multiple disabilities.* Baltimore: Brookes.

Peraino, J. M. (1992). Post-21 follow-up studies: How do special education graduates fare? In P. Wehman (Ed.), *Life beyond the classroom: Transition strategies for young people with disabilities* (pp. 27–70). Baltimore: Brookes.

Powers, M. D. (1988). A systems approach to serving persons with severe developmental disabilities. In M. D. Powers (Ed.), *Expanding systems of service delivery for persons with developmental disabilities* (pp. 1–16). Baltimore: Brookes.

Rehabilitation Act Amendments, 29 U.S.C. §701 *et seq.* (1992).

Reid, D. H., & Parsons, M. B. (1990). Assessing food preferences among persons with profound mental retardation: Providing opportunities to make choices. *Journal of Applied Behavior Analysis, 23,* 183–195.

Reid, D. H., & Parsons, M. B. (1991). Making choice a routine part of mealtimes for persons with profound mental retardation. *Behavioral Residential Treatment, 6,* 249–261.

Revell, W. G., Wehman, P., Kregel, J., West, W., & Rayfield, R. (1994). Supported employment for persons with severe disabilities: Positive trends in wages, models and funding. *Education and Training in Mental Retardation and Developmental Disabilities, 29*(4), 256–264.

Roper, P. A. (1990). Special olympics volunteers' perceptions of people with mental retardation. *Education and Training in Mental Retardation, 25,* 164–175.

Schalock, R., Stark, J., Snell, M., Coulter, D., Polloway, E., Luckasson, R., Reiss, S., & Spitalnik, D. (1994). The changing conception of mental retardation: Implications for the field. *Mental Retardation, 32*(3), 181–193.

Schleien, S., & Meyer, L. (1995). *Lifelong leisure curriculum.* Baltimore: Brookes.

Shevin, M., & Klein, N. (1984). The importance of choice-making skills for students with severe disabilities. *Journal of the Association for Persons with Severe Handicaps, 9,* 159–166.

Sileo, T. W., Rude, H. A., & Luchner, J. L. (1988). Collaborative consultation: A model for transition planning for handicapped youth. *Education and Training in Mental Retardation, 23,* 333–339.

Smull, M. W., & Bellamy, G. T. (1991). Community services for adults with disabilities: Policy challenges in the emerging support paradigm. In L. H. Meyer, C. A. Peck, & L. Brown (Eds.), *Critical issues in the lives of people with severe disabilities* (pp. 527–536). Baltimore: Brookes.

Steere, D. E., Wood, R., Pancsofar, E. L., & Butterworth, J. (1990). Outcome-based school-to-work transition planning for students with severe disabilities. *Career Development for Exceptional Individuals, 13*, 57–70.

Summers, J. A. (1986). Who are developmentally disabled adults? A closer look at the definition of developmental disabilities. In J. A. Summers (Ed.), *The right to grow up. An introduction to adults with developmental disabilities* (pp. 3–16). Baltimore: Brookes.

Szymanski, E. M., Hanley-Maxwell, C., & Parker, R. M. (1990). Transdisciplinary planning for supported employment. In F. R. Rusch (Ed.), *Handbook of supported employment: Models, methods, and issues* (pp. 199–214). Chicago: Sycamore.

Szymanski, E. M., King, J., Parker, R. M., & Jenkins, W. M. (1989). The state-federal rehabilitation program: Interface with special education. *The Exceptional Child, 56*, 70–76.

Szymanski, E. M., Linkowski, D. C., Leahy, M. J., Diamond, E. E., & Thoreson, R. W. (1993). Human resource development: An examination of perceived training needs of certified rehabilitation counselors [special issue]. *Rehabilitation Counseling Bulletin, 37*(2), 163–181.

Tarjan, G. (1989). Mental retardation revisited. *Psychiatric Annals, 19*(4), 176–178.

Taylor, L., Adelman, H. S., Nelson, P., Smith, D. C., & Phares, V. (1989). Perceptions of control at school among students in special education programs. *Journal of Learning Disabilities, 22*, 439–443.

Thompson, L., Powers, G., & Houchard, B. (1992). The wage effects of supported employment. *Journal of The Association for Persons with Severe Handicaps, 17*(2), 87–94.

Timothy W. v. Rochester, N.H. School District 875 F. 2d 954 (1st C in 1989).

Turnbull, A. P., & Turnbull, H. R. (1990). *Families, professionals, and exceptionality: A special partnership* (2nd ed.). Columbus, OH: Merrill.

U.S. Department of Education. (1993). *Fifteenth annual report to Congress on the implementation of the Individuals with Disabilities Education Act.* Washington, DC: Department of Education, Office of Special Education and Rehabilitative Services.

Vandercook, T. (1991). Leisure instruction outcomes: Criterion performance, positive interactions, and acceptance by typical high school peers. *Journal of Special Education, 25*(3), 320–329.

Wacker, D. P., Wiggins, B., Fowler, M., & Berg, W. (1988). Training students with profound or multiple handicaps to make requests via microswitches. *Journal of Applied Behavior Analysis, 21*, 331–343.

Ward, M. J. (1993). [Forward]. In P. Wehman (Ed.), *The ADA mandate for social change* (pp. xv–xix). Baltimore: Brookes.

Wehman, P. (1990a). *A national analysis of supported employment growth and implementation.* Richmond: Virginia Commonwealth University, Rehabilitation Research and Training Center on Supported Employment.

Wehman, P. (1990b). School to work: Elements of successful programs. *Teaching Exceptional Children, 23*, 40–43.

Wehman, P. (1992). *Life beyond the classroom.* Baltimore: Brookes.

Wehman, P. (1993). *ADA: A Social Mandate.* Baltimore: Brookes.

Wehman, P. (1995). *Individual transition plans: The teachers curriculum guide for helping youth with special needs.* Austin, TX: PRO-ED.

Wehman, P., & Kregel, J. (1990). Supported employment for persons with severe and profound mental retardation: A critical analysis. *International Journal of Rehabilitative Research, 13*(2), 93–108.

Wehman, P., & Kregel, J. (1995). At the crossroads: Supported employment ten years later. *Journal of the Association for Persons with Severe Handicaps, 20*(4), 286–299.

Wehman, P., Kregel, J., & Seyfarth, J. (1985a). Employment outlook for young adults with mental retardation. *Rehabilitation Counseling Bulletin, (29)*2, 90–99.

Wehman, P., Kregel, J., & Seyfarth, J. (1985b). Transition from school to work for youth with severe handicaps: A follow-up study. *Journal of the Association for Persons with Severe Handicaps, 10*, 132–136.

Wehman, P., Sale, P., & Parent, W. (1992). *Supported employment: Toward integration of workers with disabilities.* Austin, TX: PRO-ED.

West, M. D., & Parent, W. S. (1992). Consumer choice and empowerment in supported employment services: Issues and strategies. *Journal of the Association for Persons with Severe Handicaps, 17*, 47–52.

White, W. J., Alley, G. R., Deshler, D. D., Schumaker, J. B., Warner, M. M., & Clark, F. L. (1982). Are there learning disabilities after high school? *Exceptional Children, 49*, 273–274.

Williams, R. R. (1991). Choices, communication, and control: A call for expanding them in the lives of people with severe disabilities. In L. H. Meyer, C. A. Peck, & L. Brown (Eds.), *Critical issues in the lives of people with severe disabilities.* Baltimore: Brookes.

Wolfe, P. S. (1994). Judgment of the social validity of instructional strategies used in community-based instructional sites. *Journal of the Association for Persons with Severe Handicaps, 19*(1), 43–51.

Wolfensberger, W. (1972). *The principle of normalization in human services.* Toronto, Canada: National Institute on Mental Retardation.

Wolfensberger, W. (1991). Reflections on a lifetime in human services and mental retardation. *Mental Retardation, 29*(1), 1–15.

Yan, X., Mank, D., Sandow, D., Rhodes, L., & Olson, D. (1993). Co-workers' perceptions of an employee with severe disabilities: An analysis of social interactions in a work setting. *Journal of the Association for Persons with Severe Handicaps, 18*(4), 282–291.

Early Intervention

Rebecca Anderson Weissman and David C. Littman

LEARNING GOALS

Upon completion of this chapter the reader will be able to

- provide a rationale for early intervention;
- discuss five guiding philosophies in providing services;
- describe in sequential detail the child assessment process; and
- discuss issues of transition planning, cultural sensitivity, and transdisciplinary staffing.

I f all young children with developmental disabilities and their families had the same resources, priorities, and concerns, then providing state-of-the-art early intervention services would be easy. In such a scenario, a few simple research studies would answer the relatively few questions about how best to serve the uniform population, and turning the research results into practical information would be a straightforward, one-time-only exercise. Curriculum material for teaching early interventionists would be developed, and preparation programs using the material could be established wherever and whenever needed.

The reality is, of course, that the resources, priorities, and concerns of young children with developmental disabilities are incredibly diverse. Early interventionists cannot rely on a few simple research studies that can be easily translated into practical guidelines. Rather, numerous complex studies of families, children, preparation methods for early interventionists, and specific intervention strategies are needed to determine how to serve effectively the diverse population of these young children and their families. Because of the quantity and complexity of the information required to provide early intervention, building the bridge between research and practice is an immense task that cannot be accomplished either by researchers or by practitioners alone.

As a combination team of a practitioner and a researcher, we have tried to consolidate key information about early intervention in a concise, practical, ready-to-use reference. Our goal is to inform practitioners about what information is needed to provide early intervention services to young children with developmental disabilities, where to obtain this information, and how to use it.

The chapter begins with a review of four of the primary reasons we are committed to providing early intervention services. Following this review is a description of five guiding philosophies that appear over and over in models of early intervention services. Then comes the focus of the chapter: content information organized around a four-phase model of service delivery in which assessment, program design, delivery, and program evaluation form a cycle, which starts over when the results of the evaluation are used as part of the assessment for the subsequent trip through the cycle.

WHY PROVIDE EARLY INTERVENTION SERVICES?

- *It's the law.* The Individuals with Disabilities Education Act Amendments of 1991, or IDEA (P.L. 99-457, amended by P.L. 102-119), requires all states to provide a free and appropriate education for children aged 3 through 5 years with disabilities. In addition, it requires states that accept Part H funds to provide services to infants and toddlers, from birth through 2 years of age, with disabilities (Thiele & Hamilton, 1991).

- *It's the best time to begin.* Early intervention focuses on treatment of identified developmental delays and prevention of developmental delays secondary to the identified delays (e.g., reduced cognitive development due to a motor delay or lack of exploration opportunities). Both research results and demonstrated practice show that the earlier a problem is detected and the earlier treatment is begun, the more effective intervention is. Early intervention can alter, in a positive direction, overall development and learning (Lilly & Shotel, 1987).

- *It's cost effective.* Because we are a society with limited resources, we must be concerned with obtaining the most benefit for our expenditures in early intervention. Large-scale research efforts have clearly shown that the longer help is delayed, the more it costs (Ramey & Landesman-Ramey, 1992). Shearer and Mori (1987) put it well: "Early education models funded by the Handicapped Children's Early Education Program (HCEEP) and research findings have amply demonstrated the cost effectiveness of early intervention in terms of ameliorating the effects of handicapping conditions and in *preventing secondary problems* [italics added] that compound the original deficit" (p. 161).

- *It works.* There is no longer any question that early intervention can be effective. There is, of course, controversy about just how effective particular types of early intervention may be for particular types of disabilities (Dunst, 1986; Ramey & Landesman-Ramey, 1992). Clearly, however, well-considered, professionally delivered early intervention services can help virtually any child with a disabling condition, and early intervention saves time, money, and pain.

GUIDING PHILOSOPHIES

This section provides a brief description of five primary guiding philosophies that are integral to successful early intervention. Of course, these philosophies portray the ideal: Programs manifest each of these philosophies to a greater or lesser degree depending on the number of employees, staff preservice and in-service training, and program budget limitations. For example, many teams use consultants who are available for only a small number of hours. This factor may make functioning as a team difficult. Nonetheless, the primary guiding philosophies are important components of early intervention service delivery and deserve special consideration. They are described in more detail in the section on service delivery.

- *Family Involvement.* Early intervention must (according to the intent of IDEA) include the family (Cardinal & Shum, 1993; Diamond & Squires, 1993). Key areas for family involvement include assisting the parents in adapting to the special needs of their young child, assisting the parents to utilize needed community resources, and facilitating mutually satisfying parent–child interactions (Niños Especiales Program, 1986). Support for the parental caregiving role should be a primary focus for services.

- *Service Coordination.* No single professional discipline or agency has all the necessary resources to address all of the needs of a young child with a disability and his or her family. Therefore, service coordination, previously referred to as case management, is meant to provide a coordinated network of service delivery within and across community agencies specific to the needs of each young child and family (see Chapter 15). A single service coordinator, preferably someone who works directly with the young child and family, should be identified for coordinating service delivery.

- *Transdisciplinary Approach.* A transdisciplinary approach requires team members from multiple disciplines and the child's parents as equal team members, all working together as an interdisciplinary team (Orelove & Sobsey, 1992). In addition, active teaching and learning across disciplines should occur as a result of the team process in its delivery of early intervention services (Niños Especiales Program, 1986). This not only enhances service delivery but also reduces the number of personnel directly handling infants and young children, as well as the number of personnel who visit the home. Benefits of the transdisciplinary approach include a more holistic approach to the provision of early intervention services and less intrusion into the daily routines of young children and their families.

- *Transition Planning.* Transition planning requires that intervention goals and instructional strategies reflect the development of skills that will be needed for success in each child's subsequent environment (Chandler, 1993). Transitions frequently encountered in early intervention include (a) hospital to home, (b) home-based services to center-based services, and (c) center-based services to elementary school.

- *Cultural Competence.* Cultural competence is an important issue when a provider of early intervention services is of a cultural heritage different from that of the family and young child receiving services (Lynch & Hanson, 1992). Caretaking and child-rearing practices can differ enormously. Family members will be most responsive to suggestions and strategies that are consistent with their cultural values. Language barriers, cultural roles and norms, and socioeconomic factors are all important considerations for the provision of early intervention services (Barrera, 1993; Bernstein & Stettner-Eaton, 1994).

In the following section, we incorporate these five guiding philosophies into the service delivery cycle. The critical focus for the remainder of this chapter is not why professionals need to provide early intervention services but how.

ASSESSMENT

Monitoring, screening, and assessment, the starting points in early intervention, represent the beginning of the service delivery cycle, which may begin at birth (Diamond & Squires, 1993). If an infant is at risk for a developmental disability, he or she should be monitored by hospital staff or by personnel in local follow-up clinics. Infants are typically monitored at regular intervals, such as every 3 or 4 months, for any signs of delayed development. Children with identified risk factors require more frequent observation. For example, a premature infant born with a very low birth weight of 2 pounds and respiratory distress syndrome needs intense developmental monitoring, even if the outcome, medically, is positive. Infants with medical complications or questionable birth histories who require a stay in the neonatal intensive care unit or who are born to a substance-abusing mother need to be monitored.

The goals of screening in early intervention are to determine quickly whether administration of a complete assessment battery (comprehensive testing in all developmental domains) is necessary and, if so, to determine which assessment tool would be most useful. It is important to note that interventionists who test very young children need significant training (Meissels & Provence, 1990).

On the basis of the screening, infants and young children with poor or questionable results typically are referred to early intervention programs. It is important that early intervention programs have well-established eligibility criteria and referral procedures in place. Early intervention programs should not duplicate screening or assessment activities already performed but should extend the testing and establish services promptly when they are indicated. Sources of referrals may include professionals from medical, educational, and social agencies as well as family members.

The goal of assessment in early intervention is the collection of sufficient information about the child's developmental status, medical status, and related family resources, priorities, and concerns so that needed services can be delivered. Results from an initial assessment battery indicate whether intervention services are necessary and provide a foundation of information on which the Individualized Family Service Plan (IFSP) or Individualized Education Program (IEP) can be built.

The next step of the service delivery cycle—program design—depends largely on the results of the assessment and the additional information collected. To design a service plan, the professional must have extensive knowledge not only of the child's status but also of the family's need for information and support and of the goals they have for their infant or young child. The initial assessment battery provides a baseline against which to compare future health status, developmental growth, and achievement of both child- and family-related goals.

Tools Needed in Early Intervention

Professionals have available to them different types of assessment tools, several developmental domains to test in, and a variety of standardized and criterion-referenced tools (Bricker, 1993; Linder, 1993). It is important not only that the selected instruments demonstrate high levels of validity and reliability but also that interpretation of standardized assessments take into account cultural norms. For example, our experience suggests that for young children of Puerto Rican her-

itage social skills are often slightly above the norm and independent feeding skills are often slightly below the norm (for tests normed on children from an Anglo culture). We believe that cultural differences (not biologic ones) in teaching social and feeding skills are responsible. Whenever possible, the practitioner should use tools that are already normed on the target population with which one intends to use them. When such a match is not possible, the practitioner should note this in the report.

To eliminate some confusion and to expedite the assessment process, we have recommended types of tools to use in an assessment battery and, in some cases, a sample tool that, on the basis of our experience, may be the most helpful to begin with. Table 2.1 provides a sample assessment battery with specific recommendations. The table is intended to assist practitioners and teams of practitioners to develop an early intervention assessment battery. The information is only a beginning point and should in no way be considered complete for all children and families. Table 2.1 includes tools for use with young children aged birth through 5 years and tools for practitioners to use collaboratively with families. The table begins with the category of general information. Before any testing takes place, the assessment battery and its purpose should be fully explained to the family, and written permission should be obtained. When possible, the practitioner should test the child in a familiar environment with familiar objects and ask a family member to help elicit desired behaviors. When either or both conditions are not possible, the practitioner should rely more heavily on parent report than on the behavior (or lack of it) elicited by unfamiliar people in an unfamiliar environment.

Demographic information (e.g., names of family members, their ages, their relationship to the child) should then be collected, along with current medical information (e.g., diagnosis, medications) and a birth history (e.g., length of gestation, weight at birth, APGAR scores, complications).

The next step is to administer a normative assessment tool. With normative assessment tools a

Table 2.1. Sample Assessment Battery in Early Intervention

Type of Tool	Purpose	Specific Recommendations
1. Tools for infants/young children		
General information	Permission slips signed by legal guardian (consent and release of information)	Self-made forms specific to population and program needs are best
	Collect demographic data (child and family)	
	Collect current medical information and birth history	
Normative	Provides a standard score	*Battelle Developmental Inventory* (screening tool included) (Newborg et al., 1984)
	Determines eligibility	
	Overall program evaluation	
Play based	Assists with designing intervention plan for natural environment	*Transdisciplinary Play-Based Assessment* (Linder, 1990)
Criterion referenced	Provides current levels of skill acquisition in all domains	*Carolina Curriculum for Handicapped Infants and Infants At Risk* (0–2) (Johnson-Martin et al., 1986)
	Assists with designing intervention plan	*Carolina Curriculum for Preschoolers with Special Needs* (2–5) (Johnson-Martin et al., 1990)
Language specific	Specifically measures skill acquisition of receptive and expressive language (few language items on other tests at this age)	*Receptive and Expressive Emergent Language Scale* (Bzoch & League, 1970)
	Assists with designing intervention plan	
Behavior specific	Measures general behavioral characteristics (items not on other tests)	*Carolina Record of Individual Behavior* (Simeonsson, 1979)
	Assists with designing intervention plan	
Clinical evaluations	Conducted by specialists as needed	Team decision after reviewing previous test results; for example, team decides clinical physical-therapy evaluation is necessary
	Answers remaining questions	
	Assists with designing intervention plan; for example, motor items tested within normal limits but quality of movement is poor	
2. Family tools		
Community resources	Identifies services received from other local agencies and frequency of contact	Self-made checklist consisting of all local medical, educational, and social agencies, name of contact person, phone number, and frequency of use
	Identifies gaps in services	
	Facilitates service coordination and interagency communication	
	Assists with designing intervention plan	
Information	Allows caretakers to request and utilize information of current importance to them	Self-made checklist specific to population served
	Assists with designing intervention plan	Need corresponding written pamphlets to distribute
Support	Primary caretaker identifies resources, priorities, and concerns regarding routine child-care tasks	*Family-Focused Intervention Rating Scale* (Dunst, 1983)
	Assists with designing intervention plan	

child's developmental status can be compared with that of other children at the same chronological age. A standard or percentile score of 100 is considered average (mean). A normative tool helps practitioners determine eligibility for services by indicating how far away from the mean a given child's score is. Over time, a normative tool establishes a pattern indicating whether a child is progressing closer to the mean or moving farther from it. When combined with other sources, these data can be a valuable measure of a program's effectiveness (e.g., at preventing secondary causes of developmental delays). Note that young children with severe disabilities or progressive diseases will most likely move farther away from the mean as they age. For these populations, one should expect this pattern and use the information to describe the population (e.g., when seeking additional resources). Normative tools (typically) are not the best for purposes of program planning. They often contain test items (e.g., standing on one foot) that are not functional skills to teach. Therefore, it is necessary to use play-based observation and/or criterion-referenced tools.

Play-based observation is an assessment process that is dynamic and ongoing. It occurs in a natural setting with people and materials with which the child is already comfortable. It is a flexible, useful measure that provides an individual set of characteristics needed for program planning. The transdisciplinary play-based assessment model is developmental, transdisciplinary, and holistic. A team consisting of the child's parents and professionals from representative disciplines, knowledgeable about all areas of child development, gathers information about the child that includes developmental level, learning style, interaction patterns, and other relevant behaviors. Ongoing communication between the parents and team members is a key component (Linder, 1990).

Criterion-referenced tools provide specific information on the skills a child can and cannot do. Many criterion-referenced tests include all developmental domains, and some include a correlating curriculum. These instruments are helpful for program planning as well as for documenting the achievement of new skills.

A language-specific tool is an important inclusion in an early childhood assessment battery. Language delays are common, as evidenced by the numerous language-based preschool programs in existence. Also children with expressive language delays often receive poor scores on cognition measures because test items in this area may require a verbal response. It is important for the practitioner to determine whether assistive technology will be needed to facilitate interactive communication. A language-specific tool may help provide a more accurate picture.

Behavior-specific items may be observed during a play observation but typically are not included on the other types of tools previously mentioned. A measure of behavioral characteristics (e.g., ability to console the self) provides helpful information for the development of intervention strategies.

Clinical observations, usually conducted by a specialist, should be utilized when any questions remain unanswered. For example, a child might obtain test results within normal limits for motor development (e.g., walks independently but gait is abnormal). When the quality of motor movement is poor, the child should be referred for a physical-therapy evaluation.

Practitioners serving young children aged 3 through 5 years are required to develop an IEP (not an IFSP). However, we strongly recommend that practitioners serving this age group also address family resources, priorities, and concerns even though formal goals that address family-desired outcomes are not required. In our experience, when global family needs are addressed and met (e.g., obtaining food stamps or respite care), family members then actively seek specific information and skills to facilitate the development of their child. We hypothesize that as global needs are met, family members have more time, energy, and desire to devote to more specific activities that directly relate to the child's development. Practitioners must help families identify their priorities and concerns, make the appropriate referrals, and follow up on them. The following tools are helpful in achieving these goals.

A checklist of community resources facilitates service coordination and interagency coordination. It also assists with designing an intervention plan. We recommend that program personnel develop a self-made checklist specific to the community they serve. This checklist should include all medical agencies that serve young children (e.g., hospitals, clinics, private physicians), educational and intervention programs (e.g., infant programs, day-care centers, preschool programs, Head Start programs), and social agencies (e.g., agencies that provide food stamps, housing, counseling, job training). For each agency listed, the form should include the name of the contact person and his or her telephone number. An additional section should provide space for the frequency of use by the family receiving services.

In addition, we recommend an information checklist that is specific to the population served. This form allows parents to identify what written information they are most interested in receiving at that time. Obviously, the correlating written information (e.g., pamphlets) must be available. Topic areas should include specific disabilities (e.g., cerebral palsy, Down's syndrome), typical early childhood topics (e.g., feeding, bedtime, toileting), developmental information (e.g., how to facilitate key developmental milestones), and community resources.

Another support tool that is recommended is one that allows a primary caretaker to identify resources as well as priorities and concerns with regard to routine child-care tasks. This tool should focus on the family's daily routine, such as bathing, feeding, and playing. We recommend the *Family Focused Interview Rating Scale* (Dunst, 1983). This tool asks caretakers to identify which family member performs a given task and to rate how enjoyable or difficult it is. This tool is helpful for initiating dialogue with the family about the stresses in their life caused by caring for a young child with a disability.

Other possible tools include those that measure other areas of parental stress or of the home environment. A word of caution is necessary, however. It is not the practitioner's role to judge or "assess" family functioning. It is the practitioner's role to assist family members to identify their own resources (e.g., knowledge about child development) and priorities and concerns (e.g., respite care) from the family's perspective. Taking prompt, direct action to assist families to build on their resources and to address their identified priorities and concerns is a great method for establishing trust between family and practitioners.

Consolidating the Information

Once an assessment battery is completed, the next step is a team meeting. We recommend administration of all instruments within 1 month. Each team member should summarize his or her results. It is most helpful if a single summary page is completed at the meeting. A summary page should include overall test scores for the young child; identify areas needing intervention; list family-identified resources, priorities, and concerns; and indicate dates for future testing. The development of the intervention plan (whether an IEP or an IFSP) with the family and team members is now underway!

Figure 2.1 illustrates a simple checklist of items that we believe are essential. If most items are not completed for your team at this time, begin with a series of team meetings, prioritize goals and timelines, and share responsibility for completing these tasks. We have found that the checklist is a valuable roadmap to completing this process.

DESIGNING EARLY INTERVENTION SERVICES

With the advent of IDEA, an IFSP is mandatory for any family receiving services under Part H (ages birth to 3 years); IEPs are mandatory for children needing special services (ages 3 through 5 years). Because many practitioners are already

Item	Completed (yes/no)	If Not, When	By Whom
1. Written eligibility criteria (correlates with program mission, state and federal regulations)			
2. Written referral procedures A) receiving B) sending			
3. Written screening/assessment procedures a. Begins with a screening tool (unless completed before referral) b. Outlines typical sequence of tools c. Tools are valid and reliable d. Tools are culturally competent (or adjusted and reported) e. Infant/young child tools 　Normative referenced test 　Play-based assessment 　Criterion-referenced test 　Test of language acquisition 　Test specific to behavior 　Additional clinical evaluation Family tools 　Community resources 　Need for information 　Need for support			
4. Assessment summary a. Is conducted at a team meeting b. Identifies a service coordinator c. Is informative to outside agencies d. Summary report includes 　Schedule of future testing 　Present levels of functioning 　Family resources, priorities, and concerns			

Figure 2.1. Assessment checklist for early intervention programs.

familiar with IEPS, the focus of this section is on designing IFSPs.

An IFSP is required to document family status (resources, priorities, and concerns) and to develop family-oriented goals and objectives. It is important to use strategies in service delivery that build on family strengths. It is also important to assist families in their problem-solving efforts (Garshelis & McConnell, 1993). Addressing family resources, priorities, and concerns requires an

additional set of strategies and services not required by an IEP. An IFSP is a comprehensive written plan of action developed collaboratively with the family, service coordinator, and other team members (Niños Especiales Program, 1987).

Table 2.2 includes a list of the legal requirements of an IFSP, descriptions of these requirements, where applicable, tools from the sample assessment battery that provide this information, and related examples as they might appear on an IFSP.

Table 2.2. Individualized Family Service Plan (IFSP) Contents, Requirements, and Examples

IFSP Requirements	Descriptions	Related Tools	Sample Item
Present levels of child development in all domains	Domains include cognition, receptive/expressive language, gross and fine motor skills, self-help, and social–emotional development	*Transdisciplinary Play-Based Assessment* (Linder, 1990), *Battelle Developmental Inventory* (Newborg, Stock, & Wnek, 1984), *Carolina Curriculum for Handicapped Infants and Preschoolers* (Johnson-Martin, Attermeier, & Hackner, 1990; Johnson-Martin, Jens, & Attermeier, 1986)	Gross-motor skills: Jerry is able to sit independently although muscle tone is slightly low. Pull to stand is emerging.
Statement of resources, priorities, and concerns	Statement of family-desired outcomes relating to the enhancement of the child's development	Potentially all family tools used	Parents report a strong network of family and friends. Ms. Smith (mother) is interested in written information on Down syndrome. Mr. Smith (father) is interested in visiting preschool programs in the local community.
Identification of a service coordinator	Person responsible for facilitating clear communication between self, family, other team members, and community agencies		Jennifer Reilly, infant specialist.
Long-term goals and short-term objectives	Expected outcomes to be achieved by child and family, written in measurable terms including: criteria, procedures, and timelines used to determine degree of progress	Potentially all child and family tools used	Long-term goal: Jerry will walk independently. Short-term objective: Jerry will pull to stand and maintain a standing position, with support provided at hip level from Ms. Smith, for 5 consecutive minutes during three consecutive home visits.
Specific early intervention services	A list of all services that address the unique needs of child and family including: method, frequency, and dates of initiated and anticipated duration of services	Community resources checklist	Nutrition services from county child and family services agency. One visit per month.
Steps for transition	A list of activities that support the move of the child from one service delivery setting to another; includes documenting activities such as parent information, visitations and selection of new site, communication with staff at new site, follow-up phone calls	Potentially all child and family tools used (although indirectly)	Appointments will be scheduled for parents and infant specialist to visit each of the three local preschool programs within 2 months.
Parental consent			

Figure 2.2 also contains a checklist for developing an IFSP. We recommend the use of this checklist during team meetings.

DELIVERING EARLY INTERVENTION SERVICES

Three issues arise in the service delivery phase of the early intervention cycle: where services are delivered, who delivers the services, and how the five guiding philosophies appear as real concerns when delivering services.

1. Where should services be delivered? A primary concern when delivering services is location. Ideally a continuum of options exists. Three typical options include home-based service (service providers visit families at home), center-based service (preschool, day-care center), and a combination of the two.

Delivering services in the home might be the option of choice when the focus of the intervention is facilitating parent–child interactions, providing significant support services to the family, or serving an extremely medically fragile child (in some cases services may need to begin in the hospital) (Lowenthal, 1994). Center-based services are usually the option of choice when intervention emphasizes peer interaction or a primary caretaker is unavailable for home visits. Children typically make the transition from home-based to center-based services between the ages of 2 and 3 years. However, age alone should not determine the location of services because individual child and family needs should play the major role.

2. Who should deliver services? The answer to this question is complex. Medical personnel (e.g., nurse, occupational therapist), educational personnel (e.g., infant specialist, special educator), and social services personnel (e.g., social worker, psychologist) compose an interdiscipli-

Item	Comments
1. Legal requirements	
a. Present levels of performance _____	
b. Schedule of future evaluations _____	
c. Statement of resources, priorities, and concerns _____	
d. Service coordinator	
e. Goals and objectives _____	
f. Specific services _____	
g. Transition plan _____	
h. Signature of legal guardian _____	
2. Goals and objectives	
a. Assessment results _____	
b. Desired outcomes and needs of the family _____	
c. Increased independence for child and family _____	
d. Terminology used is understandable to all _____	
3. Intervention strategies	
a. Are comprehensive and collaborative _____	
b. Build on identified strengths _____	
c. Address unique priorities and concerns _____	
d. Result from team decisions _____	
e. Are culturally competent _____	

Figure 2.2.   Individualized Family Service Plan checklist.

nary team. Team members ideally provide a variety of direct services, meet regularly, and provide ongoing consultation and training to each other.

The services to be provided should be a team decision and should be documented in the intervention plan. Decisions should be based on family input, assessment results, and team discussion. The decisions should also address these questions: Which team is best equipped to provide a comprehensive set of services, including service coordination, to a specific child and family? Which team members need to be available to provide training and consultation to the primary service providers of the intervention plan? Is someone outside the team needed for a specific service?

3. What is the role of the guiding philosophies? The guiding philosophies, first mentioned in the introduction of this chapter, play a significant role in the implementation of an intervention plan. We therefore provide a goal statement for each guiding philosophy and follow it with a brief "real-life" scenario.

Family Involvement

The primary goal of family involvement is to assist each family in maintaining or developing a sense of confidence and competence with respect to their caretaking role.

....

CASE EXAMPLE: CARMEN

Part of the caretaking role includes medical appointments. Rosa, a young mother of a premature infant, Carmen, requested the support of her home visitor (an early child special educator) when attending medical visits for her daughter. Now that she was at home following a lengthy stay in the neonatal intensive care unit, Carmen needed to visit a nurse practitioner monthly (for evaluation and monitoring of health care issues, including asthma). Carmen was also scheduled to visit a neurologist (for evaluation and monitoring of neuromotor development) and

an ophthalmologist (because of retinopathy) routinely.

After further discussion, Rosa revealed that she felt intimidated and overwhelmed by so many medical appointments for her daughter. Rosa speaks English well, but it is her second language. She sometimes felt uncomfortable asking questions during these medical appointments. Rosa felt most comfortable with the nurse practitioner because they spoke on the phone frequently and had already developed a rapport.

The home visitor agreed to accompany Rosa on several visits to the neurologist and the ophthalmologist. The purpose of this level of support was to assist Rosa in feeling confident and competent in her new caretaking role. The home visitor provided initial support with her presence, reassured Rosa that her questions were appropriate and that she had a right to ask them, and faded support (e.g., called Rosa after a visit) as Rosa's comfort level with this activity increased. Note that the home visitor did not take over the caretaking function by asking questions for Rosa.

....

Service Coordination

The primary goal of service coordination in early intervention is the coordination of overall service delivery with a community focus.

....

CASE EXAMPLE: CHRISTOPHER

A 3-year-old boy, Christopher, attends a local integrated preschool program. Christopher has spina bifida, and his service providers include a nursery school teacher, a physical therapist, an occupational therapist, and a nurse. The team, including his parents, felt most comfortable with the physical therapist also serving as the service coordinator.

Service coordination services provided by the physical therapist include meeting regularly with other team members to discuss Christopher's needs (e.g., helping him learn to maneuver his new wheelchair), writing notes to his parents about his school activities, inviting the family and their social worker to important meetings, maintaining all records on Christopher, and attending medical visits as necessary (e.g., when his wheelchair needed altering; Diamond & Squires, 1993).

Transdisciplinary Approach

The primary goal of utilizing a transdisciplinary approach within an interdisciplinary team is to provide ongoing, active consultation and needed training across disciplines.

CASE EXAMPLE: JOHN

A 6-month-old infant, John, and his father have been receiving home visits from both an infant specialist and a physical therapist. The father's primary concern is John's high muscle tone. Although John responds positively to social interactions, he is not yet initiating them. The infant specialist and the physical therapist decided to train each other in specific activities and strategies necessary to facilitate increased initiations of social play and increased motor development, respectively. This transdisciplinary approach eliminated the need for two isolated intervention programs for John. A consolidated approach included joint home visits initially while the infant specialist and physical therapist trained each other. Additional features of the program were exchange of related written information; alternating home visits after training was complete (each professional taking responsibility for addressing both goal areas simultaneously with John and his father); continued consultation (meetings and by phone); and additional joint visits as needed to update activities for John.

Transition Planning

The primary goal of transition planning is to help assure success for each child when moving from one setting of service delivery to another.

CASE EXAMPLE: JANET

Janet is 4 years old and has been attending a local Head Start program as well as receiving speech and language services. She has made significant improvement in her use of spontaneous language. Some sounds, however, are still difficult to understand, and it is expected that she will continue to need speech therapy next year when she enters kindergarten.

A transition plan for Janet began 1 year prior to discharge. Transition activities included providing information to the family and the public elementary school about Janet and her expected needs; scheduling a team meeting that included the family and a representative from the elementary school, such as the principal; assisting parents in visiting recommended programs; selecting a kindergarten placement (an IEP was developed by a team that comprised parents and current and new staff); inviting the kindergarten teacher and the speech therapist to a team meeting to review Janet's current progress and to ask questions; forwarding records to the new placement site; scheduling a time for Janet to visit her new classroom; and follow-up phone calls made by the service coordinator to family and new staff working with Janet (2 weeks after class started).

Cultural Competence

The primary goals of cultural competence are to embed intervention suggestions and strategies into routine family life, maintain family involvement, and provide services consistent with the needs of a minority population.

CASE EXAMPLE: ROBERTO

Roberto is an 18-month-old boy with Down syndrome. He and his family have recently migrated from Puerto Rico. Culturally competent services to this family included a Spanish-speaking home visitor; extensive support services (instead of referrals, direct assistance dealing with other community agencies was provided such as helping the father enroll in English classes); including the aunt (a frequent caretaker) as well as the mother in decisions about intervention goals and strategies; learning about the family's culture; and respecting the family's right to maintain their language, values, and customs.

In summary, service delivery must be comprehensive. By ensuring that early intervention services are genuinely family oriented and culturally competent, by utilizing a service coordinator and a transdisciplinary approach, and by preparing for transitions, practitioners will indeed be providing services that are comprehensive.

PROGRAM EVALUATION

Everybody hates evaluation but everybody's got to do it. Fortunately, there is another way to look at evaluation, and it is the way that we suggest in this chapter: "Evaluation involves figuring out what we (the team) did well and what we can do better."

The primary viewpoint of this chapter is that early intervention is an ongoing cycle of activities that does not culminate in, but begins anew, with evaluation. Thus, rather than feeling pressured by evaluation—feeling that evaluation is the point at which one is tested to see whether one has performed well enough—practitioners should use evaluation as a device for answering the most important question that faces us all in early intervention: What should we do next? Our view of

evaluation, then, is that its primary role should be *formative* rather than *summative*.

Summative evaluation addresses questions of an early intervention program's effectiveness at the end of the program's life. That is, summative evaluation occurs only once—when the child no longer needs intervention services. Formative evaluation, on the other hand, occurs during the entire intervention process. Formative evaluation helps early interventionists determine how to improve services for individual children and is, therefore, much more important within the four-phase cycle of early intervention.

We describe here four evaluation problems that early interventionists have frequently asked us to help them with, and we give what we hope will be useful, usable answers. Table 2.3 lists each of the four evaluation problems and offers brief suggestions for addressing each from the formative viewpoint.

Evaluating Developmental Progress

The evaluation of a child's progress is crucial for the effective improvement of early intervention services. Because the goal of early intervention is progress of the child through controlled, directed change, it is necessary to monitor the child's status at frequent intervals so that change can be controlled effectively (Bricker, 1993; Bricker & Littman, 1982). Hence, formative evaluation of the child's progress must be a major emphasis. Formative evaluation information should be collected from all team members, and all team members should be aware of all the information. If all members of the team know the results of the frequent evaluations of the child's status, then the results can be used formatively when it is useful to modify or redesign the child's intervention plan. Table 2.3 suggests those aspects of a child's performance that are useful in this kind of formative evaluation and that seem best addressed by criterion-referenced measures and play-based observations.

Table 2.3. Program Evaluation Suggestions

Evaluation Program	Suggested Frequency
Child's Progress	
Individual	Frequent: Use for IFSP or IEP modification (e.g., tools listed in Table 2.1)
All enrolled	Occasional: Use to improve procedures for IFSP or IEP modifications (e.g., tools listed in Table 2.1)
Family-Desired Outcomes	
Individual	As above (e.g., tools listed in Table 2.1)
All enrolled	As above (e.g., tools listed in Table 2.1)
Consumer Satisfaction	
Families	Frequent: Use to improve trust and involvement (e.g., survey)
Other agencies	Occasional: Use to insure effective interagency coordination (e.g., survey)
Program Effectiveness	Occasional: To improve one or more phases of service delivery cycle (collective/all measures)

Note. IEP = Individualized Education Program; IFSP = Individualized Family Service Plan.

Children who are being evaluated summatively (e.g., before transition to a new service delivery setting) can be assessed with both norm-referenced and criterion-referenced assessments. The norm-referenced assessments give the subsequent service professionals an objective picture of the child compared with other children, and the criterion-referenced and play-based observation measures provide information that can be extremely useful in devising new intervention goals.

Evaluating Family-Desired Outcomes

As it is for the child, the focus of evaluation for the family is formative. Interventionists should always have the goal of supporting the family to adapt to changes within the family structure and the social environment. Because the goals specified in a family intervention plan typically focus on directed adaptive change, keeping track of

whether the intervention strategies are producing the desired change is vital (e.g., Are family-desired outcomes attained?). This approach requires formative evaluation that identifies areas in which the direction of change under the current intervention plan is appropriate and other areas of change that may benefit from shifts in intervention strategies.

Evaluating Consumer Satisfaction

If people are not happy either with the help they receive or with the people who help them, they are likely either to drop out of the service system entirely or to go "shopping" for a "better" situation. One of the most important roles of formative evaluation is, therefore, to provide practitioners a constant awareness of how families feel. Perhaps more than any of the other three evaluation problems, consumer satisfaction requires frequent monitoring (e.g., by survey).

Evaluating Overall Program Outcome

Even when the overall program outcome is evaluated and summative evaluation intuitively seems most appropriate, the evaluation should be performed with a view to program improvement. Although many evaluation techniques commonly associated with summative evaluation are used for this purpose (e.g., pre- and postintervention measurements), the interpretation of the measures can and should be used formatively with the main goal of improving the program.

Realistic, useful evaluation is conducted for one simple reason: to determine what to do next to improve whatever one is evaluating. Evaluation feeds into all four phases of the service delivery cycle described in this chapter. Indeed, formative evaluation of the evaluation procedures themselves can be an extremely valuable activity and should be undertaken whenever one has the feeling that "something is wrong (or right!) but I just cannot put my finger on it." Evaluation is the process of putting one's finger on the problem. Thus, addressing any of the four evaluation problems described previously can have a significant impact on the assessment, design, delivery, or program evaluation phase of the early intervention cycle.

FINAL THOUGHTS

We have suggested that early intervention should be viewed as a cycle of four interrelated phases. Beginning with assessment, the early intervention cycle proceeds to program design, delivery, and evaluation. Evaluation serves the purpose of providing valuable information that can be used to improve the service delivery on the next pass through the cycle. Of course, this is an abstract view of the process that is useful for presenting the material we wanted to communicate. If our readers now believe that the phases are not really laid out in a line but instead feed back and forth into one another, they are correct.

To assist readers who would like more detailed information, a brief resource list (books and journals) is provided in Appendix 2.1. The categories include assessment, families (working with them), general (early intervention), medical, parents (especially for them), and technology. Numerous resources are available at university libraries. We have selected a few that may be most helpful.

Our goal has been to help service delivery personnel see their activities as an integral part of a community-wide service delivery system. Knowledge is the key to power and if we have given you any knowledge that has empowered you (as we hope you will empower the children and families you serve), then we are satisfied.

APPENDIX 2.A
KEY RESOURCES IN EARLY INTERVENTION

Assessment

Bailey, D., & Woolery, M. (1994). *Assessing infants and preschoolers with handicaps.* Columbus, OH: Merrill.

Bergen, D. (1994). *Assessment methods for infants and toddlers: Transdisciplinary team approaches.* New York: Teachers College Press.

Gibbs, E. D., & Teti, D. M. (Eds.). (1990). *Interdisciplinary assessment of infants.* Baltimore: Brookes.

Linder, T. W. (1990). *Transdisciplinary Play-Based Assessment* (rev.). Baltimore: Brookes.

Meissels, S., & Provence, S. (1989). *Screening and assessment: Guidelines for identifying young disabled and developmentally vulnerable children and their families.* Washington, DC: National Center for Clinical Infant Programs.

Families (Working with Them)

Bailey, D. B., McWilliam, P. J., & Simeonson, R. J. (1992). *Implementing family-centered services on early intervention: A team-based model for change.* Cambridge, MA: Brookline Books.

Bennett, T., Lingerfelt, B. V., & Nelson, D. E. (1990). *Developing individualized family support plans: A training manual.* Cambridge, MA: Brookline Books.

Dunst, C., Trivette, C., & Deal, A. (1988). *Enabling and empowering families: Principles and guidelines for practice.* Cambridge, MA: Brookline Books.

Healy, A., Kessee, P., & Smith, B. (1989). *Early services for children with special needs: Transaction for family support.* Baltimore: Brookes.

Johnson, B. H., McGonigel, M. J., & Kaufman, R. K. (1991). *Guidelines and recommended practices for the individualized family service plan* (2nd ed.). Bethesda, MD: Association for the Care of Children's Health.

Lynch, E. W., & Hanson, M. J. (Eds.). (1992). *Developing cross-cultural competence: A guide for working with young children and their families.* Baltimore: Brookes.

McWilliam, R. A. (1992). *Family-centered intervention planning: A routine-based approach.* Tucson, AZ: Communication Skill Builders.

General

Bricker, D. (1989). *Early intervention for at-risk and handicapped infants, toddlers and preschool children.* [VORT Corporation, P.O. Box 60132, Palo Alto, CA 94306.]

Bricker, D., & Cripe, J. J. W. (1992). *An activity-based approach to early intervention.* Baltimore: Brookes.

Brown, W., Turman, S. K., & Pearl, L. F. (Eds.). (1993). *Family-centered early intervention with infants and toddlers: Innovative cross-disciplinary approaches.* Baltimore: Brookes.

Johnson, L. J., Gallagher, R. J., LaMontagne, M. J., Jordan, J. B., Gallagher, J. J., Hutinger, P. L., & Karnes, M. B. (Eds.). (1994). *Meeting early intervention challenges: Issues from birth to three.* Baltimore: Brookes.

Linder, T. W. (1983). *Early childhood special education program development and administration.* Baltimore: Brookes.

Meissels, S. J., & Shonkoff, J. P. (1988). *Handbook of early childhood intervention: Theory, practice and analysis.* Baltimore: Brookes.

Odom, S. L. *Journal of Early Intervention* [Division Manager, CEC, 1920 Association Drive, Reston, VA 22091.]

Odom, S. L., & Karnes, M. B. (1988). *Early intervention for infants and children with handicaps.* Baltimore: Brookes.

Topics in Early Childhood Special Education (journal). [PRO-ED, 8700 Shoal Creek Boulevard, Austin, TX, 78757.]

Parents

Dinkmeyer, D., McKay, G. D., & Dinkmeyer, J. S. (1989). *Early Childhood Step: Systematic Training for Effective Parenting of Children Under Six* [includes video]. Circle Pines, MN: American Guidance Service.

Featherstone, H. (1980). *A difference in the family: Living with a disabled child.* New York: Basic Books.

Finne, N. (1974). *Handling the young cerebral palsied child at home.* New York: Dalton.

Greenspan, S., & Greenspan, N. T. (1985). *First feelings: Milestones in the emotional development of your baby and child.* New York: Viking.

Harrison, H. (1983). *The premature baby book: A parent's guide to coping and caring in the first years.* New York: St. Martins Press.

Parks, S. (1986). *Make every step count: Birth to one year.* Palo Alto, CA: VORT Corporation.

Special Care: For Families of Preterm and High Risk Infants [magazine]. San Diego, CA: Special Care Productions.

Zipper, I. N., Hinton, C., Weil, M., & Rounds, K. (1993). *Family-centered service coordination: A manual for parents.* Cambridge, MA: Brookline Books.

Medical

Batshaw, M. L., & Perrett, Y. M. (1992). *Children with disabilities: A medical primer* (3rd ed.). Baltimore: Brookes.

Blackman, J. A. (Ed.). *Infants and Young Children: An Interdisciplinary Journal of Special Care Practices.* Frederick, MD: Aspen.

Blackman, J. A. (1984). *Medical aspects of developmental disabilities in children birth to three.* Rockville, MD: Aspen.

Ensher, G. L., & Clark, D. A. (1986). *Newborns at risk: Medical care and psychoeducational intervention.* Rockville, MD: Aspen.

Technology

Goossens, C., & Crain, S. (1986). *Augmentative Communication Assessment Resource.* Birmingham, AL: Sparks Center for Developmental and Learning Disorders.

Goossens, C., & Crain, S. (1986). *Communication Assessment Resource.* Birmingham, AL: Sparks Center for Developmental and Learning Disorders.

REFERENCES

Barrera, I. (1993). Effective and appropriate instruction for all children: The challenge of cultural/linguistic diversity in young children with special needs. *Topics in Early Childhood Special Education, 13*(4), 461–487.

Bernstein, H., & Stettner-Eaton, B. (1994). Cultural inclusion in Part H: Systems development. *Infant Toddler Intervention, 4*(1), 1–10.

Bricker, D. (1993). *Assessment, evaluation, and programming system for infants and children—Measurement for birth to three years* (Vol. 1). Baltimore: Brookes.

Bricker, D., & Littman, D. (1982). Intervention and evaluation: The inseparable mix. *Topics in Early Childhood Special Education, 1*, 23–33.

Bzoch, K., & League, R. (1970). *The Receptive–Expressive Emergent Language Scale for the Measurement of Language Skills in Infancy.* Gainsville, FL: Tree of Life Press.

Cardinal, D., & Shum, K. (1993). A descriptive analysis of family related services in the neonatal intensive care unit. *Journal of Early Intervention, 17*(3), 270–282.

Chandler, L. K. (1993). Steps in preparing for transition: Preschool to kindergarten. *Teaching Exceptional Children, 25*, 52–56.

Diamond, K., & Squires, J. (1993). The role of parental report in the screening and assessment of young children. *Journal of Early Intervention, 17*(2), 107–115.

Dunst, C. J. (1983). *Family-Focused Intervention Rating Scales.* Morganton, NC: Family, Infant and Preschool Program, Western Carolina Center.

Dunst, C. J. (1986). Overview of the efficacy of early intervention programs. In L. Bickman & D. L. Weathersford (Eds.), *Evaluating early intervention programs for severely handicapped children and their families.* Austin, TX: PRO-ED.

Education of the Handicapped Act Amendments of 1986, 20 U.S.C. § 1472.

Garshelis, J., & McConnell, S. (1993). Comparison of family needs assessed by mothers, individual professionals, and interdisciplinary teams. *Journal of Early Intervention, 17*(1), 36–49.

Individuals with Disabilities Education Act of 1990, Title 20, U.S.C. 1400–1485. *U.S. Statutes at Large, 104,* 1103–1151.

Johnson-Martin, N. M., Attermeier, S. M., & Hackner, B. (1990). *The Carolina Curriculum for Preschoolers with Special Needs.* Baltimore: Brookes.

Johnson-Martin, N. M., Jens, K., & Attermeier, S. (1986). *The Carolina Curriculum for Handicapped Infants and Infants At-Risk.* Baltimore: Brookes.

Lilly, T. J., & Shotel, J. R. (1987). Legal issues and the handicapped infant: From policy to reality. *Journal of the Division for Early Childhood, 12,* 4–12.

Linder, T. W. (1990). *Transdisciplinary play-based assessment: A functional approach to working with young children.* Baltimore: Brookes.

Linder, T. (1993). *Transdisciplinary play-based intervention: Guidelines for developing a meaningful curriculum for young children.* Baltimore: Brookes.

Lowenthal, V. (1994). Collaborative training in the education of early childhood educators. *Teaching Exceptional Children, 8,* 25–31.

Lynch, E. W., & Hanson, M. J. (1992). *Developing cross-cultural competence: A guide for working with young children and their families.* Baltimore: Brookes.

Meissels, S., & Provence, S. (1990). *Screening and assessment.* Washington, DC: National Center for Clinical Infant Programs.

Newborg, J., Stock, J., & Wnek, L. (1984). *Battelle Developmental Inventory.* Allen, TX: DLM-Teaching Resources.

Niños Especiales Program: A comprehensive guide to serving Puerto Rican families in early intervention. (1986). Unpublished manual. Farmington, CT: Pediatric Research & Training Center.

Niños Especiales Program: An introduction to individual family service plans in early childhood special education. (1987). Unpublished workbook. Farmington, CT: Pediatric Research & Training Center.

Orelove, F. P., & Sobsey, D. (1992). *Educating children with multiple disabilities* (2nd ed.). Baltimore: Brookes.

Ramey, C., & Landesman-Ramey, S. (1992). Effective early intervention. *Mental Retardation, 30*(6), 337–345.

Shearer, M. S., & Mori, A. A. (1987). Administration of preschool special education programs: Strategies for effectiveness. *Journal for the Division for Early Childhood, 11,* 161–170.

Simeonsson, R. (1979). *Carolina Record of Individual Behavior.* Chapel Hill, NC: School of Education and Frank Porter Graham Child Development.

Thiele, J. E., & Hamilton, J. L. (1991). Implementing the early childhood formula: Programs under P.L. 99-457. *Journal of Early Intervention, 15,* 5–12.

Going to School

Kathryn A. Blake, Paul Sale, and Lisa M. Ehrhart

LEARNING GOALS

Upon completion of this chapter the reader will be able to

- describe the instructional model sequence that should be used in teaching children with disabilities;

- describe the Individualized Education Program (IEP) and the process for development and implementation;

- discuss and review the merits of inclusion of students with disabilities into general education classrooms; and

- list and describe the key elements of the Individuals with Disabilities Education Act of 1990 (IDEA), such as nondiscriminating evaluation and due process.

In this chapter, we focus on ways to solve problems subsumed under the general problem of how to select and deliver the most appropriate special education services for students with developmental disabilities. At the same time, we consider a frequently occurring concurrent problem—the many times severely disabled, multiply disabled youngsters are labeled retarded or less intelligent than they really are because their disabilities and the resulting deprivation of experience prevent them from developing and expressing the intellectual abilities they have. Given this label, they are treated as less intelligent. In turn, given this treatment, they function at a less intelligent level. This sequence of labeling, lowered expectancy, and self-fulfilling prophecy can lead to some terrible mistakes. On the other hand, if the sequence is broken, there can be some incredible victories (e.g., see Brown, 1955, and Lee & Jackson, 1991).

One should consider Helen Keller as a keystone to understanding the general problem of how to select and deliver the most appropriate special education services for students with developmental disabilities and the concurrent problem of labeling, lowered expectancy, and self-fulfilling prophecy.

••

CASE EXAMPLE: HELEN

Helen was the child of well-to-do parents. She was born in rural Alabama in the late 1800s. Her case is classic. She developed normally until she was about 18 months old. Then, following a childhood illness, she developed encephalitis. In turn, the brain destruction caused by the encephalitis left her blind and deaf. In addition, she did not have speech and language because the illness occurred while she was still prelingual or while she was just beginning to learn language. The Kellers tried diligently to obtain services for Helen, but few were available in that time and place. Therefore, Helen reached middle childhood without intervention. In the parlance of the day, Helen might have been called feebleminded. She did not have speech and language, she behaved socially and emotionally at an early childhood level, and she showed little comprehension of her environment. At this point, the Kellers found Annie Sullivan. Annie recognized Helen's intellectual brilliance and potential for learning. She communicated to Helen the concept of language that symbols represent concrete and abstract entities. Given Helen's grasp of this concept of language and the technique of finger spelling in the hand, Annie helped Helen develop the strengths that helped to circumvent her limitations. Finally, Helen graduated from Radcliffe College and became a world-renowned author and lecturer. Detailed accounts of Helen Keller's life can be found in such works as Joseph Lash's *Helen and Teacher* (1990) and Helen's writings, for example, *The Story of My Life* (1903), "Three Days to See" (1933), and *The World I Live In* (1938).

More specifically then, the problem in providing special education services to students with mental retardation and other developmental disabilities is to describe the limitations caused by their disabilities, to go beyond these limitations to find their strengths, and to build a program of services that will capitalize on their strengths and circumvent their limitations. Above all, the task for professionals is not to miss the Helen Kellers among us, that is, not to use too quickly the label "severely mentally retarded" and with that label make the errors of lowered expectancies and the self-fulfilling prophecy.

This chapter is devoted to special education services that one can use to help solve problems in dealing with students with developmental disabilities. That is, we consider special education

services that are available for students with developmental disabilities and how students are placed for the delivery of these services. As we do so, we consider how special education services articulate with other services and best practices for particular problems described elsewhere in this volume. Then, we provide an overview of how special education services are organized in relation to federal laws.

We illustrate our points with the case of Maurice, a 14-year-old boy classified as developmentally disabled. He is in school at present. His diagnosis is cerebral palsy—severe, spastic, quadriplegia. His speech and hearing are normal. His receptive language is adequate within the context of his physical limitations and the ensuing restricted experiences. He is limited in expressive language. He does not articulate words—not surprisingly, because the muscles in his speech-production apparatus are spastic. At this time, he has not learned alternative modes of communication to put together messages he wishes to convey. He has some use of his right arm and hand but no use of his left. He is limited in self-care and mobility.

STUDENTS WITH DISABILITIES IN SPECIAL EDUCATION

How many students are there like Maurice or Helen Keller in the United States today? More specifically, how many children and youth are now receiving special education services? This is important information for planning purposes by the states and for funding local school programs.

According to the Office of Special Education Programs (1994), 4,633,674 students with disabilities were being served in the United States during the school year of 1992–1993. Approximately 11% were labeled as mentally retarded and over 50% with specific learning disabilities. Table 3.1 presents the total numbers of students within the 12 categories that the U.S. Department of Edu-

Table 3.1. Disability Categories and Students Aged 6 to 21 Years Served Under Part B and Chapter 1 (SOP): Numbers and Percentages, School Year 1992–1993

Disability	Part B		Chapter 1 (SOP)		Total	
	Number	Percent[a]	Number	Percent[a]	Number	Percent[a]
Specific learning disabilities	2,333,571	52.4	35,814	19.7	2,369,385	51.1
Speech or language impairments	990,718	22.2	9,436	5.2	1,000,154	21.6
Mental retardation	484,871	10.9	48,844	26.9	533,715	11.5
Serious emotional disturbance	368,545	8.3	34,123	18.8	402,668	8.7
Multiple disabilities	86,179	1.9	17,036	9.4	103,215	2.2
Hearing impairments	43,707	1.0	17,189	9.5	60,896	1.3
Orthopedic impairments	46,498	1.0	6,423	3.5	52,921	1.1
Other health impairments	63,982	1.4	2,072	1.1	66,054	1.4
Visual impairments	18,129	0.4	5,682	3.1	23,811	0.5
Autism	12,238	0.3	3,289	1.8	15,527	0.3
Deaf-blindness[b]	773	0.0	652	0.4	1,425	0.0
Traumatic brain injury	2,906	0.1	997	0.5	3,903	0.1
All disabilities	4,452,117	100.0	181,557	100.0	4,633,674	100.0

[a]Percentages sum within columns.

[b]8,404 persons from ages birth to 21 have been identified by coordinators of the State and Multi-State Services for Children with Deaf-Blindness. They are required under 20 U.S.C §§1422(c)(1) and (2) to conduct an annual census of all persons under 22 years of age that meet the federal definition for Deaf-Blindness (*Federal Registry, 1991*, p. 51585). For a full report, contact the Severe Disabilities Branch of OSEP.

Note. From *Sixteenth Annual Report to Congress on the Implementation of the Individuals with Disabilities Education Act* by Office of Special Education Programs, 1994, Washington, DC: U.S. Department of Education.

cation uses to track students. Many of these disability categories are fully or at least partially discussed in this volume under the broader category of developmental disability.

Definitions

Definitions for two sets of services are pertinent: special education services and related services, as defined in the Individuals with Disabilities Education Act of 1990.

Special Education Services

Special education services generally are the set of activities used to deliver instruction to students with disabilities. More specifically, the following definition is used in the Individuals with Disabilities Education Act (P.L. 101-476, as amended):

- *Special education* means specially designed instruction at no cost to the parents or guardians to meet the unique needs of a child with a disability, including classroom instruction, instruction in physical education, home instruction, and instruction in hospitals and institutions.

- This term includes speech pathology, or any other related service, if the service consists of specially designed instruction, at no cost to the parents or guardians, to meet the unique needs of a handicapped child, and is considered *special education* rather than *related service* under state standards.

- The term also includes vocational education if it consists of specially designed instruction, at no cost to the parents, to meet the unique needs of a child with a disability.

- *The terms in this definition are defined as follows:*

- *At no cost* means that all specially designed instruction is provided without charge, but does not preclude incidental fees which are normally charged to nondisabled students or their parents as a part of the regular education program.

- *Physical education* is defined as follows: The term means the development of: physical and motor fitness, fundamental motor skills and patterns; and skills in aquatics, dance, and individual and group games and sports (including intramural and lifetime sports). The term includes special physical education, adapted physical education, movement education, and motor development.

- *Vocational education* means organized educational programs which are directly related to the preparation of individuals for paid or unpaid employment, or for additional preparation for a career requiring other than a baccalaureate or advanced degree. (§ 300.16)

Related Services

The Individuals with Disabilities Education Act requires that professionals provide related services in coordination with special education services. Related services are defined as follows:

> *Related services* include transportation and such developmental corrective, and other supportive services as are required to assist a child with a disability to benefit from special education, and includes speech pathology and audiology, and psychological services, physical and occupational therapy, recreation, early identification and assessment of disabilities in children, medical and counseling services, including rehabilitation counseling, except that such medical services should be for diagnostic and evaluation purposes only. The term also includes school health services, social work services in schools, and parent counseling and training. (§ 300.16)

Coordination Among Services

Coordination among services is the articulation of work focused on common objectives. The activities professionals use in delivering several special education and related services to students share many elements. The use of these elements in a mutually reinforcing way facilitates work with students with developmental disabilities. Organizing this work within a case management team operation is a good technique. (See Chapter 15 for a description of case management.)

Maurice's situation provides an illustration. His expressive language is limited because of the spasticity of the muscles in his speech apparatus and because of extremely limited experience related to his severe spastic quadriplegia and legal blindness.

A prime goal of the team is to improve Maurice's expressive language so that he can communicate in academic, personal, social, and business situations. In turn, this prime aim requires that Maurice learn something to communicate and that he learn to use various speech- and language-production devices, computers, and other writing devices.

The teachers and the therapists can, and should, coordinate their services as they work with Maurice on these activities, as in the following examples:

• The special education teachers, the regular education teachers, and, in time, the vocational education teachers should focus on the content of Maurice's expressive language. As he works on this content, the teachers should have him incorporate the techniques that the therapists are teaching him.

• The speech and language therapists should focus on activities such as relaxation, breath control, correct placement of his tongue and other parts of his speech apparatus, and use of the various speech- and language-production devices. The speech and language therapists should have him practice these techniques on the content he is learning with the teachers and on the techniques he is learning with the physical and occupational therapists.

• The occupational therapists and the physical therapists should focus on such matters as increasing Maurice's hand and arm use through work on muscle relaxation and specific movements as well as through the operation of computers and other communication devices. As they do so, the physical and occupational therapists should have him practice these techniques with the content he is learning with the teachers and the techniques he is learning with the speech and language therapists.

The case manager's role is to facilitate communication and cooperation among these specialists as well as between these specialists and Maurice's family to be sure that they all reinforce each others' work. In addition, the case manager has a responsibility to ensure that all of these activities consistently focus on Maurice's movement toward more independent personal, vocational, and community-living activities.

INSTRUCTIONAL PLANNING AND PLACEMENT

Instructional planning involves the selection of components and systems for teaching a student. Placement involves the identification of a student for delivering instruction.

Figure 3.1 illustrates a model of the sequence of activities we use in instruction. We employ seven components in two phases. Phase 1 is the identification of present performance levels. Phase 2 is the development of instructional programs. Here we use six activities.

1. Selecting instructional objectives

2. Selecting instructional sequences

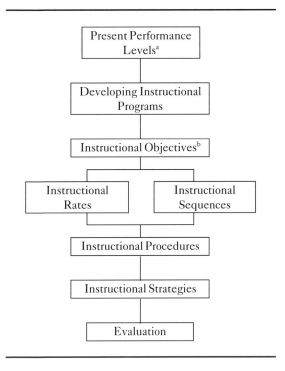

Figure 3.1. Instructional model sequence. [a]Also labeled *entering behavior* or *prerequisite skills*. [b]Also labeled *curriculum*, when collected in a set.

3. Selecting instructional rates

4. Selecting instructional procedures

5. Deciding about instructional settings

6. Evaluating results of instruction

Present Performance Levels

Present performance levels are the student's status in relation to the new behavior specified in an objective to be taught and on the knowledge and skills required to learn that new behavior. That is, the information about present performance levels indicates whether the student is ready for working on the objective.

One faces several problems in assessing the present performance levels of a student with a developmental disability. A primary problem is obtaining valid and reliable estimates of the student's present performance levels. Evaluating students with severe or multiple disabilities is extraordinarily complex. Two conditions must be met before one can use norm-referenced instruments with anyone, that is, before one can compare a student's status to that of the norm group. These requirements also apply to students with developmental disabilities.

The first condition pertains to standard procedures of testing. The students being tested and the students in the norm group must receive the same directions, use the same methods of responding, and generally receive the test under the same circumstances. The norms do not apply if this condition is violated and the test is not administered according to the standard procedures. The test may be easier or harder for the student being tested than it was for the students in the norm group. In turn, this difference could result in skewed scores and wrongly indicate what the student is able to do.

The second condition in using normative scores from norm-referenced testing pertains to the student's experience with the language and materials in the test. The students being tested must have had the same chances as the students in the norm group to learn the language used in the test and to learn how to use material like those in the test items. If the student being tested has had either restricted experience or different experiences, for him or her the test items are not accurate ways of sampling the behavior they are supposed to sample. The student may be more capable than his or her test scores indicate.

In most cases, these conditions cannot be met for students with severe disabilities. For example, their disabilities lead to restricted experiences—experiences not common with those of the norm group. In addition, their disabilities preclude their responding to the tests in the standard way that members of the norm group did when the norms were being established. As a result of these and similar problems, too often the evaluation techniques yield further measures of the disability, not measures of the characteristics of interest.

Consider Maurice's situation. A psychologist evaluated Maurice within the framework of the *Vineland Adaptive Behavior Scales* (Sparrow, Balla, & Cicchetti, 1984) and other developmental scales. Given the results, he classified Maurice as severely mentally retarded. Of course, he had no basis for this classification. He did not obtain a measure of Maurice's intellectual potential. Instead, he obtained further measures of Maurice's cerebral palsy, his speech and language impairments, and their combined effect on Maurice's experience and his ability to perform the items in the developmental scales.

A tragic error was nearly made here. Once a student is labeled, one tends to treat the student according to that label, and the student becomes the condition named in the label. The error was, however, prevented when a teacher included notes in Maurice's records indicating that he had a great sense of humor. The teacher had noticed that Maurice kept up with the activities in his surroundings. When funny things happened—often subtle things—he laughed. That is, he showed humor appropriate to the situation.

In time, monitors from the state's special education department conducted the 3-year evaluation of the special education program in which Maurice was enrolled. Monitors read the comments about Maurice in his records and interviewed Maurice's teacher further.

Maurice's show of appropriate humor raised a flag on the situation. Students with severe retardation seldom show such characteristics. Therefore, the state monitors questioned Maurice's evaluation and classification. Finally, he was referred to a long-established center organized to evaluate students with severe disabilities. The evaluators used diagnostic–prescriptive teaching methods. As a result of their work, they rejected the diagnosis of severe mental retardation and eliminated it from Maurice's records. Subsequently, teachers and therapists acted accordingly.

With the original diagnosis, those working with Maurice did not obtain an estimate of Maurice's intellectual ability. Instead, they received a further description of his cerebral palsy, his limited speech and language, and their effects on his experiences. Further evaluation eliminated this error.

The problem of reliably and validly assessing students with severe or multiple disabilities has been widely considered (e.g., see Kaufman, 1990; Luftig, 1989). When one deals with the present performance levels of students with multiple or severe disabilities, one seeks to solve the problems with procedures like the following. One should leave alone characteristics that one has to infer, such as intellectual potential. Instead, one should follow a diagnostic–prescriptive teaching model.

The diagnostic–prescriptive model involves the sequence of selecting an instructional objective, teaching it intensively, and observing how and how much the student learns. With successive approximations, the teacher can determine the appropriate levels and procedures for teaching the students. Then, the teacher sees how far and how fast the student can progress.

In assessing present performance levels, one should approach the youngster as if he or she were Helen Keller. For example, one should treat the child like a seeing child and expect him or her to act like a seeing child.

Developing Instructional Programs

Instructional programs include multiple components: instructional objectives, instructional sequences, instructional rates, instructional procedures, instructional settings, and instructional systems.

- *Instructional objectives* are statements about what the student should be able to do if he or she learns through instruction. Objectives are based on the goals for the student. They guide the selection of the instructional procedures and the evaluation procedures.

- *Instructional sequences* are arrangements of instructional objectives in the order they are to be taught. Most sets of objectives for a given topic are arranged from simple to complex. That is, the objectives with no prerequisites are learned first. In turn, they become prerequisites for learning more complex skills.

- *Instructional rates* are based on the timing for presenting the objectives, that is, how fast they are presented or how much time is spent on each objective. Instructional schedules are based on instructional rates.

- A *curriculum* is a set of instructional objectives. A scope and sequence chart for a curriculum includes the instructional objectives and the order in which they are organized.

- *Instructional procedures* are the methods, media, and equipment used to help students reach their objectives.

- *Instructional methods* are recurrent patterns of teacher behavior. They include teacher presentation (lectures, demonstrations), student problem solving (inquiry training, experimenting), group work (discussion, debate), individual work, direct experience (consultants, field trips), and behavioral techniques.

- *Instructional media* are materials and machines. They include print media (textbooks, workbooks); audio, visual, and audiovisual media (photographs, audiotapes, videotapes, three-dimensional models); prototypes (games and simulations); and programs (programmed text, computer-assisted instruction).

• *Special equipment* comprises devices to compensate for particular disabilities, such as computers and braille writers.

• *Instructional settings* are the ways personnel and space are arranged for delivering instruction to particular students or groups.

• *Personnel allocation* refers to how students, teachers, and teacher aids are organized. Common patterns are tutoring, independent study, solitary activity, small groups, and large groups.

• *Space allocation* is how facilities are arranged for instruction. Frequently used patterns are common areas, carrels, special centers, and depositories.

• *Instructional systems* are sets of activities put together to teach a particular topic. Each package includes the several instructional components just described and shown in Figure 3.1.

A problem in developing instructional programs for students with developmental disabilities is the selecting of program elements based on a student's present performance levels. In the interests of normalization, one should select as many elements as possible from the programs for nondisabled students. At the same time, as necessitated by the student's present performance levels, one makes different selections than one would make for nondisabled students.

Selections differ for each student with a developmental disability on the basis of his or her present performance level. Sometimes, one selects only different objectives, sometimes only different schedules, sometimes only different procedures, or sometimes only different settings. Further, one sometimes makes different selections for more than one instructional component. Again, the practitioner must fit the program to the student's characteristics—his or her present performance levels.

Maurice's instructional activities are focused on life-management activities such as consumer economics and academics (e.g., language-related tasks including listening to and reading literature and written composition; mathematics; social studies; and the sciences). In addition, Maurice's instructional program heavily emphasizes expressive communication through oral means and electronic assistive devices. In these latter activities, Maurice's teacher works closely with the speech, language, physical, and occupational therapists. Maurice's teachers use some of the same instructional procedures they use with other students. The difference lies in their devoting more time to individual work. In addition, they adjust Maurice's instructional schedule to allow him more time for all of his work. See *Stepping Out* (1991), Bos and Vaughn (1991), Langone (1990), McDonnell, Wilcox, and Hardman (1991), and Widerstorm, Mowder, and Sandall (1991) for more information about instructional activities for students with developmental disabilities.

Placement for Instruction

Educational placement is the locating of a student for convenient delivery of educational services to him or her. These placements are accompanied by barrier-free facilities and barrier-free transportation. There are a number of options for placing students with developmental disabilities for their special educational services. Selecting among these options is governed by the principle of the least restrictive environment, based, in turn, on the goal of normalization.

The following list includes the frequently used options for special education placement of students with developmental disabilities, arranged from least restrictive to most restrictive.

• regular class

• regular class with consultation assistance to the teacher

• regular class with assistance by itinerant specialist

• regular class plus resource-room help

• regular class with part-time special classes

- full-time special class

- full-time residential school

- hospital

- home

There continues to be a major interest by many in *how many* students are served in each of the listed environments. As we discuss later a heated debate continues in the field about the merits of full inclusion of students into general education classes.

The Office of Special Education Programs (1994) provided data on the placement of students in the 12 special education disability categories into six of the placement environments. About 35% of students were served in regular classes and another 36% in resource rooms plus regular classes during the 1991–1992 school year. Table 3.2 provides a summary of these breakdowns.

When one is selecting a placement option for a student with a developmental disability, the goal is to find the least restrictive environment. That is, on the basis of the instructional objectives in his or her Individualized Education Program (IEP), the student is placed in the least restricted, most normal environment in which instruction based on these objectives is being delivered to other students. For example, if the instructional objectives in the IEP of a 14-year-old student with a developmental disability were the social studies objectives outlined in the eighth-grade curriculum, the student could study social studies with the regular eighth-grade class. The teacher may or may not need consultant help. If, on the other hand, another 14-year-old student's IEP specified the social studies objectives of the third-grade curriculum, that student would not work with the chronologically younger (9-year-old), nondisabled third graders. Such a placement would not meet the normalization requirement. Instead, a more appropriate placement for instruction would be a resource room or a special class.

Placing students with developmental disabilities in the least restrictive environment often causes management problems. For example, a student with a developmental disability who has hand and arm involvement that precludes handwriting and handling books and papers requires special accommodation such as audiotaping or videotaping of class notes, the use of devices to hold and turn the pages of books, and the use of computers or oral presentations for preparing papers, projects, and tests.

Maurice's IEP has life-management objectives as well as academic objectives that are on grade levels of students who are chronologically younger. Therefore, he is enrolled in a special class for instruction to meet these objectives. Given his attention span and his propensity to keep up with his environment, he has objectives for music and literature on an eighth-grade level commensurate with his chronologic age. He participates with the regular eighth-grade class to pursue these objectives.

A MOVEMENT TOWARD FULL INCLUSION

A fundamental change in placement and service delivery for students in special education is underway in the 1990s. Since the passage of the Education for All Handicapped Children Act of 1975, practitioners, advocates, and professionals in the field of special education have debated about the best location for providing special education services to students with disabilities. Since the passage of the law, service provision has been occurring increasingly in the regular education classroom. Most recently there has been a movement toward *full inclusion*. In its pure form, full inclusion means that students remain in regular education settings 100% of the day and receive all services from specialists within the regular education settings. The full inclusion model of service delivery differs significantly from the more traditional mainstreaming efforts of the 1970s and 1980s. Basic tenets of the inclusion concept are provided by Stainback, Stainback, and Jackson (1992):

Table 3.2. Percentages of Students Aged 6 to 21 Years Served in Different Educational Environments: School Year 1992–1993

Disability	Educational Environment[a]					
	Regular Class	Resource Room	Separate Class	Separate School	Residential Facility	Homebound/ Hospital
Specific learning disabilities	24.7	54.2	20.0	0.9	0.1	0.1
Speech or language impairments	85.5	9.1	3.9	1.4	0.1	0.1
Mental retardation	5.1	25.4	59.2	8.8	1.2	0.3
Serious emotional disturbance	15.8	27.8	36.9	13.9	4.0	1.5
Multiple disabilities	6.2	18.1	47.1	22.6	3.8	2.2
Hearing impairments	27.0	20.5	31.2	9.6	11.5	0.1
Orthopedic impairments	32.4	21.0	34.3	7.3	0.9	4.1
Other health impairments	35.3	27.6	21.4	3.3	0.5	11.8
Visual impairments	39.6	21.2	19.6	8.5	10.6	0.4
Autism	4.7	6.9	48.5	35.9	3.1	0.9
Deaf-blindness	5.8	6.2	36.3	21.2	28.6	1.8
Traumatic brain injury	7.8	9.0	23.7	53.4	3.7	2.4
All disabilities	34.9	36.3	23.5	3.9	0.9	0.5

[a]Data for students placed in public and private separate schools and in public and private residential facilities have been combined for presentation in this table.

Note: From *Sixteenth Annual Report to Congress on the Implementation of the Individuals with Disabilities Education Act* by Office of Special Education Programs, 1994, Washington, DC: U.S. Department of Education.

- All children must be included in both the educational and social life of their schools and classrooms.
- The basic goal is to not leave anyone out of school and classroom communities from the very beginning (thus, integration can be abandoned since no one has to return to the mainstream).
- The focus is on the support needs of all students and personnel.

As we have illustrated throughout this chapter and in contrast to the full inclusion service delivery model, the mainstreaming model has students receiving some special education services within the special education setting (e.g., in a resource room or therapy room).

School districts, state boards of education, and other human service agencies across the nation are setting policies related to the inclusion of students with disabilities. In a benchmark report, the National Association of State Boards of Education (NASBE; 1992) issued a call for inclusive schools. In its report, NASBE recommended the creation of new belief systems that result in the setting of unified goals for special education and regular education students. They also recommended that the link between funding, placement, and disabling label be severed. Inclusive schools rely on heterogeneous grouping and the ability for flexible learning goals and objectives for all students, including those in special education. The strongest advocates of full inclusion believe that no services should be provided to special education students outside of the regular classroom activities. Thus, full inclusion implemented completely would negate the continuum of services models (where students may be placed in segregated settings for all or part of the day) currently in place in most school districts.

Recent litigation supports the idea of full inclusion. In *Sacramento City Unified School District v. Holland* (1994), the court supported the right of an 11-year-old girl to participate 100% of the day in a regular education classroom. The court weighed four factors when deciding the case: (a) the student's educational benefits from full-time placement in a regular education classroom, (b) the nonacademic benefits of a regular classroom placement, (c) the effect of the child with a disability on the other class members, and (d) the cost of a regular education placement with proper, supplementary aids and services (Holland, 1994).

Maurice's placement would appear vastly different under a full inclusion model. All of his learning would occur in regular eighth-grade classrooms. He would have the assistance of a part-time aide and student tutors to help with learning activities as provided in his IEP. His teachers would collaborate frequently with the special education teachers to design and implement flexible objectives for learning activities that would further his IEP goals. He would receive his related services within the regular education classroom.

Full inclusion is not supported by everyone. Although most believe that a number of students can be served effectively in regular classrooms 100% of the day, many seek to retain the continuum of services that has been the hallmark of the least restrictive environment clause of IDEA. Brown et al. (1991) advised against joining the "0% club" (no mainstreaming or inclusion for anyone) or the "100% club" (full inclusion for everyone). Illustrating these beliefs is the Council for Exceptional Children's (CEC) *Policy on Inclusive Schools and Community Settings* (1993):

> CEC believes that a *continuum* [italics added] of services must be available for all children, youth, and young adults. CEC also believes that the concept of inclusion is a meaningful goal to be pursued in our schools and communities. In addition, CEC believes children, youth, and young adults with disabilities should be served whenever possible in general education classrooms in inclusive neighborhood schools and community settings. Such settings should be strengthened and supported by an infusion of specially trained personnel and other appropriate supportive practices according to the individual child. (p. 1)

Others argue more forcefully that there will always need to be segregated classes and even segregated schools. For example, Lieberman (1992) noted that some children may, at some point in their lives, need a program outside of the regular classroom because the children need highly specialized skills taught by specially trained teachers, need a peer group whose members are more like they are, and might never respond to the demands of the academic curriculum. Diamond (1995) related the opinion of the NASBE Special Education Study Group: "... A situation in which every child is integrated and there are no choices for separate programming is as unacceptable as one in which every child is segregated and there are not choices for integration. The important issue is ... whether the child is learning" (p. 252).

Regardless of one's philosophical belief in the need for a continuum of services, it is clear that an ever-increasing number of students are being educated mainly in general education classrooms. It is a revolution. A national study of inclusive practices conducted by the National Center on Educational Restructuring and Inclusion (Lipsky, 1994) found six common factors necessary for successful inclusion to take place:

• *Visionary leadership.* This factor includes a positive view of the value of education to the students with disabilities, an optimistic view of the capacities of teachers and schools to change, and confidence that practices evolve and that everyone benefits from inclusion.

• *Collaboration.* The factor derives from the recognition that no one teacher can be expected to possess all of the knowledge and expertise needed for serving all students and thus must necessarily draw upon the knowledge and expertise of others.

• *Increased use of authentic assessment techniques.* The factor means changing from the use of assessments as screening devices to the refusal of assessment foci to an appraisal of individual student abilities and needs.

• *Supports for staff and students.* This factor includes providing systematic staff development,

allowing planning time for special and general education staff to collaborate, and providing supplementary aides and supports to students.

• *Funding.* This factor means moving away from funding formulas that encourage separate special education programs.

• *Parent involvement.* With this factor, parent participation is encouraged through family support services.

ORGANIZATION WITHIN THE LAW

Education-related legal and human rights of students with developmental disabilities are heavily protected at the federal and state levels. These legal protections are based on a solid foundation of constitutional law, common law, and statutory and regulatory law. In addition, citizens with developmental disabilities are governed by the same laws as all other U.S. citizens. Table 3.3 outlines the body of laws affecting citizens with disabilities.

Constitutional Source

Part 1 of the Fourteenth Amendment of the Constitution is the primary constitutional source for special education law. The four key clauses are the citizenship clause, the supremacy clause, the due process clause, and the equal protection clause. "All persons born or naturalized in the United States and subject to the jurisdiction thereof, are citizens of the United States and of the State wherein they reside" [citizenship clause]. "No State shall make or enforce any law which shall abridge the privileges or immunities of citizens of the United States" [supremacy clause]; "nor shall any State deprive any person of life, liberty, or property, without due process of law" [due process clause]; "nor [shall any State] deny to any person within its jurisdiction the equal protection of the laws" [equal protection clause].

Table 3.3.   The Body of Laws Affecting
U.S. Citizens with Disabilities

**All citizens including those with disabilities—the
founding documents**

- The Declaration of Independence of the Thirteen
  American Colonies
- The Constitution of the United States of America

**Only citizens with disabilities—statutes and
administrative regulations**

- Individuals with Disabilities Education Act
  (formerly known as the Education of the
  Handicapped Act), the Handicapped Children
  Protection Act, and other amendments
- Rehabilitation Act and Amendments (Services)
- Rehabilitation Act and Amendments (§§ 501, 503,
  and 504)
- Developmental Disabilities Assistance Act
- Civil Rights Act of 1964 and the Civil Rights
  Restoration Act of 1987
- Architectural Barriers Act
- Fair Housing Amendments of 1988
- Air Carriers Access Act
- Perkins Act (Vocational Education)
- Americans with Disabilities Act of 1990
- States' statutes and regulations

**Only citizens with disabilities—policy statements,
rulings, and decisions from**

- United States Supreme Court
- United States Circuit Courts of Appeal
- United States District Courts
- States' courts
- United States Office of Education, Office of Special
  Education and Rehabilitation Services (OSERS)
- United States of Education Office of Civil Rights
  (OCR)
- States' education agencies
- Other federal and state executive departments

**All students including students with disabilities—
the school laws**

- All statutes and regulations and all rulings and
  decisions regarding, for example, child abuse and
  neglect, freedom of expression

**All citizens including those with disabilities—the
general laws**

- All statutes and regulations and all rulings and
  decisions, for example, business laws, criminal laws

Common Law

The case law supporting the rights and protection of students with disabilities is strong. In the ground-breaking ruling in *Brown v. Board of Education of Topeka* (1954), the United States Supreme Court affirmed that the equal protection and due process clauses of the Fourteenth Amendment are in force in educational decisions. Capitalizing on the precedents in *Brown* and on the cultural and legal zeitgeist, advocates brought a number of cases, which were decided in favor of students with disabilities. For example, some early landmark decisions were made in *Larry P. v. Riles* (1972), *Mills v. D.C. Board of Education* (1972), *Pennsylvania Association for Retarded Children v. Commonwealth of Pennsylvania* (1972), and *Wyatt v. Stickney* (1972). Several important principles were established in such cases (e.g., the right to free public education; the right to nondiscriminatory evaluation; the right to be educated with nondisabled peers; the right to adequate consultation with parents; and the right to adequate instruction with proper goals).

The complaints and remedies in these cases pertained to specific federal jurisdictions like the Northern District of California and the Eastern District of Pennsylvania. The remedies, or principles, were nationalized, made general to all students in the United States, in the federal statutory and regulatory laws.

Statutory–Regulatory Law

Since the middle of the 19th century, federal statutes have provided for education, treatment, and care of people who have disabilities. Emphasis on all school children with disabilities, however, began in the late 1950s and early 1960s. The statutory enactments paralleled, incorporated, or negated the judicial enactments. Some landmark statutes are named in Table 3.3. Most of these laws have been amended extensively over the years.

These statutes and their accompanying regulations prescribe and guarantee a large number of specific rights and protections for people with disabilities. These can be generalized as the right to a free appropriate public education from infancy through adulthood, the right to vocational rehabilitation services and appropriate vocational education, the right to nondiscriminatory evaluation, the right to confidentiality and control over records, and the right to procedural due process.

Requirements

The Individuals with Disabilities Education Act mandates that youngsters with disabilities from infancy through age 21 receive a free appropriate public education. Implementing this mandate involves a wide range of detailed regulations for required best practices to be followed at the state and local levels. These regulations pertain to such matters as identifying eligible participants, funding services, personnel training, procedural safeguards (for guaranteeing due process, protection in evaluation, placement in the least restrictive environment, and confidentiality of information), programming for transition from school to adult roles, and legal representation in administrative and judicial disputes. Several sources have information about these regulations and their interpretation in administrative and judicial rulings. Two examples are Rothstein's (1990) *Special Education Law* and Tucker and Goldstein's (1991) *Legal Rights of Persons with Disabilities: An Analysis of Federal Law.*

The IEP exemplifies these requirements. (For more details, see Larsen & Poplin, 1980; Strickland & Turnbull, 1990.) The IEP is the keystone to a free appropriate public education. Simply, in a student's IEP, the practitioner should start with the student's present level of performance, set goals, and then marshall whatever services are needed to help the student move from his or her present performance level to the goals established. In more detail, the IEP encompasses the following requirements:

- a written statement for each student with a disability

- developed in a meeting by:

  - a representative of the local education agency or of an intermediate education unit who is qualified to provide, or supervise the production of, specifically designed instruction to meet the student's unique needs.

  - the teacher

  - the student's parents or guardians

  - whenever appropriate, the student

- and including:

  - the student's present levels of educational performance

  - annual goals, including short-term instructional objectives

  - the specific educational services to be provided to the student (that is, instructional services, nonacademic services, related services, and services to insure procedural safeguards)

  - the extent to which the student will be able to participate in regular education programs

  - a statement of the needed transition services for students beginning no later than age 16 and annually thereafter (and, when determined appropriate for the individual, beginning at age 14 or younger), including, when appropriate, a statement of the interagency responsibilities or collaboration before the student leaves the school setting

  - the projected date for initiation of and anticipated duration of the services

  - appropriate objective criteria and evaluation procedures

  - a schedule for determining, at least annually, whether the student is achieving the instructional objectives

An IEP must be developed for all identified students regardless of their placement during instruction—public school, private school, hospital, residential school, or home. The conference to plan the IEP must be conducted within 30 days after the beginning of the school year or 30 days after the student becomes eligible for special education services.

We use 17 steps to design an IEP according to the preceding guidelines and to specify the student's placement for receiving the IEP (see Figure 3.2). IEPs developed in depth, with frequent evaluations and revisions, are extremely important to students with developmental disabilities. For example, the core of Maurice's IEP is the selection of elements considered in the sections on Coordination of Services and on Instructional Planning and Placement. That is, the developers (the parents/advocates, the special educators, and the related service providers) work together to plan specific activities for Maurice, ways these activities can be coordinated, and how they can be evaluated.

Accountability

Given that judicial decisions and statutes/regulations are general rules, honorable people often disagree about how these rules should be applied in specific cases. In addition, because of the pressures of day-to-day situations and variations in the levels of personnel training, professionals sometimes take actions that may constitute negligence or malpractice. Consequently, one must be concerned about accountability. Three major areas of accountability are monitoring programs, dealing with individual disputes, and deciding about personnel liability.

Program Monitoring

The IDEA requires and has procedures for ensuring that special education programs are monitored at least every 3 years. The federal Office of Special Education and Rehabilitation Ser-

vices (OSERS) monitors programs in state departments of education. In turn, the state departments of education monitor programs in local school districts.

The monitoring essentially involves investigating whether the requirements of the laws are being observed. Procedural due process is observed. Deficient programs are given ample time to remedy problems. Failure to remedy problems can result in loss of funding.

Program monitoring is especially important for special education programs in which students with developmental disabilities are enrolled because some students with developmental disabilities have complex problems. As a result, their special education services can be complicated and long term. Lapses from legally required standard practices can occur. For example, inappropriate instruments were used to evaluate Maurice's present performance levels, and Maurice was inappropriately classified as severely intellectually retarded. The state department of education monitors found the problem. The IDEA and the state requirement for nondiscriminatory evaluation clearly had been violated. That is, Maurice had been subjected to a discriminatory evaluation. As a result of the monitors' work, the legal violation in Maurice's situation was recognized and rectified. Again, program monitoring is crucial.

Individual Disputes

IDEA includes requirements and procedures for dealing with disputes about actions with respect to an individual student. A parent/advocate who disagrees with a decision may request an administrative hearing at the local school district level. Either party may appeal the decision of the local hearing officer to the state education agency level. In turn, appeals may be made to the federal level, either to the OSERS or to the Office of Civil Rights (OCR).

A case may be moved to the federal courts once administrative remedies are exhausted, or,

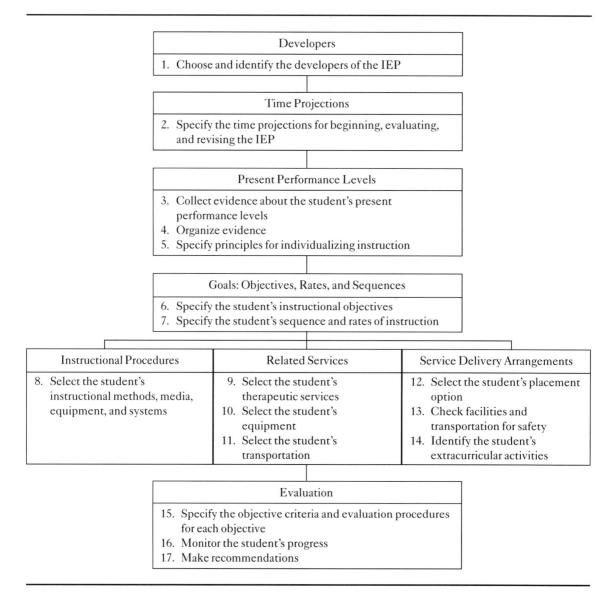

Figure 3.2.   Relationship among components and steps in the Individualized Education Program (IEP).

in some specified cases, before administrative remedies are exhausted. Within the federal court system, the route is the district courts, the circuit courts of appeal, and the Supreme Court. The use of attorneys' services is allowed in all of these actions. Prevailing plaintiffs in court disputes may claim reimbursement for attorneys' fees and other litigation expenses.

The courts also may award prevailing plaintiffs reimbursement for expenses such as cost of private placement while disputes about placement are being resolved. This is so if it is reasonable to expect that so much time will be required to resolve the dispute that the student will be harmed by remaining in his or her current placement until a final decision is made.

The courts also may award funds for compensatory education. That is, school districts may have to pay the costs of programs to rectify losses resulting from programs not supplied when they should have been supplied or losses resulting from incorrect practices.

The complexity of the limitations of students with developmental disabilities may lead to ambiguity about the nature of the best decisions or to decisions that are costly to implement. Consequently, disputes arise frequently. The procedures for resolving disputes through administrative hearings and the federal courts are extremely important for students with developmental disabilities. The provisions in the Handicapped Children's Protection Act for awarding costs to the prevailing plaintiffs makes these avenues more widely available to parties who have legitimate complaints.

Consider again Maurice's initially being subjected illegally to discriminatory testing. The monitors from the state department of education found the problem, and it was rectified without dispute. However, Maurice's parents/advocates also had another avenue for resolving the problem. They could have disputed the initial evaluation procedures. In turn, they could have sought redress through administrative hearings ranging from the local school level, through the state level, to the federal level in the U.S. Department of Education. Lacking a satisfactory resolution, they could have sought redress in the federal court system.

The plaintiffs (Maurice's parents/advocates) could have asked that the discriminatory evaluation cease and that nondiscriminatory evaluation be used. They also could have asked that funds be supplied for compensatory programs to make up for time lost and errors made as a result of the original incorrect evaluation.

Personnel Liability

Can a student, or his or her parent/guardian, recover monetary damages from personnel whose failure to act (dereliction of duty) or whose wrongful action (malpractice) caused harm to the student? At present, the answer to this question is unclear.

The relevant federal statute is in the Civil Rights Act, § 1983, Civil Action for the Deprivation of Rights. This section holds that "every person who subjects, or causes to be subjected, any citizen of the United States or other person within the jurisdiction thereof to the deprivation of any rights, privileges, or immunities secured by the Constitution and laws, shall be liable to the party injured in an action at law, suit in equity, or other proper proceeding for redress."

The body of tort law also may pertain. Persons claiming to be harmed have brought a number of suits for damages. In some cases, the courts have awarded monetary damages, but in other cases, they have not.

The doctrine of sovereign immunity is one major reason for this ambiguity or inconsistency even in cases in which fault was obvious. The doctrine of sovereign immunity ("the king can do no wrong") has its roots in English common law. Extended to present-day U.S. law, sovereign immunity means that one cannot sue the government. However, there are two exceptions. The first exception applies when a Constitutional right is violated. Cases brought under § 1983 fall in this category.

The second exception pertains to claims based on statutes. Governmental immunity generally is based on common-law precedent and the Thirteenth Amendment of the U.S. Constitution. This immunity can be abrogated in two ways: A state can specifically waive immunity in a case, and Congress can write a waiver into a particular statute.

It is fairly clear, as we considered earlier, that a person can successfully claim reimbursement for expenses incurred in rectifying errors. On the other hand, the extent to which one can claim damages for harm caused by personnel dereliction of duty or malpractice is unclear. This matter probably will be clarified in the near future, in view of the increasing numbers of cases occurring, the laws providing for the award of expenses to prevailing plaintiffs, and the highly specific standards for best right practices being enacted in the laws and their amendments.

The option of recovering monetary damages for harm is important to students with developmental disabilities and their parents or guardians for three reasons. One, some students with developmental disabilities have such severe and complex problems that they can come to harm quickly if they are not carefully supervised and treated with correct procedures. Two, the IDEA has long required and provided for comprehensive personnel training; so, personnel working with students with developmental disabilities can learn right practices and precautions. Three, the IDEA and several other laws specifically prescribe certain standard best practices, as do researchers and widely disseminated practitioners' handbooks.

Consider once again the example of Maurice's situation. The IDEA's system for ensuring accountability led to the discovery and remediation of the problem. However, Maurice did lose opportunity for development while he was being incorrectly educated as a severely intellectually retarded student. In addition, the problems of evaluating students with severe disabilities and the dangers of misclassification and of the self-fulfilling prophecy have long been known. Training programs and publications have widely disseminated this knowledge. As a result, Maurice's parents/advocates could explore the possibility of a liability action for damages.

FINAL THOUGHTS

Students with mental retardation or other developmental disabilities have had an increasingly available array of educational services in the last two decades. There continue to be efforts, sometimes opposing efforts, to fine tune how education is delivered to these students. Although the debate regarding service delivery location is currently on center stage, the future holds even

greater challenges. What, for example, will be the effects of an increasingly fiscally and philosophically conservative Congress on education in general and on special education in particular? Will the move toward increased state control of education result in more disparate programs and differential rights to an education across the nation? Will the aging population continue to support the extra fiscal support that made Maurice's program possible? In the future, educators, parents, advocates, and policy makers will necessarily have to become more active to advance, even maintain, the great advances already made in special education.

REFERENCES

Bos, C., & Vaughn, S. (1991). *Strategies for teaching students with learning and behavior disorders.* Boston: Allyn & Bacon.

Brown, C. (1955). *My left foot.* New York: Simon & Schuster.

Brown, L., Schwartz, P., Udvari-Solner, A., Kampschroer, E., Johnson, F., Jorgensen, J., & Gruenewald, L. (1991). How much time should students with severe intellectual disabilities spend in regular education classrooms and elsewhere? *Journal of the Association for Persons with Severe Handicaps, 16,* 39–47.

Brown v. Board of Education of Topeka, 347 U.S. Code 483, 493, 1954.

Council for Exceptional Children. (1993). CEC policy on inclusive schools and community settings. *Teaching Exceptional Children, 25*(Suppl.), 1.

Diamond, S. C. (1995). Special education and the great God, inclusion. In J. M. Kauffman & D. P. Hallahan (Eds.), *The illusion of full inclusion: A comprehensive critique of a current special education bandwagon.* Austin, TX: PRO-ED.

Education for All Handicapped Children Act of 1975, 20 U.S.C. § 1400 *et seq.*

Education of the Handicapped Law Report. Horsham, PA: LRP Publications.

Holland, R. (1994, March). Ninth Circuit upholds regular classroom placement (1994, March). *Inclusive Education Programs, 2,* 1.

Individuals with Disabilities Education Act of 1990, 20 U.S.C. § 1400 *et seq.*

Kaufman, A. S. (1990). *Assessing adolescent and adult intelligence.* Boston: Allyn & Bacon.

Keller, H. (1903). *The story of my life.* New York: Doubleday.

Keller, H. (1933). Three days to see. *Atlantic Monthly, 151,* 34–42.

Keller, H. (1938). *The world I live in.* New York: Appleton-Century.

Langone, J. (1990). *Teaching students with mild and moderate learning problems.* Boston: Allyn & Bacon.

Larry, P. v. Riles, 343 F. Supp. 1306 (N.D. Cal. 1972), *aff'd*, 502 F2d 963 (9th Cir. 1974).

Larsen, S. C., & Poplin, M. S. (1980). *Methods for educating the handicapped: An individual education program approach*. Boston: Allyn & Bacon.

Lash, J. (1990). *Helen and teacher*. New York: Dell.

Lee, C. M., & Jackson, R. (1991). *Faking it: A look into the mind of a creative learner*. Portsmouth, NH: Heinemann, Boynton & Cook.

Lieberman, L. E. (1992). Preserving special education . . . for those who need it. In W. Stainback & S. Stainback (Eds.), *Controversial issues confronting special education: Divergent perspectives* (pp. 13–25). Boston: Allyn & Bacon.

Lipsky, D. (1994). National survey gives insight into inclusive movement. *Inclusive Education Programs, 1(3)*, 4–7.

Luftig, R. L. (1989). *Assessment of learners with special needs*. Boston: Allyn & Bacon.

McDonnell, J., Wilcox, B., & Hardman, M. (1991). *Secondary programs for students with developmental disabilities*. Boston: Allyn & Bacon.

Mills v. D. C. Board of Education, 348 F. Supp. 866 (D.D.C. 1972).

National Association of State Boards of Education. (1992). *Winners all: A call for inclusive schools*. Alexandria, VA: Author.

Office of Special Education Programs. (1994). *Sixteenth annual report to Congress on the implementation of the Individuals with Disabilities Education Act*. Washington, DC: Department of Education.

Pennsylvania Association for Retarded Children v. Commonwealth of Pennsylvania, 334 F. Supp. 1257; 343 F. Supp. 279 (E.D. Pa. 1971, 1972).

Rothstein, L. F. (1991). *Special education law*. New York: Longman.

Sacramento City Unified School District v. Holland, 786 F. Supp. 874 (E.D. Cal. 1992), *aff'd*, No. 92-15608, slip op. (9th Cir. March 1993).

Sparrow, S. S., Balla, D. A., & Cicchetti, D. V. (1984). *Vineland Adaptive Behavior Scales*. Circle Pines, MN: American Guidance Service.

Stainback, S., Stainback, W., & Jackson, H. J. (1992). Toward inclusive classrooms. In S. Stainback & W. Stainback (Eds.), *Curriculum considerations in inclusive classrooms: Facilitating learning for all students* (pp. 3–17). Baltimore: Brookes.

Stepping out: A dynamic community based life skills program. (1991). Verona, WI: Attainment.

Strickland, B., & Turnbull, A. P. (1990). *Developing and implementing special education programs* (3rd ed.). Columbus, OH: Merrill.

Tucker, B. P., & Goldstein, B. A. (1991). *Legal rights of persons with disabilities: An analysis of federal law*. Horsham, PA: LRP Publications.

Widerstorm, A. H., Mowder, B., & Sandall, S. R. (1991). *At risk and handicapped newborns and infants: Development, assessment, and intervention*. Boston: Allyn & Bacon.

Wyatt v. Stickney, 344 F. Supp. 373, 387, 396 (M.D. Ala. 1972).

Transition from School to Adulthood

Katherine Inge, Paul Wehman, Tom J. Clees, and Stacy Dymond

LEARNING GOALS

Upon completion of this chapter the reader will be able to

- define *transition services* in terms of who should participate, when they should participate, and who should provide the services;

- describe critical changes that need to occur so that people with severe disabilities can access the rehabilitation system;

- analyze the components needed to develop a collaborative transition program in any community;

- describe the relationship between an Individualized Education Program and an Individual Transition Plan;

- explain the value of community-based vocational programs; and

- identify four service related and four politically related advocacy activities.

The concept of transition as it relates to students with mental retardation is frequently referred to in the literature as transition from school to the work setting or as employment outcomes (Clark & Kolstoe, 1994; Wehman, 1992). However, transition is naturally a process that begins at birth and extends over the life span. Students with mental retardation are continuously *transitioning* physically and instructionally. The concept of transition is analogous to a piece of cloth that requires many threads to develop. There are also many issues closely interwoven into the transitioning process.

Helping the *student* prepare to transition into an adult world begins many years prior to the adolescent years. The transition process for many students begins during their early years as they move from one setting to the next. Students mainstreamed from a self-contained setting are concerned more about social or transitional issues than about academic issues. Educators will be faced not only with instruction in the issues of social changes, academic stresses, and transition but also with assisting the student with mental retardation in coping with these concern.

A second factor in the transition of students into new environments is the *attitude* of teachers. Numerous factors affect teachers' attitudes toward students with disabilities. Participation in quality in-service training, previous course work related to disabilities, comfort level in working with the student, and class size are but a few. Many factors are beyond the control of the teacher who is trying to support a student in transition. Working collaboratively with the receiving teacher becomes a major factor. Frequently, general education teachers are unsure of their skills, and a strong support base is lacking. Special education teachers can help the general educator teacher by

- providing a list of relevant learning and social/behavioral characteristics of the child to be mainstreamed;

- helping the general education teacher understand how the child learns, especially the rate and level as they relate to those of the nondisabled child;

- helping develop a parallel program to be implemented within the general education setting;

- offering to co-teach with the teacher; and

- providing ongoing instructional and emotional support for the teachers.

The most recent reauthorization of the Education for All Handicapped Children Act occurred during the 101st Congress. Public Law 101-476 became law in September of 1990 and is now known as the Individuals with Disabilities Education Act (IDEA). IDEA defined transition services as follows:

> A coordinated set of activities for a student, designed within an outcome oriented process, which promotes movement from school to postschool activities, includes postsecondary education, vocational training, integrated employment (including supported employment), continuing adult education, adult services, independent living, or community participation. The coordinated set of activities shall be based upon the individual student's needs taking into account the student's preferences and interests and shall include instruction, community experiences, development of employment and other postschool adult living objectives, and when appropriate acquisition of daily living skills and functional vocational evaluation. (20 U.S.C. §1401[a][19])

Prior to this legislation, transition had been described within the special education process, but it had never been defined in terms of who should participate, when they should participate, and who would provide the services. IDEA mandated that transition services for students with severe disabilities include "*community experiences*, the development of employment, and other postschool adult living objectives" (§1401[b][5], italics added). In addition, a transition plan must be developed for a student no later than age 16 and, in some cases, at age 14 or younger. Interagency responsibilities and linkages also must be included before the student graduates. IDEA resulted from the increased focus on efforts to facilitate the successful movement of youth with disabilities from school to adult settings. IDEA requires local education agencies to include transition planning and implementation in the Individualized Education Program (IEP) process for all students with disabilities. Thus, for the first time, legislation spells out a requirement for providing transition services to support youth in their movement into postschool settings.

The plan for transition services *must* be included on the IEP of *all* students receiving special education by the time they reach 16 years of age and must be reviewed annually thereafter. The law and the regulations state that transition services should be addressed at a younger age when determined appropriate for the individual.

Practitioners and experts agree that age 16 may be too late, particularly for those students with complex transition needs and for those students at risk of dropping out of school. A logical time to begin long-range transition planning is when students are in or are preparing to leave middle school. This is the time when students traditionally make decisions regarding their course of study in high school.

Transition services may be any service or program that promotes a student's successful movement into postsecondary education, employment, and independent living. These services may be special education or general education or related services. Some students with disabilities will not require specialized transition services. Some will require services only in one area or only at one time during their high school career. Some students will require complex interagency cooperation to meet their transition goals. In Table 4.1 is an IEP Transition Checklist on which the educational team can draw.

All IEP meetings must include the student's teacher, parent or parents, and administrator. When transition planning is being discussed, the student is to be invited to participate. If students cannot or choose not to attend the IEP meeting, then the IEP team will be expected to seek other means of acquiring student input. Parents must be informed that the student will be invited to the IEP meeting.

REHABILITATION ACT OF TRANSITION AMENDMENT OF 1992

Another important piece of legislation that affects the transition of students from school to work is the Rehabilitation Act Amendments of 1992 (P.L.

102–569). The definition of transition services included in the amendments *duplicates* the one found in IDEA. The Amendments recognize that many students with the most severe disabilities will exit school systems, requiring rehabilitation services. Consequently, the new regulations mandate a state plan that requires the state rehabilitation agency to address the development of policies that will assure coordination between the rehabilitation agencies and state education agencies (see Figure 4.1). The outcome is to assure that students exiting the schools who require rehabilitation services receive those services with no interruption in service (Inge & Brooke, 1993).

It is also important for consumers, advocates, and professionals to know that the new Amendments are guided by the presumption of ability: A person with a disability, *regardless of the severity of the disability,* can achieve employment and other rehabilitation goals, if the appropriate services and supports are made available. Therefore, the primary responsibilities of the vocational rehabilitation system are to

• assist the individual with a disability to make informed choices about potential employment

Table 4.1.   IEP Transition Checklist

IEP Components	Questions To Be Answered
Present Level of Performance	What transition-related skills does the student demonstrate?
Desired Postsecondary Outcomes	What are the long-range goals, dreams, and hopes held by the student and the family for further education? for employment? for adult living?
Annual Goals	What goal(s) are appropriate for this year that will improve the present level of performance relative to the desired outcome?
Objectives	What short-term objectives or activities need to be accomplished in order to achieve the annual goal(s) for transition areas?
Services	How, where, when, and with whom will transition services take place? Are community experiences an appropriate option?
Linkages	Does this transition service require linkage or referral to another service provider?

Note. Adapted from *Project UNITE Newsletter* (p. 11), by S. deFur, 1994, Alexandria: Virginia Department of Education. Adapted with permission.

GOALS AND PUBLIC EDUCATION. Each state plan must

... contain plans, policies, and procedures to be followed (including entering into a formal interagency cooperative agreement ... with education officials responsible for the provision of a free appropriate public education to students who are individuals with disabilities) that are designed to:

A) facilitate the development and accomplishment of

  (i)   long-term rehabilitation goals;
  (ii) intermediate rehabilitation objectives; and
  (iii) goals and objectives related to enabling a student to live independently before the student leaves a school setting, to the extent the goals and objectives described in clause (i) through (iii) are included in an individualized education program of the student, including the specification of plans for coordination with the educational agencies in the provision of transition services;

B) facilitate the transition from the provision of a free appropriate public education under the responsibility of an educational agency to the provision of vocational rehabilitation services under the responsibility of the designated State unit, including the specification of plans for coordination with educational agencies in the provision of transition services authorized under section 103(a)(14) to an individual, consistent with the individualized written rehabilitation program of the individual; and

C) provide that such plans, policies, and procedures will address

  (i)   provisions for determining State lead agencies and qualified personnel responsible for transition services;
  (ii) procedures for outreach to and identification of youth in need of such services; and
  (iii) a timeframe for evaluation and follow-up of youth who have received such services (Sec. 101(a)(24)).

Figure 4.1.　Rehabilitation Act Amendments of 1992.

outcomes that result in integration and inclusion in the community;

• develop an individualized rehabilitation program with the full participation of the person with a disability;

• match the needs and interests reflected in the individualized programs with the appropriate services and supports including rehabilitation technology and supported employment;

• proactively foster cooperative working relationships with other agencies and programs, including local education authorities, to unify the service system; and

• emphasize the quality of services and the accountability that service representatives have to honor the dignity, participation, and growth of persons with disabilities as their employment interests develop over time.

The transition provisions added to the act do not shift the burden for transition planning from education to rehabilitation. Instead, they promote coordination and collaboration between the two systems so service for eligible students is not interrupted. The state plan requirements for transition under the Rehabilitation Act Amendments include the following elements.

Eligibility

Prior to the Rehabilitation Act Amendments of 1992, an individual had to have evaluations to determine his or her rehabilitation potential and the feasibility for employability. Often these evaluations concluded that persons with the most severe disabilities were not eligible for services. However, because of advances in technology and supported employment, disability can no longer be equated with an inability to work (Inge & Brooke, 1993). With the assumption that people with disabilities can work, several critical changes will occur:

• The notion of feasibility is removed.

• The rehabilitation counselor must demonstrate that *no* employment outcome is possible in order to determine that a person is ineligible.

- The burden of proof for accessing the system shifts from the individual to the rehabilitation system.

A two-part process essentially determines a person's eligibility for rehabilitation services. First, does the person have a disability? Second, does he or she require assistance from the vocational rehabilitation system to achieve an employment outcome? The presumption of ability changes the emphasis from an evaluation of rehabilitation potential to an assessment of eligibility and rehabilitation needs.

Eligibility determinations must now focus first on existing data, particularly on information provided by the individual with a disability and his or her family or advocates. Other sources may include education agencies, social security agencies, the individual's personal physician, previous or current employer(s), community organizations such as United Cerebral Palsy affiliates, and any organization or person referring the individual. The use of existing data for determining eligibility for rehabilitation services has major implications for school systems. If students participate in school programs that provide community-based vocational training and paid work experiences prior to graduation, data will be available to establish eligibility for rehabilitation services after graduation. Students will have developed resumes and references from previous and current employers to demonstrate the feasibility of employment outcomes. In the sections that follow the importance of creating meaningful collaborations between counselors, educators, students, and the family is emphasized; these collaborations are key to ensuring an unbroken flow of services to the student.

Transition and Collaboration

As we noted previously, recent legislation has mandated that transition goals be addressed in students' IEPs. One way to improve transition planning is through collaborative planning between agencies such as states' departments of vocational rehabilitation, vocational education programs, and special education and general education programs. Dick (1987) reported the efforts of a consortium of personnel from public school districts, private special education agencies, and vocational rehabilitation agencies. The teachers were provided in-service training in vocational assessment terms, administration of assessment instruments, and interpretation of assessment results. As another means of collaboration, the teachers compiled a list of over 600 objectives from curricula such as that by Brolin (1978). These were eventually compiled into a bank of objectives that contained four broad goals with a total of 24 objectives and numerous subobjectives under those. These goals are presented in Table 4.2. These goals were then used by a vocational evaluator to generate a list of vocational recommendation items that matched the language used in the bank of objectives. This list helped reduce confusion regarding the jargon employed by different professional groups. In addition, it afforded the opportunity for individuals to open a dialogue to establish future collaborative efforts such as coordinating services and delineating roles and responsibilities of teachers, evaluators, and other individuals responsible for the transition process. Table 4.3 outlines objectives and corresponding assessment instruments and available curricula related to the objective. No evaluation of the quality of the assessment procedures or curricula was offered; the list merely represented readily used or available programs. More individuals with severe disabilities should be taught within the community as much as possible, and assessment of students' skills should be referenced to relevant present and future settings through ecological inventories. The assessment, objective, and curriculum items in Tables 4.2 and 4.3, however, are examples of a comprehensive system for identifying transition objectives and corresponding instruction.

Table 4.2.   Transitional Goals and Objectives

GOAL 1.0: IMPROVE DAILY LIVING SKILLS

Objectives

1.1   Increase consumer skills and ability to handle money.
    1.1.1   Increase life reading skills.
    1.1.2   Increase life math skills.
    1.1.3   Improve purchasing and consumer skills.
    1.1.4   Improve budgeting skills.
1.2   Increase knowledge of foods and nutrition.
    1.2.1   Increase knowledge about food buying and meal planning.
    1.2.2   Practice food preparation.
1.3   Improve ability to maintain clothing.
1.4   Improve ability to select housing and to manage a home.
    1.4.1   Improve ability to select housing.
    1.4.2   Improve ability to do home management.
1.5   Increase knowledge about community and government.
    1.5.1   Learn about community.
    1.5.2   Learn about government.
1.6   Increase awareness of leisure time and family activities.
1.7   Develop good health practices.
1.8   Improve mobility and traveling skills.

GOAL 2.0: IMPROVE PERSONAL–SOCIAL SKILLS

Objectives

2.1   Improve appearance.
2.2   Improve self-concept and awareness of emotions.
2.3   Improve verbal and written communication skills.
2.4   Improve information processing and problem solving.
2.5   Improve ability to interact with others.
2.6   Improve self-control.
2.7   Demonstrate male–female–friend social status.

GOAL 3.0: INCREASE PREVOCATIONAL SKILLS (DICK, 1987)

Objectives

3.1   Learn more about careers and work in preparation for jobs.
    3.1.1   Increase awareness about careers.
    3.1.2   Gather information about careers.
3.2   Develop a career plan.
3.3   Improve job-related communication skills.
    3.3.1   Improve job-related verbal communication.
    3.3.2   Improve job-related reading skills.
    3.3.3   Improve job-related writing skills.
3.4   Improve ability to do job-related math.
    3.4.1   Practice math related to jobs.
    3.4.2   Practice time and measurement related to jobs.
3.5   Improve perceptual motor skills related to occupations.

GOAL 4.0: INCREASE VOCATIONAL SKILLS

Objectives

4.1   Demonstrate skills needed to hunt for and acquire a job.
    4.1.1   Practice filling out applications.
    4.1.2   Demonstrate job interviewing.
    4.1.3   Demonstrate job hunting.
4.2   Know basics about equipment.
4.3   Improve needed job behaviors.
    4.3.1   Improve time on task.
    4.3.2   Improve following directions.
    4.3.3   Improve dealing with authority.
    4.3.4   Improve getting along with others.
    4.3.5   Improve accuracy of work.
    4.3.6   Improve job attitudes.
4.4   Learn advanced job knowledge/information.
4.5   Demonstrate ability to leave a job appropriately.

Collaboration Model

An excellent model for developing collaboration among agencies, the community, families, and disabled individuals is that provided by Lombard (1989). Although this model is built primarily around organizing activities to assist school, agency, and other service providers and advocates to facilitate successful transitions from school to postschool employment, it is equally applicable

Table 4.3.   Sample of Transition Objectives with Assessment and Curriculum Materials

GOAL 1.0: IMPROVE DAILY LIVING SKILLS
OBJECTIVE 1.1: INCREASE CONSUMER SKILLS AND ABILITY TO HANDLE MONEY

Assessment	Objectives	Curriculum
1.1.1 Life Reading Skills Brigance Inventory of Essential Skills, Section D—Functional Word Recognition Best Best—Reading and language arts section	1.1.1 Life Reading Skills a. Read and use sale ads to locate used car, furniture, apartments, or houses for rent. b. Read and complete commonly used forms and applications. c. Read and interpret insurance terms. d. Read newspaper for informational-consumer purposes. e. Read directions on boxes. f. Identify basic price labels, weights, measurements, expiration dates, and "in store" survival words.	1.1.1 Life Reading Skills P—School Specialty Developing Everyday Reading Skills ($3.25) Coping Skills—Using the Newspaper ($1.95)
1.1.2 Life Math Skills Brigance Inventory of Essential Skills, Section R—measurement, Section S—metrics	1.1.2 Life Math Skills a. Identify money and make change. b. Know how to handle a paycheck. c. Use the metric system related to shopping skills. d. Interpret sale prices. e. Interpret unit pricing of food items. f. Understand monthly income including types of financial assistance.	1.1.2 Life Math Skills P—Weekly Reader Figure It Out ($2.30) Math That Pays ($2.30) P—Janus Paychecks ($3.30) P—Publisher

Note. From "Translating Vocational Assessment Information into Transition Objectives and Instruction," by M. Dick, 1987, *Career Development for Exceptional Individuals, 10,* pp. 76–84. Reprinted with permission.

to all areas of community functioning. The model consists of the following components: steering committee, core change team, community survey, and community action plan. These components can be viewed as a task analysis for developing a transition program in any community.

Steering Committee. A steering committee is a small group of individuals who will coordinate the formation of the transition model and form a core change team. Individuals on this committee should include representatives from school districts, agencies, and other service programs. An additional suggestion is to include highly visible community members who can stimulate publicity and garner additional support (e.g., a political figure), as well as persons with disabilities or a parent or guardian of a person with a disability (Clees, 1991).

Core Change Team. This team is an expansion of the steering committee and includes all members of the committee plus individuals with disabilities;

their parents or guardians; rehabilitation personnel; administrators; individuals providing postsecondary services; medical personnel; vocational educators; and representatives from technical schools, colleges, social services, mental health services, and other agencies; and interested parties. The function of this team is to coordinate the remaining components of the model. This coordination is vital to providing the full range of support services that an individual requires to maintain status within the community. Without such collaboration, typical problems associated with uncoordinated services and isolated service providers (e.g., replication of services or service voids) are likely to occur (Everson, 1995).

Community Survey. This part of the model includes the identification of public school services and curricula, postsecondary training and employment options, and the continuum of adult support services. The support services that are integral to supported living and employment, as discussed earlier in this chapter, would be the target of such a survey. Surveys of recreation and leisure options and of supports as well as of public transportation and supported mobility options would also be needed. Table 4.4 is an example of a survey of public and private agencies and programs serving individuals with disabilities in Georgia. This survey was conducted by phone and personal interviews.

Some of the programs were discovered by the surveyors only after speaking to another agency or program. This survey, although not comprehensive, demonstrates what can be accomplished with little prior knowledge and with little time. The service providers were identified through the telephone directory or by referral from one agency or program to another, and only 1 to 2 hours per day over a 2-week period were needed to complete the survey (including interviews). This information could also be compiled through a mailed survey. In-person interviews, however, provide exposure to the agencies or programs.

Community Action Plan. A community action plan includes a plan to fill the voids in existing services (e.g., mobility training, development of a home support model) by conducting training to familiarize parents with available services and how to access them, developing interagency collaboration and cooperation (e.g., interagency service agreements regarding shared costs, delineation of responsibilities), and training school personnel to teach functional skills in all community living areas. Postschool service providers also need to develop these same skills.

Develop Plan for Individual Transition Process

This plan includes development of procedures for the in-school transition process, including the use of ecologic vocational surveys to identify skill strengths and deficits, the development of vocational and other transition goals (both within school and to the postschool world), the provision of instructional supports in vocational classes, and the identification of postschool follow-up procedures. The Individual Transition Plan (ITP) is not legally required in the same way as an IEP, nor does it hold the specificity of structure that the IEP holds. Transition planning needs to occur in the context of the IEP. In frequent communication with many teachers and other educational personnel, it becomes patently clear that the ITP is all too often only a stepchild to the IEP. It is not uncommon in a school system for the IEP meeting to last an hour to an hour and a half and then be followed by a 15- to 30-minute ITP meeting. In those school systems where these are the practices, it is most unfortunate because the whole idea of the ITP is to create a design or blueprint with a future orientation and in collaboration with the student and family. This purpose can hardly be accomplished in 15 to 20 minutes.

As an example of an ITP, we have provided the case of Sid, a 20-year-old with mental retardation (see Wehman, 1995). A detailed ITP is presented in Figure 4.2.

Table 4.4. Community Survey: Public and Private Agencies and Programs Serving Children, Youth, and Adults with Disabilities in Georgia

Agency/ Program	Responsibilities (as stated in interview)	Funding	Referred	Eligibility Requirements
Adult- Centered Education	1. Prepare for GED 2. Teach basic reading and math (illiteracy)	State	By self or advocate	16 years and older drop-outs, age-outs
Youth Detention Center	1. Holding facility—detention— waiting for court date Hold up to 90 days 2. Short-term treatment •Academics •Socialization skills •Wilderness skills	State	By juvenile court system To youth services	Court assigned Juvenile
Youth Services	1. Treatment and rehabilitation 2. Alternative placement (16 years and younger) 3. 16 years and older (Gainesville) •Provides on-the-job training •6 to 8 months average on job •Probation until court sentence completed	State	By Courts, OTP, YDC To Kelly Diversified work programs (Warm Springs)	Committed by courts; 16 years and younger Committed by courts; 16 years and older drop-outs
Troubled Children Committee	1. "Trouble shooter" 2. Family intervention	State	By Youth Services	Consistent problems in schools or with court system Juvenile
Joint Training Partnership Act	1. Private company receives up to one half of wages for placement of client •6-month requirement 2. Trainer—2 weeks on-the-job training	State and federal (grant programs)	By schools to companies in community	14 years and older Economic needs Handicapping condition Potential drop-out or has dropped out
Jobs for Georgia	1. 6 schools in state 2. State employee works with student (job specialist); serves as middle person between student and employer 3. Job specialist identifies 50 students •Must place 80% •6 months to place •Verbal contact every 2 weeks until placed	State Department of Labor	To companies in community	Graduating but not college bound
Division of Vocational Rehabilitation	1. Counselor works 1:1 •Sets up work experience in school setting (janitorial) •On-the-job training (e.g., florist, nursing home) 2. Work with family and school personnel 3. Teacher responsible for imple- mentation within school setting	State and federal	By school or agencies To Athens Technological Institute, colleges, companies in the community	16 years and older Disabilities

Individual Transition Plan 7

I. Career and Economic Self-Sufficiency

1. Employment Goal	Sid will work part time at a local library as a book filer with supported employment.
Level of present performance	Sid works 2½ hours per day in the library.
Steps needed to accomplish goal	(1) Apply to VR; (2) assist Sid in applying for the job; (3) provide on-site training as needed for Sid; (4) arrange for transportation; and (5) meet with appointed VR counselor to prepare for transition of support from school to VR.
Date of completion	6/1/95
Person(s) responsible for implementation	teacher and VR counselor
2. Vocational Education/Training Goal	Sid will work initially 4 hours per day at the school library with minimal supervision, and expand this number throughout the year.
Level of present performance	Sid performs required tasks at his current school-supported job site with minimal supervision.
Steps needed to accomplish goal	(1) Develop relationship with school librarian; (2) provide individualized training to Sid at the site; (3) fade support; and (4) arrange for observation of Sid at the site by Department of Rehabilitative Services (DRS) counselor.
Date of completion	10/1/94
Person(s) responsible for implementation	teacher
3. Postsecondary Education Goal	N/A
Level of present performance	

Figure 4.2. Example Individual Transition Plan. From *Individual Transition Plans: The Teacher's Curriculum Guide for Helping Youth with Special Needs* by P. Wehman, 1995, Austin, TX: PRO-ED. Copyright 1995 by PRO-ED, Inc. Reprinted with permission.

Individual Transition Plan 7

Steps needed to accomplish goal	
Date of completion	
Person(s) responsible for implementation	
4. Financial/Income Needs Goal	Sid will be financially independent of his sister/guardian.
Level of present performance	Sid is receiving SSI and a small paycheck. His sister handles all finances and takes care of Sid's basic needs. He does not have access to his funds.
Steps needed to accomplish goal	(1) Assist Sid in opening a bank account; (2) assist him in budgeting for clothes and recreation; and (3) assist Sid in maintaining his account.
Date of completion	3/1/95
Person(s) responsible for implementation	case manager and guardian with Social Security representative if available

II. Community Integration and Participation

4. Independent Living Goal	Sid will live in a supervised apartment with one or two roommates.
Level of present performance	Sid demonstrates basic self-care skills. He can do simple household chores and prepare cold foods.
Steps needed to accomplish goal	(1) Apply for residential services; (2) train Sid how to look for apartments; (3) continue instruction in self-care; and (4) continue instruction in simple cooking/shopping.
Date of completion	3/1/95
Person(s) responsible for implementation	teacher *(continues)*

Figure 4.2.   continued

Individual Transition Plan 7

6. Transportation/Mobility Goal	Sid will independently utilize special transportation services (STAR).
Level of present performance	Sid does not have access to public transportation. He spends evenings and weekends at home and travels by school bus to current work site.
Steps needed to accomplish goal	(1) Apply for transportation; (2) assist Sid in budgeting for transportation; (3) provide training in meeting and departing from van; (4) program phone for one-touch dialing for STAR; and (5) provide Sid with word and picture list of recreational sites to request.
Date of completion	5/1/95
Person(s) responsible for implementation	case manager, VR counselor, teacher, and Center for Independent Living
7. Social Relationships Goal	Sid will develop a relationship with a male peer or elder.
Level of present performance	Sid does not engage in activities with peers outside of school and does not have the presence of a male in his family.
Steps needed to accomplish goal	(1) Access volunteer from Sid's church or a community organization; and (2) budget for recreational activities.
Date of completion	5/1/94
Person(s) responsible for implementation	case manager and guardian
8. Recreational/Leisure Goal	Sid will obtain personal recreation items as needed.
Level of present performance	Sid loves music and enjoys listening to a Walkman at school. He has few items of his own other than clothes.
Steps needed to accomplish goal	(1) Assist Sid in accessing his funds; (2) take Sid in stores and continue instruction in making small leisure purchases in the community; and (3) teach Sid to use and maintain purchased recreational equipment. *(continues)*

Figure 4.2.   continued

Individual Transition Plan 7

Date of completion	4/1/95
Person(s) responsible for implementation	teacher and guardian

III. Personal Competence

9. Health/Safety Goal	Sid will receive routine medical attention.
Level of present performance	Sid has never visited a dentist and receives doctor check-ups only when mandatory.
Steps needed to accomplish goal	(1) Make appointments through community services; (2) identify appropriate dentist(s); (3) arrange for transportation; (4) help Sid know what to ask dentist; and (5) assist Sid in budgeting for fees.
Date of completion	4/1/95
Person(s) responsible for implementation	case manager and guardian
10. Self-Advocacy/Future Planning	Sid will obtain personal guardianship and alternative trusteeship.
Level of present performance	Sid can clearly express his desires. He is dependent in all financial matters. Current guardianship is not optimal.
Steps needed to accomplish goal	Seek legal counsel to assist in planning for alternative guardianship and trusteeship.
Date of completion	8/1/95
Person(s) responsible for implementation	case manager

Student Career Preference

Working in a library

Figure 4.2. continued

COMMUNITY-BASED VOCATIONAL PROGRAMS

Once the local community and individual student transition planning is underway, implementation of real-life functioning skills should be heavily emphasized. Cronin and Patton (1993) have observed the importance of infusing functional life skills into the daily curriculum. Falvey (1989) has written eloquently about how to teach these skills in community environments, and Chapter 16 of this book is devoted entirely to this important way of teaching persons with developmental disabilities.

A major outgrowth of interdisciplinary collaboration for transition must be established by providing students with community-based vocational experiences that take place in local businesses and industries. Vocational training must reflect a community's local economy in order to prepare students with severe disabilities for paid jobs by the time of graduation (Moon & Inge, 1993; Moon, Inge, Wehman, Brooke, & Barcus, 1990; Renzaglia & Hutchins, 1988; Wehman, 1992, 1995). Each school system's vocational curriculum will differ according to the community in which the students reside. Development of the curriculum will entail continual assessment of the local labor market to determine the major employers in the community, the types of employment most commonly available, and the type of employment that has been obtained by individuals with disabilities (Everson, 1995; Moon et al., 1990).

School systems are cautioned to analyze carefully the types of training experiences selected. For instance, it may be easy to develop a horticultural program on the school grounds or to obtain collating work from the school office for vocational training purposes. However, if these training experiences do not reflect future job possibilities, the students may have difficulty with their transition from school to work. In addition, teachers should limit simulated work in the classroom setting because such simulation does not provide the needed coworker/social integration training

that is critical for job success. Work experiences on the school grounds should be for younger students under 14 when community-based training is not an option (Moon, Kiernan, & Halloran, 1990; Renzaglia & Hutchins, 1988). Finally, as students near graduation, time in real job settings should increase until the majority of the school day is spent in the community (Brown et al., 1991; Sailor et al., 1986; Wehman, 1992, 1995). The following list details the sequence of the steps involved in designing a community-based instructional program:

1. Conduct a community job-market analysis.

2. Identify businesses with the targeted jobs and contact the personnel director or employer.

3. Select and analyze appropriate jobs for community-based training.

4. Schedule community-based training.

5. Design individual systematic instruction programs.

More information on this important topic is presented later in Chapter 16.

ADVOCACY

Advocates can play a vital role by acting on behalf of individuals with disabilities to maintain current levels of support in some areas while establishing or increasing the level of support in others. Advocates can be nearly anyone, including parents and relatives, coworkers, organization representatives, friends, service delivery personnel and professionals, other persons with disabilities, and the person with a disability serving as self-advocate. Advocacy activities are equally varied. They can be undertaken on behalf of an individual with a disability or in the interests of persons with disabilities in general. Numerous types of advocacy activities have been identified by Biklen (1979):

• service-related advocacy activities

- communicating goals to teachers, parents, employers, and coworkers

- coordinating services such as education or training, benefits, medical care, transportation, and recreation

- taking an active role in transition planning, beginning as early as possible during or after the school years

- training the individual at home, at work, or in the community

- training parents and others, such as group home and apartment supervisors, in skills such as performing ecologic inventories and task analytic instruction

- delivering instruction or services related to any or all settings

- providing emergency support related to health, transportation, and interpersonal factors

- politically related advocacy activities

  - demonstrating publicly on behalf of a person(s) with a disability

  - making demands

  - writing letters

  - developing newsletters and other communications

  - lobbying

  - boycotting businesses and organizations that are not accessible to or that support policies that discriminate against individuals with disabilities

  - litigating and providing or procuring legal advocacy

  - negotiating

  - providing model program demonstrations

Advocates may, in addition, provide reinforcement to programs, politicians, teachers, and agencies for providing beneficial supports and for being advocates themselves. This reinforcement may take the form of public recognition, letters to their supervisors, celebrations, and so forth (Clees, 1991).

Many advocates may lack the skills and the time to engage in all of the activities listed. The professions, interests, and other commitments of advocates will determine the type and extent of their advocacy activities. As Clees (1991) noted, advocates should, however, be willing to commit whatever strengths they have in a consistent manner over some period of time, particularly if the advocacy involves forming a personal relationship with a person who happens to have a disability. Even advocates who have no skills related to the disabilities of the persons for whom they advocate can provide valuable support, whether related to daily survival (e.g., grocery shopping, transportation) or given in the form of friendship.

FINAL THOUGHTS

In many ways, the future lives of young adults with disabilities will be influenced by the economic, social, and political forces in American society more than by any specific technological or instructional breakthroughs. More than ever, teachers and other helping professionals know how to help individuals with disabilities gain employment, enter the community successfully, and look forward to a good quality of life. The fact that this knowledge is not more significantly implemented is due more to certain dynamics in American society and local communities than to anything else. For example, those young people with disabilities who have learned what their rights are and how to advocate for those rights are more likely to be able to take advantage of the opportunities that exist in many communities today. Those young adults with disabilities who live in communities with thriving businesses and industry and a growing economy that calls for a diverse labor force are more likely to share in the fruits of meaningful employment than those who live in impoverished economic areas. Those young people with disabilities who have had the benefits of stable families and progressive schools and communities are more likely to have a greater degree of hope and courage to try new ideas and innovations.

The future can be very rich indeed for young adults with disabilities, but they face similar challenges as all youths in American society. The future can be as rich and positive for young people with disabilities as they themselves wish to work toward in conjunction with their families and teachers. This generation of young people has spawned a Miss America, Heather Whitestone, who is hearing impaired; it has lifted Chris Burke, a young person with Down syndrome, into the national media spotlight as a star of *Life Goes On;* and there are many other examples of young people with disabilities achieving great success. The challenge awaits people with disabilities, their families, and teachers to help them fully attain their potential.

REFERENCES

Biklen, D. (1979). *Community imperative: A refutation of all arguments in support of deinstitutionalizing anybody because of mental retardation.* Syracuse, NY: Human Policy Press.

Brolin, D. (1978). *Life centered career education: A competency-based approach.* Reston, VA: Council for Exceptional Children.

Brown, L., Swartz, P., Udvari-Solner, A., Kampschroer, E. F., Johnson, F., Jorgensen, J., & Gruenewald, L. (1991). How much time should students with severe intellectual disabilities spend in regular education classrooms and elsewhere? *Journal of the Association for Persons with Severe Handicaps, 9*(4), 262, 269.

Clark, G., & Kolstoe, O. (1994). *Career education and transition.* Boston: Allyn & Bacon.

Clees, T. (1991). Community living. In P. J. McLaughlin & P. Wehman (Eds.), *Developmental disabilities* (pp. 228–267). Austin, TX: PRO-ED.

Cronin, M., & Patton, J. R. (1993). *Life skills for individuals with special needs.* Austin, TX: PRO-ED.

deFur, S. (1994). *Project Unite Newsletter.* Alexandria: Virginia Department of Education.

Dick, M. (1987). Translating vocational assessment information into transition objectives and instruction. *Career Development for Exceptional Individuals, 10*(2), 76–84.

Everson, J. (1995). *Supporting individuals with deaf-blind impairment in the community.* Baltimore: Brookes.

Falvey, M. A. (1989). *Community-based curriculum: Instructional strategies for students with severe handicaps* (2nd ed.). Baltimore: Brookes.

Individuals with Disabilities Education Act, 20 U.S.C. §§1400–1485 (1990).

Inge, K. J., & Brooke, V. (Eds.). (1993, Winter). *Rehabilitation Act Amendments of 1992 Newsletter.* Richmond: Virginia Commonwealth University, Rehabilitation Research and Training Center on Supported Employment.

Lombard, R. (1989). *Collaborative community based transition model: An implementation manual.* Paper presented at the 67th annual convention of the Council on Exceptional Children, San Francisco.

Moon, M. S., & Inge, K. J. (1993). Vocational training, transition planning, and employment for students with severe disabilities. In M. Snell (Ed.), *Systematic instruction of persons with severe disabilities* (4th ed., pp. 117–132). Columbus, OH: Merrill.

Moon, M. S., Inge, K. J., Wehman, P., Brooke, V., & Barcus, J. M. (1990). *Helping persons with severe mental retardation get and keep employment: Supported employment issues and strategies.* Baltimore: Brookes.

Moon, M. S., Kiernan, W., & Halloran, W. (1990). School-based vocational programs and labor laws: A 1990 update. *Journal of the Association for Persons with Severe Handicaps, 15*(3), 177–185.

Rehabilitation Act Amendments, 29 U.S.C. § 101(c) (1992).

Renzaglia, A., & Hutchins, M. (1988). A community-referenced approach to preparing persons with disabilities for employment. In P. Wehman & M. S. Moon (Eds.), *Vocational rehabilitation and supported employment* (pp. 91–112). Baltimore: Brookes.

Sailor, W., Halvorsen, A., Anderson, J., Goetz, L., Gee, K., Doering, K., & Hunt, P. (1986). Community intensive instruction. In R. H. Horner, L. H. Meyer, & H. D. B. Fredericks (Eds.), *Education of learners with severe handicaps: Exemplary service strategies* (pp. 251–288). Baltimore: Brookes.

Wehman, P. (1992). *Life beyond the classroom: Transition strategies for young people with disabilities.* Baltimore: Brookes.

Wehman, P. (1995). *Individual transition plans: The teacher's curriculum guide for helping youth with special needs.* Austin, TX: PRO-ED.

Growing Older

Michael Malone and Nancy Kropf

LEARNING GOALS

Upon completion of this chapter the reader will be able to

- discuss the population characteristics of older individuals with lifelong disabilities;

- discuss how quality-of-life issues affect older individuals with lifelong disabilities;

- identify critical components of the "Bill of Rights" for older individuals with lifelong disabilities;

- discuss various health care needs of older individuals with lifelong disabilities;

- identify and discuss various residential placement options and the issues that are critical to consider in relocation efforts that affect the lives of older individuals with lifelong disabilities; and

- identify various types of services and supports and discuss the relative merits of each relative to older individuals with lifelong disabilities.

CASE EXAMPLE: NANCY

Nancy is a friendly and outgoing 59-year-old woman who lives with her elderly mother. Nancy has been diagnosed as having mild mental retardation and experiences seizures. For the last 15 years she has been employed at a local sheltered workshop, performing a variety of jobs. Although Nancy concentrates on her work, her job performance and earnings are only 40% of the current rate paid to 100% performance workers in the same job. In her free time, Nancy likes to listen to music, watch television, and go shopping. She occasionally socializes with friends from the sheltered workshop but considers her mother to be her best friend. Nancy's mother assists her with her fi-

nances, transportation, purchases, and the acquisition of health care services. What will be Nancy's future when her mother is no longer able to provide the type of support that Nancy currently receives? Will Nancy be able to continue a similar lifestyle? How will Nancy meet the financial obligations of maintaining the same quality of life she currently enjoys?

CASE EXAMPLE: DON

Don is a 64-year-old who has been diagnosed as having moderate mental retardation, has limited communication skills, and demonstrates deficits in daily living skills. Don lived at home with his parents until his father passed away, at which time Don was 45 years old. After his father's death, Don's mother felt she could no longer care for Don by herself and had him admitted to a nearby institution. Prior to his move to the institution, Don was not required to assist in his own care nor was he engaged in any out-of-the-home work experiences. Don has been working as a housekeeper in the building where he lives for the past 5 years. Lately, Don has begun showing resistance when prompted to get ready to go to work. He chooses to lounge on the sofa, watching the television. Numerous prompts by staff are needed to get Don to go to work. Staff who know Don believe that he wants to retire. Given that Don has made excellent progress in learning new daily living and job-related skills, should he be encouraged to maintain his current working status? To what would Don retire? What would Don's quality of life be if he remains working? If he retires?

••

To address the issues of best practices that benefit individuals such as Nancy and Don, just profiled, one must begin with the seemingly simple question, Who are Nancy and Don? Such inquiry must take two forms: the general *who* relative to descriptions of the population to which individuals such as Nancy and Don belong and the specific *who* relative to individual characteristics and needs. Comprehension of the general *who* provides professionals with information that enables them to understand and address issues related to the specific *who*. Indeed, failure to comprehend general population descriptions and trends relative to individuals with developmental disabilities (hereafter referred to as lifelong disabilities) as they enter into late life limits our ability to develop best practices in service delivery. In this chapter, we attempt to provide material that will contribute to efforts to provide services and supports to individuals with lifelong disabilities as they enter into late life. Specifically, we discuss identification of the aging segment of our society who have lifelong disabilities and relevant issues associated with quality of life,

health care, service provision, placement and supported living, finance, regulations and legal considerations, and, finally, daily activities and programs.

DEMOGRAPHIC PROFILE

With the "graying" of our society, we have witnessed great changes in the national population profile (*Aging America*, 1991; Schaie & Willis, 1986). Projections indicate that, as we move into the 21st century, the proportion of our society composed of people who have made the transition into late life will increase substantially. This continued expansion in the ranks of individuals within the general population who are elderly is paralleled by the growth in numbers of individuals with lifelong disabilities who are also aging (Lubin & Kiely, 1985; Maaskant, 1993). Efforts to estimate the prevalence of individuals with lifelong disabilities who have made the transition from midlife to late life have been limited by several factors. These include estimating only those individuals with diagnoses of mental retardation and excluding other lifelong disability diagnoses, including only older individuals who are connected to formal service systems, and the lack of precision that exists in defining the lower limit of *aged* for this population (M. Seltzer, 1992).

Although the definition of lifelong disabilities put forth in the Developmental Disabilities Assistance and Bill of Rights Act of 1993 identifies various conditions that may impact on an individual's ability to function independently, most of what is known regarding individuals with lifelong disabilities in the later years is based on individuals with mental retardation. As M. Seltzer (1992) suggested, little is known regarding service provision to those individuals with noncognitive lifelong disabilities. Increases in the numbers of individuals with lifelong disabilities who are elderly may be attributed to a variety of factors including the shift in the population profile discussed previously; identification efforts at the state level resulting from increased awareness and attention from federal agencies; and improved health care, which has substantially extended life expectancies of individuals with certain lifelong disabilities (Cotten, Sison, & Starr, 1981; DiGiovanni, 1978; M. Seltzer & Seltzer, 1985; Thurman, 1986).

To develop services for an aging population, one must determine what constitutes a transition from midlife to late life for this group. The most widely used marker defining late life has been chronologic age. The lower limit of "old age" used by professionals has ranged from 30 years of age to 65 years of age (Segal, 1977; M. Seltzer & Seltzer, 1985; Thurman, 1986; Tymchuk, 1979; Walz, Harper, & Wilson, 1986). Age 60 is considered the point of transition in the Older Americans Act of 1965 (1989). Age 55 appears frequently in the literature and is consistent with many federal programs (Segal, 1977). Although chronologic age, especially that of 55 years, may be useful as an arbitrary marker for entrance into old age for individuals with extended life expectancies, it proves to be a less than adequate marker for individuals who are more severely involved, have limited adaptive skills, or whose medical background is associated with a life expectancy below 55 years (Eyman & Borthwick-Duffy, 1994). As suggested by Seltzer and Krauss (1987), a more useful approach may be to identify certain life stages or functional abilities that alert one to an individual's transition to late life. A number of alternatives to chronologic age have been proposed, including Thurman's (1986) suggestion of subtracting 10 years from the average life expectancy of specific groups to determine eligibility for designated elder services and Eisdorfer's (1983) four life stages identified in Table 5.1.

Finally, other indexes of aging that have been discussed in the literature include biological aging focused on the physical aspects of aging; social aging focused on societal expectations related to productivity and attitudes toward aging in general; and psychological aging focused on intellectual functioning, emotional adjustment, and individual perceptions of aging (Birren, 1959; M. Seltzer, 1985b; Thurman, 1986).

Table 5.1. Eisdorfer's Life Stages

Stage	Description
1	*Early Life:* Resources are invested in youth with the expectation that future societal benefits will follow.
2	*Midlife:* Adult workers contribute goods and services to benefit society.
3	*Post Work:* Individuals retire healthy and remain functionally independent.
4	*Late Life:* Less-than-healthy individuals become functionally dependent on others.

Note. Based on information in "Conceptual Models of Aging: The Challenge of a New Frontier" by C. Eisdorfer, 1983, *American Psychologist, 38,* pp. 197–202.

Each of these approaches has its merits relative to alerting professionals to an individual's transition into late life, but no single measure of the transition period from midlife to late life appears entirely satisfactory. The use of chronologic age as a marker is limited due to the variability of life expectancies among subgroups. Dependence on either life-stage or domain-specific aging indexes to determine eligibility for aging services is problematic because both rely on functional limitations in life activities as a diagnostic marker. In light of the apparent limitations of each of the preceding approaches, the reliance on multiple indicators would seem to have the greatest utility to service providers. A definition including chronologic age to satisfy agency requirements and qualifiers related to functional aspects of society and aging would be most useful. This definition should include those characteristics described in the Older Americans Act Amendments and measures of the aging process relative to physical change, change in cognitive ability related to performing daily activities, emotional change, and change in social skills, any of which may impact negatively on the quality of life and longevity of an individual.

For such an approach to be viable, efforts must be made to collect specific demographic and epidemiological data to guide decisions related to services appropriate for a heterogeneous group of individuals with lifelong disabilities as they age. At the present time, little information of this type exists except possibly for individuals with mental retardation, and, even for this group, definitive data are not available. A 1% to 3% prevalence rate is typically applied to figures on the general population to estimate the number of individuals with lifelong disabilities in late life (M. Seltzer & Krauss, 1987; Sison & Cotten, 1989; Tymchuk, 1979; Walz et al., 1986). These prevalence estimates typically refer to individuals with mental retardation and differ dramatically from estimates (e.g., 12% to 13%) made of the total population of individuals with disabilities in various states (Jacobson, Sutton, & Janicki, 1985; Walz et al., 1986).

As interest in older individuals with diagnoses other than mental retardation increases (Gold & Whelan, 1992; Turk & Machemer, 1993), efforts should be made to include these older adults in prevalence estimates. Indeed, the inclusion of all relevant individuals in these efforts would result in a more accurate estimate of the number of elders with lifelong disabilities than that which we currently have based on only individuals with mental retardation. Combining prevalence rates used by the United Cerebral Palsy Association (0.3%), the Epilepsy Foundation of America (0.4%), the National Society for Children and Adults with Autism (0.032%), and the rate suggested by Baroff (1982) of 0.396% for individuals with mental retardation results in a total prevalence rate of about 1%. This 1% prevalence estimate and the population projections reported in Rice and Feldman (1983) result in the estimated number of individuals with lifelong disabilities who are 65 years or older shown in Table 5.2.

Such figures should be viewed with caution because mortality rates for any given subgroup are not considered when prevalence rates are applied to the general population. Research has shown that individuals who are not severely involved and who demonstrate adaptive skills related to toileting, eating, and mobility are more likely to live longer than are individuals who are severely involved and have substantial deficits in adaptive skills (Eyman & Borthwick-Duffy, 1994). In addition, it is believed that, as in the general population, the rate of disability accelerates with age after age 50 to 55 (Blake, 1981; Janicki & Jacobson, 1986). Increased disability may be associated with a loss of function and death (Anderson, 1989; Eyman, Call, & White, 1989). Although trends may be discussed, the individual differences in experience, in etiology and functional ability, in gender, and in residential history must not be overlooked.

Although the lack of specific demographic and epidemiological data limits the extent to which professionals can obtain precise figures, reliance on liberal estimates may lead to a service system better prepared to handle the actual population expansion. Error in this direction is preferable to error in a more conservative direction, for example, error resulting from reliance on estimates derived from actual service recipients because many older individuals are outside or minimally involved with mental retardation/developmental disabilities (MR/DD) services (Smith, Fullmer, & Tobin, 1994). A conservative error could result in the service system's being inadequately prepared to accommodate the increasing numbers of individuals with lifelong disabilities as they reach late life.

Table 5.2. Estimated Number of Individuals with Lifelong Disabilities, 65 Years and Older

Year	Prevalence Estimate
1980	258,920
1990	315,580
2000	362,520
2020	526,530
2040	672,560

QUALITY OF LIFE

The phrase "quality of life," widely used in the field of mental retardation in this past decade (Landesman, 1986), seems on the surface to be self-defining. One's quality of life may be viewed as a function of those ingredients in one's life that enhance personal growth, independence, health, and overall happiness. Attainment of optimum quality of life is facilitated through the protection of rights and the receipt of needed services. The definition of quality of life becomes less clear, however, when service providers working with individuals with lifelong disabilities in later life attempt to specify those elements that contribute to personal growth, independence, health, and happiness and how to guarantee rights and services to this group. Thus, the definition and the understanding of the concept of quality of life have become great challenges in developing best practices for service delivery to individuals such as Nancy and Don (profiled at the beginning of this chapter).

As discussed by Schalock, Keith, Hoffman, and Karan (1989), the concept of quality of life may be defined from three perspectives: social, psychological, and social policy. From the social perspective, quality of life may be defined in terms of influences external to the individual. Such environmental influences include social welfare, standard of living, formal and informal supports, education, housing, public services, health services, safety, and leisure programming. Edgerton and Gaston's (1991) study of older individuals who had been deinstitutionalized demonstrated how an array of these factors must be present to support older individuals with lifelong disabilities in community settings. Although this list is not exhaustive, it provides direction to addressing quality-of-life issues from a community standpoint.

In contrast to this perspective, the psychological perspective of quality of life represents those things that hold personal relevance to an individual in maintaining or improving life conditions such as independence, productivity, and accep-tance. These personal perceptions include satisfaction with the environmental influences discussed previously as well as general, perceived happiness and well-being. An increase in one's satisfaction with personal–social resources seems to be related to increases in life satisfaction, a sense of well-being, and feelings of personal competence.

The final perspective, noted by Schalock and coworkers (1989), from which the concept of quality of life can be understood is that of social policy. The social policy perspective relates to the documentation of needs that can be used to allocate fiscal resources. As defined by Murrel and Norris (1983), quality of life is a function of the degree to which human and environmental resources complement one another. Best practices in service delivery cannot be developed without an understanding of both the needs of individuals with lifelong disabilities as they enter into late life and the means with which to provide the services to address those stated needs.

How can service providers help elderly individuals with lifelong disabilities continue to grow as individuals and maintain health and happiness in relation to the social, psychological, and social policy perspectives? This challenge can be met in a number of ways. Professionals must be aware of and understand the rights of older individuals as fellow human beings and as recognized by law. A number of these rights, summarized in Table 5.3, have been outlined by Cotten and Spirrison (1986), Walker (1985), Malone (1993), and others. Such a bill of rights is applicable to all individuals with lifelong disabilities as they enter into late life.

Acknowledgment and comprehension of these rights, however, are not enough. As service providers, we must take the appropriate steps to guarantee that individual rights are respected and enforced. Although organizations advocating the rights of individuals with lifelong disabilities exist (e.g., United Cerebral Palsy Association, American Association on Mental Retardation, Epilepsy Foundation of America, National Society for Children and Adults with Autism), a need exists for advocacy groups that focus on issues impor-

Table 5.3.   Bill of Rights for Individuals
with Lifelong Disabilities

- The right to be considered a person first, not a condition or diagnosis

- The right to be recognized as an individual with likes and dislikes, strengths and weaknesses, and good days and bad days

- The right to an adequate standard of living and economic security

- The right to have the opportunity for self-expression

- The right to individualized and personalized services that promote full personal potential

- The right to an array of services that is generally available to other groups

- The right to live as independently as one wishes in the community of one's choice and in as typical a manner as is possible

- The right to participate in and contribute to the community

- The right to supported well-being and to qualified care when required

- The right to be personally involved in setting goals and making decisions affecting one's own life

- The right to occupy one's leisure time in personally satisfying ways

- The right to pursue spiritual satisfaction

- The right to succeed and fail on one's own terms

- The right to a positive future, with appropriate levels of involvement, freedom, and choice, regardless of age

- The right to enjoy typical family relationships, companionship, and romance

- The right to appropriate levels of activity and attention to permit continued integrity of self, individual identity, and purpose

- The right to an interesting environment and lifestyle, with an availability of options to provide a variety of surroundings

- The right to choose to retire, at an appropriate age, and to be able to look forward to postwork life and experiences that are rewarding

- The right to dignity in life and death

tant to those individuals who are aging (Sison & Cotten, 1989; Tymchuk, 1979; Walz et al., 1986). The basic rights that protect and enhance the quality of life of elderly citizens should be the same for both the general population and for the population of citizens with lifelong disabilities. We must recognize, however, that the latter group may require additional consideration to ensure they have the opportunity to experience life at its fullest. In providing such assurances, we must be careful to provide a balance between the role of guardian and respect for autonomy of the individual (Howell, 1988). All too often, professionals fail to ask for input from the individual with a lifelong disability when making decisions that will affect that individual's life. We must be careful not to abuse the rights and freedoms of those individuals we are intending to help. As we noted previously, individuals with lifelong disabilities who reach old age typically are not severely involved and have strengths in skills related to daily living. These individuals have the capacity and deserve the opportunity to have input into decisions that will directly affect the quality of their lives. The acknowledgment of rights such as those identified in this chapter will likely promote and enhance feelings of personal relevance and self-direction within the individual with a lifelong disability and his or her family.

In addition to acknowledging, understanding, and guaranteeing the rights of older individuals with lifelong disabilities, professionals must also be aware of the basic needs of this group. Tibbits (1979) suggested that all older individuals have a need

- to render some socially useful service

- to be considered a part of the community

- to occupy increased leisure time in satisfying ways

- to enjoy normal companionship

- for recognition as an individual

- for opportunity for self-expression

- for health protection and care
- for suitable mental stimulation [and emotional support]
- for living arrangements and family relationships
- for spiritual satisfactions

A primary medium through which rights and needs of older individuals with lifelong disabilities are addressed is the support system, both formal and informal. These issues are discussed later in this chapter. In brief, service providers attuned to the multifaceted nature of quality of life will be better able to develop best practices to benefit individuals with lifelong disabilities who are aging. One must be aware of and work to protect the rights and needs of these individuals. Issues related to underutilization of services and supports must be addressed. These efforts will do much to enhance the quality of life of individuals with lifelong disabilities as they age.

HEALTH CARE

Individuals with lifelong disabilities who attain late life (by traditional markers) typically are less severely disabled, are ambulatory, do not have major physical or behavioral limitations, and have adequate self-care skills (Eyman & Borthwick-Duffy, 1994). Richards (1975) noted that death in this group as it ages may be related more to risk factors particular to a severe disabling condition than to the aging process itself. Although some factors are physiological (e.g., early onset of Alzheimer's disease in individuals who have Down syndrome), other risk factors are a result of social issues such as barriers to adequate medical services, lack of trained health professionals to provide services to older individuals who have lifelong disabilities, and previous negative experiences with health care professionals (G. Seltzer & Luchterhand, 1994). Even for those individuals who are not affected by such risk factors, health issues play an important role. In general,

individuals with lifelong disabilities experience physiologic and physical changes associated with aging similar to those experienced by individuals without lifelong disabilities (Hand, 1993).

Although there are similarities between individuals with and without lifelong disabilities that are associated with the aging process, age-related health changes may occur earlier in the lives of individuals with lifelong disabilities (M. Seltzer & Seltzer, 1985). The most dramatic example of the early onset of an age-related health problem is the diagnosis of Alzheimer's disease in many individuals with Down syndrome while they are 30 to 40 years old (Wisniewski & Hill, 1985).

Care Issues

There do not appear to be any specialized best practices associated with the provision of health services to citizens with lifelong disabilities. There is a general perception, however, that older individuals with lifelong disabilities are underserved in health care and that many health providers have little training in, understanding of, or sensitivity to health issues of this group of older adults (G. Seltzer & Luchterhand, 1994). The Department of Health and Human Services (DHHS; 1987) noted that the use of health and medical services by elderly individuals with lifelong disabilities may be related to an individual's level of independence. An individual who has been relatively independent all his or her life is likely to have used and will continue to use regular health services. Such an individual may require additional assistance from others as he or she ages. Individuals who are less independent (e.g., individuals living in a supervised residential setting) will most likely use generic health services but will require, depending on their needs, a larger array of supports than will individuals with greater degrees of independence. As individuals with less independence age, they may require certain specialized services (e.g., vision screening). Individuals with the least independence, typically individuals with severe disabilities, have historically lived in larger residential care facilities (e.g., intermediate care facilities for individuals with mental retardation [ICFs/MR]) that staff medical personnel. Given the availability of health services at the facility, these individuals are the least likely to seek out generic health care services. This pattern may change as the deinstitutionalization process continues and some individuals with the most severe disabilities take advantage of community-based supports.

A national survey of facilities for individuals with lifelong disabilities revealed that individuals aged 63 to 74 years experienced health problems comparable to their cohorts without lifelong disabilities. High blood pressure, arthritis, and heart disease proved to be the most common ailments for both groups (Anderson, 1989). Anderson also found, as did Krauss and Seltzer (1986), that individuals living in institutional settings are perceived to need more medical care than do those living in community residences. Community residents were noted to have a greater number of unmet needs by Krauss and Seltzer (1986). However, Anderson (1989) speculated that the institutionalized group is not more medically needy, but that service availability is often translated into the concept of need in developmental centers.

Alzheimer's Disease

Dementia is defined as a symptomatologic diagnosis whereby there is a loss of intellectual functioning severe enough to interfere with occupational or social functioning (American Psychiatric Association, 1987). Dementia indicates reduced functional abilities in all aspects of an individual's life. Dementia may follow a rapid, slow, or erratic course. Sometimes the dementia stops temporarily, allowing the individual to enjoy a period of stability.

Diagnosis of dementia among individuals without disabilities nominally focuses on four different areas of performance (Wisniewski & Hill,

1985). Intactness of short-term memory, decrease in ability to think abstractly, inflexibility in thinking, and overall slowing of activity manifested in all areas of life are the primary areas of intellectual decline noted. Diagnosis of dementia is particularly difficult with individuals who experience a lifelong disability. The difficulty increases as the severity of disability increases. Apathy, abrupt emotional changes, lack of care in grooming and hygiene, decreased expressive abilities, and the detection of abnormalities during neurologic evaluations have been reported in individuals with Down's syndrome and Alzheimer's disease.

Although some question has been raised on the issue, current evidence suggests a link between Down syndrome and Alzheimer's disease. Studies have indicated incidence rates that range from 20% to 45% of the groups studied. Rasmussen and Sobsey (1994) discussed the difficulties in dementia diagnosis in Down syndrome. Complicating factors include a lack of early detection and an imperfect correlation between physiological changes in the brain and corresponding behavioral changes. The problem in estimating prevalence is further complicated by the functional and residential status of participants in many studies, that is, individuals who tend to have severe or profound mental retardation and who reside in institutional settings (Wisniewski & Hill, 1985).

Individuals with Down syndrome aged 30 or older should complete a mental status evaluation on a yearly basis. This evaluation can be completed in conjunction with a recommended annual physical examination. A mental status evaluation typically focuses on abilities associated with concentration, orientation, and memory. Intelligence tests should also be administered regularly to examine constancy of intellect. Careful observation by caregivers should reveal any changes in daily living skills. Early signs of dementia require referral to specialists for further diagnosis. Indeed, locating an instrument to assess mental status for individuals with lifelong disabilities can be problematic.

The care of an individual with lifelong disabilities and Alzheimer's disease is essentially the same as that for a person with Alzheimer's disease without a lifelong disability. Reality orientation can provide a routine to help structure the individual's day. The goal is to encourage independence while ensuring safety of the person involved. Respite care is an important part of the intervention plan for the caregivers. Participation in a support group that focuses on the families of patients with Alzheimer's disease is also helpful for many caregivers.

Mental Health

Information-processing problems; associated medical, physical, or sensory disorders; an inability to express one's feelings adequately; and cultural influences are associated with the development of mental health issues in individuals with mental retardation. Although families and service providers may believe that shielding individuals with lifelong disabilities from painful or complicated facts is preferable, incorrect or misleading information has the consequence of confusing or provoking anxiety (see Yanok & Beifus, 1993). Individuals with mental retardation develop severe mental illness or difficult behaviors at a rate almost twice the rate of individuals without mental retardation (Menolascino & Potter, 1989).

In a study of mental illness in individuals with retardation, Menolascino and Potter (1989) identified the major types of mental illness encountered. Of 76 elderly individuals with mental retardation evaluated for 9 months in a psychiatric hospital, almost one third exhibited schizophrenic behaviors. Other diagnoses were dementia (both senile and Alzheimer's type), affective disorders such as depression, adjustment disorders such as brief reactive psychoses, personality disorders including schizoid type, and anxiety disorders (Menolascino & Potter, 1989).

A fundamental requirement in the delivery of services to elderly individuals with mental retardation and mental illness is the provision of an intensive schedule of intervention (Menolascino & Potter, 1989). Thoughtful caregivers who show individuals how to express themselves and who prompt individuals to learn new coping behaviors are critical to the intervention process. In addition, interventions may involve the use of psychoactive medications. Psychopharmacology in the older population has been controversial for many years because many biological processes important to effective pharmacological intervention (e.g., the absorption, transport, metabolic integration, and excretion of drugs) change with advancing age. As a result, many drugs affect elderly individuals differently than they affect younger cohorts. When psychoactive medications are combined with other medications used to treat physical ailments, the interaction of the drugs can produce unexpected side effects. In addition, psychotropic drugs sometimes produce serious side effects such as heart rhythm changes or involuntary movements as a result of tardive dyskinesia (Rinck & Calkins, 1989). In spite of all these considerations, older individuals with lifelong disabilities are prescribed and consume more psychoactive drugs than younger individuals (Anderson & Polister, 1993; Pary, 1993).

Vision

Most people lose some visual function with age (DiStefano & Aston, 1986). Loss of visual acuity (sharpness of image at a distance), loss of ability to focus quickly, inability to see clearly closely, sensitivity to glare, need for increased light, and difficulty seeing well at night are some of the more common difficulties encountered. Each of these occurs as a function of age. The most common causes of visual deterioration are cataracts, senile macular degeneration, diabetes mellitus, and glaucoma (DiStefano & Aston, 1986). Cataracts, which cloud the lens, are the most common cause of reduced vision in elderly individuals. Recommended medical intervention includes the surgical removal of the cataract. Macular degeneration, a second cause of visual deterioration, is the major cause of blindness in elderly individuals. The part of the retina that allows the perception of fine detail and color deteriorates slowly. Blurring and clouding of vision are common complaints. Although laser treatment can be a successful intervention, early diagnosis and prompt treatment of the condition are critical. A third consideration, diabetes, may cause a variety of visual dysfunctions, many of which are caused by uncontrolled blood sugar levels. Prompt medical intervention is a must if any visual irregularities occur, because many of these conditions are irreversible. Finally, service providers must consider glaucoma as a causal agent of visual impairment. Although glaucoma is not directly related to the aging process, the slow progression of the disease may result in late identification, after serious damage has occurred. Glaucoma is associated with increased pressure within the eye, which results in nerve damage and permanent loss of peripheral vision. The individual is left with what is commonly called tunnel vision (DiStefano & Aston, 1986).

These vision-related limitations affect the elderly regardless of disability status. However, the person with a lifelong disability may not be able to adequately describe the symptoms and receive appropriate and timely intervention. Unfortunately, assessment of visual impairments has been a neglected area of research and practice for older individuals with lifelong disabilities (G. Seltzer & Luchterhand, 1994). It is imperative for caregivers and others close to the individual with a disability to be attentive to the symptoms of these conditions and to the behavior of the elderly individual with a disability. A person with a lifelong disability may appear to lose some functional daily living skills with no apparent cause. The diminishment of such skills may be associated with visual deterioration and should prompt appropriate screening efforts.

Assistive devices and adjustments to daily routines may allow individuals with visual impairments to capitalize on their remaining vision. Magnifiers can be used for image enlargement; field-expanding devices allow those with tunnel vision to increase their mobility; large-print books are now available; and higher wattage light may be beneficial. Contrasting colors of electrical wall plates, dishes and placemats, combs and brushes, and stairs (by placing contrasting tape on steps) may also assist individuals in leading a life to which they are accustomed. Devices such as the Kurzwell Reading Machine, which translates printed words into synthesized speech via computer and talking books, are available. Finally, mobility training may be warranted (DiStefano & Aston, 1986).

Hearing

Hearing loss is so common in elderly individuals that it is rarely evaluated (Glass, 1986). There is no evidence that older individuals with lifelong disabilities experience symptoms of hearing loss more frequently than the general population of elderly individuals. Presbycusis is the term used to describe normal hearing loss due to aging. Inability to hear speech clearly, even though the enunciation and volume are adequate (speech discrimination), an increased sensitivity to certain sounds or pitch that sound especially loud (recruitment), and sounds within one's ears (tinnitus) are characteristic of age-related hearing loss. Any or all of these characteristics may be present in elderly individuals. Ear wax buildup, an inner ear mechanism malfunction, central nervous system changes, trauma due to loud noise, or the auditory mechanism damage due to certain drugs are the most common reasons for presbycusis (Glass, 1986).

If an older person with a lifelong disability seems to be unusually preoccupied and inattentive, his or her hearing should be evaluated (Evenhuis, van Zanten, Brocaar, & Roerdinkholder, 1992). Because the individual may not be able to clearly communicate problems that he or she might have experienced prior to or during the evaluation, professionals must be keenly aware of any cues and reactions to environmental stimuli that the individual may provide. Several options are available for individuals with hearing impairments including hearing aids, cochlear implants, and aural rehabilitation. A variety of techniques are usually used.

Other devices are available to help individuals with hearing impairments function independently and safely. Flashing lights can be attached to the telephone, doorbell, or fire alarm. Personal care dogs may be trained to assist in physical guidance and to alert their human companion to important sounds and environmental situations. Closed-captioned television, amplified telephones, and telecommunication devices for the deaf (TDD) systems that use the telephone lines to send and receive printed messages are available. The TDD system is now used by elderly individuals with hearing impairments as well as by deaf individuals (Glass, 1986).

Nutrition

Physiologic changes that occur as a result of the aging process affect the way the body uses nutrients (Huber, 1985). As the body ages, the proportion of lean body mass decreases, resulting in reduced energy, or caloric, needs. If intake is not adjusted, weight is gained. Taste is decreased, dental problems may lessen food intake, nutrients may not be absorbed efficiently, digestive disturbances become commonplace, large-bowel disorders often intensify, and conditions such as osteoporosis and vascular disease may emerge (Huber, 1985).

Huber (1985) noted that these conditions are common to all elderly individuals. Nutritional status is also affected by medications, disease, and the individual's eating skills. Caregivers and friends should be observant of weight changes and the person's ability to feed himself or herself while maintaining a desirable weight. If physical disability encroaches on an individual's ability to eat independently, investigation into a variety of adaptive utensils and other eating devices should be made.

FINANCIAL AND LEGAL ISSUES

Legislative action has caused aging and developmental disability agencies to begin integrated planning, funding, and delivery of services for the elderly with lifelong disabilities (Janicki, 1994). The Developmental Disabilities Act as amended in 1993 requires more collaborative work between the developmental disability and aging groups. This act also includes fiscal appropriations to support university programs that focus on training personnel to work with individuals who are aging and who have lifelong disabilities.

The Older Americans Act, as amended in 1987, called particular attention to the needs of older individuals with lifelong disabilities. In 1992, the Older Americans Act became even more explicit and authorized additional supports for community involvement of older adults and their care providers (Janicki, 1993). The Administration on Aging was directed to develop collaborative relations with the Administration on Developmental Disabilities. This relationship encourages the developmental disability and aging networks at the state and local levels to focus on need rather than on category of recipient. The recent amendments specifically targeted providing elderly individuals with lifelong disabilities access to the services offered by the Older Americans Act such as home helpers, legal services, transportation, and congregate meals (Older Americans Act as amended through December 1988). Federally funded agencies have been directed to promote research and to sponsor educational opportunities as an incentive to encourage entry into the field as a profession (Special Committee on Aging, 1989). Although more options are becoming available for elderly individuals with lifelong disabilities, the individual and his or her caregivers must move through a maze of legal and financial choices, which may often seem impenetrable, in search of the best fit between individual needs and programs.

Braddock, Hemp, Fujiura, Bachelder, and Mitchell (1990) found the average daily cost of maintaining an individual in an intermediate care facility for individuals with mental retardation (ICF/MR) was $153.54 in 1988. They also found that approximately 85% of all federal funding for residences of individuals with lifelong disabilities is spent on congregate (16 or more beds) living settings, ICFs/MR. The costs have crept upward over the last decade despite a decrease in the number of individuals living in institutional settings. As the percentage of federal expenditures has increased, the states have significantly reduced their contributions to residential care.

The Home and Community Based Services Waiver created by the Omnibus Budget Reconciliation Act of 1981 (P.L. 97-35) is sometimes used to enable individuals with lifelong disabilities to avoid institutionalization by providing a residential exception to the Medicaid-funded ICF/MR. The cost of supporting the individual in the community under this waiver cannot be more than would be spent for the care of the individual in an ICF/MR. Because each state determines which services it will reimburse under the waiver, a lack of uniformity of services exists from state to state (Castellani, 1987). Use of the waiver option for individuals with lifelong disabilities is slowly increasing, however. Braddock et al. (1990) reported that approximately 30,000 individuals with mental retardation received waiver services nationally in 1988 at a cost of $248 million dollars. This number represents an increase of approximately 3,000 individuals since 1986.

Pensions are of interest both to the families who have a member with a lifelong disability and to the individuals themselves. The state of New York (Ross, 1989) has studied the feasibility of several pension options. Ross found that the majority of individuals with lifelong disabilities are supported by Supplemental Security Income (SSI) or Social Security Disability Income (SSDI). Although many individuals work, their jobs are often low paying and part-time, and in settings such as sheltered workshops. In such cases, pension benefits are typically not available.

A monthly paycheck is an important symbol of independence. However, because most individuals with lifelong disabilities have likely not paid into a pension program, there are no funds from which they can draw (Ross, 1989). Several options are still possible. For example, one chapter of the Association for Retarded Citizens (ARC) in New York pays each retiree with a lifelong disability a bonus of $10 monthly for a maximum of 24 months after retirement. Because the money is not a pension or a fringe benefit, the bonus is not considered income and does not disrupt the SSI support being received.

Sheltered workshops could also charge their customers a nominal surcharge of 1% or 2% to finance their employees' retirement. This method could be undertaken at the local, regional, or state level. A statewide pension program administered by a statewide agency or association of agencies is another option. Although the provision of tax-deferred annuities as pensions is currently being explored, the question arises as to whether this plan might put the worker in an employee status and cause legal difficulties (Ross, 1989). The idea of helping the individual with a lifelong disability open an individual retirement account (IRA) is also under consideration. This option, however, is limited to those individuals with financial resources beyond their job earnings, because SSI recipients cannot maintain over $2,000 worth of assets without jeopardizing their need status. Some proponents believe that the IRA option is the most reasonable. However, existing laws regulating IRAs would have to be modified to accommodate large numbers of individuals who experience lifelong disabilities and who fall into the lower income brackets. If such an instrument were noninheritable by anyone other than the worker or his or her children, there may be an incentive to modify the existing laws.

A final option, one explored by the state of New York, is to use a private insurance company to administer pension plans. Payroll deductions of as little as $10 per month can be deposited into a tax-free annuity account for the individual. One possible limitation to this option is the irregular schedule of earnings often experienced by individuals with lifelong disabilities.

A related area of concern is that of permanency planning. As discussed by Howell (1988), such planning has associated practical and ethical considerations. Individuals who experience physical, intellectual, or social-emotional challenges also may experience varying degrees of stability in their service and support networks throughout their lifetimes. The various individual and family transitions that these people experience as they age, although not necessarily significantly different from the transitions that are experienced by people without disabilities, are potentially more complex given (a) the individual's level of functioning and (b) a decreasing array of support options. For instance, there typically is a greater density of individual and family supports geared toward the earlier years than the later years. Further, individuals with disabilities will experience what all of us experience: the death of parents. Unlike the rest of us, however, such a loss may represent critical financial and functional support.

Attention is now being directed at how families plan for the future of the member with a disability (Kaufman, Adams, & Campbell, 1991). Unfortunately, many families cope with the stress of future planning by denying the need for preparation or by assuming that other family members (e.g., siblings) will assume care at some future point (Heller & Factor, 1988). Preparation for future care is an especially critical concern of older parents due to anxieties about quality of care or the perception of "uncompleted parenting" that can compromise the planning process (Jennings, 1987; Kelly & Kropf, 1995; Kropf & Greene, 1993; Smith & Tobin, 1993).

An exploratory study of adults with lifelong disabilities who live with their parents showed that the economic status of the family is a major factor in whatever long-term plans are made. In addition, the higher the adaptive functioning level of the child and the child's gender (female), the greater was the likelihood of permanency planning. It was particularly interesting that over 500 of the parents surveyed had not made concrete plans for their child's future (Kaufman, Campbell, & Adams, 1990).

The financial and legal aspects of the life of an individual with a lifelong disability are, for many individuals, vague at best. Permanency planning should be a priority, especially when one considers the likelihood that an individual with a lifelong disability will outlive his or her parents. A host of legal issues arise that warrant consideration when developing permanency systems. Will the individual be able to decide and communicate his or her wishes regarding health, finances (including estates and investments), and life direction? As additional services become available, such as the impetus for supported living and home ownership options (O'Brien, 1994), mechanisms to help older adults and their families with learning options and decision making must be instituted and refined. Another issue involves competency for independent decision making. Can the older individual make competent decisions or will he or she require assistance due to the inability to conceptualize the situation and its possible outcomes? These are the issues of guardianship. Are competent individuals with lifelong disabilities giving powers of attorney to individuals they trust so their wishes can be carried out in the future if they are unable to do so themselves? Wishes regarding issues such as refusal of medical intervention, resuscitation orders, advocacy desires, management of financial matters, and life direction might be specified. These are the issues confronted by elderly individuals without disabilities. These are the identical issues elderly individuals with lifelong disabilities should confront. An attorney knowledgeable in estates, guardianship, and powers of attorney should be consulted.

SERVICES

As previously discussed, formal and informal support systems serve as a primary medium through which rights and needs of older individuals with lifelong disabilities are addressed. The organization and supervision of formal and informal supports leads to increased activity on the part of the person receiving support as that person's needs are met. This outcome is important given that increased activity level is clearly predictive of quality of life in elderly individuals without lifelong disabilities (Osberg et al., 1987). Because individuals with lifelong disabilities experience physical or mental impairments that result in life situations that are more constricted than those of individuals without disabilities, the importance of the development of a strong support network becomes apparent.

Formal Supports

Formal supports may be the most easily observed, although not necessarily the most effective, of the two types of supports that we discuss. This support generally includes a variety of services moderated from outside the personal social network. Formal supports may include services related to health, vocational training, transportation, recreation or leisure, counseling, and information and referral (Clements, 1991; Hamilton & Segal, 1975; Keller, 1991; Segal, 1978; Tymchuk, 1979). Unfortunately, such services are often underutilized by those individuals in greatest need. A number of factors may contribute to poor utilization of formal support by individuals with lifelong disabilities in late life (Segal, 1978). First, the level of awareness of service availability among this group is generally low. Efforts must be made to increase this awareness and to ensure positive attitudes toward accessing services once they are made known. Second, inconsistency of services across areas (e.g., city, county, state) may limit access by individuals in need. Such inconsistency can engender confusion and frustration that can lead individuals to "drop out" of the service delivery system. Third, inadequate distribution of services necessarily affects their usage by a large number of individuals. Services may be inaccessible because of location, increased case loads that create waiting lists, and an inadequate system of identifying the population membership. Fourth, personnel who provide services are often not adequately trained to address older individuals' needs. In response to this need for trained personnel, funding has been made available such as that from the Administration on Developmental Disabilities to University Affiliated Programs for training initiatives in the area of aging and lifelong disabilities (cf. Kropf, Malone, & Welke, 1993).

The MR/DD and aging networks provide a multitude of services. Historically, each has served a specific group, with minimal overlap. As administrative priorities have changed and fiscal resources have diminished, however, the emphasis for program development has shifted to linking these disparate service sectors (Ansello & Eustis, 1992). Legislative action in both areas requires more collaboration and information exchange among agencies. The MR/DD and aging networks are not insensitive to this pressure. Age discrimination was the impetus for establishing the aging network. Those involved in the aging system focus on creating services that are not specially geared to the elderly but are responsive to the needs of older people in general. The focus has shifted from a specific age, income status, or disability status to the individuals' need for resources (McDowell, 1988). The Older Americans Act is one means of providing services to older individuals. The funding of programs through this act gives state and regional agencies on aging the authority to coordinate and tailor the services they offer according to identified needs (Quirk & Aravanis, 1988).

Much of the current discussion on services for older individuals with lifelong disabilities focuses on the administrative provision of the service rather than on quality, appropriateness, or rationale. Many states have conducted surveys in an attempt to determine the needs of this population of citizens. M. Seltzer and Krauss (1987) have identified three primary means of service provision for elderly individuals with lifelong disabilities: to receive services with other individuals who have lifelong disabilities in an age-integrated group; to receive services with non-age-integrated groups of individuals who are elderly and who experience similar disabilities; or to access aging programs that are designed to serve seniors without lifelong disabilities. The state of Massachusetts conducted a survey of how the state's services were being used. They found that almost two thirds of the elderly with mental retardation received services in age-integrated, disability-segregated settings. One third received generic senior services whereas approximately 5% participated in segregated age and disability programs. The individuals with lifelong disabilities involved were recipients of MR/DD network services (M. Seltzer, 1988). One can only speculate about the number of elderly individuals with lifelong disabilities using generic elder programs. Such information is largely unknown to the MR/DD network.

One area of concern for many advocates is the improvement of individual access to aging programs. Referral to aging programs by interdisciplinary teams, with admission contingent on a successful trial period, is discussed as one means of incorporating older individuals with lifelong disabilities in elder programs (Cotten & Spirrison, 1986). Cross-training of service providers is a necessity to ensure effective and comprehensive programs that meet the needs of the older population of individuals with lifelong disabilities (Gibson, 1991). Coordinated interagency projects, including financial sharing, are another critical area (Cotten & Spirrison, 1988; Hawkins & Eklund, 1990). Case management, advocacy, day services, home care, and respite services are also commonly mentioned as important services (Hawkins & Eklund, 1989, 1990; Jacobson, Stoneman, & Kropf, 1994).

Caregivers

When services are viewed from the perspective of the caregiver rather than from that of the service provider, satisfaction with services seems to be moderated by the caregiver's perception of stress and his or her ability to maintain the caregiver role. High levels of maladaptive behaviors are associated with more intense feelings of stress and burden by the parents. Interestingly, the age of the caregiver does not seem to be related to the perception of burden (Kaufman et al., 1990) or to the assessment of the ability to perform caregiving chores. Caregiver perception of no longer being able to provide appropriate care is the impetus to access formal services (Engelhardt, Brubaker, & Lutzer, 1988). Some of the more available services are discussed briefly.

Attention to the needs of care providers is becoming more prominent, with the recognition that parents of older children now experience extended parenting due to longer life expectancies for both the parents and the offspring. Examples of parents who are 70 and 80 years of age are not uncommon (Kelly & Kropf, 1995). Jennings (1987) has described these older caregivers as "perpetual parents" due to the extended caregiving responsibilities, which usually begin at the birth of their child with a disability and cease at their own incapacitation or death. The needs of older care providers include both concrete services (e.g., respite care or home maintenance) and psychosocial interventions to address perceptions of uncompleted parenting or excessive worries and fears about the future (Kropf & Greene, 1993).

Specialized Services

The most commonly available services are those provided by the Older Americans Act (as amended, 1988). Included are congregate meals at nutrition sites, housekeeping services, advocacy, case management, legal assistance, socialization, and leisure activities through senior centers. Less commonly found, but valuable, are adult day-care programs and respite care programs. Although these services are generally thought of as part of the aging network, many of the same services are duplicated as part of the MR/DD network.

Case management, the organization and coordination of activities for another, has long been used by professionals working with individuals with lifelong disabilities to assist the individual in meeting his or her obligations and receiving services as needed. The case manager provides many different functions that can assist both the older individual with a lifelong disability and his or her family. Examples of specific tasks undertaken by case managers include linkage to other programs, advocacy on behalf of the individual, and auxiliary support to the individual or family such as arranging or providing transportation. Case management is essential in the lives of many individuals with lifelong disabilities because this practice approach provides a sense of structure and provides a checks-and-balances system to assure accountability by other service providers (Greene & Kropf, 1995). A recent trend is private case management, which is reimbursable by insurance.

Informal Supports

Formal support systems should not exist in a vacuum. Ideally, formal support should be balanced by informal, or personal/social, support. Simply defined, informal support is the exchange of emotional, tangible, or instrumental assistance based on the relationships of particular individuals, not on formalized roles. Such support exchanges take place between family members, friends, or neighbors and may include a sharing or coordination of emotional, leisure, and financial resources. In these types of relationships, no formalized agreements are made between the individuals involved (Hooyman, 1983). It is not unusual to find that individuals who have lifelong disabilities who are elderly have limited informal support systems. Reports by individuals with lifelong disabilities indicate difficulties associated with finding friends, maintenance of friendships, and loneliness (Bostwick & Foss, 1981). Understandably, barriers in this area will negatively affect one's self-efficacy and quality of life.

The significance of informal support to older persons with lifelong disabilities is underscored by the results of a study conducted by Edgerton (1988). The tremendous success in independent functioning demonstrated by the older participants in the study was attributed in part to the strength of the informal supports enjoyed by the participants. Although small support systems can be high in quality and beneficial to the recipient of support, the small size of the support network may place the recipient at greater risk when the system eventually breaks down (e.g., from the death of a parent). Because individuals with lifelong disabilities may be unmarried and childless, they are often limited in the breadth of familial support that they can receive (Seltzer, 1985a). Although many of these aged individuals are now outliving their parents, who are often their strongest advocates (DiGiovanni, 1978), the strength of sibling relationships must not be ignored.

Although family members serve as the primary informal supports for aging individuals with lifelong disabilities who are living in the family home, the number of such persons who are actually residing with family members is unclear (Krauss & Seltzer, 1986). Across the lifespan, however, families are the nations' "largest 'service provider' for individuals with MR/DD" (Fujiura, Roccoforte, & Braddock, 1994, p. 250). These individuals may receive no support from professionals and have few friends to count on for support. In contrast, individuals living in the community receive support from family, friends, and professionals (Krauss & Erickson, 1988). Not surprisingly, the support networks (formal and informal) for the individuals living in the family home are significantly smaller than for those living in community settings (Krauss & Erickson, 1988). Although siblings often provide much support, it is unclear whether they are willing and able to assume the role of primary resource or caregiver when the parent can no longer fill this capacity. Kaufman and colleagues (1990) found that some aged parents have unspoken expectations that their children without disabilities will care for siblings with lifelong disabilities when the parent is no longer able.

Finally, the prevailing social trend of the dissolution of the family network may negatively impact the family support system of individuals with lifelong disabilities. Family members who would otherwise be called upon to accept caregiving responsibilities when the parents are no longer able may not be a stable source upon which the individual can rely. Regardless of the reason for potential restriction of informal supports, the threat of losing a critical form of emotional and substantive support is very real to older individuals with lifelong disabilities (M. Seltzer & Seltzer, 1985). The importance of the complementary interaction between types of supports and services becomes evident when one becomes aware of the potentially limited personal support available to older individuals with lifelong disabilities and the potential risks that are faced by the individual should the informal supports that are available erode. When relationships become limited, the importance of community supports is increased. This interaction underscores the importance of the need for an interdependence of supports and services (Carswell & Hartig, 1979; Famighetti, 1979; M. Seltzer & Krauss, 1987; Thurman, 1986) that will allow greater flexibility in the provision of services that address the needs of the older individual in the event that restrictions are imposed, by whatever means, upon any part of the system. Such an interdependence of supports would also facilitate more positive transitions and subsequent adjustments than would likely be the case should the older individual remain reliant on any one particular source of support.

RESIDENTIAL PLACEMENT ISSUES

Any discussion of residential placement issues related to individuals with lifelong disabilities is likely to elicit a diverse array of responses and viewpoints that reflect a broad continuum of beliefs and values. Without a doubt, the potential placement options for older individuals with lifelong disabilities are varied and range from public residential facilities (i.e., institutions) to private community options in which individuals own their homes. Many self-advocates and their supporters (e.g., family members and friends) have fought for full community inclusion and associated placement considerations. Other advocates have fought equally hard to protect that which they consider their rights—to have a range of placement options available that include public residential facilities. For example, a small but vocal lobbying group, the Voice of the Retarded, has attempted to dismantle the Developmental Disabilities and Assistance Bill of Rights Act because of its support of full community inclusion. Our intent for this section is not to address the philosophical and emotional differences that are evident in the field with regard to placement issues but to highlight important considerations that should be a part of the decision-making process, regardless of philosophical leanings. Interested readers are also referred to Heller (1985), M. Seltzer and Krauss (1987), and O'Brien (1994).

During this century, we have witnessed an increasingly negative social reaction to the short- and long-term placement of individuals with lifelong disabilities in public residential facilities. The mass warehousing of this group of individuals through the first half of this century created such social disdain that the word *institution* has been attributed highly negative connotations. Since 1960, in fact, 25 states have reduced or totally closed the state-run institutions for individuals with lifelong disabilities (Lakin, Braddock, & Smith, 1994).

This movement to deinstitutionalize individual placement options has been, in part, a result of and, in part, a contributor to the expansion of the continuum of residential options for persons with lifelong disabilities. As indicated by Clees in Chapter 18, a host of residential options are available for individuals with lifelong disabilities including public and private residential facilities, nursing homes, group homes, foster homes, family homes, and numerous independent, supported options, such as apartments and owned homes. M. Seltzer and Krauss (1987) provided an informative resource on residential typologies (see Table 5.4). The residential

Table 5.4. Residential Typologies

Author	Typology	Dimensions Used for Classification
Baker, Seltzer, & Seltzer (1977)	1. Small group homes (≤ 10 residents) 2. Medium group homes (11–20 residents) 3. Large group homes (21–40 residents) 4. Mini-institutions (41–80 residents) 5. Mixed-group homes 6. Group homes for older adults 7. Foster family care 8. Sheltered villages 9. Workshop dormitories 10. Community preparatory programs 11. Semi-independent units 12. Comprehensive systems	• Type of administrative structure • Population characteristics • Program philosophy • Program size
Butler & Bajaanes (1977)	1. Custodial 2. Maintaining 3. Therapeutic	• Presence of habilitative programming • Degree of community contact • Level of activity within the residence • Intensity of caregiver involvement

Campbell & Bailey (1984)	1. Family oriented placements
	   a. Natural family
	   b. Foster family
	   c. Boarding homes
	2. Client-directed placements
	   a. Independent living options
	3. Agency-directed placements
	   a. Group homes
		• Type of program sponsorship

Hill & Lakin (1986)	1. Specialized foster home 2. Small group residence (1–6/7–15) 3. Large private group residence (16–63/64–299/300+) 4. Large public group residence (16–63/64–299/300+) 5. Semi-independent 6. Board and supervision 7. Personal care 8. Specialized nursing	• Program model • Program size • Program sponsorship
Scheerenberger (1983)	1. Natural family home 2. Foster family home 3. Group home 4. Private residential facility 5. Semi-independent living 6. Independent living 7. Boarding home 8. Community psychiatric program 9. General medical hospital	• Discrete service type

(continues)

Table 5.4. *Continued*

Author	Typology	Dimensions Used for Classification
	10. Public residential facility	
	11. Hospital for the mentally ill	
	12. Nursing home	
	13. Correctional facility	
	14. School for the blind	
	15. Intermediate care facility	
	16. Rest home	
	17. Work placement	

Seltzer & Krauss (1987)	1. Community-based residential programs:
	  a. Foster homes
	  b. Group homes
	  c. Group homes with nurses
	  d. ICFs/MR
	  e. Apartment programs
	  f. Mixed residential programs
	2. Institutional residential programs
		• Program setting
		• Program type

Note. Adapted from *Aging and Mental Retardation: Extending the Continuum* (pp. 54–55) by M. M. Seltzer and M. W. Krauss, 1987, Washington, DC: American Association on Mental Retardation. Copyright 1987 by the American Association on Mental Retardation. Adapted with permission.

options identified by Clees (Chapter 18, this volume) and M. Seltzer and Krauss (1987) represent a continuum from most restrictive to least restrictive options currently available.

Although a variety of residential options for persons with lifelong disabilities exist, professionals must be careful to identify program options that are designed to meet the needs of an aging population of individuals. Professionals must not assume that a program that supports younger adults is necessarily equipped to meet the needs of older individuals. Paralleling a growth in national interest and need, the development of community and institutional residential programs that specifically address the needs of elderly individuals occurred on any significant level in the mid-1980s (M. Seltzer & Krauss, 1987). Many of these programs evolved into the position of serving and supporting older individuals with lifelong disabilities as a function of the aging of the program's resident base.

Many individuals with lifelong disabilities, especially those who are elderly, appear to fall victim to the "relocation shuffle." As institutional residential facilities are closed, residents are moved to other residential placements. As individuals age and as other life or agency circumstances change (e.g., the diminishment of functional ability, the loss of informal support systems, change in administrative priorities), individuals are at risk for transferral from one program to another. In spite of the range of residential placement options and the reduction in the numbers of institutional residential programs, there appears to be a disproportionate increase in the rate of admission and readmission of individuals with lifelong disabilities into institutional residential programs as they grow older. Given this trend and other relocation efforts, professionals must address questions about the appropriateness of relocation (i.e., is it truly in the best interests of the individual who is relocated?) and the impact of the relocation on the individual concerned.

Before any relocation effort is undertaken, one must weigh the potential benefits against the potential risks for the individual, independently of professional beliefs. Although relocation trauma was at one time considered to be a critical factor, it is now known that such risk may be minimal for many individuals (Heller, 1985). Individuals in good health may experience short-term physical, emotional, and behavioral change; however, with such individuals it is believed that the benefits outweigh the potential risks. As suggested by Heller (1985) and O'Brien (1994), quality of residential life and the impact of relocation on any one individual is likely to be influenced by the following factors:

- individual characteristics related to strengths, vulnerabilities, physical and psychological health;

- individual perceptions related to familiarity with residence, preparation prior to relocation, control allowed, power in decision making related to residence and relocation;

- level of social support, both formal and informal;

- characteristics of the program environment related to individual suitability, degree of restrictiveness, parallels with previous residence, physical design, and social climate and orientation; and

- management of the relocation process, especially preparatory efforts; respect for the individual involved; and overall administration of the change process.

Tantamount to these discrete issues is the goodness of fit between each, with an emphasis placed on the individual's needs, desires, and health (physical and psychological) condition. Relocation is most detrimental to individuals in poor health.

An often neglected factor, independent of specific setting characteristics, is the desire of the individual being considered for relocation. For example, many individuals who have maintained long-term residence in an institutional residential program have developed routines, adjusted to the safety of the program, created a social network, and developed a sense of permanency and stability (Dickerson, Hamilton, Huber, & Segal, 1979; M. Seltzer & Seltzer, 1985). The disruption of a life situation caused by relocation may be severe (DiGiovanni, 1978; Heller & Factor, 1988; Rago, 1985; Thurman, 1986) if, in fact, an individual expresses a desire to maintain his or her residence in the program from which he or she is to be moved. In one study, 18 of the 23 individuals interviewed expressed a preference to stay in the institutional residential program (Dickerson et al., 1979). This is not to say that these elderly individuals cannot or will not adjust to other, less restrictive programs or that they will not realize benefits in their overall functioning. Indeed, evidence supports positive outcomes to this effect. However, as professionals we are faced with a social and philosophical dilemma. On the one hand, we support personal independence and opinions. On the other hand, we are faced with a situation in which the personal independence and opinion of the individual whose life will be affected are contradictory to our beliefs about best practice. The outcome in such cases is often that the opinion of the individual or his or her primary agents is devalued by assignment of a lesser degree of importance than that assigned to the celebrated cause (whatever it may be) of the person(s) with the true power of decision making. We have put forth this extreme, although not unrealistic, example, not as a statement in favor of institutional residential facilities, but to underscore the dilemmas that professionals may face if they sincerely attempt to put in practice that which they espouse. Although this issue of true personal rights and options in decision making may not be reconciled, professionals must be aware of the potential effect of this issue on relocation efforts and must develop means to alleviate the effect on the individual (Jacobson & Kropf, 1993).

ACTIVITIES AND PROGRAMS

As we have discussed in earlier sections, the majority of money spent on individuals with lifelong disabilities is spent within the ICF/MR setting. Certain criteria must be met for an agency to qualify for this money whether it is in a large or small community setting. A brief history reveals the background and reasoning for the criteria used for activities conducted in ICF/MR-funded settings.

The ICFs/MR are funded through Title XIX/ Medicaid of the Social Security Act (1990). The funding itself is channeled from Medicaid through the Health Care Financing Administration (HCFA). Medicaid, having a medical orientation, takes the perspective that the individuals receiving the funding need medical or rehabilitation intervention (Braddock et al., 1990). The intervention for individuals with lifelong disabilities is to present them with the opportunity to acquire new knowledge and skills. The goal is that all experiences should be quality learning opportunities that are objective and measurable. Thus, the term *active treatment* was born. Active treatment means that each individual must participate in daily activities that will increase or maintain the individual's current level of functional independence.

In recent years, active treatment has been redefined to include more flexible intervention options for older individuals who are ready to retire from work or continuous skill-building activities. The standards focus on the wishes of the individual, his or her quality of life, and maintenance of existing skills. Rather than discuss specific activities in detail in this section, we will briefly discuss the issues associated with activities of elderly individuals with lifelong disabilities. Perhaps at no other time in their lives do individuals with and without lifelong disabilities have more in common. Many individuals of both groups have spent a significant period of their lives working and are looking forward to retirement. There are those who want to work forever and cannot imagine retirement. There are also those who have never been employed but are aging and feeling the effects of the aging process.

The literature on activity and older individuals with lifelong disabilities does not provide a dominant program model. Both disability-segregated and disability-integrated programs have been used with success (M. Seltzer & Krauss, 1987). Some fear that individuals with lifelong disabilities will be isolated as they age due to the combination of two conditions, aging and disability, often the basis of discrimination in our society. However, elderly individuals with lifelong disabilities qualify, as do those in the general population, for many government-sponsored services such as those funded by the Older Americans Act.

Although hesitation and resistance may be encountered when elderly individuals with mental retardation begin participating in generic senior centers, M. Seltzer and Krauss (1987) found general acceptance by the seniors without mental retardation and senior center staff to be the norm. Good health and the age of the individual with the lifelong disability were the most important factors that influenced acceptance in the generic senior centers. An important point noted by M. Seltzer and Krauss (1987) is that the use of generic senior centers is not desirable for all elderly individuals with lifelong disabilities. An individualized approach to this decision is recommended.

Common elements to many elder services programs are health awareness, physical exercise, independent living skills, reality orientation, counseling, nutrition, and leisure–recreation activities. Additionally, some elders with lifelong disabilities may need assistance or prompting in the areas of self-help skills (Catapano, Levy, & Levy, 1985). One suspects that older individuals with lifelong disabilities have the desire for socialization, including romance with others; participation in spiritual or religious activities; age-appropriate activities; intergenerational contact; and meaningful activities in their lives. Little investigation has been conducted with this group to identify and explore their desires. Creative approaches to obstacles will enable sensitive professionals to help them achieve their wishes.

FINAL THOUGHTS

Over the life course of the current cohort of older people with developmental disabilities, numerous medical, social, and political changes have occurred. As with the general aging population, the number of older people with developmental disabilities who live as members of their families and communities is expected to greatly increase in the coming century. Unfortunately, the developmental disabilities, aging, social welfare, and health care service networks have paid limited attention to the unique needs of this segment of our older population. Indeed, with the current political atmosphere—one of program reduction, diminishing fiscal resources, and a shifting of attention away from social service programs—this already neglected population stands at even greater risk for being "lost between the cracks." As people with developmental and other lifelong disabilities (e.g., physical, psychiatric) live longer lives, service providers will need to creatively develop and bridge resources across service networks to provide support and assistance to these older adults.

In addition to changes in formal services, greater attention needs to be given to the informal support systems of older people with lifelong disabilities. Greater emphasis must, and will, be placed on grass roots groups composed of families and other community advocates in order for individual needs to be met. Families often bear sole responsibility for providing care to people with disabilities across the life span. The cumulative stresses of lifelong caregiving can compromise families' coping strategies, economic resources, and physical and emotional health of the care providers. Macrolevel changes, such as legislative and financial support for family caregivers, increased flexibility in employment options, and accessible and affordable respite care options, are necessary.

With the coming decades, our older population will become more diverse. Although diversity is usually conceptualized as ethnic/racial plurality, people with lifelong disabilities will also be members of the older generations and bring to late life unique experiences, resources, and needs. Our formalized service systems need to include greater numbers of practitioners, administrators, educators, and politicians who are aware and concerned about the older people who have lifelong disabilities.

REFERENCES

Aging America: Trends and projections. (1991). Prepared by the U.S. Senate Special Committee on Aging, American Association of Retired Persons, Federal Council on the Aging, and U.S. Administration on Aging. Washington, DC: U.S. Senate Special Committee on Aging.

American Psychiatric Association. (1987). *Diagnostic and statistical manual of mental disorders* (3rd rev.). Washington, DC: Author.

Anderson, D. J. (1989). Healthy and institutionalized: Health and related conditions among older persons with developmental disabilities. *The Journal of Applied Gerontology, 8,* 228–241.

Anderson, D. J., & Polister, B. (1993). Psychotropic medication use among older adults with mental retardation. In E. Sutton, A. R. Factor, B. A. Hawkins, T. Heller, & G. B. Seltzer (Eds.), *Older adults with developmental disabilities: Optimizing choice and change* (pp. 61–76). Baltimore: Brookes.

Ansello, E. F., & Eustis, N. N. (Eds.). (1992). *Aging and disabilities: Seeking common ground.* Amityville, NY: Baywood.

Baker, B. L., Seltzer, G. B., & Seltzer, M. M. (1977). *As close as possible: Community residences for retarded adults.* Boston: Little, Brown.

Baroff, G. S. (1982). Predicting the prevalence of mental retardation in individual catchment areas. *Mental Retardation, 20,* 133–135.

Birren, J. E. (1959). Principles of research on aging. In J. E. Birren (Ed.), *Handbook of aging in the individual* (pp. 3–42). Chicago: University of Chicago Press.

Blake, R. (1981). Disabled older persons: A demographic analysis. *Journal of Rehabilitation, 47,* 19–27.

Bostwick, D. H., & Foss, G. (1981). Obtaining consumer input: Two strategies for identifying and ranking the problems of mentally retarded young adults. *Education and Training of the Mentally Retarded, 16,* 207–212.

Braddock, D., Hemp, R., Fujiura, G., Bachelder, L., & Mitchell, D. (1990). *The state of the states in developmental disabilities.* Baltimore: Brookes.

Butler, E. W., & Bajaanes, A. T. (1977). A typology of community care facilities and differential normalization outcomes. In P. Mittler (Ed.), *Research to practice in mental retardation. Vol. 1. Care and intervention* (pp. 337–347). Baltimore: University Park Press.

Campbell, V. A., & Bailey, C. J. (1984). Comparison of methods for classifying community residential settings for mentally retarded individuals. *American Journal of Mental Deficiency, 89,* 44–49.

Carswell, A. T., & Hartig, S. A. (1979). *Older developmentally disabled persons: A survey of impairments.* Unpublished manuscript.

Castellani, P. J. (1987). *The political economy of developmental disabilities.* Baltimore: Brookes.

Catapano, P. M., Levy, J. M., & Levy, P. H. (1985). Day activity and vocational program services. In M. P. Janicki & H. M. Wisniewski (Eds.), *Aging and developmental disabilities: Issues and approaches* (pp. 305–316). Baltimore: Brookes.

Clements, C. (1991). *The arts/fitness quality of life project: Creative ideas for working with older adults in group settings.* Baltimore: Health Professions Press.

Cotten, P. D., Sison, G. F. P., & Starr, S. (1981). Comparing elderly mentally retarded and non-mentally retarded individuals: Who are they? What are their needs? *The Gerontologist, 21,* 359–365.

Cotten, P. D., & Spirrison, C. L. (1986). The elderly mentally retarded developmentally disabled population: A challenge for the service delivery system. In S. J. Brody & G. E. Ruff (Eds.), *Aging and rehabilitation* (pp. 159–187). New York: Springer.

Cotten, P. D., & Spirrison, C. L. (1988). Development of services for elderly persons with mental retardation in a rural state. *Mental Retardation, 26,* 187–190.

Dickerson, M., Hamilton, J., Huber, R., & Segal, R. (1979). The aged mentally retarded client: A challenge to the community. In D. P. Sweeney & T. Y. Wilson (Eds.), *Double jeopardy, the plight of the aging and aged developmentally disabled persons in mid-America* (pp. 8–35). Ann Arbor: University of Michigan Press.

DiGiovanni, L. (1978). The elderly retarded: A little-known group. *The Gerontologist, 18,* 262–266.

DiStefano, A. F., & Aston, S. J. (1986). Rehabilitation for the blind and visually impaired elderly. In S. J. Brody & G. E. Ruff (Eds.), *Aging and rehabilitation: Advances in the state of the art* (pp. 203–218). New York: Springer.

Edgerton, R. B. (1988). Aging in the community—A matter of choice. *American Journal of Mental Retardation, 92,* 331–335.

Edgerton, R. B., & Gaston, M. A. (1991). *I've seen it all: Lives of older persons with mental retardation in the community.* Baltimore: Brookes.

Eisdorfer, C. (1983). Conceptual models of aging: The challenge of a new frontier. *American Psychologist, 38,* 197–202.

Engelhardt, J. L., Brubaker, T. H., & Lutzer, V. D. (1988). Older caregivers of adults with mental retardation: Service utilization. *Mental Retardation, 26,* 191–195.

Evenhuis, H. M., van Zanten, G. A., Brocaar, M. P., & Roerdinkholder, W. H. M. (1992). Hearing loss in middle-age persons with Down syndrome. *American Journal on Mental Retardation, 97,* 47–56.

Eyman, R. K., & Borthwick-Duffy, S. (1994). Trends in mortality rates and predictors of mortality. In M. M. Seltzer, J. W. Krauss, & M. P. Janicki (Eds.), *Life course perspectives on adulthood and old age* (pp. 93–108). Washington, DC: American Association on Mental Retardation.

Eyman, R. K., Call, T. L., & White, J. F. (1989). Mortality of elderly mentally retarded persons in California. *Journal of Applied Gerontology, 8,* 203–215.

Famighetti, R. A. (Ed.). (1979). *Aging and aged developmentally disabled: An exploration into issues and possibilities.* Union, NJ: Kean College.

Fujiura, G. T., Roccoforte, J. A., & Braddock, D. (1994). Costs of family care for adults with mental retardation and related developmental disabilities. *American Journal on Mental Retardation, 99,* 250–261.

Gibson, J. W. (1991). Aging and developmental disabilities: Service provider health-care training needs. *Educational Gerontology, 17,* 607–619.

Glass, L. E. (1986). Rehabilitation for deaf and hearing-impaired elderly. In S. J. Brody & G. E. Ruff (Eds.), *Aging and rehabilitation: Advances in the state of the art* (pp. 218–239). New York: Springer.

Gold, N., & Whelan, M. (1992). Elderly people with autism: Defining a social work agenda for research and practice. In F. Turner (Ed.), *Mental health and the elderly: A social work perspective* (pp. 102–114). New York: Free Press.

Greene, R. R., & Kropf, N. P. (1995). A case management approach with Level I families. In A. Kilpatrick & T. Holland (Eds.), *Working with families* (pp. 85–104). Needham Heights, MA: Allyn & Bacon.

Hamilton, J. C., & Segal, R. M. (1975). *A consultation-conference on developmental disabilities and gerontology.* Ann Arbor, MI: University Park Press.

Hand, J. E. (1993). Summary of national survey of older people with mental retardation in New Zealand. *Mental Retardation, 6,* 424–428.

Hawkins, B. A., & Eklund, S. J. (1989). Aging and developmental disabilities: Interagency planning for an emerging population. *The Journal of Applied Gerontology, 8,* 168–174.

Hawkins, B. A., & Eklund, S. J. (1990). Planning processes and outcomes for an aging population with developmental disabilities. *Mental Retardation, 28,* 35–40.

Heller, T. (1985). Residential relocation and reactions of elderly mentally retarded persons. In M. P. Janicki & H. M. Wisniewski (Eds.), *Aging and developmental disabilities: Issues and approaches* (pp. 379–389). Baltimore: Brookes.

Heller, T., & Factor, A. (1988). Permanency planning among Black and white family caregivers of older adults with mental retardation. *American Journal on Mental Retardation, 26,* 203–208.

Hill, G., & Lakin, K. C. (1986). Residential support systems. *American Journal of Mental Deficiency, 91,* 162–168.

Hooyman, N. (1983). Social support networks in services to the elderly. In J. K. Whittaker, J. Garbarino, & Associates (Eds.), *Social support networks: Informal helping in the human services* (pp. 133–164). New York: Aldine.

Howell, M. C. (1988). Ethical dilemmas encountered in the care of those who are disabled and also old. *Educational Gerontology, 14,* 439–449.

Huber, A. M. (1985). Nutrition, aging, and developmental disabilities. In M. P. Janicki & H. M. Wisniewski (Eds.), *Aging and developmental disabilities: Issues and approaches* (pp. 257–268). Baltimore: Brookes.

Jacobson, J. W., Sutton, M. S., & Janicki, M. P. (1985). Demography and characteristics of aging and aged mentally retarded persons. In M. P. Janicki & H. M. Wisniewski (Eds.), *Aging and developmental disabilities: Issues and approaches* (pp. 115–142). Baltimore: Brookes.

Jacobson, S., & Kropf, N. P. (1993). Facilitating residential transitions of older adults with developmental disabilities. *Clinical Gerontologist, 14,* 79–94.

Jacobson, S., Stoneman, Z., & Kropf, N. P. (1994). *The consumer discovery process: Aging individuals with developmental disabilities.* Athens, GA: Governor's Council on Developmental Disabilities and University of Georgia.

Janicki, M. P. (1993). *Building the future: Planning and community development in aging and developmental disabilities*. Albany: New York State Office of Mental Retardation and Developmental Disabilities.

Janicki, M. P. (1994). Policies and supports for older persons with mental retardation. In M. M. Seltzer, J. W. Krauss, & M. P. Janicki (Eds.), *Life course perspectives on adulthood and old age* (pp. 143–165). Washington, DC: American Association on Mental Retardation.

Janicki, M. P., & Jacobson, J. W. (1986). Generational trends in sensory, physical, and behavioral abilities among older mentally retarded persons. *American Journal of Mental Deficiency, 90*, 490–500.

Jennings, J. (1987). Elderly parents as caregivers for their adult dependent children. *Social Work, 32*, 430–433.

Kaufman, A. V., Adams, J. P., & Campbell, V. A. (1991). Permanency planning by older parents who care for adult children with mental retardation. *Mental Retardation, 29*, 293–300.

Kaufman, A. V., Campbell, V. A., & Adams, J. P. (1990). A lifetime of caring: Older parents who care for adult children with mental retardation. *Community Alternatives: International Journal of Family Care, 2*, 39–54.

Keller, M. J. (Ed.). (1991). *Activities with developmentally disabled elderly and older adults*. New York: Haworth.

Kelly, T. B., & Kropf, N. P. (1995). Stigmatized and perpetual parents: Older parents caring for adult children with lifelong disabilities. *Journal of Gerontological Social Work, 24*, 3–16.

Krauss, M. W., & Erickson, M. (1988). Informal support networks among aging persons with mental retardation: A pilot study. *Mental Retardation, 26*, 197–201.

Krauss, M. W., & Seltzer, M. M. (1986). Comparison of elderly and adult mentally retarded persons in community and institutional settings. *American Journal of Mental Deficiency, 91*, 237–243.

Kropf, N. P., & Greene, R. R. (1993). Life review with families who care for developmentally disabled members. *Journal of Gerontological Social Work, 21* (1/2), 25–40.

Kropf, N. P., Malone, D. M., & Welke, D. (1993). Teaching about older people with mental retardation: An educational model. *Educational Gerontology, 19*, 623–634.

Lakin, K. C., Braddock, D., & Smith, G. (1994). Trends and milestones. *Mental Retardation, 32*, 77.

Landesman, S. (1986). Quality of life and personal life satisfaction: Definition and measurement issues. *Mental Retardation, 24*, 141–143.

Lubin, R. A., & Kiely, M. (1985). Epidemiology of aging in developmental disabilities. In M. P. Janicki & H. M. Wisniewski (Eds.), *Aging and developmental disabilities: Issues and approaches* (pp. 95–113). Baltimore: Brookes.

Maaskant, M. A. (1993). *Mental handicap and aging*. Dwingeloo, The Netherlands: KAVANAH.

Malone, D. M. (1993). *Bill of Rights*. (Available from Interdisciplinary Training Program and Core Curriculum, The University Affiliated Program for Persons with Developmental Disabilities, Dawson Hall, The University of Georgia, Athens, GA 30602.)

McDowell, D. (1988). Aging and developmental disability: Personal reflections on policy for persons. *Educational Gerontology, 14*, 465–470.

Menolascino, F. J., & Potter, J. F. (1989). Mental illness in the elderly mentally retarded. *The Journal of Applied Gerontology, 8*, 192–202.

Mueller, B. J., & Porter, R. (1969). Placement of adult retardates from state institutions in community care facilities. *Community Mental Health Journal, 5*, 289–294.

Murrell, S. A., & Norris, F. H. (1983). Quality of life as the criterion of need assessment and community psychology. *Journal of Community Psychology, 11*, 88–97.

O'Brien, J. (1994). Down stairs that are never your own: Supporting people with developmental disabilities in their own homes. *Mental Retardation, 32*(1), 1–6.

Older Americans Act of 1965 as Amended Through December 1988. (U.S. House of Representatives Committee Print Serial No. 101-A and U.S. Senate Special Committee on Aging Serial No. 101-B). Washington, DC: U.S. Government Printing Office (1989).

Older Americans Act Amendments. (1987). (U.S. House of Representatives Committee on Serial Print No. 101-A and U.S. Senate Special Committee on Aging Serial No. 101-B). Washington, DC: U.S. Government Printing Office.

Older Americans Act Amendments. (1992). (U.S. House of Representatives Committee on Serial Print No. 101-A and U.S. Senate Special Committee on Aging Serial No. 101-B). Washington, DC: U.S. Government Printing Office.

Omnibus Budget Reconciliation Act of 1981, §2176, *United States Statutes at Large, 95*, 812–813. Washington, DC: U.S. Government Printing Office.

Osberg, J. S., McGinnis, G. E., DeJong, G., & Seward, M. L. (1987). Life satisfaction and quality of life among disabled elderly adults. *Journal of Gerontology, 42*, 228–230.

Pary, R. (1993). Psychoactive drugs used with adults and elderly adults who have mental retardation. *American Journal on Mental Retardation, 98*, 121–127.

Quirk, D. A., & Aravanis, S. C. (1988). State partnerships to enhance the quality of life of older Americans with lifelong disabilities. *Educational Gerontology, 14*, 431–437.

Rago, W. V. (1985). The impact of technology on the delivery of mental retardation services in the year 2000: A research perspective. In C. M. Gaitz, G. Niederehe, & N. L. Wilson (Eds.), *Psychosocial and policy issues* (Vol. 2, pp. 209–218). New York: Springer.

Rasmussen, D. E., & Sobsey, D. (1994). Age, adaptive behavior, and Alzheimer disease in Down syndrome: Cross-sectional and longitudinal analyses. *American Journal on Mental Retardation, 99*, 151–165.

Rice, P. R., & Feldman, J. F. (1983). Living longer in the United States: Demographic changes and health needs of the elderly. *Health and Society, 61*, 362–396.

Richards, B. W. (1975). Mental retardation. In J. G. Howells (Ed.), *Modern perspectives on the psychiatry of old age* (pp. 171–189). New York: Academic Press.

Rinck, C., & Calkins, C. F. (1989). Pattern of psychotropic medication use among older persons with developmental disabilities. *The Journal of Applied Gerontology, 8*, 215–227.

Ross, D. M. (1989). *A report to the New York State Developmental Disabilities Planning Council on the feasibility of different pension support systems for New York State residents with a developmental disability*. Unpublished manuscript.

Schaie, K. W., & Willis, S. L. (1986). *Adult development and aging* (2nd ed.). Boston: Little, Brown.

Schalock, R. L., Keith, K. D., Hoffman, K., & Karan, O. C. (1989). Quality of life: Its measurement and use. *Mental Retardation, 27*, 25–31.

Scheerenberger, R. C. (1983). *Public residential services for the mentally retarded, 1982.* Madison, WI: National Association of Superintendents of Public Residential Facilities for the Mentally Retarded.

Segal, R. (1977). Trends in services for the aged mentally retarded. *Mental Retardation, 15*, 25–27.

Segal, R. (1978). Services for the aged developmentally disabled person: A challenge to the community. In M. G. Rose, D. Berstein, & L. Plotnick (Eds.), *Conference proceedings on the aging/developmentally disabled person* (pp. 5–13). College Park: University of Maryland.

Seltzer, G. B., & Luchterhand, C. (1994). Health and well-being of older persons with developmental disabilities: A clinical review. In M. M. Seltzer, J. W. Krauss, & M. P. Janicki (Eds.), *Life course perspectives on adulthood and old age* (pp. 109–142). Washington, DC: American Association on Mental Retardation.

Seltzer, M. M. (1985a). Informal supports for aging mentally retarded persons. *American Journal of Mental Deficiency, 90*, 259–265.

Seltzer, M. M. (1985b). Research in social aspects of aging and developmental disabilities. In M. P. Janicki & H. M. Wisniewski (Eds.), *Aging and developmental disabilities: Issues and approaches* (pp. 161–173). Baltimore: Brookes.

Seltzer, M. M. (1988). Structure and patterns of service utilization by elderly persons with mental retardation. *Mental Retardation, 26*, 181–185.

Seltzer, M. M. (1992). Aging in persons with developmental disabilities. In J. E. Birren, R. B. Sloane, & G. D. Cohen (Eds.), *Handbook on aging and mental health* (2nd ed., pp. 583–599), San Diego, CA: Academic Press.

Seltzer, M. M., & Krauss, M. W. (1987). Aging and mental retardation: Extending the continuum. *Monographs of the American Association on Mental Deficiency, 9*, 3–187.

Seltzer, M. M., & Seltzer, G. B. (1985). The elderly mentally retarded: A group in need of service. In G. Getzel & J. Mellor (Eds.), *Gerontological social work practice in the community* (pp. 99–119). New York: Haworth Press.

Sison, G. F. P., & Cotten, P. D. (1989). The elderly mentally retarded person: Current perspectives and future directions. *Journal of Applied Gerontology, 8*, 151–167.

Smith, G. C., Fullmer, E. M., & Tobin, S. S. (1994). Living outside the system: An exploration of older families who do not use day programs. In M. M. Seltzer, J. W. Krauss, & M. P. Janicki (Eds.), *Life course perspectives on adulthood and old age* (pp. 19–38). Washington, DC: American Association on Mental Retardation.

Smith, G. C., & Tobin, S. S. (1993). Practice with older parents of developmentally disabled adults. *Clinical Gerontologist, 14,*(1), 59–77.

Thurman, E. (1986). Maintaining dignity in later years. In J. A. Summers (Ed.), *The right to grow up: An introduction to adults with developmental disabilities* (pp. 91–115). Baltimore: Brookes.

Tibbits, C. (1979). Can we invalidate negative stereotypes of aging? *The Gerontologist, 19*, 10–20.

Turk, M. A., & Machemer, R. H. (1993). Cerebral palsy in adults who are older. In R. H. Machemer & J. C. Overeynder (Eds.), *Understanding aging and developmental disabilities: An in-service curriculum* (pp. 111–130). Rochester, NY: Strong Center for Developmental Disabilities.

Tymchuk, A. J. (1979). The mentally retarded in later life. In O. J. Kaplan (Ed.), *Psychopathology of aging* (pp. 197–209). New York: Academic Press.

Walker, B. R. (1985). Presidential address 1985: Inalienable rights of persons with mental retardation. *Mental Retardation, 23*, 219–221.

Walz, T., Harper, D., & Wilson, J. (1986). The aging developmentally disabled person: A review. *The Gerontologist, 26*, 622–629.

Wisniewski, K., & Hill, A. L. (1985). Clinical aspects of dementia in mental retardation and developmental disabilities. In M. P. Janicki & H. M. Wisniewski (Eds.), *Aging and developmental disabilities: Issues and approaches* (pp. 195–210). Baltimore: Brookes.

Yanok, J., & Beifus, J. A. (1993). Communicating about loss and mourning: Death education for individuals with mental retardation. *Mental Retardation, 3*, 144–147.

Developmental Disabilities

Mild Mental Retardation

John Langone

LEARNING GOALS

Upon completion of this chapter the reader will be able to

- define and discuss the 1992 American Association on Mental Retardation definition of *mental retardation;*

- outline the effects of limited or intermittent support on the perceptions that society may have of people with developmental disabilities;

- discuss the major learning and cognitive characteristics of persons with mild mental retardation;

- discuss and give examples of important concepts such as generalization, self-direction, and work ability;

- discuss the importance in striving to help adults with mental retardation reach economic self-sufficiency;

- describe the need for using task analyses as a technology of teaching; and

- discuss the importance of teaching independent living skills.

FUNCTIONAL DESCRIPTION

A widely used definition of mental retardation is the one originally developed for and updated by the American Association on Mental Retardation (AAMR). In 1992, the AAMR published the most recent revision of the definition that includes significant changes from the one published a decade earlier (AAMR, 1992).

Traditionally, the definition of mental retardation emphasized the differences of people with this disability from those without cognitive deficits by using two criteria: intellectual capacity and adaptive behavior. In essence these two com-

ponents still exist in the current definition (D. J. Smith, 1994). In the 1983 revision of its *Manual on Terminology and Clarification in Mental Retardation,* the AAMR defined mental retardation as "significantly subaverage general intellectual functioning existing concurrently with deficits in adaptive behavior and manifested during the developmental period" (Grossman, 1983, p. 11). For the purpose of the 1983 definition, the developmental period included birth through age 18 and was characterized by slow, arrested, or incomplete development of a person's intellectual functioning.

The 1992 definition maintains a phrase similar to the one used in the previous revision that stated "significantly subaverage intellectual

113

functioning" (p. 1). Also remaining in the newest revision is the requirement that the onset of mental retardation occur before age 18.

The major changes from the 1983 to 1992 definitions address three areas. First, the global term *adaptive behavior* has been expanded and now includes 10 specific adaptive skill areas. The current definition states, "existing concurrently with related limitations in two or more of the following applicable skill areas: communication, self-care, home living, social skills, community use, self-direction, health and safety, functional academics, leisure, and work" (AAMR, 1992, p. 5).

The concept of adaptive behavior has been the definitional component that has continually caused the most controversy among professionals. In the previous definition, adaptive behavior was defined as an individual's ability to meet the standards of maturation, learning, personal independence, and/or social responsibility (Grossman, 1983) one would normally demonstrate at each of life's stages. The current definition, although maintaining this basic premise, provides a considerably more detailed description of the basic components of adaptive functioning. Each of the 10 adaptive skill areas is described in more precise behavioral terminology and thus may provide the basis for more precise measurement strategies.

Accurate measurement of adaptive behavior is important. This fact is especially crucial for those individuals whose intellectual functioning falls in the borderline range of mental retardation. For example, a person whose score falls below approximately 70 on an individually administered intelligence test would not be considered to have mental retardation if he or she did not demonstrate concurrent deficits in adaptive behavior. The importance of an accurate measurement of adaptive behavior is obvious when one considers that the outcome of this evaluation may be all that stands between an individual and the label "mental retardation."

The second major change in the 1992 definition of mental retardation involves the inclusion of four important assumptions that must be met before the definition of mental retardation can be established. An assessment *must* consider a person's cultural and linguistic diversities. In addition, assessment *must* consider differences in the forms people use to communicate as well as potential differences in the behaviors they exhibit. For example, assessment strategies should consider a person's engaging in nonverbal communication or requiring an augmentative or assistive communication device.

The second and third assumptions address the issue of adaptive behavior. The definition now includes wording that emphasizes the need to assess adaptive behavior in the context of the community where the individual being assessed lives. Specific consideration should be given to comparing the adaptive skills of the target students to those of age peers who come from the same cultural or linguistic background (AAMR, 1992). Also emphasized is the need to identify a person's strengths in adaptive skills as a comparison to the deficits that have been identified.

The final assumption adds to the definition a significantly new dimension not addressed in previous revisions. Basically, a positive outlook toward mental retardation is now included in the definition, reflecting what has been proven in the literature over the past 20 years. That is, over the course of their lives persons with mental retardation will generally improve in the areas related to life functioning given the appropriate supports by service agencies, individuals, and other community settings.

This last assumption typifies the third major change in the definition of mental retardation. In the past, significantly subaverage intellectual functioning was described by severity levels (*mild, moderate, severe,* and *profound*), that is, in terms of how far an individual's measured intelligence deviated from the norm. The 1992 definition now classifies individuals with mental retardation, not by severity levels, but in terms of the varying levels of support they will need over the course of their lives. These four levels of support included as a part of the overall definition now relate to the intensity of a person's needs: (1) intermittent supports that may be episodic or short term and may be needed over a person's life span; (2) limited supports that require more consistency over longer periods of time; (3) extensive supports that involve regular involvement by service providers; and (4) pervasive supports that require constant and intense involvement by service providers and may potentially require life-sustaining assistance.

Although these four intensities of support roughly parallel the historical categories of mild, moderate, severe, and profound, they are fundamentally different in the approach the AAMR intended toward categorization. Instead of categorizing an individual solely on the basis of an IQ score, this new system in theory allows professionals, in concert with parents, to design programs based on the intensity of any given individual's needs.

Of course, as with any new effort at developing a definition of mental retardation, several concerns have been outlined by the professional community (D. J. Smith, 1994). Most of the concerns are based on what, if any, effects this definition will have on the current practices of school systems and service agencies. The effects that changes in the definition may have in the development of Individualized Education Programs (IEPs), teacher certification and training programs, and funding are still to be determined (D. J. Smith, 1994). However, two major issues have been raised that will require close monitoring by parents and professionals over the next several years.

First, the delineation of the 10 adaptive skills is a positive addition to the definition, but the tools for *accurate* measure of these skills still do not exist. For professionals, there is no lack of commercially produced adaptive behavior scales available. Unfortunately, because of the nature of these instruments, the question of subjectivity still exists. Measures of adaptive behavior can be subjective, and the ratings of the same person can vary from rater to rater. Professionals who remain cognizant of this fact can decrease the probability of misclassifying individuals by obtaining a number of adaptive behavior ratings from a variety of sources. Parents, teachers, neighbors, and relatives should all be consulted, and the information gathered from these sources should be used to formulate a more thorough profile of a person's ability to function in his or her environment.

The second concern involves the surface change of the IQ score cutoff identified in the 1992 definition as approximately 70 to 75. In practice, this change is minor because the 1983 definition included the cutoff at an IQ score of 70, which allowed for professional judgment in considering scores up to 75 on an individually administered test of intelligence if conditions warranted. Critics of this change rightfully worry that the 1983 cutoff of a 70 IQ score might have unintentionally kept down the numbers of individuals classified as mentally retarded because of potential legal ramifications (MacMillan, Gresham, & Saperstein, 1993). By adding the ". . . to 75" and eliminating the less specific language relating to professional judgment, some believe that this will encourage and increase the numbers of individuals assessed as having mental retardation.

Intermittent Supports for People with Mental Retardation

People with mild intellectual deficits demonstrate cognitive abilities and adaptive skills that probably will require intermittent supports as identified in the 1992 AAMR definition. A person's strengths and weaknesses should be described in relation to four dimensions outlined in the AAMR procedures: (1) intellectual functioning and adaptive skills; (2) psychological and emotional well being; (3) health/physical well-being and etiology; and (4) life activity environments (AAMR, 1992). Therefore, the new definition eliminates the four classifications that were based on IQ scores and moves to a single diagnostic label of mental retardation. A diagnosis might now identify a student with mental retardation with intermittent support needs in the areas of social skills, functional academics, and work. For example, Will was referred for testing by his teacher because of his poor academic achievement and lack of social skills that the teacher deemed appropriate for individuals in Will's age group. Further testing revealed that Will's IQ score fell below 70, and scores on an adaptive behavior scale indicated significant limitations in three areas—functional academics, social skills, and self-direction. His performance indicated that he needed additional assistance in the form of intermittent supports, so the psychologist, referring teachers, and remedial specialists worked together to develop strategies that could be used with Will in the general education class.

Individuals with mild cognitive deficits differ greatly from one another and will therefore require different levels of support. The possibility exists that some individuals with mild disabilities will require only intermittent supports, whereas others might require limited supports at certain periods of their lives. In reality, the question remains whether or not school systems will adopt this new classification scheme or continue to place students on the basis of more traditional IQ cutoff scores.

Over the years the number of persons identified and labeled as needing special education services has decreased considerably (Patton, Beirne-Smith, & Payne, 1990). This decrease is the result of a number of variables, including a lack of clear evidence that special education has helped these individuals to make significant academic and social gains and the identification of inappropriate testing practices that labeled a disproportionate number of students of racial/ethnic minority groups as having mild intellectual disabilities.

In any event, the population of individuals identified as having mild cognitive disabilities is smaller, and the identified individuals demonstrate more intense academic and social skills deficits than those of individuals enrolled in special education programs in the 1970s (Polloway & Smith, 1987). Individuals with mild cognitive disabilities still constitute the greatest number within the category of mental retardation. The causes of mild mental retardation are the least

understood. Heredity is certainly an important factor in the onset of mild mental retardation; however, medical researchers are currently unable to pinpoint identifiable organic causes for most cases. Other variables such as environmental pollution (e.g., lead emissions in the air), lack of environmental stimulation, little or no pre- and postnatal health care, and poor nutrition all affect the cognitive deficits experienced by some individuals. This complex interaction of heredity and environment (nature vs. nurture) results in a disproportionate number of individuals with mild mental retardation coming from families at the lower socioeconomic level of society.

Children with mild cognitive deficits develop social, motor, and language skills at a slower rate than do their peers. These developmental delays, however, often go unnoticed during the preschool years (Thurman & Widerstrom, 1990). When these children enter school, their disabilities become more pronounced, and a combination of academic and behavioral deficits causes teachers to begin the referral process (Ysseldyke & Algozzine, 1990). The case of La Tonia illustrates this pattern.

● ●

CASE EXAMPLE: LA TONIA

La Tonia's parents stated that she was always "slower" than her siblings. She began walking later than her brothers and sisters and had trouble communicating her needs until she was 3 years old. Her parents believed that these delays were normal because La Tonia was "born early" and that she would "catch up" to the other children in time. When La Tonia entered school, her teachers noticed that she exhibited deficits in preacademic readiness skills. They also estimated that her maturity level was delayed by about 1 to 2 years. After La Tonia repeated a second year of developmental kindergarten, during which she made small improvements, her teachers referred her for additional assessment and potential special education services.

● ●

Limited to Extensive Supports for People with Mental Retardation

Those children whose cognitive deficits are more pronounced are usually identified earlier, often at birth, and will probably require limited to extensive supports over the course of their lives. For example, Martin's composite IQ score on the *Stanford–Binet Intelligence Scale, Fourth Edition* (Thorndike, Hagen, & Sattler, 1986) was 38 and he demonstrated significant developmental delays (approximately 2 years) in learning to sit, crawl, and walk. He is currently 8 years old and requires help dressing and feeding himself more difficult foods such as spaghetti or soups. Martin's language continues to be delayed. He has good receptive language, but his ability to express himself verbally is limited to single words or short phrases.

A variety of clinical syndromes have observable physical characteristics (e.g., Down syndrome) that are associated with moderate mental impairments. Some individuals with moderate cognitive disabilities also have additional disabling conditions (e.g., cerebral palsy). The disabilities associated with moderate intellectual disabilities are more likely to be directly linked to a genetic or biochemical problem that manifested itself during the prenatal period.

In the past, the common outcome for individuals with more pronounced mental retardation was institutionalization. Today, professionals realize that the prognosis for community placement of these individuals is excellent. With early and continual support (i.e., limited to extensive) to families and innovative educational programs, these learners can become independent, productive citizens.

CASE EXAMPLE: CARRIE

Carrie is an 18-year-old high school student who has Down syndrome. She enjoys attending after-school activities such as football games and occasionally attends movies with a boy from her special education class. Carrie attends a self-contained special education class that emphasizes community-based instruction (Langone, 1986, 1990). Carrie spends most of her day in community settings, learning to work, shop, and live as independently as possible. She attends some classes with her regular education peers, such as physical education, participates in after school clubs such as 4-H, and eats lunch with neighborhood friends. The goal for Carrie is eventually to live in a community apartment with a nondisabled roommate and to work in a local library. Her transition plan, currently being developed, indicates that, in addition to the preceding goals, Carrie will be helped to participate in a regular bowling league whose members are not disabled and in a support group composed of individuals with disabilities.

INSTRUCTIONAL PROGRAM GOALS

Individuals with mild to moderate cognitive deficits who require intermittent to extensive supports have the same needs and desires as anyone in the general population. As a group, people with these disabilities are more alike than different in terms of the program goals set by parents and professionals and the instructional strategies designed to help them reach those goals.

The main differences among people with cognitive deficits are not between subgroups (e.g., mild compared with moderate mental retardation), but between each individual and the distance to his or her life goals (Grey, 1981). All individuals have differing needs regardless of their disabilities. The common denominator is that all people have the right to live as independently as possible. To achieve this goal, professionals must take into account the life goals of *each* individual when developing programs to teach academic, social, or vocational skills (Langone, 1990).

Activities should be offered in an environment in which the individual is expected to use the targeted skills. For example, Bobby, a student with mild cognitive deficits who needs limited supports, may have problems choosing the appropriate clothing for work or leisure settings. Sam, a student who needs more extensive supports, may have difficulty dressing himself as well as choosing appropriate clothing. Both students require assistance in learning self-care skills, each one differing only in the distance to his life goal of independently working and living in the community.

Mere labels cannot predict what individuals need to learn in relation to their life goals. Nevertheless, if individuals have mental retardation, they will need help learning the same skills. The level of skills ultimately learned and the intensity of the strategies used to teach them are dependent on each individual's needs and the distance to his or her life goals. In the remainder of this chapter, I describe a variety of curricular areas that relate to the needs of all learners with mental retardation. Each section includes a general description of characteristics that individuals with these disabilities often exhibit and suggestions for program development and instructional strategies.

Self-Care

The ability to take care of one's own personal needs is a vital component of independent living. For individuals with mild to moderate mental retardation, deficits in caring for these needs are evident. In most cases, these individuals can learn to care for their personal needs at least as well as the general population who do not have disabilities. Because of the heterogeneity of this group, self-care needs and the intensity of training required to help them master the related skills vary tremendously. For example, one student with mild cognitive disabilities might need to learn more appropriate table manners at a local restaurant. Another student with moderate mental disabilities might need to learn to use eating utensils properly when faced with a variety of foods.

Generally, self-care skills are grouped into two categories: eating and dressing/grooming. A variety of skills can be clustered under these two categories:

Eating

- Choosing foods of proper nutritional value

- Showing appropriate eating habits, such as table manners and clearing his or her place

- Ordering and eating food appropriately in different community restaurants

Dressing/Grooming

- Using a variety of electrical self-care appliances appropriately and safely (e.g., razors)

- Showering or bathing independently as needed and doing so in a variety of environments (e.g., YMCA and home)

- Matching clothing for color, style, or design

- Matching clothing to a variety of conditions (e.g., weather, work, and environment)

The preceding self-care skills are a small sample of those that might be targeted for instruction in an educational program for students with mild to moderate cognitive deficits. Regardless of the age of the learners, professionals would first determine what self-care skills the students need in their current and future environments by implementing a community needs assessment (Langone, 1986). This approach, accomplished through interviews and observations, provides information that allows professionals to determine the level at which students currently function.

Because of the heterogeneity of the group categorized as mild to moderate cognitively impaired, the range of skills addressed is broad and based on the age of the learner. A 5- or 6-year-old child with moderate cognitive delays may not be completely toilet trained or may demonstrate inappropriate toileting skills (e.g., refusal to wipe him- or herself after a bowel movement). In such cases, instructional strategies can be designed to omit the inappropriate responses and to teach the appropriate alternative behaviors.

The literature is replete with examples of interventions designed to teach basic self-care skills to younger individuals who have mild to moderate mental retardation, such as toilet training (Foxx & Azrin, 1973), dressing (Nutter & Reid, 1978), and eating (Riordan, Iwata, Finney, Wohl, & Stanley, 1984). In addition, more advanced self-care behaviors such as restaurant skills are being taught with great success (Marholin, O'Toole, Touchette, Berger, & Doyle, 1979).

•••

CASE EXAMPLE: CARMEN

Carmen, a high school student with mild mental retardation, often comes to school dressed in clothes that are both provocative and of loud colors that often do not match. During the community needs assessment process, the teacher learns that Carmen's mother also dresses in this fashion. During the needs assessment process, the teacher gathers information about the types and styles of dress appropriate for potential employment outcomes.

At this point, the teacher develops an instructional program designed to help Carmen discriminate and use appropriate dress for certain environments. The teacher attempts to do this without attaching a value judgment on Carmen's current style. Knowing that Carmen's mother also dresses in this fashion helps the teacher avoid alienating the mother and eventually Carmen. The goal is to help Carmen learn to discriminate among the environments in which specific types of clothing can be worn. The teacher does this by exposing Carmen to many appropriate role models in the community.

•••

Receptive and Expressive Language

MacMillan (1982) stated that speech and language deficiencies occur at a significantly greater frequency among learners with mild to moderate mental retardation than might be expected in the general population. This observation appears to be the result of three factors. First, more individuals with moderate mental retardation may have associated physiologic problems that adversely affect their ability to produce clear speech. Second, individuals with mild mental retardation who come from lower socioeconomic groups may not be exposed to as many good role models (e.g., their parents may not be able to talk to them as often as parents in higher socioeconomic groups). Finally, cognitive ability and language development are linked, and a decrease in cognitive ability may lead to language deficits (Fazio, Johnston, & Brandl, 1993; Patton et al., 1990).

Receptive and expressive language difficulties range in severity from problems with articulation of sounds or pronunciation of words to a significant delay in language development (Bedrosian, 1993; Spradlin, 1968). For many individuals with mild cognitive impairments, speech and language problems can be a secondary disabling condition. Epstein, Polloway, Patton, and Foley (1989) found that in a sample of 107 individuals with mild mental retardation, over half were eligible for speech pathology services. In addition, as mentioned previously, this high incidence can be attributed partly to the poor environments where these children reside. Speech and language problems in this group can also be attributed to cultural differences (Patton et al., 1990). Researchers and government statistics have demonstrated that a disproportionate number of students identified as mildly retarded come from racial/ethnic minority groups. The cultural differences and language barriers working in tandem with environmental influences possibly contribute to the language delays experienced by many of these individuals.

In addition, individuals with more moderate cognitive deficits run the risk of having secondary physical impairments that can adversely affect their speech and language development (Thurman & Widerstrom, 1990). Motor development problems and physiologic anomalies may decrease the individual's ability to produce intelligible speech. For example, a protruding tongue, a characteristic found in many individuals with Down syndrome, adversely affects the pronunciation of words (MacMillan, 1982).

Hearing problems are more common in learners with moderate cognitive deficits than in the general population of individuals without disabilities (Patton et al., 1990). These problems may be directly linked to language delays and poor speech production (Thurman & Widerstrom, 1990). Regardless of the cause, the presence of deficits or delays in speech and language development is increased for individuals with mild to moderate cognitive disabilities.

As with all other areas of the curriculum, the best place to teach appropriate use of receptive and expressive language is in a natural setting. The results of research indicate that those individuals with cognitive deficits who live in the community engage in more appropriate conversation and can use more sophisticated language than do their peers who live in institutions (Brinton & Fujiki, 1993). Over the years, researchers and educators have found that language skills learned in isolated classroom activities do not automatically generalize to other daily living activities. Younger children require more traditional language training designed to help them master basic verbal behaviors and verbal prerequisites (Bricker, 1983). These children, however, still need assistance with generalizing newly acquired language skills to play groups, family functions, and other community-based activities.

The best time to assist children with mild to moderate cognitive deficits to obtain language skills is during their early years (Thurman & Widerstrom, 1990). Language training by an early-intervention specialist should include both direct service to the child and assistance to the parents designed to help them teach and foster these skills in their children. However, as individuals become older, their language skills can continue to improve (Fujiki & Brinton, 1993; Schiefelbusch, 1993), and instruction toward that end should not cease during the elementary years.

Early instruction involves systematically teaching and reinforcing a learner's ability to imitate and discriminate gestures or vocalizations. The teacher accomplishes these objectives by using both *chaining* and *shaping* strategies. Initially, the teacher reinforces all vocalizations, thereby increasing the overall number. Gradually, only those vocalizations that more closely resemble the final objective are reinforced until the learner can reliably produce the sound or word. Eventually, the teacher reinforces only more complex vocalizations such as a statement (e.g., "Say, 'I want a drink'").

The most important component of a language and communication program and the one most often overlooked is the promotion of the generalization of these skills. As with all skills, a systematic program designed to enhance generalization is necessary because these students do not transfer learned skills easily. As the student initially acquires language and communication skills, the teacher simply increases the number of stimuli the student is exposed to during the course of instruction. For example, when teaching the student to respond to the request "Put the can in the box," the teacher can use boxes and cans of different sizes and weights or cans with different labels.

Teaching students to generalize more advanced language and communication skills requires increasing the students' exposure to naturally occurring events. Students with mild to moderate cognitive deficits appear to learn more advanced communication skills when they are in the setting where the communication demands have real-life value (Bedrosian, 1993; Fujiki & Brinton, 1993). Teaching advanced language skills in community and school environments helps learners to see that language is a way to control the environment, a realization that motivates them to master these skills. For example, Wendi might be learning to remember and repeat orally five important criteria for renting an apartment. Once she can state the five points, the teacher might ask her, on site in a model apartment, to repeat each point orally for the group and to note its significance. A final activity or test for Wendi would be to call or visit apartment managers and ask them the questions related to the criteria (e.g., How many bedrooms does the apartment have?). Generalization of Wendi's advanced communication skills continues to improve as she practices these activities in more apartments and in the presence of other apartment managers. A variety of instructional strategies are used to teach language to learners with mild to moderate cognitive handicaps. All of these individuals can learn to control their environments and to communicate with people using language. The extent to which they advance their skills depends on the types and numbers of innovative social and other community activities developed for them by their teachers.

Learning and Cognition

Individuals with mild to moderate mental retardation have pervasive limited cognitive ability (Keogh, 1988). This pervasive limited cognitive ability is not as inconsistent, in terms of intelligence versus achievement, as one might expect from students accurately identified as having learning disabilities or behavior disorders. These students have frequent "peaks and valleys" in terms of their ability to grasp new concepts and to apply new skills.

All comparisons are relevant. Although students with mild to moderate mental retardation show much less of a discrepancy between their measured intelligence and their achievement compared with nondisabled students, they differ considerably within their own group (Edgar, 1987; MacMillan, 1982). The major characteristic

shared by all categories of learners with mild to moderate disabilities is that they fall significantly behind their general education peers in tasks that require learning and using academic skills. Deshler and Schumaker (1986) found that by high school, many learners categorized as having mild disabilities had fallen *at least* 6 years behind their general education peers in academic achievement. If this finding is indeed true for those students with mild disabilities, the differences for those with moderate mental retardation are great enough that comparisons lose their meaning.

Two basic theories have been used to describe the cognitive development of individuals with mild to moderate mental retardation. The *developmental* theory, best described by Zigler (1969), postulates that individuals progress through the same developmental levels as those who do not have disabilities, but they do so at a much slower rate. Adherents to the developmental approach also postulate that the highest developmental levels reached by individuals with cognitive deficits are much lower than the highest levels reached by their peers without disabilities.

The *difference* theorists postulate that the mental capabilities of individuals with mental retardation are qualitatively different from those of their nondisabled peers (Zigler, 1969). These theorists contend that differences exist in the ability of people with cognitive deficits to process learned information.

Research supporting or refuting each theory is equivocal. Regardless of one's theoretical point of view, the results of these studies underscore the fact that individuals with mental retardation are slow to learn new skills, do not grasp concepts well at symbolic or abstract levels, are inefficient learners, and do not readily transfer learned skills to new settings or when different materials are required (Hayes & Taplin, 1993; Langone, 1986). Therefore, more recent research has focused on finding the most effective and efficient instructional strategies to use in helping these individuals overcome the deficits resulting from mental retardation.

Learning Skills

For many reasons, individuals with cognitive deficits may learn facts and lists by intensive drill, but they fail to master higher-order learning skills. Abstract concepts such as numerical reasoning, time, measurement, and use of money may be difficult skills for them to master (Langone, 1990).

Part of the question that has not adequately been answered is whether these learners cannot master advanced learning skills or whether professionals have not adequately identified and taught these skills because they overemphasize the drilling of basic facts. The trend toward improving the learning skills of individuals with cognitive deficits is to teach more advanced skills in environments where these skills have a high probability of being used. For example, high school students with mild mental disabilities may have great trouble learning to add and subtract and generally to use fractions in classroom activities involving a blackboard and paper-and-pencil tasks. These same students may be able to master the use of fractions when they are taught in cooking exercises conducted in hospital kitchens or in building-trade exercises conducted at an office remodeling project.

Having acknowledged that individuals with mental retardation have varying deficits in memory, attention, organization of material, ability to model others, and language, researchers have turned their attention to identifying and testing strategies to accommodate for these deficits (Turner, Dofny, & Dutka, 1994; Wright & Schuster, 1994). Effective teachers instruct learners how to pay close attention to the relevant parts of any task by color coding the important components of reading, mathematic, or vocational tasks. This approach helps students discriminate between what is important and what is not, thus minimizing their memory problems and improving the quality of their work.

There are many other examples of instructional strategies that can be used to help learners with mild to moderate mental retardation to minimize their weaknesses in cognition. Memory improvement devices (mnemonics) as mediators help learners with poor memories to complete a variety of advanced tasks. In addition, teaching students more socially acceptable behaviors might also assist them in developing better problem-solving skills (Healey & Masterpasqua, 1992). Finally, the use of computer-based instruction appears to be a promising medium for teaching learners higher-order cognitive skills (Gerber, 1994).

CASE EXAMPLE: PAUL

Paul, a high school–aged student with moderate mental retardation, has been taught to remember the word *state* as a mnemonic device when he goes to a restaurant. This device helps Paul remember skills he has learned in his community-based instructional activities:

Say hello to the waiter or waitress.

Tell him or her what you want.

Ask for help when needed.

Take your time eating.

Employ good manners.

Paul has learned a variety of words he uses in different situations. His teacher reinforces Paul socially for verbally modeling her by saying each letter and statement aloud at appropriate points (depending on the task). Over subsequent trials, Paul is encouraged and given reinforcement for repeating the statements in an increasingly softer voice until he eventually repeats them silently to himself. The teacher judges the use of the mnemonic by the accuracy of Paul's task completion. At some point, it becomes difficult to judge whether Paul uses the mnemonic device or completes the task because he has learned the chain of steps. The mnemonic is merely a backup device that Paul can refer to if, for some reason, the chain of skills is interrupted.

Mnemonic devices are especially useful for learners who are confronted by social situations because these devices help them remember what actions are appropriate for the conditions.

Generalization of Skills

Individuals with mild to moderate cognitive impairments have trouble generalizing skills they have learned in one setting to other settings that involve different materials, different people, and different time (Langone & Westling, 1979; Wehman, Abramson, & Norman, 1977). This problem also exists among persons in the general population; however, it appears more pronounced among individuals with mental retardation.

A number of behaviorally oriented strategies have been developed to assist these learners in overcoming most deficits they have in generalizing learned skills. Varying the settings, the time of day, the materials, and the people working with a student appears to facilitate generalization (Stokes & Baer, 1977). These seem like commonsense suggestions. Unfortunately, many educational programs that provide services to learners with cognitive deficits do not take these issues into account. Community-based instruction (Langone, 1986, 1990) helps learners to minimize their problems with generalization by allowing them to practice skills in environments where they are expected to use them.

CASE EXAMPLE: MR. CEDAR

Mr. Cedar may want his middle school–aged students with mild mental retardation to apply math skills to everyday problems such as cost-comparison shopping. He has attempted to accomplish this task over many weeks, using only classroom-based activities. On a field trip to a local grocery store, Mr. Cedar was dismayed to discover that most of his students became confused and were unable to complete their assigned problems.

At the time, Mr. Cedar did not realize that the root of the problem was the students' inability to generalize. His alternative was to teach and practice some of the skills in classroom-based activities and concurrently to allow the students frequent practice applying these skills in a variety of grocery stores in the community.

Teachers of students with moderate cognitive deficits are using these strategies more frequently to teach independent living skills. For example, when teachers want their students to order, pay for, and eat in fast-food restaurants, they teach the skills in a variety of community-based locations.

Mobility

Mobility for individuals with mild to moderate mental impairments is not a crucial issue. Most individuals who fall into this category do not have long-term physical problems that impede their ability to move from one place to another. This statement is, however, relative. For example, many children with mild deficits develop motor skills at a slower rate than do their peers (Patton et al., 1990). Similarly, most children with moderate cognitive disabilities develop motor skills (e.g., crawling and walking) at a slower rate than do their peers with mild mental disabilities (Thurman & Widerstrom, 1990).

The same relationship across categorical areas is true for multiple disabling conditions. On the basis of the variety of biomedical conditions associated with moderate mental retardation, one would expect a higher percentage of these individuals to have physical impairments compared with their peers with mild cognitive delays. In any case, the number of individuals with mild to moderate mental retardation who have mobility problems as a result of physical impairments is small compared with people who have severe mental retardation. Those students who have additional mobility problems should work with physical and occupational therapists who assist the primary program providers. For example, occupational therapists can guide teachers in choosing appropriate adaptive devices (e.g., expanded computer keyboards) and in training the students to use them, thus allowing the students to use microcomputers to complete their school work.

Self-Direction

The ability to direct one's self can be defined in many ways by different professionals. In the context of this chapter, self-direction is defined as one's ability to control the events that ultimately affect his or her life and one's belief that the control of such events is possible. Historically, individuals with mild to moderate cognitive deficits have not fared well in becoming self-directed. Seen as a variety of personality characteristics, these skills were thought to be deficient in persons with mental retardation and directly linked to their cognitive deficits (Zigler, 1966).

Many educators today tend to view these personality variables in a different light and to approach the problems that students have with self-directed behavior from a behavioral viewpoint. The reinforcement history of persons with mild to moderate mental retardation is often considerably different from that of their peers without disabilities. Because of their intensive history of failure over long periods of time, many of these individuals begin to lose confidence in their abilities, a loss causing them to overrely on the leadership and skills of others. Therefore, personality disorders exhibited by people with cognitive deficits may be the result of the complex interrelations among these individuals, their families, and the social system that provides them services (Balla & Zigler, 1979).

CASE EXAMPLE: BETSY

Betsy, who was born with moderate intellectual disabilities, was not born with personality problems. Her birth caused her family to react adversely to the increased stress placed on it by Betsy's disability and resulted in a decrease in the quality of parenting and sibling interaction she received. Over the years, her reaction to an overprotective environment caused her to demonstrate less desirable behavior, such as overdependency on others, and led to her belief that she could never do anything right.

A protracted history of failure with a variety of experiences may cause some individuals with cognitive deficits to distrust their own abilities and to become overdependent on others to direct them. Thus, individuals with mental retardation may show more outer-directed behavior than one might expect. When individuals exhibit outer-directedness, they tend to rely on external cues, rather than trusting their own problem-solving skills (Zigler, 1966).

Another characteristic of self-direction involves a person's ability to see the cause-and-effect relationship between his or her behavior and subsequent events. Locus of control is essentially a personality characteristic that causes people to judge whether or not they control many of life's events that directly affect them. People who believe they control their own lives and many of the events that surround them seem to be more intrinsically motivated and to have what theorists believe is an internal locus of control (Bialer, 1961). Conversely, those people who feel they have little or no control over their lives demonstrate an external locus of control and seem to be more extrinsically motivated.

The more classical research literature provided results supporting the theory that, compared to the general population, individuals with mental retardation tend to be more dependent on others, less trusting of their own abilities, and more motivated by extrinsic reinforcers. Obviously, within the group of individuals with mild to moderate mental retardation, the variability of these characteristics is great. When one is developing educational programs, it makes sense to view these characteristics as a behavioral paradigm rather than as intrinsic to mental retardation.

Because of their significant cognitive delays, individuals with mental retardation may be treated differently by significant others and professionals, a tendency affecting their reinforcement histories and experience with failure. For example, unless they are provided strong supports children with mild mental retardation placed in regular education classes from kindergarten may face repeated failure in trying to grasp increasingly more difficult academic content. Even after a relatively short period (kindergarten and first grade), these children might have experienced many situations of failure that over time cause them to doubt their own abilities.

One example of how reinforcement history can be affected can be traced to the overuse of tangible reinforcers (e.g., food, toys, extra play time) by professionals and family members. Because children with mental retardation are delayed developmentally, caregivers frequently reward small gains in behavior with large amounts of primary or tangible reinforcers. Over time, this practice tends to teach children that one (the learner) works only when the rewards are large enough.

The tendency of individuals with mild to moderate cognitive deficits to be less self-directed can be minimized if caregivers practice common-sense strategies (Misra, 1992). For example, by gradually fading prompts and cues, teachers assist students in relying more on their own problem-solving skills. This approach, paired with a systematic and gradual fading of tangible reinforcers, allows learners to become less reliant on external motivations. Asking students if they are proud of themselves when they accurately complete tasks while *showing* them you are proud of their efforts (using smiles, pats on the back) helps them to "internalize" reinforcers.

Task analysis, that is, breaking a task down into smaller parts, helps learners deal with more manageable tasks and allows them greater chance for success. Applying task analysis to the range of academic, vocational, and leisure and recreation skills has become the most successful curricular and instructional tool available to special educators. Breaking tasks (skills) into component parts reduces student avoidance behavior and anxiety that often accompany the presentation of activities that they perceive as being beyond their abilities.

Finally, self-direction may be helped by the move toward placing students with disabilities in inclusive classes, with regular educators teaming with special educators to provide quality instruction for all the children on their individual levels (Sailor, Gee, & Karasoff, 1993). Children with disabilities have the potential to make positive gains in social, language, and academic skills when placed in close contact with their nondisabled peers, if a well-designed program with the appropriate supports is available.

Capacity for Independent Living

The word *independence* is one that, in daily use, has many different meanings. Most professionals would agree that the major goal of all special education programs is to help people with disabilities become as independent as possible. For individuals with mild to moderate mental retardation, the definition of independence has been narrowly defined.

People who have cognitive impairments have often been relegated to positions of dependence from which they continually look to others to meet their needs. Most individuals with mild mental retardation are assimilated into society as part of the lower class, at the lowest socioeconomic level. Individuals with moderate cognitive disabilities lead dependent or semidependent lives, with the smallest proportion living in group homes or semi-independent apartments managed by state agencies. Most of these citizens are cared for by their families or are relegated to residential/institutional settings.

In either case, the quality of life for these citizens, in terms of the number of independent living activities they are taught, does not compare to what their peers without disabilities learn. This situation can be traced to the emphasis placed on academic training in school programs. People without disabilities usually learn independent living skills outside of school in the context of extracurricular clubs and groups (e.g., 4-H, scouting), through instruction in their homes, or simply through trial and error resulting from modeling the behaviors of others.

Individuals with mental retardation are included less often in extracurricular activities, come from homes less likely to provide this training, and do not have the same ability to learn through trial and error by modeling the behaviors of others. Therefore, their lack of continued exposure to out-of-context, academically based activities or, at best, to simulations of independent living skills hinders any successful transition to community living.

During the past decade, special educators became increasingly interested in teaching independent living skills to students with moderate mental retardation in environments where they ultimately would be required to use those skills. Programs were designed to teach independent shopping skills in community grocery stores, restaurant skills in fast-food establishments, and leisure skills at a variety of community-based sites (Langone, 1986). Unfortunately, programs emphasizing independent living skills have not been a top priority in classes for students with mild mental retardation (D. D. Smith, 1989). The case for teaching community-based independent living skills to all learners with mild to moderate disabilities is receiving increased emphasis in the literature (e.g., Foxx, Faw, Taylor, Davis, & Fulia, 1993; Langone, 1990; Polloway, Patton, Payne, & Payne, 1989; Schuler & Perez, 1988; Smith & Edelen-Smith, 1990).

The importance of teaching independent living skills is obvious when one considers that the major goal of special education is to assist learners in becoming independent. Students with mild to moderate mental retardation often have deficits in social skills, and these deficits can severely affect their successful integration into both the community and other school environ-ments (Margalit, 1993). Teaching social skills appears to be most effective when it is done in context with actual daily living activities (Foxx, Mc-Morrow, Bittle, & Ness, 1986; Haring & Breen, 1992; Thompson & McLaughlin, 1992). In addition, the broader area of independent living skills (e.g., home management, family care, leisure, consumer skills) can provide realistic opportunities for developing activities that help these students apply a variety of general cognitive, academic, and language skills.

Economic Self-Sufficiency

A person's worth, both in his or her own perception and in the perception of others, is often judged by his or her ability to earn a living. Status is often placed on the type of job one does, and this status may affect the individual's overall quality of life. Because of the status that society places on work, it is important for individuals with mild to moderate cognitive disabilities to enhance and increase their status by finding and maintaining employment (Burnham, 1992; Langone, 1990).

The potential for economic self-sufficiency of individuals with mild to moderate cognitive deficits is excellent. Many published research studies, project reports, and program guidelines outline successful, vocationally related programs for these individuals (e.g., Hill & Wehman, 1983; Knox & Parmenter, 1993; Szymanski & King, 1989; Wehman, 1992).

The programs that have been successful are, unfortunately, too few and have not had the most desired national impact. Rusch and Phelps (1987) cited a 1986 Senate subcommittee report indicating that at least 67% of Americans with disabilities are not working. Those people with disabilities who are employed are more likely to be employed only in part-time jobs. Finally, for those Americans with disabilities who are not working, 67% indicate they want to work. These data, although dated, remain virtually the same today.

Transition from School to Adult Roles

Developing program options that help individuals with disabilities make successful transitions from school to all aspects of life has received national emphasis over the past 5 years. Previously, only those activities that dealt with movement from school to the world of work were stressed. Professionals are now emphasizing consideration of an individual's successful transition at every important life juncture (Ianacone & Stodden, 1987). For example, children with disabilities who move from one program to another (e.g., preschool to elementary, elementary to middle school) should have transition plans developed that allow for more meaningful movement with little lost ground between programs. Transition plans should assist individuals with disabilities whenever a major program change is initiated (Wehman, 1995).

The employability potential of learners with mild to moderate cognitive deficits is dependent on the quality of their entire school program, not just on their educational opportunities in high school. The amount and quality of time students with disabilities spend participating in tasks related to work (e.g., vocational education classes or community-based work sites) appear to determine their eventual success in competitive employment (Edgar, 1987; Hasazi, Gordon, & Roe, 1985). Unfortunately, there does not appear to be a relationship between these data and what actually is taught in special education classes (Edgar, 1987). The importance of restructuring special education curricula with more emphasis on work-related and independent living skills is evident.

The emphasis on appropriate work-related skills begins in elementary school and continues throughout one's life. For example, to minimize or eliminate poor work attitudes, students beginning in elementary school can spend time in the community with their teachers learning work-related skills through job samples simplified for their needs (Langone, 1990). This process allows students to learn about the world of work in actual community settings and allows them to observe community members doing their jobs. Teachers can choose good work role models for the students to observe and talk to and generally to help them see the positive side of employment.

As students progress through middle and high school programs, the amount and sophistication of the activities increase. Students accompanied by their teachers can participate in a variety of job sites that represent a cross section of their community's employment possibilities. These activities allow the students to learn work-related behaviors (e.g., social and community skills, task behavior, and assertiveness) and allow teachers to teach academic skills related to each job (Brinton, 1994; Brinton & Fujiki, 1993).

FINAL THOUGHTS

The field of mental retardation has come a long way over the past two decades. Professionals have observed a painfully slow movement away from segregated settings for people who have mental retardation toward environments where they are fully included into daily life activities enjoyed by many citizens. Also, we have observed the application of instructional methodologies and assistive technologies that have helped people with these disabilities in becoming productive citizens and lifelong learners.

Unfortunately, we still have a long way to go. Although we know a great deal of what should be done to improve the quality of life for people with disabilities, we now must work hard to see that these advances become widespread and available to all of them. Professionals and parents must continually work together to ensure that people who need them receive assistive devices. In addition, we need to work continually with parents in helping their children receive access to high quality, community-based, and inclusive instruction as well as opportunities for lifelong learning and self-determination.

To accomplish these goals, we must first identify people who are interested in becoming professionals in education and who demonstrate a strong work ethic. The demands placed on professionals in the future will increase as the need for more cooperation between disciplines and with parents increases. Meeting these demands will require individuals who know how to work hard and are not easily distracted from their primary responsibility of providing instruction and assistance to those who have mental retardation and to their families.

REFERENCES

American Association on Mental Retardation. (1992). *Mental retardation: Definition, classification, and systems of supports* (9th ed.). Washington, DC: Author.

Balla, D., & Zigler, E. (1979). Personality development in retarded persons. In N. Ellis (Ed.), *Handbook of mental deficiency, psychological theory and research* (2nd ed., pp. 143–168). Hillsdale, NJ: Erlbaum.

Bedrosian, J. L. (1993). Making minds meet: Assessment of conversational topic in adults with mild to moderate mental retardation. *Topics in Language Disorders, 13,* 36–46.

Bialer, I. (1961). Conceptualization of success and failure in mentally retarded and normal children. *Journal of Personality, 29,* 301–333.

Bricker, D. (1983). Early communication development and training. In M. Snell (Ed.), *Systematic instruction for the moderately and severely handicapped* (pp. 269–288). Columbus, OH: Merrill.

Brinton, B. (1994). Ability of institutionalized and community-based adults with retardation to respond to questions in an interview context. *Journal of Speech and Hearing Research, 37,* 369–377.

Brinton, B., & Fujiki, M. (1993). Communication skills and community integration in adults with mild to moderate retardation. *Topics in Language Disorders, 13,* 9–19.

Burnham, S. C. (1992). Pride in work: Perceptions of employers, service providers and students who are mentally retarded and learning disabled. *Career Development for Exceptional Individuals, 15,* 101–108.

Deshler, D., & Schumaker, J. B. (1986). Learning strategies: An instructional alternative for low-achieving students. *Exceptional Child, 52,* 583–590.

Edgar, E. (1987). Secondary programs in special education: Are many of them justifiable? *Exceptional Children, 53,* 555–556.

Epstein, M. H., Polloway, E. A., Patton, J. R., & Foley, R. (1989). Mild retardation: Student characteristics and services. *Education & Training of the Mentally Retarded, 24,* 7–16.

Fazio, B. B., Johnston, J. R., & Brandl, L. (1993). Relation between mental age and vocabulary development among children with mild mental retardation. *American Journal on Mental Retardation, 97,* 541–546.

Foxx, R. M., & Azrin, N. H. (1973). *Toilet training the retarded.* Champaign, IL: Research Press.

Foxx, R. M., Faw, G. D., Taylor, S., Davis, P. K., & Fulia, R. (1993). "Would I be able to . . . ?": Teaching clients to assess the availability of their community living life style preferences. *American Journal on Mental Retardation, 98,* 235–248.

Foxx, R. M., McMorrow, M. J., Bittle, R. G., & Ness, J. (1986). An analysis of social skills generalization in two natural settings. *Journal of Applied Behavior Analysis, 19,* 299–305.

Fujiki, M., & Brinton, B. (1993). Growing old with retardation: The language of survivors. *Topics in Language Disorders, 13,* 77–89.

Gerber, B. L. (1994). Beyond drill and practice: Using the computer for creative decision making. *Preventing School Failure, 38,* 25–30.

Grey, R. A. (1981). Services for the LD adult: A working paper. *Learning Disability Quarterly, 4,* 426–434.

Grossman, H. J. (Ed.). (1983). *Manual on terminology and classification in mental retardation* (rev.). Washington, DC: American Association on Mental Deficiency [now called American Association on Mental Retardation].

Haring, T. G., & Breen, C. G. (1992). A peer-mediated social network intervention to enhance the social integration of persons with moderate and severe disabilities. *Journal of Applied Behavior Analysis, 25,* 319–333.

Hasazi, S. B., Gordon, L. R., & Roe, C. (1985). Factors associated with the employment status of handicapped youth exiting from high school from 1979–1983. *Exceptional Children, 51,* 455–469.

Hayes, B. K., & Taplin, J. E. (1993). Development of conceptual knowledge in children with mental retardation. *American Journal on Mental Retardation, 98,* 293–303.

Healy, K. N., & Masterpasqua, F. (1992). Interpersonal cognitive problem-solving among children with mental retardation. *American Journal on Mental Retardation, 96,* 367–372.

Hill, M., & Wehman, P. (1983). Cost benefit analysis of placing moderately and severely handicapped individuals into competitive employment. *Journal of the Association for the Severely Handicapped, 8,* 30–38.

Ianacone, R. N., & Stodden, R. A. (1987). Transition issues and directions for individuals who are mentally retarded. In R. N. Ianacone & R. A. Stodden (Eds.), *Transition issues and directions* (pp. 1–9). Reston, VA: Council for Exceptional Children.

Keogh, B. K. (1988). Improving services for problem learners: Rethinking and restructuring. *Journal of Learning Disabilities, 21,* 19–22.

Knox, M., & Parmenter, T. R. (1993). Social networks and support mechanisms for people with mild intellectual disability in competitive employment. *International Journal of Rehabilitation Research, 16,* 1–12.

Langone, J. (1986). *Teaching retarded learners: Curriculum and methods for improving instruction.* Boston: Allyn & Bacon.

Langone, J. (1990). *Teaching students with mild and moderate learning problems.* Boston: Allyn & Bacon.

Langone, J., & Westling, D. L. (1979). Generalization of prevocational and vocational skills: Some practical tactics. *Education and Training of the Mentally Retarded, 14,* 216–221.

MacMillan, D. L. (1982). *Mental retardation in school and society* (2nd ed.). Boston: Little, Brown.

MacMillan, D. L., Gresham, F. M., & Saperstein, G. N. (1993). Conceptional and psychometric concerns about the 1992 AAMR definition of mental retardation. *American Journal of Mental Retardation, 98*, 325–335.

Margalit, M. (1993). Social skills and classroom behavior among adolescents with mild mental retardation. *American Journal on Mental Retardation, 97*, 685–691.

Marholin, D., II, O'Toole, K. M., Touchette, P. E., Berger, P. L., & Doyle, D. A. (1979). "I'll have a Big Mac, large fries, large Coke, and apple pie," . . . or teaching adaptive community skills. *Behavior Therapy, 10*, 236–248.

Misra, A. (1992). Generalization of social skills through self-monitoring by adults with mild mental retardation. *Exceptional Children, 58*, 495–507.

Nutter, D., & Reid, D. H. (1978). Teaching retarded women a cloth selection skill using community rooms. *Journal of Applied Behavior Analysis, 11*, 475–487.

Patton, J. R., Beirne-Smith, M., & Payne, J. S. (1990). *Mental retardation* (3rd ed.). Columbus, OH: Merrill.

Polloway, E. A., Patton, J. R., Payne, J. S., & Payne, R. A. (1989). *Strategies for teaching learners with special needs* (4th ed.). Columbus, OH: Merrill.

Polloway, E. A., & Smith, J. D. (1987). Current status of the mild mental retardation construct: Identification, placement, and programs. In M. C. Wang, M. C. Reynolds, & H. J. Walberg (Eds.), *Handbook of special education research and practice: Vol. 2: Mildly handicapped conditions* (pp. 102–125). Oxford, England: Pergamon Press.

Riordan, M., Iwata, B., Finney, J., Wohl, M., & Stanley, A. (1984). Behavioral assessment and treatment of chronic food refusal in handicapped children. *Journal of Applied Behavior Analysis, 17*, 327–342.

Rusch, F. R., & Phelps, L. A. (1987). Secondary special education and transition from school to work: A national priority. *Exceptional Children, 53*, 487–492.

Sailor, W., Gee, K., & Karasoff, P. (1993). Full inclusion and school restructuring. In M. Snell (Ed.), *Instruction of students with severe disabilities* (4th ed., pp. 1–30). New York: Macmillan.

Schiefelbusch, R. L. (1993). Communication in adults with mental retardation. *Topics in Language Disorders, 13*, 1–8.

Schuler, A. L., & Perez, L. (1988). The role of social interaction in the development of thinking skills. In E. Meyen, G. A. Vergason, & R. J. Whelan (Eds.), *Effective instructional strategies for exceptional children* (pp. 259–275). Denver, CO: Love.

Smith, D. D. (1989). *Teaching students with learning and behavior problems* (2nd ed.). Englewood Cliffs, NJ: Prentice-Hall.

Smith, D. J. (1994). The revised AAMR definition of mental retardation: The MRDD position. *Education and Training in Mental Retardation and Developmental Disabilities, 29*(3), 179–183.

Smith, G. J., & Edelen-Smith, P. J. (1990). A commencement model of secondary education and training in mild mental retardation. *Education and Training on Mental Retardation, 25*, 15–24.

Spradlin, J. E. (1968). Environmental factors and the language development of retarded children. In S. Rosenberg & J. H. Koplin (Eds.), *Developments in applied psycholinguistic research* (pp. 56–79). New York: Macmillan.

Stokes, T. F., & Baer, D. M. (1977). An implicit technology of generalization. *Journal of Applied Behavior Analysis, 10*, 349–367.

Szymanski, E. M., & King, J. (1989). Rehabilitation counseling in transition planning and preparation. *Career Development for Exceptional Individuals, 12*, 3–10.

Thompson, D., & McLaughlin, T. F. (1992). Social skills coaching: The effects of social skills coaching on the social interaction of a mainstreamed TMH student and peers. *British Columbia Journal of Special Education, 16*, 212–222.

Thorndike, R. L., Hagen, E. P., & Sattler, J. M. (1986). *Stanford–Binet Intelligence Scale* (4th ed.). Chicago: Riverside.

Thurman, S. K., & Widerstrom, A. H. (1990). *Infants and children with special needs: A developmental and ecological approach* (2nd ed.). Baltimore: Brookes.

Turner, L. A., Dofny, E. M., & Dutka, S. (1994). Effect of strategy and attribution training on strategy maintenance and transfer. *American Journal on Mental Retardation, 98*, 445–454.

Wehman, P. (1992). *Life beyond the classroom*. Baltimore: Brookes.

Wehman, P. (1995). *Individual transition plans: The teacher's curriculum guide for helping youth with special needs*. Austin, TX: PRO-ED.

Wehman, P., Abramson, M., & Norman, C. (1977). Transfer of training in behavior modification: An evaluative review. *The Journal of Special Education, 11*, 127–131.

Wright, C. W., & Schuster, J. W. (1994). Accepting specific versus functional student responses when training chained tasks. *Education and Training in Mental Retardation and Developmental Disabilities, 29*, 43–56.

Ysseldyke, J. E., & Algozzine, B. (1990). *Introduction to special education* (2nd ed.). Boston: Houghton Mifflin.

Zigler, E. (1966). Research on personality structure in the retardate. In N. R. Ellis (Ed.), *International review of research in mental retardation* (Vol. 1, pp. 77–105). New York: Academic Press.

Zigler, E. (1969). Development versus difference theories of mental retardation and problems of motivation. *American Journal of Mental Deficiency, 73*, 536–556.

Severe Mental Retardation

William R. Sharpton and Michael D. West

LEARNING GOALS

Upon completion of this chapter the reader will be able to

- discuss the different teaching/supporting options that can be utilized when working with people with severe mental retardation;

- discuss how persons with severe mental retardation function in self-care skills;

- identify one good communication goal for a student with severe mental retardation;

- describe the difference between a group home and supported living in terms of the life of a person with severe mental retardation;

- discuss the importance of providing opportunities for making choices in educational and habilitative services for individuals with severe mental retardation; and

- describe the theoretical base and program components of supported employment.

FUNCTIONAL DESCRIPTION

Reference works on persons with mental retardation typically describe expectations of their abilities, capacities, and potential for development. For persons with severe and profound mental retardation, however, what one is more likely to find is a description of *in*ability, *in*capacity, and little or no expectation for growth and development. Descriptions such as these are common:

- unlikely to achieve any measure of productivity

- unable to enter into relationships

- total dependency on family or support agencies

- potential limited to self-help skills

- require lifelong supervised care

In this chapter, we take a different approach, by illustrating competencies developed by individuals with severe or profound retardation. The key to their success has been the manner in which service providers train and support persons with disabilities, which may be summarized in the following framework:

If a task can be taught, teach it.

If it can't be taught, adapt it.

If it can't be adapted, support it.

Figure 7.1 illustrates this framework, along with decision rules for the use of each option. This service delivery model can be successfully

131

Instructional Options	Decision Questions
OPTION 1: Teach the task	1. Can the task be divided into smaller steps that are easier to master?
	2. Does the learner have the capacity to complete the task as it is typically performed?
OPTION 2: Adapt the task	1. Will adaptation of the environment facilitate task completion?
	2. Will adaptation of the steps facilitate task completion?
	3. Will adaptations to the learner (prosthetics) facilitate task completion?
OPTION 3: Support the task	1. Have all other options been considered?
	2. Will support be provided in the least intrusive environment?

Figure 7.1.   Model for selection of instructional options.

used to assist persons with severe and profound mental retardation in performing meaningful, rewarding, and socially valued activities in a variety of real-life settings. First, we briefly describe the options available within this framework and introduce some fundamental concepts. Case examples presented throughout this chapter illustrate the use of these options in varying combinations and to varying degrees, based on the individual characteristics, needs, and preferences of the learners.

Option 1: Teach the Skill

Skills can be systematically taught to be performed in the same manner that a typical learner would perform them. The key to effective instruction is to provide only the level of assistance

needed by the learner to successfully complete the task, a determination that must be supported by collection of training data. Ideally, the learner will be able to complete the task without any assistance other than that provided in the natural setting. For example, in the laundromat, there are signs that explain the operation of the machines. This kind of information is called a *natural cue.* The information is not always written, however. For example, the rubber mat in front of an electric door is the cue for its operation.

In most cases, learners with severe intellectual impairment need to be provided some instructional assistance if the task is to be performed correctly. This instructional assistance is known as a *prompt.* Prompts vary in terms of type and intensity, and the prompt selected for successful instruction should offer sufficient information for correct task completion but not so much assistance that the learner is not challenged. Instructional data can be used to assist the trainer in making decisions about what types of prompts to provide. (Detailed descriptions of systematic training procedures are beyond the scope of this chapter. Interested readers are referred to these excellent sources: Falvey, Brown, Lyon, Baumgart, & Schroeder, 1980; Guess & Helmstetter, 1986; Haney & Falvey, 1989; Snell, 1993.)

Option 2: Adapt the Task

Adaptations can be designed to make the task easier or to assist an individual in task performance. Most adaptations have to be developed by the trainer, and, therefore, it is very important for trainers to know how to determine whether or not an adaptation is appropriate for the individual. These are some questions service providers should ask regarding the adaptive devices and techniques they develop to address specific tasks:

1. Is the adaptation effective? That is, does the use of the adaptation result in correct task completion?

2. Does the adaptation maintain the dignity of the individual? It is very important that service providers remember their role as advocates for the people we serve. Therefore, adaptations should be developed so that they are appropriate to the age of the individual and do not draw negative attention to him or her.

3. Is the adaptation durable? Can it be used as it was intended without quickly becoming unusable due to wear and tear? Nothing is more frustrating for the learner than to fail in the performance of a task because an adaptation is not working.

4. Is the adaptation portable? The adaptation should be designed so that it can be easily taken by the learner to the place where it is needed. Adaptations are particularly useful if they can be used in a variety of settings.

Option 3: Support the Task

Service personnel can support the learner by assisting with the difficult steps while allowing the learner to perform those that are within his or her abilities. The concept of allowing people with mental retardation to perform part of a task even though they cannot complete all of the task independently is known as *partial participation* (Baumgart et al., 1982). The alternative to partial participation is exclusion from the task until the individual has learned all of the prerequisite skills. This model of instruction often results in the instruction of isolated skills over long periods of time, with the learner still waiting to perform tasks or to engage in activities that could very well enrich their lives.

Ideally, the person providing the support or assistance should be a part of the setting in which the task naturally occurs. For example, store clerks are available to provide assistance to all shoppers, including those who have disabilities. Of course, in some cases sufficient support is not available in the natural environment, and instructional programs must be designed to provide support. In these cases, it is important for service providers to develop a plan to transfer support as soon as possible to individuals present in the natural setting or to make external supports as unobtrusive as possible.

Describing Severe Intellectual Disability

Historically there has been some disagreement over definitions of mental retardation. The American Association on Mental Retardation (AAMR) has put forth the following definition:

> Mental retardation refers to substantial limitations in present functioning. It is characterized by significantly subaverage intellectual functioning existing concurrently with related limitations in two or more of the following applicable adaptive skill areas: communication, self-care, home living, social skills, community use, self-direction, health and safety, functional academics, leisure, and work. (Luckasson et al., 1992, p. 1)

This definition recognizes the interplay and occasional incongruity between measured intelligence levels and an individual's ability to function in a relatively unhindered manner within social and cultural environments. Many individuals may score in the range of *retardation* on intelligence tests but be able to function adequately within the social norms of their own family, school, neighborhood, and other immediate environments. They are not "retarded" because no one suspects that they are, and labeling them mentally retarded would cause tremendous stigma and potential harm.

For individuals with a significant degree of retardation, inconsistency between measured intelligence and social adaptation is rarely an issue. From birth or early childhood, many of these individuals will show outward signs of an organic pathology, such as a genetic syndrome or brain damage, to account for the presence of impairment in mental functioning.

Diagnosis depends on formal assessment of general intellectual capabilities, typically derived from an intelligence quotient (IQ) or mental age level (MA). According to diagnostic standards established by the AAMR (cf. Grossman, 1973), an individual scoring at least four standard deviations below the mean on a standardized intelligence test with comparable deficits in adaptive behavior would be termed *severely retarded*, and those scoring at least five standard deviations below the mean would be termed *profoundly retarded*. Persons with severe and profound mental retardation together compose no more than 3% to 4% of all persons with mental retardation (Scheerenberger, 1983).

In contrast to these diagnostic standards, the 1992 AAMR classification manual (Luckasson et al., 1992) eschews levels of retardation and instead focuses on the types and intensities of supports needed by the individual, either intermittent, limited, extensive, or pervasive. The impetus for these modifications is the changing perceptions of mental retardation and persons who are mentally retarded, a growing social acceptance, and the evolution of the service delivery system (Luckasson & Spitalnik, 1994). Although the elimination of stigmatizing diagnostic labels is welcome, the use of the terms "severe mental retardation" and "profound mental retardation" will likely continue for many years.

According to Carr (1984), reduced intellectual capacity generally will be manifested in two ways: first, there will be limitations in the range of cognitive skills which the individual can master; second, there will be limitations in the individual's capacity to respond to environmental cues. Persons with severe intellectual impairment will exhibit significant delays or complete interruptions in the development of motor skills, language abilities, problem solving, and other aspects of learning. Their inability to respond to environmental cues may result in lack of affect or the presence of self-stimulatory, repetitive, and socially immature or inappropriate behaviors.

Persons with severe or profound mental retardation have been found to be more likely to have other disabling conditions as well. For example, the incidence rates for visual and hearing impairments, health problems, cerebral palsy and other physical handicaps, epilepsy, and psychiatric or behavioral impairments have been found to increase with level of retardation (Kelleher & Mulcahy, 1986; Kobe, Mulick, Rash, & Martin, 1994; Tager-Flusberg, 1994; Thompson & Gray, 1994). In large part, these secondary problems likely result from the organicity that also contributed to retardation.

Self-Care

Individuals with severe and profound mental retardation do not typically develop many of the self-care skills through the maturational process. However, with intensive training, adaptation, and support, all can participate to some degree in dressing, feeding, toileting, grooming, and other self-care responsibilities (Snell, 1993).

To effectively train and involve their clients, service providers must view self-care, not as the sole focus of an instructional program, but as a part of the normal routine of life. Thus, self-care skills should be taught at times they naturally occur and within the natural contexts of preparation for school, work, or bed. Too often, self-care skills are instructed apart from the natural routines during therapeutic encounters, a practice resulting in ineffective, pointless instruction.

••

CASE EXAMPLE: MARY

Mary is a young woman with severe mental retardation in her late twenties who currently lives in a group home with three other young adults. Her active treatment plan includes an intensive training program for building self-help skills. When the training program was first designed, the staff decided to provide instruction during the evening hours after dinner because more time could be spent with Mary on an individual basis. Unfortunately, Mary's ability to prepare herself in the morning when she was getting ready to go to work did not seem to improve significantly.

The group-home support staff reached a decision to change the instructional program for Mary. First, they decided that it made more sense to provide instruction on these tasks twice daily: once during the morning when Mary was preparing for work and once in the evening when she was preparing for bed. Next, they identified all of the tasks involved during her morning and evening routines. For each task, the critical steps were identified, and for each step, the staff decided whether to teach a typical performance, to design an adaptation, or to provide support. Where possible, the tasks that required the most assistance were grouped so that the staff could provide needed support for one "cluster" of tasks and Mary could complete the remaining tasks more independently. Thus, it was much easier for the staff to schedule their instruction and to provide support to the other residents of the household.

Problems still remained with Mary's moving from one self-help task to the next. The staff designed a checklist that included a picture of each critical task in the order in which it should be performed. The checklist was laminated and a grease pen attached so that Mary could mark each task as it was performed. Of course, Mary did not learn to use this adaptation independently. The support staff used prompts systematically to teach Mary to perform the critical tasks. Careful collection of instructional data over a 6-week period demonstrated that Mary had significantly improved her ability to prepare herself for work and bed. She still requires support for some steps, but the staff have noticed that it is much easier to provide assistance to Mary.

Receptive/Expressive Language

Because cognition and language development are interrelated, it is not surprising that persons with severe or profound mental retardation generally have more severe communicative disorders than do persons with lesser degrees of retardation (Schiefelbusch, 1972; Tager-Flusberg, 1994). In fact, Grossman (1983) indicated that these individuals will typically develop only minimal communication skills of any kind even with intensive training. He noted, however, that some members of this group may develop complex verbal skills, grammar, and sight word recognition.

Impaired receptive and expressive language abilities of people with severe or profound retardation originate from a number of sources, including abnormal speech mechanisms, physiological problems, potential hearing loss, poor language-learning environments, as well as impaired cognitive processes (Dodd & Leahy, 1989). In recent years, however, tremendous advances have been made in providing members of this population functional communication skills (Butler, 1994; Reichle, Piché-Cragoe, Sigafoos, & Doss, 1988). Service providers can help the person obtain these skills by conducting an ecological examination of the functions that communication serves across natural environments and by providing the learner with either training in communication skills and/or an adaptive communication system that enables him or her to fulfill those functions. Adaptive communication systems include the use of pointing, gesturing, signing, or a graphic system, such as symbols, picture cards, or communication boards or electronic system, or any combination of any of these methods. In providing speech or language intervention, service providers also need to remember that communication is a function of environment. When communication is deficient, environments should be examined and enriched where needed to promote effective communication.

Too often, language and communication are taught during prescribed times in therapeutic environments, with the expectation that the individual will transfer these skills to real-life encounters. In order to be effective, communication training, as all training activities, should occur at natural times and places and in natural contexts (Halle, 1988).

Service providers should also remember that the goal of communication training is the learner's gaining some control over his or her immediate environment. Success toward that goal can be reduced in two ways:

• Service providers teach the learner to use a single form of communication with the expectation that it will work in all settings. It is rare that a single communication board, set of picture cards, gestural language, or other communication system can be developed that the learner can master and that will work effectively in all environments in which he or she will be expected to function. To attempt to do so invites frustration and failure.

• Control over communication systems or communication opportunities is maintained by the service provider and not the learner. A classic example of this is the communication board that the student is taught to use during "speech class" but which is locked up or unavailable during other school activities or when the learner is at home.

CASE EXAMPLE: LAURA

Laura is a 13-year-old who is severely mentally retarded and attends a middle school near her neighborhood. Because she is nonverbal, her teacher, in cooperation with the speech therapist, has developed a communication board and taught her to use this system to express a variety of concepts. This year, her Individualized Education Program (IEP) has been expanded to include instruction in community settings. In particular, her parents are interested in Laura's learning how to order a meal in a fast-food restaurant, because the family tends to eat in a variety of these establishments.

Initially, her teacher decided to let Laura use her regular communication board to order food at the restaurant. Unfortunately, Laura became confused because of the large number of symbols on the board and because the personnel at the restaurant were not able to understand what Laura wanted to eat.

After carefully analyzing the problems that were occurring, the instructional team decided to create a special communication board just for the fast-food restaurant. The board was organized so that the items of food were presented within "categories" of food types (e.g., beverages). Laura was taught to identify a choice in each of the three categories and thus order a complete meal.

Through systematic instruction in the use of this adapted strategy for communication, Laura now independently orders her food in three fast-food settings. In fact, for each restaurant she uses a separate board that has been especially designed to reflect the menu of that establishment. Laura's participation in this task has been expanded to include selecting the correct order card before leaving for the restaurant. She is now able to participate much more independently with her family when they eat out.

CASE EXAMPLE: CHARLES

Charles recently entered his first year of high school on a regular campus; however, he had very little experience in performing functional tasks in community settings. In fact, instructional personnel have always set fairly low expectations for Charles because of his severe mental retardation and dual sensory impairments. His new teacher wanted to involve him in functional activities but was concerned that he attempted to communicate only with grunting noises or by reaching out with his arms. Based on his mother's report that Charles likes soft drinks, the instructional team decided to teach him to purchase a drink from a vending machine. The communication specialist used a pop top as an object cue for Charles. At first, he was given the pop top each time he was taken to the vending machine to purchase a drink. Later, the pop top was placed in a calendar box that was divided into compartments. By following a left to right sequence, Charles was able to know which activity should be performed by the object that the staff had placed in the compartment. The instructional team was particularly excited the day that Charles went to the calendar box and, instead of following the sequence in the set order, searched until he found the pop top, which he held out toward the teacher. In essence, Charles was saying, "I want to buy a drink." In this case, his language had moved from a receptive to an expressive mode.

Learning and Cognition

Impaired learning ability and capacity is, of course, the embodiment of mental retardation. According to Owens (1989), problems with learning and problem solving originate with impairments in these cognitive processes: identifying salient stimuli and attending to them for sufficient periods of time; organizing and encoding incoming sensory information into categorical groupings; storing and retrieving information in both short- and long-term memory; and transferring learning to new tasks or settings. Persons with severe or profound mental retardation will typically have significant difficulties in each of these cognitive areas.

In times past, these problems were used to point to the need for segregated, lifelong custodial care for these individuals. Now, more and more people who provide assistance to this population recognize that these deficits point to the need for specialized and individualized instruction, adaptation, and support in inclusive settings (Belfiore, 1994; Mount, 1994). A major evolutionary change is occurring in research and application of instructional technology targeted to the needs of persons with severe and profound retardation (Bradley, 1994). Past efforts have demonstrated the ability of all individuals, regardless of their level of retardation, to learn isolated tasks through competent instruction. More recently, emphasis is being placed on teaching functional skills that lead to an enhanced lifestyle for these individuals (Horner, 1989).

CASE EXAMPLE: GERALD

Gerald is a young man with severe mental retardation who is involved in a high school vocational training program. His mother expressed her concern to the instructional team during the IEP conference that her son is not very involved in household routines. In fact, he is very dependent on family members for most activities of daily living such as selection of clothing, grooming, meal preparation, and maintenance of his bedroom. Gerald is able to count to five, but has not mastered many academic skills such as color identification, reading, and typical readiness skills.

Recently, Gerald began training at a new work site that requires employees to wear uniforms. Immediately, the instructional staff noticed that Gerald was highly motivated to wear the uniform. In fact, his mother had problems with Gerald's wanting to wear his uniform every day, rather than on Tuesdays and Thursdays when he reports to the training site. The instructional team worked with the family to incorporate this new motivation in critical home routines. The teacher adapted a calendar by placing large green Xs on all of the Tuesdays and Thursdays and attaching a red marker on a string (see Figure 7.2). Now when Gerald gets up in the morning, he goes to the refrigerator with his mother to look at the calendar. He locates the current day to determine whether or not it is a uniform day. After making this decision, he takes the marker and places an X on the day so that he will know where to look for the next day. Now he is ready to assist in the selection of clothing. The instructional team also decided to teach Gerald to participate in washing the uniform. The laundering has now become a Saturday chore in the home. At this time, Gerald is not able to perform all of the steps, but he does load and unload the machine as well as operate the controls, which are adapted with colored tape.

Even though Gerald is still not independent in the performance of household tasks, he is certainly more involved than he was before.

Not only are his parents pleased with his progress, but his younger siblings have begun to comment about their older brother's going to work.

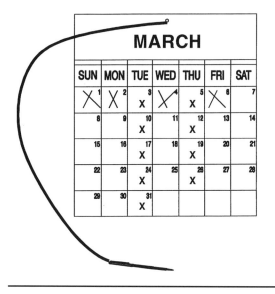

Figure 7.2. Gerald's adapted calendar for determining days to wear uniform.

Mobility

Functional mobility may be assessed along two interrelated parameters: first, as an individual's capacity for physical movement within the specific environments in which he or she functions (e.g., the workplace, the home, etc.); second, as the capacity to move from one environment to the next or through the community at large.

As mentioned previously, persons with severe or profound mental retardation frequently have physiological or neurological impairments that impair physical movement. These impairments, as well as learning deficits, will result in limited functional mobility both within and among environments.

Mobility is emerging as a critical issue for enhancing the physical integration and participation of persons with severe handicaps in work

and social activities, particularly as the field has progressed from center- and school-based services to community-based models of instruction and support. Independent ambulation may be instructed or adapted by the use of wheelchairs, walkers, handrails, and other types of aids. Community movement may be facilitated through training and adaptation in order for the person to utilize a variety of transportation modes, including family vehicle, friends' vehicles, and public transit, and independent movement by foot, bicycle, and so forth. Community movement may also be supported through the use of carpooling and other ride-sharing options.

CASE EXAMPLE: KESHA

Kesha is 25 years old and had been waiting for an integrated employment opportunity for approximately 6 months. A suitable job became available in a laundry facility within a large urban hospital. However, the job coach had concerns about her safety because Kesha is severely mentally retarded and blind. Specifically, the concern centered on the fact that Kesha must walk down a busy corridor that is used by forklifts to reach the locker rooms and the cafeteria.

Kesha did not need assistance when she was at the folding table because all of the work takes place there. The task is typically structured so that two workers fold clothes at the same station and retrieve clothes from a large bin approximately 20 feet away when all clothes on the table have been folded. The job coach has worked with management to alter the task slightly in order to accommodate Kesha's presenting needs. All of the clothes are retrieved from the bin by her coworker; however, Kesha folds a greater number of the smaller items because she does not have to interrupt her work to walk over to the bin.

Through careful planning, the job coach designed a strategy to afford Kesha maximum independence in negotiating the corridor, yet insuring her safety. Kesha typically crossed the corridor only three times daily: during her morning and afternoon breaks to get to the bathroom, and during lunch to reach the cafeteria. The job coach decided that support was necessary for Kesha to walk safely down the corridor. The job coach also believed that the most important issue besides Kesha's safety was for support to be provided in as natural a way as possible without compromising Kesha's dignity. Two coworkers were identified who would act as sighted guides for Kesha when it was time to go on break or to lunch. They simply walk over to Kesha, sign "break" into her hand, and offer their arm so that she can accept their assistance. Because these workers have the same schedule as Kesha's, there is no interruption of the work flow.

CASE EXAMPLE: JEREMY

Jeremy attends a middle school and has been learning to participate in shopping for groceries in a neighborhood supermarket. Because he uses a walker for support, he has been paired with a peer for the shopping activity. Typically, Jeremy identifies the correct item, and the peer is responsible for pushing the cart.

For the past year, the school occupational therapist has become increasingly discouraged with the use of an isolated therapy model. She works with Jeremy in the occupational therapy room twice a week and is concerned that he may or may not use newly learned skills in natural settings. When she expressed these feelings to Jeremy's teacher, they decided to incorporate the occupational therapy objective of transferring to and from the walker with the grocery shopping activity.

The therapist developed a program to teach Jeremy to leave his walker at the front of the store, transfer to the grocery cart, and use the cart for support while he shopped. At first, this task was very difficult for Jeremy since the cart would roll as he attempted to transfer. Another concern was the fact that

Jeremy could not let go of the cart when retrieving an item or he would lose his balance. Thus, he was taught to move through the aisle of the store selecting items only on the right-hand side. At the end of the aisle, he makes a U-turn so that he can pass down the aisle again to select items on the left side.

Although he still shops occasionally with a peer, Jeremy is especially proud that he can go through the store alone while his teacher waits at the front of the store or his mother completes her own shopping.

Self-Direction

Most people cherish their ability to make decisions and choices regarding the many facets of their lives: where they will live, work, and play, and with whom; the types of social and leisure activities in which they will engage; what to have for dinner; which skills are important to have in one's repertoire; what clothes to wear today; and so on. For many persons with mental retardation, these choices and many more are usually made for them, with the likelihood of imposed choices increasing with the severity of the retardation. Freedom of choice and decision making have only recently been proposed as viable and essential components in the lives of persons with severe and profound retardation (Belfiore, 1994; Guess, Benson, & Seigel-Causey, 1985; C. Kennedy & Haring, 1993; Parson, McCarn, & Reid, 1993; Shevin & Klein, 1984).

Persons with significant retardation are highly unlikely to develop sufficient abilities to achieve complete self-direction and autonomy. However, the complete absence of self-direction is undignified and frequently leads to "learned helplessness" and total dependence on others (Guess et al., 1985). Therefore, a central theme of each treatment or educational program should be that persons with significant retardation are allowed to show preferences, to make choices and decisions, and to exhibit some control over their own day-to-day activities and long-term goals (Belfiore, 1994;

Bowen, 1994). Service providers can foster self-direction in several ways:

• Individuals with significant retardation can be trained to discover their preferences and to make choices and decisions. In areas where independent choice making is not feasible or safe, choice making can be adapted or supported. As with any skill area, individuals with severe and profound mental retardation can partially participate in self-direction by exerting control over specific situations or life choices (C. Kennedy & Haring, 1993).

• Opportunities for expressing preferences and making choices and decisions should be available in all areas of service. Learning to make good decisions requires experience with the process of decision making, with alternatives, and with consequences of decisions (M. Kennedy, 1993).

• Service providers should respect the decisions that people with significant mental retardation make, even if they do not always agree with the end result. Service providers should keep in mind that making choices is a means of establishing one's own identity and individuality, not that of the service provider. They should also keep in mind that it is part of the human condition to make bad decisions on occasion and to learn from mistakes.

CASE EXAMPLE: MS. KINDRICKS

Ms. Kindricks decided to incorporate choice making in the shopping activity that her elementary students perform on Wednesdays and Fridays. To assist the children in preparing for the shopping trip to a convenience store, she developed a picture sequence board that paced the children through using the restroom, getting their coats, selecting a dollar bill, and the other tasks associated with "getting ready."

She then added a component to the sequence that assists the children in making a selection of what they want to buy at the store. She designed a "choice board" by hanging cards representing the items that the parents reported were their children's favorites. Each item is actually a wrapper affixed to a small piece of laminated cardboard, which is attached to the board with Velcro. When each child decides what he or she wants to purchase, the child takes the choice card off of the board and takes it to the store so that he or she will know what to purchase. Ms. Kindricks has made duplicates of each choice card so that each child can select from the full range of options.

CASE EXAMPLE: JANE

Jane is a young adult with severe mental retardation who has been working with support for over one year. Unfortunately, she does not appear to participate in many leisure activities even though she is now earning money. The support staff in her group home have noticed that Jane likes certain types of clothing, particularly scarves of bright colors.

The staff decided to teach Jane to shop for clothing items as a leisure activity. At first, she required a great amount of assistance in making a selection. However, by preselecting stores that have clothing in Jane's price range, teaching Jane to find the areas of the store with her favorite items, and allowing her multiple opportunities to go shopping, Jane's group home staff have enabled her to select and purchase clothing of her choice. Jane also keeps a catalog at home to get ideas of what she would like to purchase when she goes shopping.

Capacity for Independent Living

There is universal consensus that persons with severe or profound mental retardation, because of their cognitive impairments, require some form of domestic support. This support will typically include assistance with such activities as meal preparation, shopping, money management, self-care, transportation, and other day-to-day needs. Although most persons with severe or profound retardation receive this assistance from their immediate families, individuals with severe or profound mental retardation also compose disproportionately large segments of the populations of residential services, especially institutions (Seltzer & Seltzer, 1983).

Recent trends in residential placement for persons with severe and profound mental retardation have generally mirrored that of the field as a whole: away from large congregate living facilities and toward small group living or individual placement options, such as specialized foster care, adoption, or supported apartment living (Lakin, Hill, & Bruininks, 1988; Lakin, Blake, Prouty, Mangan, & Bruininks, 1993). More progressive programs are shifting focus away from funding residential services to supporting *individuals* with all levels of retardation wherever, however, and with whomever they choose to live, thereby promoting a greater degree of independence, integration, and "sense of home" (O'Brien & O'Brien, 1994). In addition, there is growing commitment by service providers and state funding agencies to provide needed and desired supports to families that have a member with severe disabilities in order to allow the family to remain intact and to prevent or delay out-of-home placement (Cohen, Agosta, Cohen, & Warren, 1989; Farber & Marcel, 1994).

CASE EXAMPLE: DAVID

After David had lived in a state institution for people with severe retardation, his family decided that they wanted him to live in the community. The case worker from the Division of Mental Retardation and Developmental Disabilities informed the family that David had a choice of two options: a group home for six residents or a supported apartment for David and one other individual.

The family very carefully thought about the two options and the impact of each on David's lifestyle. Their major concern was that David is very outgoing and enjoys being with other people, and they did not want him to be isolated without opportunities for social interactions. After great consideration, they selected the group-home option even though many professionals had advised them that it is the more restrictive residential option. The family believe that David is used to living with many people, so the group home will require less of an adjustment.

David now lives in the group home, which is located in a suburban neighborhood, with five other housemates. He enjoys participating in household tasks and is involved in numerous activities sponsored by a community church. Additionally, he is known by many of the residents throughout the neighborhood because he walks a mile and a half every evening as part of an exercise program.

CASE EXAMPLE: TINA

Tina lived at home throughout her school years and when she first became employed as an office worker. When Tina reached the age of 24, her parents began to seek an alternative residential option; however, they were not at all pleased with the concept of a group home. They believed that living with a large number of people in one household would be too much of an intrusion of Tina's lifestyle. In fact, they became frustrated with the case worker from the Division of Mental Retardation and Developmental Disabilities because she seemed to believe that Tina did not have sufficient skills to live in a less restrictive setting.

The family was fortunate in that Tina qualified for a new residential initiative for persons with disabilities that allowed for monies to be used more flexibly than in the past. Tina now resides with a nondisabled roommate in an apartment that is convenient to the bus that she takes to work. She pays for her portion of the rent with human services funds and uses part of her salary to contribute to living expenses. Her family has assisted her in decorating the apartment, a leisure activity that Tina really enjoys.

Economic Self-Sufficiency

Persons with severe and profound mental retardation historically have not been economically self-sufficient, relying on financial support from family members, public and private agencies, and income assistance programs such as Supplemental Security Income (SSI), food stamps, and the like. In addition, vocational training and employment programs for increasing economic self-sufficiency historically have excluded members of this population or have placed them in nonremunerative, therapeutic activities from which they were expected to progress to paying jobs when they were "ready."

Research and demonstration projects of the late 1970s and early 1980s established that persons with severe and profound mental retardation, generally thought to be unemployable outside of the sheltered workshop or activity center, could achieve success in competitive work through a combination of intensive training and postplacement follow-along efforts (Bellamy, Horner, & Inman, 1979; Rusch & Mithaug, 1980; Wehman, 1981; Wehman, Hill, & Koehler, 1979). A central theme to each of these efforts was the abandonment of the "readiness" model of vocational preparation, in which people were endlessly preparing to work, and the adoption of a job-placement methodology of "place first, then train and support." The vocational strategy that emerged from these early efforts, known as *supported employment*, has since grown in acceptance funding, and scope and is now a vocational rehabilitation service option for persons with severe disabilities in every state.

Supported employment became a service option by way of the 1986 Amendments to the Rehabilitation Act (P.L. 99–506). The final regulations for the amendments define supported employment as paid work for persons with severe disabilities in integrated settings with ongoing support services, such as job skills reinforcement and continuing monitoring and assessment (*Federal Register*, 1987). More recently, supported employment regulations have defined the target population as those with "the most severe disabilities" (*Federal Register*, 1992). Supported employment has dramatically improved the vocational outlook for members of a number of disability groups, including persons with severe and profound mental retardation (Wehman & Kregel, 1990). This new service delivery option is also affecting the curriculum used in many educational programs at state and local levels. Federal initiatives and funding have made competitive work available to more students and adults with severe disabilities (Wehman, Moon, Everson, Wood, & Barcus, 1988).

••

CASE EXAMPLE: MR. CLARKSON

Mr. Clarkson is a vocational rehabilitation counselor who is responsible for identifying individuals in need of supported employment services. Although he would like all persons with severe disabilities to access supported employment services, he must often select from among many individuals because a limited number of supported employment opportunities are available at one time. He has been directed to include some individuals who are exiting public school and has just received two descriptions of exiting students in two community school districts.

The first description is approximately one-half page in length and states that the student, Michael, has been involved in 2 years of work-adjustment training. Additionally, Michael has participated in an intensive prevocational program that involved assembly, sorting, and packaging a variety of items in a classroom converted into a simulated sheltered workshop. The report describes Michael's fine and gross motor skills and his ability to follow one-step, two-step, and multiple-step directions. Finally, the report includes a checklist that describes his ability to count; sort; recite his name, address, and telephone number; and perform other basic skills.

The second report is written in the format of a resume. Over a 5-year period, the student, Sara, has participated in vocational training in 10 community business sites. Each of the 10 sites represents a different occupational cluster such as food service or office/clerical work. For each cluster, the resume includes a description of the duties Sara performed and of her work accuracy and speed at the beginning and end of the training period. During her last year of school, Sara has worked on a part-time basis in a bakery.

A second part of the resume describes the adaptations and strategies that have been used to assist Sara in completing vocational tasks. In fact, she is able to follow complex sequences through the use of a picture prompting system. The resume also describes her ability to perform or participate in a variety of essential activities such as shopping, telephone use, street crossing, and the use of the public transit system. Finally, references are provided so that supervisors and coworkers who are familiar with Sara can be contacted.

It is not hard to understand why Mr. Clarkson decided to provide supported employment services to Sara first. Of course, he is charged with the responsibility of providing services to all individuals who meet the eligibility requirements. The case for serving Sara was stronger, however, because her resume clearly attested to her employability.

CASE EXAMPLE: JASON

Jason is 26 years old and has worked in a sheltered workshop for 5 years prior to taking his new job in a spice factory. Although some adult service personnel wanted to find Jason an integrated employment opportunity earlier, the fact that he was severely retarded influenced the decision to allow him to remain in the sheltered workshop. Just this year, his parents felt secure enough about the success of the supported employment program operated by the center to allow Jason to participate.

While in the sheltered workshop, Jason worked approximately 32 hours a week and earned an average of $40 per month. He was not entitled to any benefits such as health

care and paid vacation time. At this time, Jason is working 30 hours a week at his new job and earns $105 a week. He accrues 2 weeks' vacation annually and is eligible for health care benefits.

Jason has also decided to join the company bowling league. In fact, he travels to the bowling alley with a neighbor who is employed at the same company. His parents are beginning to realize the variety of opportunities available to Jason due to his entry into a typical employment setting.

DISCUSSION

When we began this chapter, we wrote that the manner in which service providers operated helped their clients achieve success. This is not intended to discount or detract from the efforts of the learners, for indeed they also had to put forth a great deal of work and enthusiasm for the learning to occur. Our closing comments concern the unifying attitudes, beliefs, and practices of the trainers.

First, each of the service providers recognized the importance of integrated opportunities for their clients in fostering normative behavior and for setting expectations of families, staff members, the students and clients themselves, and other significant individuals with whom they worked, lived, and socialized. These providers began with the belief not only that their clients *could* participate meaningfully in integrated settings and activities but also that they *should* participate as well. The service providers also recognized the value of the individual needs and preferences of their students, clients, and their families in selecting activities and settings for the instructional programs, an approach that also contributed to their clients' success.

Second, these service providers achieved success because they perceived that their clients' problems and failures existed either in the task or in the environment, not necessarily in the client. Thus, the focus of training became how to creatively manipulate those factors to meet the presenting needs of the learners. This manipulation involved training, adapting, or supporting new behavior and was firmly rooted in (a) a foundation of empirical and theoretical support, (b) a demand that outcomes be meaningful for clients and contribute to a more normal and enriched lifestyle, and (c) respect for the dignity of the learner.

Finally, service providers did not succumb to an "all or nothing" approach to inclusion in normalizing, integrated activities. That is, meaningful activities were not disregarded simply because the learner would not be able to achieve complete independence or to engage in the particular activity in the same manner as do persons without disabilities. Participation in normalizing, integrated activities, even if it must be adapted or supported, is more dignified, opens more opportunities, and enhances the dignity and quality of life for persons with significant mental retardation.

FINAL THOUGHTS

These are exciting times for individuals with severe mental retardation and their families. No longer do we ask questions like these: Can they really work at real jobs in the community? Can they go to school with their nonretarded brothers and sisters, friends, and neighbors? Can they participate in making choices and decisions about their lives? After two decades of demonstration and legislation in educational and habilitative services, the question now is how to make true community integration and participation the reality for *everyone*, including those who have severe retardation.

Many of the barriers to full inclusion for persons with severe mental retardation are systemic. For example, many educational systems operate segregated schools into which it is assumed that all students with significant retardation will be placed. Rehabilitation centers often have "prevocational" or "work activity" programs, which never lead to either real work or a vocation, for their clients with severe mental retardation. State mental retardation funding systems often use funding "slots" to predetermine the number of individuals who can enter community-based employment in any year. One of the greatest challenges ahead will be to redesign existing service systems in such ways that will allow individuals with severe mental retardation and their families to exercise true choice of where and with whom they would like to learn, live, and work.

REFERENCES

Baumgart, D., Brown, L., Pumpian, I., Nisbet, J., Ford, A., Sweet, M., Messina, R., & Schroeder, J. (1982). Principle of partial participation in educational programs for severely handicapped students. *Journal of the Association for the Severely Handicapped, 7*, 17–27.

Belfiore, P. J. (1994). *Recognizing choices in community settings for people with significant disabilities.* Washington, DC: American Association on Mental Retardation.

Bellamy, G. T., Horner, R. H., & Inman, D. P. (1979). *Vocational habilitation of severely retarded adults: A direct service technology.* Baltimore: University Park Press.

Bowen, J. N. (1994). The power of self-advocacy: Making thunder. In V. J. Bradley, J. W. Ashbaugh, & B. C. Blaney (Eds.), *Creating individual supports for people with developmental disabilities* (pp. 335–345). Baltimore: Brookes.

Bradley, V. J. (1994). Evolution of a new service paradigm. In V. J. Bradley, J. W. Ashbaugh, & B. C. Blaney (Eds.), *Creating individual supports for people with developmental disabilities* (pp. 11–32). Baltimore: Brookes.

Butler, K. G. (Ed.). (1994). *Severe communication disorders: Intervention strategies.* Gaithersburg, MD: Aspen.

Carr, T. H. (1984). Attention, skill, and intelligence: Some speculations on extreme individual differences in human performance. In P. H. Brooks, R. Sperber, & C. McCauley (Eds.), *Learning and cognition in the mentally retarded* (pp. 189–215). Hillsdale, NJ: Erlbaum.

Cohen, S., Agosta, J., Cohen, J., & Warren, R. (1989). Supporting families of children with severe disabilities. *Journal of the Association for Persons with Severe Handicaps, 14*, 155–162.

Dodd, B., & Leahy, J. (1989). Phonological disorders and mental handicap. In M. Beveridge, G. Conti-Ramsden, & I. Leudar (Eds.), *Language and communication in mentally handicapped people* (pp. 33–56). London: Chapman & Hall.

Falvey, M., Brown, L., Lyon, S., Baumgart, D., & Schroeder, J. (1980). Strategies for using cues and correction procedures. In W. Sailor, B. Wilcox, & L. Brown (Eds.), *Methods of instruction for severely handicapped students* (pp. 109–133). Baltimore: Brookes.

Farber, A., & Marcel, K. (1994). Parent power: Change through grassroots networking. In V. J. Bradley, J. W. Ashbaugh, & B. C. Blaney (Eds.), *Creating individual supports for people with developmental disabilities* (pp. 373–385). Baltimore: Brookes.

Federal Register. (1987, August 14). 52(157), 30546–30552. 34 C.F.R. 363.

Federal Register. (1992, June 24). 57(122), 28432–28442. 34 C.F.R. 363.

Grossman, H. (Ed.). (1973). *Manual on terminology and classification in mental retardation.* Washington, DC: American Association on Mental Deficiency.

Grossman, H. (Ed.). (1983). *Classification in mental retardation.* Washington, DC: American Association on Mental Deficiency.

Guess, D., Benson, H. A., & Siegel-Causey, E. (1985). Concepts and issues related to choice-making and autonomy among persons with severe disabilities. *Journal of the Association for Persons with Severe Handicaps, 10,* 79–86.

Guess, D., & Helmstetter, E. (1986). Skill cluster instruction and the individualized curriculum sequencing model. In R. H. Horner, L. H. Meyer, & H. D. Fredericks (Eds.), *Education of learners with severe handicaps* (pp. 221–248). Baltimore: Brookes.

Halle, J. (1988). Adopting the natural environment as the context of training. In S. N. Calculator & J. L. Bedrosian (Eds.), *Communication assessment and intervention for adults with mental retardation* (pp. 155–185). Boston: College Hill.

Haney, M., & Falvey, M. A. (1989). Instructional strategies. In M. A. Falvey (Ed.), *Community-based curriculum* (pp. 63–90). Baltimore: Brookes.

Horner, R. H. (1989). Editorial farewell. *Journal of the Association for Persons with Severe Handicaps, 14,* 253.

Kelleher, A., & Mulcahy, M. (1986). Patterns of disability in the mentally handicapped. In J. M. Berg (Ed.), *Science and service in mental retardation* (pp. 15–22). New York: Methuen.

Kennedy, C. W., & Haring, T. C. (1993). Teaching choice-making during social interactions to students with profound multiple disabilities. *Journal of Applied Behavior Analysis, 26,* 63–76.

Kennedy, M. (1993). Foreword. In P. Wehman (Ed.), *The ADA mandate for social change* (pp. xv–xix). Baltimore: Brookes.

Kobe, F. H., Mulick, J. A., Rash, T. A., & Martin, J. (1994). Nonambulatory persons with profound mental retardation: Physical, developmental, and behavioral characteristics. *Research in Developmental Disabilities, 15,* 413–423.

Lakin, K. C., Blake, E. M., Prouty, R. W., Mangan, T., & Bruininks, R. H. (1993). *Residential services for persons with developmental disabilities: Status and trends through 1991.* Minneapolis: University of Minnesota Center on Residential Services and Community Living, Institute on Community Integration.

Lakin, K. C., Hill, B. K., & Bruininks, R. H. (1988). Trends and issues in the growth of community residential services. In M. P. Janicki, M. W. Krauss, & M. M. Seltzer (Eds.), *Community residences for persons with developmental disabilities: Here to stay* (pp. 25–42). Baltimore: Brookes.

Luckasson, R., Coulter, D. L., Polloway, E. A., Reiss, S., Schalock, R. L., Snell, M. E., Spitalnik, D. M., & Stark, J. A. (1992). *Mental retardation: Definition, classification, and systems of support* (9th ed.). Washington, DC: American Association on Mental Retardation.

Luckasson, R., & Spitalnik, D. (1994). Political and programmatic shifts of the 1992 AAMR definition of mental retardation. In V. J. Bradley, J. W. Ashbaugh, & B. C. Blaney (Eds.), *Creating individual supports for people with developmental disabilities* (pp. 81–95). Baltimore: Brookes.

Mount, B. (1994). Benefits and limitations of personal futures planning. In V. J. Bradley, J. W. Ashbaugh, & B. C. Blaney (Eds.), *Creating individual supports for people with developmental disabilities* (pp. 97–108). Baltimore: Brookes.

O'Brien, J., & O'Brien, C. L. (1994). More than just a new address: Images of organization for supported living agencies. In V. J. Bradley J. W. Ashbaugh, & B. C. Blaney (Eds.), *Creating individual supports for people with developmental disabilities* (pp. 109–140). Baltimore: Brookes.

Owens, R. (1989). Cognition and language in the mentally retarded population. In M. Beveridge, G. Conti-Ramsden, & I. Leudar (Eds.), *Language and communication in mentally handicapped people* (pp. 112–142). London: Chapman & Hall.

Parson, M. B., McCarn, J. E., & Reid, D. H. (1993). Evaluating and increasing meal-related choices throughout a service setting for people with severe disabilities. *Journal of the Association for Persons with Severe Disabilities, 18,* 253–260.

Rehabilitation Act Amendments of 1986, P.L. 99–506, 29 U.S.C. 701 *et seq.*

Reichle, J., Piché-Cragoe, L., Sigafoos, J., & Doss, S. (1988). Optimizing functional communication for persons with severe handicaps. In S. N. Calculator & J. L. Bedrosian (Eds.), *Communication assessment and intervention for adults with mental retardation* (pp. 239–264). Boston: College Hill.

Rusch, F. R., & Mithaug, D. E. (1980). *Vocational training for mentally retarded adults: A behavioral analytic approach.* Champaign, IL: Research Press.

Scheerenberger, R. C. (1983). *A history of mental retardation.* Baltimore: Brookes.

Schiefelbusch, R. L. (1972). Language disabilities of cognitively involved children. In J. V. Irwin & M. Marge (Eds.), *Principles of childhood language disabilities* (pp. 209–234). New York: Appleton-Century-Crofts.

Seltzer, M. S., & Seltzer, G. B. (1983). Classification and social status. In J. L. Matson & J. A. Mulick (Eds.), *Handbook of mental retardation* (pp. 185–198). New York: Pergamon Press.

Shevin, M., & Klein, N. K. (1984). The importance of choice-making skills for students with severe disabilities. *Journal of the Association for Persons with Severe Handicaps, 9,* 159–166.

Snell, M. E. (1993). *Instruction of students with severe disabilities* (4th ed.). New York: Merrill.

Tager-Flusberg, H. (Ed.). (1994). *Constraints on language acquisition: Studies of atypical children.* Hillsdale, NJ: Erlbaum.

Thompson, T., & Gray, D. B. (Eds.). (1994). *Destructive behavior in developmental disabilities: Diagnosis and treatment.* Thousand Oaks, CA: Sage.

Wehman, P. (1981). *Competitive employment: New horizons for severely disabled individuals.* Baltimore: Brookes.

Wehman, P., Hill, J. W., & Koehler, F. (1979). Helping severely handicapped persons enter competitive employment. *AAESPH Review, 4,* 274–290.

Wehman, P., & Kregel, J. (1990). Supported employment for persons with severe and profound mental retardation: A critical analysis. *International Journal of Rehabilitation Research, 13,* 93–107.

Wehman, P., Moon, M. S., Everson, J. M., Wood, W., & Barcus, J. M. (1988). *Transition from school to work: New challenges for youth with severe disabilities.* Baltimore: Brookes.

Cerebral Palsy

Katherine Inge

LEARNING GOALS

Upon completion of this chapter the reader will be able to

■ describe the different types of cerebral palsy and the resulting effects on movement and posture;

■ summarize the techniques for handling and positioning students with cerebral palsy as well as the related safety precautions;

■ discuss the impact of assistive technology and give examples of low- and high-technology devices that can assist people with developmental disabilities;

■ describe how materials and programs can be adapted to facilitate participation in functional activities by students with cerebral palsy;

■ outline the steps in assessing a student's physical abilities for the completion of dressing activities and the implications for developing task analyses to teach dressing skills;

■ review the effects of proper positioning on oral motor abilities; and

■ describe a minimum of three oral motor concerns and their implications for feeding students with cerebral palsy.

FUNCTIONAL DESCRIPTION

Approximately two children per 1,000 live births are affected by some type of cerebral palsy resulting in problems with movement and posture (Copeland & Kimmel, 1989). Cerebral palsy is a *nonprogressive* disorder caused by a lesion or defect to the brain occurring prior to birth, during the birth process, or during the first 4 years of life (Bleck & Nagel, 1983; Copeland & Kimmel, 1989; Inge, 1987). Nonprogressive refers to the

fact that the actual damage to the individual's brain does not worsen over time. However, if proper programming and treatment are not provided, the individual's ability to move and perform functional activities can decrease.

The identification of the different types of cerebral palsy is based on the individual's resulting movement disorder and the portion of the body involved (see Tables 8.1 and 8.2). Information about the classification and location of the disability is helpful in program planning. Professionals are, however, cautioned not to limit individuals on the basis of their medical diagnoses.

Table 8.1. Cerebral Palsy: Classification by Type

Type	Characteristics
Spasticity	• Characterized by increased muscle tone (hypertonicity) • Muscle tone varies in response to movement, stimulation, or effort • Voluntary movement may be slow and difficult • Most common type of motor dysfunction
Athetosis	• Involuntary, uncontrolled movements • Fluctuating muscle tone is present during activity and at rest • Movements have a writhing quality
Ataxia	• Movements characterized by poor balance and coordination • More noticeable during movement/purposeful activity than at rest
Rigidity	• Muscle tone is severely rigid ("lead pipe" movement) • Interferes with the individual's purposeful movement as well as movement initiated by the caregiver
Hypotonia	• Floppy or low muscle tone • Difficulty moving against gravity • Joints are hypermobile
Mixed	• Characterized by more than one type, for example, spasticity and athetosis • One type usually is predominate

Note. The information in this table is based on the following sources: Bigge (1989), Campbell (1993), Copeland and Kimmel (1989), Dunn (1991), and Inge (1987).

Table 8.2. Cerebral Palsy: Classification by Distribution

Monoplegia	Only one extremity (limb) involved Usually rare in children with cerebral palsy
Hemiplegia	One side of the body involved, including the arm and leg on the same side
Triplegia	Three limbs of the body involved Usually one arm and both legs
Paraplegia	Only the lower extremities (legs) involved Very rare in cerebral palsy May be person with diplegia who has mild upper extremity involvement
Diplegia	All limbs involved, but legs more involved than arms and hands Usually associated with spasticity
Quadriplegia	Whole-body involvement, including the trunk and four limbs Arms may be more involved than the legs

Note. The information in this table is adapted from Campbell and Kimmel (1989) and Inge (1987).

Mobility

The foundation for all movement is postural muscle tone, which allows an individual to have postural stability while moving to complete a motor action (Campbell, 1987, 1988; Campbell & Forsyth, 1993). For example, a person can sit upright with the arm in a stable position while writing with a pen or typing on a keyboard. He or she is able to make adjustments in the position, that is, move the hand from left to right across the page without losing balance in sitting. The individual with cerebral palsy, however, usually has atypical muscle tone that can be excessive (spasticity/hypertonicity) or insufficient (hypotonia) or that fluctuates between the two (Copeland & Kimmel, 1989; Dunn, 1991).

In addition to problems with atypical muscle tone, the individual with cerebral palsy may have persistent primitive reflexes that would normally disappear as an infant matures (Copeland & Kimmel, 1989; Inge, 1987). For instance, the individual whose movements are affected by the symmetrical tonic neck reflex may have difficulty straightening his or her arm to reach for an object if the head is flexed (bent) forward. Another individual may have difficulty combing his or her hair if movement is affected by the asymmetrical tonic neck reflex. The reflex causes extension of one arm and flexion of the other upon head turning.

It is not the intent of this chapter to describe fully the influences of abnormal muscle tone and reflex movement. The following case studies, however, are provided to describe the different types of cerebral palsy and the resulting effects on movement and posture. The reader should refer to the texts listed in the reference section as well as consult with physical and occupational therapists to obtain additional information. Remember, two individuals with cerebral palsy can have the same classification and body part involvement but have very different abilities. Review and assessment through a team approach can identify each individual's strengths and limitations.

CASE EXAMPLE: BILL AND MARY (PART 1)

Bill is physically challenged by spastic cerebral palsy with right hemiplegia. This information reveals that he has increased muscle tone, or hypertonicity, on the right side of his body that includes his arm and leg. His involvement is mild, which means that he can walk with a cane and use his right arm as an assist to the left. For instance, when working on tabletop activities, Bill can hold down a piece of paper while writing with his left hand. He cannot, however, use his right hand to complete fine motor activities such as buttoning or opening packages.

Mary, Bill's friend, also has spastic cerebral palsy with right hemiplegia. Mary, however, is severely affected by her disability and is unable to walk. She uses a wheelchair that she propels, using a left, one-arm manual drive. Because she had limited programming as a young child, Mary can no longer straighten her right arm, which is held close to her body with the elbow and wrist flexed (bent). The term used for this immobility is *contracture.* Mary is unable to use her hand or fingers for any functional tasks; however, her left arm has normal muscle tone and movement.

CASE EXAMPLE: SARAH (PART 1)

Sarah is a young woman with athetoid cerebral palsy that affects her ability to perform motorically. Movements throughout her body are characterized by flailing, involuntary motions with extensor tone predominating. She is able to sit independently when positioned on the floor as well as scoot about on her buttocks. Sarah can bear weight on her legs momentarily when supported by another person, but she is unable to stand independently or walk because of fluctuating muscle tone. Sarah uses an electric wheelchair with a joystick that she pushes with her right fist.

Fine motor activities are problematic because Sarah has difficulty stabilizing her arm at the shoulder joint. Involuntary movements are noted at her elbows, wrists, and fingers. Speech is also limited because of athetosis; however, Sarah has learned to communicate by typing messages on an augmentative communication device, using a head pointer.

CASE EXAMPLE: KEITH

Keith's ability to move independently is affected by spastic quadriplegia. This information reveals that he has hypertonicity (increased muscle tone) throughout his head, trunk, and limbs. Keith has difficulty moving any part of his body for purposeful activity. His muscles always appear to be very stiff, and any movement he makes is slow and labored. Keith uses a manual wheelchair that has knobs on the rims of each wheel. He pushes the knobs with the heel of each hand, because he is unable to adequately grasp the wheel rims. His parents are currently saving funds to purchase an electric wheelchair to improve his mobility skills.

Mobility out of his wheelchair is limited to rolling over from his stomach to his back on a mat and sitting independently once someone has assisted him to that position. He loses his balance easily and falls to one side, unable to return to sitting. The effort to complete any gross motor task can be seen throughout his body with increased extensor tone.

Fine motor tasks are also completed slowly with noted spasticity. Keith is able to use his hands for activities such as self-feeding, using a built-up handled spoon; typing on a computer keyboard, using the index finger of his right hand; and completing leisure recreation tasks such as playing checkers with his friends. He is able to speak, but his speech is difficult to understand because of spasticity.

Handling and Positioning Considerations

Individuals with cerebral palsy often require lifting, handling, and positioning assistance from the many professionals who interact with them on a daily basis (Campbell, 1993). It is critical that these professionals learn to provide this assistance properly to prevent injury to themselves and to the individuals being lifted and positioned. The use of proper "body mechanics" ensures that back strain and injury do not occur when one is moving an individual with cerebral palsy. Table 8.3 provides a list of precautions for lifting and positioning.

The presence of hypertonicity, hypotonicity, or fluctuating muscle tone usually results in atypical movements and postures that limit skill development for individuals with cerebral palsy (Campbell, 1987; Campbell & Forsyth, 1993; Inge, 1987; Rainforth & York, 1991). Knowledge of proper positioning and handling techniques can assist the individual in completing an activity that he or she may otherwise be unable to perform. In addition, if an individual is allowed to persist in using abnormal movement patterns and positions, he or she may eventually be unable to move in a more normalized fashion.

The goals of proper positioning include normalizing muscle tone, maintaining proper body alignment, stabilizing the body, and promoting participation in activities (Rainforth & York, 1991). For instance, a young child with cerebral palsy

Table 8.3. Safety Precautions for Lifting and Handling

- Never try to lift someone by yourself if the person is over 1/4 of your total body weight. **If in doubt, seek assistance!**

- Keep the weight you are lifting as close to your body as possible. The farther away the person is, the "heavier" he or she will be.

- Always keep your knees bent and your back straight when lifting. **Never** lift using your back. The leg muscles are much stronger and will allow you to lift the maximum amount of weight.

- Never twist or rotate at the waist when lifting. Move your body as one unit. To change directions, step around and turn your body without twisting at the waist or lower back.

- Never lift an individual with cerebral palsy by taking an arm and leg while someone else takes an arm and leg. This is especially true of an individual with hemiplegia because weight and tone will be different on the two sides of the person's body.

- Always lock the wheelchair brakes prior to moving an individual to and from a wheelchair.

- Make sure all seat belts and straps have been unfastened prior to lifting.

- Detach removable armrests and leg rests from the wheelchair and move them out of the way.

- Clear the environment of all extraneous materials, for example, toys, that you may trip over during lifting.

- If the individual has more involvement on one side of the body than on the other, make the transfer in the direction of the stronger side. For example, if the person has left hemiplegia, transfer him or her to the right whenever possible.

- Always require the individual to assist according to his or her capabilities.

- Movements should be slow and smooth. The individual being lifted should be aware of what is going to occur and what is expected of him or her.

- If you do injure your back, be sure to have it checked by a physician.

Note. The information in this table is adapted from the following sources: Copeland et al. (1976), Copeland and Kimmel (1989), and Rainforth and York (1987).

who is unable to stand independently may be positioned in a prone stander that stabilizes the hip joint and allows him or her to stand while performing an activity. Some suggested activities include making a sandwich on the kitchen counter, drying dishes at the sink, brushing or combing hair in front of the bathroom mirror, or brushing teeth.

Many different positioning devices can be purchased or built, including wedges, side-liers, corner chairs, bolsters, and adaptive wheelchairs. It is critical that each individual's abilities are assessed and that adaptive equipment is selected for optimal functioning. Occupational and physical therapists usually assume these responsibilities in program planning. The reader is directed to Finnie (1975), Copeland and Kimmel (1989), and Rainforth and York (1991) for detailed instructions on positioning and handling techniques. Table 8.4 provides basic guidelines in this area.

Associated Problems and Cognition

Many individuals with cerebral palsy are not affected by any other disability; however, approximately two thirds have associated problems (Prensky & Palkes, 1982). These additional disabilities can include mental retardation, seizures, visual impairments, hearing loss, speech and language disorders, and learning disabilities. It is possible for an individual to be severely limited motorically yet have normal intelligence. For instance, one may assume that a child with limited mobility who is unable to speak to be severely mentally retarded, but this assumption may not be true. Professionals are cautioned not to make these assumptions but to assess thoroughly an individual's capabilities. A review of the case studies already presented may be useful in understanding the varying abilities of individuals with cerebral palsy.

Bill, the young man with spastic hemiplegia, also has a learning disability. This disability became evident when he had difficulty learning to read and spell; however, math never seemed to be a problem for him. In fact, Bill usually earned As

Table 8.4.   Positioning and Handling Guidelines

- Never leave individuals positioned indefinitely in adaptive equipment. Check them frequently and correct body alignment as needed. Remember, many of these individuals cannot move themselves and may develop pressure sores if left in the same position for extended periods of time.

- Select adaptive equipment that assists the individual in completing an activity in as normal a position as possible.

- Identify a "menu" of positioning options and rotate among them during a day's activities.

- Modify the environment to eliminate excessive noise and distractions. Overly stimulating environments can increase muscle tone and facilitate abnormal movement patterns.

- Learn to feel muscle tone changes. **Stop** if you are increasing abnormal patterns.

- Avoid quick movements when positioning and handling individuals with hypertonicity because rapid or jerky movement can stimulate spasticity. Slow, steady movement is important.

- Learn the key points of body control: the head, trunk, shoulders, hips, and pelvis.

- Never pull on a body part that is flexed. This will increase spasticity.

- Never carry the child like an infant because this limits his or her visual field and he or she will never learn head or body control.

- Increase muscle tone in individuals with low tone (hypotonicity) by bouncing or tapping a body part in the direction of the required movement.

- Provide the least amount of assistance and encourage the individual to participate whenever possible. Providing too much support or control does not allow the individual to develop motor control. Assess needs often and change as indicated.

Note. The information in this table is adapted from the following sources: Copeland and Kimmel (1989), Finnie (1975), and Sobsey (1987).

and Bs in math. Testing revealed that he had a learning disability but was of normal intelligence. With assistance from a resource teacher, Bill was able to stay in a regular education classroom throughout his school years and to receive a high school diploma.

Mary also has a diagnosis of spastic hemiplegia; however, she is severely mentally retarded. Her disability was identified early because Mary did not show an interest in people or toys as an infant. Psychological testing revealed that she has an IQ of 27, which places her in the severe range of mental retardation. Mary's school years have been spent in a program for students with severe disabilities, where she receives intensive instruction in domestic, leisure–recreation, vocational, and community skills. Her school days include community-based instruction as well as opportunities to interact with her age-appropriate, nonhandicapped peers.

Although Sarah is severely physically disabled with athetoid cerebral palsy, she has normal intelligence. As an infant she was unable to learn to speak, but Sarah was fortunate to have a speech therapist and teacher who quickly recognized her intellectual abilities. She attended regular classes but, because of her physical limitations, she received assistance with personal care and with classwork. With individualized attention, Sarah was quickly able to learn to read and to type on a computer keyboard using a head pointer. Currently she is an avid reader of mystery novels and is enrolled in a computer programmer course at her local university.

Assistive Technology

Technology has had great impact on the everyday lives of individuals with cerebral palsy and has allowed them to gain greater control and independence (Inge & Shepherd, 1995). The Individuals with Disabilities Education Act of 1990 (IDEA) and the 1994 Reauthorization of the Technology-Related Assistance for Individuals Act (Tech Act) define assistive technology device and service:

> The term *assistive technology device* means any item, piece of equipment, or product system, whether acquired commercially off the shelf, modified, or customized, that is used to increase, maintain, or improve functional capabilities of individuals with disabilities [20 U.S.C. § 140(25)].

> The term *assistive technology service* means any service that directly assists an individual with a disability in the selection, acquisition, or use of an assistive technology device [20 U.S.C. § 140(26)].

There is a continuum of complexity in technology related to the device itself and the type of materials or manufacturing techniques used to produce the device. *Low technology* usually includes devices that are passive or simple, with few moving parts (Mann & Lane, 1991). Low-technology devices that individuals with cerebral palsy may use are reachers, weighted or built-up-handled spoons, keyguards, and book stands. Velcro, dycem, and splinting materials are also low-technology materials that aid persons with cerebral palsy to complete tasks. For instance, a placemat made from dycem, a nonslip material, could assist an individual to eat by preventing his or her plate from moving around on the table. In addition, he or she may benefit from a spoon whose handle has been enlarged with splinting materials (Inge & Shepherd, 1995). Another individual could become independent in dressing when he or she purchases a pair of shoes with Velcro closures rather than shoe laces.

High technology includes devices that have greater complexity and may have an electronic component (Anson, 1993). Computers, augmentative communication devices, environmental control units, and power wheelchairs are examples of high-technology devices. Further examples of high- and low-technology devices for individuals with cerebral palsy can be found throughout this chapter under each section. The reader is referred to Flippo, Inge, and Barcus (1995) for a detailed description of assistive technology issues and applications.

Receptive and Expressive Language

Individuals with cerebral palsy, as in any area of functioning, may have normal to severe receptive and expressive language difficulties. Abnormal muscle tone can limit not only gross and fine motor abilities but also the muscles that control facial and tongue movements. These effects can result in difficulty with articulation, speech production, and breath control (Campbell, 1993; Copeland & Kimmel, 1989).

Fortunately, major advancements have been made in the area of communication for individuals with severe disabilities (Coots & Falvey, 1989; Miller, 1993; Miller & Allaire, 1987; Reichle & Karlan, 1985; Reichle, York, & Eynon, 1989; Tanchak & Sawyer, 1995). Many options are available, depending on the abilities of the individual in need of speech and language programming. Speech therapy may be indicated for those individuals who have difficulty with articulation, or an alternative system may be appropriate for individuals unable to develop speech.

Augmentative communication systems can be as simple as a picture or word board or as complicated as a computerized electronic device (Miller, 1993). Electronic boards are available with synthesized voices or message printouts that can be accessed with a variety of special input devices. Examples include head pointers, light beams, and pressure-sensitive switches that respond with the touch of any body part. The complexity of the system is matched to the individual's intellectual and physical abilities.

The selection and design of an augmentative communication system should include input from the individual with cerebral palsy, the speech pathologist, parents, teacher, and occupational and physical therapists. Together, these individuals can determine whether the person will communicate verbally or if an alternative device is needed. If the team determines that speech is not a functional option, physical and occupational therapists can help determine the optimal position and body part to be involved in using a communication system as well as determine the input device that should be utilized. The speech pathologist is most familiar with the systems available commercially and the level of abilities required to operate the various augmentative communication devices (Tanchak & Sawyer,

1995). Parents and teachers can provide information on the individual's communicative intent, which is crucial for matching skill level to an augmentative system.

In any case, language programming should occur in the natural environment during naturally occurring times of the day. For instance, the speech pathologist may accompany a student into the community to learn how to use a communication board for ordering a meal at the local fast-food restaurant. The following case studies may be useful in understanding the communication needs of individuals with cerebral palsy.

CASE EXAMPLE: MARY (PART 2)

Mary had difficulty developing speech and language due to her combined problems of cerebral palsy and severe mental retardation. As a young child, she made several sounds that were understood by her parents to indicate that she was happy, uncomfortable, or hungry. When she began school, however, her teacher, speech pathologist, and occupational and physical therapists determined that Mary would need an alternative communication system.

Because Mary had full use of her left arm, these service providers decided that she could point directly to pictures on a communication board. Initially, only three picture symbols were placed on her board to indicate *eat, drink,* and *bathroom.* Instructional sessions were scheduled during mealtime, snacks, and toileting time rather than set up as special sessions for language instruction. Mary's teacher designed a program using a time-delay procedure with a physical prompt to teach her to use the pictures on the board (Halle, Marshall, & Spradlin, 1979; Kaiser, 1993; Snell & Gast, 1981). Initially 25 trials were implemented at a 0-second delay. For instance, during snack time, the teacher would hold up Mary's cup and say "Mary, what do you want?" At the same time (0-second delay) that the teacher asked the question, she physically prompted Mary to point to the picture of drink. Mary was then given the opportunity to drink from the cup.

After the first 25 trials, the teacher gradually began to delay the physical prompt, giving Mary an opportunity to respond independently. The teacher employed this technique systematically by implementing 25 trials at 2 seconds, 25 trials at 4 seconds, and so forth, until Mary met her program objective of pointing to the picture independently. During the training procedure, the teacher designed an error-correction procedure to use if Mary made more than three consecutive errors during delay levels greater than 0. When this occurred, the teacher dropped back to 5 consecutive trials at 0-second delay before returning to a higher delay level.

CASE EXAMPLE: SARAH (PART 2)

Sarah, the young woman with athetoid cerebral palsy, never developed speech because of fluctuating muscle tone in her facial muscles and tongue. Sarah was able to make sounds and "talk" in complete sentences, but only people who were familiar with her could understand these vocalizations. Speech therapy was attempted when she was a young child but with little improvement in oral communication.

Initially, a picture communication board was developed, which was replaced with an alphabet board when Sarah learned to read and spell. Because she was unable to use her hands consistently to point to the symbols or letters, Sarah used a head pointer to spell what she wanted to say. Sarah recently received an augmentative communication device that has a synthesized female voice as well as a printout strip. Sarah uses a head pointer to type what she wants to say, and the computerized communication device "talks" for her. This particular device can be programmed to respond to commonly asked questions using codes that Sarah easily learned how to use. The code system increases her speed, because every word no longer needs to be typed. With the help of this augmentative communication system,

Sarah is able to communicate effectively in complete sentences at a good conversational pace.

Self-Care

Completion of self-care tasks is often difficult for individuals with cerebral palsy because of the sophisticated and coordinated movements required to perform even the most simple tasks (Campbell, 1993; Sobsey, 1987). Motor responses that most people take for granted, such as sitting or standing without support while dressing, are problematic for the individual whose movements are influenced by spasticity or athetosis. The child with a severe asymmetrical tonic reflex may not be able to take a spoon to his or her mouth because head turning to look at the spoon causes the arm to extend. Another individual may have difficulty with toileting due to a spastic bladder. In frustration, many care providers resort to completing self-care activities for a person with a physical disability, because they assume that it is easier and faster to do it themselves.

This tendency to complete self-care activities for individuals with cerebral palsy can be referred to as the "all or none" philosophy. In other words, if a person cannot complete all of an activity, he or she should not receive instruction on that task. The result is increased dependency and the exclusion of many skills from a training curriculum that an individual could at least partially learn to complete. Baumgart et al. (1982) and Ferguson and Baumgart (1991) have discussed the principle of partial participation and its applications for individuals with severe disabilities. They suggest using material adaptations, adapting the environment, adapting skill sequences, and using personal assistance to allow students access to activities that they otherwise would be excluded from. If caretakers implement these strategies, the individual with a physical disability can participate in age-appropriate, functional activities. Table 8.5 suggests material and environmental modifications to increase participation in self-care activities.

Table 8.5. Using the Principle of Partial Participation
for Self-Care Activities

Material Adaptations

- Utensils or swivel utensils with built-up handles
- Adaptive hand splints for holding utensils
- High-sided dishes, scoop bowls, and plate guards
- "Nosey" cutout cups
- Cup holders, two-handled drinking cups, adaptive straws
- Suction cups and nonslip mats
- Velcro closures, button hooks, and zipper pulls
- Dressing sticks, reachers, shoehorn aides, and stocking aids
- Toothbrushes, weighted and with built-up handles
- Dispenser handles on toothpaste pump containers
- Razor holders
- Deodorant and shaving cream dispenser handles to depress nozzles
- Long-handled combs and brushes
- Built-up handles or Velcro-handled combs and brushes
- Bathing mitts and bath brushes
- Soap-holder mitts and sponges
- Hand-held urinals and toileting aids

Environmental Adaptations

- Removing architectural barriers
- Lowering light switches, checking counter heights
- Rearranging furniture
- Ramps
- Doorknob extensions
- Grab bars
- Bed rails
- Tub-transfer bench, bath-support chair, shower chair
- Elevated toilet seat or toilet chair

Material Adaptations

Rainforth and York (1987, 1991) defined an adaptation as any device or material that is used to accomplish a task more efficiently. Adaptations for individuals with cerebral palsy are usually designed to decrease the physical demands of an activity and range from low to high "tech." For instance, Sarah's involuntary movements in her hands, which are related to athetoid cerebral palsy, make it impossible for her to grasp a spoon. She uses a self-feeder designed for individuals with this problem. Keith, the young man with spastic cerebral palsy, has difficulty grasping small objects. He is successful in self-feeding, using a spoon with an enlarged handle.

Both of these individuals required an assistive device for the same activity; however, two different solutions were identified. Sarah's self-feeder is an example of a high-technology solution whereas Keith's enlarged-handled spoon is an example of low technology. It is important to remember that not all individuals with cerebral palsy can use the same adaptations. When selecting and designing materials, professionals should consider several things (Copeland, Ford, & Solon, 1976; Rainforth & York, 1987, 1991; York, Nietupski, & Hamre-Nietupski, 1985): First, an adaptation should not be used if the person has the potential for learning a task without one. Second, professionals should work in teams that include the individual with cerebral palsy, the teacher, the occupational therapist, and the physical therapist. Together, they can assess the movement required to perform the task and evaluate the individual's abilities. They should then decide what type of assistive device is needed and whether it must be made or is available commercially.

The final selection should be made on the basis of the least intrusive design that allows the person to be as independent as possible. Keith, for example, is unable to perform fine motor prehension tasks due to spastic quadriplegia. One activity that he is unable to complete is turning on a lamp switch. At first, his teacher thought she should attach a microswitch to the lamp in Keith's bedroom so that he would perform this task independently. After some thought, the teacher determined that Keith could learn to use a commercially available lamp that turns on when the base is touched. With instruction, he learned to tap the lamp with his forearm and thus turn it on. The adaptation selected was more normalizing, because many homes have this type of lamp.

It should be noted, however, that the use of the microswitch would be appropriate for those individuals who cannot learn to operate a lamp in any other fashion. Clearly, the use of an adaptive switch has allowed many individuals with cerebral palsy to partially participate in many functional daily-living activities. Table 8.6 provides suggestions for microswitch use based on the physical ability of the individual. Occupational and physical therapists can provide invaluable input in this area when the service provider is determining which motor response the individual with cerebral palsy can use to activate a switch.

Adapting Skill Sequences

Often the sequence or manner in which a task is completed can be altered in order for the person with cerebral palsy to be successful in skill completion (York & Rainforth, 1991). For instance, a person with limited range of motion of the arms may not be able to reach his or her hands under the faucet of a sink. Therefore, the task of hand-washing can be modified by the positioning of a basin of water, soap, and towel within the individual's reach.

Dressing is another self-care area that can be modified for individuals with severe physical disabilities. To complete dressing and undressing tasks, a person usually needs to be able to maintain a stable base of support; shift body weight when leaning forward, backward, or side to side; reach and grasp clothing; and move arms and legs (Copeland & Kimmel, 1989). Many of these movements are problematic or impossible for the individual with severe cerebral palsy. However, modifying the way the task is completed, such as by providing an external base of support in sitting, may make it possible for a person to complete a dressing or undressing task successfully (Campbell, 1993).

The first step in determining if a task should be altered is to assess the physical capabilities of the

Table 8.6.   Examples of Motor Responses for Activating Assistive Technology Devices

HEAD/FACE

- Raise/lower eyebrows to activate switch attached to battery operated toy
- Nod head to interrupt a light beam to turn on the television
- Lift head to trigger a mercury switch that is connected to a tape recorder
- Bite switch to control an electric wheelchair
- Lift chin to operate a joystick to play video games
- "Sip and puff" switch to move an electric scooter
- Turn head to touch a pressure-sensitive switch that operates the electric blender (e.g., touch forehead, cheek, or chin to switch)
- Voice-activated computer system

ARM/HAND

- Squeeze ball/bulb switch to turn on fan
- Push joystick to play Nintendo
- Move arm/hand to touch a pressure-sensitive switch (e.g., touch elbow, palm, forearm, fingers to switch) that operates an environmental control unit
- Move arm/hand to contact skin with pad switch (no pressure required) to activate a buzzer in parents' bedroom
- Raise arm with a mercury switch cuff to turn on the radio
- Extend wrist to use a specialized splint for writing
- Clap hands to turn on/off lights on the Christmas tree
- Move arm to use a ballbearing orthosis for self-feeding
- Move arm/hand/finger to interrupt a light-beam switch that operates an augmentative communication device

LEG/FOOT

- Push foot/toes to activate pillow switch to recline electric bed or chair
- Move toe(s) to activate "splint switch" (molded foot splint with miniature paddle switch mounted near toes) that operates an electric page turner
- Push joystick with foot/toes to play with an electrical toy train
- Move leg to touch pressure-sensitive massage cushion
- Raise leg to activate mercury switch attached to CD player
- Foot/leg moves toward a proximity switch that turns on whirlpool bath (switch is activated when body part is brought within a specific range)

Table 8.7. Assessing Physical Abilities for Dressing Activities

EVALUATE THE PERSON'S UPPER BODY CONTROL

Can the person . . .

sit in a straight chair without support?

lean forward away from the back of the chair without losing his/her balance?

sit in a chair with arms and pull himself/herself forward away from the back of the chair using one hand?

reach with one or both hands overhead?

reach with one or both hands to the back of the neck, waist, and feet?

grasp with one or both hands?

do "push-ups" using the armrests in his/her wheelchair to lift the buttocks off the seat?

lean back in the wheelchair and lift buttocks off the seat? (May be contraindicated for an individual with total-body extension.)

EVALUATE THE PERSON'S MOBILITY ON THE FLOOR

Can the person . . .

roll from side to side?

lie on his/her back and independently lift buttocks off mat?

lift his/her buttocks off the mat by pushing with the feet against a stable surface such as a wall?

reach with one or both hands overhead?

place one or both hands on the back of the neck, waist, and feet?

grasp with one or both hands?

sit up from supine (back) or prone (stomach position)?

get to a kneeling position independently?

use a chair or grab bar to pull himself/herself to a kneeling position?

EVALUATE THE PERSON'S ABILITY TO STAND

Can the person . . .

stand momentarily without support?

use a chair or grab bar to pull himself/herself to standing position momentarily?

reach with one or both hands while standing to his/her neck, waist, knees?

grasp with one or both hands while standing?

individual and the demands of the activity. It is not necessary for a person to be able to stand or sit independently to complete dressing tasks without assistance or at least to participate partially. However, it is important to ensure that abnormal movement patterns are not facilitated when asking a person with cerebral palsy to participate in dressing and undressing activities (Campbell, 1987). It is recommended that the teacher, care providers, and therapists work together as a team when designing self-care programs to determine carefully which movements can be utilized that do not promote atypical patterns. Table 8.7 provides information that can serve as a guide for conducting an assessment for dressing and undressing activities.

The simplest way to modify a task for a person with a physical disability is to write a task analysis for that skill based on the person's mobility. After completing an assessment of the person's skills and comparing this to the activity demands, the team is ready to design a task analysis. The following two case studies demonstrate how this analysis can be accomplished.

The process for modifying a task with the use of a team assessment and program-planning strategy can be applied to any instructional activity. This is true for skills in all program domains, including domestic, vocational, leisure–recreation, or community. In fact, it is critical for individuals with cerebral palsy to become as independent as possible.

· ·

CASE EXAMPLE: MARY (PART 3)

Mary's mother has always been overprotective of Mary and assumed that her daughter would never learn dressing and undressing tasks because of her severe mental retardation and spastic cerebral palsy. The teacher and occupational therapist at her school evaluated Mary's capabilities for dressing and identified the following physical characteristics:

- Mary uses a wheelchair for mobility.

- She can lean forward away from the back of the chair for approximately 5 seconds.

- Mary cannot use her right arm, which is usually flexed tightly at the elbow and hand. She can, however, raise it to shoulder height.

- Her left arm and hand have normal motor functioning.

After they discussed the findings, the teacher and therapist decided that putting on a buttoned shirt or sweater would be a good first objective. They developed a task analysis based on Mary's abilities, as shown in Table 8.8.

Table 8.8.　Task Analysis for Putting on a Buttoned Shirt or Sweater

---

1. Lay sweater face up on lap (neck at knees).
2. Grasp sweater at armhold (using left hand).
3. Pull sleeve over (right) hand.
4. Pull sleeve over (right) elbow.
5. Pull sweater onto shoulder.
6. Grasp neck of sweater.
7. Lean forward from wheelchair.
8. Pull sweater across back.
9. Lean back in wheelchair.
10. Grasp neck of sweater.
11. Lean forward in wheelchair.
12. Shake sweater into position.
13. Lean back in wheelchair.
14. Put (left) arm into sleeve.
15. Straighten front of sweater.

An important point to note in this task analysis is that Mary was taught to put her right arm into the sweater sleeve before inserting her left arm. Dressing the arm or leg that is more affected by cerebral palsy first makes the task easier (Payne & Reyder, 1983). This is true whether the person is attempting to dress himself or herself or the caregiver is providing assistance.

The other consideration in developing a dressing task analysis for Mary was her abil-

ity to lean away from the back of her wheelchair for only 5 seconds. This limitation necessitated several steps in the task analysis that allowed her to lean forward, complete a portion of the activity, rest, and then lean forward again for another step in the task. Time for rest may be a necessary consideration for many individuals with cerebral palsy who have physical limitations that prohibit them from completing a task in a more typical way.

···

CASE EXAMPLE: DAVID

David is Mary's classmate with severe athetoid cerebral palsy and severe mental retardation. He is dependent on his family for all daily-living activities. No one has ever worked on dressing tasks with him before, because he is mentally retarded and is not able to sit in his wheelchair without trunk supports and a seat belt. His teacher and occupational therapist decided that David should be able to complete some dressing activities with skill-sequence adaptations and systematic instruction. The assessment of his physical capabilities revealed that David

- rolls from side to side freely when placed on a mat;

- can reach his feet in side-lying and grasp with both hands;

- rolls to his back and lifts his hips off the mat; and

- cannot sit unsupported.

On the basis of these findings, the team selected a pants-off program as David's first dressing goal. Because David had good mobility on the mat, the team believed that David could easily learn to take off a pair of stretch, pull-on pants that did not have fasteners. Undressing was selected as an easier initial task to master than dressing (Snell, 1987; Snell & Farlow, 1993).

The next step in the process was to develop a task analysis for use during instruction. The team members decided that each step should be written as a verbal prompt to ensure program consistency from one trainer to another. Regardless of whether the teacher, occupational therapist, physical therapist, or teacher's aide was providing instruction, the verbal prompts would remain the same. This was an important point to consider, because David is also severely mentally retarded. Consistency of instruction would be crucial for skill acquisition. The task analysis presented in Table 8.9 was developed.

Table 8.9. Task Analysis for Taking off Pants

Note. The trainer positions student on the mat for instruction.

1. Grasp waistband of pants with both hands.
2. Push pants down to hips.
3. Lift hips off mat.
4. Push pants below hips.
5. Lower hips to mat.
6. Roll onto side.
7. Grasp pants at waistband with both hands.
8. Push pants down onto thighs.
9. Bend leg up to chest.
10. Push pants off leg.
11. Roll onto other side.
12. Bend leg up to chest.
13. Push pants off leg.
14. Straighten out leg.
15. Roll onto back.

Once the task analysis was completed, the teacher decided to use a modified version of Azrin's "Rapid Method" of teaching dressing skills to individuals with severe and profound mental retardation (Azrin, Schaeffer, & Wesolowski, 1976; Snell, 1987). The teacher or therapist initially provided a verbal prompt for David to initiate the first step in the task analysis. If no response occurred, the teacher or therapist would point to the part of the garment involved in that step of the task. After several more seconds, the teacher or therapist molded David's hands around the pants and repeated the verbal in-

struction. Finally, if no response was initiated, physical guidance was provided to complete the step correctly. A 5-second latency was allowed between each prompt to give David time to respond independently. Continuous use of praise and touch for any attempt to complete the task composed the reinforcement strategy. Because his caregivers utilized a team approach, David began to learn skills for independence.

....

Personal Assistance for Partial Participation

Personal assistance can be an effective strategy for enabling individuals with severe physical disabilities to perform tasks they could not otherwise manage. A person with cerebral palsy, for instance, may not be able to open a drawer to remove clothing articles; however, if given a choice of two garments to wear, the person can point to the preferred item. Another individual may require assistance in transferring to and from a shower chair for bathing, assistance in washing his or her feet, and assistance in towel drying the lower part of his or her body. However, the remainder of the bathing activities might be completed independently with the use of adapted bathing mitts, long-handled brushes, soap dispensers, and oversized bath towels. Personal assistance should be the last resort to ensure partial participation in any activity. Modifying the task and supplying assistive technology devices often makes human assistance unnecessary for the individual with a physical disability.

Feeding Concerns

Mealtime is often problematic because abnormal muscle tone results in poor feeding positions; in inadequate oral motor control that leads to drooling, choking, and gagging; and in lack of motor control for self-feeding. In most cases, the occupational or speech therapist assumes the lead in designing feeding programs. As in all other programmatic areas for individuals with cerebral palsy, however, a team approach is recommended.

Many excellent resources are available for professionals responsible for planning and implementing feeding programs (Copeland & Kimmel, 1989; Finnie, 1975; Fraser, Hensinger, & Phelps, 1990; Morris & Klein, 1987; Sobsey, 1987). Specific program management encompasses many different aspects, including gross motor and positioning considerations, the presence of primitive postural reflexes, oral motor reflexes, and abnormalities (Fraser et al., 1990). A brief overview of specific feeding problems and considerations is presented in Table 8.10.

Gross Motor Concerns and Positioning Considerations

Individuals with cerebral palsy often have abnormal postural reflexes that interfere with gross motor development and successful feeding (Copeland & Kimmel, 1989; Fraser et al., 1990; Morris & Klein, 1987). The first reflex to consider that has an influence on feeding is the asymmetrical tonic neck reflex. Individuals with this reflex have difficulty in total body reactions as well as in oral motor functions. For instance, this reflex can be noted when the person turns his or her head to one side. The arm on that side of the body extends while the other arm flexes. Some individuals are so affected by this reflex that voluntary positioning of the head in midline is inhibited. This reflex makes it difficult for the caregiver to get food into the individual's mouth, and it interferes with normal oral motor control and self-feeding (Sobsey, 1987).

Another reflex that affects feeding is the tonic labyrinthine reflex. This reflex influences the positioning of the individual's head and often results in excessive head extension or flexion. Extreme flexion or extension of the head affects the person's ability to swallow in a controlled manner (Fraser et al., 1990). Neck extension is especially problematic, because it may result in food aspira-

tion, limited respiration, and inhibition of swallowing.

Another problem that may affect gross motor movement and positioning is muscle tone. Increased muscle tone, or spasticity, can result in head hyperextension and shoulder elevation. As stated previously, this head positioning causes difficulty in swallowing and, in some instances, may be life threatening to the individual who aspirates food.

A person with hypotonia, or low muscle tone, can also have poor trunk and head control. In this instance, the individual may not have the ability to lift his or her head from a flexed position. Excessive head flexion is just as problematic to the feeder as is head extension for proper swallowing (Fraser et al., 1990). Finally, the person with athetosis may be difficult to feed because of excessive involuntary movements of the head, neck, and trunk. Athetosis can result in difficulty with mouth closure as well as with involuntary tongue movements.

Morris and Klein (1987) suggested that a total-body assessment be completed to determine the individual's postural strengths and needs. Total-body assessment should include observation of total-body posture, trunk mobility and stability, shoulder position, and head control. None of these can be looked at in isolation, because one body part influences the position of another. For instance, the person who has inadequate trunk control and stability may posture in an asymmetric seated position with more weight shifted to one hip than to the other. This position results in total-body compensations that make it difficult for the person to eat properly. Another example of posture compensation is seen in the person who does not have adequate foot support in a seated position. This individual may experience an increase of postural muscle tone that is evident even in the oral motor musculature.

The service provider should also assess hip and pelvis placement during mealtimes when determining feeding problems. Forward and backward tilting of the pelvis can result in problems with head control, breathing, and mouth control (Morris

Table 8.10. Feeding Concerns and Treatments

Problem	Description	Intervention
Spasticity	An abnormal increase in muscle tone resulting in a stiffness or lack of mobility that interferes with normal patterns of movement. Jaw thrust may be a problem in individuals influenced by severe extension. A bite reflex is sometimes seen when the person's movements are dominated by flexion.	Good positioning 1. Person should be positioned securely so that he/she is supported and relaxed. 2. If possible, positioning should be upright or slightly reclined. 3. Head and trunk should be in midline. 4. Hips should be to the back of the chair with protective seat belt. 5. Trunk should be aligned over the pelvis with feet on firm foot rest. 6. Check positioning during mealtimes and correct as needed.

ORAL MOTOR PROBLEMS ASSOCIATED WITH SPASTICITY

Problem	Description	Intervention
Lip retraction	Tone is increased in upper lip so it is drawn over the teeth. The person is unable to relax and pull the lips together.	1. Manual jaw control. 2. Use firm pressure starting at the bridge of the nose to draw the upper lip over the teeth. 3. Use total-body relaxation exercises prior to mealtime. 4. Encourage the person to swallow prior to giving a bite of food. 5. Do not scrape the spoon on the person's teeth.
Poor jaw gradation	Tone is increased in facial muscles, often resulting in either exaggerated mouth opening or inability to open mouth wide enough for food presentation.	1. Manual jaw control. 2. Encourage the person to watch the feeder so he/she will correctly anticipate when to open the mouth. 3. Use relaxation techniques.
Tongue thrust	Food is pushed out of the mouth by the tongue instead of moving it to the rear of the mouth for swallowing. This is especially aggravated by improper positioning, especially head hyperextension.	1. Minimize through positioning. 2. Avoid holding spoonful of food in front of the person. 3. Provide inward/downward pressure on the tongue with spoon. 4. Jaw control, applying firm pressure to the base of tongue.
Bite reflex	A touch around or inside the mouth triggers the jaw to clamp down. Aggravated by an increase in flexor tone.	1. Minimize reflex with positioning. 2. Use oral motor exercises to desensitize oral cavity. 3. Use rubber-coated spoon. 4. If person clamps on the spoon, allow him/her to relax. Do not pull spoon out of mouth before person relaxes.

(continues)

Table 8.10.   *Continued*

Problem	Description	Intervention
Oral hypersensitivity	Adverse response to tactile stimulation that may be seen as anxiety, discomfort, or withdrawal. Can be seen in individuals with hypertonia or hypotonia.	1. Use oral motor exercises for oral desensitization. 2. Wipe the mouth area by moving toward the mouth with firm pressure.
Hypotonia	An abnormal decrease in muscle tone resulting in decreased posture and movement.	Good positioning: 1. Person should be positioned securely so that he/she is supported. 2. If possible, positioning should be upright or slightly reclined. 3. Head and trunk alignment should be in midline. 4. Check positioning during mealtimes and correct as needed.

ORAL MOTOR PROBLEMS ASSOCIATED WITH HYPOTONIA

Problem	Description	Intervention

Lip immobility	Low tone in lips results in inability to remove food from the spoon or make an adequate lip seal.	1. Use manual jaw control.
		2. Stimulate lip closure with oral motor stimulation:
		  a. Tap around the lips.
		  b. Stretch upper lip.

Tongue immobility	Low tone in the tongue results in inability to get the food back to the molars where it can be chewed or swallowed.	1. Oral motor exercises:
		  a. Tap the base of the tongue.
		  b. Stroke the side of the tongue prior to chewing.
		2. Place food on the molars to stimulate chewing and tongue lateralization.

Low tone in facial muscles	Results in reduced ability to chew.	1. Oral motor exercises:
		  a. Tapping
		  b. Stimulate masseter muscle
		2. Work on chewing during feeding.

Hypotonic gag	Absence of gag reflex, often resulting in aspiration of food.	1. Oral motor exercise. 2. Careful feeding to prevent aspiration.

& Klein, 1987). A forward or anterior tilt of the pelvis causes postural compensations throughout the body. The shoulders counterbalance the hips by pulling backward into retraction, which tightens the neck muscles, decreases jaw mobility, and inhibits swallowing. Retraction of the shoulder girdle also causes a tension that can pull the neck into hyperextension.

Fraser et al. (1990) stated that mealtime is not the time to emphasize the development of gross motor skills such as head and trunk control. Finnie (1975) stressed the need to provide proper positioning control to the "whole" person; if this is not done, the person becomes more spastic or has increased involuntary movements. Appropriate positioning allows the individual to concentrate on eating skills without attempting to maintain the stability and support of other body parts necessary for eating (Fraser et al., 1990). This approach translates into positioning provided manually by the feeder or by adaptive equipment until the individual develops better total-body control.

Head support varies based on the abilities of the individual being fed. For instance, individuals like Beth may need support from the caregiver, whereas others may benefit from a commercially available headrest on the wheelchair. Still others with severe involvement may find side-lying a functional alternative in a side-lier or on a wedge (Fraser et al., 1990). Morris and Klein (1987) as well as Finnie (1975) have provided excellent diagrams as guidelines for assessment and selection of proper feeding positions.

In any case, positioning should be a team decision made by the teacher and the occupational and physical therapists. Proper positioning helps break up abnormal muscle tone and movement and allows for isolated movements of the head, jaw, tongue, and lips. A positioning assessment determines the problems that can be addressed and minimized through adaptive devices or caregiver control (Copeland & Kimmel, 1989).

CASE EXAMPLE: BETH

Beth has severe spastic quadriplegia and requires chest and hip supports to maintain a seated position. Prior to mealtime she is positioned in her wheelchair by use of external support to ensure that her hips are flexed to the back of the chair and that she is upright rather than leaning to one side. Beth's feet are strapped to the footplates of her chair to provide increased total-body stability.

Beth also has difficulty with head control and usually holds her head in hyperextension. As previously discussed, neck extension leads to aspiration and difficulty in swallowing. Therefore, the person assisting Beth during mealtime uses manual jaw control to maintain her head slightly flexed 5 to 15 degrees. This assistance reduces extensor hypertonus (Fraser et al., 1990). The caregiver is careful not to flex Beth's head flexion greater than 15 degrees because this can inhibit swallowing.

Oral Motor Concerns

Tonic Bite. A number of oral motor problems interfere with successful mealtime experiences for individuals with cerebral palsy. One is the tonic bite pattern, which is an obligatory closure of the jaw upon tactile stimulation of the teeth and gums (Fraser et al., 1990). Several factors stimulate a tonic bite in a person with cerebral palsy: poor positioning with too much hip flexion or extension, posterior pelvic tilt, an overstimulating environment, and oral hypersensitivity (Morris & Klein, 1987).

Tom is a young child with a tonic bite associated with severe spastic cerebral palsy. His treatment team identified that poor positioning with excessive hip extension facilitated Tom's tonic bite reflex. Proper placement of his wheelchair lap strap kept Tom's hips flexed during mealtimes if the feeder checked periodically to make sure that Tom's hips had not moved into extension. If a tonic bite occurred during feeding, the caregiver learned to wait until Tom relaxed to take the spoon out of his mouth. Pulling on the spoon only served to stimulate Tom's tonic bite problem (Fraser et al., 1990). Finally, the team designed a program to decrease Tom's oral hypersensitivity. Morris and Klein (1987) provided a detailed description of oral motor desensitization exercises that can be utilized on the basis of each individual's treatment needs.

Hyperactive Gag Reflex. Individuals who have a hyperactive gag, which is stimulated by input to areas of the mouth other than the posterior tongue or soft palate, have difficulty eating. Several treatment approaches are used to assist the person in dealing with this problem (Morris & Klein, 1987). For example, Mary's mother has been shown how to use applesauce as a "binder food" to assist Mary with forming a bolus of food for swallowing. Her mother alternates a bite of hard, lumpy food with a spoonful of applesauce to bind the remaining loose pieces into a bolus. Mary then is less likely to choke on small pieces of food that she has difficulty swallowing. Her mother also learned that flexing Mary's head forward when she gags during feeding stops the response.

Next, Mary's occupational therapist designed an oral motor program to decrease her hypersensitive gag. Firm downward pressure on the tongue was applied with a spoon or tongue depressor and carefully worked to the point of Mary's tolerance. When this program was initiated, Mary would gag when even the tip of her tongue was stimulated. Over time, the therapist gradually was able to "walk" the spoon further back into her mouth without stimulating a gag response. This approach may be useful with other individuals who have a hypersensitive gag; however, each individual should have a program designed for his or her specific needs.

Jaw and Tongue Thrust. Jaw thrust is characterized by an abnormally strong downward extension of the lower jaw and is associated with head extension or total-body extension patterns (Fraser et al., 1990). Poor positioning with too much hip extension and posterior pelvic tilt contributes to an increase in jaw thrust (Morris & Klein, 1987). Therefore, program plans that include working on better sitting are indicated. The trunk and pelvis should be in alignment with the shoulder girdle forward and abduction of the scapulae. Manual jaw control during feeding to maintain jaw closure and to promote stability is also indicated. Illustrations can be found in Finnie (1975) and in Morris and Klein (1987).

Tongue thrust is an abnormally strong protrusion of the tongue that is characterized by a swallow with anterior rather than posterior movement (Fraser et al., 1990). Tongue thrust makes it difficult to insert a spoon into the individual's mouth and results in expulsion of food. Increased extensor tone, neck hyperextension, and shoulder retraction also create extensor patterns in the mouth. Therefore, an assessment of the person's positioning during mealtime and making adjustments as needed are critical. Manual jaw control is indicated for some individuals (Finnie, 1975).

It is not uncommon for an individual with cerebral palsy to have difficulty with both jaw and tongue thrust. For instance, Jimmy is a youngster who is unable to successfully feed himself because his jaw and tongue thrust are so severe. When Jimmy attempts to place food in his mouth, the combined force of these two problems causes food to be pushed forward instead of back for swallowing. An assessment of Jimmy's physical abilities revealed that he has spastic quadriplegia; however, he is able to walk with a walker and to sit in a chair independently. Because Jimmy is not dependent on a wheelchair for mobility and support, service providers assumed that positioning was not an issue for feeding. Upon closer observation, however, they noted that Jimmy had limited trunk control and that his positioning was influenced by extensor tone and spasticity. He often sat in a cafeteria chair with shoulders slumped forward, pelvis tilted backward, and legs extended at the hips. This position created increased tone in the facial muscles and tongue, resulting in increased tongue and jaw thrust during mealtime. A chair was designed for him to use for meals that ensured that his feet were supported and hips flexed. Increased support through his lower body decreased the excessive tone resulting in decreased oral motor problems. In addition, the caregiver assisted Jimmy with manual jaw control to inhibit both tongue and jaw thrust.

Lip Closure. A lack of lip closure often is associated with feeding problems for individuals with cerebral palsy and may be caused by low muscle tone or spasticity. Severe spasticity associated with increased extensor tone can cause lip retraction, which is a pulling back of the lips from the teeth. Poor lip closure causes difficulty in taking food from a spoon and problems with swallowing (Fraser et al., 1990). Treatment procedures for lack of lip closure are based on whether it is caused by increased or low muscle tone. Tapping around the mouth may be indicated for the individual with low muscle tone but contraindicated for the person with increased tone. Positioning for feeding should be assessed to decrease spasticity and extensor tone as much as possible. In addition, the feeder should use a shallow spoon and be careful not to scrape the food on the individual's teeth. Feeding should be slow so that the person can use his or her lips to remove the food from the spoon. Manual jaw control may be indicated (Finnie, 1975).

Tongue Lateralization. The final oral motor problem to be considered is lack of tongue lateralization, which inhibits the development of chewing and is identified by predominating in-and-out movements of the tongue. This problem may be caused by oral hypersensitivity, hypotonicity, or insufficient jaw stability (Morris & Klein, 1987). Positioning to reduce abnormal muscle tone should be the first consideration. Increased sensory input to the tongue should include manual stimulation as well as placement of food directly on the biting surfaces of the teeth. Foods that dissolve easily and are relatively soft, such as graham crackers, pieces of cheese, and cereal, are the items of choice for this activity. One should gradually change the types of food for chewing as the individual's ability to lateralize the tongue improves.

The oral motor problems discussed in this chapter are only a few of those faced by individuals with cerebral palsy. An attempt has been made to provide a representative sample that will serve as an initial guide to assessment and program planning. Table 8.10 provides an overview of feeding concerns and techniques for remediation. The reader is directed to Morris and Klein (1987) for additional treatment techniques.

CASE EXAMPLE: GENNY

Genny has decreased muscle tone, or hypotonia, which is noted throughout her body as well as in the oral musculature. Because she does not use her upper lip to remove food from the spoon during mealtime or attempt to chew, her mother has always fed her baby foods. This practice has only made the problem worse, because Genny has not had any experiences that would stimulate oral motor

development. Because Genny's problems stem from low tone, the occupational therapist designed a program to stimulate muscle tone. The mother and teacher were taught to tap the muscles for lip closure and chewing prior to mealtime. In addition, they were shown how to avoid scraping food on Genny's teeth by stimulating the upper lip to move in response to firm pressure during spoon removal. The next step was to introduce soft foods for chewing, such as oranges wrapped in cheesecloth, graham crackers, and cheese, by placing the food directly on Genny's molars. Tongue lateralization for this activity was encouraged by stroking the side of her tongue with a spoon or tongue depressor. The texture of Genny's food was gradually changed to replace the baby food with chopped table food. Her mother is happy to have Genny eating the same food as the other family members.

Dressing Concerns

The principle of partial participation related to dressing skills for individuals with cerebral palsy was discussed earlier in this chapter. However, it may be necessary for caregivers to provide total assistance to some individuals who have severe to profound motor involvement. A number of positioning and handling strategies are available that make assisted dressing easier for the caregiver. Finnie (1975) and Copeland and Kimmel (1989) are excellent sources for this information. Table 8.11 provides some basic ideas for dressing the individual with severe motor limitations.

CAPACITY FOR INDEPENDENT LIVING

One of the most serious barriers to community living for individuals with cerebral palsy is the lack of living options and support services. A survey conducted in Virginia (Community Services

---

Table 8.11.   Positioning and Handling Strategies for Dressing

---

- Dress and undress a young child or infant with extensor muscle tone prone (on the stomach) across the lap of the caregiver and diaper him or her on the stomach rather than on his or her back.

- Bend or flex the individual's hips, knees, and ankles to reduce excessive extensor muscle tone.

- Decrease abnormal movement patterns by side-lying. Roll the individual from side to side while dressing and undressing him or her. This slow rolling movement reduces excessive muscle tone.

- Using side-lying to lessen the individual's tendency to push back into extension, making it easier for the caregiver to bring the head, shoulders, and arms forward for dressing. The individual's feet and legs are also easier to bend.

- Use slow movement with firm pressure when moving an individual for dressing and undressing.

- Put clothes on the arm or leg that is more involved first.

- Straighten the individual's arm prior to putting on clothing. Do not try to pull by the hand through the sleeve an arm that is bent.

- Bend the individual's leg before putting on socks and shoes. Extended legs make the ankle and foot stiffer, and the toes are more likely to be flexed.

- Use fuller cut clothing with front openings, elastic waistbands, or Velcro closures when necessary.

Assistance Center, 1989) indicated the following barriers to independent living for individuals with physical disabilities:

- Housing is too expensive.

- Nothing is available in the desired locations.

- The waiting list is too long.

- Housing is not accessible.

- Home modifications are needed.

- Assistance is needed with household responsibilities.

- Personal-care assistance is needed.

Personal assistance services are perhaps the most crucial needs on the list for independent living. These services make it possible for individuals who are unable to care for their daily-living needs, such as personal hygiene, dressing, eating, toileting, mobility, and household maintenance, to live in community rather than in institutional settings. For example, John is 35 years old and a law school graduate; however, he has severe physical limitations because of spastic cerebral palsy. John would not be able to have his own apartment and work in the community if not for his full-time assistant, Mike. Mike provides assistance with dressing, feeding, toileting, household maintenance, and transportation. In addition, Mike accompanies John to work and provides physical assistance as needed.

John can afford to hire a personal assistant because he works full time as a lawyer. However, many individuals with cerebral palsy are not as fortunate and must reside in more restrictive housing situations. Cindy, who is also 35 years old, has severe spastic cerebral palsy. She has been living in a nursing home since the age of 22. At that time, her parents believed that Cindy must leave home because they were elderly and could no longer care for her physical needs. They could not afford to hire an attendant to assist with her care, so their only choice was to select a nursing home as her living arrangement.

Because most of Cindy's education took place through a homebound program, she has limited work skills. In addition, her community does not have a program to assist individuals with severe physical disabilities enter employment. Cindy relies on Medicaid to pay her nursing home expenses and to provide her with a $30-a-month allowance. In addition, Cindy lives in a state that does not have a Medicaid waiver program, so she cannot use Medicaid funds to pay for a personal-care attendant to assist her in independent living. Unfortunately, at this time, Cindy's chances for independent living appear slim.

The following issues are critical in improving the independent living options for individuals with physical disabilities (Volunteer Disability Service Planners Work Group, 1990):

- development of family-like environments in community neighborhoods with nondisabled individuals

- development of stipend programs or financial assistance for families to purchase or obtain needed services, home modifications, and adaptive equipment within the home environment

- development of incentive programs to access federal and state financial resources to increase the number of accessible and affordable housing options

- improvement of accessible and efficient transportation services

- identification of potential funding sources to expand personal assistance services

ECONOMIC SELF-SUFFICIENCY

Supported employment has made a difference in the vocational lives of many individuals with severe disabilities. To date, however, very few individuals with cerebral palsy have achieved employment nationally through the supported employment initiative (Wehman, Revell, & Kregel, 1995). This situation may be due to a perceived lack of vocational competence for this group as well as their varied physical abilities and limitations.

In addition, many professionals lack the skills to identify the physical barriers to employment and to utilize assistive technology to eliminate the problems. Franklin (1990) stated that, in the 1990s, assistive technology in combination with supported employment will redefine employability for individuals with disabilities. The passage of P.L. 100-407, the Technology-Related Assistance for Individuals with Disabilities Act in 1988 and its reauthorization in 1994, has provided support and direction for the development of model programs designed to promote employability for individuals with severe disabilities.

Assistive technology for employment may include both high- and low-technology devices as defined by Congress. For instance, a low-technology device may be blocks to raise the work area of an individual who is seated in a wheelchair. A high-technology device, on the other hand, is usually designed by a rehabilitation engineer or therapist or purchased commercially (e.g., a device for inputting information into a computer). An individual's need for technology should be carefully assessed, and adaptive equipment provided only if a person cannot function without its use. Professionals also need to assess thoroughly an individuals' capabilities and to utilize supported employment strategies to match them to appropriate job types (Sowers & Powers, 1991). Assistive technology cannot provide solutions for all limitations. For instance, it may be unwise to place a person with severe fine motor limitations in a high-production assembly job even if adaptive devices can be made to assist in task completion. Table 8.12 (see p. 169) provides a list of resources in the area of assistive technology. The following case studies demonstrate the use of supported employment and assistive technology in assisting individuals with cerebral palsy in the world of work.

CASE EXAMPLE: GINNY

Ginny is a young woman who has spastic cerebral palsy, quadriplegia. She recently began work at a parts store as an office worker. The job was identified for her by a supported employment program through a process of consumer assessment, job analysis, and job-compatibility analysis (Moon, Goodall, Barcus, & Brooke, 1986). Her employment specialist identified that Ginny had many of the basic skills to complete the job duties, which included answering the telephone, processing invoices, and filing. She was able to communicate effectively and could read in order to complete the invoice and filing tasks. At first, however, her physical limitations seemed to interfere with the completion of her job duties. Ginny was unable to raise her arms higher than shoulder height, and she tired easily from using her hands for activities. Her electric wheelchair did not fit under a standard desk, and Ginny was unable to access the file cabinets because she could not maneuver her chair close enough to open the bottom and top drawers.

After reviewing the situation, the employment specialist and an occupational therapist determined that a number of low-technology devices could be used that would aid Ginny in carrying out her job duties. The employer was willing to have the office area arranged to fit Ginny's needs as well as to assign a coworker to provide additional physical assistance as indicated. The following modifications were developed:

- Blocks were used to raise the desk to a comfortable work height.

- A headset was placed on the phone to eliminate the need for constantly picking up the receiver.

- A temporary hanging file was placed next to Ginny's desk for use during a day's worth of filing. A coworker assisted her by placing the files in the office cabinets at the end of the work day.

- An electric stapler was purchased for stapling invoices together.

- An electric typewriter was used for taking office messages and orders rather than having Ginny write on a note pad. The employment specialist designed a form for Ginny to use that made her note taking easier.

CASE EXAMPLE: SUSAN

Susan is currently in a special education program for students with severe mental retardation and physical disabilities. Because she is 20 years old, her teacher is concerned about transition from school to work and has referred Susan to a grant program designed for students who have similar disabilities. Project staff identified a job at the local university library stamping identification numbers on the spines of new books. This job is typically performed daily by graduate assistantship students in a large room of the library (Renzaglia & Hutchins, 1990). An assessment of her physical strengths and limitations identified the following characteristics:

- Susan uses a wheelchair for mobility and requires personal assistance for movement from one place to another.

- She has limited movements in both arms because of hypertonicity throughout her head, trunk, and limbs.

- Lateral wheelchair supports and a seat belt are necessary to assist Susan in sitting upright in her chair. She also requires foot support and straps.

- Susan can raise her right arm at the shoulder joint so that her forearm is parallel to and 6 inches above her wheelchair lap tray.

- She does not have any functional mobility in her fingers, which are usually tightly fisted into the palms of both hands.

- She is visually attentive and can turn her head from side to side.

- Susan is severely mentally retarded.

Because of these physical characteristics, Susan obviously would need assistive technology to complete the job of stamping books with the library identification number. Project staff worked closely with a rehabilitation engineer, and a spring-loaded device was designed to assist Susan in completing the task. The first step in the job required personal assistance from a coworker or project staff member to load the equipment with 10 books for stamping. At that point, Susan was responsible for pressing a switch to drop a book into position. She then would touch another plate that held the heat stamp in order to apply heat to the spine of the book. Susan kept this in place for 10 seconds, finally touching another switch to move the book off the work surface. Intensive systematic instruction was provided by a trainer to assist Susan in learning her job.

••

Susan's community-based work experience highlights several critical issues in the area of vocational programming for individuals with severe disabilities. First, her instruction is taking place outside of the classroom setting. Typically, students with Susan's characteristics have been limited to

---

Table 8.12.   Resources for Assistive Technology

Ablenet
1081 Tenth Avenue SE
Minneapolis, MN 55414

Apple Computer, Inc.
Office of Special Education
20525 Mariani Avenue
Cupertino, CA 95014

Assistive Devices Information Network
University of Iowa Hospital School
Iowa City, IA 52242

Assistive Technology Sourcebook
RESNA Press
Department 4006
Washington, DC 20042-4006

Creative Switch Industries
PO Box 5256
Des Moines, IA 50306

Fred Sammons, Inc.
Box 32
Brookfield, IL 60513

Helen Keller National Center
111 Middle Neck Road
Sands Point, NY 11050

IBM
National Support Center for Persons with
 Disabilities
PO Box 2150
Atlanta, GA 30301-2105

Independent Living Aids
27 East Mall
Plainview, NY 11803

J.A. Preston Corporation
60 Page Road
Clifton, NJ 07012

National Center on Accessibility
Bradford Woods/Indiana University
5040 State Road 67 North
Martinsville, IN 46151

National Information Center on Deafness
Gallaudet University
800 Florida Avenue, NE
Washington, DC 20002-3695

National Rehabilitation Information Center (NARIC)
8455 Colesville Road, Suite 935
Silver Spring, MD 20910-3319

National Technology Center American Foundation for the Blind
15 West 16th Street
New York, NY 10011

Prentke Romich Company
1022 Heyl Road
Wooster, OH 44691

RESNA (Association for the Advancement of Rehabilitation Technology)
1700 North Moore Street, Suite 1540
Arlington, VA 22209-1903

Simplified Technology for the Severely Handicapped
Linda J. Burkhart
8503 Rhode Island Avenue
College Park, MD 20740

Therapeutic Toys, Inc.
Cinta, 91 Newberry Road
East Haddam, CT 06423

Toshiba America Information Systems, Inc.
9740 Irvine Boulevard
P.O. Box 19724
Irvine, CA 92713-9724

Note. The information in this table is adapted from the following sources: Moon, Hart, Komissar, and Friedlander (1995), Rothstein and Everson (1995), and Tanchak and Sawyer (1995).

"classroom only" programs that have failed to assist students in making the transition from school to work (Moon, Inge, Wehman, Brooke, & Barcus, 1990). Professionals must be creative in providing functional, age-appropriate, vocational experiences for this group of individuals.

Second, Susan is being given an opportunity to interact with nondisabled peers. Integration, that is, physical proximity and the opportunity to interact socially with others, is a primary value of supported employment (Moon et al., 1990). It is a work characteristic that most people take for granted in their everyday lives. For individuals such as Susan, however, work usually translates into sheltered-workshop and activity-center settings where minimal access to real daily environments is provided. Expectations for individuals with severe disabilities will remain low as long as professionals continue to place them in segregated environments.

Individuals with cerebral palsy can be contributing members of America's workforce. For some, it may mean the traditional route from college to employment. Others may require assistive technology and transitional employment services to locate and perform a job. Still others, like Susan, may require job modifications, supported employment, and intensive on-site support to become employed.

FINAL THOUGHTS

The real issue for the 1990s is consumer empowerment and involvement in program planning. Empowerment means that human-service professionals must work with individuals who have disabilities rather than doing something to or for them (Nichols, 1990). An individual with cerebral palsy, regardless of the severity of disability, has the same rights to live and work in the community as do his or her nondisabled peers. It is the professionals' responsibility to identify the barriers to successful living and to provide assistance in overcoming these obstacles.

REFERENCES

Anson, D. (1993). *Rehab 487: Course syllabus.* Seattle: University of Washington, Division of Occupational Therapy, Department of Rehabilitation Medicine.

Azrin, N. H., Schaeffer, R. M., & Wesolowski, M. D. (1976). A rapid method of teaching profoundly retarded persons to dress by a reinforcement-guidance method. *Mental Retardation, 14*(6), 29–33.

Baumgart, D., Brown, L., Pumpian, I., Nisbet, J., Ford, A., Sweet, M., Messina, R., & Schroeder, J. (1982). Principle of partial participation and individualized adaptations in educational programs for severely handicapped students. *Journal of the Association for the Severely Handicapped, 1,* 17–27.

Bigge, J. L. (1989). *Teaching individuals with physical and multiple disabilities* (2nd ed.). Columbus, OH: Merrill.

Bleck, E. E., & Nagel, D. A. (1983). *Physically handicapped children: A medical atlas for teachers* (2nd ed.). New York: Grune & Stratton.

Campbell, P. H. (1987). Physical management and handling procedures with students with movement dysfunction. In M. E. Snell (Ed.), *Systematic instruction of persons with severe handicaps* (pp. 174–187). Columbus, OH: Merrill.

Campbell, P. H. (1988). Dysfunction in posture and movement in individuals with profound disabilities: Issues and practices. In F. Brown & D. Lehr (Eds.), *Persons with profound disabilities: Issues and practices* (pp. 163–189). Baltimore: Brookes.

Campbell, P. H. (1993). Physical management and handling procedures. In M. Snell (Ed.), *Instruction of students with severe disabilities* (pp. 248–263). New York: Merrill.

Campbell, P. H., & Forsyth, S. (1993). Integrated programming and movement disabilities. In M. Snell (Ed.), *Instruction of students with severe disabilities* (pp. 264–289). New York: Merrill.

Community Services Assistance Center. (1989). *Results of the board for the rights of the disabled survey of Virginians with disabilities.* Richmond: Virginia Commonwealth University, Virginia Institute for Developmental Disabilities.

Coots, J., & Falvey, M. A. (1989). Communication skills. In M. Falvey (Ed.), *Community-based curriculum: Instructional strategies for students with severe handicaps* (pp. 255–285). Baltimore: Brookes.

Copeland, M., Ford, L., & Solon, N. (1976). *Occupational therapy for mentally retarded children.* Baltimore: University Park Press.

Copeland, M. E., & Kimmel, J. R. (1989). *Evaluation and management of infants and young children with developmental disabilities.* Baltimore: Brookes.

Dunn, W. (1991). The sensorimotor systems: A framework for assessment and intervention. In F. P. Orelove & D. Sobsey (Eds.), *Educating children with multiple disabilities: A transdisciplinary approach* (pp. 33–78). Baltimore: Brookes.

Enders, A., & Hall, M. (1990). *Assistive technology sourcebook.* Washington, DC: RESNA Press.

Ferguson, D. L., & Baumgart, D. (1991). Partial participation revisited. *Journal of the Association for Persons with Severe Handicaps, 16*(4), 218–227.

Finnie, N. R. (1975). *Handling the young cerebral palsied child at home* (2nd ed.). New York: Dutton.

Flippo, K., Inge, K. J., & Barcus, J. M. (Eds.). (1995). *Assistive technology: A resource for school, work, and the community.* Baltimore: Brookes.

Franklin, K. (1990). Rehabilitation engineering and assistive technology. In S. L. Griffin & W. G. Revell (Eds.), *Rehabilitation counselor desktop guide to supported employment* (pp. 99–117). Richmond: Virginia Commonwealth University, Rehabilitation Research and Training Center.

Fraser, B. A., Hensinger, R. N., & Phelps, J. A. (1990). *Physical management of multiple handicaps: A professional's guide.* Baltimore: Brookes.

Halle, J. W., Marshall, A. M., & Spradlin, J. E. (1979). Time delay: A technique to increase language use and facilitate generalization in retarded children. *Journal of Applied Behavior Analysis, 121,* 431–439.

Individuals with Disabilities Education Act of 1990, P.L. 101–476. (October 7, 1991). Title 20, U.S.C. 1400 *et seq. U.S. Statutes at Large, 105,* 586–608.

Inge, K. J. (1987). Atypical motor development and cerebral palsy. In F. Orelove & D. Sobsey (Eds.), *Educating children with multiple disabilities: A transdisciplinary approach* (pp. 43–65). Baltimore: Brookes.

Inge, K. J., & Shepherd, J. (1995). Assistive technology: Application and strategies for school system personnel. In K. Flippo, K. J. Inge, & J. M. Barcus (Eds.), *Assistive technology: A resource for school, work, and the community* (pp. 133–166). Baltimore: Brookes.

Kaiser, A. P. (1993). Functional language. In M. Snell (Ed.), *Instruction of students with severe disabilities* (pp. 347–379). New York: Merrill.

Mann, W. C., & Lane, J. P. (1991). *Assistive technology for persons with disabilities: The role of occupational therapy.* Rockville, MD: American Occupational Therapy Association.

Miller, J. (1993). Augmentative and alternative communication. In M. Snell (Ed.), *Instruction of students with severe disabilities* (pp. 319–346). New York: Merrill.

Miller, J., & Allaire, J. (1987). Augmentative communication. In M. E. Snell (Ed.), *Systematic instruction of persons with severe handicaps* (pp. 273–298). Columbus, OH: Merrill.

Moon, M. S., Goodall, P., Barcus, M., & Brooke, V. (1986). *The supported work model of competitive employment for citizens with severe handicaps: A guide for job trainers* (rev. ed.). Richmond: Virginia Commonwealth University, Rehabilitation Research and Training Center.

Moon, M. S., Hart, D., Komissar, C., & Fiedlander, R. (1995). Making sports and recreation activities accessible: Assistive technology and other accommodation strategies. In K. Flippo, K. J. Inge, & J. M. Barcus (Eds.), *Assistive technology: A resource for school, work, and community* (pp. 187–208). Baltimore: Brookes.

Moon, M. S., Inge, K. J., Wehman, P., Brooke, V., & Barcus, J. (1990). *Helping persons with severe mental retardation get and keep employment: Supported employment issues and strategies.* Baltimore: Brookes.

Morris, S. E., & Klein, M. D. (1987). *Pre-feeding skills: A comprehensive resource for therapists.* Tucson, AZ: Therapy Skill Builders.

Nichols, J. L. (1990). The new decade dawns: The search for quality and consumer empowerment converge. *Journal of Rehabilitation Administration, 14*(3), 69–70.

Payne, J. W., & Reder, R. D. (1983). *Occupational and physical therapy home instruction manual.* Cincinnati, OH: Children's Hospital Medical Center.

Prensky, A. L., & Palkes, H. S. (1982). *Care of the neurologically handicapped child: A book for parents and professionals.* New York: Oxford University Press.

Rainforth, B., & York, J. (1987). Handling and positioning. In F. Orelove & D. Sobsey (Eds.), *Educating children with multiple disabilities: A transdisciplinary approach* (pp. 183–218). Baltimore: Brookes.

Rainforth, B., & York, J. (1991). Handling and positioning. In F. P. Orelove & D. Sobsey (Eds.), *Educating children with multiple disabilities: A transdisciplinary approach* (pp. 79–118). Baltimore: Brookes.

Reichle, J., & Karlan, G. (1985). The selection of an augmentative system in communication intervention: A critique of decision rules. *Journal of the Association for Persons with Severe Handicaps, 10,* 146–156.

Reichle, J., York, J., & Eynon, D. (1989). Influence of indicating preferences for initiating, maintaining, and terminating interactions. In F. Brown & D. Lehr (Eds.), *Persons with profound disabilities: Issues and practices* (pp. 191–212). Baltimore: Brookes.

Renzaglia, A., & Hutchins, M. (1990, October). *Supported employment for individuals with severe disabilities.* Presentation at the Virginia Commonwealth University, Rehabilitation Research and Training Center Symposium on Supported Employment, Virginia Beach.

Rothstein, R., & Everson, J. (1995). Assistive technology for individuals with sensory impairments. In K. Flippo, K. Inge, & J. M. Barcus (Eds.), *Assistive technology: A resource for school, work, and the community* (pp. 105–132). Baltimore: Brookes.

Snell, M. E. (1987). Basic self-care instruction for students without motor impairments. In M. E. Snell (Ed.), *Systematic instruction of persons with severe handicaps* (pp. 334–389). Columbus, OH: Merrill.

Snell, M. E., & Farlow, L. J. (1993). Self-care skills. In M. Snell (Ed.), *Instruction of students with severe disabilities* (pp. 380–441). New York: Merrill.

Snell, M. E., & Gast, D. L. (1981). Applying delay procedures to the instruction of the severely handicapped. *Journal of the Association of the Severely Handicapped, 5*(4), 3–14.

Sobsey, D. (1987). Mealtime skills. In F. Orelove & D. Sobsey (Eds.), *Educating children with multiple disabilities: A transdisciplinary approach* (pp. 219–252). Baltimore: Brookes.

Sowers, J. A., & Powers, L. (1991). *Vocational preparation and employment of students with physical and multiple disabilities.* Baltimore: Brookes.

Tanchak, T., & Sawyer, C. (1995). Augmentative communication. In K. Flippo, K. Inge, & M. Barcus (Eds.), *Assistive technology: A resource for school, work, and the community* (pp. 57–85). Baltimore: Brookes.

Technology-Related Assistance for Individuals with Disabilities Act of 1988, P. L. 100–407. (August 19, 1988). Title 29, U.S.C. 2201 *et seq. U.S. Statutes at Large, 102,* 1044–1065.

Technology-Related Assistance for Individuals with Disabilities Act of 1994, P.L. 103–218. (March 9, 1994). Title 29, U.S.C. 2201 *et seq. U.S. Statutes at Large, 108*, 50–97.

Volunteer Disability Service Planners Work Group. (1990). Issue papers on the service needs for persons with physical and sensory disabilities. Richmond: Virginia Commonwealth University, Virginia Institute for Developmental Disabilities.

Wehman, P. (1992). *Achievements and challenges: A five-year report on the status of the national supported employment initiative.* Richmond: Virginia Commonwealth University, Rehabilitation Research and Training Center on Supported Employment.

Wehman, P., Revell, W. G., & Kregel, J. (1995). *Supported employment from 1986 to 1993: A national program that works.* Manuscript submitted for publication, Virginia Commonwealth University, Richmond.

York, J., Nietupski, J., & Hamre-Nietupski, S. (1985). A decision making process for using microswitches. *Journal of the Association for Persons with Severe Handicaps, 10*(4), 214–223.

York, J., & Rainforth, B. (1991). Developing instructional adaptations. In F. P. Orelove & D. Sobsey (Eds.), *Educating children with multiple disabilities: A transdisciplinary approach* (pp. 259–295). Baltimore: Brookes.

Seizure Disorders

Elizabeth Perry-Varner

LEARNING GOALS

Upon completion of this chapter the reader will be able to

- define epilepsy and describe at least five myths about epilepsy;

- describe three types of seizures;

- identify issues related to the psychosocial and self-esteem implications of seizure disorders;

- understand how to provide first aid for persons with seizures; and

- recognize what the legal issues are associated with epilepsy.

FUNCTIONAL DESCRIPTION

Epilepsy is a term that covers many different types of seizure disorders, of which seizures are a symptom. Seizures occur when a change or disruption in the brain's electrical system occurs, interrupting the normal functions of the brain and the rest of the nervous system. Epilepsy is caused by many things, such as a stroke, a traumatic brain injury (TBI), scar tissue in the brain, a high fever, or meningitis, to name a few.

Epilepsy is often referred to as a "hidden" disability. Persons who have it seem perfectly "normal" between seizures. As Schacter (1993) pointed out, even if a person with epilepsy has only one seizure a year, it can have a dramatic effect on the day-to-day existence. Embarrassment often accompanies a seizure that occurs in a public place; discrimination is still prevalent among employers, friends, relatives, and so on; and strict laws against persons with epilepsy obtaining a driver's license are also commonplace.

Myths concerning persons with epilepsy are still somewhat common and are listed in Table 9.1. As pointed out by Driscoll (1988), one reason for these myths may be our society's expectation for people to be "normal" and persons with epilepsy do not fit this mold. For example, when someone has a generalized convulsion, he or she loses consciousness and twitches and thrashes. Or, someone having a complex partial seizure may pick at his or her clothes. Another society-imposed attitude is that we must at all times maintain self-control. Having a seizure violates this. It has also been hypothesized that, in comparing a person with epilepsy with one with an obvious physical disability, such as a visual impairment or cerebral palsy, the latter is not responsible for "losing control" because the person never gained it to begin with. When a seizure occurs, however, the uninformed observer may wonder how control can be

---

Table 9.1. Myths About Epilepsy

- **You might catch epilepsy through contact with someone having a seizure.** Epilepsy is not contagious.

- **Epilepsy is a form of mental illness.** Actually, the majority of persons with epilepsy have normal intelligence; many are highly intelligent. Epilepsy, mental illness, and mental retardation are all distinctly different disabilities.

- **Persons with epilepsy look different.** The only difference in appearance occurs during a seizure. Otherwise, there is no physical way to tell that someone has this disability.

- **A person having a seizure can swallow his or her tongue.** The tongue is attached to the mouth. It may drop to the back of the throat, but swallowing it is impossible.

- **To have epilepsy is to have convulsions.** Convulsions, formerly known as grand mal seizures, are only one type of seizure.

- **Epilepsy can be passed down to subsequent generations.** There is a small chance that this may happen. Conversely, epilepsy can develop in persons with no family history of it.

- **Persons with epilepsy cannot be employed.** There may be obstacles to acquiring and retaining employment, but persons with epilepsy are employed in many occupations.

---

maintained on some occasions but not on others. According to Driscoll (1988), a moral judgment is being imposed on the person with epilepsy.

According to Hauser and Hesdorffer (1990), over 2 million persons have some form of epilepsy. More than 30% of these are children under 18 years. There are 300,000 new cases of seizures, 40% of which will occur in individuals under the age of 18. Most of these newly reported cases of seizures are convulsions associated with fever. Annually, 50 of 100,000 persons will be diagnosed as having epilepsy. Of this number, 30% will be younger than 18. Men are 1.1 to 1.7 times more likely to have a newly diagnosed seizure or epilepsy than are women. Trends have shown that new cases of epilepsy in children have

dropped, whereas they have increased in the elderly population.

In about half of these cases, the cause of the seizures is unknown. Some of the causes of the other half are defects in the brain; brain injury during or after birth; infections such as meningitis, measles, mumps, diphtheria; chemical imbalances; poor nutrition; childhood fevers; brain tumors; poisons (lead or alcohol); and head trauma.

TYPES OF SEIZURES

There still exists a general misconception of exactly what qualifies as a seizure. If the general public were asked to describe their impression of what a seizure is, the response likely would be that the person loses consciousness and convulses. These symptoms describe only one of many different types of seizures.

Seizures can be as varied as a brief staring spell to what appears to be picking lint off one's clothes. Some seizures are associated with loss of speech whereas other types do not affect speech at all. There is a correlation between the area of the brain that is affected and the type of seizure(s) one experiences. In addition, some people may have one type, whereas others' epilepsy is characterized by two or more types.

The following breakdown includes the most common seizure types and the prominent characteristics of each.

Generalized Tonic/Clonic (formerly called grand mal)

The entire brain is affected with this type of seizure (hence the term *generalized*). The person will sometimes cry out, then fall to the floor or ground, unaware of what is going on around him or her. Often the seizure will happen without any warning or aura. The person may become incontinent and may bite his or her tongue or the inside of the cheek. These bites are usually not serious. There will be brief stiffness (tonic phase), then jerking of the arms, legs, or both (clonic phase). The person may experience some difficulty in breathing, due to the tongue's falling to the back of the throat. The seizure may last a minute or two. After the seizure, the person may be sleepy, confused, or both, and may have a headache or other muscle soreness.

Absence Seizures (formerly called petit mal)

This type of seizure consists of brief staring spells that usually last only a few seconds. They are usually seen in children between the ages of 6 and 14 years. The person will be unaware of surroundings, then return to full alertness, without falling or losing muscle control or consciousness. These seizures are difficult to notice because they are so brief. Parents and teachers often think these children are daydreaming or ignoring them. On occasion, there will be rapid eye blinking, mouth chewing movements, turning of the head, or waving of the arms.

Simple Partial Seizures (sometimes called Jacksonian, focal, or auras)

During this type of seizure, the person is aware of having the seizure but cannot control the movements, because the motor part of the brain is affected. The movements look like "marching" because the seizure involvement moves up the arm or leg. For example, the fingers will twitch or jerk, then the entire hand, then the wrist, and so on up the arm. Depending on what area of the brain is affected, the person may experience a feeling of fear, anger, or excitement.

Complex Partial Seizures (sometimes called psychomotor or temporal lobe seizures)

During this type of seizure, the person may look as though he or she is in a trance. There may also be repetitive behavior, such as hand rubbing, picking at clothes, or walking around in a daze. The person is not aware of his or her surroundings but may be able to follow simple, one-step commands. This type of seizure may last only a minute or two, but the recovery period may be longer, in terms of full awareness of the surroundings. There may be confusion and irritability after the seizure. This type of seizure is more common in adolescents and adults than in children.

Complex partial seizures, as well as simple partial seizures, can become secondarily generalized. That is, as a second phase of the seizure, a generalized convulsion might occur.

Status Epilepticus (SE)

Status epilepticus is a medical emergency that must be treated immediately. The main characteristic is repetitive seizures without the person regaining consciousness. An SE seizure can have a stressful effect on the respiratory, cardiovascular, and central nervous systems (Leppik, 1993a).

Sometimes seizures can be precipitated by something in one's environment or immediate surroundings as well as by physical and emotional well-being (Schachter, 1993). The following is a list of common triggers:

flickering lights

fluorescent lights

venetian blinds

stress

missing a dose of medicine

taking medications sporadically or not at a scheduled time every day

exposure to extreme heat

menstruation

Following is a short case summary of an individual with tonic–clonic seizures.

CASE EXAMPLE: RICHARD

Richard is 25 years old and has tonic–clonic seizures. He has no warning or aura before one happens. He immediately loses consciousness and convulses. His parents report that he becomes very rigid and that jerking of both his arms and legs immediately follows. The only way they know a seizure is about to happen is the loud cry Richard lets out just before he loses consciousness. Richard reports that upon regaining consciousness, his tongue is usually bleeding and sometimes he has been incontinent. He also reports having a severe headache as well as overall body aches immediately after the seizure, in addition to an overwhelming need to sleep. His speech is also affected with the seizure. He has difficulty in identifying objects for up to half an hour. Because of the lack of auras, Richard had to relinquish his driver's license until he is free of seizures for 6 months.

PSYCHOSOCIAL IMPLICATIONS

Epilepsy can have a significant bearing on one's social interactions. The intermittent occurrence of the seizures can cause some dramatic responses, with withdrawal from social situations being a major one, to avoid embarrassment should a seizure occur.

Compliance with medicines is another significant problem. Persons who are on long-term drug therapy may be considered by society in general, family members, and themselves to have a debilitating illness. Therefore, as a denial tactic, they may discontinue the drug therapy. People often rationalize that if it is not necessary to take medicine, nothing is wrong. Adolescents in particular are extremely influenced by the opinions of their peers and consequently find it very embarrassing to take medicine for fear of having to disclose the reason.

Self-Esteem

Not all persons with epilepsy have problems with self-esteem. For those that do, however, diagnosis, environmental enhancement, and self-subscription can be used as a systematic approach to addressing the self-esteem issues (Goldin, 1984).

Diagnosis determines the areas in which self-esteem is affected. There are many aspects to one's overall image of himself or herself, such as intellect, physical attractiveness, sexuality, talents, moral and ethical behavior, and vocational performance.

Environmental enhancement can be used to determine what changes need to be made to improve social acceptance. This process helps the person with epilepsy facilitate change in specific aspects of the way he or she relates to the world. An important tool to develop is coping skills, which can lead to better self-perceptions.

Finally, *self-subscription* is a tool used to identify what the person's personal strengths are so that he or she can learn to focus on them. Persons with any type of disability tend to become very focused on what they cannot do. This tool focuses on one's abilities rather than on one's disability.

Quality of Life

For a person with epilepsy, the perception of his or her quality of life is directly related to his or her level of acceptance of the disability, which in turn affects the level of self-esteem. In order to achieve this "quality" state, Santilli (1993) pointed out five important tools:

1. general information about seizures, medication, and lifestyle;

2. the ability to recognize potential dangers and determine if immediate medical attention is warranted;

3. awareness of side effects of medications;

4. awareness of the particular attitudes one might have about epilepsy; and

5. an ability to solve problems.

These tools are discussed more fully in the following paragraphs.

• *General information about seizures, medication, and lifestyle.* This aspect includes adapting one's life around the disability. If, for example, a young adult developed epilepsy, he or she would need to be aware of many potential health dangers. Staying up late, consuming alcohol, and everyday stressors can all cause seizures. Becoming aware of the stressors that affect the individual in terms of seizure activity is essential, so that they can be avoided whenever possible. Understanding the importance of taking medicines is another important aspect. Many persons with epilepsy believe that if the seizures are well controlled, there is no point in continuing with the prescribed treatment, specifically medicines. Another common mistake is doubling dosages if a dose was missed. The person should never take a double dose unless directed to do so by the physician.

• *The ability to recognize potential dangers and determine if immediate medical attention is warranted.* It is essential that a person with epilepsy understand this disability from a holistic perspective. It has not only neurological ramifications but also physical, psychological, emotional, and social ones. Self-awareness and an understanding of how epilepsy affects us individually is crucial. Only then can the most appropriate plan(s) of action be taken, medically or otherwise.

• *Awareness of side effects of medications.* An open relationship with the treating physician and pharmacist is also crucial. The person with epilepsy needs to report any unusual feelings (sleepiness, depression, anxiety, etc.) that occur. Education of the particular drug that has been prescribed should be part of the treatment plan.

• *Awareness of particular attitudes one might have about epilepsy.* These attitudes can vary widely from one person with this disability to another. Some continue to believe the myths for a long time, whereas others are more progressive in their attitudes. Some deny that the epilepsy even exists; others understand the importance of acceptance and understanding. The attitudes one holds can vary as much as the type(s) of seizures one experiences.

• *An ability to solve problems.* This ability is imperative to any disability. Avoiding or internalizing problems can only lead to the increase of stress, which increases the likelihood of the occurrence of seizures. Dealing with problems in inappropriate manners other than using systematic solving techniques can also lead to substance abuse, which is often directly related to seizure activity.

Suicide

Studies have shown that persons with epilepsy can experience psychological distress to the point of committing suicide. According to Stagno (1993), the incidence of suicide is five times greater in this population than in the general population. An overdose of antiseizure medication is the most frequent method. Phenobarbital in particular has been linked to everything from suicidal ideations to the actual act of suicide. Repeated attempts have also been shown to be likely. The incidences of suicide appear to be linked to depression.

Some medicines used for seizure control are barbiturates. It is hypothesized that these medications may induce depression, which thereby increases the possibility of suicide. There is also the question of the existence of other mental illness in those with epilepsy who ultimately committed suicide. Stagno (1993) cited a report in which 61% of those persons who overdosed had received no follow-up treatment prior to the suicide.

CASE EXAMPLE: WILLIAM

William has complex partial seizures. He might be involved in the middle of a task, such as shaving, making his bed, or working on his computer. He can usually finish the immediate task, often without any memory of having completed it. Further, he usually completes the task as well as when he is not interrupted by a seizure. After finishing what he had begun to do, he usually needs either to sit or to lie down until the seizure has run its course. However, sometimes he will attempt to go on to another task, only to discover he has forgotten the steps in completing it, because the seizure activity in his brain has interrupted that thinking process. Because of the extended auras William has, he is able to sit or lie down and to let someone know he is about to have a seizure.

•••

FAMILY DYNAMICS

The psychosocial impact on a family who has a member with epilepsy is very significant. The disability upsets the balance of the family, with each member reacting differently. Moreover, the way in which the member with epilepsy is treated by his or her spouse, parents, grandparents, children, and siblings has a direct (sometimes drastic) effect on him or her.

The initial reactions of a family member to a diagnosis of epilepsy are similar to those of a death. First, there is disbelief or denial, which is a common reaction to an unexpected event. Also, the onset of epilepsy usually has no warnings. This disbelief is based on the difficulty of accepting the fact that a loved one is having seizures. The physical appearance of some types of seizures is frightening and further causes the disbelief. This emotion is also manifested by the individual's or family's ignoring the fact that a seizure has occurred and not seeking the medical attention that may be necessary.

Anger is the second emotion. The more ramifications of which the family becomes aware, the greater the chance of anger. Guilt, depression, and a sense of rejection are all associated with this anger and therefore the chances are great that many different emotions emerge during this stage.

The third stage is demystification, which occurs when the family seeks information about the epilepsy. Learning more about the disability helps them become more familiar with it. Oftentimes, learning about epilepsy means learning more about themselves. The guilt, anger, and depression are now replaced with learning how to cope.

The final stage is conditional acceptance, which happens when there is a sense of control over the epilepsy. Life with this disability and its ramifications is more acceptable. Control is the key to this phase. Even though the seizures are not necessarily controlled, the reactions to them are controlled to a greater degree.

Usually, all family members go through these initial stages, with some exhibiting the characteristics of one phase more than other phases. However, there is a vast difference between the family members in terms of handling the disability once these stages have been experienced.

If the family member with epilepsy is one of the parents, it is extremely important that the parent talk openly about it with the children. This open discussion allows the children to adjust to the disability and, at the same time, to maintain trust in and concern for both parents. Children who are allowed to see their parents have seizures and the treatment for the seizures adapt better to the threat of illness or disability in their own lives. However, there is a fine line between involving the children in seizure care and making them overly responsible for the welfare of the parent with epilepsy.

Siblings of persons with epilepsy have an important impact on overall adjustment. It is essential that siblings interact as normally as possible, no matter how much a seizure may disrupt a daily routine. The siblings will watch their parents' reactions to the seizures very carefully. If the parents panic, so will the siblings. If they are overprotective of the child with epilepsy, the siblings will be as well. The brothers and sisters need to be allowed to care for the child when a seizure occurs. At the same time, they also need to feel free from this responsibility. Many children have special feelings for the sibling with epilepsy.

Also at times, the siblings will feel resentful of all of the attention given to the child with epilepsy. This resentment can cause arguments and fighting. It is important for parents to set rules and to be consistent with enforcement.

Grandparents are often the ones in the family who find it the most difficult to adjust. They tend to encourage the parents to be overprotective and to isolate the grandchild from normal activities. They are also the most affected by the stigma and trauma of epilepsy. Because of their older age, they tend to be the most intolerant, perhaps because their opinions were formed about this disability at a time when mainstreaming, seizure control through drugs or surgery, legislation, and advocacy were not prevalent.

However, the grandparents can be in a unique situation in terms of adjustment. If their influence is positive, they can provide much reinforcement. Whereas, if their influence is negative, ways need to be found to neutralize the inappropriate information they will use.

The most important area where any family member can help himself or herself is with self-esteem, by either developing or maintaining it. Family members must realize that the parent or the sibling is lovable and capable of many things, even though he or she may be far from perfect. This realization is an extremely necessary element for high self-esteem, but it takes much courage, energy, and work to succeed.

CASE EXAMPLE: ADRIENNE

Adrienne has absence seizures. She is 8 years old and in the third grade. For several months, her teacher was sure that Adrienne was daydreaming because she would stare into space or out the window. When she was called on in class, she seemed to be ignoring the teacher because she would not respond. Adrienne had undergone IQ testing and had scored 110. Knowing this, the teacher became very frustrated because she knew Adrienne was smart. She thought some further testing for a behavioral disorder might be appropriate. She discussed this idea with the school nurse, who offered to observe Adrienne in class. The nurse concluded that Adrienne was indeed experiencing absence seizures and referred her to a pediatric neurologist.

PROVIDING MEDICAL ASSISTANCE FOR PERSONS HAVING SEIZURES

Often, some confusion exists as to the proper first-aid procedures to administer to someone who is having a seizure. Table 9.2 provides the proper first-aid procedures for someone having a seizure.

Table 9.2.   First Aid for Seizures

- Stay calm. Help the person lie down. Remove eyeglasses and dentures. Loosen tight clothing.

- Clear the area of any hard, sharp, or hot objects. Place something soft under the head, such as a jacket or a pillow.

- Do not hold the arms or legs down to try to stop the seizure. A seizure cannot be stopped once it has started.

- **Never** place anything in the mouth. **Never** attempt to pry the mouth open to insert an object.

- When the seizure ends, roll the person over on his or her side to allow the draining of saliva.

- Wait until the person is fully awake before giving them anything to drink.

Call a doctor or 911 only if

- the person has one seizure after another without regaining consciousness;

- the person does not start breathing after the seizure. (Difficulty in breathing during the seizure is normal.)

- there are injuries; or

- this is the first seizure the person has ever had.

LEGAL ISSUES

Driver's License

Not only is receiving a driver's license an important rite of passage for adolescents, it is also often a problem for persons with epilepsy. Keeping the license if seizures begin later in life can also be a problem. Many states require a person to be seizure free for a period of 1 year; other states require a period of 6 months. Some exceptions to these seizure-free requirements include long auras (warnings that the seizure is going to happen) that allow ample time to pull off the road; nocturnal seizures; or a statement from the treating physician that a change in medication caused the seizure, but that in his or her opinion, the person will continue to have good control.

Because there are many different types of seizures, the Epilepsy Foundation of America (EFA) advocates individual evaluations of the ability to drive rather than general requirements applying to everyone with epilepsy. Side effects of medicines are an important factor as well as are nocturnal seizures and auras.

When a person with epilepsy applies for a driver's license, there needs to be complete honesty about the seizure history. Otherwise, there can be serious liability issues. If an automobile accident occurs involving a person with epilepsy who had a seizure at the time of the accident, the license can be suspended or even revoked depending on state laws and the result of the accident for the other driver and passenger(s).

Some states have a mandatory reporting law, which requires a physician treating persons with epilepsy to report them to the department of motor vehicles (DMV). According to Lehman (1993), EFA opposes this law for the following reasons:

• Epilepsy is not contagious. Therefore, it is not a threat to public health.
• The act of a physician's reporting a patient's epilepsy, which is privileged information, to a state's DMV is in direct violation of the doctor–patient privilege, inherent in the relationship.

As an alternative, EFA would rather see the person with epilepsy self-report, giving him or her responsibility for the disability and ultimately providing a tool for empowerment.

Physicians have the right to report persons with epilepsy to DMV whom they believe are a threat to the public. Such persons might include those who have been advised to report themselves or to relinquish their drivers' licenses, and it is known that they have not. Further, some states provide physicians with immunity for reporting such persons.

Employment

The perception of an employer who employs people with epilepsy is extremely important to be aware of as is the reverse. Hiring a person with epilepsy is no different from hiring a person without epilepsy. This is an extremely powerful statement that many employers refuse either to acknowledge or to understand. But in reality, epilepsy should become important if and only if it interferes in some way with job performance or job safety. Then, certain accommodations can be made to ensure good performance and safety.

Table 9.3 lists the most frequent barriers that persons with epilepsy encounter when seeking employment.

Employees with epilepsy need to learn to advocate effectively for themselves in the inter-

---

Table 9.3. Employment Barriers

Obtaining a job

Disclosing one's epilepsy

Remaining employed if or when a seizure occurs

Underemployment

Educating coworkers and employers in the proper first-aid procedures as well as in general knowledge about epilepsy

---

viewing process as well as when his or her job is threatened because of the discovery of the seizure disorder. Learning how to disclose the fact that epilepsy exists in a nonthreatening manner can be a difficult skill to learn. Table 9.4 provides a comprehensive view of the different ways one can disclose his or her epilepsy and the ramifications of each.

TREATMENTS FOR EPILEPSY

Drug Therapy

According to Penry (1993), the search for effective seizure-preventative medicine started close to 2000 years ago. Clinically speaking, it has only been about 20 years that significant advances in both diagnosis and treatment of epilepsy have taken place. To this day, antiepileptic drugs (AEDs) are the most common form of treatment for seizure disorders. However, AEDs have not gone without problems, specifically in cognitive functioning and psychological effects. Phenytoin (Dilantin), phenobarbital, and carbamazapene (Tegretol) are three well-known AEDs that have been documented to cause problems ranging from loss of memory retention to irritability and drowsiness (see Table 9.5). However, if drug levels in the blood are routinely checked and the lines of communication remain open between the physician and patient, significance of these side effects can be dramatically reduced.

Three anticonvulsant drugs have been approved by the U.S. Food and Drug Administration (FDA) in the past 2 years for use in the United States: Neurontin (gabapentin), Felbatol (felbamate), and Lamictal (almotrigine). This is very significant because the United States had not approved a single major AED in the past 15 years.

According to Leppik (1993b), noncompliance of medications is a major reason for recurring seizures. One third to one half of persons with epilepsy are noncompliant. The degree of their noncompliance may vary widely, but it interferes

with appropriate treatment. The seizure activity may also be related to the increase in the cost of health care. Ambulances necessary at times of transport, the increase in the use of emergency rooms, and the possibility of a physical injury during a seizure all contribute to this increase.

Another important aspect of noncompliance is the danger it poses to others, for example, when a person drives in violation of the required seizure-free period or a pregnant woman does not follow her prescribed regimen.

There are two types of noncompliance, according to Leppik (1993b): patient controlled and structural. The former is based on a belief system the person may have; for example, the person decides that due to the good control, the seizure is less of a risk to him or her than are the drugs. The latter occurs when the seizures are the result of a traumatic brain injury, resulting in memory problems that make it difficult to remember to take medicine.

Interventions must take place if the management of seizures is to be successful. Education is important to ensure that the person understands what epilepsy is and the importance not only of drug therapy but also of his or her own regimen. The number of visits to the physician's office may need to be increased and a particular staff member designated to monitor the progress.

Another concern is the problems that AEDs can cause for pregnant women. According to Yerby (1993), infants born to mothers who were receiving AED therapy during pregnancy run a greater risk of developing congenital malformations (birth defects), with cleft palates the most common. There is a risk of the infant's developing spina bifida when the mother takes Tegretol or Depakote. However, even though these pregnancy complications increase in women with epilepsy, close to 90% have healthy babies.

Despite the significant changes in AED therapy, it is important to remember that this type of therapy greatly depends on the individual. Each person with epilepsy differs in terms of the type(s) of drugs that best control his or her seizures. Therefore, there is much trial and error

Table 9.4.   Epilepsy Employment Disclosure Chart

Time of Disclosure	Advantages	Disadvantages	Issues
On the job application	Honesty Peace of mind Ease Lets employer decide if epilepsy is an issue	Disqualification No opportunity to present qualifications No recourse Potential discrimination	May have a harder time finding work
During the interview	Honesty Peace of mind Opportunity to respond briefly and positively Discrimination less likely to occur face to face	Too much emphasis on disability may be a potential problem Evaluation may no longer be on abilities	Are you confident in discussing your epilepsy? This is difficult, but you will be a better job candidate and person if you are.
After the interview, when the job is offered, but before beginning work.	Honesty Peace of mind If the epilepsy changes the mind of the employer and you are otherwise qualified for the job, this may be violation of the Employment Title of the Americans with Disabilities Act (ADA) Opportunity to discuss any accommodations you may need to enhance your job performance	Employer may believe you should have told him or her before job was offered	Seizures need to be examined in terms of the tasks in the job that you are applying for. Need to be able to explain how the epilepsy will not get in the way of doing job. This includes job safety.
After a seizure on the job	Opportunity to prove yourself on the job before disclosing If the seizures affect your employment status but not your ability to do the job, the employer may be in violation of the ADA	Possible employer accusation of falsifying information Coworkers might not have known seizure first aid Can perpetuate epilepsy's myths and misunderstandings	Any friendships you might have made with coworkers may be hurt if they feel you have not been truthful with them.
Never	Employer cannot react to your epilepsy until you have a seizure	If you have a seizure on the job, you might be hurt by inappropriate first aid Studies show that persons with epilepsy who do not disclose have a higher number of seizures on the job Can perpetuate myths and misunderstandings	If you have not had a seizure in a long time (over 2 years) the issue of disclosure becomes less critical.

Note. From "Issues and Answers: Exploring Your Possibilities. A Guide for Teens and Young Adults with Epilepsy," by the Epilepsy Foundation of America, 1992, p. 77. Copyright 1992 by the Epilepsy Foundation of America. Reprinted with permission.

Table 9.5. Antiepileptic Drugs (AEDs)

Brand Name	Generic Name	Seizure Type	Side Effects
Dilantin	Phenytoin	Generalized Simple partial Complex partial Status epilepticus	Rash Gingivitis Drowsiness
Tegretol	Carbamazapine	Simple partial Complex partial Generalized	Sore throat Easy bruising Drowsiness Dizziness
Depakote	Valproic acid	Absence Generalized	Liver abnormalities Hair loss Weight gain
Phenobarbital	Phenobarbital	Neonatal Febrile Generalized	Drowsiness Sexual dysfunction Paradoxical excitement

and unpredictability involved in AED therapy to reach the optimum drug(s) and dosage with the least amount of side effects.

Surgery

In choosing candidates for epilepsy surgery, the first criterion is determining that other forms of treatment have failed. Usually, the person's quality of life is deteriorating despite the treatment. This deterioration would affect employability, social interactions, academic performance, and levels of self-esteem. The next step is extensive neuropsychological testing to identify the region in the brain where the seizure activity is originating as well as to determine the candidate's psychological stability in undergoing such a complicated surgical procedure.

Some changes in cognitive abilities can occur after surgery, including memory, language, and intelligence. These changes can be either positive or negative. Often in cases in which the surgery was performed in the speech hemisphere of the brain, language skills have improved. It is thought that this improvement occurred because the neu-

rological disturbance that was causing the seizures had been removed. Some decrease in IQ scores immediately after surgery has been reported, but no long-term losses have been found. Improvement in intellectual abilities has been reported in terms of performance but not in terms of IQ scores.

ADVOCACY

An advocate is a person who defends a cause or belief. Physicians, politicians, public officials, attorneys, and human-service workers all act in some capacity as advocates for patients, constituents, or clients. Through self-advocacy the patient or client promotes a belief for oneself as well as for a group to which he or she belongs.

Language is often a very good starting point when developing advocacy skills. How we refer to persons with various disabilities is a direct reflection of our own attitudes and beliefs. Table 9.6 contains the most misused terms when speaking about persons with epilepsy.

There are also other advocacy tools that apply to persons with any disability, such as assertiveness,

---

Table 9.6. Terms Misused in Referring to Epilepsy

---

disease	Epilepsy is *not* a disease, which to many implies contagiousness or an ailment. Rather, it is a symptom of a disorder, with the main characteristic being a disruption in the electrical activity in the brain.
epileptic	A person with any type of disability should *never* be defined by that disability. The individual is a *person* first and foremost. Therefore, "person with epilepsy" is more appropriate.
fit	This term is a commonly used term for *seizure* by the medical profession in England. However, persons with epilepsy in the United States are very sensitive to this term. It implies loss of control. *Seizures* is more appropriate.

---

negotiation skills, letter writing, and other communication skills. The combination of these abilities makes for a very effective advocate.

ETHICAL CONSIDERATIONS

When clinical ethics comes to mind, one usually thinks of controversial issues such as maintaining persons on life support systems or using aborted fetuses for research. But just as important are everyday, routine aspects of health care. The mundane or frequent component to one's health care does not eliminate ethical consideration.

Occasionally a life-and-death situation concerning persons with epilepsy occurs, but it is not commonplace. For example, such a situation could stem from a "do not resuscitate" order or a severe cerebrovascular accident (stroke) following surgery to correct a seizure disorder and requiring a decision to continue life support. The more common types of ethical considerations are related to informed consent and the responsibilities of the patient, as well as of the physician, nurse, counselor, and any other health care

provider. Generally defined, *informed consent* is the reaching of decisions through a series of meetings involving respect, concurrence, and, sometimes, negotiation.

Whether the circumstances are critical or not, it is paramount to always remember, as explained by Smith (1993), that the dignity of the person with epilepsy must be emphasized and that the provider should act as a "moral agent." Oftentimes, because of the health care system's attempt to be efficient, patients and clients are no longer human beings. They are simply numbers or statistics. Consequently, they do not receive adequate explanation for the tests or treatments they are given.

Smith (1993) explained that, just as the provider has a certain area of expertise, so should persons with epilepsy. It is extremely important that they have a firm grasp of what is important to them on a personal level, in terms of values and aspirations. For example, persons with different types of epilepsy or seizure frequency will opt for different types of treatment. Some may be content with drug therapy, whereas others may opt for surgery.

Patients/clients have a responsibility to themselves, as well as to the professional treating them, to be honest in discussing seizure severity, frequency, substance abuse (or any consumption of a "recreational" drug), and any other vital piece of information. They also must be willing to cooperate with the course of treatment. For example, these responsibilities can be in violation if prescribed dosages of medicine are not taken, if the reported number of seizures is deliberately inaccurate, or if a seizure has occurred within the required time frame as set by a department of motor vehicles in order to retain a driver's license.

There are many situations that can hinder the relationship between the patient/client and the service provider. Smith (1993) pointed out that the most significant ones are communication problems, noncompliance, and ulterior motives other than personal health, such as a desire to continue to receive a financial benefit or entitlement. Appropriate measures to educate and empower persons with epilepsy should be initiated when necessary.

FINAL THOUGHTS

It is not difficult to understand why epilepsy has been a misunderstood disability. The seizures are sudden and oftentimes dramatic. In addition, there is not always an easy explanation for its occurrence. Further, quite a number of psychological, social, and emotional problems accompany the seizures, which substantially compromises one's quality of life. Continued emphasis in this area is essential for change in attitudes, both societal and personal. Dodrill (1993) cited a study of 27 groups of persons with epilepsy who were given the *Minnesota Multiphasic Personality Inventory* (MMPI). Two thirds of these groups showed various abnormalities. This statistic, although based on a relatively small population of persons with epilepsy, is nevertheless alarming. Moreover, the magnitude of its implications should not go unrecognized.

There have, however, been significant changes in diagnosing and treating epilepsy. These changes include the measuring of levels of drugs in the blood, audiovisual monitoring of seizures, and the FDA's approval of new antiepileptic medications.

Persons with epilepsy need to have choice and control in every aspect of life—education, employment, housing, and personal relationships to name a few. Without choice and control, myths will continue to prevail. The first step is to develop a personal acceptance of life with this disability, thereby taking the necessary precautions to manage it on a daily basis. This could include everything from changing sleep patterns to substance-abuse recovery. Whatever changes need to occur, unless persons with epilepsy have accepted their disability, it would be unreasonable to expect others to do the same. Therefore,

without personal acceptance, obtaining choice and control will be very difficult.

Finally, consumers, working simultaneously with physicians, counselors, politicians, but most important with each other, must advocate for both system and personal changes. President George Bush said it most succinctly upon signing the Americans with Disabilities Act: "Let the shameful wall of exclusion finally come tumbling down."

REFERENCES

Dodrill, C. (1993). Historical perspectives and future directions. In E. Wyllie (Ed.), *The treatment of epilepsy: Principles and practice* (pp. 1129–1132). Philadelphia: Lea & Febiger.

Driscoll, S. (1988). *All you really wanted to know about epilepsy but were afraid to ask.* Richmond: Medical College of Virginia, Virginia Commonwealth University, Department of Neurology.

Goldin, G. (1984, July/August). Building self-esteem in people with epilepsy. Landover, MD: Epilepsy Foundation of America.

Hauser, W. A., & Hesdorffer, D. C. (1990). *Epilepsy frequency, causes and consequences.* New York: Demos.

Lehman, C. (1993). Legal aspects of epilepsy. In E. Wyllie (Ed.), *The treatment of epilepsy: Principles and practice* (pp. 1168–1177). Philadelphia: Lea & Febiger.

Leppik, I. (1993a). Compliance in the treatment of epilepsy. In E. Wyllie (Ed.), *The treatment of epilepsy: Principles and practice* (pp. 810–816). Philadelphia: Lea & Febiger.

Leppik, I. (1993b). Status epilepticus. In E. Wyllie (Ed.), *The treatment of epilepsy: Principles and practice* (pp. 678–685). Philadelphia: Lea & Febiger.

Penry, J. (1993). Historical perspectives and future directions. In E. Wyllie (Ed.), *The treatment of epilepsy: Principles and practice* (pp. 709–711). Philadelphia: Lea & Febiger.

Santilli, N. (1993). Psychosocial aspects of epilepsy: Education and counseling for patients and families. In E. Wyllie (Ed.), *The treatment of epilepsy: Principles and practice* (pp. 1163–1167). Philadelphia: Lea & Febiger.

Schachter, S. (1993). *Brainstorms: Epilepsy in our words.* New York: Raven Press.

Smith, M. (1993). Ethical considerations in the treatment of epilepsy. In E. Wyllie (Ed.), *The treatment of epilepsy: Principles and practice* (pp. 1178–1183). Philadelphia: Lea & Febiger.

Stagno, S. (1993). Psychiatric aspects of epilepsy. In E. Wyllie (Ed.), *The treatment of epilepsy: Principles and practice* (pp. 1149–1162). Philadelphia: Lea & Febiger.

Yerby, M. (1993). Treatment of epilepsy during pregnancy. In E. Wyllie (Ed.), *The treatment of epilepsy: Principles and practice* (pp. 844–857). Philadelphia: Lea & Febiger.

Behavioral Disabilities

Elaine Clark

LEARNING GOALS

Upon completion of this chapter the reader will be able to

- explain the difference between the terms *socially maladjusted* and *behaviorally disabled*;

- describe the advantages of a multidimensional classification system for behavioral disabilities;

- discuss the major self-care and independent living problems for individuals with behavioral disabilities; and

- discuss the major language and learning problems for individuals with behavioral disabilities.

Considerable differences of opinion exist about how certain developmental disorders should be defined and treated. This is especially true of emotional and behavioral disabilities. As Kazdin (1985) pointed out, beyond agreement that these impairments need to be conceptualized from a developmental and contextual framework, there is little consensus. In this chapter, I make no attempt to arrive at a consensus; rather, I have sought to describe what is generally meant by "behavioral disability," what areas of function are impaired, and what are considered to be the best practices for intervening.

According to the most recent edition of the *Diagnostic and Statistical Manual of Mental Disorders* (DSM–IV) of the American Psychiatric Association (1994), individuals with mental retardation and developmental disabilities are three to four times more likely than the general population to have mental disorders. Some sources estimate the rate to be even higher, in some cases seven times higher, when more serious disturbances are

present (Koller, Richardson, Katz, & McLaren, 1982). Although no particular behavioral feature is unique to this group of children, the nature and severity of the problems they face are often affected by the degree of their intellectual impairment as well as its cause. For example, a traumatic brain injury may result in both diminished cognitive capacity and emotional and behavioral disturbances. Although these problem behaviors may be a secondary feature, that is, a reaction to the cognitive deficits that the injury caused, these may also be a function of the neurologic damage to the brain. Children with developmental disabilities, such as mental retardation, are, however, a heterogeneous group. It is somewhat surprising to find that the interventions commonly used are quite homogeneous. In fact, in most instances, treatment will consist of behavior therapy (Cole & Gardner, 1993). In this chapter, best practices for intervention will be discussed in the context of the type of behavioral and emotional disturbances these children face.

FUNCTIONAL DESCRIPTION

Special Education Definition

In 1990, the federal law mandating special education services was reauthorized as the Individuals with Disabilities Education Act (IDEA, 1990). Although traumatic brain injury and autism were added as new disability categories, relatively few other changes were included in the criteria for children with disabilities. As with prior legislation, there is no category for behavioral disabilities; instead, the category is termed *severe emotional disturbance* (SED). According to IDEA, SED is defined as

> (i) a condition exhibiting one or more of the following characteristics over a long period of time and to a marked degree that adversely affects a child's educational performance:
>> (a) an inability to learn that cannot be explained by intellectual, sensory, or health factors;
>> (b) an inability to build or maintain satisfactory interpersonal relationships with peers and teachers;
>> (c) inappropriate types of behaviors or feelings under normal circumstances;
>> (d) a general pervasive mood of unhappiness or depression; or
>> (e) a tendency to develop physical symptoms or fears associated with personal or school problems.
> (ii) The term includes schizophrenia. The term does not apply to children who are socially maladjusted, unless it is determined they have a serious emotional disturbance. (§ 34 C.F.R. 300.5)

Because the federal definition typically serves as a model for state classification systems due to funding requirements, considerable continuity exists between the federal law and the state rules and regulations. State classifications, however, are ultimately defined by state boards of education and are to be used by local school districts to ensure proper funding for educational programs. Because funding to schools is tied to the number of children classified with a particular disability, state definitions are generally broader in coverage. According to the special education rules in the State of Utah, for example, the term *behavioral disordered* (BD) is used instead of seriously emotionally disturbed. Briefly, *behavior disorders* means that a student has a behavioral or emotional condition that persists over a long period of time and is severe enough to adversely affect school performance (Utah State Office of Education, 1993). Although children with emotional disturbances are also included under Utah rules, those who are considered to be socially maladjusted are not included unless it can be determined that they are also behavior disordered or emotionally disturbed.

The exclusion of children who are "socially maladjusted" from services under SED or BD has caused considerable debate. These children are often the most disruptive and seriously disturbed and are also the largest subgroup of children referred for special education services in SED/BD classes (McGinnis & Forness, 1988). As a result of this problem and a general lack of clarity in the definition of SED and BD, a coalition comprising 30 educators and mental health specialists was formed to work on the definition for IDEA (Council for Children with Behavioral Disorders, 1989). The coalition proposed that *emotional disorder* or *behavioral disorder* be used to broaden the definition and better represent the fact that behavioral disturbances may have underlying emotional problems. The proposed definition, which borrowed heavily from other definitions including the one used for mental retardation (Forness & MacMillan, 1989), emphasized that the disability be characterized by behavioral or emotional "responses" that are markedly different from appropriate age, cultural, or ethnic norms. These responses would need to be evident in one or more settings besides the school and be shown to adversely affect educational performance (i.e., academic, social, vocational, and personal). Unfortunately, this proposal was not included in the reauthorization of the public law in 1990. Although it is unclear if these changes will be adopted when IDEA is reauthorized, one can be certain that the special education definition will, by necessity, continue to be used in school settings to determine eligibility for services. Professionals working in and outside the schools, however, often prefer to use other classification systems, such as the DSM–IV.

DSM–IV

The *Diagnostic and Statistical Manual* (DSM) is a widely accepted and frequently used classification system. As an atheoretical approach that places emphasis on symptoms rather than on causes, the most recent version published in 1994, or the DSM–IV, does not differ much from its predecessor, the DSM–III-R, in terms of disorders that are usually diagnosed first in infancy, childhood, or adolescence. The authors of the manual did, however, include a new category, Feeding Disorder, and also specified certain subtypes of pervasive development disorders (e.g., Retts, Childhood Disintegrative Disorder, and Aspergers Syndrome). Most of the remaining disorders were unchanged except for the addition or subtraction of certain criteria. For example, symptoms of a conduct disorder are now grouped according to four categories: aggression toward people and animals, property destruction, deceitfulness or theft, and serious rule violation. A couple of items were also added to increase the category's applicability to female clients (i.e., items pertaining to staying out at night and intimidating others). The fact that the DSM–IV is a multiaxial system that lends itself to the assessment of the context of the problem as well as to the problem itself, makes it particularly well suited to the diagnosis of children and adolescents. Further, as a multiaxial system, the DSM–IV also affords clinicians the opportunity to make multiple diagnoses, something that is clearly needed when identifying childhood psychopathologic conditions, and to determine the severity of psychoso-

cial and environmental stressors and functional level, both current and past. The disorders are defined in a descriptive manner, with specific criteria for diagnoses provided. Table 10.1 lists the disorders that tend to become evident in childhood.

Despite a number of strengths, the DSM has been a frequent target of criticism. Perhaps the most common criticism has to do with its psychometric properties, in particular, problems reliably diagnosing a disorder, especially in childhood (Gresham & Gansle, 1992). There are also concerns about its validity. Gresham and Gansle (1992) argued that the DSM is inadequate as a source of information about particular childhood syndromes and has little relevance for special education placements or educational services. The psychometric shortcomings of the DSM have been attributed by some to the manner in which the categories were derived (Achenbach, 1982). That is, instead of identifying diagnostic categories, the authors used expert opinion and consensus. Multivariate procedures, on the other hand, have used sophisticated statistical techniques to empirically define behavioral patterns of interrelated characteristics of behavioral and emotional impairments.

Other Diagnostic Systems

Like IDEA and the DSM–IV, the goal of the multivariate technique is the identification of a syndrome from a dimensional approach rather than from a categorical one. Instead of an assessment of the presence or absence of a disorder, the degree and severity of demonstrable symptoms are quantified along a behavioral gradient (Kazdin, 1985). If desired, classification is possible. Cluster analytic techniques have often been used to achieve the goal of classifying individuals according to similar patterns of symptoms. The most extensive research of this type has been conducted by Achenbach and Edelbrock (1978, 1979). Factor analytic studies of children with and without referral concerns for emotional and behavioral problems have yielded two broad factors:

Table 10.1. DSM–IV Disorders Usually First Diagnosed in Infancy, Childhood, or Adolescence

---

MENTAL RETARDATION

Mild Mental Retardation
Moderate Mental Retardation
Severe Mental Retardation
Profound Mental Retardation
Mental Retardation, Severity Unspecified

LEARNING DISORDERS

Reading Disorder
Mathematics Disorder
Disorder of Written Expression
Learning Disorder NOS

MOTOR SKILLS DISORDER

Developmental Coordination Disorder

COMMUNICATION DISORDERS

Expressive Language Disorder
Mixed Receptive–Expressive Language Disorder
Phonological Disorder
Stuttering
Communication Disorder NOS

PERVASIVE DEVELOPMENTAL DISORDERS

Autistic Disorder
Rett's Disorder
Childhood Disintegrative Disorder
Asperger's Disorder
Pervasive Developmental Disorder NOS

ATTENTION-DEFICIT AND DISRUPTIVE BEHAVIOR DISORDERS

Attention-Deficit/Hyperactivity Disorder

Combined Type
Predominantly Inattentive Type
Predominantly Hyperactive-Impulsive Type
Attention-Deficit/Hyperactivity Disorder NOS
Conduct Disorder
Oppositional Defiant Disorder
Disruptive Behavior Disorder NOS

FEEDING AND EATING DISORDERS OF INFANCY OR EARLY CHILDHOOD

Pica
Rumination Disorder
Feeding Disorder of Infancy or Early Childhood

TIC DISORDERS

Tourette's Disorder
Chronic Motor or Vocal Tic Disorder
Transient Tic Disorder
Tic Disorder NOS

ELIMINATION DISORDERS

Encopresis
Enuresis

OTHER DISORDERS OF INFANCY, CHILDHOOD, OR ADOLESCENCE

Separation Anxiety Disorder
Selective Mutism
Reactive Attachment Disorder of Infancy or Early Childhood
Stereotypic Movement Disorder
Disorder of Infancy, Childhood, or Adolescence NOS

Note. Adapted from *Diagnostic and Statistical Manual of Mental Disorders* (4th ed.) by American Psychiatric Association, 1994, Washington, DC: Author.

---

externalizing and internalizing. Whereas the former typically reflects behavioral excesses that are directed outwardly toward the environment, such as noncompliance, cruelty, hyperactivity, delinquent behaviors, and aggression, the latter tends to involve behavioral deficits or problems that are inwardly directed such as anxiety, phobias, social withdrawal, depression, immaturity, and obsessive–compulsive behaviors (Edelbrock & Achenbach, 1980).

Multidimensional classification systems have a number of advantages including the capability of covering multiple behavioral characteristics and empirically determining the salience of particular areas of dysfunction. These systems, however, also have weaknesses. One of the greatest weaknesses has to do with low-frequency problem behaviors, which are likely to be overlooked because empirically derived systems rely on data that reflect more common behavior problems. Nonetheless, diagnosis is central to understanding the multiple facets of a disorder, including the cause(s) and the course.

In the remainder of this chapter, I address the functional limitations of individuals with emotional and behavioral impairments. The following functional limitations are discussed: self-care, language, learning, mobility, self-direction, capacity for independent living, and economic sufficiency.

FUNCTIONAL LIMITATIONS

Self-Care

Individuals with behavioral or emotional disorders typically possess the necessary cognitive and motor skills to care for their personal needs, even some persons with mental retardation and developmental disabilities. As a result of emotional or behavioral problems, however, these persons are often unable to care properly for themselves. The problem is frequently one of neglect. In fact, preventive health care is virtually nonexistent. This is especially disturbing given the fact that individuals with behavioral disorders, or mental illnesses, are often more susceptible to disease and injury than are their "mentally healthy" counterparts (Barkley, 1985). The problem of self-care may also be related to difficulty in complying with prescribed medical treatments, including medications.

Pharmacologic agents have been used to treat emotional and behavioral problems of children and adolescents since the 1930s. The first psychotropic medication was a stimulant, or an amphetamine. This was followed 15 years later by the introduction of two antipsychotics, chlorpromazine and thioridazine. Antidepressants and anxiolytic medications were added later. Although psychotropic medications have been used

successfully to treat some of the behavioral concomitants of emotional impairments, the underlying disturbance is typically not changed (Cepeda, 1989). Further, problems with adverse side effects continue to plague the medication user despite the proliferation of new medications on the market. Age also seems to affect the responses, including the development of side effects. Research has shown that the younger the person is (that is, under 10 years), the greater is the variability of response to medication (Gualtieri, Golden, & Fahs, 1983) and the greater is the difference in side effects.

Although all medications have side effects, that is, pharmacologic actions that occur in addition to the intended action for relieving target symptoms, some side effects can seriously interfere with a person's functioning. In many cases, the ability of a person to care for his or her own needs is affected by this. Sedation is a common side effect of many psychotropic medications. Although sedation is more often associated with initial use, it is also a frequent complaint of individuals on higher doses. Other side effects that are not uncommon yet that have the potential to influence self-care, include impaired visual–motor coordination, blurred vision, dizziness, appetite disturbance, and tremors. Even side effects such as dry mouth and constipation can affect a person's functional capacity. Despite the fact that children generally adapt to medications rather quickly, it is important to ensure that prescribed medications are of sufficient benefit to risk the potential adverse side effects. Especially when treating children, one should use an adjunctive treatment with nonmedication therapies, such as behavioral therapy (see Hutchens, 1987, for a review).

In addition to the problems with prescribed medications, individuals with emotional or behavioral difficulties also have problems associated with using nonprescribed substances such as alcohol and other drugs. Whereas many individuals, especially younger persons, only experiment with alcohol and drugs, many are chronic users and abusers. Persons with emotional or behavioral problems tend to be at greater risk for engaging in a pattern of abuse (Millman & Botvin, 1983). Chronic drug use not only poses health risks from the drugs themselves but often leads to other serious health concerns that have the potential to interfere with a person's ability to care for personal needs. Some of the effects from commonly abused drugs like alcohol, stimulants, opiates, cannabis, psychedelics, and inhalants include stimulated or depressed central nervous system function, depressed cardiac and respiratory activity, insomnia, nausea and vomiting, hyperactivity, seizures, and unconsciousness (Forman & Randolph, 1987). Further, alcohol and drug use have been associated with increased risk of accident-related injuries, some fatal. For adolescent populations, alcohol consumption has been shown to contribute to death rates as high as 45% for motor vehicle accidents (Mayer, 1983).

Although school-based prevention programs that stress the development of adaptive coping skills hold the greatest promise in attacking the problem, targeting potential abusers and gaining their cooperation in treatment is difficult. Therefore, a variety of outpatient and residential treatment programs exists. Although these programs all stress the importance of associated problem behaviors in addition to the substance abuse itself, many have different philosophies and approaches to treatment (e.g., total abstinence vs. controlled use).

Suicide is another serious concern for individuals with emotional impairments. Whereas studies have shown that a disturbingly high rate of adolescent suicides are alcohol related (Lewinsohn, Rohde, & Seeley, 1994), data have also shown that the majority of adolescents who committed suicide had serious behavioral disorders (Lewinsohn et al., 1994). Many individuals with internalizing disorders, such as depression and schizophrenia, also complete suicides. Obviously, prevention is the only treatment of choice. Some ways to work toward the goal of prevention include reducing the prescribed dosages of medications and limiting the availability of lethal weapons. To be effective, however, prevention efforts must focus on

improving the mental health atmosphere of the school as well as that of the home and must be implemented as early as possible. The Fairfax County Public Schools have developed an excellent prevention program aimed at the adolescent. For information about the program, contact the Fairfax County School District in Fairfax, Virginia. For a comprehensive volume on child suicide, Pfeffer's (1986) *The Suicidal Child* is recommended.

••

CASE EXAMPLE: NATHAN

Nathan is a 17-year-old boy with a history of developmental as well as accident-related problems. Beginning in early childhood, he was frequently taken to the emergency room for injuries that his brothers never seemed to incur. On more than one occasion, Nathan had a broken leg set and his head stitched for cuts he sustained during falls. To his parents' dismay, Nathan did not take care of himself any better when he became an adolescent. In fact, in many ways things became worse. When he learned to drive, his impulsive nature resulted in a number of accidents with the family car. Nathan wanted friends so badly that he took dares and needless risks to impress them. He would take alcohol from the bar in his own home and rifle through medicine cabinets in the homes of friends and relatives looking for drugs. Although he gave a lot away, he also began abusing drugs and alcohol himself. His last admission to the emergency room was for a drug overdose.

••

Receptive and Expressive Language

A number of problems can put an individual at risk for self-destructive behavior, and perceived incompetence is one. Studies of children with speech and language problems indicate a high incidence of other emotional and behavioral impairments, including anxious and avoidant disorders, oppositional defiant behaviors, conduct disorders, and attention-deficit/hyperactivity disorders (Beitchman, Nair, Clegg, Ferguson, & Patel, 1986). Regardless of whether a language problem is primary or secondary to an emotional impairment, it places an individual at risk for developing other problems. Whereas some individuals overcome their language problems with little residual effects, many continue to experience language difficulties that further compound their situation. Language problems not only have the potential to disrupt interpersonal communication and thus affect social functioning, but can also cause problems with a person's capacity to function independently, including achieving financial self-sufficiency.

The disturbance of language is frequently seen in some of the more pervasive developmental disorders, such as autism (DeMyer, Hingtgen, & Jackson, 1981). In fact, many children with autism who are verbal exhibit pronominal reversals, immature grammar, and difficulties with abstract language. The language of the child with autism clearly distinguishes him or her from other seriously disturbed children with language disorders, such as children with schizophrenia. The structure of language for those with schizophrenia may be normal but the content is not. Often the inappropriateness of logic and oddities of thought are reflected in the expressive language (American Psychiatric Association, 1994). Although it is beyond the scope of this chapter to describe remediation techniques, perhaps a reminder is in order that intervening with language problems from a social-context perspective may reap the greatest benefit for this population (Kretschmer, 1986). Conant, Budoff, and Hecht (1983) devised materials and activities for this purpose that closely adhere to rules of discourse. Individuals who limit their verbalizations or who do not respond in self-selected situations (e.g., are electively mute) may be more likely to benefit from interventions based on social learning theory. For example, in the electively mute child, increases in verbalization have been achieved with self-modeling techniques (Kehle, Cressy, & Owen, 1990).

•••

CASE EXAMPLE: ADAM

Adam, a third-grade student, has always had trouble in school. His parents were aware of his problems, most notably with peers, even before he entered kindergarten. The other children often made fun of the way Adam talked. The more he struggled to express himself, the more he was ridiculed. The speech therapist recently informed Adam's parents that he has a serious speech-articulation and language problem. Adam has resisted working on his problems; in fact, he becomes angry when others offer to help. This response has seriously impaired his interactions with his teachers and with the other children. Adam is a loner. He is the last to be asked to participate in games or to be invited to sleep over at another child's house. He has recently begun complaining about stomach pains and headaches and is having problems sleeping. The school psychologist who evaluated Adam is worried that he might be depressed. The psychologist plans to meet individually with Adam and to involve him in a social skills training group.

•••

Learning and Cognition

Academic skills deficits, especially in the area of reading, have been shown to be one of the strongest correlates with emotional and behavioral disorders in children and adolescents (Wells & Forehand, 1985). Studies have shown that learning problems are correlated with a higher rate of aggression (Lewis, Shanok, Balla, & Bard, 1980), as well as being related to a lack of participation in school due to truancy and absenteeism. These findings do not mean, however, that emotional and behavioral problems inevitably lead to learning problems. It is just as likely that the reverse is true: Learning problems and academic failure may lead to the emotional and behavioral problems of this population. In this case, the focus of intervention needs to be on improved learning.

Although pharmacologic therapy aimed at improving learning has been tried when behaviors are interfering with academic performance, especially with children who have attention-deficit/hyperactivity disorders, its effectiveness in improving learning has not been demonstrated (Chase & Clement, 1985). Instead, direct, behaviorally oriented interventions have been shown to be most effective in improving academic performance (Elliott & Shapiro, 1990; Kesler, 1987). These interventions have the advantage of potentially reducing some of the disruptive behavior problems while enhancing learning. Hoge and Andrews (1987) reviewed a number of studies that examined the effectiveness of modifying academic performance and of managing specific classroom behaviors to improve learning. Attempts to modify academic performance typically are made by increasing the amount of work completed, whereas modifying classroom behavior is affected by manipulating behaviors that might facilitate or detract from learning (e.g., on- or off-task behaviors). Hoge and Andrews concluded that manipulating academic performance compared with modifying classroom behavior resulted in far greater improvement in learning. Although attempts at modifying classroom behavior were successful, that is, the behaviors changed in the desired direction, this change did not have the anticipated effect on achievement.

Shapiro (1986) drew similar conclusions from his review of this research. He found that academic achievement was more improved by increasing the content mastered and the amount of time engaged in academic tasks than by other means. Although the diverse learning styles of individuals should not be overlooked (see Polce, 1987, for a review), it is widely known that "time on task" serves as a good predictor of how much is learned. In fact, it is unlikely that increases in the amount of content learned will occur if time engaged in academic tasks is not increased. Homework can be used to extend this time. Although many expect homework to yield academic benefits, research has shown that much of the homework that is assigned not only is inconsistent with validated instructional techniques (Keith, 1986; McDermott, Goldman, & Verenne, 1984), but also is improperly implemented (Olympia, Jenson, Clark, & Sheridan, 1992; Rhode, Jenson, & Reavis, 1993). Regularly scheduled, appropriate homework is an important intervention with individuals who have learning problems. To conform to the best teaching practice, homework assignments should be (1) designed to parallel classroom curriculum and instruction, (2) properly introduced, (3) allowed sufficient time for mastery of a given instructional step, and (4) graded immediately for feedback.

In addition to homework, a number of other methods are used to enhance academic performance. Although it is beyond the scope of this chapter to provide a comprehensive analysis of these techniques, a brief description is warranted. Many researchers have examined the effectiveness of self-management, that is, the application of contingencies to one's own behavior. Self-management, which typically involves self-monitoring, self-evaluation, and self-reinforcement, is an extremely effective method for improving academic skills (Childs, 1983; Shapiro, 1986). This method not only has the advantage of being more efficient (the reinforcer is always present) but also has been shown to increase generalization in a variety of settings (Rhode, Morgan, & Young, 1983). Another unique feature of self-management is its potential to increase independent learning. Self-management incorporates techniques for contingency control and involves the use of self-instruction, a strategy that has been documented to be effective in improving learning (Fox & Kendall, 1983).

Manipulating group contingencies is another useful method. Several studies have shown that group control of contingencies can be an effective means of improving academic achievement (Shapiro & Goldberg, 1986). Other effective techniques include cooperative learning (Slavin,

Madden, & Leavey, 1984), peer tutoring (Greenwood et al., 1984), and parent training (O'Leary, Pelham, Rosenbaum, & Price, 1976).

Elliott and Shapiro (1990) stated that one component underlying the various methods that have been effective in improving academic performance is contingent reinforcement. It is, therefore, critical that opportunities for reinforcement be made available, regardless of the method selected. Even with this approach, some individuals with emotional and behavioral impairments will not benefit. When emotional or behavioral problems (e.g., depression, anxiety, or psychosis) are the primary deterrents to learning, the most effective interventions are those aimed directly at improving the emotional status of the individual. For example, in cases in which anxiety plays the key role, counterconditioning procedures (e.g., relaxation training, anxiety hierarchy construction, systematic desensitization, and forced exposure), modeling, operant procedures (e.g., shaping and positive reinforcement), and self-control procedures (e.g., self-monitoring, relaxation, self-reinforcement and self-punishment, self-instruction, and stimulus control) can be used.

CASE EXAMPLE: DAVID

Basic reading and arithmetic have been problems for David for several years. Being in junior high school has not changed things. He will not follow the teacher's directions and argues when required to complete his work. Even when David does his homework, he often fails to turn it in. The teacher really cares about David and works hard to teach him basic academic skills. She even works after school for several hours each week, teaching him reading and arithmetic skills. Unfortunately, David seems to forget these the next day. He is extremely frustrated and has begun referring to himself as a "retard." Over the past several weeks, David has started to skip school. He is often found riding his skateboard around shopping mall parking lots. His classroom teacher has decided

to structure the curriculum in a way that ensures that there are well-sequenced steps that require mastery before moving onto the next and that he has multiple opportunities to respond. Frequent feedback and rewards for performance will also be planned.

Mobility

Individuals with emotional impairments rarely experience mobility problems. These individuals generally have no difficulty ambulating unless gross motor impairment exists in addition to the emotional problems. Problems with ambulation that are related to emotional impairment may, however, be the result of medication side effects. Emotional problems rarely immobilize a person, but immobilization is seen with a catatonic-type schizophrenic disorder (American Psychiatric Association, 1994). In either case, medication adjustment may relieve the problem. There is little doubt that psychotropic agents can affect motor capacity (Nicholson & Ward, 1984). Even with individuals who elect not to ambulate (e.g., those with phobias and anxiety disorders), medication therapy may have positive effects, especially when used in conjunction with nonmedication, or behavioral, therapy techniques (Hutchens, 1987).

Self-Direction

Lack of self-direction, which plagues many individuals with emotional impairments, is rarely the primary referral concern, but it can have serious ramifications for learning and daily functioning. Although most individuals display dependency during development, a fact that is considered a crucial stepping-stone for normal, independent behavior later in life (Ainsworth, 1979), most people eventually assume responsibility for their own lives. Some people, however, passively allow others to assume this responsibility. These individuals not only show excessive reliance, or dependence, on the environment for direction but also show a lack of self-initiated motivation. Children may have difficulty starting or finishing academic tasks without a great amount of assistance. This behavior, of course, has the potential to become avoidant or manipulative. These problems tend to cluster with other problems that reflect internalizing disorders, such as anxiety, withdrawal, poor peer relations (may show a tendency to interact with persons younger then themselves), and fearfulness (Achenbach & Edelbrock, 1978). Other associated behaviors include lack of self-confidence, avoidance and manipulative behavior, poor independent-work habits, and basic skills deficits (McBride & McFarland, 1987). The lack of independent decision-making behavior may, therefore, be a function of any of these deficits.

It is important to assess the actual deficit, whether it is a cognitive or a learning deficit, a social skill deficit, or a behavioral problem. Interventions that focus on the deficiency area will be most effective. *Skillstreaming the Elementary School Child* by McGinnis and Goldstein (1984) and Swift and Spivack's (1978) *Alternative Teaching Strategies* may be helpful for dealing with skill deficiencies, but they do not present the proper intervention for individuals whose lack of self-direction is rooted in a lack of secure attachment or is fostered by parent behaviors that encourage dependency and discourage self-initiative (Schaefer & Millman, 1981).

Capacity for Independent Living

Deficits in what Barkley (1985) referred to as "rule-governed behavior" make it difficult for these individuals to live independently. They respond more readily to the immediately available reinforcers in the environment and are what Skinner (1954) called "contingency governed." They show greater concern for what will happen to themselves than for how their behavior affects others. Such persons are delayed in the development of basic social skills and are uncooperative and extremely competitive. They also tend to be rejected by peers. Whereas they are not necessarily disliked by peers, even individuals who do not

show "retarded development" in basic social skills are often neglected socially. The fact that individuals with emotional and behavioral problems have serious social skills problems (either skill or performance deficits) means that they often have no significant, or meaningful, relationships. This situation, combined with a lack of basic academic skills, can easily lead to decreased independence.

Traditional approaches to therapy, such as catharsis and insight-oriented treatments, have not been particularly effective in improving the social deficits (Kazdin, 1985). Whereas deficits in rule-governed behavior are difficult to remedy, programs have been developed that emphasize problem solving, conflict negotiation, aggression control, and social skills training (Goldstein, Glick, Reiner, Zimmerman, & Coultry, 1987; Morgan & Jenson, 1988). Behavioral therapy that modifies both parent and child behaviors within the context of the home and community have shown the greatest effects (Wells & Forehand, 1985), particularly those using time out, point systems, reinforcement, and precision request making (Forehand & McMahon, 1981; Gelfand, Jenson, & Drew, 1988).

The capacity for independence, however, is not only determined in the social arena. In addition to lacking the basic academic skills, many of these individuals lack the capacity to learn independently. Learning how to learn is a critical element to success, regardless of academic ability (Davenport, 1984). Research has shown that these skills are not acquired naturally nor are they specifically taught in schools (Gettinger & Knopik, 1987). Helpful guidelines for teaching study skills and improving homework compliance have been written for both teachers and parents (see Olympia et al., 1992).

Economic Self-Sufficiency

As mentioned previously, individuals with emotional and behavior problems often lack the requisite academic skills necessary for employment as an adult. Not only have they failed to develop the proper study skills to facilitate independence in learning, but they also have serious deficits in basic subject matter areas. Reading difficulties are particularly noteworthy because reading is critical for employment and for other daily activities (Gelfand et al., 1988). As discussed in an earlier section (learning and cognition), direct behavioral treatment programs are likely to be most effective in improving these academic skills deficits.

Improving basic skills, however, is a small part when planning for the integration of this population into the workforce. It is critical that vocational skills are taught in secondary educational programs and that transition planning be a part of the individual's educational plan. It is critical that job placement match the strengths of the individual seeking the work; therefore, it is important to solicit the assistance of guidance counselors, special educators, and vocational specialists who know the individual and know the work sites.

Far too often individuals are placed in jobs in which they have no interest or for which they lack the skills to perform the required job tasks. One of the most typical job sites is a fast-food restaurant. Although these businesses are often willing to hire individuals with disabilities, the job that is required of them is often inappropriate for them. Fast-food restaurants require employees to work fast and to relate well to the customers. Oftentimes individuals with intellectual disabilities perform tasks rather slowly, and many are not adept in social interactions, especially those with high demands. Frustration and, thus, increased behavior problems and job terminations often result from such mismatches. Careful planning and the development of closer relationships with the work sites can alleviate this problem. Goodman and Iseman (1992) also recommended that the individuals' job interests be explored further and that the individuals be provided with more information about job opportunities. Further, these individuals need to be taught how to advocate for themselves more on the job (and for the job) and learn about proper work habits (i.e., being on time

and dressing appropriately), work attitudes (i.e., responding appropriately to authority), and work behaviors (i.e., working for their pay rather than sitting down on the job).

Despite the fact that some funds have been made available to financially assist individuals with developmental disabilities throughout their lifetime, resources are scarce and often difficult to find. Besides, the personal and societal costs are too great to ignore the need for these individuals to participate in the workforce.

CASE EXAMPLE: JAMES

James is a disappointment to his parents. Although he tests well, he has never applied himself in school. Most family members are also bright, but high achievers. His parents are both physicians, and his sister is a law student. James has never lived up to family expectations. He lived at home until he was 23 years old. James probably would not have moved out then, but his father insisted that he find his own apartment. One of James's basic problems is that he cannot keep a job. Just as he had difficulty with his teachers' and parents' requests, he has had difficulty taking orders from his employers. Although he does not talk back to the boss, he often insults customers with curt comments. James was fired from his last job. He was suspected of stealing tires from the back warehouse. Just last week, James made a near fatal suicide attempt with a handgun. James's parents deny that he is depressed but admit that their son does not have any present, or future, goals.

FINAL THOUGHTS

A large number of children with mental retardation and developmental disorders have significant behavioral disabilities. It has become increasingly apparent over the past two decades, in particular, since the development of the Primary Mental Health Project (Cowen et al., 1975), that the treatment of serious behavior and emotional problems is a complex task and one that is often unsuccessful. Individuals who have been identified as being at risk for developing problems that can be resistant to treatment, such as children with mental retardation, should, therefore, be provided with the opportunity to learn skills that facilitate adjustment. Although little can be done to reverse the course of the intellectual disability, there are effective ways to reduce the chances of a child's developing further problems. If service providers are to have any chance of complying with the legislative mandate for a least restrictive environment and of working toward the goal of including these children in the mainstream, then attention must be paid to their special emotional and behavioral needs.

REFERENCES

Achenbach, T. M. (1982). *Developmental psychopathology* (2nd ed.). New York: Wiley.

Achenbach, T. M., & Edelbrock, C. S. (1978). The classification of child psychopathology: A review and analysis of empirical efforts. *Journal of Consulting & Clinical Psychology, 78,* 1275–1301.

Achenbach, T. M., & Edelbrock, C. S. (1979). The Child Behavior Profile: II. Boys aged 12–16 and girls 6–11 and 12–16. *Journal of Consulting & Clinical Psychology, 47,* 223–233.

Ainsworth, M. D. S. (1979). Infant–mother attachment. *American Psychologist, 34,* 932–937.

American Psychiatric Association. (1994). *Diagnostic and statistical manual of mental disorders* (4th ed.). Washington, DC: Author.

Barkley, R. A. (1985). Attention deficit disorders. In P. H. Bornstein & A. E. Kazdin (Eds.), *Handbook of clinical behavior therapy with children* (pp. 158–217). Homewood, IL: Dorsey Press.

Beitchman, J. H., Nair, R., Clegg, M., Ferguson, B., & Patel, P. G. (1986). Prevalence of psychiatric disorders in children with speech and language disorders. *Journal of the American Academy of Child Psychiatry, 25,* 528–535.

Cepeda, M. L. (1989). Nonstimulant psychotropic medication: Side effects of children's cognition and behavior. In C. R. Reynolds & E. Fletcher-Janzen (Eds.), *Handbook of clinical child neuropsychology* (pp. 475–485). New York: Plenum Press.

Chase, S. N., & Clement, P. W. (1985). Effects of self-reinforcement and stimulants on academic performance in children with attention deficit disorder. *Journal of Clinical Child Psychology, 14,* 323–333.

Childs, R. E. (1983). Teaching rehearsal strategies for spelling to mentally retarded children. *Education and Training of the Mentally Retarded, 18,* 318–320.

Cole, C., & Gardner, W. (1993). Psychotherapy with developmentally delayed children. In T. R. Kratochwill & R. J. Morris (Eds.), *Handbook of psychotherapy with children and adolescents* (pp. 426–471). Boston: Allyn & Bacon.

Conant, S., Budoff, M., & Hecht, B. (1983). *Teaching language-disabled children: A communication games intervention.* Cambridge, MA: Brookline.

Council for Children with Behavioral Disorders. (1989). *A new proposed definition and terminology to replace "serious emotional disturbance" in Education of the Handicapped Act.* Reston, VA: Council for Children with Behavioral Disorders, Council for Exceptional Children (1920 Association Drive, Reston, VA 22091).

Cowen, E. L., Trost, M. A., Lorion, R. P., Dorr, D., Izzo, L. D., & Isaacson, R. V. (1975). *New ways in school mental health: Early detection and prevention of school maladaption.* New York: Human Sciences Press.

Davenport, E. (1984). Study skills: Tools of the trade to make studying easier and more efficient. *Early Years, 15,* 43–44.

DeMyer, M. K., Hingtgen, J. N., & Jackson, R. K. (1981). Infantile autism reviewed: A decade of research. *Schizophrenia Bulletin, 7,* 388–451.

Edelbrock, C. S., & Achenbach, T. M. (1980). A typology of Child Behavior Profile patterns: Distribution and correlates for disturbed children aged 6–16. *Journal of Abnormal Child Psychology, 8,* 441–470.

Elliott, S. N., & Shapiro, E. S. (1990). Intervention techniques and programs for academic performance problems. In T. B. Gutkin & C. R. Reynolds (Eds.), *The handbook of school psychology* (pp. 635–660). New York: Wiley.

Forehand, R., & McMahon, R. J. (1981). *Helping the noncompliant child: A clinician's guide to parent training.* New York: Guilford Press.

Forman, S. G., & Randolph, M. K. (1987). Children and drug abuse. In A. Thomas & J. Grimes (Eds.), *Children's needs: Psychological perspectives* (pp. 182–189). Washington, DC: National Association of School Psychologists.

Forness, S., & MacMillan, D. (1989). Mental retardation and the special education system. *Annals of Psychiatry, 19,* 190–196.

Fox, D. E. C., & Kendall, P. C. (1983). Thinking through academic problems: Applications of cognitive behavior therapy to learning. In T. R. Kratochwill (Ed.), *Advances in school psychology* (Vol. 3, pp. 269–301). Hillsdale, NJ: Erlbaum.

Gelfand, D. M., Jenson, W. R., & Drew, C. J. (1988). *Understanding child behavior disorders.* New York: Holt, Rinehart, & Winston.

Gettinger, M., & Knopik, S. N. (1987). Children and study skills. In A. Thomas & J. Grimes (Eds.), *Children's needs: Psychological perspectives* (pp. 594–602). Washington, DC: National Association of School Psychologists.

Goldstein, A. P., Glick, B., Reiner, S., Zimmerman, D., & Coultry, T. M. (1987). *Aggression replacement training: A comprehensive intervention for aggressive youth.* Champaign, IL: Research Press.

Goodman, B., & Iseman, S. (1992). *Transition services and IEP technical manuscript.* Unpublished manuscript.

Greenwood, C. R., Dinwiddie, G., Terry, B., Wade, L., Stanley, S. O., Thibadeau, S., & Delquadri, J. C. (1984). Teacher versus peer-mediated instruction: An ecobehavioral analysis of achievement outcomes. *Journal of Applied Behavior Analysis, 17,* 521–538.

Gresham, F. M., & Gansle, K. A. (1992). Misguided assumptions of DSM–III–R: Implications for school psychological practice. *School Psychology Quarterly, 7*(2), 79–95.

Gualtieri, C. T., Golden, R. N., & Fahs, J. J. (1983). New developments in pediatric psychopharmacology. *Developmental Behavioral Pediatrics, 4,* 202–209.

Hoge, R. D., & Andrews, D. A. (1987). Enhancing academic performance: Issues in target selection. *School Psychology Review, 16,* 228–238.

Hutchens, T. A. (1987). Children and medication. In A. Thomas & J. Grimes (Eds.), *Children's needs: Psychological perspectives* (pp. 356–364). Washington, DC: National Association of School Psychologists.

Individuals with Disabilities Education Act of 1990, 20 U.S.C. §1401 (1992).

Kazdin, A. E. (1985). Alternative approaches to the diagnosis of childhood disorders. In P. H. Bornstein & A. E. Kazdin (Eds.), *Handbook of clinical behavior therapy with children* (pp. 3–43). Homewood, IL: Dorsey Press.

Kehle, T. J., Cressy, E. T., & Owen, S. V. (1990). The use of self-modeling as an intervention in school psychology: A case study of an elective mute. *School Psychology Review, 10,* 115–121.

Keith, T. Z. (1986). *Homework.* Kappa Delta Phi Classroom Practice Series: West Lafayette, IN: Kappa Delta Phi.

Kesler, J. (1987). *Corrective reading: A method for changing the learning rate of behavior disordered children.* Unpublished master's thesis, University of Utah, Salt Lake City.

Koller, H., Richardson, S., Katz, M., & McLaren, J. (1982). Behavior disturbance in childhood and the early adult years in populations who were and were not mentally retarded. *Journal of Preventive Psychiatry, 1,* 453–468.

Kretschmer, R. (1986, April). *Language as a communication process: Implications for assessment and programming.* Paper presented at the convention of the National Association of School Psychologists, Hollywood, FL.

Lewinsohn, P. M., Rohde, P., & Seeley, J. R. (1994). Psychosocial risk factors for future adolescent suicide attempts. *Journal of Counseling and Clinical Psychology, 62*(2), 297–305.

Lewis, D. O., Shanok, S. S., Balla, D. A., & Bard, B. (1980). Psychiatric correlates of severe reading disabilities in an incarcerated delinquent population. *Journal of the American Academy of Child Psychiatry, 19,* 611–622.

Mayer, W. (1983). Alcohol abuse and alcoholism: The psychologist's role in prevention, research, and treatment. *American Psychologist, 38,* 1116–1121.

McBride, C. K., & McFarland, M. A. (1987). Children and dependency. In A. Thomas & J. Grimes (Eds.), *Children's needs: Psychological perspectives* (pp. 151–156). Washington, DC: National Association of School Psychologists.

McDermott, R. P., Goldman, S. V., & Verenne, H. (1984). When school goes home: Problems in the organization of homework. *Teachers College Record, 85*(3), 391–405.

McGinnis, E., & Forness, S. R. (1988). Psychiatric diagnosis: A further test of the special education hypothesis. *Monographs in Behavioral Disorders, 11,* 3–10.

McGinnis, E., & Goldstein, A. P. (1984). *Skillstreaming the elementary school child.* Champaign, IL: Research Press.

Millman, R. B., & Botvin, G. J. (1983). Substance use, abuse and dependence. In M. D. Levin, W. B. Carey, A. C. Crocker, & R. T. Gross (Eds.), *Developmental behavioral pediatrics* (pp. 683–708). New York: Saunders.

Morgan, D., & Jenson, W. R. (1988). *Teaching behaviorally disordered children: Preferred practices.* Columbus, OH: Merrill.

Nicholson, A. N., & Ward, J. (1984). Psychotropic drugs and performance. *British Journal of Clinical Pharmacology, 18*(Suppl. 1).

O'Leary, D. K., Pelham, W. E., Rosenbaum, A., & Price, G. H. (1976). Behavioral treatment of hyperkinetic children. *Clinical Pediatrics, 15,* 510–515.

Olympia, D., Jenson, W. R., Clark, E., & Sheridan, S. (1992). Training parents to facilitate homework completion: A model for home–school collaboration. In S. L. Christenson & J. C. Conoley (Eds.), *Home–school collaboration: Building a fundamental educational resource* (pp. 309–331). Washington, DC: National Association of School Psychologists.

Pfeffer, C. R. (1986). *The suicidal child.* New York: Guilford Press.

Polce, M. E. (1987). Children and learning styles. In A. Thomas & J. Grimes (Eds.), *Children's needs: Psychological perspectives* (pp. 325–335). Washington, DC: National Association of School Psychologists.

Rhode, G., Jenson, W. R., & Reavis, H. K. (1993). *The tough kid book.* Longmont, CO: Sopris West.

Rhode, G., Morgan, D. P., & Young, K. R. (1983). Generalization and maintenance of treatment gains of behaviorally handicapped students from resource rooms to regular classrooms using self-evaluation procedures. *Journal of Applied Behavior Analysis, 16,* 171–188.

Schaefer, C. E., & Millman, H. L. (1981). *How to help children with common problems.* New York: Van Nostrand Reinhold.

Shapiro, E. S. (1986). Behavior modification: Self-control and cognitive procedures. In R. P. Barrett (Ed.), *Severe behavior disorders in the mentally retarded* (pp. 61–97). New York: Plenum Press.

Shapiro, E. S., & Goldberg, R. (1986). A comparison of group contingencies in increased spelling performances among sixth grade students. *School Psychology Review, 15,* 546–559.

Skinner, B. F. (1954). *Science and human behavior.* New York: Macmillan.

Slavin, R. E., Madden, N. A., & Leavey, M. (1984). Effects of team assisted individualization on the mathematics achievement of academically handicapped and nonhandicapped students. *Journal of Educational Psychology, 76,* 813–819.

Swift, M. S., & Spivack, G. (1978). *Alternative teaching strategies.* Champaign, IL: Research Press.

Utah State Office of Education. (1993). *The Utah state board of education special education rules.* Salt Lake City, UT: Author.

Wells, K. C., & Forehand, R. (1985). Conduct and oppositional disorders. In P. H. Bornstein & A. E. Kazdin (Eds.), *Handbook of clinical behavior therapy with children* (pp. 218–265). Homewood, IL: Dorsey Press.

Autistic Disorder

Ronald C. Eaves

LEARNING GOALS

Upon completion of this chapter the reader will be able to

■ define and describe autism;

■ describe three major characteristics of persons with autism;

■ discuss treatment ideas for self-injurious behavior, aggression, and language development;

■ review the key issues related to cognition and especially to language; and

■ define facilitated communication and discuss its strengths and weaknesses as an intervention.

FUNCTIONAL DESCRIPTION

Autistic disorder, or autism, has had a relatively brief history marked by confusion, controversy, and change. More than 50 years ago, when Kanner first described it, autism was considered a rare type of childhood psychosis. Today, it represents the most prevalent severe emotional disorder of childhood.

Many different terms have been used to describe individuals who are now commonly diagnosed as having autistic disorder. Originally, Kanner (1943) argued that autism represented no more than 10% of children then broadly considered to be suffering from childhood psychosis. At the time, the most common form of childhood psychosis was termed *childhood schizophrenia*. Through the years, other terms were suggested, sometimes offering a unique classification system (e.g., primary and secondary autism), but

often simply fractionating the population into smaller segments [e.g., atypical personality development (Rank, 1949), symbiotic psychosis (Mahler,1953)]. Following Rimland's (1964) synthesis of the knowledge base, *autism* became a more commonplace label, ultimately supplanting alternative rubrics.

Unfortunately, the confusion over terminology did not end with Rimland's (1964) work. As the research base grew, writers proposed a variety of new diagnostic labels for children who seemed to manifest features that were distinctive from classic autism. The progression of revisions of the *Diagnostic and Statistical Manual of Mental Disorders* (DSM; American Psychiatric Association, 1980, 1987, 1994) illustrates this development. The third edition of the DSM included the umbrella term, Pervasive Developmental Disorders (PDDs). This classification included infantile autism, childhood onset PDD, and atypical PDD as subcategories. A revision of the third edition of the DSM (DSM–III–R; American Psychiatric Association, 1987) contained just two subcategories: autistic disorder and PDD not otherwise specified (NOS). Just recently, the fourth edition of the DSM has been published (DSM–IV; American Psychiatric Association, 1994). In this nosology, autism is one of five PDDs; the others are Rett's disorder, childhood disintegrative disorder, Asperger's disorder, and PDD NOS. Although Rett's disorder has a relatively distinctive set of diagnostic features, the last three subcategories share many features with classic autism. For instance, childhood disintegrative disorder is manifested after a period of normal development lasting for at least the first 2 years of life; autistic disorder must be manifested prior to 3 years of age. Asperger's disorder is distinguished from autistic disorder by its general lack of delay in cognitive and language development. The subcategory, PDD NOS, remains for use with individuals who fail to meet the criteria for other subcategories but who clearly exhibit pervasive disorders of development.

Differential Diagnosis

Autistic disorder represents a reasonably distinct gestalt to those who have actually worked with an array of individuals with autism over a long period of time. Yet, there are at least four reasons that the disorder is often misdiagnosed:

1. Because the condition is rare (roughly 2 to 15 per 10,000 in the population), few professionals have extensive experience with it.

2. Autism shares a number of characteristics with other disorders; in fact, Wing and Attwood (1987) offered reasons for confusing autism with 16 other conditions. For instance, about 75% of people with autism and all people with mental retardation exhibit low IQs and both may manifest stereotypic body movements. The person with autism may appear to be hearing impaired and thus be confused with that population. Speech and language disorders (including mut-

ism) are quite common among individuals with autism.

3. Because they usually demonstrate severe disorders in more than one domain, children with autism are often simply labeled *multidisabled.* However, the placement in facilities for people with multiple disabilities is frequently motivated by a lack of an appropriate alternative placement rather than by ignorance of the actual condition.

4. The inability of the professional community to establish a stable classification system has undoubtedly caused confusion among practitioners with little or no personal experience with people with autism.

Characteristics

Eaves and Hooper (1987–88) and Eaves (1990) completed factor analyses of behavior commonly ascribed to children with autism. They found evidence to suggest five factors: (a) Affective and Cognitive Indifference, (b) Expressive Affect, (c) Passive Affect, (d) Anxiety/Fear, and (e) Cognition. In a more recent analysis (Eaves, 1994) the Expressive Affect, Passive Affect, and Anxiety/Fear factors aggregated into a single Affect factor.

Affective and Cognitive Indifference

According to Eaves (1990), affective and cognitive indifference was the primary feature of people who clearly met the diagnostic criteria of autism in his studies. For instance, individuals labeled *atypical*—a label assigned to those who share some of the features of autism but differ from it in important ways—or simply, pervasive developmentally disordered, generally received their lowest scores on the Affective and Cognitive Indifference factor. Eaves (1990) speculated that this factor reflected lower-order arousal controlled by the brain stem and cerebellum.

Among the dimensions and behavior contributing to the Affective and Cognitive Indifference factor were

- autism (e.g., avoidance of eye contact, blank expression, lack of emotion, preference for being left alone, dislike for hugging);

- hand and body use (e.g., finger flicking, hand shaking, rocking, staring at hands close up);

- sensory stimulation (e.g., spinning jar lids, plates; playing with spinning tops; fascination for rushing air and "crinkly" sounds; unusual interest in texture);

- peculiar mannerisms (e.g., unwillingness to use hands, unusual sensitivity to smells, making peculiar sounds inside the mouth);

- fascination for objects (e.g., saving or hoarding materials; carrying one particular object at all times; fascination for elevators, fans, lawn mowers, etc.); and

- no response to pain.

It should be mentioned that the majority of these symptoms involve motor behavior and four of the five senses: vision, hearing, touching, and tasting.

Affect

This factor characterized individuals with autism who were relatively outgoing and readily interacted with the environment, but in quite distorted ways. It was related more closely to the Affective and Cognitive Indifference factor than to the Cognitive factor. Among the dimensions and behavior contributing to the Affect factor were

- eating (e.g., not eating everything on the plate, unusually picky eater);

- aggression and conduct (e.g., biting, pulling hair, or scratching others; banging head, biting own hand; whining, crying, or screaming when desires were not met; noncompliant);

- distorted affect (e.g., crying on "happy" occasions; crying without vocalizing);

- anxiety/fear (e.g., overreacting to changes in the environment, believing harmless entities

to be dangerous, excessive fear of loud noises, anxiety around water, fearfulness in crowds); and

- noncommunicative vocalizations (e.g., uttering vocalizations as if they were real words, using little or no functional speech).

Cognition

This factor exhibited a positively skewed distribution among the participants in Eaves's (1990) sample. This result is consistent with two common findings: About 75% of autistic people exhibit low levels of cognitive ability (i.e., IQs ≤ 70), and a sizable proportion of the autistic population remains mute. Among the dimensions and behavior contributing to the Cognition factor were

- savant behavior (e.g., extreme skill in one area, memorization of commercials and advertisements);

- speech (e.g., misusing pronouns, monotonal or "wooden" speech, echolalia, switching from normal to monotonal or glottal speech, loud speech); and

- skill development (e.g., spontaneous use of skill that lags behind elicited use of skill, uneven skill development, exhibiting surprising skill at times).

The factors of autism reflect the three major human attributes: the arousal, affective, and cognitive domains. Unlike many other disabilities, the condition is not characterized by slow development that mirrors the usual developmental sequence. Instead, the individual with autism displays a unique behavioral topography that may be fairly described as strange, distorted, even bizarre. No person with autism demonstrates the full range of the behavioral topography; indeed, it is the individual who exhibits only a few of the relevant symptoms who continues to be difficult to diagnose accurately. However, among those properly labeled as autistic, there are some rough rules of thumb regarding prognosis. First, the individual who shows more social and emotional contact has a better prognosis than one who shows little or no inclination to interact with others. Second, the person who has relatively good cognitive ability has the best prognosis among the population of individuals with autism.

In the remainder of this chapter, I describe treatment approaches for three individuals with autism. Their characteristics place them in the levels just briefly defined. The first youngster, John, is operating at a fundamental autistic level. His behavior may be characterized as manifesting little affective and cognitive content. The second individual, Shaka, displays a more emotional nature but one that is socially unacceptable by virtue of extreme aggression. Finally, there is Rodney, whose relatively high intelligence marks him as a good bet for a happy future in the mainstream of society.

CASE ONE: AFFECTIVE AND COGNITIVE INDIFFERENCE

CASE EXAMPLE: JOHN

John's unusual development was noticed at an early age by his parents. Almost from birth he seemed remote from and uninvolved with the world around him. His mother, Barbara, became concerned early on when John failed to engage in the bonding characteristics she had so enjoyed when nurturing his two older siblings. For instance, he was an indifferent eater, often nursing only a few moments at a time; sometimes he rejected his mother's breast entirely, even when he should have been hungry. In addition, when he was picked up by one or the other of his parents, he showed neither the usual anticipatory response nor the infant smile familiar to every parent. Instead, he seemed entirely content to be left alone in his cradle.

Other early signs of affective development were also absent. Both Barbara and her husband, Tom, agreed that their son seldom made eye contact with either of them. Even when they positioned themselves directly in front of his gaze, they had the chilling sensation that John was looking "through" them rather than at them. His lack of interest in social contact with his parents—indeed, with all human contact—was manifested in many other ways. His usual facial expression was described by his family as "unconcerned," or "just a blank." Although he didn't usually resist hugging and cuddling by his family, there was no mistaking that such expressions of affection held little attraction for him. At other times, particularly when some solitary activity was interrupted, John showed displeasure by resisting; on rare occasions, he displayed true affect through crying and temper tantrums when an activity was interrupted. Although he had considerable exposure to his age peers, as well as his two siblings, John showed no interest in them, preferring his solitary activity to cooperative play.

As John grew into childhood, peculiar physical symptoms began to characterize his behavior. He spent long periods staring intently at the palm of one hand. Gradually, he would become agitated and, with a wide-eyed, hysterical look in his face, begin shaking both hands up and down rapidly. He often held his fingers and hands in a stiff, distorted posture; such behavior was frequently accompanied by an odd flicking motion of his index finger. Other common physical activities included rocking back and forth or side to side, mouthing unfamiliar objects, and an activity that his family members referred to as "dangling." John usually dangled his mother's hair, which was often worn in a ponytail style, but he was attracted to any similar hanging material. For instance, he often grasped a venetian blind cord, jerking it up and down, causing it to bounce or "dance."

Objects had always captured John's attention more readily than did people. Yet, he seldom manipulated objects in expected ways (e.g., toy cars and dolls were held upside down as often as right side up). Also, the objects that John cherished most were often far outside the realm of usual childhood playthings. For John, the opportunity to listen to the sound made by a piece of cellophane was the equivalent of a day in the park to most children. Further, he generally showed far more interest in the texture of objects than would most children. In fact, he spent a significant proportion of time touching materials or rubbing them against his cheek. A favorite texture was that of pencil erasers and other rubbery objects, but soft, cloth fabrics were also favored. It was a rare occasion when he did not have either an eraser or a piece of cloth within easy reach.

Although John's physical appearance was normal, even attractive, and people attributed to him an "intelligent look," as he grew older it become all too obvious that his cognitive development was severely diminished when compared to his age peers. For instance, he did not develop speech; he was entirely mute. Nor did he show any real interest in activities demanding cognition at any level. For instance, magazines, books, movies, and television rarely engaged his attention more than momentarily.

A more troubling attribute was John's increasingly severe self-injurious behavior. As a child of 4 or 5 years of age, he developed a tendency to strike his chin with a closed fist. At first, the blows carried little force and were not alarming. By the time he was 9 years of age, his repertoire of self-destructive behavior had grown to a shocking extent. He continued to hit himself in the chin (and other parts of his face and head), but the force of the blows had become much more severe. Further, he now frequently banged his head against any available stationary object. Beyond that, he bit the back of his right hand so often that he had developed a thick callous.

Observation revealed that John's self-injurious behavior was most often displayed when his parents or his teacher asked him to engage in behavior that he disliked. Examples of requests that marked occasions of self-injury included (a) cleaning up around his desk at school, (b) making eye contact with an adult, (c) eating with appropriate utensils,

(d) changing an activity, and (e) bedtime preparations. The list of occasions was extensive; the common thread seemed to be John's (usually successful) attempt to gain control over others in his environment by exhibiting rather alarming self-injurious behavior.

....

Treatment of Self-Injurious Behavior

Preliminary Considerations

Before the practitioner plans a treatment strategy for self-injurious behavior, it is important to investigate several factors known or presumed to stimulate self-injury. Carr (1982a) developed a screening sequence for this purpose. First, the individual should undergo genetic screening to determine whether or not an anomaly exists. For instance, Lesch-Nyhan and de Lange syndromes have been strongly associated with lip, finger, and tongue biting. In the case of Lesch-Nyhan syndrome, drug treatment using L-5 hydroxytryptophan and carbidopa has been reported to show promising results (Nyhan, 1976). Screening for other biophysical abnormalities should also be conducted. For example, chronic otitis media has been associated with relatively high levels of head banging (de Lissovoy, 1963).

Aside from organic causes, three environmental explanations have been postulated for self-injury and other unwanted behavior: (a) positive reinforcement, (b) negative reinforcement, and (c) self-stimulation. In terms of screening, one first looks for evidence that self-injury serves as a means for obtaining positive reinforcement from the environment. Most commonly, the behavior results in attention from others, particularly when milder, less extreme behavior provides little attention for the individual. In such circumstances, it is anticipated that self-injurious behavior will occur at higher levels in the presence of significant others but may be nonexistent when the person is alone.

Negative reinforcement occurs when an aversive stimulus is removed as a consequence of the person's self-injurious behavior. In this instance, self-injury often serves to avoid aversive demands that are placed on the person (e.g., demands to complete work, attend a task, make eye contact). Given the extreme nature of self-injury and its obvious connection to the demand stimulus, the timid parent or practitioner usually quickly withdraws the demand. Thus, the person is negatively reinforced for the self-injurious behavior and the probability of its repetition on similar, future occasions is increased. This certainly appeared to be the explanation for John's behavior.

Finally, some theorists believe that self-injurious behavior serves as its own reinforcer by providing the individual with sensory stimulation. Cogent parallels have been drawn by Carr (1982a) between self-injury in autistic individuals and similar behavior observed in other mammals raised in isolation (cf. Harlow & Harlow, 1962). Indeed, studies of both normal people and those with disabilities indicate that self-injury is elevated under conditions of environmental deprivation. For instance, Levy (1944) reported that head banging disappeared among institutionalized orphans confined to their cribs after toys were introduced. Likewise, Collins (1965) reduced the head banging of a restrained adult with mental retardation by introducing stimulation in the forms of toys, activities, and a radio.

Selecting Treatment Variables

The treatment of choice depends on the practitioner's ability to identify the causes underlying self-injurious behavior. As previously mentioned, genetically determined self-injury may best be treated through drug therapy. The primary objective regarding self-injury associated with disease states (e.g., otitis media) is to gain control over the disease medically. Self-injury associated with both positive and negative reinforcement has been modified environmentally through a variety of operant-conditioning approaches: extinction, time out, differential reinforcement of other behavior (DRO), differential reinforcement of incompatible behavior (DRI), positive punishment, and response cost. Finally, alternative sources of stimulation have most often been used to gain control over self-injury considered to be motivated by self-stimulation.

Several considerations led to the selection of differential reinforcement of incompatible behavior and response cost as procedures to gain control over John's self-injury. Extinction was eliminated as a primary strategy because it works slowly and often results in temporarily elevated levels of the behavior to be modified. Because John's parents and teacher were to be trained to implement the intervention, a procedure that could plausibly demonstrate early positive results was desirable.

Time out is a mild punitive procedure by which the person is removed from a setting following an inappropriate behavior (e.g., head slapping). Consequently, the opportunity to gain reinforcers (e.g., adult attention) available in the setting is also removed. Time out has often been used effectively to reduce self-injurious behavior, but it was not chosen in this case because it would serve to reinforce the very behavior the treatment team sought to eliminate. If the team's judgment was correct, John used self-injurious behavior to avoid aversive demands placed on him. Presumably, time out would provide him with a guaranteed avoidance mechanism.

Positive punishment was not eliminated entirely as a method because it often obtains dramatic results quite quickly (Lovaas, 1969). However, it was selected as a last resort for three reasons. First, other, milder forms of intervention had not been systematically attempted; consequently, the team hoped that the use of positive punishment would prove unnecessary. Second, although John's behavior was initially alarming to see, the team knew that he had engaged in the activity for at least 3 years without serious mutilation or permanent damage. Therefore, the team doubted that there existed a significant risk of such damage during the intervention. Third, because John's parents were uncomfortable with the idea of punishing their severely disabled child, it was doubtful that they could apply any punitive procedure consistently. To the extent that they and his teacher applied the intervention inconsistently, there would be little hope for success.

Finally, the team preferred the use of DRI over DRO because the former offered John a specific, reinforceable, alternative behavior in which to engage that prevented the display of self-injurious behavior. In addition, some research (Tarpley & Schroeder, 1979) has indicated the superiority of DRI over DRO schedules, though both have proven effective in decreasing this target behavior.

Defining Treatment Procedures

Although it is highly desirable to design a treatment plan that is explicit, simple, and clear, that objective is usually met only after a period of trial and error. It is during this early phase that an awareness of alternative procedures is valuable. Although the team knew that an overall goal of the intervention was to remove John's control over the environment and to place that control back with his parents and teacher, the selection of the specific technique within a particular situation was an ongoing determination.

The treatment team decided to begin by placing arbitrary demands on John that they expected might normally precipitate self-injurious behavior. Initially, the team chose tasks that they knew John could perform easily because the team would also be demanding that he not physically abuse himself during the activity. Time periods were kept short (30 seconds) for the same reason. Had the team demanded more challenging and therefore, more aversive activities from John, they could not seriously expect him to control his self-injury. Early attempts to reinforce John with crackers for playing catch with a volleyball (and with no self-injury) failed rather miserably. Although he sometimes managed to complete a 30-second session and to obtain a reinforcer, it re-

mained clear that John was in control of the environmental contingencies. As expected, attempts to extinguish John's self-abusive tantrums had no apparent effect.

At this point the team members hit upon the idea of removing a highly desirable object from John's possession for 5 minutes whenever he injured himself. The procedure is called *response cost*. The primary object removed was John's eraser or cloth, whichever he had with him at the time. It will be recalled that he relished the texture of these objects and seldom went anywhere without them. At first he demonstrated an uncanny ability to find substitute materials (e.g., rubber ball, wash cloth), but the team soon managed to remove all conceivable substitutes from the setting. Under this added contingency, John learned to control his inappropriate self-injurious behavior, ultimately replacing it with a variety of previously aversive behaviors (e.g., counting to 10, picking up toys in a messy room, brushing his teeth). After experiencing success in controlling John's behavior under highly structured circumstances, his parents and teacher were well able to transfer the principles they had learned to a wide variety of situations.

CASE TWO: EXPRESSIVE AFFECT

•••

CASE EXAMPLE: SHAKA

Little information could be gleaned from the records regarding this 23-year-old girl's history. Aside from scant demographic data, all that was known was that she was given up for adoption by her natural mother at birth. Shaka had spent her entire life in state facilities, moving from one mental hospital to another as she grew older. She developed good language skills, though her communication was often disconnected, self-centered, and riddled with profanity.

Like many individuals with autism, Shaka maintained only a tenuous contact with her surroundings. Often, she appeared not to hear when spoken to but clearly did hear sounds within the speech range at other times. Her primary physical manifestation of autism was persistent pacing; usually she wandered in wide circles at a very brisk pace. Other physical symptoms, such as hand gazing, finger posturing, and rocking, were not in evidence.

Unlike John, Shaka was not remote from and indifferent to others. Indeed, she displayed a wide variety of facial expressions, which covered the spectrum from happiness to deep sorrow and violent rage. Yet, her emotions tended to be distorted, frequently failing to conform to environmental circumstances. For instance, during a party when others were decidedly enjoying themselves, Shaka broke into tears. In contrast, Shaka once closed a car door on her hand, breaking two fingers in the process but neither cried nor even grimaced. Similar events indicated that Shaka felt little physical pain.

Shaka's most problematic behavioral displays were gross and socially, quite unacceptable, as well as unhygienic. For instance, she was prone to remove her clothes and masturbate at odd times and places throughout the day. Attempts by hospital staff to interfere with this behavior nearly always resulted in violent physical rejoinders from Shaka. Her physical violence was accompanied by shouted profanities. Indeed, profane language was Shaka's medium; she used it as a painter uses oils. Most of the staff were convinced that Shaka enjoyed the reaction of mortification she frequently received when she undressed, masturbated, and shouted profane epithets at anyone nearby.

During her circular pacing, everyone in the vicinity soon learned to keep an eye on Shaka's location. It was her practice to walk up behind a person and, on passing the individual, to turn swiftly and try to scratch the person in the eyes. She never attacked an individual from the front; apparently, the element of surprise was a key to her tactic. Shaka also howled frequently, as if in pain, without apparent reason. Her howling was so common (some 50 to 100 times each day) that staff and patients alike soon learned to

discriminate Shaka's howl from those signaling genuine emergencies. Finally, Shaka exhibited a deep attraction to odors, most particularly the odor of feces. One of her less endearing habits was to enter a bathroom and wipe her hand around every toilet seat. She also used her hand to gouge her own anal area. Following such behavior, Shaka spent considerable time sniffing the hand that was covered with the scent of fecal matter.

....

Treatment of Aggression, Noncompliance, and Profanity

Preliminary Considerations

The treatment team's decision to begin by improving Shaka's social conduct hinged on four facts. First, some of the targets identified represented a physical danger to other patients and staff members. Second, even when no one was physically hurt as a result, her episodes of aggression, noncompliance, and profanity were very disruptive to ongoing programs, not to mention the emotional equanimity of those around her. Third, extreme behavior such as Shaka's prevented her from making much progress in other areas. For instance, she had never been seriously considered as a candidate for a vocational skills program because of her inappropriate social responses. Last, but quite important in its own right, the team believed that the staff would benefit by learning a procedure that would ultimately place Shaka under their verbal control, thus greatly reducing the need to use rather violent, physical intervention.

Selecting Treatment Variables

Neuropsychological research has demonstrated that affective behavior is under the control of an elaborate neurological system interconnecting all four major units of the brain (i.e., the brain stem, cerebellum, limbic system, and cerebrum; LeDoux & Hirst, 1986). It is currently widely assumed that behavior such as Shaka's is caused by anomalous neurological pathways or chemical aberrations within the system. Like many other patients in her institution, Shaka received drug therapy in the form of Haldol, a neuroleptic, designed to reduce psychotic symptomatology.

The team's environmental analysis of Shaka's behavior led them to believe that she used aggression, noncompliance, and profanity to gain control over her surroundings. For instance, she seemed to take pleasure in asserting her dominance, often placing her face inches away from a staff member while shouting at him or her in an intimidating manner. Also, because the team could identify no eliciting antecedent events that stimulated her behavior, they concluded that most disruptive episodes were provoked by Shaka herself. To be sure, she often sought out groups of people prior to these episodes even though she could have remained apart from the group. The team therefore believed her behavior to be a source of positive reinforcement.

On the basis of the conclusion that Shaka gained gratification from her inappropriate social behavior, the team selected time out as the procedure to reduce its occurrence. Because she rarely spent time alone, the team hoped that isolation would motivate her to comply with their requests in order to rejoin the group. At the same time it was important that Shaka be taught that there were other, more gratifying ways to obtain reinforcement. The team decided to use a DRO to strengthen appropriate behavior.

Defining Treatment Procedures

In keeping with their desire to develop an explicit, simple, and clear treatment plan, the team first drew up a list of aggressive acts, instances of noncompliance, and profane terms that would lead to Shaka's immediate isolation from the group. Next, the team established a set of alternative (DRO) behaviors that would be expected and systematically reinforced by the staff. Essentially, the alternative behaviors were designed to reflect standard rules of comportment: approaching others from the front, saying "please" to make a request, saying "thank you" when a request was granted, using appropriate salutations when joining and leaving a group, and rapid compliance to reasonable requests from the staff. Finally, the team selected a set of activities in which Shaka often participated (e.g., singing, eating, simple board games, building with Duplo blocks). The team intended to use these activities as the forum for their intervention.

Time out requires an area (usually a room) with particular characteristics. In this case, a relatively barren, but clean environment that would produce no reinforcement to its occupant was needed. In addition, the room had to be structurally able to withstand considerable physical violence without falling apart. At the same time the team wished to be able to observe and interact with Shaka at all times when she was placed in time out. Because only a single room with the necessary characteristics was available for use, the team could not implement the treatment program throughout the institutional environment. This limitation meant that special arrangements might be required to ensure that Shaka transferred gains observed in the treatment location to other sites within the institution. On the other hand, by conducting the treatment in a single, well-designed location, the team members were able to control the treatment variables much more effectively.

Intervention began with a series of activities in the treatment room with participation from Shaka, two well-behaved patients, and three staff members. Each patient was prompted to use the standard rules of comportment outlined previously, and each instance of their use was reinforced verbally by one or more of the staff. If a staff member perceived that Shaka was about to exhibit any of the undesirable behaviors, he or she warned Shaka about the consequences of such behavior. When Shaka actually manifested any one of the unacceptable behaviors included in the list, she was immediately told, "Shaka, you're going to time out for (explication of the misdeed)." Upon being placed quickly and efficiently in the time-out room, she was told, "You can come out when you've calmed down."

Rather than specify an exact amount of time during which Shaka remained calm (i.e., no kicking, howling, etc.) as the contingency for rejoining the group, the team varied the required duration from 30 seconds up to 10 minutes. The criterion duration of calm behavior for any given instance of time out was based on the staff's estimate of the degree of violence exhibited by Shaka on that occasion. More violent reactions led to longer requirements of calm.

After these procedures, Shaka showed a marked decrease in the target behaviors and a parallel increase in good comportment. As the treatment progressed, a new, and as it turned out, important activity was spontaneously added to the sessions: the Good Behavior Game, which emphasized the rules of comportment outlined previously. It consisted of role-playing situations invented by the staff and patients with the object of determining what would be the "correct" thing to do in the given situation. The staff believed that the inclusion of this game added significantly to the success of the treatment. Practitioners should be alert to such serendipitous events. They often significantly strengthen well-designed programs.

Transfer of Shaka's new behavioral repertoire to other locations on the institutional campus did not occur automatically. Often the learner must be specifically schooled to recognize the similarities between the treatment-setting conditions and those in other locations that call for the same behavior. Consequently, after the treatment program was well under way and significant improvement had occurred, the team made jaunts to other settings that Shaka habitually frequented: the cafeteria, gymnasium, dormitory, and so on. Although an ideal room for time out was usually not available, the team made the best of available facilities (e.g., the gymnasium equipment room, an empty dorm room). Happily, Shaka quickly transferred her new social comportment skills as soon as she discovered that similar contingencies were applied across all settings.

Of course, Shaka continued to exhibit bizarre behavior that was not specifically addressed in the treatment plan. For instance, her fascination with the smell of feces required a unique program to obtain substantial gains. She was allowed to maintain her pacing because it was not considered a danger and seemed to fulfill a need to expend energy. However, all staff agreed that subsequent treatment programs owed much of their success to elimination of Shaka's aggression, noncompliance, and profanity.

CASE THREE: COGNITIVE BEHAVIOR

••

CASE EXAMPLE: RODNEY

Perhaps because he had always been a handsome, physically healthy child, and one with extremely good fine motor coordination, Rodney's parents, Anne and Bob, failed to attach much significance to his delayed speech and language development. He seldom cried as an infant and rarely produced the cooing, gurgling, and babbling sounds familiar to the parents of normal children. Because he was their first child, neither parent had much prior experience to guide them, and Rodney's pediatrician seemed to think that his lack of vocabulary would eventually be reversed.

As time passed, Anne became more concerned. Not only had Rodney's language skills continued to lag (his speech vocabulary contained some 15 words at age 4 years), his other behavior seemed odd as well. Still, Anne could convince neither Bob nor Rodney's pediatrician that he had any genuine problems. They both admonished Anne not to "smother" the child but to let him develop in his own good time. Eventually Anne became so exasperated, she gathered Rodney's dishes, jar lids, and pot covers and arrived at the physician's office demanding to see the doctor. When he entered the examination room, he was convinced that, indeed, Rodney was not a simple case of developmental delay. For there on the floor, Rodney kept seven jar lids, pot covers, and dishes all spinning simultaneously! His dexterity was amazingly advanced for a child of any age, much less one of 4 years.

Although family physicians often fail to detect the telltale signs of autism, professionals considerably experienced with this population usually have little difficulty in making the correct diagnosis. Such was the case when Rodney was seen by Dr. Largent, the director of a nearby school that specialized in working with children with autism. Along with his language delay and spinning ability, Rodney exhibited many of the symptoms of classic autism. For instance, he was fascinated by water play and rushing air (whether generated by wind, fan, or air conditioning). He rarely stacked his blocks; instead he placed them in horizontal lines. He spent considerable time whirling his body, and he tended to walk on his toes. Finally, he exhibited approach–avoidance behavior toward several objects: fans, elevators, escalators, soft-drink machines, and food. One moment he would seem to be attracted to these objects; the next, he would run away as if frightened by them. Later, when he became interested in drawing, the mechanical objects would maintain a central position in his artwork.

• •

A nonverbal intelligence test administered at the school indicated an IQ of 81—rather low by general population standards but quite high among individuals with autism. This news was presented with enthusiasm by Dr. Largent because fully 75% of children with autism have IQs in the *retarded* range. Further, low IQs are associated with a failure to develop speech; in fact, about 50% of all people with autism do not develop communicative speech (Rimland, 1964). Poor language skills are associated with a poor prognosis and all too frequently, a life outside of mainstream society. Given encouragement by Dr. Largent and the staff they met, Bob and Anne immediately enrolled Rodney in the school.

Speech and Language Acquisition

Preliminary Considerations

A large number of approaches have been used to help people with autism acquire speech and language skills. Without doubt, the most common, broad method employed has been operant conditioning. Lovaas's (1977) work is probably the most widely disseminated and best documented of the operant methodology, but many others have contributed to its literature. Used in isolation, operant techniques have attained mixed results. Although a large proportion of children make significant gains with the approach, many others either fail to learn usable speech or make only minimal gains (Carr, 1982b). In addition, transfer of skills to settings in the general environment and maintenance of skills across time have both been problematical. Although there are many indications that these problems can be addressed within the behavioral approach, others have been led to search for alternative methodologies.

Perhaps the most common alternative during the 1970s and 1980s was the use of sign language. The rationale stemmed from evidence that a significant number of children with autism exhibit auditory dysfunctions in the central nervous system (Paul, 1987). It seemed to follow that, because autistic visual processing tended to be a relative strength for many individuals, the use of visual cues (i.e., signs) would enhance the development of communication. Several researchers (e.g., Barrera, Lobato-Barrera, & Sulzer-Azaroff, 1980; Clarke, Remington, & Light, 1988; Konstantareas, 1987) have debated the virtue of using simultaneous communication, in which the instructor presents both speech and signs together, or sign-alone procedures. At present, empirical results seem to favor the simultaneous approach, at least for higher functioning individuals, but both continue to be used. As with operant approaches, the use of sign language has obtained mixed results; that is, communication skills are sometimes acquired with the use of sign language and sometimes they are not. Also, as with operant technology, individuals with autism often fail to transfer and maintain the skills that they do acquire. Finally, they usually fail to use the communication skills they acquire spontaneously, and there is often an absence of generative signing (i.e., the creation of sign combinations that have not been specifically taught).

A third alternative that has received much publicity during recent years is facilitated communication (Biklen, 1990). Originally developed by Rosemary Crossley in Australia, the objective of facilitated communication is to teach severely impaired individuals to communicate by developing a clear, unambiguous pointing response to an array of alternatives. The array used may take many forms. In some cases, real objects are used. In other cases, two-dimensional images, words, or letters on a language board represent the array of response choices. The most sophisticated devices include speech synthesizers and wrist-mounted keyboards. A critical feature of facilitated communication is the use of a trained adult, who provides a minimum of facilitation needed to compensate for the student's impaired pointing response. As described by Crossley and Remington-Gurney (1992), "The degree of facilitation that was needed varied, ranging from an encouraging hand on the shoulder boosting a client's confidence to the shaping of a client's hand to enable him or her to isolate and extend an index finger for pointing" (p. 33).

Since its introduction in the United States by Douglas Biklen, hundreds of children with autism have received facilitated communication training. Such widespread application soon evoked the interest of television news-magazine broadcasts and the popular print media. Not surprisingly, professionals expressed skepticism toward the approach (Calculator, 1992; Silliman, 1992) and outright alarm that it should have been adopted so broadly without validation through research (Shane,

1993). Indeed, there *have* been serious consequences in the form of legal allegations of sexual abuse brought by children with autism through their facilitators (Bligh & Kupperman, 1993; Prior & Cummins, 1992; Shane, 1993). One critic has argued that advocates of facilitated communication resort to "emotional blackmail" (Schopler, 1992, p. 337) when they admonish facilitator trainees that they will fail unless they have trust in the procedure. Most damning, however, have been the denunciations of four professional groups against the practice: American Psychological Association, Academy of Child and Adolescent Psychiatry, American Association of Mental Retardation, and American Academy of Pediatrics ("APA Denounces Facilitated Communication," 1994).

More recently, experimental research has begun to shed some light on the efficacy of facilitated communication. To date, some 13 publications have sought, in a variety of ways, to evaluate the ability of individuals with severe disabilities to communicate using the Crossley–Biklen approach (Bligh & Kupperman, 1993; Cabay, 1994; Calculator & Singer, 1992; Eberlin, McConnachie, Ibel, & Volpe, 1993; Hudson, Melita, & Arnold, 1993; Klewe, 1993; Moore, Donovan, & Hudson, 1993; Moore, Donovan, Hudson, Dykstra, & Lawrence, 1993; Regal, Rooney, & Wandas, 1994; Smith & Belcher, 1993; Smith, Haas, & Belcher, 1994; Szempruch & Jacobson, 1993; Walker, Jacobson, Paglieri, & Schwartz, 1993). The results of these studies may be summarized in three points:

1. Only one investigation has provided any substantial support for facilitated communication (Calculator & Singer, 1992).

2. Twelve studies indicated that under controlled conditions, individuals were unable to produce literate output using facilitated communication.

3. Many studies provided evidence that facilitators were effectively, though unconsciously, controlling the responses of their disabled charges.

Neither Crossley nor Biklen has responded to the recent spate of experimental research. However, it is likely that they will repeat their earlier admonitions that the rigor demanded in controlled experiments mitigates against the feeling of trust and emotional support that is necessary for clients to use the technique effectively. For instance, Biklen, Morton, Gold, Berrigan, and Swaminathan (1992) described several students who "explained that they cannot type with particular people who do not believe they can type" (p. 14). Another weakness in the current research that Crossley and Biklen will surely mention is the fact that most of the studies included participants with relatively little experience in facilitated communication. Advocates generally consider the technique to require up to 3 years of training to achieve independence of communication. In conclusion, regardless of the continuing debate that is surely ahead, there is presently little reason to reject the advice of Smith et al. (1994) that the "clinical and educational uses of the procedure should be curtailed, and its application restricted to experimental protocols" (p. 366).

Recently, there has been a heightened interest in the *pragmatics* of both signs and speech among individuals with autism (Carr, 1982b). Pragmatics refers to the way one *uses* his or her language and communication skills, in contrast to static estimates of vocabulary size, ability to construct appropriate syntax, and so on. An emphasis in this approach has been incidental teaching, which occurs throughout the environment, in contrast to structured teaching, which occurs primarily in the classroom. The approach has stirred excitement among those who work with people with autism because it addresses some of the most nettlesome problems so far encountered with this population: the transfer of acquired skills, the maintenance of those skills, and the development of generative communication.

Selecting Treatment Variables

As might be evident from the previous discussion, the methodologies in common use are not mutually exclusive. Rather, they represent an historical progression over the past 25 to 30 years that, it is hoped, will culminate in an effective but quite complex systematic program for the improvement of the communication skills of individuals with autism.

The staff at Dr. Largent's school, being well trained, experienced, and quite familiar with the research literature regarding their charges, have developed a long-term speech and language program that includes operant conditioning, sign language, and pragmatics. Given his young age, his modest but nonetheless existent speech vocabulary, and his relatively good cognitive ability, Rodney was a perfect candidate for the program.

Defining Treatment Procedures

The development of speech and language in youngsters with autism is a long, involved process. Therefore, practitioners (and family members) must learn to appreciate very small gains over relatively long periods. For instance, Lovaas, Berberich, Perloff, and Schaeffer (1966) noted that 84 instructional hours were required to teach the first two words to one of their participants. However, as an individual's vocabulary grows, the acquisition of new words increases very rapidly.

Staff at Dr. Largent's school adopted the procedure reported by Koegel and Traphagen (1982) to select the initial words for Rodney's speech training. The procedure first required the collection of a 30-minute sample of Rodney's spontaneous vocalizations. The vocalizations were then transcribed according to the International Phonetic Alphabet. Next, Rodney was given a consonant-imitation test and a vowel-initiation test. By combining these assessment data, staff were able to identify phonemes that were of high occurrence in Rodney's spontaneous and tested vocalizations. From these phonemes, words were constructed that would also meet the criterion of having a high degree of functional use in the home and school environments.

The structured teaching component of Rodney's initial program consisted of operant methodology. In Step 1, he was taught to attend to task on request. In Step 2, he learned to imitate, first large motor movements, and later, fine motor movements of the mouth and tongue. In Step 3, verbal imitation was trained with the use of modeling and a series of graded physical and visual prompts. In this step, Rodney's vocalizations were shaped by reinforcing him for successive approximations of the modeled vocalization. Gradually, all prompts were faded. In Step 4, Rodney moved from imitative speech to functional speech, in which he learned to label actual objects (and later, actions) in the environment. Of course, Rodney's successful attempts throughout these steps were consistently reinforced to maintain a high level of motivation.

After 4 weeks of training, the staff discussed Rodney's achievement of speech and language objectives through the oral medium alone. Children who display difficulty using the auditory mode are introduced to a simultaneous communication approach that combines oral presentations and responses with signed presentations and responses. In Rodney's case, the discussion was brief. Their optimistic prognosis was supported by the good progress he had made during the early weeks of his program. Nevertheless, the staff continued to meet at intervals to consider his progress and to make any adjustments they deemed necessary.

As soon as Rodney developed a working speech vocabulary, the staff began to emphasize the pragmatics of his communication. An important component of this part of his program was the training of Anne and Bob. It was important for Rodney to use his newly developed skills both at school and at home. Because the words he had learned were selected to be highly functional, it was not difficult to identify everyday situations to promote their use. In this component of the program, two principles were applied as often as possible. First, Rodney was encouraged to *initiate* communication rather than to depend on others to initiate interactions. This procedure tended to promote spontaneous speech. Second, Rodney was encouraged to *broaden* his use of speech beyond the restricted stimulus–response arrangement used in structured teaching. For instance, he had learned to discriminate the concepts *big* and

little using a limited number of objects in the structured classroom. After being prompted to apply the same concepts to a wide variety of environmental objects, he learned to transfer the narrow skill learned in the classroom to the environment at large. Also, Rodney was prompted to combine words he had learned in as many unique ways as possible. Thus, he was reinforced strongly when he first combined the words *big* and *ball* because he had never been taught that particular sequence of words in the classroom. Combining words to form multiple-word communication and generating combinations of words not specifically taught both work against a common characteristic of autistic speech: the person's tendency to telegraph communication by reducing, rather than embellishing, the words he or he uses to communicate.

Unfortunately, a fuller description of Rodney's program cannot be presented here. However, it may be said that Rodney was one of the lucky youngsters who, because of the effort of competent practitioners, caring parents, and his own hard work, has succeeded in making the transition to a normal life. Today, he is a solid *B* student in a regular classroom in his home community. The reader is encouraged to refer to the contributions of Koegel, Traphagen, and Carr in *Educating and Understanding Autistic Children* (Koegel, Rincover, & Egel, 1982) for a comprehensive description of this general approach.

FINAL THOUGHTS

Tremendous progress in the development of treatment programs for the population with autism has occurred during the last 25 years. Although treatment outcomes continue to fall short of cures for the vast majority of those with this condition, it seems safe to assert that carefully implemented programs now result in happier, more fulfilled individuals. Such improvement has been the consequence of the work of a growing band of professionals and nonprofessionals who are dedicated to improving the lives of people with autism. Through their effort, we now have a bona fide technology to guide decision making and program planning.

On the darker side, it must be noted that the available technology is not being implemented uniformly across the nation. Too few parents and service delivery personnel have information and training that would allow them to maximize the outcomes of their work. It was the purpose of this chapter to lay a foundation on which interested readers can build. Those who pursue this field will, I believe, find both challenge and satisfaction in helping people who truly deserve our best effort. Finally, they will never be bored.

REFERENCES

American Psychiatric Association. (1980). *Diagnostic and statistical manual of mental disorders* (3rd ed.). Washington, DC: Author.

American Psychiatric Association. (1987). *Diagnostic and statistical manual of mental disorders* (3rd ed., rev.). Washington, DC: Author.

American Psychiatric Association. (1994). *Diagnostic and statistical manual of mental disorders* (4th ed.). Washington, DC: Author.

APA denounces facilitated communication for autistic students. (1994, September 7). *Special Education Report, 20*(18), 5.

Barrera, R. D., Lobato-Barrera, D., & Sulzer-Azaroff, B. (1980). A simultaneous treatment comparison of three expressive language training programs with a mute autistic child. *Journal of Autism and Developmental Disorders, 10*, 21–37.

Biklen, D. (1990). Communication unbound: Autism and praxis. *Harvard Education Review, 60*, 291–314.

Biklen, D., Morton, M. W., Gold, D., Berrigan, C., & Swaminathan, S. (1992). Facilitated communication: Implications for individuals with autism. *Topics in Language Disorders, 12*(4), 1–28.

Bligh, S., & Kupperman, P. (1993). Facilitated communication evaluation procedure accepted in a court. *Journal of Autism and Developmental Disorders, 23*, 553–557.

Cabay, M. (1994). A controlled evaluation of facilitated communication using open-ended and fill-in questions. *Journal of Autism and Developmental Disorders, 24*, 517–527.

Calculator, S. (1992). Perhaps the emperor has clothes after all: A response to Biklen. *American Journal of Speech-Language Pathology, 1*, 18–20.

Calculator, S., & Singer, K. M. (1992). Preliminary validation of facilitated communication [Letter to the editor]. *Topics in Language Disorders, 12*(5), ix–xvi.

Carr, E. (1982a). The motivation of self-injurious behavior. In R. L. Koegel, A. Rincover, & A. L. Egel (Eds.), *Educating and understanding autistic children* (pp. 158–175). San Diego, CA: College-Hill.

Carr, E. (1982b). Sign language. In R. L. Koegel, A. Rincover, & A. L. Egel (Eds.), *Educating and understanding autistic children* (pp. 142–157). San Diego, CA: College-Hill.

Clarke, S., Remington, B., & Light, P. (1988). The role of referential speech in sign learning by mentally retarded children: A comparison of total communication and sign-alone training. *Journal of Applied Behavior Analysis, 21*, 419–426.

Collins, D. T. (1965). Head banging: Its meaning and management in the severely retarded population. *Bulletin of the Menninger Clinic, 4*, 205–211.

Crossley, R., & Remington-Gurney, J. (1992). Getting the words out: Facilitated communication training. *Topics in Language Disorders, 12*(4), 29–45.

de Lissovoy, V. (1963). Head banging in early childhood: A suggested cause. *Journal of Genetic Psychology, 102*, 109–114.

Eaves, R. C. (1990, May). *The factor structure of autistic behavior.* Paper presented at the Alabama Conference on Autism, Birmingham.

Eaves, R. C. (1994). *The factor structure of autistic behavior: A replication.* Unpublished manuscript.

Eaves, R. C., & Hooper, J. (1987–88). A factor analysis of psychotic behavior. *Journal of Special Education, 21*, 122–132.

Eberlin, M., McConnachie, G., Ibel, S., & Volpe, L. (1993). Facilitated communication: A failure to replicate the phenomenon. *Journal of Autism and Developmental Disorders, 23*, 507–530.

Harlow, H. R., & Harlow, M. K. (1962). Social deprivation in monkeys. *Scientific American, 207*, 136–146.

Hudson, A., Melita, B., & Arnold, N. (1993). A case study assessing the validity of facilitated communication. *Journal of Autism and Developmental Disorders, 23*, 165–173.

Kanner, L. (1943). Autistic disturbances of affective contact. *Nervous Child, 3*, 217–250.

Klewe, L. (1993). An empirical valuation of spelling boards as a means of communication for the multihandicapped. *Journal of Autism and Developmental Disorders, 23*, 559–566.

Koegel, R. L., Rincover, A., & Egel, A. L. (1982). *Educating and understanding autistic children.* San Diego, CA: College-Hill.

Koegel, R. L., & Traphagen, J. (1982). Selection of initial words for speech training with nonverbal children. In R. L. Koegel, A. Rincover, & A. L. Egel (Eds.). *Educating and understanding autistic children* (pp. 65–77). San Diego, CA: College-Hill.

Konstantareas, M. M. (1987). Autistic children exposed to simultaneous communication training: A follow-up. *Journal to Autism and Developmental Disorders, 17*, 115–131.

LeDoux, J. E., & Hirst, W. (Eds.). (1986). *Mind and brain. Dialogues in cognitive neuroscience.* Cambridge, England: Cambridge University Press.

Levy, D. M. (1944). On the problem of movement restraint: Tics, stereotyped movements, and hyperactivity. *American Journal of Orthopsychiatry, 14*, 644–671.

Lovaas, O. L. (Producer). (1969). *Behavior modification: Teaching language to psychotic children* [Film]. New York: Appleton-Century-Crofts.

Lovaas, O. L. (1977). *The autistic child: Language development through behavior modification.* New York: Irvington.

Lovaas, O. L., Berberich, J. P., Perloff, B. F., & Schaeffer, B. (1966). Acquisition of initiative speech in schizophrenic children. *Science, 151*, 705–707.

Mahler, M. (1952). On child psychoses and schizophrenia: Autistic and symbiotic infantile psychosis. *Psychoanalytic Study of the Child, 7*, 286–305.

Moore, S., Donovan, B., & Hudson, A. (1993). Facilitator-suggested conversational evaluation of facilitated communication. *Journal of Autism and Developmental Disorders, 23*, 541–552.

Moore, S., Donovan, B., Hudson, A., Dykstra, J., & Lawrence, J. (1993). Evaluation of eight case studies of facilitated communication. *Journal of Autism and Developmental Disorders, 23*, 531–539.

Nyhan, W. L. (1976). Behavior in the Lesch-Nyhan syndrome. *Journal of Autism and Childhood Schizophrenia, 6*, 235–252.

Paul, R. (1987). Communication. In D. J. Cohen & A. M. Donnellan (Eds.), *Handbook of autism and pervasive developmental disorders* (pp. 61–84). Silver Springs, MD: Winston & Sons.

Prior, M., & Cummins, R. (1992). Questions about facilitated communication and autism. *Journal of Autism and Developmental Disorders, 22*, 331–338.

Rank, B. (1949). Adaptation of the psychoanalytic technique for the treatment of young children with atypical development. *American Journal of Orthopsychiatry, 19*, 130–139.

Regal, R. A., Rooney, J. R., & Wandas, T. (1994). Facilitated communication: An experimental evaluation. *Journal of Autism and Developmental Disorders, 24*, 345–355.

Rimland, B. (1964). *Infantile autism.* New York: Appleton-Century-Crofts.

Schopler, E. (1992). Editor's note. *Journal of Autism and Developmental Disorders, 22*, 337.

Shane, H. C. (1993). The dark side of facilitated communication [Letter to the editor]. *Topics in Language Disorders, 13*(2), ix–xv.

Silliman, E. A. (1992). Three perspectives of facilitated communication: Unexpected literacy, Clever Hans, or enigma? *Topics in Language Disorders, 12*(4), 60–68.

Smith, M. D., & Belcher, R. B. (1993). Facilitated communication with adults with autism. *Journal of Autism and Developmental Disorders, 23*, 175–183.

Smith, M. D., Haas, P. J., & Belcher, R. G. (1994). Facilitated communication: The effects of facilitator knowledge and level of assistance output. *Journal of Autism and Developmental Disorders, 24*, 357–367.

Szempruch, J., & Jacobson, J. W. (1993). Evaluating facilitated communications of people with developmental disabilities. *Research in Developmental Disabilities, 14*, 253–264.

Tarpley, H. D., & Schroeder, S. R. (1979). Comparison of DRO and DRI on rate of suppression of self-injurious behavior. *American Journal of Mental Deficiency, 84*, 188–194.

Walker, D. L., Jacobson, J. W., Paglieri, R. A., & Schwartz, A. A. (1993). An experimental assessment of facilitated communication. *Mental Retardation, 31*, 49–60.

Wing, L., & Attwood, A. (1987). Syndromes of autism and atypical development. In D. J. Cohen & A. M. Donnellan (Eds.), *Handbook of autism and pervasive developmental disorders* (pp. 3–19). Silver Springs, MD: Winston & Sons.

Self-Injurious Behavior

David Pitonyak

LEARNING GOALS

Upon completion of this chapter the reader will be able to

- define and describe self-injurious behavior;

- describe Carr's five hypotheses to explain self-injurious behavior;

- give three examples of how self-injurious behavior has been treated by operant techniques;

- give eight ways to provide positive behavioral support to individuals with self-injurious behavior;

- explain why it is important to develop multi-element support plans for individuals who engage in self-injurious behaviors; and

- explain why it is important to help an individual develop supportive relationships.

CASE EXAMPLE: JUNE

In a sterile room, she bites the bandages wrapped around her arms and hands. A staff person tells her to stop, but she continues, pulling harder and harder until one bandage unravels. Soon she is biting into her flesh, opening old sores that bleed profusely. She is drenched in perspiration and crying when the nurse arrives.

The nurse applies new bandages and administers another dosage of medication. June will fall asleep soon. It has been a hard day—a hard day for June and a hard day for staff. Now that she is sleeping, everyone can breathe a sigh of relief . . . until morning.

When June was 10 years old, a social worker from the state came to the family home and told her that she had come to take her out for ice cream. She secretly placed June's yellow suitcase in the trunk of her car and took her to an institution. A doctor had told her mother, "There is no point in sacrificing your entire life for June. She needs to be with her own kind."

June's mother visited her every Sunday afternoon for nearly 10 years, until she became suddenly ill and died. No one ever explained to June why her mother's visits ceased. "It would only upset her," said the social worker. Over the next 15 to 20 years, June's self-biting became worse and she developed a reputation as the "most difficult client" in the institution. As her self-injurious behaviors worsened, the procedures to stop them became more extreme. She was subjected to various forms of punishment, from denial of basic privileges to seclusion in a "quiet room" with her arms in splints. Eventually, her front teeth were removed, but somehow she managed to dig at her flesh with the teeth that had not been pulled. Various medications had little or no effect on her behaviors.

After years of failure, June participated in a research study to determine if her self-biting helped her to communicate important needs. Using functional analysis techniques described in this chapter, researchers learned that June used self-biting as a way of escaping unpleasant tasks and people. They also learned that she used the behavior to obtain things she wanted but was told she could not have. Information about the communicative functions of June's behavior was then used to teach her alternative ways to accomplish the same ends. In a relatively short time, the frequency and rate of her self-biting was reduced significantly. Sadly, however, the intervention did not go far enough.

Even after dramatic improvements in June's behavior, people failed to see her as a human being who needed ordinary things like good relationships, fun, security, choice, and appropriate health care. In the months following the research study, June was severely abused by two staff members. An investigation resulted in arrests, but little changed for June. Instead she was confined to "client status," and any hope of her leaving the institution was squashed by bureaucratic excuses such as "There are other people more deserving."

What follows is a description of the progress researchers have made in understanding self-injurious behaviors. It is also a description of the road ahead. After 30 years of interventions that measure the success of an intervention by whether or not it reduces behavior, we are finally realizing that it is also important to consider the quality of a person's life.

••

Self-injury can result in physical harm and even death to the individual displaying the behavior (Schroeder, Bickel, & Richmond, 1986).

Self-hitting, self-biting, self-induced vomiting, eye-gouging, and consuming nonedible substances (PICA) are examples of self-injurious behaviors that can occur at frequencies ranging from several hundred times per hour to sporadic events occurring over a sustained period (Favell et al., 1982; Ricketts, Goza, & Matese, 1993).

Self-injury has been reported in a variety of individuals, including normally developing children (de Lissovoy, 1963; Ilg & Ames, 1955), persons with psychiatric impairments (Frankel & Simmons, 1976), and persons who have sustained brain damage (Carr, 1977). However, self-injury is said to occur most frequently in persons with severe or profound mental retardation (Baumeister & Rollings, 1976; Griffin et al., 1987; Schroeder, Schroeder, Smith, & Dalldorf, 1978). Johnson and Day (1992) reported that 14.1% of institutionalized persons with developmental disabilities exhibit self-injurious behaviors; similar results have been reported elsewhere with incidence rates ranging from 10% to 15%.

It has been estimated that from 20,000 to 25,000 people with developmental disabilities exhibited a "significant degree" of self-injurious behavior in 1988. The costs of providing care to these individuals is said to be in excess of $100,000 per year per person [National Institutes of Health (NIH), 1989; Repp & Singh, 1990].

Self-injury can be devastating to the individual. In addition to the obvious physical risks, the individual may be denied access to "educational and humanizing activities" when the behavior is frequent or particularly intense (Favell et al., 1982, p. 531; Williams, Kirkpatrick-Sanchez, & Iwata, 1993). Caregivers often have little time to teach the individual adaptive or social behaviors because self-injury demands so much intervention time. Individuals are often separated from family and peers, and this isolation can itself lead to the onset of personality disorders involving "hysterical and explosive behaviors" (NIH, 1989, p. 9). The use of mechanical restraint devices such as bed restraints, camisoles, helmets, and arm splints is common during intense episodes of self-injury (Griffin, Ricketts, & Williams, 1986); ironically, these devices, if used for prolonged periods, can result in muscular atrophy, demineralization of bones, and shortening of tendons (Richmond, Schroeder, & Bickel, 1986). Individuals who exhibit self-injury may also face prolonged exposure to psychotropic medications (Singh & Millichamp, 1985). Neuroleptic drugs, such as thioridazine and haloperidol, are commonly used because they diminish motor activity (NIH, 1989). Studies suggest that long-term exposure to these drugs can depress adaptive functioning (Aman & Singh, 1983) and lead to a variety of drug-induced movement disorders including tardive dyskinesia (Gualtieri & Hawk, 1980).

In addition to the devastating impact of self-injury on the individual displaying the behavior, the individual's caregivers are also at risk. Almost anyone—professionals and nonprofessionals alike—is troubled by the sight of someone engaging in self-injury (Meyer & Evans, 1989). As Lovaas and Simmons (1969) pointed out, an individual who engages in self-injury "poses major psychological problems for those who take care of him in the form of anxiety, demoralization, and hopelessness" (p. 466). Sadly, it is not uncommon for individuals who engage in self-injury to be subjected to physical abuse from their caregivers (Furey, 1989). Self-injury is considered a significant "abuse provoking" characteristic among institutionalized adults with severe or profound disabilities (Rusch, Hall, & Griffin, 1986).

The volume of literature concerning self-injurious behavior has increased significantly in the last 25 years (Johnson & Rea, 1986). Although a significant portion of this literature deals with the possible causes of self-injury, the bulk of the literature is concerned with treatment. This emphasis on treatment is not surprising in light of the serious nature of these behaviors and the need to develop effective interventions (Johnson & Baumeister, 1978). Indeed, the seriousness of self-injury often dictates that the intervention be direct and precludes extended analysis of causal variables.

As Favell and her colleagues (1982) pointed out, little is known about the causes of self-injurious

behavior. Self-injury is strongly associated with medical conditions such as the Lesch–Nyhan syndrome, but specific causal relationships have yet to be established (Cataldo & Harris, 1982). Severity of self-injury is related to institutionalization, history of chronicity, and a number of organic disorders (Schroeder et al., 1978). There is evidence that impoverished environments may cause self-injury, but the principal evidence to support such claims is based on research with primates; any generalization of these findings to humans must be done with caution (Schroeder et al., 1986).

HYPOTHESES TO EXPLAIN SELF-INJURIOUS BEHAVIOR

Carr (1977), in a careful review of the literature, arrived at five possible hypotheses concerning the origins of self-injurious behavior:

1. Self-injury is a learned behavior maintained by positive reinforcement.
2. Self-injury is a learned behavior maintained by negative reinforcement (avoidance of or termination of an unpleasant event).
3. Self-injury is a self-stimulatory behavior that provides tactile, vestibular, and kinesthetic input.
4. Self-injury is the result of an aberrant physiologic process.
5. Self-injury is used to reduce guilt and to establish ego boundaries.

Each of Carr's hypotheses is discussed here.

The Positive Reinforcement Hypothesis

The positive reinforcement hypothesis claims that self-injury "is a learned operant, maintained by positive social reinforcement, which is delivered contingent upon the performance of the behavior" (Carr, 1977, p. 801). Lovaas, Freitag,

Gold, and Kassorla (1965) showed that self-injurious behavior could be affected by the laws of operant behavior. They demonstrated that the self-injurious behaviors of a 9-year-old girl increased when caregivers responded to those behaviors with social attention. They also showed that the behaviors decreased when social attention was withheld.

In a later report (Lovaas & Simmons, 1969), the social reinforcement hypothesis was tested by physically and socially isolating the participants. Each participant's self-injury was gradually reduced to negligible levels when this procedure was used. At the beginning of the isolation period, there was an increase (over baseline levels) in the frequency and intensity of self-injury. This increase was similar to the extinction-burst phenomenon reported in the animal literature (Skinner, 1938). These studies demonstrate that the discontinuation of reinforcement for a previously reinforced response results in a temporary increase in the frequency or magnitude of the response. The presence of an extinction burst has been suggested as further support of the positive reinforcement hypothesis (Carr, 1977). A number of subsequent investigations have also shown that social reinforcement can serve to maintain self-injurious behavior (Carr & McDowell, 1980; Durand, 1982; Durand & Crimmins, 1988).

Social reinforcement is not the only form of reinforcement that may maintain self-injury. Other reinforcers, such as tangible reinforcers, have also been shown to affect the frequency and intensity of self-injury (Durand & Crimmins, 1988; Edelson, Taubman, & Lovaas, 1983). The precise form of positive reinforcement can differ widely from individual to individual; that is, individuals may engage in self-injury for very different—even aberrant—forms of reinforcement (Favell et al., 1982). For example, for some individuals physical restraint is reinforcing (Favell, McGimsey, & Jones, 1978; Foxx & Dufresne, 1984), and its use as a contingency for self-injury may actually strengthen and maintain the behavior (Favell, McGimsey, & Jones, 1978).

The Negative Reinforcement Hypothesis

The negative reinforcement hypothesis claims that self-injury "is maintained by the termination or avoidance of an aversive stimulus following the occurrence of a self-injurious act" (Carr, 1977, p. 805). This hypothesis suggests that "individuals may expose themselves to aversive stimulation—like self-injury—in order to avoid even more aversive consequences" (Schroeder, Schroeder, Rojahn, & Mulick, 1981, p. 65).

Several authors have reported anecdotally that individuals may engage in self-injury to escape from unpleasant situations. For example, Freud and Burlingham (1949) described an institutionalized girl who engaged in head-banging to escape being put to bed. Jones, Simmons, and Frankel (1974) described a 9-year-old girl with autism who forcefully thrust the back of her hand into her upper front teeth whenever demands were placed on her. Her self-injury resulted in the immediate termination of demands and the application of mechanical restraints.

Evidence for the negative reinforcement hypothesis also comes from a number of studies in which the effects of task demands on self-injury were investigated. The purpose of this research was to show that self-injury may serve as an escape response. Carr, Newsome, and Binkoff (1976), for example, observed that self-injury was far more likely when difficult versus easy tasks were presented to an 8-year-old boy with childhood schizophrenia. They reasoned that the boy's self-injury would decrease during high-demand situations if his teacher said, "OK, let's go," a signal that normally ended the situation. In contrast, they reasoned that a signal such as "The sky is blue" (a signal that never resulted in the termination of a demand situation) would have no effect on the rate of self-injury. Both of these hypotheses were substantiated. Gaylord-Ross, Weeks, and Lipner (1980) showed that the self-injury of a 16-year-old girl varied when she was asked to perform different tasks. When she was asked to assemble a puzzle (easy), little or no self-injury occurred, but presentations of a button-sorting task (difficult) produced high rates of self-injury. In more recent studies, researchers have confirmed these early findings (Durand, 1982; Durand & Crimmins, 1988; Iwata, Dorsey, Slifer, Bauman, & Richman, 1982).

The Self-Stimulation Hypothesis

The self-stimulation hypothesis holds "that a certain level of stimulation, particularly in the tactile, vestibular, and kinesthetic modalities, is necessary for the organism, and that, when such stimulation occurs at an insufficient level, the organism may engage in stereotyped behaviors, including self-injurious behavior, as a means of providing sensory stimulation" (Carr, 1977, p. 806). In this view, some persons are thought to be insensitive to normal levels of environmental stimulation and engage in self-injury to fulfill that need (Cataldo & Harris, 1982). Although few experimental studies have been conducted to confirm this hypothesis (Edelson et al., 1983), various anecdotal and experimental reports lend credence to the hypothesis.

Levy (1944) noted that orphan children who were restricted to their cribs without toys engaged in self-injury. When these infants were given toys to play with, their self-injurious behavior disappeared, presumably because of the increased tactile and kinesthetic stimulation. Dennis and Najarian (1957) discussed similar behaviors among a group of orphan children who were left alone in their cribs because of understaffing, attributing the self-injury to "stimulation hunger." Experimental evidence for the self-stimulation hypothesis includes interesting evidence from animal studies (Berkson, 1968; Harlow & Griffin, 1965; Harlow & Harlow, 1971). Berkson (1968), for example, observed groups of monkeys who were separated from their mothers at birth to assess the influence of separation on the development of stereotyped behaviors. In addition to a variety of stereotyped behaviors observed in the monkeys (e.g., self-sucking, crouching, and body rocking), Berkson observed a number of self-injurious behaviors, including eye poking, self-biting, and body rubbing. Monkeys raised with their mothers rarely showed any stereotyped or self-injurious behaviors. Berkson concluded that stereotyped behaviors are self-stimulatory in nature, occurring when there is an absence of adequate stimulation.

Research has also shown that certain forms of self-injury in humans (e.g., eye poking) may be maintained by sensory reinforcers (e.g., visual). Favell and colleagues (1982) taught institutionalized children to manipulate toys that provided sensory input thought to be similar to input the children were achieving through self-injury. The reinforcement value of the toys was thought to compete with the reinforcement value of the children's self-injury, resulting in decreases in these behaviors. The authors wrote, "It may be argued that the pervasive deficiencies of these clients kept them in a chronic state of sensory deprivation" (p. 101).

Repp, Felce, and Barton (1988) suggested that self-injury may function as an individual's "adaptive" way of controlling the level of activity in his or her total environment. They found that the mere presence of tasks resulted in decreased levels of self-injury and self-stimulation among three students with profound mental retardation. "Interestingly," they wrote, "this is the opposite procedure suggested by the negative reinforcement hypothesis" (p. 288), which assumes that the individual engages in self-injury to escape task demands.

The Aberrant Physical Process Hypothesis

It is known that self-injury can result from aberrant physiologic processes such as the Lesch–Nyhan syndrome (Nyhan, 1976), Cornelia de

Lange syndrome (Bryson, Sakati, Nyhan, & Fish, 1980), and otitis media (de Lissovoy, 1963). For example, destructive biting of lips, tongue, and fingers is often associated with the Lesch–Nyhan syndrome, which results from a genetic flaw in purine metabolism (I. Jones, 1982). Purine is a chemical compound produced by the body during normal activity, the metabolic end product of which is uric acid. Because the biting of lips, tongue, and fingers is prevalent in individuals afflicted by the syndrome, it has been hypothesized that self-injury results from a specific biochemical abnormality (Seegmiller, 1972). To date a specific abnormality has not been identified, though biochemical studies do point to abnormalities involving the neurotransmitter serotonin and dopamine (Cataldo & Harris, 1982).

Carr (1977) has argued that several lines of evidence mitigate against a purely organic explanation of self-injury. First, there are reports of individuals with Lesch–Nyhan syndrome who do not engage in self-injury (Nyhan, 1968; Seegmiller, 1972). Second, operant techniques such as extinction, time out, and differential reinforcement of other behaviors (DRO) have been shown to be effective in treating the self-injurious behaviors of individuals with Lesch–Nyhan syndrome (Duker, 1975). One would not expect such individuals to respond to operant procedures if their self-injury was controlled by biochemical abnormalities. Finally, Duker (1975) noted that children with Lesch–Nyhan syndrome have been observed to engage in self-injury more frequently with adults who paid attention to the behavior(s). Given these observations, it seems likely that self-injury is controlled by both organic and environmental factors (Carr, 1977).

Psychotropic medications have been used widely to treat self-injurious behavior in persons with developmental disabilities (Singh & Millichamp, 1985). Despite their widespread use, little exists in the way of hard data to support the treatment of self-injury with psychotropic medications (Singh & Millichamp, 1985). In one study of the long-term effects of treatment on the self-injurious behavior of persons living in a state facility

for mental retardation, for example, Schroeder and coworkers (1978) reported sobering results; they found that only 26% of the persons treated exclusively with psychotropic medications showed improvement. This figure compares with figures obtained in studies of individuals who were treated with behavior modification alone (90% showed improvement) and individuals who received no treatment at all (21% showed improvement). As Singh and Millichamp (1985) pointed out,

> The most notable aspect of research in this area is that the data are so meager. While drugs are used extensively with the mentally retarded, there is little empirical evidence attesting to the efficacy of these drugs in the treatment of self-injury. What little data there is suggests that drugs may not be as effective as some clinicians may assume. For example, an observational study of physician's drug prescriptions for self-injury suggested that clinicians may prescribe a series of different drugs and/or the same drug in different doses in the belief that eventually a drug or dosage will be effective. (p. 263)

In conclusion, despite research that links self-injury with aberrant physiologic processes, it is generally believed that a purely organic basis for self-injury is untenable. Instead, an interaction of organic and environmental variables is suggested (Carr, 1977). From this viewpoint, the successful treatment of self-injury will require the manipulation of organic and environmental events. The use of psychotropic medications to treat self-injury has little empirical support. Researchers have called for controlled studies that isolate the effects of psychotropic medications on self-injury (Cataldo & Harris, 1982; Singh & Millichamp, 1985).

The Psychodynamic Hypothesis

Prior to the 1960s, a major body of literature concerning self-injury was psychodynamic in nature (Johnson & Rea, 1986). Proponents of psychodynamic approaches have proposed that individuals have a difficult time distinguishing the self from the external world and that self-injury is an attempt to create a "body reality" (Carr, 1977). Beres (1952) suggested that self-injury was an individual's means of alleviating guilt, and Menninger (1938) suggested that children engaging in the behavior do so because they must displace anger toward their mothers. Hoffner (1950), describing self-biting as "oral aggressiveness," suggested that self-injury could result from a variety of events, including a mother's refusal to breast-feed her child and the absence of a "pain barrier" that regulates such behavior in normal children. Others have suggested that self-injury serves an "autoerotic" and "auto-aggressive" function (Freud, 1954; Freud & Burlingham, 1949; Klein, 1932). Klein (1932), for example, suggested that the nighttime head banging of a young girl "meant having sadistic coitus with her mother, in which she played the part of her supposedly sadistic father" (p. 214).

A major problem with psychodynamic theory has been the difficulty of operationalizing concepts such as body reality, guilt, and anger displacement (Carr, 1977). Few treatment strategies based on the approach have produced meaningful outcomes when studied empirically (Bachman, 1972; Favell et al., 1982). Indeed, in a widely cited study, Lovaas, Freitag, Gold, and Kassorla (1965) demonstrated that strategies designed to alleviate guilt in an individual who engaged in self-injurious behavior actually resulted in a worsening of the problem. In contrast, the use of reinforcement and extinction strategies (described later) resulted in significant improvements in both the frequency and intensity of the individual's behaviors.

TREATMENT OF SELF-INJURIOUS BEHAVIORS BY OPERANT PROCEDURES

Since the 1960s, operant procedures have been used widely to treat the behavior problems of persons with developmental disabilities (Berkson & Landsman-Dwyer, 1977). Despite the relatively low incidence of self-injury, a great amount of the operant literature has been concerned with its reduction (Johnson & Rea, 1986). Comprehensive reviews of this literature are available (e.g., Gorman-Smith & Matson, 1985; Horner & Barton, 1980; Romanczyk, 1986; Schroeder et al., 1981).

What follows is a selective review of the operant literature related to the reduction of self-injury. Studies reported in this review have been chosen because they are representative of a specific type of operant procedure or procedures used within the last 20 years to reduce these and other problem behaviors. This review is divided into two sections: the reduction of self-injury by the use of aversive procedures and the reduction of self-injury by the use of nonaversive procedures.

Reduction of Self-Injury by Aversive Procedures

Most of the behavior-reduction strategies reported in the operant literature have emphasized the use of aversive procedures (LaVigna & Donnellan, 1986). Mesaros (1983), for example, in an extensive review of the major behavioral journals from 1968 to 1982, found that of the 96 articles dealing with autism, 85% of the behavior-reduction strategies were punitive. More recently, Lennox, Miltenberger, Spengler, and Erfanian (1988) were "surprised at the number of aversive procedures . . . still being evaluated in the literature relative to the number of positive approaches" (p. 499). In their review of seven major behavioral journals from 1981 to 1985, 65% of the strategies used to treat self-injury were considered aversive.

My purpose in this section is to review selectively the use of procedures to reduce self-injurious behaviors. These procedures can be grouped into five major categories: extinction, time out from positive reinforcement, overcorrection, electric shock, and other punishers.

Extinction

Extinction involves the withholding of the reinforcer maintaining the self-injury. The effectiveness of the extinction procedure depends on an ability to identify and control the reinforcer (Horner & Barton, 1980). If that reinforcer is caregiver attention, the use of the extinction procedure requires ignoring episodes of the behavior. If that reinforcer is the escape from an unpleasant activity, the extinction procedure involves preventing escape from the activity.

Lovaas, Schaeffer, and Simmons (1965) and Tate and Baroff (1966) found that simple extinction had no effect on the frequency of self-injury. These results are difficult to interpret, however, because no measure of adult attention was reported in either study. Carr (1977) has suggested that adults may have inadvertently paid attention to the self-injurious behavior on an intermittent basis: "This situation is likely because of the difficulty of ignoring an individual when that individual is engaging in dangerous high-frequency head banging or face slapping" (p. 802).

Lovaas and Simmons (1969) attempted to remedy the problem of inadvertent adult attention by arranging for the noncontingent isolation of two boys with severe mental retardation. The boys were isolated separately in an observation room for 1.5 hours per day to test the effectiveness of the extinction procedure. One boy produced 2,750 self-injurious responses, and the other, 900 responses in the first session. There were 25,000 and 9,000 total responses, respectively, before the behaviors were extinguished. Notably, there was no change in the frequency of self-injury for either boy in other settings.

Watson (1967) cautioned that extinction could be inappropriate in treating severe forms of self-injury. Bucher and Lovaas (1968) abandoned an extinction procedure because a young girl "could have inflicted serious self-injury or even killed herself during an extinction run" (p. 91). Because of these problems, extinction was abandoned as a strategy in a number of studies (Corte, Wolf, & Locke, 1971; Myers, 1975; Wolf, Risley, Johnson,

Harris, & Allen, 1967); the investigators in each case replaced extinction with other techniques. In a relatively small number of cases, simple extinction has been used effectively (F. Jones et al., 1974; Ross, Meichenbaum, & Humphrey, 1974; Wright, Brown, & Andrews, 1978). Wright and coworkers (1978), for example, instructed caregivers to leave the room whenever a 9-month-old baby engaged in ruminative vomiting. The vomiting gradually disappeared over a 2-month period, and these results were maintained for an 18-month period.

Despite the success of the extinction procedure in a limited number of studies, it is generally thought that the risks to individual safety are too great to warrant its use in severe cases of self-injury (Horner & Barton, 1980; Schroeder et al., 1981). Additionally, problems with generalization, durability, and substitution of other behaviors have been reported (Duker, 1975; Jones et al., 1974; Miron, 1971).

Time Out from Positive Reinforcement

Time out from positive reinforcement consists of "removing an individual from the opportunity to obtain reinforcement contingent upon each occurrence of self-injury" (Favell et al., 1982, p. 538). The forms of time out vary widely (e.g., contingent observation, withdrawal time out, seclusion time out, response cost), but all involve the removal of the individual from reinforcement or vice versa (Schroeder et al., 1981). This removal period typically ranges from several seconds to 30 minutes.

One of the earliest reports of time out for self-injury was by Wolf, Risley, and Mees (1964). The study involved a boy 3½ years old who engaged in head banging, face slapping, hair pulling, and face scratching. His mother reported that the boy "was a mess, black and blue and bleeding" after these episodes. Previous attempts to treat the behaviors with drugs and restraint had failed. The boy was placed in his room contingent upon episodes of self-injury and left alone until he stopped. His behaviors were decreased to near-zero levels in 5 months. Wolf and colleagues (1967) treated the same boy again 3 years later for face slapping. The boy's behavior was particularly troublesome to the boy's preschool teachers. Efforts to use an extinction technique failed, and the authors implemented a time-out program (removal to a separate room) where the behavior reached near-zero levels after three time-out periods.

Nunes, Murphy, and Ruprecht (1977) withdrew vibratory stimulation contingent upon self-injury from a 16-year-old boy with mental retardation. Self-injurious behavior was reduced to zero in three home and school environments in 31 days. No generalization data were presented. The study is unique in that it introduced vibratory stimulation to the boy first and then used the vibrator as a reinforcer that could easily be withdrawn.

It is important to note that time out is effective only when the individual is functioning in an environment in which reinforcement is available (Birnbrauer, 1976; Solnick, Rincover, & Peterson, 1977). Thus, most procedures should be accompanied by efforts to enrich the environment (Favell et al., 1982). Similarly, the success of a time-out program depends on the amount of reinforcement an individual is able to obtain while in time out. For individuals who find self-stimulatory behaviors to be reinforcing, the opportunity to go to a room and self-stimulate may be rewarding rather than punishing (Solnick et al., 1977). Likewise, an individual who is attempting to escape from an unpleasant or uncomfortable activity may find time out reinforcing. Both of these issues were addressed in a study by Rolider and Van Houten (1985). The self-biting behavior of a 9-year-old boy with autism was treated by a procedure termed "movement suppression time out." The authors described the procedure:

> Movement suppression consisted of telling the child to go immediately to the corner while guiding or forcing him into the corner as quickly as possible. [Tom] was positioned with his chin against the corner, both hands behind his back, with one hand on top of the other and both feet close together touching the wall. Whenever the child moved or made a verbalization, the parents said "Don't move" or "Don't talk" in a very firm, loud voice while pressing the child into the corner by placing one hand against the child's upper back between the shoulder blades . . . this procedure was applied even if the child only moved a small amount such as wiggling a finger or shifting weight from one leg to the other. The parent stood behind the child very closely so the procedure could be implemented following any movement or verbalization. This procedure lasted approximately three minutes, and the child was then told he could leave the corner. (p. 564)

The procedure was implemented after a less intrusive procedure—differential reinforcement of other behaviors (DRO)—had failed to reduce the self-biting. DRO is defined as "reinforcement for engaging in any response other than the target behavior for a specified interval of time" (Reynolds, 1961, p. 58). After 14 administrations of the program, the self-injury was nearly eliminated. In five follow-up sessions 2 and 3 months after the program was initiated, the self-biting was at the zero level. In their discussion, Rolider and Van Houten (1985) noted that the procedure, which includes physical restraint, was relatively easy to administer. They cautioned against the use of the procedure with larger persons, however. "The procedure might be less effective or safe when applied to strong combative adults or adolescents. Under these conditions the corner should be padded" (p. 573).

In addition to the problems of removing an individual to time out and holding him or her when he or she is struggling, care must be exercised to ensure that the individual will not hurt himself or herself if left alone. Favell et al. (1982) recommended that if the individual cannot be protected from self-harm, time out should not be used.

Overcorrection

Overcorrection is a complex combination of procedures that "require the misbehaving individual (a) to overcorrect the environmental effects of the inappropriate act, and (b) to practice overly correct forms of relevant behavior in those situations where the misbehavior commonly occurs" (Foxx, 1978, p. 97). When an individual engages in self-scratching, for example, he or she might be required to keep the hands open while extending them over the head at right angles to the body (e.g., Azrin, Gottlieb, Hughart, Wesolowski, & Rahn, 1975). The procedure requires the individual to practice such movements for extended periods of time. If necessary, the caregiver uses manual guidance to ensure compliance. Another form of overcorrection has been applied to individuals who engage in rumination (chewing and reswallowing vomitus; e.g., Foxx, Snyder, & Schroeder, 1979). In these cases, the individual would be required to cleanse his or her mouth with mouthwash and clean his or her face for extended periods of time.

Epstein, Doke, Sajwaj, Sorrell, and Rimmer (1974) have identified several components in overcorrection: negative feedback; time out from positive reinforcement; verbal reeducative instructions; compliance training, such as gradual guidance or shadowing; and negative reinforcement. Schroeder and coworkers (1981) stated that these procedures should be related directly to the self-injury, be applied immediately following the self-injury, and be performed in a rapid manner so as to be inhibiting.

Azrin and Wesolowski (1975) manually guided a woman with mental retardation through a clean-up procedure after she vomited, and taught her to vomit in the toilet. The procedure was successful in reducing the vomiting to near-zero levels. Prior to the use of the overcorrection program, a time-out and required relaxation program had failed. Borresson (1980) noted that adult attention and demands were both motivational variables in the self-biting of a 22-year-old man with mental retardation. After several attempts to control this behavior with alternative procedures (including extinction, mechanical restraint, and DRO) had failed, a forced running program was implemented. The procedure involved guiding the man up and down a four-step stairway on each occurrence of self-biting. Physical guidance was provided to increase the rate of stair climbing beyond a normal rate. A minimum of two staff persons was necessary to implement the procedure, which took less than 1 minute. Additionally, edible reinforcers were delivered for compliance, toy play, and appropriate social behaviors. The procedure was effective in reducing the self-biting from baseline levels in excess of 1,000 times per day to less than 2 times per day after 34 days. A reversal was conducted in which the behavior returned at frequencies in excess of baseline levels (more than 2,000 times per day). When treatment was reinstated, the self-biting was reduced to 3.7 times per day after 10 days.

Foxx and coworkers (1979) used a combination of satiation and oral hygiene procedures to reduce the rumination behaviors of an adult man and woman, both of whom were mentally retarded. The satiation condition simply consisted of allowing both individuals to have double portions of lunch. During the satiation and oral hygiene condition, the authors required both individuals to cleanse their mouths with an oral antiseptic for 2 minutes if rumination occurred. Both were required to swab or brush the insides of their mouths with the antiseptic and then to wipe their lips with a cloth that had been dipped in the antiseptic. When necessary, the caregiver used manual guidance to ensure compliance. When the individual was resistant, the caregiver performed the oral hygiene procedure. The results of the study revealed that satiation alone reduced the ruminating behaviors of these two individuals by 45% and 84%, respectively. The addition of the oral hygiene procedure resulted in near-zero levels of the behavior. Maintenance of these results after 4 months was reported. This procedure, without the satiation condition, was used by Singh, Manning, and Argell (1982) with monozygous twins, both profoundly retarded, who engaged in ruminative behaviors. The authors reported success in treating rumination but also noted collateral increases in self-stimulatory behaviors (e.g., rocking, waving, or rubbing parts of the body).

Several authors have warned that overcorrection may be inappropriate for self-injury and other problem behaviors (Foxx & Bechtel, 1982; Kelly & Drabman, 1977; Rapoff, Altman, & Christophersen, 1980; Zehr & Theobald, 1978). Rapoff and colleagues (1980), for example, found that overcorrection resulted in an immediate increase in self-injury to levels that were unacceptable. They indicated that, even had the procedure proved effective, "it was quite time consuming and impractical" (p. 43). Kelly and Drabman (1977) reported a similar finding: "Discontinuance had little to do with the staff's judgments of the treatment's effectiveness. The teachers simply did not like to perform the procedure. Although we strongly reinforced their efforts, the response cost of overcorrection outweighed any reinforcers we could practically provide" (p. 39).

Foxx and Bechtel (1982) warned that overcorrection may not be appropriate with individuals who are physically strong enough to combat their caregivers; this warning is echoed by others as well (Favell et al., 1982; Kelly & Drabman, 1977).

Electric Shock

There have been more published reports on the use of electric shock to control self-injury than on any other single technique (Favell et al., 1982). It is considered one of the most effective procedures for reducing self-injury (Carr & Lovaas, 1983) and also one of the most controversial (Mauer, 1983).

Electric shock is typically delivered from a hand-held device sometimes referred to as a "shock rod." These devices are designed to deliver a peak shock of 1,400 volts at 0.4 rnA (Harris & Ersner-Hershfield, 1978). The top of the shock rod typically includes two protruding terminals through which the shock travels to the surface of the skin. Carr and Lovaas (1983) de-

scribed the pain delivered by the shock rod this way: "Subjectively, the pain has been described as being similar to that experienced when one is hit with a leather strap or a willow switch. However, shock is not as dangerous as either of these events nor does it leave a durable, radiating pain. In fact, the pain is localized and stops as soon as the shock is terminated" (p. 221).

Contingent application of shock has been shown to result in an immediate and dramatic reduction of self-injurious behavior (Corte et al., 1971; Lovaas & Simmons, 1969; Risley, 1968; Tate and Baroff, 1966). The study by Lovaas and Simmons (1969) is representative of the effects of shock on self-injury. An 8-year-old boy, diagnosed as severely retarded, was treated for head banging. His head banging, which began when he was 2 years old, involved the beating of his temples and forehead with closed fists. At the time of treatment, he was in full restraints in an institution. Various psychotropic medications had been tried but had failed. During the baseline condition, the boy engaged in an average of 250 blows to the head in a 5-minute session. When the treatment condition was introduced, the behavior declined to a near-zero level after 12 administrations of shock over four sessions. In conditions in which shock was not introduced, however, self-injury remained high.

Generalization of treatment effects outside of the experimental situation is a significant problem with electric shock (Horner & Barton, 1980). The reduction of self-injury tends to occur only in the presence of the shock rod; thus, some researchers have suggested that the procedure be implemented in all situations (Corte et al., 1971; Foxx, Plaska, & Bittle, 1986). Another problem with shock is that individuals have been known to "show marked aversion to the sight of the hand-held shock stick" (Lichstein & Schreibman, 1976, p. 233); one report told of a boy who cried and shivered whenever the experimenter approached him (Bucher & King, 1971). The use of electric shock is also associated with the development of other undesirable behaviors. For example, Bucher and

Lovaas (1968) reported that one child became aggressive toward other children during nonexperimental time periods.

It should be noted that there have been positive emotional side effects to shock. Lovaas and colleagues (1965), for example, observed that many of the children exposed to shock in their study seemed more alert, smiled, and appeared happy. Others have reported similar findings (Carr & Lovaas, 1983; Lovaas & Simmons, 1969; Merbaum, 1973; Tate & Baroff, 1966).

Finally, discussions of the effectiveness and ethics of using shock have a long history (Johnson & Rea, 1986). Shock is an extremely restrictive procedure that is highly subject to abuse (Favell et al., 1982). Therefore, a number of guidelines have been established for its use (e.g., Foxx et al., 1986). Additionally, a number of regulations governing shock and other punishment techniques have emerged as a result of increased litigation in the mental health field (Griffith, 1983). A number of advocacy groups, including the Association for Persons with Severe Handicaps and the Association for Retarded Citizens (ARC) have called for the cessation of electric shock as a treatment option.

Other Types of Punishment

Several other procedures have been demonstrated to be effective punishers of self-injury. These procedures include forced inhalation of ammonia capsules (Baumeister & Baumeister, 1978; Tanner & Zeiler, 1975), lemon juice sprayed into the mouth (Becker, Turner, & Sajwaj, 1978; Simpson & Sasso, 1978), water mist to the face (Murphy, Ruprecht, Baggio, & Nunes, 1979), and forced swallowing of vomitus (Simpson & Sasso, 1978). As Favell and colleagues (1982) pointed out, "Some of these events are associated with possible physical side effects, ranging from chapped skin (with water mist) to mucous membrane damage (with ammonia)" (p. 541).

Concluding Remarks on Punishment

The contribution of the operant literature to the understanding and treatment of self-injury is undeniable. Prior to the emergence of operant conditioning as a major approach to the behavior problems of persons with severe disabilities, behaviors such as self-injury were thought to be "untreatable" (Johnson & Rea, 1986). As stated previously, however, the use of aversive procedures to reduce self-injury and other problem behaviors has come under increasing scrutiny (NIH, 1989).

In a comprehensive review of the "aversive" literature, Guess, Helmstetter, Turnbull, and Knowlton (1987) examined 38 studies published between 1964 and 1985 that employed aversive procedures (punishment and overcorrection). The studies represented 115 experiments and 364 individuals who exhibited a variety of problem behaviors, including self-injury. (*Note:* The authors also examined studies employing negative reinforcement procedures, but none of these involved self-injury.) Each study was evaluated in terms of treatment effectiveness or efficiency, maintenance of effects; generalization of effects, side effects, and acceptability of experimental design.

Punishment procedures (e.g., electric shock, ammonia tablets under the nose, or lemon juice sprayed into the mouth) were used to treat self-injury far more often (49%) than any other behavior type [e.g., self-stimulation (26%), disruptive behaviors (8%), aggression toward other people (5%)]. These procedures were said to be 90% to 100% effective in reducing problem behaviors overall (data were not provided for self-injury specifically), and most were said to bring about such effects quickly (the average for self-injury was 9 hours). Of the self-injury studies, 71% reported maintenance of effects; however, data were rarely reported beyond a 12-month period. Fewer than half of the studies reported generalization; of those that did, less than one third (29%) reported generalization of effects to nontreatment settings. Both positive and negative side effects were reported in 71% of the studies. Positive side effects included increases in "learning, performance and other adaptive behaviors" and negative side effects included resistance to instruction and avoidance behaviors. Finally, Guess et al. (1987) concluded that 64% of the studies were inadequately designed or contained no description of an experimental design.

Guess and coworkers (1987) also examined the effects of overcorrection (e.g., forced body movement, restitution) on self-injury. Although most of the studies in their review targeted stereotyped or self-stimulatory behaviors (45%), many targeted self-injurious behaviors (30%). Overcorrection, like punishment, was shown to be effective in reducing problem behaviors (90% to 100% reductions in over half the studies). These effects were said to occur with a mean time of 35 hours for self-injury. It should be noted, however, that there was considerable variability in the number of hours required (1 to 480 hours). Maintenance was reported in an average of 53% of the studies; however, 94% of these were for 12 months or less. Less than one third (32%) of the studies reported generalization of effects to nontreatment settings. Side effects were noted in 42% of the studies. Positive side effects included increased attention to tasks and persons, whereas negative side effects included increases in resistant behaviors and aggression toward others. Eight of the 12 studies regarding self-injury used adequate designs. The four remaining studies "had unacceptable designs (AB) or were confounded by order effects (ABC)" (p. 11).

In summary, punishment and overcorrection proved to be effective procedures for reducing self-injury *in the short term*. Few studies provided follow-up data beyond a 12-month period. Most researchers failed to report data on the generalization of effects, and of those that did, almost half found no degree of transfer across settings. Negative side effects were noted in a significant number of studies, including severe emotional reactions and resistance and avoidance behaviors. Positive effects included increases in learning and

adaptive behaviors. Most punishment studies were faulted for poor experimental design.

According to LaVigna and Donnellan (1986), the literature is "biased" toward aversive procedures. They pointed out that "punishment is the way we have been shown and taught to solve behavior problems" (p. 178) since childhood; this applies to researchers and practitioners alike. They pointed out that "neophytes" entering the profession "are likely to emulate their peers and colleagues" (p. 179) and model the use of punishment. The widespread attention that punishment has received as an effective procedure might have led some to a false impression that punishment is superior to nonaversive techniques.

Guess and colleagues (1987) raised questions concerning the effects of punishment on the perceived value of persons with developmental disabilities. A fundamental concern is, Do the interventions that are intended to enhance the well-being of the individual actually detract from the individual's worth and value in society? The authors asserted that aversive procedures may lead to the depersonalization of the individual receiving treatment. Depersonalization "involves the separation in the therapist's view of the person from the technology to treat an aspect of that person" (p. 32). Finally, critics have questioned the short- and long-term effects of aversive procedures on the caregiver (e.g., Turnbull et al., 1987). They questioned the effects of aversive procedures on the therapeutic relationship. As Bucher and King (1971) reported, one boy cried and shivered whenever the experimenter approached him. In the NIH's (1989) position paper on self-injurious behaviors, the authors stated:

> Less visible side effects associated with behavior reduction approaches include the potential for abuse in the application of these procedures, the psychological effects on staff, and most important, the negative and demeaning social image that the use of some of these procedures conveys to the general public about persons with developmental disabilities.

The Reduction of Self-Injury by Nonaversive Procedures

As stated previously, most of the behavior-reduction strategies reported in the operant literature have been punitive in nature (LaVigna & Donnellan, 1986). Although the literature related to nonaversive alternatives to punishment is expanding (e.g., Evans & Meyer, 1985; LaVigna & Donnelan, 1986; McGee, Menalascino, Hobbs, & Menousek, 1987), it is generally agreed that empirical support for these methods is scarce (Axelrod, 1987a; Snell, 1987). My purpose in this section is to review the use of nonaversive procedures to reduce self-injury. The section is divided into four parts: treatment of self-injury by rearrangement of antecedent stimulus conditions; treatment by differential reinforcement strategies; treatment based on a functional analysis of self-injury; and treatment as a comprehensive, composite approach.

Rearrangement of Antecedent Stimulus Conditions

This class of nonaversive procedures is based on the principle of stimulus control. This principle refers to the fact that self-injury is much more likely to occur in some situations than in others. Determining which situations control self-injury allows the interventionist to manipulate relevant antecedents (such as high demands) rather than consequences. Favell and colleagues (1982) pointed out:

> Which specific situations control high or low rates of self-injury depends on the individual's reinforcement history in those situations. In many cases, self-injury tends to occur when reinforcement that has previously been given is not forthcoming or when demands are placed on the individual. In such situations, the self-injury is likely to have been reinforced by the resumption of reinforcement or the withdrawal of demands, respectively. (pp. 536–537)

Procedures based on the stimulus control principle can be divided into two approaches. One approach involves identifying the stimulus conditions that are associated with low rates of self-injury and then providing the individual with access to these conditions. For example, Carr and coworkers (1976) determined that an 8-year-old boy's self-injurious behaviors increased when he was presented with commands to perform a task. In contrast, telling the boy a story did not result in an increase in self-injury. By mixing commands in with "storytelling," the authors noted a reduction in the overall frequency of self-injury without reducing the level of commands. Similarly, Weeks and Gaylord-Ross (1981) noted that demand situations resulted in significantly higher rates of self-injury than did low-demand or no-demand situations. By providing the individuals with assistance for difficult tasks (errorless learning), the rates of self-injury were significantly reduced during difficult task periods. Other examples of this approach include the provision of vibratory stimulation (Bailey & Meyerson, 1970; Dura, Mulick, & Hammer, 1988) and opportunities for toy play (Favell et al., 1982; Mulick, Hoyt, Rojahn, & Schroeder, 1978).

A second approach to self-injury based on the stimulus control procedure involves identifying and then rearranging the conditions associated with high rates of the behavior(s). As Favell et al. (1982) pointed out, the research in support of this approach is "scant": "Although research in this area is scant, the clinical value of eliminating or changing situations which are reliably associated with self-injury is clear. Such situations will differ across clients, but may include barren environments with few activities, little reinforcement for appropriate behavior or lack of social contact of any kind" (p. 537).

Touchette, MacDonald, and Langer (1985) offered an interesting case study that involves this second approach. They identified, through the use of their scatter plot diagram, a strong association between a patient's self-injury and a particular staff person. When the schedule of this staff person was altered, the rates of self-injury were significantly reduced. They also showed that the aggressive behaviors of a 14-year-old girl were strongly associated with demands; activities associated with low rates of the behaviors were alternated with demands, and significant reductions in her aggressive behaviors were achieved.

Differential Reinforcement Strategies

The principle of differential reinforcement is key to a number of nonaversive procedures. Baumeister and Rollings (1976) suggested that the principle of differential reinforcement should be the "backbone" of any behavioral treatment program; its use in the treatment of self-injury requires that reinforcement be provided for appropriate, noninjurious behaviors, whereas less (ideally no) reinforcement is provided for self-injury (Favell et al., 1982).

Two specific forms of differential reinforcement are discussed here: DRO and the differential reinforcement of alternative responses (ALT–R). It should be noted that DRO and ALT–R strategies have been applied in many studies, typically as components of treatment packages that contain aversive procedures (Woods, 1980). Thus, it is difficult to assess the effectiveness of the DRO and ALT–R contingencies alone because of the confounding effects of other procedures (e.g., Repp & Deitz, 1974). Nevertheless, there are studies in which each procedure was applied by itself to self-injury.

DRO is a popular technique with high public acceptability (Horner & Barton, 1980). In DRO, reinforcement is provided following periods of time in which self-injury is absent. In other words, the individual receives reinforcement for refraining from self-injury.

Repp, Deitz, and Deitz (1976) used a DRO procedure to reduce hand-biting in a 14-year-old girl with severe mental retardation. They began by reinforcing the absence of self-injury for 1-second intervals and gradually increased these intervals over time. They did not report generalization. Luiselli, Helfen, Colozzi, Donnellon, and Pemberton (1978) used DRO to treat, across three school environments, the self-biting of a 10-year-old boy with moderate mental retardation. Starting with 1-minute intervals, the authors were able to delay reinforcement for the nonoccurrence of self-injury to 20-minute intervals in fewer than 25 days. The authors did not report results beyond the 25-day period.

Frankel, Moss, Schofield, and Simmons (1976) reduced aggression and head banging in an 8-year-old girl by reinforcing a variety of task and play behaviors with candy and praise. Although the authors did not report results beyond a 40-day period (the girl was moved to another institution where a different type of program was carried out), the behaviors were reduced to near-zero levels. The authors also noted that the procedure was implemented after two time-out programs had failed to reduce the girl's self-injury. Also, "a surprising by-product of this approach was the reinstatement and perhaps enhancement of the social reinforcement properties of the teachers. The disappearance of these properties might well have been responsible for the failure of the isolation booth program . . . as teachers were cast in the role of dispensers of aversives" (pp. 847–848).

One of the most interesting studies using DRO to reduce self-injury was conducted by Favell and colleagues (1978). The authors determined that mechanical restraints were reinforcing to three individuals who engaged in self-injury. Restraints were subsequently used to reinforce differentially the nonoccurrence of self-injury. This procedure was implemented after aversive techniques, including the contingent use of lemon juice, had failed. The authors did not report results beyond 14 weeks.

Finally, Lockwood and Bourland (1982) used DRO and the availability of toys to reduce the self-injury of two nonambulatory children with profound mental retardation. They found that the availability of toys was not sufficient to reduce self-injury, but that the availability of toys and reinforcement for the absence of self-injury was effective. The authors did not report results beyond 80 treatment sessions, each lasting approximately 1 hour.

ALT–R is among the most widely recognized and used of the alternatives to punishment (LaVigna & Donnelan, 1986). This procedure calls for the differential reinforcement of behaviors that are topographically incompatible with self-injury.

Saposnek and Watson (1974) taught a 10-year-old boy to slap the experimenter's hand rather than his own. Reinforcing the hand slapping reduced the levels of self-injury significantly and enabled the boy to participate in a variety of educational and recreational activities. Heidorn and Jensen (1984) reported the effects of an ALT–R procedure in which the head gouging of a 27-year-old man was successfully treated. This procedure included the prevention of escape from unpleasant activities. After initial success with the program, the individual's daily dosage of chloral hydrate was reduced, but the self-injury increased; however, the behavior was gradually reduced to previous levels after the procedure was reinstated. A similar increase in self-injury occurred when the man moved to another living unit, but again the self-injury returned to a low frequency when the procedure was implemented in the new setting. The study utilized information gathered through a functional analysis, and it was hypothesized that the man engaged in his self-injurious behavior for social attention (positive reinforcement) and to escape demands (negative reinforcement). Similarly, Carr and Durand (1985) determined that adult attention and high-demand situations maintained a variety of disruptive behaviors in school-aged children, including self-injury. They taught the children how to solicit adult attention and assistance that significantly reduced their disruptive behaviors.

Functional Analysis of Self-Injury

The basic premise underlying differential reinforcement strategies is that the reinforcement of appropriate behaviors relative to problem behaviors should result in a decrease of the latter. An emerging concept, that of "functional equivalence," is based on the premise that the treatment

of problem behaviors may require more than the reinforcement of alternative or incompatible behaviors; instead, treatment may depend on the reinforcement of behaviors that serve the same *function* as the problem behavior (Favell & Reid, 1988). In this view, self-injury is seen as a form on nonverbal communication that helps the individual to achieve positive ends. For example, it is thought that self-injury may help some individuals escape from unpleasant activities. The self-injury of these individuals may be functionally equivalent to saying, "I need to take a break." In view of this, it should be possible to teach the individual appropriate ways to communicate a need for breaks. In this way, the reinforcer maintaining self-injury (the termination of demands) is used to reinforce a communicative alternative (Dunlap, Johnson, Winterling, & Morelli, 1987).

Teaching functionally equivalent behaviors depends on the identification of the reinforcers maintaining the individual's self-injury. In recent years, a number of studies have attempted to isolate systematically the reinforcers that maintain self-injury; this process, which often includes an analysis of the antecedent conditions that precipitate problem behaviors, has been referred to as "functional analysis" (Axelrod, 1987b). O'Neill and colleagues (1990) have stated that a functional analysis is designed to define operationally the problem behavior; to determine the "times and situations" when the problem behavior "will and will not be performed across the full range of typical daily routines" (p. 6); and to delineate the maintaining reinforcers of the problem behavior.

Iwata and colleagues (1982) showed that the self-injurious behaviors of nine children with developmental disabilities, ranging in ages from 1 to 17 years, were motivated by one or more of the following variables: escape from demands (negative reinforcement); social attention (positive reinforcement); and a sensory variable (self-stimulation). The authors argued that the treatment of self-injury should be based foremost on an understanding of the variables that maintain the behavior(s).

In several studies researchers have used functional analysis techniques to develop interventions for self-injury. Carr and colleagues (1976) showed that the self-injurious behaviors of an 8-year-old boy were more frequent in the presence of demands and less frequent when simple declarative statements were made. When the authors reduced or modified the demands (by interspersing stories about familiar activities), the boy's self-injury was reduced. The authors suggested that the interspersing of low- and high-demand tasks, coupled with positive teacher interactions, would result in low levels of self-injury and task participation. Gaylord-Ross and coworkers (1980) showed that by substituting difficult tasks with easy tasks and by using errorless learning teaching strategies, they could reduce the self-injurious behaviors of a 16-year-old girl with severe mental retardation. Bird, Dores, Moniz, and Robinson (1989) taught a 27-year-old man with profound mental retardation to communicate his need for breaks by handing his teacher a token that signaled the termination of demands. As he became more proficient at communicating his need to take breaks, the authors gradually increased task demands while consistently honoring his requests for breaks.

Researchers have also used functional analysis techniques to develop treatment programs for self-injury motivated by positive reinforcement. Carr and Durand (1985) taught three children with severe disabilities to ask for assistance in completing their school work. The children were taught to ask, "Am I doing good work?" or to say, "I don't understand" to solicit adult attention. The authors showed that these communicative responses, which were followed by adult attention, led to reductions of self-injurious, aggressive, and destructive behaviors. Durand and Kishi (1987) reported similar results in a study using a technical assistance model that focused on the use of functional analysis techniques. In their study, students with profound disabilities were taught to let their teachers know that they needed help or attention. The functional assessment used in this study was the *Motivation Assessment Scale* (Durand, 1988), a 16-item questionnaire.

Favell and coworkers (1982) hypothesized that the self-injurious behaviors of six young adults with profound mental retardation were motivated by "visual, tactile, gustatory or other sensory consequences" (p. 85). The authors provided these individuals with toys that presumably provided similar consequences" (e.g., a chew toy) as their self-injury (e.g., hand mouthing) and showed significant reductions in their behaviors. An interesting finding from this study and other studies is that a lack of stimulation in the environment may be a significant factor contributing to the development and maintenance of self-injurious behaviors (e.g., Horner, 1980; Iwata et al., 1982; Repp et al., 1988).

A number of authors have suggested that the use of functional analysis techniques may lead to a reduction in the use of aversive techniques (Axelrod, 1987b; Durand, 1987; Favell et al., 1982; O'Neill, Horner, Albin, Storey, & Sprague, 1990). Durand (1987) has asserted that treatment approaches, whether aversive or nonaversive, that ignore the function(s) of problem behaviors may fail to produce lasting results. He wrote,

> Suppose an individual is hitting herself to escape tasks because they are difficult or unchallenging. Techniques that involve punishing her for her self-injury or reinforcing her for not hitting herself both fail to provide her with appropriate means of leaving work, and they do not address the issue of whether the tasks themselves are appropriate. Thus, conceptually, these types of interventions may not be able to produce lasting reductions in problem behavior. Using the case described above, the individual will presumably continue to escape from tasks, and may attempt novel responses (e.g., aggression, destroying materials) toward this end. (p. 301)

At present, a relatively small number of researchers are employing functional analysis techniques, despite the clear utility of understanding what a behavior means before intervening (Gardner & Cole, 1983; Johnson & Rea, 1986). Lennox and coworkers (1988) reported that nearly two thirds (64%) of the studies they reviewed from 1981 through 1985 did not report a pretreatment functional analysis.

A Comprehensive, Composite Approach to Treatment

Treatment of self-injury often involves single interventions such as DRO, time out, or overcorrection. Favell and Reid (1988) pointed out that "such a focus on singular and relatively narrow interventions undoubtedly reflects the appropriate scientific mandate of attempting to isolate the effects of single interventions or elements of treatment" (p. 179). The effective treatment of self-injury, however, may demand changes to a variety of variables in the individual's "social and physical environments." In 1982, the Association for the Advancement of Behavior Therapy called on researchers and practitioners to move away from the "sequential application of single techniques" (Favell et al., 1982, p. 542) toward the development of multifaceted intervention packages that take into account biologic and environmental influences on behavior. This emphasis on comprehensive treatment packages reflects a growing understanding that self-injurious behaviors may serve multiple functions.

Berkman and Meyer (1988) successfully treated the self-injurious behaviors of a man named Mr. Jordan who had been institutionalized for 39 years because his behaviors were thought to be untreatable in the community. Treatment consisted of a comprehensive array of "program and placement changes," including movement from the institution to a community residence, participation in a community job placement, and access to a variety of community recreational activities. The intent of this treatment "package" was to "modify the circumstances associated with his self-injurious behaviors and replace them with functional alternatives" (p. 77). According to the authors, the key to the program's success was allowing Mr. Jordan to make decisions about the intervention package itself; that is, he was asked to make decisions about where he wanted to live, work, and recreate: "Although Mr. Jordan's self-injury was clearly related to the institutional setting, to have *imposed* [sic] community living upon him might have resulted in a similar negative pattern. Instead, the emphasis

was upon both the different environments and activities as well as upon increasing his own decisions and choices in the context of meaningful and more normalized social relationships" (p. 84).

Despite the lack of experimental control in their study, Berkman and Meyer (1988) argued that their treatment package was probably responsible for the changes, given Mr. Jordan's long history of self-injurious behaviors and his resistance to other treatment efforts. They encouraged practitioners to consider major changes in the individual's "lifestyle" *before* intervening with individual behaviors. The Rehabilitation Research and Training Center on Community-Referenced Nonaversive Behavior Management in Oregon (R. Horner, personal communication, June 8, 1989) initiated a similar study in which several people with long histories of institutionalization and treatment-resistant behavior problems are involved. The purpose of their study is to delineate, if possible, the critical variables in such intervention packages.

It seems clear that researchers and practitioners are "moving away from a time when the expectation is that manipulation of a single variable will produce dramatic, durable, and generalizable changes in the behavior of persons with very severe behavior problems" (R. Horner, personal communication, June 8, 1989). The emphasis on comprehensive, composite approaches to self-injury may reflect the field's growing awareness that singular approaches to such problems may be "clinically misleading" and "contrary to good clinical practice" (Carr, 1994; Favell & Reid, 1988).

The focus of the chapter shifts to a more general discussion of these challenging behaviors. First, it is hoped that the suggestions that follow will be helpful to people who are supporting problem behaviors. Second, it is hoped the reader will better understand the broader lifestyle issues that should be considered whenever an intervention or support plan is developed.

Supporting a person who exhibits severe challenging behaviors requires us to get to know the person as a complex human being who has a complex personal history. Although it is tempting to look for a "quick fix" to the problem, which usually means to attack the person's behavior to reduce its frequency, suppressing a person's behavior without understanding something about the life that he or she is living is unwise and often futile. Table 12.1 presents 10 ideas that are highly practical and down-to-earth suggestions.

Think about someone you know who engages in challenging behaviors. Ask yourself, "What kind of life is this person living?" Consider how you would feel if you lived the person's life. How would you behave?

The techniques in Table 12.1 can be used to support a person whose behavior is troubling you. It is not a list of quick-fix strategies or recipes for stopping unwanted behavior. It is a list of ideas for uncovering the real things that people need in life so that you can help them to find a life worth living.

FINAL THOUGHTS

The volume of literature concerning self-injurious behavior has grown considerably over the last 20 years as has the way we look at helping to support persons with challenging behaviors. Because of the serious nature of the behavior, most of the published studies have dealt with treatment versus theoretical issues. Few studies have dealt with the causes of self-injurious behavior.

A number of hypotheses concerning the factors that cause and maintain self-injury have been described. These include the positive reinforcement hypothesis, in which self-injury is viewed as a learned behavior that is maintained by positive reinforcement; the negative reinforcement hypothesis, in which self-injury is viewed as a learned behavior maintained by the termination of unpleasant stimuli following the behavior; the self-stimulation hypothesis, in which self-injury is viewed as a means of achieving sensory stimulation; the aberrant physical process hypothesis, in which self-injurious behavior is said to result from an aberrant physiologic process such as the Lesch–Nyhan syndrome; and the psychodynamic

hypothesis, in which self-injury is said to result from a variety of intrapsychic phenomena such as the need to establish ego boundaries.

The use of operant techniques to treat self-injury has been widely documented since the 1960s, with most of these techniques involving aversive components. Increasingly, questions are being raised about the use of aversive procedures with persons who are severely disabled. Unfortunately, the number of studies supporting nonaversive approaches to self-injurious behavior are few, and those that do exist tend to involve persons who exhibit the least serious forms of the behavior. Professionals, advocates, and consumers alike are calling for research concerning nonaversive approaches to serious forms of self-injurious behavior.

An emerging concept, that of functional equivalence, is based on the premise that treating problem behaviors may require more than the reinforcement of alternative or incompatible behaviors; instead, treatment may depend on the reinforcement of behaviors that serve the same *function* as the problem behavior (Favell & Reid, 1988). In this view, self-injury is seen as a form of nonverbal communication that helps the individual to achieve positive ends. A growing number of researchers are exploring the use of functional analysis techniques to determine how the social and physical environments affect self-injury. Researchers are also calling for comprehensive, composite approaches to self-injury that involve multiple treatment components.

REFERENCES

Aman, M. G., & Singh, N. H. (1983). Pharmacological intervention. In J. L. Matson & J. A. Mulick (Eds.), *Handbook of mental retardation* (pp. 317–337). Elmsford, NH: Pergamon Press.

American Psychiatric Association. (1987). *Diagnostic and statistical manual of mental disorders* (3rd ed. rev.). Washington, DC: Author.

Axelrod, S. (1987a). Book review: Doing it without arrows. *The Behavior Analyst, 10,* 243–251.

Axelrod, S. (1987b). Functional and structural analysis: Approaches leading to reduced use of punishment procedures? *Research in Developmental Disabilities, 8,* 165–178.

Table 12.1.   Supporting a Person with Severe Challenging Behavior

Simple Things You Can Do	Reason(s) Why	Example
1. Spend time with the person.	Often the people who design an intervention do not know the person in any meaningful sense.	Spend time with the person in a place the person enjoys and feels comfortable (e.g., take a walk in the park, have lunch at a restaurant, etc.).
2. Listen carefully.	Challenging behaviors are "messages" that can tell us important things about the person and the quality of his or her life.	Conduct a functional analysis to determine how the behavior might help the person to communicate important needs.
3. Develop a support plan.	The reduction of challenging behaviors is often the focus of interventions. Helping the person to find quality and happiness in his or life is important, too.	Ask, "How can we help the person to establish meaningful relationships? How can we help the person to have more fun? more choice and control? etc.?"
4. Develop a support plan for the person's supporters.	Even the best laid support plan will fall to pieces if the people providing the support are not supported.	Ask yourself, "What do I need when this person is having a difficult time?"
5. Don't assume anything.	It is easy to underestimate what people can understand.	Always remember that people are people first. Be respectful of the person in every conversation.
6. Remember that relationships make all the difference in the world.	Loneliness may be the most significant disability of our time.	Help the person to develop relationships with nonpaid community members.
7. Help the person to develop a positive identity.	People are often known as the sum total of their labels.	Avoid assumptions about people based on their labels. Help the person find ways to make a contribution to his or her friends, family, and community.
8. Instead of ultimatums, give choices.	People with challenging behaviors are often powerless over their environment.	Help the person to exercise meaningful choices each and every day. Help the person to be powerful *without* his or her challenging behaviors.
9. Help the person to have more fun.	Fun is a powerful antidote to challenging behaviors.	Make a list of the things a person enjoys doing. Do them more often!
10. Establish access to primary health care.	Many people exhibit problem behaviors because they don't feel well or because they are experiencing psychiatric distress.	Help the person to establish a good relationship with a primary health care physician.

Azrin, N. H., Gottlieb, L. H., Hughart, L., Wesolowski, M. D., & Rahn, T. (1975). Eliminating self-injurious behavior by educative procedures. *Behavior Research and Therapy, 13,* 101–111.

Azrin, N. H., & Wesolowski, M. D. (1975). Eliminating habitual vomiting in a retarded boy by positive practice and self-correction. *Journal of Behavior Therapy and Experimental Psychology, 6,* 145–148.

Bachman, J. A. (1972). Self-injurious behavior: A behavioral analysis. *Journal of Abnormal Psychology, 80,* 221–224.

Bailey, J., & Meyerson, L. (1970). Effect of vibratory stimulation on a retardate's self-injurious behavior. *Psychological Aspects of Disability, 17,* 133–137.

Baumeister, A. A., & Baumeister, A. A. (1978). Suppression of repetitive self-injurious behavior by contingent inhalation of aromatic ammonia. *Journal of Autism and Childhood Schizophrenia, 8,* 71–77.

Baumeister, A. A., & Rollings, J. P. (1976). Self-injurious behavior. In N. R. Ellis (Ed.), *International review of research in mental retardation* (Vol. 8, pp. 1–34). New York: Academic Press.

Becker, J., Turner, S. M., & Sajwaj, T. (1978). Multiple behavioral effects of the use of lemon juice with a ruminating toddler-age child. *Behavior Modification, 2,* 267–279.

Beres, D. (1952). Clinical notes on aggression in children. In R. S. Eissler (Ed.), *The psychoanalytic study of the child.* New York: International Universities Press.

Berkman, K. A., & Meyer, L. H. (1988). Alternative strategies and multiple outcomes in the remediation of severe self-injury: Going "all out" nonaversively. *Journal of the Association for Persons with Severe Handicaps, 13,* 76–86.

Berkson, G. (1968). Development of abnormal stereotyped behaviors. *Developmental Psychology, 1,* 118–132.

Berkson, G., & Landsman-Dwyer, S. (1977). Behavioral research on severe and profound mental retardation (1955–1974). *American Journal of Mental Deficiency, 81,* 428–454.

Bird, F., Dores, P. A., Moniz, D., & Robinson, J. (1989). Reducing severe aggression and self-injurious behaviors with functional communication training. *American Journal of Mental Retardation, 94,* 37–48.

Birnbrauer, J. S. (1976). Mental retardation. In H. Leitenberg (Ed.), *Handbook of behavior modification.* New York: Appleton-Century-Crofts.

Borresson, P. M. (1980). The elimination of self-injurious avoidance response through a forced running exercise. *Mental Retardation, 18,* 73–77.

Bucher, B., & King, L. (1971). Generalization of punishment effects in the deviant behavior of a psychotic child. *Behavior Therapy, 2,* 68–77.

Bucher, B., & Lovaas, O. I. (1968). Use of aversive stimulation in behavior modification. In M. R. Jones (Ed.), *Miami Symposium on the Prediction of Behavior, 1967: Adversive Stimulation* (pp. 77–145). Coral Gables, FL: University of Miami Press.

Bryson, Y., Sakati, N., Nyhan, W. L., & Fish, C. H. (1980). Self-mutilative behavior in the Cornelia de Lange syndrome. *American Journal of Mental Deficiency, 76,* 319–324.

Carr, E. G. (1977). The motivation of self-injurious behavior: A review of some hypotheses. *Psychological Bulletin, 84*(4), 800–816.

Carr, E. G. (1994). Emerging themes in the functional analysis of problem behavior. *Journal of Applied Behavior Analysis, 27,* 393–399.

Carr, E. G., & Durand, M. V. (1985). Reducing behavior problems through functional communication training. *Journal of Applied Behavior Analysis, 18,* 111–126.

Carr, E. G., & Lovaas, O. I. (1983). Contingent electric shock as a treatment for severe behavior problems. In S. Axelrod (Ed.), *The effects of punishment on human behavior* (pp. 221–245). New York: Academic Press.

Carr, E. G., & McDowell, J. J. (1980). Social control of self-injurious behavior of organic etiology. *Behavior Therapy, 11,* 402–409.

Carr, E. G., Newsome, C. D., & Binkoff, J. A. (1976). Stimulus control of self-destructive behavior in a psychotic child. *Journal of Abnormal Child Psychology, 4,* 139–153.

Cataldo, M. F., & Harris, J. (1982). The biological basis for self-injury in the mentally retarded. *Analysis and Intervention in Developmental Disabilities, 2,* 21–39.

Corte, H. E., Wolf, M. M., & Locke, B. J. (1971). A comparison of procedures for eliminating self-injurious behavior of retarded adolescents. *Journal of Applied Behavior Analysis, 4,* 201–213.

de Lissovoy, V. (1963). Head banging in early childhood. *Journal of Genetic Psychology, 102,* 109–114.

Dennis, W., & Najarian, P. (1957). Infant development under environmental handicap. *Psychological Monographs, 71,* 1–13.

Duker, P. (1975). Behavior control of self-biting in a Lesch-Nyhan patient. *Journal of Mental Deficiency Research, 19,* 11–19.

Dunlap, G., Johnson, J., Winterling, V., & Morelli, M. A. (1987). The management of disruptive behavior in unsupervised settings: Issues and directions for a behavioral technology. *Education and Treatment of Children, 10,* 367–382.

Dura, J. R., Mulick, J. A., & Hammer, D. (1988). Rapid clinical evaluation of sensory integrative therapy for self-injurious behavior. *Mental Retardation, 2,* 83–87.

Durand, V. M. (1982). Analysis and intervention of self-injurious behavior. *Journal of the Association for the Severely Handicapped, 7,* 44–53.

Durand, V. M. (1987). In Response: "Look homeward angel" A call to return to our (functional) roots. *The Behavior Analyst, 10,* 299–302.

Durand, V. M. (1988). The Motivation Assessment Scale. In M. Hersen & A. S. Bellack (Eds.), *Dictionary of behavioral assessment techniques.* New York: Pergamon Press.

Durand, V. M., & Crimmins, O. B. (1988). Identifying the variables maintaining self-injurious behavior. *Journal of Autism and Developmental Disorders, 18,* 99–117.

Durand, V. M., & Kishi, G. (1987). Reducing severe behavior problems among people with dual sensory impairments: An evaluation of a technical assistance model. *Journal of the Association for Persons with Severe Handicaps, 12,* 2–10.

Edelson, S. M., Taubman, M. T., & Lovaas, O. I. (1983). Some social contexts of self-destructive behavior. *Journal of Abnormal Child Psychology, 11,* 299–312.

Epstein, I. H., Doke, L. A., Sajwaj, T. E., Sorrell, S., & Rimmer, B. (1974). Generality and side effects of overcorrection. *Journal of Applied Behavior Analysis, 7,* 385–390.

Evans, I. M., & Meyer, L. H. (1985). *An educative approach to behavior problems: A practical decision model for interventions with severely handicapped learners*. Baltimore: Brookes.

Favell, J. E., Azrin, N. H., Baumeister, A. A., Carr, E. C., Dorsey, M. F., Forehand, R., Foxx, R. M., Lovaas, O. I., Rincover, A., Risley, T. R., Romanczyk, R. G., Russo, D. C., Schroeder, S. R., & Solnick, J. V. (1982). The treatment of self-injurious behavior. *Behavior Therapy, 13,* 529–554.

Favell, J. E., McGimsey, J. F., & Jones, M. J. (1978). The use of physical restraint in the treatment of self-injury as a positive reinforcer. *Journal of Applied Behavior Analysis, 11,* 225–241.

Favell, J. E., McGimsey, J. F., Jones, M. J., & Cannon, P. R. (1981). Physical restraint as positive reinforcement. *American Journal of Mental Deficiency, 85,* 425–432.

Favell, J. E., & Reid, D. H. (1988). Generalizing and maintaining improvement in problem behavior. In R. Horner, G. Dunlap, & R. Koegel (Eds.), *Generalization and maintenance* (pp. 175–195). Baltimore: Brookes.

Foxx, R. (1978). An overview of overcorrection. *Journal of Pediatric Psychology, 3,* 97–101.

Foxx, R. M., & Bechtel, D. R. (1982). Overcorrection. *Progress in Behavior Modification, 13,* 227–228.

Foxx, R. M., & Dufresne, D. (1984). "Harry": The use of physical restraint as a reinforcer, timeout from restraint, and fading restraint in treating a self-injurious man. *Analysis and Intervention in Developmental Disabilities, 4,* 1–13.

Foxx, R. M., Plaska, T. G., & Bittle, R. G. (1986). Guidelines for the use of electric shock to treat aberrant behavior. *Progress in Behavior Modification, 20,* 1–34.

Foxx, R. M., Snyder, M. S., & Schroeder, F. A. (1979). A food satiation and oral hygiene punishment program to suppress chronic rumination by retarded persons. *Journal of Autism and Developmental Disorders, 9,* 399–412.

Frankel, F., Moss, D., Schofield, S., & Simmons, J. Q. (1976). Case study: Use of differential reinforcement to suppress self-injurious and aggressive behavior. *Psychological Reports, 39,* 843–849.

Frankel, F., & Simmons, J. Q. (1976). Self-injurious behavior in schizophrenic and retarded children. *American Journal on Mental Deficiency, 80,* 512–522.

Freud, A. (1954). Problems of infantile neurosis: A discussion. *The Psychoanalytic Study of the Child, 9,* 40–43.

Freud, A., & Burlingham, D. (1949). *Infants without families*. New York: International University Press.

Furey, E. (1989). Abuse of adults with mental retardation: A continuing shame. *Cuap Brief: Connecticut's University Affiliated Program on Developmental Disabilities, 3*(2). New Haven, CT: University Affiliated Program.

Gardner, W. I., & Cole, C. L. (1983). Selecting intervention procedures: What happened to behavioral assessment? In O. C. Karan & W. I. Gardner (Eds.), *Habilitation practices with the developmentally disabled who present behavioral and emotional disorders*. Madison, WI: Rehabilitation Research and Training Center in Mental Retardation.

Gaylord-Ross, R., Weeks, M., & Lipner, C. (1980). An analysis of antecedent response, and consequence events in the treatment of self-injurious behavior. *Education and Training of the Mentally Retarded, 15,* 35–42.

Gorman-Smith, D., & Matson, J. L. (1985). A review of treatment research for self-injurious and stereotyped responding. *Journal of Mental Deficiency Research, 29,* 295–308.

Griffin, J. C., Ricketts, R. W., & Williams, D. E. (1986). Reaction to Richmond et al.: Propriety of mechanical restraint and protective devices as tertiary techniques. In K. D. Gadow (Ed.), *Advances in learning and behavioral disabilities* (pp. 109–116). Greenwich, CT: JAI Press.

Griffin, J. C., Ricketts, R. W., Williams, D. E., Lock, B. J., Altmeyer, B. K., & Stark, M. T. (1987). A community survey of self-injurious behavior among developmentally disabled children and adolescents. *Hospital and Community Psychiatry, 38,* 959–963.

Griffith, R. G. (1983). The administrative issues: An ethical and legal perspective. In S. Axelrod (Ed.), *The effects of punishment on human behavior* (pp. 317–338). New York: Academic Press.

Gualtieri, G. T., & Hawk, B. (1980). Tardive dyskinesia and other drug-induced movement disorders among handicapped children and youth. *Applied Research in Mental Retardation, 1,* 55–69.

Guess, D., Helmstetter, E., Turnbull, R. H., & Knowlton, S. (1987). *Use of aversive procedures with persons who are disabled: An historical review and critical analysis*. Seattle, WA: Association for Persons with Severe Handicaps.

Harlow, H. F., & Griffin, G. (1965). Induced mental and social deficits in rhesus monkeys. In S. F. Osler & R. E. Cooke (Eds.), *The biosocial basis of mental retardation*. Baltimore: Johns Hopkins Press.

Harlow, H. F., & Harlow, M. K. (1971). Psychopathology in monkeys. In H. D. Kimmel (Ed.), *Experimental psychopathology*. New York: Academic Press.

Harris, S. L., & Ersner-Hershfield, R. (1978). Behavioral suppression of seriously disruptive behavior in psychotic and retarded patients: A review of punishment and its alternatives. *Psychological Bulletin, 85,* 1352–1375.

Heidorn, S. D., & Jensen, C. C. (1984). Generalization and maintenance of the reduction of self-injurious behavior by two types of reinforcement. *Behavior Research and Therapy, 22,* 581–586.

Hoffner, W. (1950). Oral aggressiveness and ego development. *International Journal of Psychoanalysis, 31,* 156–160.

Horner, R. D. (1980). The effects of environmental "enrichment" program on the behavior of institutionalized profoundly retarded children. *Journal of Applied Behavior Analysis, 13,* 473–491.

Horner, R. D., & Barton, E. S. (1980). Operant techniques in the analysis and modification of self-injurious behavior. *Behavior Research of Severe Developmental Disabilities, 1,* 61–69.

Horner, R. H. (1990). Nonaversive behavior. *Newsletter from RRTC on Community-Referenced Non-Aversive Behavior Management in Oregon*. Richmond: Rehabilitation Research and Training Center, Virginia Commonwealth University.

Ilg, F. L., & Ames, L. B. (1955). *Child behavior*. New York: Harper.

Iwata, B. A., Dorsey, M. F., Slifer, K. J., Bauman, K. E., & Richman, G. S. (1982). Toward a functional analysis of self-injury. *Analysis and Intervention in Developmental Disabilities, 2,* 3–20.

Johnson, W. L., & Baumeister, A. A. (1978). Self-injurious behavior: A review and analysis of methodological details of published studies. *Behavior Modification, 2,* 465–487.

Johnson, W. L., & Day, R. M. (1992). The incidence and prevalence of self-injurious behavior. In J. K. Luiselli, J. L. Matson, & N. N. Singh (Eds.), *Self-injury: Analysis, assessment, and treatment* (pp. 21–56). New York: Springer.

Johnson, W. L., & Rea, J. A. (1986). Self-injurious behavior treatment and research: A historical perspective. *Advances in Learning and Behavioral Disabilities, 5,* 1–23.

Jones, F. H., Simmons, J. Q., & Frankel, F. (1974). An extinction procedure for eliminating the self-destructive behavior in a 9-year-old autistic girl. *Journal of Autism and Childhood Schizophrenia, 4,* 241–250.

Jones, I. O. (1982). Self-injury: Toward a biological basis. *Perspectives on Biologic Medicine, 26,* 137–143.

Kelly, J. A., & Drabman, R. S. (1977). Overcorrection: An effective procedure that failed. *Journal of Clinical Child Psychology, 6,* 38–40.

Klein, M. (1932). An obsessional neurosis in a six-year-old girl. In A. Strachey (Ed.), *The psycho-analysis of children* (pp. 35–57). New York: Delacorte Press/Seymour Lawrence.

LaVigna, G., & Donnellan, A. (1986). *Alternatives to punishment: Solving behavior problems with nonaversive strategies.* New York: Irvington.

Lennox, D. B., Miltenberger, R. G., Spengler, P., & Erfanian, N. (1988). Decelerative treatment practices with persons who have mental retardation: A review of five years of the literature. *American Journal of Mental Deficiency, 92,* 492–501.

Levy, D. M. (1944). On the problems of movement restraint: Tics, stereotyped movements and hyperactivity. *American Journal of Orthopsychiatry, 14,* 644–671.

Lichstein, K. L., & Schreibman, L. (1976). Employing electric shock with autistic children. *Journal of Autism and Childhood Schizophrenia, 6,* 163–173.

Lockwood, K., & Bourland, G. (1982). Reduction of self-injurious behaviors by reinforcement and toy use. *Mental Retardation, 20,* 169–173.

Lovaas, O. I., Freitag, G., Gold, V. J., & Kassorla, I. C. (1965). Experimental studies in childhood schizophrenia: I. Analysis of self-destructive behavior. *Journal of Experimental Child Psychology, 2,* 67–84.

Lovaas, O. I., Schaeffer, B., & Simmons, J. Q. (1965). Building social behavior in autistic children by use of electric shock. *Journal of Experimental Research in Personality, 1,* 99–109.

Lovaas, O. I., & Simmons, J. Q. (1969). Manipulation of self-destruction in three retarded children. *Journal of Applied Behavior Analysis, 2,* 143–157.

Luiselli, J. K., Helfen, C. S., Colozzi, G., Donnellon, S., & Pemberton, B. (1978). Controlling the self-inflicted biting of a retarded child by the differential reinforcement of other behavior. *Psychological Reports, 42,* 435–438.

Mauer, A. (1983). The shock rod controversy. *Journal of Clinical Child Psychology, 12,* 272–278.

McGee, I. J., Menalascino, F. J., Hobbs, D. C., & Menousek, P. E. (1987). *Gentle teaching: A nonaversive approach to helping persons with mental retardation.* New York: Human Services Press.

Menninger, K. (1938). *Man against himself.* New York: Harcourt, Brace & World.

Merbaum, M. (1973). The modification of self-destructive behavior by a mother-therapist using aversive stimulation. *Behavior Therapy, 4,* 442–447.

Mesaros, R. A. (1983). *A review of the issues and literature regarding positive programming and contingency management procedures for use with autistic children.* Unpublished manuscript, University of Wisconsin, Madison.

Meyer, L. H., & Evans, I. M. (1989). *Nonaversive interventions for problem behaviors.* Baltimore: Brookes.

Miron, N. B. (1971). Behavior modification techniques in the treatment of self-injurious behavior in institutionalized retardates. *NIMH Bulletin of Suicidology, 8,* 64–69.

Mulick, J., Hoyt, R., Rojahn, J., & Schroeder, S. (1978). Reduction of a "nervous habit" in a profoundly retarded youth by increasing toy play: A case study. *Journal of Behavior Therapy and Experimental Psychology, 9,* 381–385.

Murphy, R., Ruprecht, M., Baggio, P., & Nunes, D. (1979). The use of mild punishment in combination with reinforcement of alternate behavior to reduce the self-injurious behavior of a profoundly retarded individual. *American Association for the Education of Severely/Profoundly Handicapped Persons, 4,* 187–195.

Myers, D. V. (1975). Extinction, DRO, and response-cost procedures for eliminating self-injurious behavior: A case study. *Behavior Research and Therapy, 13,* 189–191.

National Institutes of Health. (1989). *Consensus development conference statement: Treatment of destructive behaviors in persons with disabilities.* Washington, DC: U.S. Government Printing Office.

Nunes, D. L., Murphy, R. J., & Ruprecht, M. L. (1977). Reducing self-injurious behavior of severely retarded individuals through withdrawal of reinforcement procedures. *Behavior Modification, 1,* 499–514.

Nyhan, W. L. (1968). Lesch-Nyham syndrome: Summary of clinical features. *Federal Proceedings, 27,* 1034–1041.

Nyhan, W. L. (1976). Behavior in the Lesch-Nyhan syndrome. *Journal of Autism and Childhood Schizophrenia, 6,* 235–252.

O'Neill, R. E., Horner, R. H., Albin, R. W., Storey, K., & Sprague, J. R. (1990). *Functional analysis: A practical assessment guide.* Sycamore, IL: Sycamore.

Rapoff, M. A., Altman, K., & Christophersen, E. R. (1980). Suppression of self-injurious behavior: Determining the least restrictive alternative. *Journal of Mental Deficiency Research, 24,* 37–46.

Repp, A. C., & Deitz, S. (1974). Reducing aggressive and self-injurious behavior of institutionalized retarded children through reinforcement of other behaviors. *Journal of Applied Behavior Analysis, 7,* 313–325.

Repp, A. C., Deitz, S. M., & Deitz, D. E. D. (1976). Reducing inappropriate behaviors in classrooms and in individual sessions through DRO schedules of reinforcement. *Mental Retardation, 14,* 11–15.

Repp, A. C., Felce, D., & Barton, L. E. (1988). Basing the treatment of stereotypic and self-injurious behaviors on hypotheses of their causes. *Journal of Applied Behavior Analysis, 21,* 281–289.

Repp, A. C., & Singh, N. N. (1990). *Perspectives on the use of nonaversive and aversive interventions for persons with developmental disabilities.* Sycamore, IL: Sycamore.

Reynolds, G. S. (1961). Behavior contrast. *Journal of Experimental Analysis of Behavior, 4,* 57–71.

Richmond, G., Schroeder, S. R., & Bickel, W. (1986). Tertiary prevention of attrition related to self-injurious behavior. In K. D. Gadow (Ed.), *Advances in learning and behavioral disabilities* (pp. 97–108). Greenwich, CT: JAI Press.

Ricketts, R. W., Goza, A., & Matese, M. (1993). A 4-year follow-up treatment of self-injury. *Journal of Behavior Therapy and Experimental Psychiatry, 24,* 57–62.

Risley, T. R. (1968). The effects and side effects of punishing the autistic behaviors of an autistic child. *Journal of Applied Behavior Analysis, 1,* 21–34.

Rolider, A., & Van Houten, R. (1985). Movement suppression time-out for undesirable behavior in psychotic and severely developmentally delayed children. *Journal of Applied Behavior Analysis, 4,* 275–288.

Romanczyk, R. G. (1986). Self-injurious behavior: Conceptualization, assessment, and treatment. In K. D. Gadow (Ed.), *Advances in learning and behavioral disabilities* (pp. 29–56). Greenwich, CT: JAI Press.

Ross, R. R., Meichenbaum, D. H., & Humphrey, C. (1974). Treatment of nocturnal head-banging by behavior modification techniques: A case report. *Behavior Research and Therapy, 9,* 151–154.

Rusch, R. G., Hall, J. C., & Griffin, H. C. (1986). Abuse-provoking characteristics of institutionalized mentally retarded individuals. *American Journal of Mental Deficiency, 90*(6), 618–624.

Saposnek, D. T., & Watson, L. S. (1974). The elimination of self-destructive behavior of a psychotic child: A case study. *Behavior Therapy, 5,* 79–89.

Schroeder, S. R., Bickel, W. K., & Richmond, G. (1986). Primary and secondary prevention of self-injurious behaviors: A life-long problem. In K. D. Gadow (Ed.), *Advances in learning and behavioral disabilities* (pp. 63–85). Greenwich, CT: JAI Press.

Schroeder, S. R., Schroeder, C. S., Rojahn, J., & Mulick, J. A. (1981). Self-injurious behavior: An analysis of behavior management techniques. In J. L. Matson & J. R. McCartney (Eds.), *Handbook of behavior modification with the mentally retarded* (pp. 61–115). New York: Plenum Press.

Schroeder, S. R., Schroeder, C., Smith, B., & Dalldorf, J. (1978). Prevalence of self-injurious behavior in a large state facility for the retarded. *Journal of Autism and Childhood Schizophrenia, 8,* 261–269.

Seegmiller, J. E. (1972). Lesch-Nyhan syndrome and the X-linked uric acidurais. *Hospital Practice, 7,* 79–90.

Simpson, R. L., & Sasso, G. M. (1978). The modification of rumination in a severely emotionally disturbed child through an overcorrection procedure. *American Association for the Education of the Severely/Profoundly Handicapped Review, 3,* 145–150.

Singh, N., Manning, P., & Argell, M. (1982). Effects of an oral hygiene punishment procedure on chronic rumination and collateral behaviors in monozygous twins. *Journal of Applied Behavior Analysis, 15,* 309–314.

Singh, N. N., & Millichamp, C. J. (1985). Pharmacological treatment of self-injurious behavior in mentally retarded persons. *Journal of Autism and Developmental Disorders, 15*(3), 256–267.

Skinner, B. F. (1938). *The behavior of organisms.* New York: Appleton-Century-Crofts.

Snell, M. (1987). In Response: In response to Axelrod's review of "Alternatives to punishment." *The Behavior Analyst, 10,* 295–297.

Solnick, I. V., Rincover, A., & Peterson, C. R. (1977). Some determinants of reinforcing and punishing effects of time out. *Journal of Applied Behavior Analysis, 10,* 415–424.

Tanner, B. A., & Zeiler, M. (1975). Punishment of self-injurious behavior using aromatic ammonia as the aversive stimulus. *Journal of Applied Behavior Analysis, 8,* 53–57.

Tate, B. G., & Baroff, G. (1966). Aversive control of self-injurious behavior in a psychotic boy. *Behavior Research and Therapy, 4,* 281–287.

Touchette, P. E., MacDonald, R. F., & Langer, S. N. (1985). A scatter plot for identifying stimulus control of problem behavior. *Journal of Applied Behavior Analysis, 18,* 343–351.

Turnbull, R. H., Guest, D., Backus, L. H., Barber, P. A., Fielder, C. R., Helmstetter, E., & Summer, J. A. (1987). A model for analyzing the moral aspects of special education and behavioral intervention: The moral aspects of aversive procedures. In P. R. Dokecki & R. N. Zaner (Eds.), *Ethics of dealing with persons with severe handicaps: Towards a research agenda* (pp. 167–210). Baltimore: Brookes.

Watson, L. S. (1967). Application of operant conditioning techniques to institutionalized severely and profoundly retarded children. *Mental Retardation Abstracts, 4,* 1–4.

Weeks, M., & Gaylord-Ross, R. (1981). Task difficulty and aberrant behavior in severely handicapped students. *Journal of Applied Behavior Analysis, 14,* 449–463.

Williams, D. E., Kirkpatrick-Sanchez, S., & Crocker, W. T. (1994). A long-term follow-up of treatment for severe self-injury. *Research in Developmental Disabilities, 15*(6), 487–499.

Williams, D. E., Kirkpatrick-Sanchez, S., & Iwata, B. A. (1993). A comparison of shock intensity in the treatment of long-standing and severe self-injurious behavior. *Research in Developmental Disabilities, 14,* 207–219.

Wolf, M., Risley, T., Johnson, M., Harris, F., & Allen, K. E. (1967). Application of operant conditioning procedures to the behavior problems of an autistic child: A follow-up and extension. *Behavior Research and Therapy, 5,* 103–111.

Wolf, M., Risley, T., & Mees, P. (1964). Application of operant conditioning procedures to the behavior problems of an autistic child. *Behavior Research and Therapy, 1,* 305–312.

Woods, T. S. (1980). Bringing autistic self-stimulatory behavior under S-Delta stimulus control. *Journal of Special Education, 4,* 61–70.

Wright, D. R., Brown, R. A., & Andrews, M. E. (1978). Remission of chronic ruminative vomiting through a reverse of social contingencies. *Behavior Research and Therapy, 16,* 134–136.

Zehr, M. D., & Theobald, D. E. (1978). Manual guidance used in a punishment procedure: The active ingredient in overcorrection. *Journal of Mental Deficiency Research, 22,* 263–272.

Deaf-Blind

JoAnn M. Marchant

LEARNING GOALS

Upon completion of this chapter the reader will be able to

■ define and describe deaf-blindness as a severe disability;

■ discuss the importance of ecologic assessment and orientation/mobility training;

■ discuss in detail functional vision programming;

■ discuss techniques for enhancing communication; and

■ list and describe five examples of how games can be used to promote learning.

Federal legislation and regulations continue to refer to "deaf-blind" individuals, but current best practice in the field of special education dictates that such individuals be viewed as having dual sensory impairments or multiple sensory impairments. These terms are more accurate because the label *deaf-blind* has usually included not only students who are deaf and blind but also those who are visually and auditorially impaired.

It has always been difficult to determine the actual number of students in the United States with both vision and hearing impairments. Reporting systems vary from state to state and such students may be labeled as *deaf-blind, multihandicapped, severely/profoundly handicapped,* or *blind* or *deaf.* A national registry of students with multiple sensory disabilities has been established, but concern exists at the state and national levels that the available data are not accurate. It is significant to note that federal legislation in 1968 established 16

deaf-blind centers around the nation to serve children. In 1968, the estimates were that 250 children were served. In 1980, the 16 centers reported serving close to 6,000 children through 300 regional service centers. A more recent estimate of children and youth aged 0 to 21 who are deaf-blind puts the count at 7,839 (Baldwin, 1991).

In 1982, federal funding was expanded to individual states that have desired to manage their own programs for these students. In 1985 and 1986, other federal monies (Title VI–C) were targeted toward nonserved populations such as preschool students and students over 18 years of age. These Title VI–C funds have also been utilized to provide technical assistance centers to assist professionals and families.

Although residential and public school programs serve larger numbers of students with severe multiple sensory disabilities than they did in the 1960s (Benson & Turnbull, 1986), many students are still found in institutional settings. The question regarding the definition of a student who is deaf-blind remains, as do problems related to appropriate curriculum, staff development, and instructional strategies. In this chapter, I focus on these issues and present case studies of several students with dual sensory impairments.

FUNCTIONAL DESCRIPTION

Students who have dual sensory impairments may be blind and deaf, or have visual and auditory impairments. The Helen Keller National Center estimates that about 94% of such individuals have residual hearing or residual sight that can facilitate their educational programs. Because of the severity of their disabling conditions, it is nearly impossible to assess these persons with formalized testing procedures to measure visual and auditory acuity and intellectual functioning. Many of these students are *functionally* vision and hearing impaired and demonstrate mental deficits. Model programs have demonstrated that instructional strategies utilized with students who are visually impaired, hearing impaired, and severely/profoundly disabled are often effective with students with dual sensory impairments.

Program Components

As noted previously, the curriculum for students with dual sensory impairments should include components that have been shown to assist students with a single disabling condition. Such components are found in curricula for programs for individuals who are blind, deaf, multiply disabled, and severely/profoundly disabled.

Ecologic Assessment

Skills that are taught to students with dual sensory disabilities should be those that the student needs to function in all the different environments in his

or her daily life. An assessment for such skills must involve teachers, therapists, parents, and other significant individuals who work with each student. This team of persons must prioritize and agree to goals and objectives that will be implemented for each student. The educational program needs to be individualized so that each student learns skills that will be utilized in daily activities with his or her family. [See Appendix 13.A for an assessment instrument for use with families in developing an Individualized Education Program (IEP).] Table 13.1 lists steps to be used in the ecologic curriculum development process.

This process represents a "top–down" approach that focuses on the skills an individual needs to function independently in a variety of environments such as home, school, and community (Brown, Branston, Hamre-Nietupski, Pumpien, & Certo, 1979). This is a very different approach from the developmental approach, which attempts

---

Table 13.1.   Steps in Curriculum Design

Step 1.   Delineate curriculum domains (vocational, domestic, community, recreation/leisure).

Step 2.   Delineate the variety of current and subsequent natural environments in each domain in which students function or might function.

Step 3.   Inventory and delineate the subenvironments within each environment.

Step 4.   Inventory and delineate the activities performed by nondisabled persons in those subenvironments.

Step 5.   Prioritize activities to delineate goals of the Individualized Education Program.

Step 6.   Delineate the skills needed to perform the activities.

Step 7.   Conduct a discrepancy analysis to determine required skills not currently in the student's repertoire.

Step 8.   Determine necessary adaptations.

Step 9.   Develop an instructional program.

to move students along normal developmental sequences in areas such as language development and fine and gross motor and cognitive skills. Students with multiple disabilities often acquire new skills at a slow rate, so they may never acquire skills needed for adult life if the developmental model is utilized.

Orientation and Mobility Training

Welsh and Blasch (1980) defined orientation and mobility as the task of teaching persons with visual impairments to move independently, safely, and purposefully through the environment. Orientation skills refer to the processes of utilizing remaining senses to establish one's position and relationships to all other significant objects in the environment. Mobility skills refer to one's ability to navigate from one's fixed position to another position in the environment.

Table 13.2 provides a basic outline of the orientation and mobility skills taught to a person who is totally blind. The outline progresses from simple skills to advanced techniques for complex, independent travel in many environments. Students with severe sensory disabilities may follow this traditional developmental sequence but at a slower rate.

This developmental approach may not be appropriate for all students with dual sensory impairments. If progress is not noted, a functional orientation and mobility program should be developed according to the six-step model in Figure 13.1; this is an ecologic approach with four main principles.

The first principle involves having orientation and mobility skills take place within and across the daily activities in which a student engages. Specific training takes place when travel is necessary, and instructional trials for an objective are performed in several locations. For example, a child practices using a cane on the way from the bus and on the path to the cafeteria.

The second principle involves the use of interspersed training trials. A student may be expected

Table 13.2.   Scope and Sequence of Orientation and Mobility

Concept development

Basic techniques
  Sighted guide
  Protective and information gathering
  Forearm technique
  Trailing
  Lower body protective technique
  Independent room orientation

Introduction to cane techniques
  Touch technique
  Training with the touch technique
  Diagonal cane technique
  Touch-and-slide technique
  Stair travel
  Congested area cane technique
  Entering and exiting doorways, cars, and so forth
  Touch-and-drag technique
  Three-point touch technique

Residential travel

Light business travel

Major metropolitan travel

Rural travel

Snow travel and other adverse conditions

to complete independently only two skills involved in getting from one place to another. He or she will be physically prompted through the other skills. Instruction is provided when the skills designated for training are required. As the student masters the initial objectives, more of each route is added to his or her performance criteria.

The third principle involves setting up a functional motivation for travel. This principle incorporates a "context instruction" phase whereby the teacher sets up an expectation that, at the end of the route, is an activity like riding the bus or eating lunch. In doing this, the teacher provides a context in which the student can perceive travel as necessary.

The fourth principle involves the use of systematic, databased procedures. Fading, or systematic

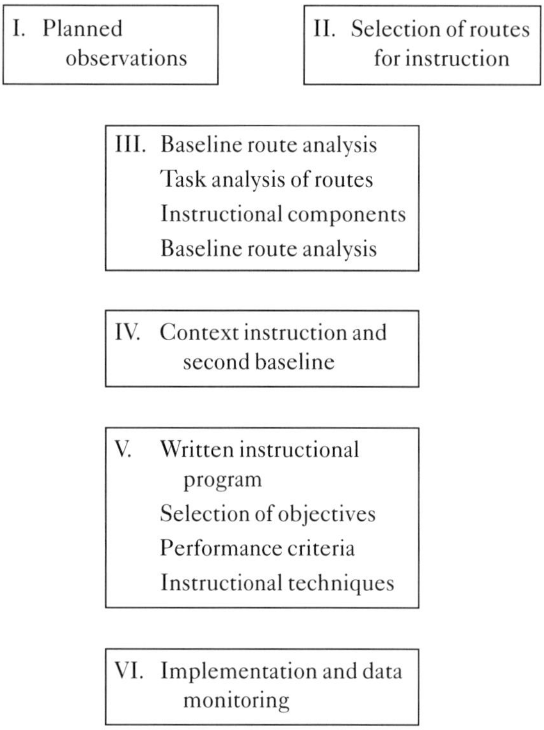

Figure 13.1. Functional orientation and mobility model.

use of most-to-least assistance, is used for initial instruction whereas least-to-most prompts and time delay are used in later stages of acquisition.

These instructional strategies allow traditional orientation and mobility skills to be taught as part of the functional education program. The student with dual sensory impairments benefits when all members of the transdisciplinary, Individualized Education Program committee work together to teach orientation and mobility skills during the regular daily travel routes. This model demands continual communication among orientation and mobility instructors, vision specialists, and classroom teachers. Such collaboration results in more effective orientation and mobility training for these students in different school and community settings.

CASE EXAMPLE: JOHN

John is a 19-year-old man with dual sensory impairments. He is profoundly deaf and has significant visual deficits. A transdisciplinary team has worked with him for many years. Team members include a special education teacher, job coach, orientation and mobility instructor, teacher for the hearing impaired, audiologist, and vision teacher.

A transition plan was begun when he was 15 years of age. The focus has been to prepare him to work independently in the community while residing in the home of foster parents with whom he has lived for many years. He has been taught to get around the community using a public bus. He is employed at the post office as a mail sorter. His hearing loss presents no problem on this job, and magnification devices are used to alleviate his vision difficulties. A job coach helped him to learn the job, and the special education teacher assists in money management and social skill development. An interagency agreement is in place to ensure that the local community service board will provide follow-up services when he completes his public school program. In addition to this support, a number of nondisabled employees at the post office have learned sign language to communicate with John on the job site. Although John has moderate mental retardation, his social skills are excellent, and he is nicely accepted by other workers.

CASE EXAMPLE: MARY

Mary is a 10-year-old with profound mental retardation and multiple sensory physical disabilities. She is cortically blind, but she does respond to sounds with gazes and turns her head toward sounds on occasion. She smiles and coos when stimulated by touch and she seems to enjoy music. A team of professionals, utilizing modern technology, has devised switches that allow Mary to activate toys and musical devices by eyebrow and tongue movements. She is also physically prompted to use switches to control devices in her environment such as the toaster. This technology allows her to participate partially in daily activities.

Staff members also communicate with her by telling her what is happening and by using tactile prompts during all activities. Different staff members wear different colognes to facilitate her identification of them.

Opportunities for choice are constantly presented to Mary. For example, two flavors of toothpaste are offered as well as two scents of soap during daily activities. Many instructional activities take place in community settings such as the mall or fast-food restaurants. The family and professionals plan together to be sure that everyone exposes Mary to multiple sensory experiences.

Constant communication among staff members, respite workers, and parents is required to assist Mary in interacting with her environment in all settings.

FUNCTIONAL VISION PROGRAMMING

Four methods traditionally have been used to enhance residual vision: optical aids, contrast effects, vision stimulation, and vision training (Lundervol, 1987). Students with dual sensory impairments benefit most from structured vision training. Such training is based on the sequential application of operant principles and database instruction (Snell, 1978). In this approach, visual behaviors are learned in naturally occurring situations so that the use of residual vision results in specific, desirable, and functional consequences. Visual skills are not taught as isolated skills but rather in the context of learning other age-appropriate tasks and activities. This approach is very different from the traditional visual-stimulation approach of using bright blinking lights in massed trials to stimulate visual skills.

This functional-context vision training involves five steps:

1. Determine the targeted visual skill.

2. Select a training context.

3. Develop an instructional strategy for the visual skill.

4. Develop an instructional strategy for the other skills to be used as the training context for the visual skill.

5. Implement the programs and monitor progress on the basis of data.

Residual vision in students with multiple disabilities can be evaluated in a number of ways. Classroom teachers should enlist the assistance of visual specialists in program development (Gee & Goetz, 1985).

Such assessment data allow the team to identify what vision skills the student has and to understand what visual behaviors he or she lacks. Table 13.3 presents a list of different visual functions and possible measures of responses that a teacher may want to consider in setting objectives (Lundervol, 1987).

When a specific vision objective has been pinpointed, the next step involves choosing a functional context in which to teach the desired skill. The skill should be taught in a functional setting with age-appropriate materials. It is also important to set up training activities that will motivate the student.

The team should develop the instructional activities using current strategies for severely/profoundly disabled programming. Reinforcers should be naturally occurring events whenever possible, and teaching activities should be carried out in as nonobtrusive a manner as possible in community-based settings. An example is teaching scanning skills at the candy bar counter in the local grocery store during hours when the store is not crowded.

Table 13.3.   Visual Functions and Responses

Visual Function	Possible Responses Forms
Orient to presence of stimulus	Head turn, gaze shift, brief fixation (less than 1 second)
Fixation (bifoveal or monofoveal)	Sustained eye contact, presence of corneal light reflection
Accommodative convergence	Continuous fixation on object as it approaches nose; typically, fixation is broken as object moves within 4 inches of nose
Gaze shift	Fixation on one object, then on second object, without smooth tracking
Tracking	Smooth eye movement to follow object, both eyes aligned, head typically follows eyes
Scanning	Systematic search of visual display
Peripheral vision	Gaze shift to find object located on peripheral visual field

FUNCTIONAL HEARING PROGRAMMING

Audiometric assessment is used to determine the presence and intensity of a hearing loss and to ascertain whether the loss is conductive or sensorineural in nature. Students with multiple sensory impairments are often difficult to test.

The single most useful test for audiologists is the auditory brain-stem response (ABR). This test is utilized when a student does not respond to a behavioral test. Behavioral tests use voluntary responses, whereas the ABR measures physiologic responses of the auditory mechanism. The ABR tests the general functional status of the auditory mechanism but does not provide an audiogram because it is not really a hearing test.

It is of value with individuals who are severely delayed because it assesses the auditory system without any need to involve behavioral responses (Martin, 1978).

Behavioral testing should be conducted in conjunction with physiologic assessment whenever possible. Visual reinforcer audiometry (VRA) procedures are useful because they require only primitive head-turn responses. Bright lights and mechanical toys are paired with sounds to elicit responses. Teachers can work closely with audiologists to test students with multiple sensory disabilities because the teachers know what tangible objects or activities are reinforcing for individual children.

Once a hearing loss has been identified, the transdisciplinary team must decide whether to attempt use of a hearing aid and when to do so. Some children must be programmed to reduce tactile defensiveness or self-abusive behaviors before hearing-aid amplification can be used.

If hearing aids are ruled out, or if additional input is needed, vibrotactile units can be utilized. These devices provide sensory input through vibrations on the skin. A microphone picks up sounds, and an amplifier amplifies and filters them. The signal is sent to a small vibrator that is attached to the arm or finger of the student. These units have proved most beneficial when used to supplement visual information (Martin, 1978).

ESTABLISHING COMMUNICATION

Teachers working with students who have dual sensory impairments must develop systematic methods of communication with them. The communication strategies should capitalize on the individual strengths identified in the assessment of each child. The focus of establishing communication skills should be to enable each student to exert some control over his or her environment and to assist him or her in interacting with other people. These skills permit the student to bond with others and to feel comfortable in the classroom.

Cooley (1987) suggested that teachers use a variety of techniques to communicate with students who have dual sensory impairments. One technique is to give the student opportunities to make choices during all activities. Two or more options should be presented whenever food, toys, or activities are selected. The student can be guided through touching each item and then prompted to make a choice.

A second strategy is to force each student to be as independent as possible. The teacher can guide students through part of a task and then wait for them to complete the activity independently. For example, the teacher helps the student stand in front of a chair and feel the edge of the seat, then waits for him or her to seat himself or herself independently.

Another suggestion involves having the teacher use physical prompts or signs to let a student know when he or she is approaching or leaving the student. A gentle touch on the arm or hand can signal arrival and a different handshake or pat on the shoulder can indicate that the teacher is leaving the student.

Special prompts should also be utilized to let the student know who is approaching. These can involve the student's feeling the person's hair or eyeglasses. Another suggestion is to have the teacher always wear the same perfume.

Staff can use object prompts to let the student know what is about to happen. At lunchtime, the student can feel the plate and utensils. Other specific prompts can indicate when an activity is completed and when it is time to do something else. Many teachers find it helpful to use the sign for "finished" to help students move from one activity to another. It is important that these strategies be carried out consistently across all environments and by all persons who interact with a student if they are to become functional for the child.

LEARNING SKILLS THROUGH GAMES

One of the most effective vehicles for teaching new skills to students with severe visual and hearing impairments is through games. Developing activities that are fun can be an excellent means of holding the student's attention. Fun is an essential ingredient for leisure-time program success. In addition to facilitating socialization, games can foster acquisition and retention of other target behaviors.

Games are valuable tools for teachers of exceptional children who realize that students need repeated exposure to material in order to learn and retain it. Carefully chosen games can provide practice that fosters acquisition and retention of the skill. An example of this is the use of a "lotto" game, instead of repeated seat work, to practice matching or visual–perceptual skills. Another example is "a-tisket-a-tasket" to practice skipping. A creative teacher can easily involve game activities in all aspects of daily planning but must take care to ensure that the games used are on the correct developmental level of the student and that the student possesses the necessary game skills, such as the ability to use dice or to read the game cards.

Selecting Games for Individuals with Developmental Disabilities

The selection of games to use with persons who are developmentally disabled is a twofold process. First, the developmental or academic level at which the student is functioning must be considered; second, the level of game skills at which the student is functioning must be assessed. The developmental or academic functioning level of the student is assessed by the interdisciplinary team that formulates the IEP for that student. Developmental assessment devices are employed in addition to the standard intelligence tests normally used to evaluate students with disabilities. Once the general assessment of the student is completed, the teacher must then determine the specific skills to be taught or reinforced by the use of games in the classroom.

Skill Areas For Which Games Can Be Used

Valett (1968) has proposed six skill areas of basic learning abilities: gross motor development, sensorimotor development, perceptual motor skills, language skills, conceptual skills, and social skills. Each ability area is defined and broken down into component skills, which are also defined. The skill areas and definitions as formulated by Valett are presented in Tables 13.4 through 13.6. Representative samples of commercial and group games that might facilitate acquisition of skills in each area are included.

No attempt is made in these tables to define which developmental or academic level each game represents. Rather, an attempt is made to point out the many skill areas in which games can play a role in an educational setting. A teacher who has assessed a class can determine relevant games to introduce, on the basis of the objectives that have been set for individual children. The teacher must take care, however, that the skills being reinforced are neither too simple nor too difficult for the individual child involved. For example, once a student has mastered the number concepts being practiced in a bingo game, playing the game is no longer educational in nature, and the teacher may wish to introduce a flashcard game involving simple addition facts or a board game involving addition of the two sets of numbers rolled on dice if addition is the next skill to be developed. Bingo can still be used for recreational and leisure-time purposes by the child, but the arithmetic lesson should include new game activities.

The teacher of individuals who are severely developmentally disabled with severe sensory disabilities can also make use of the ability areas presented by Valett (1968) but may have to plan games on a lower ability level. For example, for those games suggested for use in training body–spatial organization, if the child with dual sensory disabilities does not have game skills necessary to move through an obstacle course, the teacher may want to plan the game to initially involve moving only through one item, such as a tunnel. Another example of such adaptation involves games for developing auditory acuity. "Touch What You Hear" is a game in which each child is blindfolded and moves about the room looking for the spot where the drum or cymbals are being played, with the winner the one who finds the noise the quickest. A teacher of students with dual sensory disabilities may adapt this game by hiding behind the students and having them turn to the noise. The winner would be the student who turns first.

In conclusion, games are an excellent learning medium for individuals who have serious sensory impairments. Games can enhance motor skills, socialization, and academics, and even provide indirect assistance in work preparation.

FINAL THOUGHTS

Educational programming for students with dual sensory disabilities has changed drastically in recent decades. Many of the strategies included in current best practices for this population parallel the programming suggested for students with severe or profound disabilities.

Such programming demands a commitment to systematic, databased instruction. It requires teachers to be attuned to a student's attempts to communicate or to interact with things around him or her. Programming for these students provides a real challenge to professionals from a variety of disciplines who must form working partnerships to design a truly individualized program to assist each student.

Table 13.4. Games for Gross Motor Development

Skill	Definition	Games/Hobbies
Rolling	Ability to roll one's body in a controlled manner	line games obstacle courses
Sitting	Ability to sit erect in normal position without support or constant reminding	"Simon Says" circle sitting games
Crawling	Ability to crawl on hands and knees in a smooth and coordinated way	line and circle games obstacle courses
Walking	Ability to walk erect in a coordinated fashion without support	line and circle games nature walks hikes
Running	Ability to run without a change of pace	line and circle games relays "Squirrels in Trees" jogging
Throwing	Ability to throw a ball with a reasonable degree of accuracy	line and circle games relays dribbling and "throwing baskets"
Jumping	Ability to jump simple obstacles without falling	line games imitative games "Jack Be Nimble" jumping rope
Skipping	Ability to skip in normal play	"A Tisket a Tasket" "Follow the Leader"
Dancing	Ability to move one's body in a coordinated response to music	"Statues" dancing
Self-identification	Ability to identify one's self	"Who Knows Where ____ Is?" simple rhythms
Body Localization	Ability to locate parts of one's body	"Simon Says Touch" "Put Your Finger"
Body Abstraction	Ability to transfer and generalize self-concepts and body parts	"Funny Face" "Mr. Potato Head" "Cootie"
Muscular Strength	Ability to use one's muscles to perform physical tasks	all active games "Indian wrestling" gymnastics
General Physical Health	Ability to understand and apply principles of health and hygiene and to evidence good general health	"Go and Grow Game" "Circulation Game"

Table 13.5.   Games for Sensorimotor Integration

Skill	Definition	Games/Hobbies
Balance and Rhythm	Ability to maintain gross and fine motor balance and to move rhythmically	hopscotch "A Tisket a Tasket" "Pat-a-Cake" dancing swimming
Body-Spatial Organization	Ability to move one's body in an integrated way around and through objects in the spatial environment	"Follow the Leader" obstacle courses relays walking biking
Reaction-Speed Dexterity	Ability to respond efficiently to general directions or assignments	"Simon Says" "Boggle" candle or sculpture making
Tactile Discrimination	Ability to identify and match objects by touching and feeling	"Feeley Meely" making collages
Directionality	Ability to know right from left, up from down, forward from backward, and directional orientation	"Simon Says" "Tic-Tac-Toe" hopscotch square dancing biking
Laterality	Ability to integrate one's sensorimotor contact with the environment through establishment of homolateral hand, eye, and foot dominance	"Simon Says" line and circle games "Twister"
Time Orientation	Ability to judge lapses in time and to be aware of time concepts	"Tell Time" "Quizmo" hide and seek cooking TV watching pet care

Table 13.6. Games for Perceptual–Motor Skills

Skill	Definition	Games/Hobbies
Auditory Acuity	Ability to receive and differentiate auditory stimuli	"Turn to the Noise" "Touch What You Hear" listening to records
Auditory Decoding	Ability to understand sounds or spoken words	"Simon Says" "Bingo" exercise records
Auditory–Vocal Association	Ability to respond verbally in a meaningful way to auditory stimuli	spelling bee "Go to the Head of the Class" poetry or story reciting
Auditory Sequencing	Ability to recall in correct sequence and detail prior auditory information	"I'm Going On a Trip" "Instructo" storytelling games acting puppet shows singing
Visual Acuity	Ability to see and differentiate meaningfully and accurately objects in one's visual field	"Spin and Say" car traveling games collecting groups of items
Visual Coordination and Pursuit	Ability to follow and track objects and symbols with coordinated eye movement	"Busy Bee" ball games electric screen games cutting bowling
Visual-Form Discrimination	Ability to visually differentiate the forms and symbols in one's environment	"Lotto" matching card games "Tic-Tac-Toe" checkers reading coloring collections
Visual Figure–Ground Differentiation	Ability to perceive objects in foreground and background to separate them meaningfully	"GNIP GNOP" hide and seek dominoes electric screen games star watching use of word-game books
Visual Memory	Ability to recall accurately prior visual experiences	"Memory" "Jack in the Beanstalk Memory Game" coloring and painting about experiences
Visuomotor Fine Motor Coordination	Ability to coordinate fine muscles such as those required in eye–hand tasks	"Lotto" "Jumbo Tiddledy Winks" "Qubic" all board games painting pasting cutting needlework

(continues)

Table 13.6. Continued

Skill	Definition	Games/Hobbies
Visuomotor Spatial Form Manipulation	Ability to move in space and to manipulate three-dimensional materials	"Blockhead" relays jacks craft and shop projects
Visuomotor Speed of Learning	Ability to learn visuomotor skills from repetitive experience	"Pick Pairs" obstacle courses knitting weaving
Visuomotor Integration	Ability to integrate total visuomotor skills in complex problem solving	checkers "Connect Four" foosball pinball machines poker charades taking trips playing musical instruments letter writing

APPENDIX 13.A
ECOLOGICAL SURVEY

_____   _____
Student   Date

_____   _____
Date of Birth/Current Age   Interviewer

I. FAMILY INFORMATION

	Mother	Father
Name	_____	_____
Occupation	_____	_____

Persons Living in Household:

Name	Age	Relationship	How do they get along with son/daughter? (circle one)
_____	_____	_____	Good Fair Poor
_____	_____	_____	Good Fair Poor
_____	_____	_____	Good Fair Poor
_____	_____	_____	Good Fair Poor
_____	_____	_____	Good Fair Poor
_____	_____	_____	Good Fair Poor

Relatives outside the household with whom your son/daughter has regular contact:

Name	Age	Relationship	How do they get along? (circle one)
_____	_____	_____	Good Fair Poor
_____	_____	_____	Good Fair Poor
_____	_____	_____	Good Fair Poor

Medical problems of son/daughter or immediate family members:

_____

_____

Is son/daughter currently taking medication(s)? _____

If so, what is (are) the name(s) of the medication(s) and dosage(s)? _____

_____

Child care provider(s)   (circle one)

Day care center/   In-home care/   Other _____

Name, address, phone number _____

Does your child have a case manager from Dept. of MH/MR? _____

Name and phone number _____

Do you use respite services? _____

Where? _____

Does your son/daughter have a pet(s)? _____

Name(s) _____

What would you like for your son/daughter to be able to do by the end of the year that he/she does not do now? _____

_____

_____

II. DAILY ROUTINES/DOMESTIC/LEISURE

What does your son/daughter do to help at home? _____

Does your son/daughter go to the bathroom independently? _____

_____

Does your son/daughter dress him/herself? _____

_____

How does your child feed him/herself (spoon only, finger feed, and so forth)? _____

_____

How does your child drink (cup, straw, bottle)? _____

What does your son/daughter do to occupy his/her leisure time? _____

_____

III. COMMUNITY

Do you take your son/daughter with you when you go out? _____

Where do you go? _____

_____

Does your son/daughter participate in family activities? _____

What types (picnics, birthday parties)? _____

_____

VI. VOCATIONAL

What are your plans for your son/daughter after graduation? _____

_____

_____

Are you aware of what the school's vocational program has to offer? _____

What living arrangements would you like for your son/daughter after graduation? _____

_____

Where would you like to see your son/daughter work? _____

_____

How do you think your child will get to work? _____

_____

Do you know if your child is eligible to receive Supplemental Security Income and/or Social Security Disability Insurance? _____

V. COMMUNICATION

How do you communicate with your son/daughter? (circle one or more)

Verbal   Sign/Gesture   Augmentative Device   Other _____

Would you be willing to try any of these methods? _____

If so, which ones? _____

How do you want your child to communicate? _____

_____

Does your son/daughter have any patterns of behavior we should know about (that is, Does she/he jump up and down before needing to use the bathroom? Does she/he moan before displaying an inappropriate behavior? _____

_____

VI. BEHAVIOR MANAGEMENT

What does your son/daughter do that you are proud of? _____

_____

What does your son/daughter do that you wish she/he would stop? _____

_____

How do you usually discipline your child? _____

_____

In general, does your son/daughter usually listen to you—or do you have to punish him/her first to get him/her to listen? _____

_____

What does your son/daughter do after being praised? _____

_____

After being punished? _____

_____

VII. ADDITIONAL COMMENTS:

VIII. ADDITIONAL QUESTIONS (to be used when appropriate)

Does your son/daughter partially participate in self-care? _____

If yes, which tasks and to what extent? _____

_____

_____

Does your son/daughter display a sucking action? _____

Does your child use a wheelchair? _____   walker? _____

What mobility assistance do you feel your child will need as an adult? _____

_____

Does your son/daughter understand the meaning of   yes? _____   no? _____

Does your son/daughter turn his/her head when spoken to? _____

Toward a sound other than voice? _____

Does your son/daughter smile in response to a voice or presence of others? _____

Does your son/daughter react to everyday cues? _____

If so, how? _____

Does your son/daughter initiate/terminate activities with the use of

body language? _____   switch? _____

verbalization? _____   other? _____

REFERENCES

Baldwin, V. (1991). Understanding the deaf-blind population census. *Traces*. Monmouth, OR: Western Oregon State College, Teaching Research Division, Traces Project.

Benson, H. A., & Turnbull, A. P. (1986). *Education of learners with severe handicaps*. Baltimore: Brookes.

Brown, L., Branston, M., Hamre-Nietupski, S., Pumpien, I., & Certo, N. (1979). A strategy for developing chronologically age-appropriate and functional curricular content for the severely handicapped. *Journal of Special Education, 13*, 81–90.

Cooley, E. (1987). *Getting in touch: Communicating with a child who is deaf-blind* [Videotape]. Champaign, IL: Research Press.

Gee, K., & Goetz, L. (1985). Outcomes of instructing orientation and mobility across purposeful travel routes in natural environments. *Journal of the Association for Persons with Severe Handicaps, 11*, 1–11.

Lundervol, D. (1987). Rehabilitation of visual impairments. *Clinical Psychology Review, 7*, 169–185.

Martin, F. (1978). *Pediatric audiology*. Englewood Cliffs, NJ: Prentice-Hall.

Snell, M. (1978). *Systematic instruction for the moderately and severely handicapped*. Columbus, OH: Merrill.

Welsh, R., & Blasch, B. (Eds.). (1980). *Foundation of orientation and mobility*. New York: American Foundation for the Blind.

Learning Disabilities

William N. Bender

LEARNING GOALS

Upon completion of this chapter the reader will be able to

- discuss the definitional issues associated with learning disabilities and the attention-deficit/hyperactivity disorder (ADHD);

- describe the behavioral skills and deficits that are exhibited by children with learning disabilities;

- review the major language, learning, and cognitive challenges for students with learning disabilities and give one example of each;

- present the psychological and social–emotional problems faced by many individuals with learning disabilities;

- describe the classroom behaviors that are displayed by students with ADHD; and

- describe the postschool outcomes for students with learning disabilities.

FUNCTIONAL DESCRIPTION

The Definitions Problem

In the most general sense, a learning disability (LD) represents an unexplained inability to master learning-related tasks. By definition, a learning disability, or inability to learn, cannot be the result of low intelligence, socioeconomic factors, or poor sensory skills. Learning disabilities differ, and diagnosing two individuals as "learning disabled" does not mean that the learning problems of those individuals are the same. In fact, a consistent finding in research on learning disabilities is the amazing heterogeneity of learning problems

included under the term (Bender & Wall, 1994). This finding is quite understandable when the history of this term is considered.

Beyond this general definition, difficulty arises because of the number of different definitions used in the field in recent decades. Definitions differ because of different theoretical perspectives on what a learning disability is. Theorists who focus on language delay have written definitions that focus on that aspect. Theorists who focus on visual–motor performance have written definitions based on that aspect. Finally, the federal and state governments, as well as professional organizations, have proposed definitions designed to satisfy everyone, and in the process have satisfied very few concerned practitioners or researchers.

Learning Disabilities as a Developmental Disability

With these different definitional problems in mind, some researchers have suggested that our classification paradigms may not be well founded. Specifically, a number of researchers, over the years, have argued that the overall similarity of students with various mild disabilities may be greater than the differences (Lilly, 1979; Polloway, Patton, Smith, & Buck, in press; Ysseldyke & Algozzine, 1984). Hallahan and Kauffman (1977), as one early example, suggested that students with mild mental retardation, mild behavioral disorders, and mild learning disabilities demonstrated significant overlap in learning characteristics. Although definitions that focus on static indicators (i.e., an IQ score or a discrepancy score between IQ score and achievement) allow for no overlap between various disabilities, a more functional approach that focuses on the functional or academic skills of individuals, or both, indicates similarity between students with mild disabilities. Also, the social skills of individuals with LD seem to be somewhat impaired (Haager & Vaughn, 1995), an impairment indicating another similarity to individuals with mental retardation, behavioral disorders, and other developmental disabilities. Further, as adults many students with LD are served by the same social service agencies as those that serve individuals with developmental disabilities. From this perspective then, perhaps learning disabilities should be conceptualized along the continuum of developmental disabilities, as one of the less severe forms of disability, as suggested by Polloway and his coworkers (in press).

Of course, an immediate disclaimer is necessary; by less severe, I do not mean that individuals with LD have fewer problems to contend with or that the burden is lighter. In contrast, the burden associated with a learning disability would seem to be greater in that the societal expectations for individuals with LD may exceed those for an individual with severe depression or profound retardation. Rather, by less severe, in this context, I intend the reader to focus on the relatively normal prognosis for individuals with LD. These individuals will marry, hold jobs, raise children, and live a relatively normal life in most cases, though the impairment associated with the learning disability will be felt throughout life (Adelman & Vogel, 1993). In this functional sense, then, individuals with LD may be very similar to individuals with mild mental retardation, behavioral disorders, and other developmental disabilities.

Learning Disabilities and ADHD

Within the last decade, another group of students with attention problems has been identified, and some practitioners believe that this group—students with ADHD—may be a subgroup of students with LD. Other researchers suggest that this is a subgroup of students with behavioral disorders. Researchers have attempted to document differences between students with ADHD and those with LD with only limited success (Stanford & Hynd, 1994). Korkman and Pesonen (1994) did demonstrate that students with ADHD were more impulsive than students identified as LD, and Stanford and Hynd (1994) indicated that parents and teachers view these groups as different in some respects, though a great deal of suspicion remains that there may be a great similarity between LD and ADHD.

From a more empirical perspective, Barkley (1992) studied the comorbidity (i.e., the coexistence of) these disabilities. He indicated that approximately 40% of students with ADHD also met the criteria for placement as learning disabled. Even using a more rigorous definition of learning disabilities, he estimated that between 19% and 26% of students with ADHD were learning disabled. This high overlap of categories suggests that some reclarification may be necessary. At the very least, the recent research focus on ADHD has fueled the flames in the ever-present definitional problems in the field of learning disabilities. Needless to say, there is, at present, considerable debate about the existence of ADHD as a separate category or placement of these students within the existing categories of LD or be-havioral disorders (Reid, Maag, & Vasa, 1994). It is hoped that research may stipulate the relation-ship between these classifications more accu-rately in the future.

Regardless of the conceptualization, a learn-ing disability is still a significant developmental insult in a child's or adolescent's life (Bender & Wall, 1994). Also, although the definitional con-siderations just discussed are crucial for research purposes, a practitioner in the developmental disabilities field is well advised to use the defini-tion provided by the state in which he or she practices. Although some consistency based on federal legislation has emerged, definitions of learning disabilities do vary from one state to an-other. Generally, the state's department of educa-tion can provide a set of rules and regulations for special education services that includes the state definition of learning disability.

For purposes of this chapter, I will describe students with learning disabilities from the more traditional perspective, related to research that focuses on "pure" LD groups—that is, on stu-dents with only a diagnosis of LD and no comor-bid diagnosis. However, information on students with ADHD is provided in the few limited areas where such information is available. The reader is advised to watch the development of research on ADHD (most of the research is less than 10 years old) and continually consider how this dis-ability may affect the field of learning disabilities in particular and the field of developmental dis-abilities overall.

THE DEFINITIONS OF LEARNING DISABILITIES

Operationalization

A number of terms are used to denote learning dis-abilities. Chalfant (1985) found at least five terms in different states, including *learning disabilities, learning disabled, specific learning disabilities, percep-tually impaired*, and *perceptual/communication disor-*

dered. One other term that has recently been used in the research literature is *dyslexia* (Brachacki, Nicolson, & Fawcett, 1995), but no state reports a specific category with that title. As alluded to pre-viously, ADHD has been identified as a disability that may often coexist with a learning disability, though few researchers use these terms synony-mously (students with ADHD who do not also manifest the other characteristics associated with LD are typically lumped together as "other health impaired" when states report counts of students with disabilities to the federal government). Despite this diversity in terms, there are several common aspects to most definitions of LD. Ex-amination of these components provides an orga-nizational structure for understanding the current assessment procedures in the field.

The Discrepancy Criteria

The most frequently used method of identifying LD is to measure the discrepancy between ability and achievement. The assumption that students with LD are not performing as well academically as they should has led to the development of mathematical formulas for identifying students with disabilities. These formulas are used to determine the degree of difference between in-telligence, as measured on standardized IQ as-sessments, and achievement in academic subject areas.

At least five major types of ability–achieve-ment discrepancy calculations have been used historically (Chalfant, 1985; Schuerholz et al., 1995). First, practitioners calculated a discrepancy between grade placement and achievement level by subtracting the latter from the former. The re-sult from this procedure suggested that a fifth grader who was reading at a second-grade level must be disabled, a hypothesis that was clearly in-adequate because intelligence level was not con-sidered. Also, many children would be classified by that process who were merely unmotivated or failed to turn in homework, or both. This particu-lar system fell into disuse in the 1970s.

The "formula" calculations were the next to evolve. Because the foregoing procedure did not take into account the child's intelligence level, theorists developed formulas that did. These formulas usually involved calculation of an "expected achievement" level, based on an intelligence score and grade placement, compared to actual achievement. If the observed discrepancy was large enough, the child was considered learning disabled. This formula calculation, like the earlier system, fell into disuse in the early 1980s.

Standard-score calculations were developed next because the formulas just described were based on mathematical manipulation of grade-equivalent scores (e.g., a 3.5 in reading), and such calculations were inappropriate mathematically. When scores from different tests are used, the means and standard deviations of the scores must be the same in order for the scores to be mathematically tractable, and the standard deviations of the different grade-equivalent scores are different across the grades. Consequently, the concept of a standardized score comparison was developed, whereby the practitioner derives an IQ score and an achievement score based on tests that have the same mean and standard deviation and that thus yield scores that are mathematically comparable. Today, standard-score calculation is the most common method of identifying children with LD.

Schuerholz and her coworkers (1995) described a recent innovation on the standard-score discrepancy concept that takes into account any error associated with the standardized scores. By including the reliability of the scores in the overall calculation, some of the error associated with this method may be reduced (Schuerholz et al., 1995), and these researchers recommended that procedure.

The final type of calculation is the regression-score calculation, which was developed from the standard-score procedure. Repeated tests, resulting in scores that are either very high or very low, tend to yield scores that regress toward (or fall back toward) the mean. This phenomenon is called *regression* and can create error in simple subtraction of standardized scores. Thus, some states use "regression tables," which are basically standard-score comparisons that take this regression phenomenon into account.

In addition to the discrepancy between ability and achievement, other types of discrepancies have been used to identify a learning disability. For example, many psychologists believe that different levels of scores on IQ tests, or different patterns of scores on the subtests of IQ tests, indicate a learning disability. It is not uncommon for practitioners to identify children as LD on the basis of this type of discrepancy.

In 1976, the U.S. Department of Education indicated that a discrepancy that was unexplained by other factors was the only useful indicator of a learning disability. Also, Chalfant's (1985) report indicated that certain discrepancy procedures may be considered indicators of a learning disability, and most states to date still utilize the discrepancy criteria in their state definitions.

However, there is some degree of dissatisfaction with the discrepancy-score process. For example, the Council for Learning Disabilities (1987) recommended that the use of discrepancy formulas be phased out, but the report did not recommend any type of alternative identification procedure. Despite this recommendation, the Council for Learning Disabilities did endorse the regression method for calculating discrepancy for states in which some measure of discrepancy was required. Finally, research has shown that practitioners regularly use discrepancies to identify learning disabilities (Chalfant, 1985; Valus, 1986).

A related problem was noted when researchers and parents inquired about identification of learning disabilities during the preschool years. To date, the use of discrepancies has resulted in identification of children with LD only after they enter school. Specifically, if a state's definition of LD stipulates a standard-score discrepancy between IQ and reading achievement of 20 points as indicative of a learning disability, the identification of children with LD at the age of 4 (prior to the use of school achievement tests) becomes problematic if not impossible because no school achievement score would be available for that aged child.

Consequently, most children with LD are identified after the school years begin. In fact, the available data indicate that most students are identified as learning disabled when they are at the third- and fourth-grade levels.

The Psychological Process Criterion

The early assumption inherent in the definition of a learning disability was that some type of disability in perception, language, or cognition prevented an individual from learning. Numerous assessments of copying skills—referred to as visual–motor performance—and motor movement skills have been used over the years, as have various language tests. A more common method for measuring "basic psychological processes" is to use standardized intelligence tests and to examine the discrepancies between various subscale scores on the tests based on visual perception and language skills. Thus, discussion of these mental or psychological processes includes terms such as *perception; visual learning deficit*, or *auditory learning problems; receptive/expressive language* (to be discussed in a later section); *memory processes; attention;* and *sensory integration*, or the ability to combine information obtained from several senses, notably hearing and vision.

This component of the definition has always been problematic because the theorists disagree on what the processes are that are basic to learning and on how those processes should be measured (Ysseldyke, 1983). To date, no exhaustive list of these processes has been proposed. Also, the measurement devices used as indicators of different types of perception are not adequate technically (Coles, 1978). For these reasons the Council for Learning Disabilities (1987) recommended that measurement of such processes be terminated.

Nevertheless, many practitioners still routinely perform assessments of psychological processes in some fashion, and it is not uncommon to find assessments of visual–motor performance, as one example, on many assessment reports today. Because there are no specifics as to what these processes entail, states vary greatly in required assessment practices. The best advice for the practitioner is to adhere to the rules and regulations published by the state department of education for assessment practices in his or her state. These procedures can usually be obtained by interested professionals from the department of education in question.

The Exclusionary Criteria

The last part of the federal definition attempts to state what a learning disability is not rather than what it is. Early definitions of LD included a phrase that suggested that learning disability was not a form of retardation and that children with mental retardation should not be considered learning disabled. At that point, during the early and mid-1960s, it was necessary to differentiate LD from mental retardation, not because of major dissimilarity of the conditions, but for political reasons: That is to say, the political expedient of securing funding for research and services for these children necessitated separation from populations who had already attracted national attention—those with mental retardation.

Of course, defining a population by what it is not rather than by what it is always results in problems; it is like trying to define the color red by pointing to things that are not red. Such attempts at definition inevitably suggest a real problem in the definition of the term. Again, during that period, securing funding by differentiation of the overall types of disabilities was the driving force. Also during the 1960s, the exclusionary clause was expanded to include children who are culturally deprived or behaviorally disturbed. These exclusions also resulted in assessment problems because it is often difficult to tell different types of disabilities apart. For example, a child with learning disabilities and a child with behavioral disorders often behave similarly, and many students with learning disabilities also manifest social or emotional problems or both (Bender & Wall, 1994). Also, no criteria are provided to make the distinction between LD and behavioral disorders.

This problem is further compounded in comparisons between students with learning disabilities and those with ADHD. Bender and Wall (1994) suggested that, minus the discrepancy criteria previously discussed, many students with ADHD may be considered learning disabled, because the attentional problems and organizational skills problems seem to be the root of the problem for both types of children. To date, the exclusionary clause for the definition of learning disabilities does not specify ADHD, and approximately 40% of students with ADHD also demonstrate a learning disability (Barkley, 1992).

Here again, a functional perspective that concentrates on the functioning of individuals within schools and society may well lead to differing conclusions concerning what disabilities exist (Polloway et al., in press). As discussed previously, on a functional level there are few demonstrable differences between students with learning disabilities, mental retardation, behavioral disorders, and ADHD, and from that perspective, the problems associated with the exclusionary clause in the definition of LD are moot.

Even in light of these problems, the vast majority of state definitions still include some form of exclusionary clause. In most cases, both students with retardation and students with behavioral disorders are excluded.

CHARACTERISTICS

In view of the heterogeneity among children referred to as learning disabled, the identification of functional characteristics that are universal to this population is difficult. Still, general characteristics that may be found in children with LD can be identified and used to illustrate the types of school problems that are characteristic of this group. The practitioner is referred to the summary at the end of the chapter for a complete list

Table 14.1. Behavioral Characteristics of Students with Learning Disabilities

Excessive distractibility, or inability to concentrate on a learning task for the same length of time as other children

Awkwardness in use of one's hands for either gross motor or fine motor tasks

Difficulty in reading words on the blackboard, even with corrective lenses

Excessive hyperactivity, or inability to stay in his or her seat in the school room

Neurologic impairment caused by impairment in cranial nerve function, demonstrated by a neurologic exam

Awkwardness of step or gait when walking

of characteristics that may be found in most children and youth with LD.

Table 14.1 presents the types of behavioral characteristics frequently discussed as indicative of a learning disability. It is, however, merely a list of "potential" characteristics and should not be taken as a checklist for identification purposes. The research evidence clearly demonstrates the profound heterogeneity of LD populations, and no characteristics list can be used as a single criterion for identification.

One of the best ways to understand this disability is to review the types of academic, emotional, and social behavior problems that are associated with the condition. The basis for the following descriptions are taken from Bender (1991).

∙∙∙

CASE EXAMPLE: BOBBY

Bobby has failed several subjects in the fourth grade, and his mother believes that this is related to his low reading skill. Although he passes reading, he usually passes it with a *D* or a *C*. His parents are concerned and have spoken to the fourth-grade teacher. The teacher has indicated that Bobby is in the lowest level reading group but that he still seems to be having problems. She also mentioned several other problem areas, including spelling and handwriting. He does not seem to be "with it" in class and is often staring out the window or moving about the class when he should not be. His homework is rarely turned in, and he seems to be somewhat disorganized in his long-term projects. The teacher also reported that Bobby has difficulty in writing a paragraph when one is assigned in class. Despite these difficulties, Bobby seems to have no difficulty with math, and he usually earns a *B* for that subject. His parents do not understand this, because they see that Bobby spends at least 1½ hours in his room each night for homework.

CASE EXAMPLE: ALPHONSO

Alphonso is in the tenth grade and has recently transferred into the local high school. The history teacher noted that he has a problem reading the text as well as reading questions on the unit tests. His homework, when he has it at all, is disorganized and indicates a problem understanding the material. His written work is barely readable, and his syntax is often confused. He writes in short sentences, and any understanding of paragraph structure seems to be totally lacking. Finally, Alphonso seems to realize that he is having significant problems with his work, and his self-concept has suffered. He is a proud teenager and does not like the other students to know that he has problems reading. Consequently, he does not like to share his work with the class, either verbally or in written form. After about a month, during which Alphonso received barely passing grades, the teacher asked for help.

CASE EXAMPLE: THOMAS

Thomas never read well and had problems with handwriting since he was in first grade.

When he entered the fourth grade, the teacher decided that he needed help in both of these areas, so she began to work with him during class. When she began, she was sure that the extra work would help, because Thomas seemed to be motivated to improve his reading. As she worked with him, she noted that he would often say one word when he meant another. Also, sometimes his thoughts were confused, and he was unable to communicate as clearly as the typical fourth-grade child. It became apparent that the extra work did not help, so in desperation, the teacher approached the special education teacher to discuss having Thomas tested.

CASE EXAMPLE: JESSICA

Jessica earned below-average grades during her first year of school, but when she entered the second grade, she began to have problems with some of her work. She could not recognize words and did not understand the stories she read during reading time. She also had trouble when other students or the teacher read the story. Even though she could name the characters in a story, she could not remember the plot of the story very well, and if she had to tell the story to someone else, she tended to get the facts confused and could not recall the sequence of events. Despite this problem, Jessica was doing low-average work in math and could complete simple math operations as well as any other student.

In each of the preceding descriptions, there was some indication of relative strengths and weaknesses. Students with LD tend to have some areas in which they do acceptable school work. Most of these students have difficulty with reading, language arts, written expression, or reading-based content subjects, and some students with learning disabilities may be as much as 4 to 6 years behind in academic achievement in the language arts area. However, there are students whose only disability seems to be in math. The types of memory problems that were evident when Jessica heard a story read are common, as are the organizational problems discussed as a characteristic of both Bobby and Alphonso.

The characteristics attributed to Bobby in the description could well be attributed to any child with ADHD as well as to a child with learning disabilities. Note the attention problems, the lack of organization, and the noncompletion of homework, which are characteristics of both ADHD and LD. Note also that the parents merely assumed that Bobby worked in his room each night, and there was no apparent monitoring to assure that the time in the room was really spent on homework.

Finally, with older students such as Alphonso, there is often some degree of emotional or personality disturbance because the older students realize that they are different from their peers and they do not usually cope well with those differences (Bender & Wall, 1994). Students with LD are often reported to have poor social skills and lower social acceptance by their peers than do nondisabled students (Haager & Vaughn, 1995). This low social acceptance can result in decreased self-concept and lower self-expectations. Also, these social–emotional problems frequently become so severe that students with learning disabilities may be coidentified as either ADHD or behaviorally disordered. Again, the overlap of these categories suggests that perhaps a broader developmental disabilities perspective may be more appropriate for many students with LD (Polloway et al., in press).

SELF-CARE

Self-care is not a major problem for most individuals with LD. As indicated previously, most of these students are identified after the school years begin. Most parents report that children with LD seem to learn rudimentary self-care skills as quickly as do their siblings. For example, tying shoes at the age of 3 or 4 years is not a problem (as it usually is for a child with moderate

mental retardation) nor is helping around the home difficult for children with LD.

Subtle differences probably exist, however, because of the lack of organizational abilities on the part of the child who is learning disabled. Disorganization is often a problem reported by parents of students diagnosed with ADHD, also. This deficit may result in an inability to follow directions for making the bed or for bringing out all the white and light-colored clothes for washing.

Dyslexic individuals, who represent one subgroup of the total LD population (probably less than 10%), may need additional training in self-care skills throughout life. The person with true dyslexia will probably never read beyond the second- or third-grade level and will need special training for driving an automobile (because of the need to read road signs) or using a city transportation system (Brachacki et al., 1995). Other self-care adjustments may also be necessary before an individual with dyslexia is truly independent.

Individuals with ADHD may also demonstrate problems throughout life. There are numerous reports of individuals with ADHD who experience extreme difficulties as adults, when managing work schedules or merely arriving at work on time becomes increasingly important. Although few of these problems are severe enough to warrant daily residential care, it is not uncommon to find adults with ADHD whose spouses manage their schedules of daily appointments.

RECEPTIVE AND EXPRESSIVE LANGUAGE

As it is in most children, receptive language is more developed in students with LD than is expressive language. There is typically some language delay but not usually enough to determine that a disability exists during the language-learning period characteristic of the second and third years of life. Consequently, the scanty research on early language development in children who are eventually diagnosed as having LD has not shown any potential for identifying this disability at an early stage.

Still, children with learning disabilities tend to have the more sophisticated types of language problems (Roth, Spekman, & Fye, 1995). Typically, these children produce recognizable sentences and can participate, though minimally, in conversations from the early ages. Whereas the problem in students with moderate to severe retardation may be eliciting rudimentary forms of language, the problems among children with LD concern use of language in academic and social situations. Thus, although some deficiencies exist in syntax and semantics of students with LD, most of the problems involve pragmatic use of language in the real world.

Syntax and Semantics

The early research on language development among students with LD has concentrated on syntax, semantics, and pragmatic language. *Syntax* refers to the formal relationships between words in phrases or sentences. Examples of such relationships include the subject–verb relationship or the relationship between the verb and the direct object. *Semantics* refers to knowledge and comprehension of words. Ability in this area is often measured by receptive vocabulary tests.

Most research on syntax and semantics has demonstrated deficits in children with LD (Boucher, 1986; Wiig, Lapointe, & Semel, 1977; Wiig, Semel, & Crouse, 1973). Children with learning disabilities demonstrate deficits in the ability to apply morphologic rules (e.g., formation of plurals, verb tenses, and possessives) and difficulty in both comprehension and expression of syntactic structures such as relationships between words in sentences and phrases. Understanding exactly who a pronoun applies to and what function is served by a direct object or an indirect object are examples of this syntactic skill. These deficits are apparent both in the child's understanding of the language of others and in his or her own production of spoken language. Finally, at least one of

these studies demonstrated that oral language production did not automatically improve with age among students with learning disabilities, as it does in most children (Wiig et al., 1977).

Pragmatic Use of Language

Pragmatics is the other level of language and the most recent area to receive research attention. *Pragmatics* is the use of language in context. This aspect of language encompasses the social and cultural roles of the participants in the conversation (Boucher, 1986; Roth et al., 1995). Theorists who study pragmatic language emphasize the ecologically based study of language in real communication situations rather than scores on a test that may not indicate true communicative skill. Researchers in this area tend to measure the actual utterances a child makes when he or she communicates with other children and adults.

An important aspect of pragmatic language is the ability to adjust one's language to the speaker to enhance communication. For example, a person generally uses a more simplistic language with a young child than with an older person. This language adaptation is referred to as *code switching*. Such adaptations may be made in a number of ways, including using more simple sentences or using fewer modifiers in each complete thought.

Early research suggested that children with learning disabilities did not code switch as frequently as did non–learning-disabled children (Boucher, 1984; Bryan, Donahue, & Pearl, 1981). Asking questions, responding to inadequate messages, and persuasion were noted as difficult skills to master for children with learning disabilities (Boucher, 1986; Bryan et al., 1981). The lack of these skills was cited as a possible reason for inadequate social skills among these children (Bryan et al., 1981).

Referential communication, another aspect of pragmatic language, requires that a child communicate specific information to another and evaluate the adequacy of communication from another. Giving or receiving instructions is one example of referential communication. Referential communication skills, therefore, include awareness of accurate and inadequate messages as well as of communication choices, such as selection of specific terms, which are based on such communication.

Roth et al. (1995) compared students with learning disabilities to normally achieving students on reference cohesion in oral narratives. *Reference cohesion* refers to the understanding and utilization of pronouns (e.g., *he, she, it*), possessive adjectives (e.g., *mine*), demonstratives (e.g, *this, there, now*), and comparatives (e.g., *same, different*; Roth et al., 1995). Students with learning disabilities were compared with their age mates at three ages between 8 years and 13 years, because more sophisticated understanding of reference cohesion developed during those years. Oral narrative stories were collected and compared. At every age group, students with learning disabilities were less successful at reference cohesion than were nondisabled peers.

Several studies have suggested that children with learning disabilities are deficient in understanding and responding to inadequate communication (Donahue, Pearl, & Bryan, 1980; Feagans, 1983; Wiig, Semel, & Abele, 1981). For example, Spekman (1981) created dyads, or paired groups, some of which included a child with a disability and some of which did not. Each child in each dyad was to communicate information and to act on information received from the partner in the dyad. This research design allowed for comparison of referential communication skills as well as of listening competence. The children were told they could ask questions regarding incomplete communications. Although no differences were found in their abilities to follow directions, to complete the task, or to ask appropriate questions, the children with learning disabilities gave less task-relevant information. Consequently, these dyads demonstrated less success in completion of the task than did the dyads that included only normally functioning children.

The implications of this research for the practitioner are relatively straightforward. If a child with a learning disability demonstrates a pragmatic language disability in referential communication skills, that student will be less capable of giving instructions to his or her classmates and playmates. Consequently, this disability will affect the student's performance in group projects that require verbal participation of each group member. Also, the child will have problems responding to instructions given by the teacher or by other members of the group. Clearly, disability in referential communication presents real problems in the typical elementary or secondary school classroom.

A number of educational activities may be used to expand a child's success in pragmatic language skills. Any projects that require a child to communicate information to others utilizing referential communication skills can be a learning experience for these children. In giving directions to others, a child has to plan what the other needs to know, the order in which information should be presented, and the speed with which information should be given. By placing children with learning disabilities in that position and then discussing with them their efforts at communication, a more sophisticated level of pragmatic language may be obtained. However, merely assigning these children to group projects without appropriate postcommunication follow-up will not result in improved communication skill. Alternatively, the communication must be examined and reconstructed so that the child understands the strengths and weaknesses of his or her communication efforts.

Impact of Language Deficits

Deficits in semantics, syntax, and pragmatic language skills in both the receptive and expressive areas often create additional problems in school performance. For example, such deficits often result in difficulty with written assignments, reading assignments, or group projects. The teacher and other practitioners must be sensitive to these language problems and to the effects of these problems on school tasks, and expectations for school work should be adjusted accordingly.

Adjustments that language deficits require may be simple or extensive. Many students with LD take tests orally rather than in written form. By allowing this form of testing, the teacher can obtain a true picture of the student's comprehension rather than a measure of comprehension that may be unduly influenced by the child's ability to read the test and to write an answer. Other modifications that lessen the impact of language deficits include use of alternative texts, use of alternative reading materials that cover the same content but that are written at a lower reading level, use of graphic aids during lectures that students must listen to and determine the important information that should be included in the notes, and the frequent checking of notes taken by the student to ensure that the notes are complete. Many of these adaptations are useful for students with ADHD, also, in addition to other students in the class who may be having difficulty.

Summary of Language Deficits

Although little evidence exists of major delays in expressive or receptive language in children with LD, more sophisticated language problems are well documented (Boucher, 1986; Roth et al., 1995). Students with learning disabilities have deficits in both syntax and semantics that negatively affect their school performance in many spoken and written tasks. Perhaps a more debilitating disability is the deficit in pragmatic language. Students with learning disabilities do not have the pragmatic language skills to adapt their language to the situation or to use referential communication skills—either receptive or expressive—in a fashion commensurate with their age group. Finally, some evidence suggests that, unlike for nondisabled children, these language problems are not overcome with age. To alleviate these pragmatic language problems, specific instructional techniques, such as frequent use of

and feedback on referential communication skills, are necessary.

LEARNING AND COGNITION

Several major areas of research involve cognition of students with LD. Cognition may include a host of different variables, but most researchers would include, at a minimum, intelligence, attention, and memory as three major cognition areas. The practitioner should be aware of the recent findings in each of these domains.

Intelligence

The definition of LD stipulates that children so diagnosed have average or above-average intelligence, and studies over the years have indicated that the anticipated IQ level for children with learning disabilities is approximately 90 to 93 (Bender, 1985; Gajar, 1979; Webster & Schenck, 1978). This range probably reflects several things. First, intelligence, as measured today in Western culture, is heavily dependent on verbal skills, and this dependence may deflate the average IQ levels reported. If children with LD do demonstrate deficits in syntax, semantics, and pragmatics—as the research cited previously indicates—a depressed score on verbal intelligence would be expected, even for children with normal intelligence in other areas.

In addition, these intelligence figures are based on samples of students with LD identified by the public schools, and identification procedures in public schools are not exact and may be quite different from identification procedures in research clinics (also definitions may differ from state to state). At present, the average level of intelligence for students with LD remains unclear. However, because of the exclusion of students with mental retardation in most state definitions of LD, most states will identify students as LD only if their intelligence is 70 or above (i.e., the cutoff score for mental retardation), and some states identify students as LD only if their IQ is 85 or above (i.e., the traditional "normal" IQ range).

Some students with LD have a level of intelligence in the "gifted" range. These students are known as "gifted–learning-disabled" students. Some students with IQs above 130, or 2 standard deviations above the mean, also demonstrate an ability–achievement discrepancy, as discussed previously. Although these students may be at or above grade level academically, if there is a large discrepancy between their IQ and their achievement, they may be classified as learning disabled or as gifted–learning disabled. Research studies that examine the characteristics of this group are recent and relatively rare. As a result, little is known about this group of students.

Attention

The construct of attention is more complex than it seems and involves at least three different types of skills. On-task behavior indicates the persistence or length of time a student can remain concentrated on a task. This attention variable is usually measured by observation of the student's eye contact with an assigned task and results in a measure of the percentage of on-task behavior.

Focus of attention indicates the student's ability to inhibit distracting stimuli. This variable is typically measured by a teacher rating of a child's tendency to distractibility (to be drawn off-task by competing stimuli in the educational environment).

Finally, selective attention is a cognitively based process that involves choosing which aspects of a stimulus to attend to. This variable is typically not measured on the standard assessment battery. However, various research tasks that compare a student's recall of important versus unimportant stimuli may be used to measure this attention variable in certain research studies.

Research in each of these areas has indicated that students with LD suffer deficits compared with their age mates (Bender, 1991; Bender & Wall, 1994; McKinney & Feagans, 1983). Also, students with ADHD are identified primarily as having deficits in attention, and this is one factor that has suggested that there may be substantial overlap between LD and ADHD. For example, whereas the average on-task rates for nondisabled children range between 80% and 95%, the average rates of on-task behavior typically reported in the literature indicate that children with LD are on-task between 35% and 65% of the time (Bender, 1985, 1991). This level of on-task behavior is also characteristic of students identified as having ADHD (Barkley, 1992). This deficit in on-task behavior, the first attention variable just discussed, obviously has a negative affect on academic achievement, regardless of the terminology used to describe the child. In short, if students cannot concentrate on an education task during a seatwork assignment, those students will be less successful in school.

Research has indicated that many children with LD, ADHD, or both can be trained to stay on-task for longer periods of time. This training, usually referred to as self-monitoring, was developed by Hallahan, Lloyd, and Stoller (1982) at the University of Virginia. The training involves a simple procedure that forces the child to ask himself or herself the question, "Am I paying attention?" on a periodic basis during a learning task. When such a procedure is utilized each day for a period of weeks, the child apparently forms the habit of monitoring his or her on-task skills. This training is relatively simple, and parents of children with disabilities have actually conducted this type of self-monitoring training with their own children during nightly homework sessions. Instructions are available in several sources (Bender, 1991; Hallahan et al., 1982). Also, this self-monitoring procedure has been successfully employed with students with ADHD (Fowler, 1992).

Typically, behavioral ratings are used to indicate the levels of distractibility behaviors for both students with LD and students with ADHD (McKinney, Montague, & Hocutt, 1993). Other diagnostic procedures that are used for measuring distractibility behavior of students with LD or ADHD include anecdotal reports from teachers and classroom observations of behavior, conducted by either school psychologists or teachers.

Research on the distractibility of students with LD is somewhat equivocal. In studies that used teacher perceptions of distractibility—the polar opposite of focused attention—as the measure of attention, the data typically indicate that students with LD are highly distractible, thus indicating a general inability to focus on a task (Bender, 1985; McKinney & Feagans, 1983). However, in experimental studies in which the distracting stimulus is presented in a controlled fashion, such as distracting light shown on the page that the child is reading, students with LD seem to be no more highly distractible than are nondisabled students (Zentall, 1986; Zentall, Zentall, & Booth, 1978). More research, using both of these methods, is necessary before conclusions can be drawn regarding distractibility of students with LD.

Selective attention involves a conscious choice of particular aspects of the stimuli that deserve attention, and the research results indicate that children with LD are not able to make consistently correct choices about the importance of competing stimuli (Bender, 1991). Typically, students with LD and ADHD answer questions more impulsively than do others and do not make the effort to attend selectively to the discriminative aspects of the stimuli that are used to answer the question. Research, at present, indicates that this deficit in selective attention is not due to a lack of desire to complete the problem correctly but rather to a lack of knowledge about the cognitive steps necessary for good selective attention, that is, concentration on what to attend to and what to ignore.

Selective attention skills may be developed for educational tasks by teachers who assist the child in the thought process. When a child gives an answer that indicates incorrect thinking, the teacher should take a moment and reconstruct the child's selective attention process. Sometimes the teacher can accomplish this by merely asking the child why that answer seems to be correct. The teacher may then be in a position to indicate to the child certain errors in attending to unimportant aspects of the problem or ignoring vital information in the formulation of the answer. This type of teaching requires small classes and a teacher who is highly responsive to the thought processes of the child. Also, it is rarely (if ever) advisable to embarrass a child by such questions in front of peers. Still, this questioning technique can illuminate how children reach the conclusions they reach, and that information can assist a sensitive teacher in making appropriate educational suggestions for the child.

Memory

The research on memory abilities of children with LD has also indicated problem areas (Torgesen, 1984). Memory may be divided into short-term memory, holding a stimulus in one's memory for a few seconds; and long-term memory, holding a stimulus anywhere from a few minutes to many years. Memory problems in children with LD tend to be associated with short-term memory. Once a child with LD learns something, that information is retained in a manner comparable to that of nondisabled children. Children with LD, however, have problems with short-term memory and with the cognitive strategies that are used to transfer stimuli into long-term memory (Ross, 1976; Torgesen, 1984).

To transfer a piece of information from short-term into long-term memory, most individuals develop some type of memory strategy. Many of us use verbal rehearsal to memorize names of persons we have just met. As another common example, when nondisabled children are required to memorize pictures of various stimuli, they typically develop a classification system, place the pictures in the different classes or groups, and memorize the pictures in each group. Children with LD are much less likely to use these common strategies than are nondisabled children (Torgesen, 1984). Unfortunately, very little study of the memory processes for students with ADHD has been done.

However, memory research on students with LD is optimistic because it indicates that, once a child with LD has been trained in an age-appropriate memory strategy, that child can usually use that strategy and improve his or her memory performance. A number of instructional strategies, generally referred to as "cognitive strategy training" or "learning strategies" instruction are being used to enhance the performance of children with LD on a wide range of memory tasks. These learning strategies generally include an acronym in which each letter represents a step for the student to perform. For example, the "RAP" strategy is a learning strategy that enables a child to memorize the major points from a paragraph of written text. The letters stand for the following steps: R—read the material, A—ask questions concerning the material, and P—paraphrase the material. When students with LD are trained to complete these steps, their ability to memorize important details from written material increases. Research of this nature has led to a large body of information on teaching strategies for students with LD. Sometimes this body of literature is referred to as learning strategies research or metacognitive research. This research is one of the more influential areas of research in the learning disabilities field today, and teachers should regularly review the professional journals seeking instructional ideas that use learning strategies of this nature to enhance memory skills of students with LD.

Summary of Cognition

Research has shown that, in almost every aspect of cognition, children with LD demonstrate some deficits, as summarized in Table 14.2. The intelligence of these children seems to be lower than the norm. Deficits are consistently demonstrated in both on-task attention measures and selective attention, and memory research has consistently indicated problems in memory transfer and mem-

Table 14.2. Cognitive Characteristics

Characteristic	Description
IQ	Many students with LD demonstrate lower than normal IQs, perhaps because IQ is heavily dependent on language skills.
Memory	Short-term memory problems seem to be the basis of much learning difficulty for students with LD. These problems are apparent in memory strategies for academic tasks. Long-term memory does not seem to be a problem.
Focusing Attention	Students with LD are on task less than others. Typical on-task averages for LD groups range from 35% to 65% on-task time.
Distractibility	Whereas teachers rate students with LD as more distractible in class, laboratory studies have failed to demonstrate higher distractibility.
Selective Attention	Students with LD manifest problems attending to the appropriate aspect of the stimuli. However, once selective attention strategies are taught to students with LD, their selective attention improves dramatically.

ory strategies. With these deficits in cognitive skills that are intimately related to academic performance, it is not surprising that the cognitive deficits negatively affect the school work of these children. Although the attention problems associated with ADHD are well documented, very little research on memory, intelligence, and other cognitive processes is currently available.

These summary statements are, however, based on research on groups of children, and no automatic assumptions should be made regarding the cognition of a particular child with LD.

For example, some children may have a disability based on memory deficit and still be able to perform educational tasks in a fashion similar to that of nondisabled children. Before making assumptions concerning the particular disability of a child, teachers and practitioners should conduct a thorough assessment to identify the type of disability that may be present in the individual case.

CAPACITY FOR INDEPENDENT LIVING

Among students with LD, the capacity for independent living is not usually in question. These students typically live independently after completing school, and many have families, hold jobs, and lead relatively normal lives. Several factors result from the disability, however, that may impair their capacity to function independently during their adult lives, including academic and social–emotional outcomes from the schooling process.

Academic and Cognitive Outcomes

Although long-term follow-up studies of students with LD are rare—and follow-up studies of students with ADHD as adults are even more rare—there are some indicators that the types of academic and cognitive difficulties that students with LD experience during school persist after the school years (Adelman & Vogel, 1993; Gregory, Shanahan, & Walberg, 1986; C. Johnson, 1984). In a recent summary of postschool outcomes for students with LD, Adelman and Vogel (1993) indicated that many young adults with LD were limited to low-paying or entry-level positions. Approximately 58% of students with LD were working during the 2 years after graduation from high school, and this approaches the employment rate for individuals without disabilities (i.e., 61%; D'Amico, 1991). However, there are significant gender differences that indicate that women with LD have much higher unemploy-

ment rates than do men with LD (Adelman & Vogel, 1993).

In an earlier comprehensive study, Gregory and colleagues (1986) conducted a retrospective study in which they compared outcome measures for high school seniors with and without learning disabilities. Gregory and his coworkers used a data set designed to predict outcomes for all high school seniors in the secondary schools in America. Over 26,000 students completed a survey with information about themselves, and 439 of these students identified themselves as learning disabled. This group was compared to the nondisabled group on various academic variables, and the results demonstrated that the academic deficits of students with LD in reading, math, and language arts are apparent as late as the last year in school.

Research on reading and academic skills has demonstrated that many students with LD finish school with academic performance around the fifth-grade level. The reading level of adolescents with LD seems to peak at around the fifth- or sixth-grade level and to improve little thereafter. Also, research indicates that the IQ–achievement discrepancy is still relatively large for most of these students. C. Johnson (1984) identified deficits in reading comprehension, written work, and verbal language problems that continue to plague adults who are learning disabled after the postschool transition period. These levels of achievement performance present problems either in further schooling or in entrance into the workforce.

Because years of remedial schooling have failed to alleviate these academic problems, more schooling probably will not help. At this point, it is most beneficial for practitioners to assist the youth with LD to identify coping strategies that make normal independent-living skills possible. Use of a functional-skills curriculum during the later years of schooling seems to offer the best remedy for recurring academic problems. In a functional-skills curriculum, daily-living skills, such as completion of tax return forms, job applications, and medical insurance forms, compose the curriculum. With the student's practice in those types of skills, the problems of living independently after school are alleviated somewhat.

Emotional and Social Outcomes

Another set of variables that may impair independent-living skills of students with LD includes social and emotional variables such as self-concept, peer relationships, and social interactions (Bender & Wall, 1994). Horn, O'Donnell, and Vitulano (1983) reviewed a number of studies that suggested that the self-concept of adults with LD was lower than that of non–learning-disabled comparison groups. Several more recent studies of self-satisfaction support this deficit in self-concept among older students and adults with LD (Bender & Wall, 1994; Gregory et al., 1986; Pihl & McLarnon, 1984).

However, not all of the research is consistent on this point. Lewandowski and Arcangelo (1994) compared the self-concept of 40 young adults who had received services for LD in the public schools to 40 adults who did not receive any special education services. That study demonstrated no differences in the self-concept of these two groups. Further, the groups compared favorably on overall social adjustment. Clearly, these recent results are much more optimistic than is the body of earlier studies.

The study by Gregory and coworkers (1986) compared the locus of control of seniors with LD and non–learning-disabled students. Locus of control involves the perception of control that one has over one's environment. A high level on "internal" control typically indicates that one feels fairly secure that one's actions can result in positive occurrences in one's environment, whereas a high level of "external" locus of control indicates that one feels rather helpless to effect change in one's own life circumstances. The data indicated that youth with LD demonstrate higher levels of external locus of control than would be desirable and that level of external control may have negative repercussions for independent-living skills. This finding of higher external locus of control

has been supported in other research (Pintrich, Anderman, & Klobucar, 1994).

Finally, a number of emotional and social variables have been studied among the young adult LD population that have not been studied in younger groups, including emotional adjustment, legal troubles, depression, and suicide. This research indicates that students with LD do not compare favorably with nondisabled students in these areas (Huntington & Bender, 1993; Bender & Wall, 1994; Gregory et al., 1986). For example, Huntington and Bender (1993) indicated that youths with LD were more at risk for depression and, possibly, suicide, than nondisabled youths, though these conclusions must be regarded as tentative, given the relative lack of studies on those variables.

The study by Gregory and colleagues (1986) measured several other social and emotional variables including overall adjustment, self-ratings of personal attractiveness, satisfaction with peer group, trouble with the law, parental interests in the student's activities, adequacy of home-study facilities, and mother's absence from the home. On each variable, the seniors with LD demonstrated less positive outcomes than did the comparison group of nondisabled seniors.

Clearly, these results, summarized in Table 14.3, do not demonstrate positive outcomes of special education interventions during the adolescent years. Further, these results indicate potential problems that young adults with LD may find in independent living. For example, trouble with the law, in the form of a simple parking ticket, requires reading; that is, it includes instructions on when and where to pay the fine, and some effort is necessary on the part of the person, or mistakes will be made in that process. Students with limited reading ability or inappropriate understanding of language may be more inclined to get into trouble of this type or to respond inappropriately when they do get into such trouble.

Unfortunately, concern with emotional development and social skills among students and young adults with LD is relatively recent, and re-

---

Table 14.3. Emotional and Social Outcomes

Variable	Research Findings
Self-Concept	Many students with LD have lower self-concept than do nondisabled students.
Locus of Control	Students with LD generally have higher external locus of control and do not attribute success in their endeavors to their own efforts.
Depression	Research has suggested that some students with LD manifest higher levels of depression and may possibly be at higher risk for suicide than other students.
Social Success	Some research indicates that adolescents with LD engage in fewer social outings and enjoy less satisfaction with peer relationships.
Legal Problems	Some students with LD have more minor legal problems than do other students, a finding that may indicate less-than-satisfactory social adjustment.

---

search on effective interventions for independent-living skills is, at present, nonexistent. Although some research on social relationships during the school years has been conducted, little is known about how to increase social skills to facilitate independent living during the postschool period.

ECONOMIC SELF-SUFFICIENCY

Economic self-sufficiency in our society depends to a large extent on successful schooling in either a vocational program or a higher education program, and adults with LD frequently do attend college or vocational training programs after high school. In one study, D. Johnson and Blalock (1987) re-

ported that 23 of 93 adults with learning disabilities attended college, and 19 obtained degrees.

Yost, Shaw, Cullen, and Bigaj (1994) investigated the types of programs that colleges offer for students with disabilities. They surveyed service providers in 2-year, 4-year, and graduate institutions to determine the basic outlines of service that are provided for young adults with LD who attend postsecondary schools. Overall, although almost all the responding institutions indicated that services were available, there was no underlying philosophical basis for services, and services often seemed to be uncoordinated. However, a wide variety of services were offered in varying degrees at different institutions, including tutoring, reading assistance, note-taking skills, and waivers for particular classes.

We would anticipate that the number of students attending college will increase as most colleges establish programs for students with LD. Of course, to date few studies have been conducted on postcollege employment of students with LD. Despite this lack of data, one may tentatively conclude that completing college indicates some degree of economic self-sufficiency for a sizable minority of adults with LD.

Additional data do exist on the overall vocational outlook for adults with LD. Schalock and coworkers (1986) showed, in a 5-year follow-up study of postsecondary schools, that 72% of the students with LD were employed after school, and as mentioned previously, other research has shown employment rates that are similar to those of nondisabled individuals (D'Amico, 1991). However, most of the available data indicate that students with LD, although employed, may be trapped in lower-paying jobs and may receive fewer advancement opportunities than other workers (Adelman & Vogel, 1993). Also, a sizable minority of persons with LD are, apparently, not employed even 5 years after school. Thus, the economic picture is not entirely positive for these students. These data are supported by several other studies of children with disabilities (see Adelman & Vogel, 1993; or Bender, 1991, for review).

Still, based on these data, the prognosis for economic self-sufficiency for most adults with LD appears to be somewhat positive, and practitioners should let parents and the individuals with disabilities themselves know this. Further, practitioners should endeavor to make vocational educational opportunities available for most students with LD during the secondary school years and thereafter. The content of such programs should focus on job-related skills as well as on work-related skills (e.g., getting to work on time, punching the time clock) and interpersonal skills needed on the job (e.g., getting along with other workers, supporting newer employees, requesting assistance as necessary). Only by providing a complete vocational training program such as this can the practitioner hope to improve the outlook for economic self-sufficiency for his or her clients.

SUMMARY

One major factor in any discussion of characteristics of an intervention program for children and youth with LD, or ADHD, is the heterogeneity of each population. For example, whereas most students with LD may have problems in pragmatic language, not all students with this disability do. Most of these students have problems in selective and sustained attention, but not all of them do. Many students with ADHD are hyperactive, but not all students diagnosed with ADHD are. Consequently, the following list of characteristics is not intended to be used as a diagnostic checklist but rather as a rough guide to the types of problems that may be noted in this population of students.

In light of this caveat, some characteristics can be stipulated that may be found in many children with LD. The types of characteristics are those that are presented in most introductory texts about LD. The types of interventions that alleviate each problem are also mentioned.

1. The ratio of male to female individuals identified as learning disabled ranges from 2:1 to 5:1. Many more male students than female students are identified as learning disabled. This is also true of students who may be diagnosed as ADHD.

2. Self-care is not usually a problem with most students with LD, though higher order, self-care skills that involve sequencing and organizational abilities may present problems.

3. Deficits exist among children and adolescents with LD in almost every area of language—semantics, syntax, and pragmatics—in both reception and expression. These deficits often result in difficulties in written language, speaking communication, and listening skills. Interventions are generally aimed at providing training in pragmatic language skills with frequent feedback about the adequacy of the spoken or written communication.

4. The average IQ of populations in public schools identified as learning disabled is approximately 90 to 93, or several points lower than the population norm for nondisabled children, even though the definition of LD stipulates that children identified as learning disabled have average or above-average IQs.

5. Attention deficits are frequently demonstrated by students with both LD and ADHD. Research has shown that on-task time among students with LD or ADHD is lower than that among nondisabled students. Also, the selective attention capabilities of students with LD are less developed than those of normal children. Interventions for these attention skills include self-monitoring training of on-task behavior and direct cognitive strategy training in attention to various stimuli. These self-monitoring interventions are also recommended for students with ADHD.

6. Students with learning disabilities have problems with short-term memory skills and with memorization ability. Educational interventions for these skills include memory strategies that include memorization of learning-strategy acronyms and use of verbal rehearsal and visual imagery to improve memory of textual material.

7. Neither mobility nor self-direction seems to be a major problem for students with LD or

ADHD. Although each of these disabilities may, on occasion, be associated with an unusual body carriage or unusual gait, this is not apparent in every individual with LD or ADHD.

8. Although most persons with LD do live independently after the school years, problems in both academic and emotional and social skills persist and may lead to complications during the postschool adjustment period. Functional-skills curricula may alleviate some of the problems associated with low academic functioning. However, no research has been conducted on interventions to improve social and emotional functioning of young adults with LD.

9. Most students with LD are economically self-sufficient after the school years, and a sizable minority pursue higher education, either in a 4-year college program or in a vocational program. Increased attention to postsecondary vocational or college training should assist the young adult with LD to attain economic self-sufficiency.

10. Approximately 40% of students with ADHD also manifest a learning disability, based on a significant discrepancy between IQ and achievement in one or more areas. This finding has led some to postulate that these disabilities may represent merely a continuum of developmental disability rather than two separate conditions.

FINAL THOUGHTS

A number of movements on the present educational scene, some of which have been discussed in this chapter, will certainly impact the future of the field of learning disabilities. As more information becomes available on ADHD, we will begin to understand more concretely the relationship between these two disabilities.

Also, the inclusion movement—the efforts to serve all students with disabilities in mainstream classes—may make differentiation of specific types of disabilities moot. That is, why differentiate categories of disabilities such as LD, mental retardation, behavioral disorders, and ADHD when the services for all of them are functionally

similar and take place in the same mainstream class setting?

Regardless of how these issues are resolved, almost every teacher should be well prepared to deal with the types of functional problems represented by students with LD. Learning characteristics such as increased inappropriate behaviors, poor attention skills, and poor short-term memory skills do necessitate certain types of instructional approaches, and teachers usually find that the instructional innovations that they attempt for students with LD make them more effective teachers for all of their students. This, then, is the challenge and the joy of teaching students with LD: to be the most effective teacher one can be and to watch the positive effects of those teaching skills for all students.

REFERENCES

Adelman, P. B., & Vogel, S. A. (1993). Issues in the employment of adults with learning disabilities. *Learning Disability Quarterly, 16*, 219–232.

Barkley, R. A. (1992). *Attention-deficit hyperactive disorder: A handbook for diagnosis and treatment.* New York: Guilford Press.

Bender, W. N. (1985). Differential diagnosis based on the task-related behavior of learning-disabled and low-achieving adolescents. *Learning Disability Quarterly, 8*, 261–268.

Bender, W. N. (1991). *Introduction to learning disabilities: Identification, assessment, and teaching strategies.* Needham Heights, MA: Allyn & Bacon.

Bender, W. N., & Wall, M. E. (1994). Social-emotional development of students with learning disabilities. *Learning Disability Quarterly, 17*, 323–341.

Boucher, C. R. (1984). Pragmatics: The verbal language of learning disabled and nondisabled boys. *Learning Disability Quarterly, 7*, 271–286.

Boucher, C. R. (1986). Pragmatics: The meaning of verbal language in learning disabled and nondisabled boys. *Learning Disability Quarterly, 9*, 285–295.

Brachacki, G. W. Z., Nicolson, R. I., & Fawcett, A. J. (1995). Impaired recognition of traffic signs in adults with dyslexia. *Journal of Learning Disabilities, 28*(5), 297–301.

Bryan, T., Donahue, M., & Pearl, R. (1981). Learning disabled children's peer interactions during a small-group problem solving task. *Learning Disability Quarterly, 4*, 13–22.

Chalfant, J. C. (1985). Identifying learning disabled students: A summary of the national task force report. *Learning Disabilities Focus, 1*(1), 9–20.

Coles, G. S. (1978). The learning disability test battery: Empirical and social issues. *Harvard Educational Review, 48*, 313–340.

Council for Learning Disabilities. (1987). The CLD position statement. *Journal of Learning Disabilities, 20*, 349–350.

D'Amico, R. (1991). The working world awaits: Employment experiences during and shortly after secondary school. In M. Wagner, L. Newman, R. D'Amico, E. D. Jay, P. Butler-Nalin, C. Marder, & R. Cox (Eds.), *Youth with disabilities: How are they doing? The first comprehensive report from the national longitudinal transition study of special education students* (pp. 8–55). Menlo Park, CA: SRI International.

Donahue, M., Pearl, R., & Bryan, T. (1980). Learning disabled children's conversational competence: Responses to inadequate messages. *Journal of Applied Psycholinguistics, 1*, 387–403.

Feagans, L. (1983). Discourse processes in learning disabled children. In J. D. McKinney & L. Feagans (Eds.), *Current topics in learning disabilities* (Vol. 1, pp. 87–115). Norwood, NJ: Ablex.

Fowler, M. (1992). *CH.A.D.D. educator's manual: An in-depth look at attention deficit disorders from an educational perspective.* Fairfax, VA: CASET Associates.

Gajar, A. (1979). Educable mentally retarded, learning disabled, emotionally disturbed: Similarities and differences. *The Exceptional Child, 45*, 470–472.

Gregory, J. F., Shanahan, T., & Walberg, H. (1986). A profile of learning disabled twelfth-graders in regular classes. *Learning Disability Quarterly, 9*, 33–42.

Haager, D., & Vaughn, S. (1995). Parent, teacher, peer and self-reports of the social competence of students with learning disabilities. *Journal of Learning Disabilities, 28*, 205–215.

Hallahan, D. P., & Kauffman, J. M. (1977). Labels, categories, behaviors: ED, LD, and EMR reconsidered. *Journal of Special Education, 11*, 129–149.

Hallahan, D. P., Lloyd, J. W., & Stoller, L. (1982). *Improving attention with self-monitoring: A manual for teachers.* Charlottesville: University of Virginia.

Horn, W. F., O'Donnell, J. P., & Vitulano, L. A. (1983). Long-term follow-up studies of learning disabled persons. *Journal of Learning Disabilities, 9*, 542–554.

Huntington, D., & Bender, W. N. (1993). Adolescents with learning disabilities at risk? Emotional well-being, depression, and suicide. *Journal of Learning Disabilities, 26*, 159–166.

Johnson, C. L. (1984). The learning disabled adolescent and young adult: An overview and critique of current practices. *Journal of Learning Disabilities, 7*, 386–391.

Johnson, D. J., & Blalock, J. W. (1987). *Adults with learning disabilities: Clinical studies.* Orlando, FL: Grune & Stratton.

Korkman, M., & Pesonen, A. E. (1994). A comparison of neuropsychological test profiles of children with attention deficit-hyperactivity disorder and/or learning disabilities. *Journal of Learning Disabilities, 27*, 383–392.

Lewandowski, L., & Arcangelo, K. (1994). The social adjustment and self-concept of adults with learning disabilities. *The Journal of Learning Disabilities, 27*, 598–605.

Lilly, M. S. (Ed.). (1979). *Children with exceptional needs.* New York: Holt.

McKinney, J. D, & Feagans, L. (1983). Adaptive classroom behavior of learning disabled students. *Journal of Learning Disabilities, 16*, 360–367.

McKinney, J. D., Montague, M., & Hocutt, A. M. (1993). *A synthesis of research literature on the assessment and identification of attention deficit disorder.* Miami, FL: Miami Center for Synthesis of Research on Attention Deficit Disorder.

Pihl, R. O., & McLarnon, L. D. (1984). Learning disabled children as adolescents. *Journal of Learning Disabilities, 17*, 96–100.

Pintrich, P. R., Anderman, E. M., & Klobucar, C. (1994). Intraindividual differences in motivation and cognition in students with and without learning disabilities. *Journal of Learning Disabilities, 27*(6), 360–370.

Polloway, E. A., Patton, J. R., Smith, T. E. C., & Buck, G. H. (in press). *Mental retardation and learning disabilities: Conceptual and applied issues.*

Reid, R., Maag, J. W., & Vasa, S. F. (1994). Attention deficit hyperactivity disorder as a disability category: A critique. *Exceptional Children, 60*, 198–214.

Ross, A. O. (1976). *Psychological aspects of learning disabilities and reading disorders.* New York: McGraw-Hill.

Roth, F. P., Spekman, N. J., & Fye, E. C. (1995). Reference cohesion in the oral narratives of students with learning disabilities and normally achieving students. *Learning Disability Quarterly, 18*(1), 25–40.

Schalock, R. L., Wolzen, B., Ross, I., Elliot, B., Werbel, G., & Peterson, K. (1986). Post-secondary community placement of handicapped students: A five-year follow-up. *Learning Disability Quarterly, 9*, 295–303.

Schuerholz, L. J., Harris, E. L., Baumgardner, T. L., Reiss, A. L., Freund, L. S., Church, R. P., Mohr, J., & Denckla, M. B. (1995). An analysis of two discrepancy-based models and a processing-deficit approach in identifying learning disabilities. *Journal of Learning Disabilities, 28*(1), 18–29.

Spekman, N. (1981). Dyadic verbal communication abilities of learning disabled and normally achieving fourth and fifth grade boys. *Learning Disability Quarterly, 4*, 193–201.

Stanford, L. D., & Hynd, G. W. (1994). Congruence of behavioral symptomatology in children with ADD/H, ADD/WO, and learning disabilities. *Journal of Learning Disabilities, 27*, 343–353.

Torgesen, J. K. (1984). Memory processes in reading disabled children. *Journal of Learning Disabilities, 18*, 350–357.

Valus, A. (1986). Achievement-potential discrepancy status of students in LD programs. *Learning Disability Quarterly, 9*, 199–205.

Webster, R. E., & Schenck, S. (1978). Diagnostic test pattern differences among LD, ED, EMH, and multihandicapped students. *Journal of Educational Research, 72*, 75–80.

Wiig, E. H., Lapointe, C., & Semel, E. M. (1977). Relationships among language processing and production abilities of learning disabled adolescents. *Journal of Learning Disabilities, 9*, 292–299.

Wiig, E. H., Semel, E. M., & Abele, E. (1981). Perception and interpretation of ambiguous sentences by learning disabled twelve-year-olds. *Learning Disability Quarterly, 4*, 3–12.

Wiig, E. H., Semel, E. M., & Crouse, M. A. B. (1973). The use of English morphology by high-risk and learning disabled children. *Journal of Learning Disabilities, 6*, 457–464.

Yost, D. S., Shaw, S. F., Cullen, J. P., & Bigaj, S. J. (1994). Practices and attitudes of postsecondary LD service providers in North America. *Journal of Learning Disabilities, 27*, 631–640.

Ysseldyke, J. E. (1983). Current practices in making psychoeducational decisions about learning disabled students. *Journal of Learning Disabilities, 16*, 226–233.

Ysseldyke, J. E., & Algozzine, B. (1984). *Introduction to special education*. Boston: Houghton Mifflin.

Zentall, S. S. (1986). Effects of color stimulation on performance and activity of hyperactive and nonhyperactive children. *Journal of Educational Psychology, 78*, 159–165.

Zentall, S. S., Zentall, T. R., & Booth, M. E. (1978). Within task stimulation: Effects on activity and spelling performance in hyperactive and normal children. *Journal of Educational Research, 71*, 223–230.

Service and Program Issues

Case Management

Susan Neal and Beth Gilson

LEARNING GOALS

Upon completion of this chapter the reader will be able to

- describe the guiding principles of case management;

- list the components in case management and give examples of maintaining flexibility to meet consumers' and families' needs;

- discuss how the guiding principles affect the way case management services are provided;

- discuss the importance of the family's role in decision making;

- review the importance of evaluation in case management at the individual, agency, and system levels; and

- describe the role of the case management supervisor and the need for providing ongoing training and technical assistance to staff.

Case management provides a central point of contact for individuals with disabilities and their families as they identify resources and plan to meet their needs. There currently exist many readings, definitions, approaches, and names for case management. It can be referred to as service coordination; it can be based on a "broker" or a "direct" model of service delivery; it can be provided as either an internal or external agency service. No matter the name, model, or administrative function, case management is the one service that assists in pulling all services together and making sure that they provide what the consumer and family say they need. This chapter is our attempt to share what we have learned in our years of direct service with other case managers. We understand that case manage-ment will look different in different settings but believe the underlying principles and activities shared in this chapter will be useful to anyone interested in learning about or providing case man-agement to children and adults with developmental disabilities.

Many different opinions exist as to what case management for people with developmental disabilities should be. These opinions have been operationalized into an array of service models, many claiming to be state of the art or best practice. In this chapter, we have chosen not to discuss the models that exist but rather to focus on the tools that case managers need to facilitate the integration of people who are developmentally disabled with their personal environments. Looking at people as individuals is repeatedly emphasized throughout the chapter. The focus in the following pages is on the values needed to provide the most effective and least obtrusive support for consumers as they go about meeting the challenges in their day-to-day lives.

When case managers are clear as to the values held regarding the people with whom they are working, they find it possible to face the job with enthusiasm, energy, and creativity. If the values are not clear, the potential for continuing frustration and eventual professional burnout exists. Case managers develop and test their values through experience rather than through any specific educational training. People usually do not go to college with the goal of becoming a case manager, but case management skills are increasingly being taught within the curriculums of many different professions. Any professional can hold and practice the values inherent in case management. Therefore, the information in this chapter is intended for any person acting in the capacity of a case manager regardless of his or her formal academic training.

CASE MANAGEMENT: WHAT IT HAS BEEN, WHAT IT IS, WHAT IT CAN BE

The label *case management*, given to what can be considered the most important support service for consumers with developmental disabilities, too often connotes depersonalization and control. For years, professionals in all of the social services have designated the people who are on the receiving end of services as nameless, faceless cases, cases that are in need of being "managed." Professionals tend to forget that human beings sooner or later resist control and show their resistance, either appropriately or inappropriately, through their behavior. In the past the people whose behavior was perceived as being inappropriate, usually those people who were argumentative, injurious, or not considered socially appropriate in their actions, were prioritized as needing case management. These were the people who did not easily fit into the system, who were not easily amenable to existing rules and control. Yet, these same people were the ones who were given more control, more case management. Thus, the cycle tended to perpetuate itself, managing the people who needed to be managed.

People with developmental disabilities have traditionally been targeted as needing case management. Usually it is their behavior excesses or deficits or just the fact that they are considered less than capable that gets them and their families into the service system. People with developmental disabilities are deemed to belong to a group of people with similar characteristics and needs who are incapable of negotiating service systems to meet their needs. Thus, each "case" belonging to this disability group has often been deemed to need case management provided by a case manager (i.e., someone who is faster than a speeding discharge plan and able to leap tall bureaucratic mazes in a single bound).

The myths of disability "groups" and "super" case managers are slowly being dispelled within the field of developmental disabilities. Each person with a disability label is considered an individual who is challenged by specific barriers because of the characteristics of his or her disability. Instead of being labeled as *clients*, people are being referred to as persons or, sometimes, as consumers of the supports and services that will assist in eliminating the barriers created by their disabilities. As professionals gain more experience in the delivery of services, they see the efficacy and cost effectiveness of providing the level of support the individual needs rather than fitting the individual into existing programs.

Although those in the field are slowly recognizing that not everyone who has a developmental disability needs case management, case managers are seen as the key that links the consumer with the needed supports. Professionals who are providing case management are seen less and less as managers and more as facilitators. Case managers cannot provide and do everything as a "superperson," but they can coordinate a team consisting of the consumer, professionals, family, and friends who can identify and put in place the supports that are needed. Therefore, the responsibility of service provision is spread among the team members, with the case manager providing the quality assurance that what team members say is needed is actually delivered and that it has the intended effect in the day-to-day life of the consumer.

Case management is not a paper-shuffling, administrative function. Neither is it a daily skill-training, direct-care, or pure advocacy service. Rather, it is the nucleus of the system of support that is provided to and received by a person who wants such a service. Case management does not have to be provided to or on behalf of every consumer of the developmental disability service system. It can be conducted by the consumer or his or her family or caregiver or both as long as the support that may be needed at any time as the consumer lives, learns, works, and socializes within the community is available.

When it works well, case management is the hub of services and the focus of support. It can facilitate the efficiency and effectiveness of a system while it meets the individualized needs of consumers. Case management can improve the responsiveness of service providers and the satisfaction of consumers, their families, and service providers. Beyond its own activities, case management has the potential to enhance the quality of programming throughout the service delivery system. In most systems, case management activities take place from the time of entry to successful completion of programming. Through these activities, case management can affect program planning and development, implementation and coordination of services, and evaluation of programming and support.

The success of case management in promoting quality services often depends greatly, sometimes solely, on who is fulfilling the role of case manager. For example, because it is the case manager who identifies resources to meet the needs of a consumer, the options are usually limited to his or her scope of awareness of resources and to what he or she sees as appropriate given the abilities of the consumer. If a case manager is working with an 18-year-old woman who is severely mentally retarded and believes that work experience is unrealistic and currently not important, then transition services with supported employment will not be seen as an option. Another case manager working with this same woman might see work experience as important and refer her to transitional services. In this example, what the consumer receives depends on the person providing the case management. Agency policies and procedures, team process, and supervision can all affect the quality of case management, but the values and abilities of the case manager are the major factors for success. How a case manager perceives the people who are served, the job responsibilities, and the role within the agency determines the quality of interactions and interventions. These perceptions are directly tied to values.

GUIDING PRINCIPLES

A case manager needs a set of values that respects and supports the lives of consumers and their families. Before continuing to address the idea of what case management can be, we believe it will be helpful to identify some of the values that make case management successful. These values help establish a framework from which responsive case management can be developed. This framework is not a prioritized, inclusive list of values that guarantee good case management; instead, it is a foundation for best practice.

All People Are Individuals

The value that all people are individuals is essential for quality case management. We work in a world of categories and too often determine needs based on diagnosis and disability. Checklists, standardized tests, and other resources that can help case managers be more efficient in their work are becoming more popular. As case loads become larger, case managers do not have the time to really know the people they are serving. Formalized assessments give ranges, but spending time with a person, and his family, in natural settings, exposes the person's uniqueness. A standardized test can indicate that a woman is mildly mentally retarded. It does not, however, indicate that she likes to embroider, that she has a brother she is very close to, that she can cook but cannot tell time, and that she usually sleeps 10 hours a night. All of this information is useful as programs are planned and activities are suggested. Her level of mental retardation will be less significant in her day-to-day life. This day-to-day life is where case management takes place. When a case manager does not know the uniqueness of the people he or she is working with, services are not supportive.

The majority of outcomes through case management services depend on the relationship between the case manager and the consumer and his or her family. A case manager who enjoys a rapport with a consumer and his or her family will be more successful than the case manager who has a poor relationship. A positive relationship with a consumer and his or her family can facilitate the case manager's obtaining better information about the person's uniqueness and therefore enable him or her to do a better job of matching needs to services. It can also provide the mutual respect and understanding that is necessary for a working partnership, which is important to quality case management.

CASE EXAMPLE: KATIE

An example of what can happen when a case manager does not take the time to know the consumer and family is reflected in the case of Katie, a 12-year-old girl who is developmentally disabled. A case manager had been working with Katie and her family for about a year. On several occasions the case manager spoke with the mother, whose main concern is friendship for her daughter. Katie has also stated to the case manager that weekends away from her friends at school were boring. The case manager began looking for a recreation program that would provide socialization for Katie on weekends. It took many months for the case manager to find an appropriate program. The case manager was determined to find an integrated program that would provide opportunities for friendships with children with disabilities and children without disabilities. Finally, after having many telephone conversations with staff and administrators, placing Katie on a waiting list, and securing transportation, the case manager arranged for Katie to attend a Saturday afternoon recreation program at a local community center. The case manager, pleased with success, called to give the family the good news. The case manager's excitement ended when she learned from the girl's mother that the family was Jewish and that Saturday is their day of worship. The family preferred that their children not participate in outside activities on Saturdays. The case manager felt frustrated that so many months of work had gone to waste and felt embarrassed that she had not known this basic fact about the family. The family was shocked at how little the case manager knew about their daughter's life and were distressed at not being informed of the case manager's plans earlier in the process. This case clearly demonstrates that the best intentions and plans can be inappropriate if family lifestyles and preferences are not considered.

Families Make Decisions

Getting to know consumers and their families well takes time. All successful relationships in our lives develop over time through many face-to-face interactions. Relationships between case managers and the people they serve are no exception. It is impossible to know the likes and dislikes of people or how they spend their days through letters, staff meetings, and telephone conversations. A relationship with the consumer develops through visiting in the home, eating together, shopping together, or participating in daily activities. One creative case manager uses Christmas shopping as an excellent way to get to know the people in her program. Through this one activity, she obtains information on family transportation, decision making, fiscal management, traditions, and individual interests and likes as gifts are selected. She arranges this shopping trip to be informal and as close to what the family would do as possible. The case manager then uses the information gathered from this trip to support activities in the future. For example, if the consumer feels unable to find transportation for an activity, the case manager will remind the family of how they were able to find transportation for Christmas shopping. She reinforces their resourcefulness and supports their decision making and problem solving as a family. This case manager is able to do her job well because she takes the time to know the people she serves.

All consumers come to case management services with some type of support system. That system can include the natural family or foster parents, siblings, other relatives, neighbors, a landlady, or roommates. These support persons cannot be ignored; in fact, they can be the most useful resource to the case manager. These people usually remain constant in the consumer's life, whereas case managers come and go. Members of this support system offer advice and suggestions to the consumer throughout involvement with the case manager. Through experience, case managers realize that final decisions are made in families or in other support groups, not in meetings. Consumers and families who may not verbalize their feelings in meetings do let case managers know in some way what they will, and will not, do. Involving members of the support system in program planning helps case managers offer appropriate assistance. This is not to say that the final decision should be left to family and friends in all cases. For some consumers, the final decision must be their own. The value expressed here is that the role of family and friends must be clearly seen, respected, and supported by case managers. The case manager can realize this goal by keeping the support individuals informed, providing opportunities for input, and using them as resources. The case manager cannot do so by inviting family or friends to participate only in periodic, formal staff meetings. Involvement of the support persons should be a partnership with the case manager as all activities are planned, implemented, and monitored.

In case management, a significant value is that all services are accountable, first and foremost, to consumers and their families. Services exist for consumers, not vice versa. The case manager must consider the consumer's welfare and dignity when making program decisions. Issues such as maintaining confidentiality, setting criteria for admission and discharge, charging fees, referring to other services, and keeping records can all greatly affect the lives of consumers. Case managers must address these issues by upholding the personal worth of consumers and respecting their differences. Policies and procedures for operating programs cannot be based on the premise that the population being served is a homogeneous group. Case managers must be responsive to people by adhering to approaches that support the individual, not approaches that simply make the office run better.

All People Have Basic Wants

The final value to be discussed is that people with disabilities want the same basic things from life that people without disabilities want. They want to live in a home with family or housemates, have friends and neighbors, go to school, work, and socialize within their community. Much has been written about community integration and the importance of family and friends. Along with promoting integration, case management can also provide consumers with challenges that help them grow as individuals. In any setting, case managers can challenge consumers with activities such as making decisions, encouraging self-direction, developing personal preferences, and using their natural support system effectively. Case management has not evolved at the same pace as other programs, such as vocational and residential services, that have improved by accepting the abilities of consumers and challenging them to enhance their abilities. In some case management services, consumers work in supported employment and participate in supported living arrangements yet continue to have case managers who, instead of the consumer, make all doctors' appointments, provide transportation, and remain the direct contact with the physician. Case management services that do not support the consumer's existing skills and that do not promote learning new skills can put the entire service delivery off balance. Case managers must consistently encourage consumers to use their own skills.

CASE MANAGEMENT CHALLENGE

Such a framework built of these values makes obvious the tremendous potential for case management. Case management is the key to coordinated, responsive services, across programs and agencies. A level of quality assurance is provided by case managers through their partnership with consumers and families and their sharing of information on resources throughout the service delivery system and community. As case managers promote the importance of family, friends, and community participation for all people, they support integration through all of the activities. Finally, case managers can facilitate learning of new skills and maintenance of existing skills for consumers in areas imperative for successful community integration. Skills such as making choices, communicating, solving problems, and advocating for oneself can be naturally taught and encouraged by case managers in their day-to-day interactions with consumers and families.

The challenge for case managers and their supervisors is to adopt these values and to operationalize them within their systems. This attempt is often complicated by agency policies and procedures, standards and regulations, and, unfortunately, sometimes by other staff in the system. It helps to remember that everything will not change overnight. Change may be a slow process that initially occurs with a few consumers. For case management to meet its full potential, however, all of its activities, or components, must be assessed to ensure that these values are reflected in the work.

COMPONENTS OF CASE MANAGEMENT

The components of a case management service delivery system must allow for flexibility in meeting individual needs and must take into consideration consumer preference in choosing how the service components will be used. In other words, what a case manager offers to a consumer should be unique to that person, and the consumer should have a say in the type, frequency, location, and extent of involvement by the case manager in his or her life. What is undesirable is a rigid system in which a consumer must meet an exact criterion to be eligible for and remain a recipient of the service. Too often, eligibility and service criteria become exclusionary rather than inclusionary, and consumers become the square pegs trying to fit into case management round holes.

There must also be flexibility in identifying who the consumer of the case management service really is. When an individual is served outside of the context of family, friends, neighbors, and caregivers, often conflict arises between what the case manager wants for the consumer and what others see as needed. The following description of Sarah's situation is an example of what can happen when the case manager is required to question whose interests need to be represented.

In this example, conflict between Sarah's family and the team will, in all certainty, be the entire focus of the upcoming meeting unless the case manager can convince everyone that Sarah is not the only consumer whose interests need to be represented. It would do no good for the case manager to decide that Sarah is the consumer and to alienate her family by saying that because Sarah is her own guardian, what she wants should occur. On the other hand, neither would it help Sarah if the case manager represents her parents' interests and thus prevented her from taking advantage of a less restrictive service option. The role of the case manager must be that of facilitating compromise so that the consumer receives what he or she desires and agrees is needed, while not alienating any potential support provider who is needed for maximizing achievement of success.

The function or role of the case manager is not only that of facilitator but also that of coordinator, advocate, team leader, and provider of service linkage and quality assurance. But what does a case manager do to accomplish all of these roles? Most activities of a case manager fall into four primary categories: assessment, planning, implementation, and review. Table 15.1 presents some examples of the components of case management.

CASE EXAMPLE: SARAH

Sarah is a 36-year-old woman who has lived all her life with her parents, Mr. and Mrs. Smith, who are now approaching retirement age. Although they have never filed a petition to become Sarah's court-appointed guardians, Mr. and Mrs. Smith have always acted in this capacity, insisting that they sign every document on Sarah's behalf. Sarah has cerebral palsy, which has severely limited her physical and expressive communication abilities. For the past year, the staff at the sheltered workshop that Sarah has attended since graduating from school have targeted her for supported employment services. The staff have shown Sarah various job sites and feel extremely confident that her nonverbal communication indicates that she wants to work at the local YMCA. Sarah's parents refuse to give permission or to sign release forms for the supported employment program because they fear that if the job does not work out, Sarah will have lost her space at the workshop and will have to wait at home until a new job site is available. Mr. and Mrs. Smith are both still working and will not consider leaving Sarah home alone. The workshop and supported employment program want to accept Sarah's signature mark on a release form so that they can go ahead with the transfer. They are absolutely sure that they have Sarah's informed consent and that she knows the risks involved. The case manager has decided to call a team meeting before Sarah is transferred from the workshop.

Assessment

A case manager must have adequate information about the consumer and his or her personal environment before any other service delivery can effectively occur. Case managers have traditionally not had available an assessment protocol designed specifically for their use. Instead, they have had to rely on formal assessments done by other professionals and on the verbal information provided by the consumer and current caregivers. Often all that is available is medical information, intelligence testing, and educational–vocational evaluations. This information usually is not current, nor have the results and recommendations been compared with each other.

What is most revealing about a consumer is a situational assessment that combines verbal and observational information about what the person is actually able to do at home and in the community. A case manager does not have to be the one who actually conducts such an assessment, but it is extremely helpful for the case manager to be a part of the process and have firsthand knowledge of the consumer's capabilities.

An assessment barrier that is frequently identified is that there are not enough professionals in

Table 15.1. Case Management Components

Function/Role	Example
Facilitator	Makes sure that the consumer, family, and service providers are all communicating to each other the pertinent information needed to resolve the issue
Coordinator	Ensures that the consumer is receiving the services identified within a plan and serves on behalf of the consumer as the point of contact for all providers
Advocate	Assures that the consumer's "voice" is heard in all decision making
	Responsible for identifying when service providers and others need to meet with the consumer and family to plan service delivery and resolve issues. Schedules and facilitates the meeting
Service Linkage	Assists the consumer in identifying and applying for specific services and in transitioning from one service to the next
Quality Assurance	Makes sure that the consumer is receiving the services that are wanted, that the consumer is satisfied with them, and that they are accomplishing what the consumer needs

a given community with experience in evaluating people with developmental disabilities. Obtaining a psychologic evaluation that includes an assessment of adaptive behavior in addition to an intelligence score is often difficult. Rather than go without this information, case managers themselves can use an adaptive behavior assessment tool and use the information in conjunction with a narrative summary that describes the consumer's current status. If nothing else, a good narrative description of what a person does at home, in school or the workplace, in social situa-

tions, and with family and friends can suffice. Table 15.2 presents four common barriers to appropriate assessment.

After all of the assessment information is collected, it must be compared, and from it, the consumer's strengths and limitations identified. It is best if the consumer and the care providers who know the consumer best are the ones who identify the strengths and limitations with the case manager. These are the people who form the basis of a program-planning team that directs the focus of all services and supports that a consumer receives.

Planning

The strengths and limitations of a consumer serve as the framework upon which services and supports are planned. Supports are needed both to maintain and to strengthen what a person does well and also to assist the person in developing the skills and competencies needed in his or her life. The case manager is essential to ensuring that the supports identified as needed are what the consumer has agreed are needed and wanted and that they are neither too restrictive nor too broad to be effective. To accomplish this, the case manager serves as the team leader or at least as a team member with major monitoring responsibilities.

Table 15.2. Common Barriers Encountered During Assessment

Lack of a comprehensive assessment protocol specific to case management

Inadequate information about the issue available from previous assessments or as initially reported by the consumer

Information that is available is biased or not current

Not enough professionals in the community with experience in evaluating people with developmental disabilities

Services and supports are identified in conjunction with goals and objectives. In addition to the consumer himself or herself, the case manager should have the best overall understanding of what the consumer wants and needs to accomplish. The case manager must ensure that the team establishes a long-range goal on which all other service providers base their goals and objectives. Sometimes the most sensible strategy is to have a team meeting at least once a year during which a mutually agreed on overall goal for the consumer is set and potential objectives and program strategies are discussed. Then each provider of the supports or services that have been set as priorities works at a later time with the consumer to establish specific, short-range (i.e., less than 1 year) program goals and objectives. The case manager must make sure that all of the program goals and objectives fit into the framework of the overall goal set by the team.

At times, a case manager does not have a team within which to work. In these instances, the team becomes the consumer, others chosen by or who are acting on behalf of the consumer (i.e., family, legal guardian, advocate), and the case manager. Service planning occurs whether or not an interdisciplinary team is present, but when the team is small, the case manager has a greater responsibility for knowing the availability of potential services and supports and subsequent linkage activities.

Implementation

Not only does the case manager provide coordination and direction for the consumer's planning team, he or she also must frequently develop goals and objectives for the case management activities. The case manager is usually responsible for what are called service coordination objectives, which specify what the case manager will do on behalf of the consumer. Service coordination objectives are different from behavioral objectives, which focus on what the consumer will achieve. Both types of objectives should be written so that progress can be measured (i.e., who will do what, by when, and with what kinds of supports).

It is important for the case manager to have written documentation of what activities are being done. Documentation is kept either in an activity log, which is summarized periodically, or as narrative notes that are placed in the record each time the case manager does something on behalf of the consumer. The activities must be tied back to the goals and objectives. If they are not, there must be reassessment of and any necessary revisions made to the objectives.

Review

Case managers have the responsibility of providing the quality assurance that all services and supports being received by the consumer are having the intended effect. The case manager has many ways of accomplishing quality assurance, from regular, on-site observations of the consumer to a paper review of data submitted by other service providers. No single way of review can be recommended, but what is done must be consistent and least invasive in the lives of the consumer and the caregivers. The maximum time frame in which a review process occurs should be semiannually. A quarterly review is recommended. If a case manager's review of services and interventions is not seen as needed at least once every few months, then the question must be raised as to whether the consumer actually needs case management services.

The periodic review of a consumer's service plan provides part of the assessment information upon which future goals and objectives are set. The information gathered from the reviews regarding progress, or lack of progress, should be shared with the consumer as well as with all other team members.

The necessary components of case management (i.e., assessment, planning, implementation, and review) remain the same, regardless of whether the consumer is a child, an adult, or a senior citizen. Nor do they change in relation to where the person lives: within a family, in a supervised setting, or independently in his or her own home. What does change is how each of the components is delivered by the case manager and how the consumer interacts and grows within the process. The next section provides guidance to case managers in evaluating the effectiveness of what they do.

PROGRAM EVALUATION

Services delivered to individuals with developmental disabilities traditionally have been evaluated according to standards set by national accreditation bodies, by state and local licensing authorities, or by a combination of both. Case management is usually not a licensed service, and only recently have standards evolved specific to the activities of a case manager. Evaluation strategies other than the standards for measuring service delivery outcomes can provide more qualitative information for use in evaluating how case management is being received by consumers and their families. This approach is important because it is no longer enough to justify the effectiveness of case management activities to funding sources, agency administrators, and utilization reviewers by presenting data that specify numbers served, frequency of contacts, documentation deficiencies corrected, and goals accomplished.

Evaluation of case management service delivery should always be approached from the perspective of the consumer. The question, "What kind of success is being evaluated?" must be asked and answered in terms of the success of the consumer, not just in terms of what the case managers have accomplished. Evaluation strategies should measure the successes of the individual consumer, as well as the successes of all who are served within a given service delivery system. The following suggestions for evaluation strategies can be built into the assessment of case management at the individual consumer, agency, and service system levels.

The Individual

Most of the time, an individual's achievement, or lack of achievement, of the goals and objectives listed on his or her individual service plan is what constitutes evaluation of progress. Case managers are responsible for monitoring the implementation of program strategies and often share in the blame when the consumer does not respond as expected. To avoid this failure, the case manager can influence the development of program goals and objectives so that they are written narrowly enough to ensure success yet, at the same time, broadly enough to challenge the consumer. One must always remember that success is what motivates individuals to continue to achieve. People with developmental disabilities are not exceptions to this rule.

In addition to assuming responsibility for monitoring consumers' responses to specific skill training, and equally important, the case manager must look at how well consumers are integrated into their homes and family activities; whether they are involved in the same activities as their peers who are not disabled; and whether, as shown by their behavior, they like what they are doing. Perhaps most important is the need to look at whether the individuals are making choices on a day-to-day basis. If the case management is effective, then not only will the individuals have the opportunity for making choices, they will also demonstrate their ability to make decisions regardless of how basic their choices are or how challenging their disabilities.

The Agency

Administrators of service agencies focus not only on the effectiveness of the service provided but also on whether the outcomes justify the cost of delivering the service. One of the best ways of looking at this is to examine how case managers spend their work time. It is suggested that the administrator look beyond the ratio of direct and indirect service hours to a more qualitative assessment of what case management activities are actually required to achieve a particular outcome (e.g., the transition of a student from school into employment or of an adult from living with his or her family to another setting). The time that a case manager spends handling the behavior crisis of a person living with elderly parents is probably significantly different from that spent with a person living in a staff-supervised setting. Examining the actual case management activities done with specific consumers reveals trends in case loads. These trends can provide objective indicators for planning and resource allocation purposes.

The System

The effectiveness of case management within a service delivery system can be evaluated on the basis of how well people with developmental disabilities are integrated into the community. It is helpful to determine the number of segregated preschools, schools, day support programs, apartment buildings, recreational programs, church groups, boy or girl Scout troops, and senior citizen programs. This type of evaluation is important, not as a value judgment against segregated settings, but rather as an indication of the level of integration and participation of people with developmental disabilities in day-to-day community activities. One way the case manager can determine the level of integration is to ascertain who the friends of people with disabilities are. If the friends of consumers are limited only to caregivers or to other consumers with whom they live or with whom they spend the school or work day, then case management is not being effective in facilitating community integration.

It is important for case managers to remember that evaluation is not just an activity that occurs every so often. Assessment of case management service delivery should begin at the planning stage, before service is initiated with any consumer. The same approach used with individual program planning can be applied to overall case management service delivery: The need for case management is assessed by identifying strengths and limitations; goals and objectives are developed, and services are implemented; outcomes are reviewed and used for further modifications in the delivery of the service. Approaching evaluation as an evolving process ensures that case management is "doing what it should be doing."

PREPARATION AND SUPERVISION

The role of case managers is increasing in importance as the service delivery system improves. Best practice, such as community integration and family-centered services, relies heavily on successful case management. These new challenges and responsibilities will be met by case managers who have the values, knowledge, and skills necessary to do the job well. Ensuring that case managers are competent and comfortable in their roles demands that attention be given to preservice and in-service training, technical assistance, and ongoing supervision. All areas of personnel preparation and work evaluation need to reflect and support creative, responsive case management. A match must occur between what is known about case management and its potential and the activities that teach, monitor, and evaluate the components of case management.

Case management is no longer perceived as a single activity within all staff roles, but rather as a role that involves many activities. It is becoming a position with a career track for professionals, not an entry level position that serves as a stepping stone to other jobs within an agency. For example, in Virginia it is not difficult to find case managers who have been in this role for 10 to 15 years. The knowledge and skills needed to do case management are increasing as the service evolves. Training in topics such as communication, negotiation, assessment, group interaction, team leadership, and family dynamics has become important to prepare case managers for their work. In addition, case managers can benefit from training that defines their role, discusses current best practice, and describes the potential of case management services. Case management is emerging as a curriculum in preservice training, but currently these courses are few in number and are not part of a specific degree program.

The time is right for colleges and universities to begin offering course work and specialized degrees in case management. This training should be interdisciplinary because no one discipline is best suited for the role and because the work of the case manager is interdisciplinary in nature. Preservice training for case managers also needs to provide many hours of contact with consumers and families in their homes and communities. A practicum, for example, could be for all students to provide 6 hours per week of free respite to families with children who are disabled. This simple change from agency-based to a family-based field experience is invaluable to students who are preparing for the case manager role. Students would experience firsthand family dynamics and interactions with parents, siblings, and consumers; and at the same time, provide an invaluable support to these families through respite services. This practicum could be ongoing, free service to families as students enter the curriculum year after year.

On the job, case managers face many challenges and demands that make ongoing training and supervision necessary. Case managers need training and technical assistance that help them understand their community, agency, and role within the organization. They need to be encouraged to be inquisitive and creative but to also know their limits of authority and of responsibilities. Technical assistance is needed to help case managers use their time wisely, stay on track with their activities, and expand their knowledge of resources to meet individualized needs of consumers. As case management continues to develop, it is important regularly to expose case managers to current trends through training opportunities.

The case manager's supervisor will, in most agencies, be the key source of information and skill development. It is the supervisor who will be asked for assistance in prioritizing activities; identifying resources; clarifying policies, procedures, and regulations; and solving problems. The supervisor's role is a balance between administration and the case manager, always keeping consumer satisfaction as a priority. For example, a case manager currently working in early intervention services uses a family-centered approach whereby families are making many of the decisions that professionals have made in the past. If this case manager works in an agency whose administration believes all final decisions need to be made by staff, the family-centered approach will be in conflict with agency policy. The supervisor of case management services will need to educate the administration about this approach and its importance and, at the same time, support the work of the case manager.

To promote quality case management, the supervisor needs to commend case managers when integration occurs and dependence on the case manager decreases. Supervisors are the key to stopping the superperson syndrome of case management. Case managers need to ensure that as much autonomy and decision making as possible are left to the consumer and family. A supervisor can help the case manager assume the role of facilitator and maintain the values important to successful case management, as described in this chapter. It is easy to become overly helpful in providing case management services. Supervisors and coworkers can provide objective insights and useful suggestions as case managers adapt services to meet the changing needs of consumers and their families. It is sometimes difficult to draw the line between encouraging independence and "dumping" on the family and consumer. Supervisors need to guide case managers as they address these difficult issues on an individual-consumer basis.

The importance and demands of the supervisors of case management services have also increased. There are in-service training needs for supervisors, because many of these supervisors were case managers who were promoted because of a job well done. Training that addresses team leadership, policy analysis, current trends in services, management, and staff development will help supervisors in their roles.

FINAL THOUGHTS

The success of case management is not determined by the discipline of the case manager, the model of the service, or the type of agency administering the service. The success depends on the values of the people providing the service, the provision of services that facilitate community life, and agency administration that supports its case managers. It is time to be creative and innovative in case management services and to break with tradition. Questions about size of case load, preferred model, and which discipline makes the best case manager will, unfortunately, keep the system in its traditional, outdated approach. Instead, it is now time to question whether there is sufficient time for interactions, whether services are flexible enough to meet changing needs, and whether collaboration is occurring among many disciplines to provide the best services possible.

Community-Based Vocational Training

Katherine Inge, Stacy Dymond, and Paul Wehman

LEARNING GOALS

Upon completion of this chapter the reader will be able to

- describe what community-based instruction is and why it is an effective way to help train individuals with developmental disabilities;

- list and briefly describe the five major steps in developing community-based training sites;

- describe the key components of instructional strategies for implementing community-based instruction; and

- discuss the importance of utilizing several different training sites in the community-based instruction process.

Community-based vocational training provides functional-skills training in an integrated business setting, addressing the production, quality, and social demands of the natural work environment. A community-based approach to training has been recognized by many as a best practice for teaching individuals with developmental disabilities (e.g., Falvey, 1989; Wehman & Revell, in press). The emphasis is on *training*, not field-trip experiences. The first major component is assessment of the local labor demands to determine the employment trends and to identify current and future job openings (Inge, Dymond, et al., 1993). Once these have been determined, job training sites can be established in businesses.

Training in a real work environment is particularly important for those students with severe disabilities, because they do not generalize work skills learned in segregated school programs to community sites (Wehman, 1992). Due to this in-ability to generalize from one setting to another and to difficulties in learning new skills, the individual with developmental disabilities must be increasingly exposed to community-based training as he or she progresses through the school program (Renzaglia & Hutchins, 1988). The more difficulties displayed in skill transferral by an individual, the more he or she can benefit from instruction in the natural or community environment.

Although community-based instruction has been identified as a needed curriculum component for students with developmental disabilities, many school systems continue to exclude students with the most significant disabilities. The presence of challenging behaviors may be one of the reasons that teachers hesitate to take some students into the community (Wehman, 1992). Issues of concern include the safety of the teacher, employees, as well as the student if he or she becomes "uncontrollable" on a job site and liability for damages to individuals or the environment. The simple solution for school districts, in some instances, is to continue training within the school setting rather than providing the much needed exposure to community work experiences.

The steps in developing community-based training sites include (1) conducting a job-market analysis, (2) identifying businesses with the targeted jobs and contacting the personnel director or employer, (3) selecting and analyzing appropriate jobs for community-based training, (4) scheduling community-based vocational instruction, and (5) designing individualized instructional programs. Teachers may first want to contact adult service agencies within their communities to determine the location of supported employment placements. These sites may not be appropriate for community-based vocational training experiences, because the presence of unpaid students could confuse the employers and result in inappropriate work expectations and labor law violations (Moon & Inge, 1993). A detailed listing of the steps and activities involved in developing community-based training sites is provided in Table 16.1.

Step 1: Conduct a Job-Market Analysis

Initially, a school system may want to identify a task force of teachers to develop procedures for completing a community job-market analysis (Pumpian, Shepard, & West, 1988). In some instances, the task force may appoint the transition coordinator to complete business contacts, or a special education teacher at the secondary level may take the lead. In any case, a plan of action should be developed to prevent duplication of effort.

Once school personnel have been identified to complete the market analysis, they may begin by surveying their local chamber of commerce or economic development office, looking in the telephone directory, reading the newspaper want ads, interviewing potential employers, complet-

ing follow-up contacts with school graduates, and contacting adult service agencies and supported employment programs to determine job placements for individuals with severe disabilities. A list of contacts might include the following:

- State Economic Development Office
- State Employment Commission
- Chamber of Commerce
- Trade Associations
- Better Business Bureau
- City and County Employment Offices
- Department of Labor
- Telephone Book/Newspaper Classifieds
- Business Newsletters
- Vocational Rehabilitation Agencies
- Supported Employment Providers
- Civic Clubs and Organizations
- Friends and Associates

Step 2: Identify Businesses with the Targeted Jobs and Contact the Personnel Director/Employer

Once the local economy has been assessed to determine the possible job types for students with severe disabilities, the teacher(s) must determine where instruction will occur. Each student should have the opportunity to experience a variety of jobs in a number of different settings to assist the student in developing a work history, determine his or her job preferences, identify future training needs, and determine skill characteristics for future job matching. The task force that completed the community job-market analysis should also identify the individual(s) who will approach employers regarding use of their businesses for community-based training sites.

Table 16.1. Steps and Activities for Developing a Community-Based Vocational Training Program

Steps	Activities
1. Conduct a community job-market analysis.	1. Identify a school task force and/or individual(s) who will be responsible for completing the analysis. 2. Survey the telephone directory yellow pages. 3. Read the classified section of the newspaper. 4. Contact local business organizations (i.e., Chamber of Commerce). 5. Survey school graduates to determine jobs held by individuals with disabilities in the community. 6. Create a list of potential jobs, by job type, that are available to students with severe disabilities.

2. Identify businesses with the targeted jobs and contact the personnel director or employer.	1. Establish a school policy for contacting employers/businesses.
	2. Identify school personnel responsible for business contacts.
	3. Review and revise (as needed) school insurance/liability policy to cover community-based training sites and transportation.
	4. Outline school policy for meeting labor law regulations.
	5. Develop a contract for meeting the labor law requirements.
	6. Contact the business . . . by letter and/or telephone.
	  a. Briefly describe the school's community-based program.
	  b. Discuss jobs that may be appropriate for training.
	  c. Schedule a time to visit and explain the program further.
	7. Visit the business in person.
	  a. Describe the purpose of vocational instruction.
	  b. Discuss the employer, teacher, and student responsibilities on the job site.
	  c. Explain the labor law regulations for nonpaid work experiences.
	  d. Discuss liability issues.
	  e. Develop a community-based training agreement.
	  f. Identify possible job tasks for training.
	  g. Schedule a time to observe the identified tasks to develop task analyses.
	  h. Send a thank-you note.
	8. Compile a file for each business visited.

3. Select and analyze appropriate jobs for community-based training.	1. Visit the job site. 2. Discuss the identified jobs with the site supervisor. 3. Discuss the job-site rules and regulations. 4. Observe the coworkers performing the job duties. 5. Select the tasks best suited for students with severe disabilities.

(continues)

Table 16.1. *Continued*

Steps	Activities
	6. Develop a job duty schedule and task analyses for the activities selected.
	7. Identify available times with the employer or department supervisor for training.
	8. Request at least 1- to 2-hour blocks of time for each site identified.
	9. Agree on a start date.
4. Schedule community-based training.	1. Identify students to receive vocational training.
	2. Hold IEP/ITP meetings for students.
	a. Identify student training needs.
	b. Discuss purpose of community-based vocational training with transition team members.
	c. Write vocational goals/objectives.
	3. Match students to available sites.
	4. Sign community-based training agreements [student, parent(s), employer, school representative].
	5. Develop a daily schedule.
	6. Develop a transportation schedule.
	7. Send a copy of the schedule to the school principal, special education supervisor, parents, employers, etc.
	8. Provide parents with information on individual insurance coverage for liability.
5. Design individual systematic instruction programs.	1. Modify job duty schedules and task analyses based on student characteristics.
	2. Select a data collection procedure.
	3. Take a baseline of student performance on all tasks to be taught.
	4. Select an instructional procedure.
	5. Select a reinforcer.
	6. Implement the training program.
	7. Take probe data on student performance.
	8. Routinely review student data and modify program format as needed.
	9. Review student goals and objectives for training and update as needed.

Note. This table is adapted from Moon and Inge (1993); Moon, Inge, Wehman, Brooke, and Barcus (1990); Moon, Kiernan, and Halloran (1990); and Pumpian, Shepard, and West (1988).

Initial information to identify potential jobs within a business can be obtained from the personnel director or employer. Often this individual will be able to provide written job descriptions that can be useful in identifying job types.

However, observation of the actual work sites usually is more beneficial for job identification (Moon, Inge, Wehman, Brooke, & Barcus, 1990). When selecting nonpaid work experiences, the teacher must be careful not to displace a worker within the job site in order to meet labor law requirements (Inge, Simon, Halloran, & Moon, 1993). Therefore, the tasks targeted should provide enough space for the student and teacher to work alongside the regular employees.

Another issue the teacher must consider is the number of tasks that should be targeted for instruction. There is some debate whether it is more beneficial to provide students experience with many tasks, or to limit experience to one or two tasks (Sowers & Powers, 1991). This decision should be based on the characteristics of specific students. However, it may be more appropriate to limit the number of tasks for students with severe disabilities. Sowers and Powers (1991) suggested that providing instruction on a number of different tasks or moving students from task to task before skill learning may not allow them to experience a sense of accomplishment.

Contacts with the personnel director or a company manager can be made by phone or letter to set up an appointment to discuss the school's program in detail. Additional methods for initial contacts may include visits to local business association meetings, employer breakfasts, visits to regional business offices, and so on (Pumpian et al., 1988). "Dropping in" on employers without an appointment is not recommended.

Step 3: Select and Analyze Appropriate Jobs for Community-Based Training

Often, the initial contact made with a business is with an employer or management-level individ-

ual who will not be able to specifically assist the teacher in identifying jobs for training. The teacher will be referred to a supervisor who, in turn, will be the actual contact person for community programming.

Activities during this phase of setting up a community-based training site include observing the coworkers as they perform the job duties available, selecting tasks that are appropriate to the students who will be receiving training, and actually working the selected job duties. A tentative schedule of the activities that the student(s) will be performing should be developed, as well as task analyses for skills targeted. Both the schedule and the analyses may need modification once specific students are assigned to the work site. Finally, the teacher should negotiate the times for the student(s) to be on site and a start date.

Job Duty Schedule

A job duty schedule outlines the specific work tasks that will be performed by the students, as well as the time the tasks will be performed. Figure 16.1 is a sample job schedule for a community-based training site.

In addition to the job duty schedule, the teacher/trainer needs to determine if there are any special requirements that the employer has for the student(s) on the job site. Answers to the following sample questions should be determined (Moon & Inge, 1993):

- Does the employer/supervisor want the student(s) to wear a uniform or specific clothing (e.g., white shirt with black pants)?

- What entrance should be used?

- Is it important to report to the supervisor or to a coworker upon arrival?

- Do employees have assigned lockers and can one be available to the student(s)?

- Is there an identified break area and employee bathroom?

Community-Based Training Site:	Discount Clothing Store - Stock Room
Area Supervisor:	Mrs. Mary Miller
Teacher Completing Form:	Stacy D.

☑ Daily
(Training tasks remain
the same from day to day)

☐ Varies day to day
(If checked here, complete a
separate form for each day's
schedule)

If above box is checked, indicate day for which this form is completed:

☐   ☐   ☐   ☐   ☐
Mon   Tues   Wed   Thurs   Fri

Vocational Training Tasks	Approximate Time
1:00 P.M.–1:15 P.M.	Punch in, set up work area
1:15 P.M.–1:30 P.M.	Open clothing boxes
1:30 P.M.–2:00 P.M.	Put clothes on hangers
2:00 P.M.–2:15 P.M.	Break in employee lounge
2:15 P.M.–3:00 P.M.	Unpack boxes, fold items, put on shelves in stock room
3:00 P.M.–3:30 P.M.	Punch out - Go to McDonald's - Return to School

Comments: Students should wear dark blue pants and a white shirt for this training site. Report to Mrs. Miller upon arrival. If she is not in the stock room, call ext. 75 and report to security. Students will work with Bill and Laura (coworkers) on all tasks.

SIGNATURE/TITLE: _____   DATE: _____

Figure 16.1.   Sample community-based training schedule. From *Designing Community-Based Instructional Programs for Students with Severe Disabilities*, by K. Inge and P. Wehman (Eds.), 1993, Richmond, VA: Rehabilitation Research and Training Center on Supported Employment.

- Are there specific break times for employees?

- Are there any company benefits that may be available to the students (e.g., free lunch or soda)?

- Are there any restricted (hazardous) areas or activities that can be identified?

- Is there a company policy or procedure for reporting accidents on the job?

All of this information can then be recorded and placed in a file that can be accessed by all school personnel. This file would be particularly impor-tant during teacher absences when another school employee must supervise the site.

Task Analysis

Whatever activities are included in the job duty schedule, the teacher needs to complete a thorough task analysis of each activity prior to bringing the student(s) to the work site. He or she should observe the coworkers performing the task; identify each step that is completed; and then perform the job, modifying the steps as necessary. Finally, the teacher should check with the supervisor to ensure that the task is being performed correctly.

Each step of a task analysis should consist of one observable behavior that can be taught individually (Barcus, Brooke, Inge, Moon, & Goodall, 1987; Moon, Inge, et al., 1990; Moon & Inge, 1993). The steps should be worded in the second person so they may be used as verbal prompts during instruction (e.g., "Wipe the lid of the toilet"), as well as making references to things that are observable (e.g., "Push the green button"). A good task analysis assists the teacher in organizing instruction, providing consistent training, and evaluating the student's performance. Figure 16.2 is a sample task analysis for cleaning a toilet.

There are several tips for developing and individualizing task analyses for vocational instruction in order to facilitate a student's skill acquisition and quality performance. First, the teacher should analyze a job to determine if *discrimination* is part of the task and, if so, how can this be "built" into the task analysis. For instance, many individuals with severe disabilities may be unable to distinguish clean versus dirty. In the task analysis, the teacher could analyze cleaning the toilet and determine a pattern of wiping the top, sides, seat, and inside of the toilet that would always result in a clean surface. These steps would then be broken down into smaller steps for instruction. For a student with discrimination difficulties, a sample step in the task analysis may be further analyzed as shown in Figure 16.3.

Another area that the teacher has addressed in the task analysis for cleaning the toilet is chaining of activities or work tasks. For instance, the last three steps of the task are the first three steps of cleaning the next toilet. In this manner, the teacher can write all of a student's task analyses to interconnect in order to sequence the work activities. This sequencing will help the student learn to move from one task to another and ultimately be independent on the job site.

Efficiency should also be considered when writing a task analysis. For instance, students with severe disabilities may avoid reaching across the midline of their body, using two hands together, or using one hand consistently. The teacher should observe the student and determine the most efficient way to complete the task based on

---

Task Analysis: Clean the Toilet

1. Put toilet brush in bucket.
2. Pick up cleanser.
3. Push bucket to first toilet.
4. Squirt cleanser in toilet.
5. Set down cleanser.
6. Pick up brush.
7. Tap brush two times on side of bucket.
8. Brush top of toilet.
9. Brush sides of toilet.
10. Brush front of toilet.
11. Dip brush in bucket.
12. Tap brush two times on side of bucket.
13. Brush seat of toilet.
14. Raise seat of toilet.
15. Brush inside seat of toilet.
16. Dip brush in bucket.
17. Tap brush two times on side of bucket.
18. Dip brush inside toilet.
19. Brush inside of toilet four times.
20. Tap brush two times on seat.
21. Put toilet brush in bucket.
22. Pick up the cleanser.
23. Push bucket to next toilet.

Figure 16.2.   Sample task analysis: Clean the Toilet.

---

8. Brush top of toilet. (Student wipes top one time, always working left to right.)

> Place brush at back corner.
> Move brush across top of toilet.
> Place brush at front corner.
> Move brush across top.

Figure 16.3.   Sample step analysis. The information placed in parentheses serves as a cue to the trainer for consistency of prompting but is not used as a verbal cue to the student.

his or her physical abilities. For instance, if no physical limitations prohibit the student's using both hands to complete a task, the task analysis should require the student to do so (e.g., picking up an armful of laundry with both arms vs. using one hand only). Systematic instruction then can be implemented to teach the student the physical requirements of the activity.

The use of *natural cues or material prompts* can also be built into the task analysis to facilitate skill acquisition. For instance, the student can be taught to use work supplies as a cue for task completion or assistance in moving from one step or work duty to another. An example might be putting the "pink" cleanser in all toilets that need to be cleaned as the first step in the task analysis. The presence of cleanser in the toilet provides a cue that a bathroom stall has not been cleaned.

Completing a job to *production standards/speed* often will be an issue when teaching students with severe disabilities. Initial consideration when designing a task analysis can assist in eliminating this problem. For instance, students may continue to perform a step in a task even though it is not necessary (e.g., cleaning the inside of a toilet, scrubbing a pot, etc.). Observation of the student may reveal that he or she is perseverating on steps in the task. In the sample task analysis of cleaning the toilet, for instance, the teacher could write the task analysis to provide structure to the steps that are being repeated (e.g., "Tap the brush two times on side of bucket"). Even though most students with severe disabilities will not understand the concept of a number of movements, repetition through systematic instruction can result in skill performance.

Step 4: Schedule Community-Based Instruction

Creative use of school personnel to schedule and transport students for community-based instruction will clearly be the greatest challenge for administrators and teachers of students with severe disabilities. A number of model demonstration programs across the country have identified solutions for scheduling and transportation issues (Baumgart & Van Walleghem, 1986; Hutchins & Talarico, 1985; Nietupski, Hamre-Nietupski, Welch, & Anderson, 1983; Wehman, Moon, Everson, Wood, & Barcus, 1988). Staffing solutions have included team teaching; use of volunteers, paraprofessionals, peer tutors, graduate students, and student teachers; heterogeneous grouping of students; staggered student training schedules; and utilization of support personnel providing integrated therapy services. Transportation issues have been resolved by the use of volunteers' or parents' cars with mileage reimbursement, coordination of training schedules with regular school bus schedules, use of public transportation, use of school district vehicles, and walking to sites within short distances. Each school system must select procedures that are effective for their specific needs. A rule of thumb to follow for scheduling purposes is no more than four students per training site per instructor; however, fewer would be more effective for skill development (Wehman et al., 1988).

Scheduling should also focus on providing a variety of experiences across the students' school year. Each transition team should decide what experiences are appropriate to a student's long-term objectives and make recommendations concerning training in the community. Keep in mind that the labor law regulations require that a student's program for nonpaid work experiences should not exceed the following in a given school year:

- Vocational exploration—*5* hours per job experienced

- Vocational assessment—*90* hours per job experienced

- Vocational training—*120* hours per job experienced

Tables 16.2 and 16.3 show how the training schedule and job duties can be established for one group of students with severe disabilities who participate in community-based instruction.

Table 16.2. Vocational Job Duties for Community-Based Instruction

Training Site	Job Duties
Hechingers (Hardware Store)	1. Stock the shelves
	2. Front (organize) the shelves
	3. Straighten the bins
	4. Break down boxes
	5. Clean the bathrooms
	6. Straighten the battery section
Shoney's (Restaurant)	1. Empty the buspan
	2. Wash the dishes
	3. Unload the dishwasher
	4. Bus the tables
	5. Roll the silverware
	6. Wipe tables
Howard Johnson's (Hotel)	1. Clean the vending machine area (wiping vending machines, sweeping and mopping the floor)
	2. Clean the restroom (sinks, toilets, sweeping and mopping the floor)
	3. Vacuum the lobby
	4. Fold linen
	5. Wash windows

Step 5: Design Systematic Instructional Procedures

Once the sites have been identified and a schedule for student placement determined, the teacher must design instructional programs outlining how each student will be taught job skills and other related vocational activities. Included in the design should be (a) specific training objectives, (b) individualized task analyses, (c) data collection guidelines, (d) instructional strategies, (e) reinforcement procedures, and (f) program modifications. The following sections outline each of these components in detail.

Write Vocational Training Objectives

Training objectives are written to include the observable behaviors that will be taught, the conditions under which they will occur, and the criteria that will be used to evaluate the student's performance (Snell & Grigg, 1986; Wehman et al., 1988). Each skill that is being taught on a job site should have a program objective included in the student's Individualized Education Program (IEP) or Individualized Transition Plan (ITP). Figure 16.4 is an example of one student's objective for folding a bath towel.

Individualized Task Analyses

Although the teacher developed task analyses when he or she negotiated with the employer to set up the training site, each student will need them custom designed for his or her training needs. This customizing will occur during the first several days that the teacher and student(s) are on a job site. For instance, the teacher may determine that a task needs to be broken down into more detailed steps or designed to eliminate a particular discrimination that the student cannot make. The process of altering or modifying a task analysis can be facilitated by the use of data collection. Data can point to a step(s) in the task that the student is not learning and indicate that a change needs to be made in this area.

Collect Baseline and Probe Data

Data collection is an important part of any instructional program because it is necessary for monitoring a student's skill acquisition. However, it is a critical portion of community-based instruction, because the teacher/trainer must be able to demonstrate that a student's vocational placement is for training purposes in order to meet the U.S. Department of Labor regulations for nonpaid work experiences. In other words, data can indicate when the student is able to perform a work task to the standards/requirements

Table 16.3.   Student Training Schedule

Student	Location	Time	Instructor
OCTOBER 22–DECEMBER 7			
R. M.	Shoney's	7:30–9:15 A.M.	Curtis
J. G.	Shoney's	9:45–11:45 A.M.	Curtis
L. R.	Shoney's	12:45–2:45 P.M.	Curtis
M. L.	Hechingers	7:30–9:15 A.M.	Chris
G. A.	Hechingers	9:45–11:45 A.M.	Chris
H. R.	Hechingers	12:45–2:45 P.M.	Chris
C. S.	Howard Johnson's	9:45–11:45 A.M.	Stacy
P. P.	Howard Johnson's	12:45–2:45 P.M.	Stacy
DECEMBER 10–JANUARY 18			
P. P.	Shoney's	7:30–9:15 A.M.	Stacy
J. A.	Howard Johnson's	9:45–11:45 A.M.	Stacy
H. R.	Howard Johnson's	7:30–9:15 A.M.	Curtis
M. L.	Howard Johnson's	12:45–2:45 P.M.	Curtis
L. R.	Hechingers	7:30–9:15 A.M.	Chris
R. M.	Hechingers	9:45–11:45 A.M.	Curtis
J. G.	Hechingers	12:45–2:45 P.M.	Chris
C. S.	Shoney's	9:45–11:45 A.M.	Chris
JANUARY 8–MARCH 8			
J. A.	Shoney's	7:30–9:15 A.M.	Stacy
M. L.	Shoney's	9:45–11:45 A.M.	Chris
H. R.	Shoney's	12:45–2:45 P.M.	Chris
J. G.	Howard Johnson's	7:30–9:15 A.M.	Curtis
L. R.	Howard Johnson's	9:45–11:45 A.M.	Curtis
R. M.	Howard Johnson's	12:45–2:45 P.M.	Curtis
P. P.	Hechingers	9:45–11:45 A.M.	Stacy
C. S.	Hechingers	7:30–9:15 A.M.	Chris

of the work site. At this point in training, the student must receive payment for work completed or he or she needs to be moved to another site for additional work experiences (Inge, Simon, Halloran, & Moon, 1993).

Once training begins, data collection is referred to as a *probe* and should be collected at least one time a week prior to the beginning of a training session. The critical component of both baseline and probe assessments is that the student is allowed to perform the task *independently without feedback, reinforcement, or prompting* (Moon & Inge, 1993; Moon, Inge, et al., 1990). Typically, a skill is

considered learned when the student performs the task correctly for three or four consecutive probe trials without any assistance from the trainer (Wehman et al., 1988).

Select an Instructional Strategy

Least Prompts. The majority of the literature on teaching vocational tasks to individuals with severe disabilities focuses on the use of least prompts as the teaching strategy of choice (Barcus et al., 1987; Cuvo, Leaf, & Borakove, 1978;

Component	Example
Condition under which behavior will occur	Given a laundry basket of bath towels and the cue, "Fold the towels,"
Observable behavior	Janet will fold the towels
Criteria for evaluation of student performance	with 100% accuracy according to the steps in the task analysis for three consecutive probe trials.

Figure 16.4. Sample behavioral objective.

Test, Grossi, & Keul, 1988). This strategy is also referred to as a *response-prompt hierarchy*, because the trainer progresses from the least amount of assistance (usually a verbal prompt) to the most intrusive (usually a physical prompt) until one prompt stimulates correct responding.

Use of a least-prompt strategy can be very effective for teaching skills on community job sites. Teachers are encouraged to consider various types of prompts to use in addition to the traditional verbal–model–physical sequence. For instance, as a student becomes more proficient on a site, the teacher might try using an indirect verbal prompt in the sequence such as, "What do you do next?" before using the verbal prompt specific to the step in the task analysis. This technique may be effective also for training students who have long been dependent on teachers for verbal instruction. In addition, gestures can be used instead of a full model prompt or partial physical assistance such as touching the student's arm.

Regardless of the types of prompts selected, the teacher should establish a latency period or time that he or she will wait for the student to respond before providing the next level of assistance. Usually a student should be given approximately 3 to 5 seconds to respond independently. Students with physical disabilities, however, may require longer latency periods based on their movement limitations, and this requirement

should be determined on an individual basis (Inge, 1992; Sowers & Powers, 1991). Finally, the teacher is cautioned to deliver each prompt only once before moving to the next, more intrusive prompt. The following is a list of steps for using a least-prompt strategy.

Guidelines for Using a Least-Prompt Hierarchy

1. Have the student move to the appropriate work area unless movement is part of the task analysis (TA).

2. Stand behind or beside the individual so that you can quickly provide prompts when necessary.

3. Provide the cue to begin the task (e.g., "Clean the mirror," "Sort the coathangers," etc.).

4. Wait 3 seconds for self-initiation for Step 1 of the TA.

5. If the student completes the step independently, provide reinforcement and proceed to Step 2 of the TA. Score + or – on the data sheet.

6. If the student is incorrect or does not respond within 3 seconds, provide a verbal prompt specific to Step 1 of the TA (e.g., "Pick up the Windex.")

7. If the student completes the step with a verbal prompt, provide reinforcement and move to Step 2. Record *V* (for *verbal*) on the data sheet.

8. If the student is incorrect or does not respond within 3 seconds, model the response (e.g., teacher picks up the Windex).

9. If the student completes the step with a model prompt, provide reinforcement and move to Step 2. Record *M* (for *model*) on the data sheet.

10. If the student is incorrect or does not respond within 3 seconds, physically guide him or her through the response (e.g., teacher guides the student's hand to pick up

the Windex). Record *P* (for *physical*) on the data sheet.

11. Begin instruction on Step 2 of the TA.

12. Repeat this procedure for each step in the TA until the task is completed. *Always interrupt an error* with the next prompt in the least-prompt system.

Time Delay. The use of time delay on vocational training sites is another option for teachers of students with severe disabilities (Inge, Moon, & Parent, 1993; Moon, Inge, et al., 1990). There are several critical components to a time-delay procedure (Gast, Ault, Wolery, Doyle, & Belanger, 1988; Snell & Gast, 1981). First, the teacher must select a prompt that will consistently assist the student to perform the task correctly. Initially, the prompt is given simultaneously with the request to perform the job duty. Gradually, increasing amounts of time (usually seconds) are waited between giving the request to perform the task and providing the prompt to complete the task correctly. The number of trials at each delay level and the length of the delay should be determined prior to initiation of the program. By the teacher's pairing the prompt with the request to perform a work task, the student is not allowed to make errors initially. The delay procedure allows the teacher to gradually fade assistance until the student performs without prompting. For example, a set number of trials are designated for 0-second delay, the next set at 2 seconds, the next at 4 seconds, and so forth, until the student performs without assistance.

Unlike the system of least prompts, time delay requires that the teacher select one prompt for use during the instructional program. Therefore, the procedure would be particularly useful if a student has consistently demonstrated a preference for one type of prompt. For example, if a student has shown that he or she always responds to a model prompt without making errors, the teacher can select it to place on delay (Moon, Inge, et al., 1990).

If an error occurs during time delay, the teacher should implement an error-correction procedure. Typically an error may occur as increasing amounts

of time are waited before the prompt is provided. Usually error correction consists of immediately interrupting the student's mistake and providing the prompt. If the student makes three or more errors in a row, the teacher may consider reverting to a number of trials at 0 seconds before again delaying the prompt. Monitoring of the training data is essential to ensure that the student is not constantly making errors during the procedure. If this is the case, the teacher should consider selecting another prompt in order to provide an errorless learning experience.

Identify Reinforcers and Determine Schedule of Delivery

Selection of reinforcers as well as the systematic delivery of reinforcement is critical for student success on community-based vocational sites. The most effective reinforcers are those that arise as a natural consequence to a given task or situation within the work environment (Wilcox & Bellamy, 1982). Therefore, the teacher should begin by attempting to identify items that are available in a specific community-based setting. For example, there may be a vending machine located within the employee break room which can be used to reinforce the student at the end of a training period or an employee cafeteria where he or she can get a snack. However, it should be remembered that not all individuals will be reinforced by the same items and that even the most preferred reinforcer used too frequently will lose its effectiveness (Falvey, 1989). Only after failing to identify a natural reinforcer should the teacher select more artificial items (Moon, Inge, et al., 1990). Teachers are also cautioned to select only age-appropriate materials for use on community sites. The following information may be helpful in identifying potential reinforcers for students (Barcus et al., 1987; Falvey, 1989; Moon, Inge, et al., 1990).

1. Survey individuals familiar with the student to determine likes and dislikes. Include

leisure activities, tangible items, types of verbal reinforcement, and so forth.

2. Observe the student in several natural environments during his or her free time and record what he or she does.

3. Offer the student a chance to interact with several novel items and record what he or she does. Repeat the experience over several days and determine if there is a pattern to item selection.

4. Select an item and use it as a reinforcer for a behavior the student already performs independently. Observe to see if that behavior increases.

Timing. After items have been identified for use on community-based sites, a schedule of reinforcement should be determined. Ideally, all reinforcement should be given quickly and immediately following the occurrence of the desired behavior. However, it usually is not feasible on a job site to provide tangible or edible reinforcement immediately after a behavior occurs (Moon, Inge, et al., 1990). In addition, most students with severe disabilities will not understand the connection between work well done during the training session and the soda purchased at McDonald's before returning to school. In these instances, the teacher must develop a training program that utilizes exchangeable reinforcers on predetermined schedules. Exchangeable items include money, tokens, points on a card, checks on a calendar, and so forth.

Schedule of Delivery. Teachers can choose to reinforce students using two types of schedules: a predetermined number of responses/ratio schedule of reinforcement or a predetermined period of time/interval schedule (Moon, Inge, et al., 1990). When delivering reinforcement on a ratio schedule, the teacher may use a fixed-ratio or variable-ratio schedule. In a fixed schedule, reinforcement is provided after a set number of responses (e.g., after every 3 steps in the task analysis, after every 5 towels folded). It may be preferable to design programs with a variable ratio schedule that requires

delivery after an average number of responses. With this strategy, the student is reinforced on the average of a number of responses (e.g., on the average of every 3 steps in the task analysis, on the average of every 3 towels folded). In this manner, the student is not able to anticipate when reinforcement will be delivered, a condition that may approximate that in the natural environment.

Use of an interval schedule is similar to a ratio schedule in that it too can be delivered on a fixed or variable basis. In this instance, the teacher designs the program to provide reinforcement based on time intervals. Using the fixed interval schedule, the teacher may select to reinforce a student after every 5 minutes, at the end of the training session, at the end of the work week, and so forth. A variable schedule would occur on the average of a set period of time, such as on the average of every 10 minutes.

Regardless of the type of schedule the teacher selects, he or she must design a plan for fading the reinforcement to naturally occurring items on the job site. For instance, the teacher should always pair verbal praise with the delivery of a tangible item, fading the reinforcement to supervisor or coworker approval over the course of the program.

Program Modifications

Community-based instruction provides an excellent opportunity for teachers to determine the most effective training strategies to use with specific students in real work sites. By monitoring a student's progress through data collection, the teacher often can pinpoint what changes need to be made in an instructional program to assist a student in skill acquisition. Occasionally, it is difficult to determine exactly what needs to occur to facilitate success. In these instances, we suggest that several teachers or the student's transition team brainstorm solutions to problems encountered. Figure 16.5 represents a list of brainstorming questions that can assist in program modifications.

Finally, the information generated during community-based vocational training should be

1. Analyze the effectiveness of the training strategy.

   • Does the prompting procedure (i.e., least prompts, time delay) match the learning style of the student?
   • Is the student responding to the type of prompt(s) selected?
   • Is the student distracted by noise or people in the environment? Is he or she attending to task?
   • Can you reduce the number of skills being taught in order to provide repeated practice on a specific job duty?

2. Has the task analysis been individualized to match the student's abilities?

   • Has the task been broken down into small enough steps?
   • Have the physical limitations of the student been taken into consideration?
   • Does the task analysis eliminate the need to make quality judgments?
   • Can several steps of the task be taught rather than the whole task analysis?
   • Would the student benefit from a backward-chaining procedure?
   • Do the steps in the task analysis include any external cues or extra prompts that have been added to the task (i.e., turning the pages in a picture book)?

3. Have all the components of delivering reinforcement been considered?

   • Is the reinforcer individualized to the student's needs?
   • Has the student satiated to the selected reinforcer?
   • Is the timing of the reinforcer correct?
   • Is the schedule of reinforcement appropriate?
   • Have the naturally occurring reinforcers become meaningful to the student?

4. Can the task be modified for the specific problem area(s)?

   • Are there simple equipment adaptations that can be added to assist the student?
   • Can extra cues (e.g., visual or tactile) be added to the task?
   • Can coworkers provide assistance during a difficult portion of the task?
   • Can the location of task completion be modified to decrease distractions?

Figure 16.5.   Brainstorming solutions to training problems.

shared with future teachers and adult service agencies to facilitate the transition process from school to work. The following case study is a description of *how* this type of training can be directly used to help a student with severe disabilities.

CASE STUDY IN COMMUNITY-BASED INSTRUCTION

Bobby was 21 years old with an IQ of 36 as measured by the *Stanford–Binet Intelligence Scale* (Thorndike, Hagen, & Sattler, 1986). This score placed him in the range of severe mental retardation. His teacher described him as rarely interacting with others appropriately and as physically aggressive with self-stimulatory behaviors. Mellaril was prescribed for these behaviors. It was also noted that Bobby had a great difficulty with any change in his routine and required daily consistency to be successful. His strengths were his good fine and gross motor skills and his ability to speak in clear sentences. Bobby's vocational program had included working on cleaning tasks and collating, stapling, and folding paper within the school building. He had also been included in a janitorial crew that received training at a residential facility for youth with emotional disturbances. At the time of the program, Bobby lived at home with his mother who had chronic mental illness and who received services from the local mental health program.

Phase 1: Initial Training Placement

Initially, Bobby was placed at a hotel, folding laundry and cleaning a small vending machine area from 12:45 to 2:45 P.M. on Mondays, Tuesdays, Wednesdays, and Thursdays for his community-based training. A structured instructional program based on a time-delay strategy with a physical prompt (Moon, Inge, et al., 1990) and reinforcement schedule were developed for him; however, within 5 days of placement, the teacher/trainer reported uncontrollable behaviors. These included running from the instructor and laughing, clinging to her arm, and running to the pool area of the motel.

A behavior management program was implemented in an attempt to keep Bobby at the training site. This included a strategy of differential reinforcement of other behaviors with checks that earned edible reinforcement. The data showed that Bobby was on task only for 5% of his training session by the fifth day of his community experience. His behaviors included:

- swinging his body against the motel stair railings,

- running down the guest corridors,

- screaming,

- climbing on cars in the parking lot, and

- physically resisting instruction.

The staff met, discussed the problem, and determined that the behaviors had escalated to a level that could result in physical harm to the trainer or to Bobby. The team decided that he must be removed from the training site. A brainstorming session generated the following possibilities for consideration in designing a new program and training experience for Bobby.

The first step was to initiate instruction for Bobby within the school complex. The decision to return to school was based on two factors. First, it was necessary to *immediately* break the negative training cycle that was occurring between Bobby and the instructor at the job site. Second, with Bobby's return to school, the trainer could work with Bobby in a familiar environment and provide one-on-one training while designing a new instructional program for returning to the community. This plan was seen as the better alternative to discontinuing training until a new program could be developed. *Returning to the school environment was not seen as a necessary step to get Bobby "ready" for the community.*

The community-based instructor identified several training activities for Bobby to complete at school: wiping down the vend-

ing machines, washing windows, cleaning tables, and sweeping the sidewalks. Time of day was changed to the first activity of Bobby's morning, and training time was decreased to 30 minutes. The primary objective was to provide time in a *familiar environment* for Bobby to adjust to the trainer/teacher. During the school-based training period, the instructor also changed her systematic instruction procedure from physical assistance on time delay to a system of least prompts. The team believed that Bobby did not respond well to the more intrusive physical assistance. Bobby's on-task behavior increased across an 8-day period to 90% on the 13th day of his first training experience.

At this point, the team decided that the new instructional procedures appeared effective and that Bobby should begin to resume his training in the community. A brainstorming session resulted in the decision to combine in-school instruction with the community component. Bobby would receive 2 hours of training, daily, beginning as soon as he arrived at school. Initially, he would start work in this familiar environment, because he seemed to have the greatest amount of difficulty initiating activities with the trainer. Near the end of the 2 hours, Bobby and the trainer would leave school and finish the session at Howard Johnson's.

Initially, the plan called for Bobby to stay at the hotel and work for only 5 minutes. As he was successful (with no occurrence of the behaviors), this time period would be increased by 3 to 4 minutes. The team projected that a gradual increase in time spent in the community would result in Bobby's success with his vocational program. Bobby's on task behaviors began to decrease as the training moved from school to include community programming. On day 14 of his program, Bobby was on task for approximately 75% of the 5-minute training session. Day 15 showed a decline to 50% on-task behavior during a 12-minute training session. By day 18, the trainer was unable to get Bobby in her car to go to the community training site.

This refusal to work coincided with the end of Bobby's first training experience, because the employer had agreed to provide a vocational training site for an 8-week period. At this time, the team decided that a new strategy was needed in order for Bobby to be successful in community-based training. Several issues were discussed during a planning session for Bobby:

- Bobby now associates the community-based trainer with work (something he does not like to do). The trainer and Bobby need to develop a positive relationship with no demands for work performance placed on Bobby.
- Although changes were made in his instructional program, the tasks remained the same at the hotel training site. A new site needs to be developed with different job types/responsibilities.
- Intensive one-on-one instruction needs to be reduced from the current 2-hour block of time. Reduce interaction with community-based instructor to ½ or 1 hour maximum.
- Initiate a training period that focuses on identifying and developing community reinforcers for Bobby. Currently, he does not appear to enjoy community access or activities.

After this discussion, the team decided to discontinue vocational training for a 6-week period and to substitute community instruction in nondemanding, "fun" activities. This time period would allow the trainer to identify community activities that could be used as reinforcers during later vocational training.

Phase 2: Community-Based Training

During this phase of instruction, the primary objective was to provide successful experiences within the community while placing limited demands on Bobby. In other words, the main requirement was for him to stay within close physical proximity to the trainer without clinging to her body, throwing his body, or running from her. Tasks focused on low-demand activities that could provide an element of fun in order to build a rapport between the trainer and Bobby. Initially, he was only required to remain with the instructor for brief periods of time (i.e., 5 to 10 minutes) in

the grocery store. As Bobby became successful in staying with the trainer, the number and type of community training sites as well as the number of demands to participate in the activity were expanded. Gradually, over the course of 6 weeks, he began to participate in shopping, going to fast-food restaurants, and using the post office. Whenever Bobby began to get excited or to laugh inappropriately, the trainer was able to calm him by looking at him and speaking a few words (i.e., "Settle down Bobby" or "Do you want to stay here?"). At the end of the 6-week period, it was determined that Bobby was able to remain with the trainer in a community setting for up to 30 to 45 minutes and to participate in activities without engaging in challenging behaviors. Some of the activities that were focused on during this community training are shown in Figure 16.6.

Morning Schedule: 7:30 A.M.

Tasks:

- Waiting in grocery line
- Putting items on checkout counter
- Paying for items
- Waiting for change
- Browsing in stores
- Sitting quietly in a fast-food restaurant
- Eating a snack
- Using a self-serve soda machine
- Posting a letter
- Crossing the street

Figure 16.6. Community training activities for Bobby.

Throughout this phase of community-based instruction, the trainer kept a diary of anecdotal notes on Bobby's behavior. The following is an excerpt from this diary:

12/21 - Ukrops Cafe - 30 minutes: Another super day for Bobby! I asked him what he wanted to get for breakfast before we left his house, and he said "sausage biscuit." It was raining today so it was hard to spend much time looking for cars before we crossed the road. Bobby waited in line for

4 minutes before placing his order. With a cue "what do you want?" from me (not the store person) Bobby was able to say sausage biscuit. When we got to the drink section, Bobby said he wanted a soda. (O.J. and milk were in front of him along with cups for soda/coffee. Soda/coffee were on the other side of the wall out of view. Bobby was able to request something he couldn't see!) He needed assistance using the self-serve drink bar. I physically assisted him to press his cup against the ice dispenser and Coke. (He wanted to use his finger to push the lever.) It took Bobby about 20 minutes to eat breakfast. Most of the time was spent drinking the soda and chewing all of the ice in the container. Half-way through eating (he was done with the biscuit and just working on his drink), he started to laugh loudly. I asked him if he was ready to go, and he quieted down immediately and remained quiet for the rest of the time we were there. When we got back to school, Bobby did something he's never done before. We've been working on locking my car door. He usually remembers to push the button down, but always forgets to hold the handle up when we close the door. I started to redirect him back to fix the door when I noticed that he'd done it correctly before I had gotten around to his side of the door! How Exciting!! I used gestures and some physical assistance to teach that skill.

Phase 3: Community-Based Vocational Training at Hechingers

Setting, Time, and Training Tasks

A training placement at a large hardware store, Hechingers, was identified as the next vocational training placement for Bobby. This site was selected because the manager was extremely supportive and had already supported several students at his work site. In addition, the manager was receptive to having Bobby at Hechinger's with the understanding that he had numerous challenging behaviors and would be receiving training primarily on increasing his ability to remain in a community environment. The employer agreed to have Bobby work, beginning at 9:45 A.M. on Mondays, Tuesdays, Thursdays, and Fridays. The employee who was normally responsible for maintaining the bathrooms continued to perform this function in order to

meet the Department of Labor's regulations for a nonpaid work experience.

Training tasks included cleaning the men's and women's bathrooms: wiping the sinks, counters, mirrors, urinals, toilets; and mopping the floors. The bathrooms were targeted because the instructor believed that she would have better control over Bobby's behaviors in a small, enclosed work environment. For instance, by positioning herself between Bobby and the door to the bathroom, she was able to prevent him from running out of the room. This setting was in contrast to that of his previous community experience at Howard Johnson's, where he could easily move about in large work areas and "escape" the environment.

•••

Discussion

Critical to a review of this case study is a discussion of the continual brainstorming sessions and subsequent program revisions that led to Bobby's eventual success in community-based instruction. The instructor persisted in identifying reinforcers, changing instructional procedures, modifying expectations, and changing training sites until Bobby was able to respond to training for a 2-hour block of time on a community job site. Several key factors led to Bobby's success. First, the trainer was able to identify a *community* reinforcer, the soda break at McDonalds. Bobby learned to associate work with earning money that he could use to have access to a preferred activity.

The other critical element of this program was the gradual increase in expectations that occurred during Bobby's time at multiple work sites. All too often, trainers/teachers set objectives that students are unable to meet, a situation that subsequently results in failure and denied access to reinforcement. In this case study, Bobby was always successful in meeting his goal, and he learned to rely on the timer as a prompt to help him meet his goal for reinforcement. It should be mentioned, however, that criterion or goal levels would have been decreased if he had encountered problems. For instance, if Bobby had been unable to meet a specified goal for 2 consecutive days, the time would have been lowered in order for him to experience success.

When training in the community, teachers should not become discouraged if their students do not respond as successfully as in this example. Again, constant monitoring of the program data will provide information regarding how the student is performing in different community sites. It is hoped that Bobby's case study example can provide guidelines and ideas for other students who previously have been denied access to community-based instruction.

FINAL THOUGHTS

Within the past decade, researchers and practitioners alike have determined the effectiveness of community-based training. This chapter has provided the details and guidelines for how to go about the program implementation in a local agency or school. We have used schedules, real job sites, and a real person as examples of how successful this approach is, yet how much time and planning is involved. Students will enter adulthood with more competency if they learn skills in the community.

REFERENCES

Barcus, M., Brooke, V., Inge, K., Moon, S., & Goodall, P. (1987). *An instructional guide for training on a job site: A supported employment resource*. Richmond: Virginia Commonwealth University, Rehabilitation Research and Training Center.

Baumgart, D., & Van Walleghem, J. (1986). Staffing strategies for implementing community-based instruction. *Journal of the Association for Persons with Severe Handicaps, 11*(2), 92–102.

Cuvo, A. J., Leaf, R. B., & Borakove, L. S. (1978). Teaching janitorial skills to the mentally retarded: Acquisition, generalization and maintenance. *Journal of Applied Behavior Analysis, 11*, 345–355.

Falvey, M. A. (1989). *Community-based curriculum: Instructional strategies for students with severe handicaps* (2nd ed.). Baltimore: Brookes.

Gast, D. L., Ault, M. F., Wolery, M., Doyle, P. M., & Belanger, J. (1988). Comparison of constant time delay and the system of least prompts in teaching sight word reading to students with moderate retardation. *Education and Training in Mental Retardation, 23*, 117–128.

Hutchins, M., & Talarico, D. (1985). Administrative considerations in providing community integrated training programs. In P. McCarthy, J. Everson, S. Moon, & M. Barcus (Eds.), *School to work transition for youths with severe disabilities* (Monograph, pp. 111–121). Richmond: Virginia Commonwealth University, Project Transition Into Employment.

Inge, K. J. (1992). Cerebral palsy. In P. McLaughlin & P. Wehman (Eds.), *Developmental disabilities: A handbook for best practices* (pp. 30–53). Fort Washington, PA: Andover Medical Publishers.

Inge, K. J., Dymond, S., Wehman, P., Sutphin, C., Johnston, C., & Fiana, M. (1993). Community-based vocational preparation for students with severe disabilities: Designing the process. In K. J. Inge & P. Wehman (Eds.), *Designing community-based vocational programs for students with severe disabilities* (pp. 1–50). Richmond: Virginia Commonwealth University.

Inge, K. J., Moon, M. S., & Parent, W. (1993). Applied behavior analysis in supported employment settings. *Journal of Vocational Rehabilitation, 3*(3), 53–60.

Inge, K. J., Simon, M., Halloran, W., & Moon, M. S. (1993). Community-based vocational instruction and the labor laws: A 1993 update. In K. Inge & P. Wehman (Eds.), *Designing community-based vocational programs for students with severe disabilities* (pp. 51–80). Richmond: Virginia Commonwealth University, Rehabilitation Research and Training Center on Supported Employment.

Inge, K., & Wehman, P. (Eds.). (1993). *Designing community-based instructional programs for students with severe disabilities*. Richmond: Rehabilitation Research and Training Center on Supported Employment.

Moon, M. S., & Inge, K. J. (1993). Vocational training, transition planning, and employment for students with severe disabilities. In M. Snell (Ed.), *Systematic instruction of persons with severe disabilities* (4th ed., pp. 556–587). Columbus, OH: Merrill.

Moon, M. S., Inge, K. J., Wehman, P., Brooke, V., & Barcus, J. M. (1990). *Helping persons with severe mental retardation get and keep employment: Supported employment issues and strategies*. Baltimore: Brookes.

Moon, M. S., Kiernan, W., & Halloran, W. (1990). School-based vocational programs and labor laws: A 1990 update. *Journal of the Association for Persons with Severe Handicaps, 15*(3), 177–185.

Nietupski, J. A., Hamre-Nietupski, S., Welch, J., & Anderson, R. J. (1983). Establishing and maintaining vocational training sites for moderately and severely handicapped students: Strategies for community/vocational trainers. *Education and Training of the Mentally Retarded, 18*(3), 169–175.

Pumpian, I., Shepard, H., & West, E. (1988). Negotiating job-training stations with employers. In P. Wehman & M. S. Moon (Eds.), *Vocational rehabilitation and supported employment* (pp. 177–192). Baltimore: Brookes.

Renzaglia, A., & Hutchins, M. (1988). A community-referenced approach to preparing persons with disabilities for employment. In P. Wehman & M. S. Moon (Eds.), *Vocational rehabilitation and supported employment* (pp. 91–112). Baltimore: Brookes.

Snell, M., & Gast, D. L. (1981). Applying delay procedures to the instruction of the severely handicapped. *Journal of the Association of the Severely Handicapped, 5*(4), 3–14.

Snell, M., & Grigg, N. C. (1986). Instructional assessment and curriculum development. In M. E. Snell (Ed.), *Systematic instruction of persons with severe handicaps* (pp. 64–109). Columbus, OH: Merrill.

Sowers, J., & Powers, L. (1991). *Vocational preparation and employment of students with physical and multiple disabilities.* Baltimore: Brookes.

Test, D. W., Grossi, T., & Keul, P. (1988). A functional analysis of the acquisition and maintenance of janitorial skills in a competitive work setting. *Journal of the Association for Persons with Severe Handicaps, 13*(1), 1–7.

Thorndike, R. L., Hagen, E. P., & Sattler, J. M. (1986). *Stanford–Binet Intelligence Scale: Fourth Edition.* Chicago: Riverside.

Wehman, P. (1992). *Life beyond the classroom: Transition strategies for young adults with disabilities.* Baltimore: Brookes.

Wehman, P., Moon, M. S., Everson, J. M., Wood, M., & Barcus, M. (1988). *Transition from school to work: New challenges for youth with severe disabilities.* Baltimore: Brookes.

Wehman, P., & Revell, W. G. (in press). Transitioning best practices. In R. Turnbull (Ed.), *National Organization on Disability Report to Congress on IDEA.* Washington, DC: National Organization on Disability.

Wilcox, B., & Bellamy, G. T. (1982). *Design of high school programs for severely handicapped students.* Baltimore: Brookes.

CHAPTER 17

Supported Employment

Paul Wehman and Wendy Parent

LEARNING GOALS:

Upon completion of this chapter the reader will be able to

- define supported employment and explain how it is used to help individuals with severe disabilities;

- discuss what the role of a job coach is in designing community and workplace supports;

- describe the importance of integration for workers with disabilities into the workplace; and

- provide an overview of national implementation of supported employment.

Within the past decade there has developed a major interest in many states for supported employment as a vocational outcome for adults with developmental disabilities who have never worked before or have been considered to be employed (Kregel & Wehman, 1989; Wehman & Kregel, 1995; Wehman, Sale, & Parent, 1992). A vast majority of these individuals who have been labeled developmentally disabled spent their time at home, in segregated workshops, or in day activity centers (Buckley & Bellamy, 1985; Hayden & Abery, 1994).

Several supported employment models ranging from individual placement models, enclaves, and mobile work crews to entrepreneurial models have been developed to provide a wider range of vocational options for persons with severe disabilities. Individuals with developmental disabilities have been major beneficiaries of supported employment as they have historically not been employed in competitive settings.

Less than one third of working age Americans with disabilities are employed, according to the *National Organization on Disability (NOD)/Harris Survey of Americans with Disabilities.* Conducted by Louis Harris and Associates in early 1994, it is called "the most comprehensive survey of adults with disabilities concerning work and employment issues" by NOD. Furthermore, the U.S. Bureau of the Census (1992) reported an increase of 6 million Americans with disabilities, now numbering 49 million. The Bureau reports that of that number, about half, or 24 million, have severe disabilities. Persons who are completely unable to perform everyday tasks are considered severely disabled by the Bureau.

Of interest to supported employment advocates and professionals are two main findings:

- Only 23% of working-age persons with severe disabilities were employed, whereas the NOD survey, which sampled all working-age people with disabilities, reported that 31% were employed.
- Only half of working-age persons with severe disabilities had health insurance, compared with

80% for persons without disabilities, according to the U.S. Bureau of the Census (1992) report.

These are dramatic data in that they show the crushing challenge faced by people with disabilities and, despite the best efforts of many, a very long road ahead to careers and employment for people with disabilities.

With these data in mind, we present this chapter, which focuses on three areas. First, we define the characteristics of various supported employment models that are presented. Second, we describe a way that natural community and business supports can be used to enhance supported employment outcomes. Finally, we summarize the success level of people with different disabilities who are participating in supported employment with the use of nationally collected data as well as case studies.

WHAT IS SUPPORTED EMPLOYMENT?

According to the *Federal Register* (1992), supported employment is "Paid work in a variety of settings, particularly regular work sites, especially designed for handicapped individuals: (i) for whom competitive employment has not traditionally occurred; and (ii) who, because of their disability, need intensive ongoing support to perform in a work setting" (p. 36). Within this definition, several key components of supported employment exist. We further define these components in order to clarify the concept of supported employment.

Paid Employment

In order for a job to be considered supported employment, compliance with wage and hour regulations must be met. Some individuals are paid at minimum wage or above, although provisions can be made to pay on a commensurate wage according to the individual's productivity level.

Integration

Integration is an essential feature to better ensure that workers will have the same opportunities as others for physical and social contact with nondisabled coworkers and the general public. Two important factors for the practitioner to consider are the capacity of the setting and the level realized by nondisabled workers.

Ongoing Support

A key characteristic that distinguishes supported employment from other vocational services is the ongoing support offered. This support can include but is not limited to direct training, indirect intervention at the work site, and advocacy issues away from the work site. The amount of ongoing support is individually based according to the worker; however, by federal guidelines, an employment specialist must physically visit the work site at least two times per month.

Workers with Severe Disabilities

Supported employment is specifically designed to serve those individuals who because of the severity of their disability cannot obtain or maintain employment without ongoing support; persons who are able to sustain employment independently would not be candidates for supported employment. According to Bellamy, Rhodes, Mank, and Joyce (1988), the term *severe disabilities* is used to describe individuals who need intensive, ongoing support in order to live and work in community settings. These are individuals who are typically not served by vocational rehabilitation and other job-training programs.

Supported employment is a program that reflects a variety of models such as enclaves, mobile work crews, individual placements, and entrepreneurial models. Supported employment is characterized by the inclusion of individuals with the most severe disabilities in a place and training model where both integration and wages are highly valued (Kiernan & Stark, 1986; Rusch, 1986; Wehman et al., 1992). Implementing supported employment programs requires coordinated efforts from several groups, each of which has different responsibilities and outlooks toward the success of the individual's employment opportunities. Employers provide the job opportunities; vocational rehabilitative agencies fund, regulate, and evaluate employment programs; employment specialists or job coaches provide the intensive training, job development, and ongoing support; significant others advocate for the services needed; and the individual with a disability has the power to choose the type of supported employment model and the type of work to perform (Bellamy et al., 1988).

The role of the employment specialist or job coach is very diverse and challenging. This person is responsible for providing initial community screening, client screening, job placement, intensive job site training, task analysis, data collection, assessment, orientation and training of coworkers, coordination of transportation, ongoing follow-along and advocacy, and so on (Bellamy et al., 1988; Rusch, 1986; Wehman, 1981). With such a diverse role, the employment specialist must have the flexibility to wear many hats at one time. He or she not only possesses the ability to present the supported employment program to the business community and train individuals with disabilities in a variety of work settings but also possesses the stamina to be effective in advocacy and follow-along services.

DESCRIPTION OF SUPPORTED EMPLOYMENT MODELS

Individual Placement Model

The individual placement model is an employment approach for individuals with moderate and severe disabilities that enables them to be placed and trained and provided support in integrated community competitive jobs with the assistance of an employment specialist or job coach. In this model, one individual with a disability is hired at minimum wage or above by a community business or industry. The employment specialist provides intensive job training, advocacy, and support from the first day of employment (Moon, Goodall, Barcus, & Brooke, 1986). As the employee gains the necessary skills to work independently and performance reaches the employer's standards, the employment specialist gradually reduces the time and intensity of training provided to the employee. At any time during employment, the employment specialist can provide additional training, advocacy, and support whenever necessary to maintain employment. Additional training usually occurs if there has been a change of job duties, added job duties, change of equipment used, or change of supervisor and coworkers. All of these factors can indirectly or directly affect the employee's work performance and, in turn, may require training or support from the employment specialist. A major factor to consider is the job match. When the employment specialist considers a job for an individual they must consider the individual's job preference, because if that individual does not like the type of work he or she will not put forth the necessary effort to succeed. In addition, the employment specialist must look at the individual's physical ability, social skills, behavioral problems, safety skills, shift hours, and transportation issues.

Benefits of the Individual Placement Model

- It allows the target employee maximum choice for job selection that meets his or her individual preference and abilities.

- It offers the greatest opportunity for integration among nondisabled workers and the general public because the workplace is centered in the community. In addition, the individual with the disability is not grouped with other individuals with disabilities, grouping that would reduce the likelihood of coworker involvement.

- It allows the individual to earn competitive wages (Kregel, Wehman, Revell, & Hill, 1990).

- It offers flexibility in jobs, limited only in what the community has to offer. Jobs may include computer work, warehouses, secretarial, landscaping, dishwashing, and so on.

Mobile Work Crews

In the mobile work crew model, the crew consists of a number of workers with severe disabilities (generally 4 to 8) and one supervisor, who is usually a human services worker with a supported employment agency. The crew typically travels from one business to another performing custodial work, grounds maintenance, housecleaning, janitorial duties, and other needed services in the community. Work contracts are drawn up between the different agencies, and the human services worker provides the training, supervision, and transporting from site to site and never fades from the job site. Potential for contact with the general public is an important consideration in work-site selection to ensure optimal integration opportunities. Integration usually takes place when the crew interacts with the general public during breaks and lunchtime. This model is flexible to the local job market and is able to meet the needs of urban, suburban, or rural areas (Bellamy et al., 1988; Bourbeau, 1985; Mank, Rhodes, & Bellamy, 1986).

Benefits of the Mobile Work Crew

- It has flexibility in program design. In rural areas, the program may be operated by a single crew serving 4 to 6 individuals. In more populous areas, the program may utilize multiple crews and include 24 to 28 individuals.

- It provides flexibility in work performed. Workers may stay on one specific crew or rotate among crews to experience a variety of working conditions.

- Wages earned by crew members are usually higher than those earned on a piece-rate basis, depending on the contract developed between the business and supported employment agency (Bourbeau, 1985).

Enclaves in Industry

The enclave is one of the most commonly accepted supported employment models. It is characterized by a group generally of 8 or fewer workers with severe disabilities who are trained and supervised by a human services worker within a local business. The individuals are employed in an integrated host business or industry and have access to employment opportunities provided to all employees of the host business or industry. Enclaves pay wages commensurate with the individuals' productivity and may be paid directly by the host business or industry or by the human services support organization (Rhodes & Valenta, 1985). The human services worker does not fade from the job site. The ability to provide continuous supervision and flexible and shared decision making between the host business or industry and the human services support organization is one of the advantages of the enclave model (Bellamy et al., 1988).

Benefits of the Enclave Model

- It provides real job opportunities structured within a company, so program employees experience the full range of employment outcomes, including reasonable income for work performed, integration among nondisabled coworkers, and good working conditions.

- It provides ongoing support that allows persons with severe disabilities to perform their work (Rhodes & Valenta, 1985).

THE ROLE OF THE JOB COACH: ORCHESTRATING COMMUNITY AND WORKPLACE SUPPORTS

As has been noted already, supported employment has contributed to improved employment outcomes for thousands of individuals with severe disabilities who were unable to work successfully within the traditional vocational rehabilitation model. Characterized by individualized support on and off the job site, initial and ongoing employment services, and assistance from a skilled job coach, supported employment has become widely recognized as the most effective approach for achieving meaningful employment for individuals with a variety of disability labels (Albin, 1992; Rusch, 1990; Wehman et al., 1992). Supported employment has provided the mechanism that has allowed many persons to enter the competitive labor force for the first time and to experience the outcomes of work that are well known to the general population. Individuals who are working with assistance from supported employment are reported to be earning increased wages (Revell, Wehman, Kregel, West, & Rayfield, 1994; Wehman, 1992), maintaining regular hours (Rehabilitation Services Administration, 1993), receiving company benefits (West, Kregel, & Banks, 1990), performing a wide variety of jobs (Rehabilitation Services Administration, 1993; State of New York, 1993), and experiencing some degree of integration at their job sites (Chadsey-Rusch, Gonzales, & Tines, 1988; Parent, Kregel, Metzler, & Twardzik, 1992; Parent & Wehman, 1994). Perhaps most important, individuals working in supported employment tend to be highly satisfied and report that they like their jobs, the services they have received, and the type and amount of assistance provided by their job coaches (Parent, 1994; Test, Hinson, Solow, & Keul, 1993).

The success of supported employment can be directly attributed to two important and unique features that distinguish this approach from other vocational options. One is the provision of individualized supports to assist persons with severe disabilities with becoming equal participants in the competitive labor force. This support is generally aimed at identifying individuals' skills and interests (consumer assessment), finding them a job (job development), making the necessary start-up arrangements (job placement), teaching them how to do the job (job-site training), and providing needed assistance for as long as the worker is

employed (ongoing follow-along services; Moon et al., 1986; Wehman & Kregel, 1985). Although these five components of the supported employment model remain the same, the level and intensity of support for each person is likely to vary, depending on the individual and his or her specific situation. The second feature is the role of a job coach or employment specialist, who functions as trainer, advocate, and facilitator in providing and coordinating these supports (Sale, Wood, Barcus, & Moon, 1988; Wehman & Melia, 1985). The responsibilities of the job coach are varied, with primary emphasis on ensuring the delivery of whatever work and work-related assistance individuals need in order to become employed and to maintain their jobs. This assistance includes addressing issues on and away from the job site, such as transportation, case management, Social Security, interpersonal relationships, skill training, grooming, lunch and breaks, supervision, and career advancement. The individualized nature of the model in the delivery of needed supports and the services of a professional job coach have been the major reasons why supported employment has been so widely accepted and promoted by consumers (Brooke, Barcus, & Inge, 1992; Parent, 1994), parents (Beckett & Fluke, 1988; Moore, 1988), employers (Kregel & Unger, 1993; Shafer, Hill, Seyfarth, & Wehman, 1987), and job coaches (Association for Persons in Supported Employment, 5001 West Broad Street, Suite 34, Richmond, VA 23230).

Despite the tremendous number of people who were unemployed and are now working with the help of supported employment, thousands more continue to be sitting at home, attending day activity programs, or working in sheltered workshops. Recent efforts have focused on developing additional support technologies aimed at enhancing service delivery practices in order to better meet the needs of all individuals interested in community-based employment. Identifying new and effective approaches for better supporting workers with severe disabilities and assisting greater numbers of persons who would like to enter the work force is a critical element in the continued growth and expansion of supported employment services (Kregel & Wehman, 1989). Innovations, such as assistive technology, rehabilitation engineering, compensatory strategies, natural supports, job modifications, "job carving," and personal assistant services, have opened the door to employment for many persons previously considered too severely disabled to work (Hagner & Dileo, 1993; Mank, 1994; Nisbet, 1992; Wehman et al., 1992). As a result, job coaches now have a much more extensive array of tools, in addition to behavioral training techniques, with which to support workers with severe disabilities in competitive jobs in the community.

Unfortunately, these advancements in technology have not always translated into practice at the direct service level, as evidenced by inconsistencies in supported employment implementation nationwide (Murphy, Rogan, & Fisher, 1994; Wehman & Kregel, 1995). The use of new innovations and support strategies is all too often based on the philosophy of the programs, the knowledge of the providers, or the skills of the job coaches rather than on the needs and preferences of consumers (Brooke et al., 1992). Decisions about specific supports are frequently dictated by an individual's disability label: rehabilitation engineering, assistive technology, or personal assistant services for persons with physical disabilities; compensatory strategies for persons with traumatic brain injury; job modifications or job carving for persons with mental retardation or mental illness; and natural supports for persons with mild to moderate disabilities. Actually, anyone participating in supported employment could potentially benefit from any support technology and should have access to whatever type of assistance he or she chooses to receive at the time that he or she would like to use it. This support can include natural and human services supports provided by the workplace, community, family, friends, or job coaches, depending on the choice of each individual participant. The bottom line in the delivery of supported employment services is the provision of any and all supports selected by the consumer in a manner of his or her own choosing to whatever degree of assistance he or she prefers.

As supported employment evolves to incorporate consumer-choice initiatives and a variety of new support technologies, the job coach's role becomes even more critical as greater responsibilities and expectations are demanded (Kregel, 1994). In addition to being adept in traditional supported employment service methodologies, job coaches must also have the knowledge and skills to develop business and community support resources, facilitate informed choices, assist with accessing preferred supports, provide a variety of individualized supports, coordinate and monitor all types of assistance, and respond to any changes over time. The major difference between the model of the 1990s and traditional supported employment is the way problems and issues are perceived and addressed by the job coach. Rather than responding to a support need by first providing the assistance themselves, job coaches should assess the situation with the consumer, share information about all possible support options, assist the individual with accessing the support of his or her choice, and provide ongoing assistance with whatever help is desired.

In the following sections a model of supported employment service delivery is described, one that enhances the role of the job coach by maximizing the use of employer, coworker, community, and family supports to enable an individual to obtain, learn, and maintain a job of his or her own choosing. First, strategies for identifying and developing support resources including specific examples from each of the five categories of support options is presented. Second, a systematic process for accessing community and workplace supports as well as specific strategies for utilizing support options is discussed. This general process is applicable for any support need that is identified during all phases of supported employment service delivery.

Developing Support Resources

The job coach's first step in utilizing an array of support options is finding out what type of assistance is potentially available in the community and in different employment settings. The job coach can accomplish this only by becoming familiar with the local community and the many support resources available to and used by individuals with and without disabilities. Similar to the community job-market analysis typically conducted by most supported employment programs, identifying community and workplace support options requires that personal contact be made with various agencies, organizations, associations, and businesses (Moon et al., 1986; Parent, Sherron, Stallard, & Booth, 1993).

Ideas of organizations or agencies to investigate can be identified from a variety of sources. Those found to be the most productive include personal connections through friends, acquaintances, or experiences; the telephone directory; the consumer and his or her friends; the newspaper; and other colleagues. Five general types of support categories have been identified: (1) employer supports, (2) transportation supports, (3) community supports, (4) personal and independent-living supports, and (5) recreation and social integration supports.

Choosing and Accessing Community and Workplace Supports

Taking full advantage of all the support resources available to assist an individual with achieving his or her employment goals does not typically happen for persons with severe disabilities (Hagner & Dileo, 1993). Just because a support is available at the workplace or in the community does not necessarily mean that the consumer will automatically access it or benefit from its use. It is not uncommon for an individual not to know that potential supports are available to him or her, how to choose among the alternatives, or how to go about accessing a desired support. A critical factor in the use of a variety of supports is the role of the job coach, who helps the consumer with identifying, choosing, and accessing needed supports at whatever level of assistance he or she prefers. A systematic process for utilizing community and

workplace supports in supported employment includes the following components: (1) determining individual needs and preferences, (2) brainstorming potential options, (3) assessing job and community supports, (4) identifying individual choices, (5) developing strategies for accessing supports, (6) evaluating support effectiveness, and (7) arranging provisions for ongoing monitoring. Table 17.1 highlights these steps to be followed for any support need that is identified during all phases of the supported employment model. Each of the steps in this process is briefly described in the following sections.

Determining Individual Needs and Preferences

It is important for the job coach to identify the types of assistance that a consumer needs or would like to receive in order to gain and maintain employment. These can be related to finding a job, learning how to do the job, maintaining work performance, developing social relationships, or other work- and non–work-related issues both on and off the job site. For example, an individual may be concerned over not having transportation to and from work, being shy and having difficulty making friends, not being able to perform the job as fast as coworkers doing the same task, or not knowing how to cash a paycheck and count money.

Table 17.1.   A Systematic Process for Utilizing Community and Workplace Supports

---

1. Determine individual needs and preferences.

2. Brainstorm potential options.

3. Assess job and community supports.

4. Identify individual choices.

5. Develop strategies for accessing supports.

6. Evaluate support effectiveness.

7. Arrange provisions for ongoing monitoring.

The best strategy for determining an individual's job and support preferences is to ask him or her directly. Meeting with the individual and, if possible, with his or her family, provides an excellent opportunity to introduce yourself, explain the types of services offered by your program, "break the ice" and get acquainted, begin identifying their interests, and arrange other times to meet again. For example, one individual indicated that he could not handle working full-time hours, another stated that she preferred a job with physical activity to help keep her weight down, another person said that he had trouble remembering things and would need assistance to prevent him from forgetting, and another reported that she had difficulty getting up in the morning and needed help preparing for work. Multiple visits, either by telephone or in person, are helpful in establishing rapport and a trusting working relationship so critical for successful employment. Ongoing communication is essential for determining if an individual's support needs or preferences have changed so that new or additional supports can be arranged.

Brainstorming Potential Options

For every support need that is identified, a variety of support resources that could be available for assistance should be selected. This is a good time to return to the "cookbook" of support options investigated during the community analysis and to consider any other ideas that come to mind. However, caution should be used to prevent being limited to considering only these supports and not pursuing other new ideas that may be more specifically related to the person or situation. Perhaps the individual's church, neighbors, or the community club to which a family member belongs may be available to assist in a multitude of ways.

Assessing Job and Community Supports

All of the ideas that are generated should be discussed with the consumer, and the discussion should include a clear and detailed explanation of just what utilizing a support of this nature would entail. The availability of the support option, the pros and cons of each, and the level of interest expressed by the individual can be explored at this time. Assessing these factors can provide some direction in which to go when pursuing supported employment activities. For example, an individual in need of transportation who generally can choose between the bus, a taxi, carpooling with coworkers, or riding her bicycle but who refuses to ride the bus, does not have taxi service, and can only ride her bicycle within a 2-mile radius of her home would require specific job development emphasizing a close location or other coworkers with whom to ride.

Identifying Individual Choices

Individuals may have difficulty selecting the job they would like to have and the supports they would like to use without sufficient information presented to them in a manner that they can understand. Some individuals may not know what the different options are, others may not know their preferences, and others may lack the skills to make a choice among the alternatives. The job coach can help by providing concrete information either verbally, in written form, or through hands-on experience, or by all these means. One idea for assisting with choosing a job is to have the individual accompany the job coach when making employer contacts during job development. Not only does this strategy allow the individual to directly look at the job and to assess its desirability, but it also provides the opportunity to get his or her "foot in the door" and to make that critical first impression with the employer.

Developing Strategies for Accessing Supports

Just because a community or workplace support is available does not necessarily ensure that an individual interested in using it will automatically have access to it. Our experience suggests that a more formalized process for accessing supports must be initiated. This process typically involves assisting the individual with contacting the support resource and making the specific arrangements for its use. Often, accessing supports requires giving the individual specific steps to follow, guiding him or her through the process, and accompanying him or her during the initial meeting or use of the support. For example, asking the individual to pick up job applications or to contact any interesting employers about a job opening may not be as productive as having him or her come to your office, decide on specific employers to call, and providing a telephone to actually make the calls. Similarly, an individual employed by a company that offers a coworker mentor may need help in linking up with that coworker, expressing his or her support needs, learning how to communicate with the coworker, and indicating his or her preferences if a more compatible coworker is desired.

Evaluating Support Effectiveness

Once a support has been arranged, provisions must be made to determine its effectiveness at meeting the individual's support needs. The receipt of assistance alone is not an assurance that the intended outcome has been achieved. Rather, multiple measures of the quality, stability, and desirability of the support need to be obtained from all persons potentially affected, such as the consumer, employer, coworkers, family, and members of the community. For example, one company indicated at the time of hiring that typical practices were to pair a senior coworker mentor with a new employee until he or she was able to perform the job. On the first day, the assigned mentor was pulled away after 15 minutes because of the heavy workload and because two employees had called in sick. The individual requested assistance from the job coach who was available on site to help the mentor or worker as needed. Discussions with the employer revealed that he did not realize the importance of constant training for an extended period of time and agreed to schedule the worker during slower shifts to ensure that a coworker could be available the entire time.

Arranging Provisions for Ongoing Monitoring

The stability and dependability of community and workplace supports on an ongoing basis are critical issues affecting employment success. Regardless of what supports are in place throughout the individual's employment tenure, provisions for ongoing monitoring must be made in an effort to proactively ensure that the necessary support is maintained. A multitude of factors can influence the reliability of an ongoing support, such as a change in the needs and preferences of the individual, coworker and supervisor turnover on the job site, a modification in work procedures or job duty responsibilities, a geographical change in the individual's living situation, or a desire by a community volunteer to terminate the previously arranged helping relationship. For example, an individual who had previously been employed at a variety of jobs and lost them due to difficulties in getting ready for work every day, chose a job as a busperson for his favorite restaurant, which also offered the hours, location, job duties, and coworkers that he was interested in. He asked the job coach to assist him with getting up and ready for work because he liked this job and did not want to lose it. He and the job coach brainstormed many different options, and, after trying them all, the individual selected the following in order of priority: (1) paying a peer to help, (2) arranging a student volunteer, and (3) hiring a paid attendant. A list of each person's name, telephone number, and hours of availability was developed for the individual and arrangements made with a friend to contact them on the day work schedules were posted to arrange weekly assistance.

KEY POINTS TO REMEMBER IN DESIGNING A SUPPORT SYSTEM

The use of community and workplace supports in the provision of supported employment services represents the state of the art of what we know today in how best to support individuals with severe disabilities in the competitive jobs of their choice. Built on the knowledge and successes of the last decade, the development and utilization of a variety of innovative support technologies further enhance service delivery practices to better meet the needs of all persons who would like to work and receive assistance from supported employment. However, as the field of supported employment moves to this next level, several critical points must be kept in mind.

1. The utilization of community and workplace supports is not a panacea for correcting all of the shortcomings observed in supported employment implementation. It will not fix all of the inconsistencies in service delivery, the lack of funding resources, the shortages of skilled job coaches, the disincentives for conversion, the interagency "turf" issues, the large numbers of persons on waiting lists for services, or the poor quality outcomes reported for some supported employment participants (e.g., low wages, minimal integration, few hours, lack of career advancement). What it will do is place consumers in the driver's seat, allowing them to direct their careers and truly choose the type and amount of assistance they would like to receive to make them happen.

2. The basic premises on which supported employment was established have not changed despite the expansion to include new service technologies. People with disabilities want to work in real jobs, and supported employment offers the means for achieving this goal. No support strategy or methodology, regardless of how good it sounds, should compromise the values on which this vocational model was based. Individuals have the right to be employed by community businesses where they earn comparable wages, work side by side with their coworkers, receive worthwhile hours, and experience all of the same benefits as other employees of the company. Most important, they should be able to choose these characteristics of their jobs and change their minds as their needs and preferences dictate.

3. The reliance on community and workplace supports is not an all-or-nothing approach but rather one of the supportive features of the existing supported employment model. The job coach is responsible for implementing all of the services characteristic of the consumer assessment; job development; job placement; job-site training; and ongoing, follow-along phases of supported employment. However, each individual needs different types of assistance, and the same individual will need varying levels of support at different times in the employment process. The type of support an individual receives to meet each of these needs and the way it is provided are decided by that person, using the systematic process outlined in this chapter. For example, an individual with extensive job-site training needs may choose to have a coworker teach one task, the job coach teach another job duty, her parents arrange transportation, the rehabilitation counselor purchase uniforms, a friend assist with managing her paycheck, the cafeteria personnel help with taking lunch and breaks, the job coach accompany her for social events on the job and after work hours, the supervisor monitor work performance, and a Social Security consultant assist with writing a Plan for Achieving Self-Support (PASS). (See Chapters 1 and 18 also.)

4. With the advent of new and creative support technologies, the job coach's role is not eliminated but instead remains more than ever an essential element of the model. It is evident that community and workplace supports do not automatically meet the support needs of individuals with severe disabilities. People were not working before the establishment of supported employment and many more still are unemployed due to a lack of services. However, this situation does not mean that individuals cannot benefit from the assistance provided by different support resources, but only that some kind of help is needed in order to solicit that assistance in a meaningful way to meet particular support needs. The job coach is the one constant person who possesses the skills to be able to identify and develop support resources, assist with accessing their services, evaluate their effectiveness, and arrange alternative provisions as the need arises.

In the next section are two case studies that describe how supported employment is implemented with individuals who have a severe developmental disability. The exciting aspect of each case study is that each individual greatly reduced his level of mental retardation due to support in the workplace.

CASE STUDIES OF COMPETENCY IN SUPPORTED EMPLOYMENT

. . . .

CASE EXAMPLE: TAYLOR

Employee Characteristics. Taylor is a 22-year-old man who has been assessed by school psychologists as having severe mental retardation according to his scores on standardized intelligence tests (IQ score of 24). Medical records indicate that he has Trisomy 21 with ventricular septal defect, a serious cardiac defect. Taylor takes heart medication daily and is not allowed to lift over 25 pounds or work in excessive heat. He has no sensory or motor impairments and is overweight. His speech is unclear and difficult to understand. Psychological evaluations indicate significant deficits in language develop-

ment with verbal understanding assessed at the 5-year level. School records and observations reveal that Taylor initiates interactions frequently and is often immature, with excessive touching and flirting.

Taylor has lived with his family for 9 years and, prior to that, lived in a residential institution for persons with severe and profound mental retardation. His educational program since leaving the institution has been a self-contained classroom in an integrated high school. Taylor's school curriculum provided community-based training in janitorial and food-service jobs at a local manufacturing center, supply center, and the school cafeteria. His training included dusting, bussing tables, sweeping, operating a dish machine, trash disposal, mopping, and pot scrubbing. His teachers report that he can perform the tasks correctly and that he works at a slow rate.

Employment Record. With the help of a special university project and local school personnel, Taylor was placed as a dishwasher at a restaurant 8 months before his graduation. He was hired to work 16 hours a week on Friday and Saturday nights. His schedule increased to approximately 20 hours a week after 5 months. Taylor was paid $3.50 an hour beginning the first day of employment. Additional benefits included medical insurance, a free meal, and a bonus incentive plan. Taylor has received one bonus check of $100.00 for working 500 hours. His family transports him to and from work.

Taylor's job duties are operating a dish machine, putting dishes away, sweeping, mopping, and emptying trash. A copy of a detailed task analysis of daily activities used for training necessary job skills is provided in Table 17.2.

After one year of employment, the supervisor changed Taylor's job tasks to wrapping potatoes for baking, making french fries, operating a dish machine, and emptying trash. Two other dishwashers work during the same hours, and Taylor assists them as needed. The supervisor and coworkers trained Taylor to perform the new job tasks without assistance from the employment specialist.

Table 17.2.   Individualized Task Analysis and Special Training Strategies

Trainee: Taylor Employment Specialist: Shelia M.		Job Site: Western Sizzlin Restaurant Job Title: Dish Machine Operator
Approximate Times	**Task Performed**	**Task Analysis-Diagrams- Special Training Techniques**
4:55–5:00	1. Put on uniform.	1a. Put on apron and tie. b. Put on hat.
	2. Punch time card.	2a. Locate card in rack. b. Locate "in" on card. c. Line "in" up with red nozzle on clock. d. Pull black lever to clock in.
5:00–7:00	3. Load dishes onto racks.	3a. Pick up plates; hold in left hand. b. Shake apart; put in rack. (black behind silver in same row) c. Repeat until all black plates are removed from table. d. Remove salad plates and bowls from bus pan. e. Put dishes in rack. f. Repeat *d* and *e* until rack is full.
	4. Place full rack over sink. 4a. Rinse with hose.	4a. Life rack and carry to sink area. b. Use water hose to rinse dishes.
	5. Load dishes onto racks.	5. Repeat Step 3.
	6. Place full rack over sink.	6. Repeat Step 4. If busy, it is better to load rack, place over sink area and spray both racks at one time.
	7. Put two racks into dish machine.	7. Take racks over to sink and push or slide into dish machine.
	8. Close machine door.	8. Take handle with hand and pull door completely down.
	9. Turn on dish machine.	9a. Use index finger and push white button to the right. b. Hold for approximately 2 to 3 seconds. c. Release button.
	10. Load glasses, cups, and soup bowls.	10a. Remove glasses, cups, and soup bowls from bus pan. b. Carry and load into racks located above sink area. c. Repeat *a* and *b* until the racks become full. (This is to be done throughout the loading process. It may be an hour before the rack is full.)
	11. Put classes, cups into dish machine.	11a. When one of the racks is filled with glasses, cups, or soup bowls, put in dish machine. b. Repeat Step 7.
	12. Close machine door.	12. Repeat Step 8.
	13. Turn machine on.	13. Repeat Step 9.
7:00–8:00	14. Continue loading racks with dirty dishes.	14. Repeat Steps 3 to 13.

(continues)

Table 17.2. *Continued*

Trainee: Taylor	Job Site: Western Sizzlin Restaurant
Employment Specialist: Shelia M.	Job Title: Dish Machine Operator

Approximate Times	Task Performed	Task Analysis-Diagrams-Special Training Techniques
	15. If caught up on work (loading), wash pans and plastic containers.	15a. Go to sink and remove dirty pans. b. Bring pans to work area near sink. c. Spray the inside of pans with water hose. d. Scour with green pad if needed. (This is to loosen food only.) e. Put pans on flat rack. f. Slide through dish machine. (Make sure two racks are in the machine before turning it on.) g. Turn machine on. Repeat Step 9.
	16. Wash silver. 16a. Locate push cart.	16a. When silver rack bottom is covered with knives, forks, and spoons, carry rack to sink. b. Rinse with hose. c. Push rack of silver into dish machine. Make sure two racks of dirty dishes are in machine. d. Turn machine on. Repeat Steps 8 and 9.
8:00–9:00	17. Catch clean dishes.	17a. When machine cuts off, lift machine door. b. Pull out two racks of dishes. c. Stack dishes at end of counter (bowls, cups).
	18. Catch clean silver.	18a. Pull rack with silver out of machine. b. Pour silver on counter. c. Sort knives and put into round containers. d. Sort forks and put into round containers. e. Sort spoons and put into round containers. f. Sort soup spoons and put into round container.
	19. Wash silver second time.	19. When silver containers become at least half full, push silver back into machine and wash again (two racks needed in machine).
	20. Load clean dishes onto push cart.	20a. When caught up, put black plates on top of cart. b. Put smaller dishes on second and bottom rows. c. Continue until all clean dishes are on cart.
	21. Carry clean dishes to front line and store.	21a. Push loaded cart to front (grill area). b. Unload black plates first. Place on top of counter behind grill. c. Repeat *b* for remaining dishes. Place red plates, potato plates, salad bowls, and small bowls along under table behind french fry area. Salad plates belong on counter beside desserts.
	22. Load glasses, bowls.	22. If down time, repeat Step 10.

(continues)

Table 17.2. *Continued*

| Trainee: Taylor | Job Site: Western Sizzlin Restaurant |
| Employment Specialist: Shelia M. | Job Title: Dish Machine Operator |

Approximate Times	Task Performed	Task Analysis-Diagrams-Special Training Techniques
9:00–9:30	23. BREAK. a. Order meal, continue to work, then punch out.	23a. Order meal at cashier stand. b. Carry meal ticket to order desk. c. Go to time clock; locate time card. d. Locate "out" on card just under the punched "in" 5:00. e. Line "out" up with red nozzle on clock. f. Pull black lever to clock out. g. Go to very back of restaurant and eat meal.
9:30	24. Punch in.	24. Follow Step 2. Punch directly under time he punched out.
9:30–Closing	25. Load or catch dishes, pans, silver, plastic containers.	25. Follow Steps 3 to 22.
	26. Sweep visible trash from floor.[a]	26a. Use broom to collect debris. b. Use dust pan to collect debris. c. Discard in trash can.
	27. Put Tide and water in bucket.	27a. Put 2 cups of Tide in bucket. b. Use hose to fill bucket with water.
	28. Scrub floor with scrub brush and Tide solution.	28a. Start in prep area; dip brush in solution. b. Pull out and scrub floor. c. Repeat *a* and *b* when brush becomes dry. d. Continue until floor is completely scrubbed.
	29. Hose floor down.	29. Repeat Step 27.
	30. Remove excess water from floor with squeegee.	30. Use squeegee to push excess water into floor drain.
	31. Before leaving, all pans and dishes must be washed and put away.[b]	31. Repeat Steps 3 to 22.

[a]Step 26 is exchanged with second dishwasher. One cleans floor and the other continues to do dishes. Pans will be coming from salad and potato bar.
[b]Make sure dish room is clean before leaving.

Problems Presented and Nature of Intervention. Taylor was trained by the employment specialist to perform the job tasks, to use the time clock, to order his meal at break time, and to socialize appropriately with coworkers. As the task analytic data indicated that Taylor was completing the job to the company's standards, the employment specialist gradually reduced her time on the job site. Initial training during the first month required 89 hours of trainer-intervention time. The employment specialist began fading support the second month, and reduced her time to 1 hour per shift during the third month. The total intervention time after 18 months of employment is 161 hours. Taylor continues to receive ongoing, follow-along services by the employment specialist. His work performance is monitored through job-site visits, supervisor evaluations, and phone calls to the family.

Taylor's supervisor evaluations during the first 2 months on the job indicated that he needed improvement in speed and consistency. The employment specialist used behavioral training strategies to teach skill acquisition and production rate before fading support from the job site. Two additional supervisor evaluations indicated that he was frequently tardy and absent. The employment specialist identified the problem as a change in scheduling that resulted in an increase in Taylor's hours. Taylor's employer verbally notified him of the change. To prevent future such occurrences, arrangements were made so that the employer would send a note home to the family, notifying them of schedule changes.

After Taylor had been employed for 11 months, the employment specialist made a follow-along visit to the job site and observed him lifting potato boxes weighing 50 pounds. Coworkers reported that they volunteered to provide assistance but that Taylor repeatedly initiated the task independently. After lifting the boxes, Taylor would grasp his chest and close his eyes. The coworkers and supervisors would respond by asking Taylor if he was all right and suggesting he take a break. The employment specialist intervened and modeled initiating requests for assistance when the opportunity to lift the boxes occurred. Reinforcement was provided by the coworkers and employment specialist for requesting assistance. After several weeks of training, the behavior was eliminated.

Outcome Measures. Taylor has earned over $5,000 in wages and has paid $1,235 in taxes after 18 months of employment. Since Taylor has been employed, he has lost over 8 pounds, a significant improvement. His family, teachers, and employment specialist state that his immature social behaviors have reduced. Taylor's family reports that he is allowed to stay home alone now, which was not permitted before he began working. Assessment data indicate that Taylor's work rate

has increased from a slow to an average pace. In addition, the performance evaluations show that Taylor adapts to task changes more easily since the beginning of his employment. The employer consistently rates Taylor's work performance positively on supervisor evaluations and states that "he reduces the tension in the kitchen."

··

CASE EXAMPLE: JOHN

Employee Characteristics. John is a 23-year-old man whose primary diagnosis is autism. His psychological test data suggest wide discrepancies in John's abilities. His mental age at 18 was reported at 8 years (*Peabody Picture Vocabulary Test–Revised;* Dunn & Dunn, 1981). Intelligence test records place him in the moderate range of mental retardation with an IQ of 45. Reading and math skills at eighth- and third-grade levels, respectively, according to the *Slosson Oral Reading Test* (Slosson, 1990) and the *Wide Range Achievement Test–Revised* (Jastak & Jastak, 1984), which were also administered at age 18.

He is described as "highly active" and deficient in social and language skills. His movements are very quick and abrupt. His verbalizations are inappropriately loud and composed of one- to three-word staccato phrases. He avoids eye contact, making very short repeated glances at people when forced to interact with them. He sometimes hums or uses language in a self-stimulatory manner. Other inappropriate behaviors observed of John include walking too fast, pushing people out of his way, perseverating on words and phrases, and flipping objects with his fingers. When upset or frustrated, John has been observed to walk to and fro at a fast pace, sometimes around in circles repeating a word or phrase over and over again.

John's school services included a period in a residential program for individuals with autism from age 12 to 18. His vocational training consisted of assembling food packets, shelving books in the library, and filing papers. At age 18, he returned home and was provided school services outside of the classroom, which consisted of one-to-one instruction provided by a homebound instructor in the school central office building. His educational program focused on vocational training and applied academic skills. Vocational training involved sorting mail in the central office mail room and reshelving books in the professional library. John was described as being difficult to train and extremely dependent on teachers' verbal and physical prompting.

Employment Record. The year before John's last year in school, he was selected for participation in a supported, competitive employment program. Through this program, a supported work employment specialist located a 28-hour-per-week position for John at a local bank operations center as a proof operator in September of his last year in school. The job involved John's using a specialized computer terminal to enter bank transaction items into the bank's main computer system.

After 2½ months of training, the employment specialist decided that John would not be able to complete the job duties in the proof operator position without ongoing, constant supervision because of the high number of variations and exceptions that occurred in the work and that would require judgment decisions to be made by John. John's employer at the bank identified another position at the bank that he believed might be a more appropriate match to John's abilities. After the employment specialist completed a thorough analysis of the position, John was started in the second position.

This position, called a lockbox clerk, required the sorting and processing of installment loan payments, which included separating the payment coupons from the checks, determining if the payment arrived by the due date, and then balancing the amounts paid using an electronic calculator. John was also responsible for deciding when items needed to be rejected and routed to the loan department. Handwriting was required to mark items or batches of items to

indicate the actions to be taken. Sample portions of the task analyses for both the proof operator and lockbox clerk positions are provided in Table 17.3.

Problems Presented and Nature of Intervention. The first position of proof operator was determined not to be an appropriate job match due to incomplete job-analysis information. Because of the nature of the job, many details were identified after several weeks of doing the job. After deciding that the job was too difficult, the work supervisor along with the employment specialist identified the second position of lockbox clerk.

Standard job-site training procedures as practiced included use of an ecological and task analytic approach with behavioral and systematic instructional procedures being applied (Moon et al., 1986). The employment specialist provided intensive one-to-one training of all job and social skills, all work-related communication with coworkers and supervisors necessary for the completion of job duties (e.g., asking for more work, notifying a supervisor of equipment malfunction, etc.), transportation using the city buses, ordering lunch in the employee cafeteria, and ways of spending break time appropriately.

In this position, the particular problems presented during training were fading prompts, dealing with exceptions, communicating with supervisor and coworkers, and printing legibly and small enough to fit into spaces on forms.

To fade prompts, the employment specialist implemented a question-prompt procedure (i.e., "John, what do you do?") followed by a period of withholding any verbal interaction until John finally began to initiate the behaviors independently. Positive reinforcement was given in the form of verbal praise for independent initiating. The job specialist took care to deliver reinforcement intermittently in order to avoid transferring the dependence to the reinforcer, which would inhibit John's initiation of the subsequent behavior required in the task sequence.

To help John respond correctly to the exceptions that occurred in processing the loan installments, the employment specialist de-

---

Table 17.3.   Proof Operator and Lockbox Clerk Jobs in a Bank

---

CLOSING A PROOF MACHINE

1. *Look* on the journal tape; *find* the last sequence number (on the left side).
2. *Write* this number on your Batch Log Sheet (END SEQUENCE NUMBER _____).
3. Press *ND* key, *DN* key, 5 and the ____ key.
4. Press *ADD* key and __*__ key.
5. *Add* up all of the batches from the Batch Log Sheet (hit debit key after each number).
6. *Press* ____ key.
7. The two subtotals should be the same. *Write* numbers on Log Sheet–TOTAL BATCHES.
8. *Press* __*__ key and *release* ADD key.
9. *Press ND* key, *DN* key and __*__ key.
10. *Press* 1, 9, *PROG* key and ____ key. *Write* two numbers on Log Sheet–ITEM COUNT.
11. *Tear* off top proof journal tape. *Circle* total and *put* your name and the date on it.
12. *Tear* off second proof journal tape. *Fold* it up. *Circle* the total and *put* your name and the date on it. *Put* a rubber band around the tape.
13. *Sign* Batch Log Sheet and *fill* in STOP TIME _____.
14. *Fill* in Time Sheet.
15. *Turn* Time Sheet, Batch Log Sheet, Proof Journal Tapes (both), first practice item, and adding machine tapes in to *supervisor.*
16. *Turn* the machine off and *cover* the machine. Be sure your work area is clean.

LOCKBOX CLERK TASK

1. Compare check with document.
2. Decide action to take with items.
    If check matches, put in "accept" stack.
    If check is slightly larger, put in "accept" stack.
    If check is much larger, put in "reject" stack.
    If check is less, put in "reject" stack.
3. Write correct department on other bank mail.
4. Send items to loan department.
5. Decide when check is a deposit or loan payment with no document.
6. Keep all correspondence.
7. Write *AN* on front of envelope (if not listed on Corr).
8. Check for date and final payment written on document.
9. Check for bank name and signature on check.
10. If either is missing, pass to coworker to stamp.
11. Write correct description on front of envelope (Corr, Ck Reject, Ck/No Doc, Final Payment/CK Reject).
12. Stop to add up stacks of checks and documents.
13. If adding machine tapes match, rubber-band stacks.
14. If adding machine tapes do NOT match, search for error.
15. Correct error.

veloped a checklist of procedures with "if–then" routines for processing irregular items. John's reading skills were utilized to train him to read brief instructional cues, placed on his desk blotter, that told him what action to take for a given type of exception. Each time an exception occurred, the employment specialist prompted John to refer to the written instructional cues, match the type of exception, and carry out the action as instructed. After many repetitions of this training to recognize an exception, refer to written cues, and complete the action as written, John was able to handle the exceptions independently. The prompt-fading procedure was also used. There was one exception for which John was unable to be trained: making a judgment about how much over or under the required loan payment amount that the check amount could be in order to be accepted or rejected. This part of the job was negotiated out of the job duties to a coworker.

Interactions with coworkers and supervisors were trained by the employment specialist with systematic procedures. As the employment specialist began to fade intervention time, she began prompting John to ask the room supervisor for more work or assistance rather than asking her. As well, she assisted the supervisor and coworkers in asking John for items or giving him instructions by modeling the behaviors and then having John ask for them. Prompt fading in this instance was achieved by the employment specialist's gradually becoming less available to John and coworkers and supervisors. Handwriting problems were solved by modifying some forms to accommodate John's very large printing and by teaching John to use abbreviations.

The total number of intervention hours required for John's ultimate success as a bank employee was very high. Obviously, the majority of the hours were required during the first 6 months of John's employment, with the first 3 months being used on an incompatible job match.

In the second position, John began to perform job duties and other work-related behaviors according to preestablished criteria based on the employer's standards. Eventually, the employment specialist began to gradually reduce intervention time from the job site. The supervisory role of the employment specialist was transferred to the work-site supervisor during the gradual reduction of time from the job site. The employment specialist made frequent phone contact with the parents and employer as well as once-a-week visits to the job site.

Two reasons can be offered to explain the high number of intervention hours. First, job development and job analysis in the high-technology business world is somewhat more complex than the typical employment settings that have been common for supported employment consumers. Supported employment professionals need more experience in employment settings other than service industries, such as food services and janitorial services. Far fewer hours might have been possible in a simpler job placement. However, to place John in a position that did not utilize his higher level skills would be to underemploy him for the sake of programmatic efficiency. Second, the wide discrepancies evident in John's abilities and inabilities made consumer assessment information difficult to translate for an appropriate job match.

Outcome Measures. Beginning the first day of employment in the lockbox clerk position, John earned $4.80 per hour working 20 hours per week. His cumulative wages earned at the time of this report was over $8,700 with over $2,000 paid in taxes. His supervisor at the bank has said that John is one of his more accurate workers: "He never makes a mistake." In addition to the primary financial gains, marked improvements in John's adaptive behavior are evident.

By the time John graduated from school, he was performing the job at above 95% accuracy, and his production rate was approaching the standards of the employer. Employer evaluations indicated a high level of satisfaction with John's performance.

NATIONAL IMPLEMENTATION OF SUPPORTED EMPLOYMENT

With this background of how supported employment programs operate and how they can benefit individuals with developmental disabilities, it is now relevant to ask: How widespread are these programs? Are they effective? Who do they help? In this next section, we provide some answers to these questions and more.

Over the past decade, there has been steady growth in the supported employment program initiative nationally (Powell et al., 1991; Rusch, 1986; Wehman et al., 1992) and away from sheltered workshops (e.g., McGaughey, Kiernan, McNally, Gilmore, & Keith, 1994). One of the main vehicles for this stimulus has been the systems-change grants awarded to state vocational rehabilitation (VR) agencies under Title III of the Rehabilitation Act (Shafer, Revell, & Isbister, 1991; Wehman, Kregel, & Shafer, 1989; West, Revell, & Wehman, 1992). These grants have been documented as an effective way to promote change (Shafer et al., 1991). As of January 1994, 38 states and the District of Columbia had received these grants, which allowed state VR programs to increase supported employment capacity. Strategies for developing this capacity included fee-for-service arrangements, interagency agreements, provision of consumer database systems for evaluation, and technical assistance to provider agencies. Supported employment case service funds have also been made available to the states on a formula basis through Title VI, Part C of the Rehabilitation Act Amendments of 1992.

The federal investment in supported employment has produced remarkable dividends for the program over a relatively short period of time. For example, Wehman et al. (1989) reported a total of 32,342 supported employment participants nationally in 1988. Several years later, this figure had jumped to 74,000 (West et al., 1992). Sale, Revell, West, and Kregel (1992) reported that in 1990, funding of supported employment from non-VR sources, such as state departments of mental retardation, developmental disabilities, mental health, and education, exceeded VR sources by more than a two-to-one margin. They concluded that for every $1 spent in VR funds for time-limited services, $2 from other federal, state, and local funding sources were leveraged in order to fund extended services for supported employment consumers.

In addition, Sale et al. (1992) reported that Title I case service funds and state general revenue funds accounted for over 70% of VR funds being used for supported employment services. Title I funds are the largest source of VR dollars; they can be used for all aspects of vocational rehabilitation to achieve employment outcomes for persons with disabilities. In comparison, Title VI, Part C funds can be used only for the provision of supported employment services. The use of substantial amounts of non-Title VI, Part C VR funds indicates that supported employment is being increasingly viewed as a viable service option by VR counselors and is becoming integrated into state VR service delivery systems.

Despite the substantial growth in supported employment participants, providers, and funding, and despite the documented benefits that supported employment participants experience (Helms, Moore, & McSweyn, 1991; Kiernan, McGaughey, & Schalock, 1986; Noble & Conley, 1987; Thompson, Powers, & Houchard, 1992), there is a critical need to further expand the program. Mank (1994) noted that supported employment has not fulfilled its promise to people with severe disabilities. He and others (Wehman & Kregel, 1995) are especially concerned that many states have yet to seriously address and overcome the regulatory and financial disincentives that inhibit local day programs from converting into supported employment programs. There is justifiable concern that nearly a decade of systems-change efforts have generally failed to bring about a substantial shift away from segregated vocational services (Mank, 1994; McGaughey, Kiernan, Mc-Nally, & Gilmore, 1993; Wehman & Kregel, 1994). Furthermore, it is clear that individuals with severe mental retardation or physical impairments continue to be underserved in supported employment programs (Corthell & Yarman, 1992; West et al., 1992), as well as those with significant behavioral or functional impairments (Kregel & Wehman, 1989).

In similar fashion, Revell and his colleagues (1994) decided to identify and analyze national programmatic and outcome data associated with implementation of supported employment by each state in the United States. Supported employment outcome data were assessed from the vocational rehabilitation state agencies as were the strategies that some states have undertaken that might positively influence the development of supported employment. They found that approximately 74,000 persons were reported to be in supported employment as of 1991, with a total of 42 states providing data; 62% were people with mental retardation, and 22% with mental illness.

Several positive findings emerged from the Revell et al. (1994) study. First, there continues to be a steady growth in the number of individuals participating in supported employment. Although the rate of growth has slowed somewhat from the dramatic pace in the late 1980s, a total of 74,000 participants for 40 of the 50 states plus the District of Columbia and the Virgin Islands is still impressive, particularly when compared with the fiscal year 1988 data of 32,342 (Wehman et al., 1989). The 32,342 figure reflects supported employment participation in 48 states. It is reasonable to assume that the dramatic rate of growth experienced earlier has been slowed because of a very difficult recession that most regions of the United States experienced during the 1990–1992 period. The work by Walter, Liacopoulos, and Sasnett (1993) supported the adverse effect that negative economic conditions have had on supported employment participants. By most accounts, the 1990–1992 recession was among the worst in the United States in decades, with hundreds of thousands of jobs lost due to corporate restructuring. Despite these economic

strains, supported employment programs continued to survive and even thrive.

A second very interesting finding from this survey is the expanding use of the individual placement model in supported employment programs. This is an approach that invariably leads to competitive employment in work settings where the majority of the workers do not have disabilities. The use of an employment specialist and natural supports is clearly gathering momentum as the supported model of choice. As recently as 1988, the small business model was selected as the model of choice by approximately 7.3% of the respondents (Wehman et al., 1989); the most recent survey now shows that less than 1% of respondents use this choice. Clearly, the more normalizing and better paying model of individual placement is the supported employment service option of choice for consumers, advocates, and professionals.

Interestingly, results from the present study indicated a national mean average weekly wage of $111.44 for supported employment participants. These data reflect a dramatic increase of about 500% in salary level of participants before supported employment to after supported employment. These data are consistent with the earlier findings of Kregel, Wehman, and Banks (1989) as well as those of Thompson et al. (1992).

FINAL THOUGHTS

In closing, we should note that most recently Revell et al. (1994) presented an update of this just-mentioned study with all 50 states for the 1993 year. The number of people participating in supported employment has continued to grow to now over 105,000 nationally. These data provide a dramatic extension of how well received supported employment is as a program that meets the vocational needs of individuals with disabilities. It is reasonable to assume that there will be increasing growth toward integrated employment throughout the 1990s.

Our purpose in this chapter has been to provide a review of how supported employment programs are affecting persons with developmental disabilities. As we have shown, people with many different disabilities increasingly are being involved in supported employment. Long-term funding, coordination of services, and expanded business relations continue to be strong needs. The national data show that this is a very popular program, which continues to grow, yet over 1 million people still sit in adult activity centers and other supported, segregated day programs who would like to work. Supported employment is an excellent way for people who have been unemployed to finally attain competitive employment.

REFERENCES

Albin, J. (1992). *Quality improvement in employment and other human services.* Baltimore: Brookes.

Americans with Disabilities Act of 1990, P.L. 101-336. (July 26, 1990). Title 42, U.S.C. 12101 *et seq. U.S. Statutes at Large, 104,* 327–378.

Beckett, C., & Fluke, D. (1988). Supported employment: Parental involvement. *Exceptional Parent,* January/February, 20–26.

Bellamy, G. T., Rhodes, L. C., Mank, D. M., & Joyce, A. (1988). *Supported employment: A community implementation guide.* Baltimore: Brookes.

Bourbeau, P. (1985). Mobile work crews: An approach to achieve long-term supported employment. In P. McCarthy, J. M. Everson, M. S. Moon, & J. M. Barcus (Eds.), *School to work: Transition youth with severe disabilities* (pp. 68–78). Richmond: Virginia Commonwealth University, Rehabilitation Research and Training Center on Supported Employment.

Brooke, V., Barcus, M., & Inge, K. (1992). *Consumer advocacy and supported employment: A vision for the future* [Monograph]. Richmond: Virginia Commonwealth University, Rehabilitation Research and Training Center on Supported Employment.

Buckley, J., & Bellamy, G. T. (1985). *National survey of day and vocational programs for adults with severe disabilities: A 1984 profile.* Unpublished manuscript, Johns Hopkins University, Baltimore.

Chadsey-Rusch, J., Gonzalez, P., & Tines, J. (1988). Social ecology of the workplace: A study of interactions among employees with and without mental retardation. In J. Chadsey-Rusch (Ed.), *Social ecology of the workplace* (pp. 27–54). Champaign: University of Illinois at Urbana-Champaign, Secondary Transition Intervention Effectiveness Institute.

Corthell, D., & Yarman, D. (1992). *Serving the underserved: Principles, practices and techniques.* Stout: University of Wisconsin at Stout, Nineteenth Institute on Rehabilitation Issues.

Dunn, L. M., & Dunn, L. M. (1981). *Peabody Picture Vocabulary Test–Revised.* Circle Pines, MN: American Guidance Service.

Federal Register, 57(189), 447794–44852 (1992, September 29). 34 C.F.R. 300–301.

Hagner, D., & Dileo, D. (1993). *Working together: Workplace culture, supported employment, and persons with disabilities.* Brookline, MA: Brookline Books.

Hayden, M., & Abery, B. (Eds.). (1994). *Challenges for a service system in transition.* Baltimore: Brookes.

Helms, B. L., Moore, S. C., & McSweyn, C. A. (1991). Supported employment in Connecticut: An examination of integration and wage outcomes. *Career Development for Exceptional Individuals, 14,* 159–166.

Jastak, J. F., & Jastak, S. R. (1984). *Wide Range Achievement Test–Revised.* Wilmington, DE: Jastak Associates.

Kiernan, W., & Stark, J. (1986). *Pathways to employment for adults with severe developmental disabilities.* Baltimore: Brookes.

Kiernan, W. E., McGaughey, M. J., & Schalock, R. C. (1986). *National employment survey for adults with developmental disabilities.* Boston: Children's Hospital, Training and Research Institute for People with Disabilities.

Kregel, J. (1994, Fall). Natural supports and the job coach: An unnecessary dichotomy. *Rehabilitation Research and Training Center at VCU, 1.*

Kregel, J., & Unger, D. (1993). Employer perceptions of the work potential of individuals with disabilities: An illustration from supported employment. *Journal of Vocational Rehabilitation, 3*(4), 17–25.

Kregel, J., & Wehman, P. (1989). Supported employment: Promises deferred for persons with severe handicaps. *Journal of the Association for the Severely Handicapped, 14*(3), 293–303.

Kregel, J., Wehman, P., & Banks, P. D. (1989). The effects of consumer characteristics and type of employment model on individual outcomes in supported employment. *Journal of Applied Behavior Analysis, 22,* 407–415.

Kregel, J., Wehman, P., Revell, W. G., & Hill, M. (1990). Supported employment in Virginia 1980–1988. In J. Kregel, P. Wehman, & M. Shafer (Eds.), *Supported employment for persons with severe disabilities: From research to practice* (Monograph, Vol. 3, pp. 15–30). Richmond: Virginia Commonwealth University, Rehabilitation Research and Training Center on Supported Employment.

Louis Harris & Associates. (1994). *N.O.D./Harris Survey of Americans with Disabilities.* New York: Author.

Mank, D. (1994). The underachievement of supported employment: A call for reinvestment. *Journal of Disability Policy Studies, 5*(2), 1–24.

Mank, D. M., Rhodes, L. E., & Bellamy, G. T. (1986). Four supported employment alternatives. In W. E. Kiernan & J. A. Stark (Eds.), *Pathways to employment for adults with developmental disabilities* (pp. 418–422). Baltimore: Brookes.

McGaughey, M. J., Kiernan, W. E., McNally, L. C., & Gilmore, D. S. (1993). *National perspectives on integrated employment: State MR/DD agency trends.* Boston: Children's Hospital, Training and Research Institute for People with Disabilities.

McGaughey, M., Kiernan, W., McNally, L., Gilmore, D., & Keith, G. (1994). *Beyond the workshop: National perspectives on integrated employment.* Boston: Institute for Community Inclusion.

Moon, M. S., Goodall, P., Barcus, M., & Brooke, V. (1986). *The supported work model of competitive employment for citizens with severe handicaps: A guide for job trainers.* Richmond: Virginia Commonwealth University, Rehabilitation Research and Training Center on Supported Employment.

Moore, C. (1988). Parents and transition: "Make it or break it." *The Pointer, 32*(2), 12–14.

Murphy, S., Rogan, P., & Fisher, E. (1994). National survey of natural support practices in supported employment. *Info-Lines, 5*(4), 1, 3.

Nisbet, J. (1992). *Natural supports in school, at work, and in the community for people with disabilities.* Baltimore: Brookes.

Noble, J., & Conley, R. (1987). Accumulating evidence on the benefits and costs of supported and transitional employment for persons with severe disabilities. *Journal of the Association for Persons with Severe Handicaps, 12,* 163–174.

Parent, W. (1994). *Consumer satisfaction and choice at the workplace: A survey of individuals with severe disabilities who receive supported employment services.* Unpublished doctoral dissertation, Virginia Commonwealth University, Richmond.

Parent, W. S., Kregel, J., Metzler, H. M. D., & Twardzik, G. (1992). Social integration in the workplace: An analysis of the interaction activities of workers with mental retardation and their coworkers. *Education and Training in Mental Retardation, 27*(1), 28–38.

Parent, W., Sherron, P., Stallard, D., & Booth, M. (1993). Job development and placement, strategies for success. *Journal of Vocational Rehabilitation, 3*(3) 17–26.

Parent, W., & Wehman, P. (1994). *Integration in the workplace: What employment specialists need to know.* Unpublished manuscript.

Powell, T., Pancsofar, E., Steere, D., Butterworth, J., Hurowitz, J., & Rainforth, B. (1991). *Supported employment.* New York: Longman.

Rehabilitation Act Amendments of 1992, P.L. 102-569, Title 29, U.S.C. 701 §101[c].

Rehabilitation Services Administration. (1993). *Series A1 preliminary tabs fiscal year 1991.* Unpublished report. Washington, DC: Author.

Revell, W. G., Wehman, P., Kregel, J., West, M., & Rayfield, R. (1994). Supported employment for persons with severe disabilities: Positive trends in wages, models and funding. *Education and Training in Mental Retardation and Developmental Disabilities, 29,* 256–264.

Rhodes, L. E., & Valenta, L. (1985). Enclaves in industry. In P. McCarthy, J. Everson, S. Moon, & M. Barcus (Eds.), *School-to-work transition for youth with severe disabilities* (Monograph). Richmond: Virginia Commonwealth University, Rehabilitation Research and Training Center on Supported Employment.

Rusch, F. R. (1986). Competitive employment issues and strategies. In G. T. Bellamy, L. Rhodes, D. M. Mank, & J. M. Albin (Eds.), *Supported employment: A community implementation guide.* Baltimore: Brookes.

Rusch, F. R. (Ed.). (1990). *Supported employment models, methods, and issues.* Sycamore, IL: Sycamore.

Sale, P., Revell, W. G., West, M., & Kregel, J. (1992). Achievements and challenges II: An analysis of 1990 supported employment expenditures. *Journal of the Association for Persons with Severe Handicaps, 17,* 236–246.

Sale, P., Wood, W., Barcus, M., & Moon, M. S. (1988). The role of the employment specialist. In B. Kiernan & B. Schalock (Eds.), *Economics, industry, and disability: A look ahead* (pp. 432–442). Baltimore: Brookes.

Shafer, M. S., Hill, J., Seyfarth, J., & Wehman, P. (1987). Competitive employment and workers with mental retarda-tion: Analysis of employers' perceptions and experiences. *American Journal of Mental Retardation, 92*(3), 304–311.

Shafer, M. S., Revell, W. G., & Isbister, F. (1991). The national supported employment initiative: A three-year longitudinal analysis of 50 states. *Journal of Vocational Rehabilitation, 1*(1), 9–17.

Slosson, R. L. (1990). *Slosson Oral Reading Test.* East Aurora, NY: Slosson Educational Publications.

State of New York. (1993). *Integrated employment implementation plan, chapter 515, the laws of 1992.* New York: Author.

Test, D. W., Hinson, K. B., Solow, J., & Keul, P. (1993). Job satisfaction of persons in supported employment. *Education and Training in Mental Retardation, 28*(1), 38–46.

Thompson, L., Powers, G., & Houchard, B. (1992). The wage effects of supported employment. *Journal of the Association for Persons with Severe Handicaps, 17,* 87–94.

U.S. Bureau of the Census. (1992). *Selected social characteristics: 1990.* Washington, DC: Department of Labor.

Walter, D., Liacopoulos, G., & Sasnett, G. (1993). *The impact of prevailing economic conditions on supported employment programs in the 1990's: An examination of service delivery.* Washington, DC: St. John's Community Services.

Wehman, P. (1981). *Competitive employment: New horizons for severely disabled individuals.* Baltimore: Brookes.

Wehman, P. (1992). *Achievements and challenges: A five-year report on the status of the national supported employment initiative.* Richmond: Virginia Commonwealth University, Rehabilitation Research and Training Center on Supported Employment.

Wehman, P., & Kregel, J. (1985). A supported work approach to competitive employment of individuals with moderate and severe handicaps. *Journal of the Association for Persons with Severe Handicaps, 10*(1), 3–9.

Wehman, P., & Kregel, J. (1994). Toward a national agenda for supported employment. *Journal of Vocational Rehabilitation, 4*(4), 3–12.

Wehman, P., & Kregel, J. (1995). At the crossroads: Supported employment ten years later. *Journal of the Association for Persons with Severe Handicaps, 20*(4), 286–299.

Wehman, P., Kregel, J., & Shafer, M. S. (Eds.). (1989). *Emerging trends in the national supported employment initiative: A preliminary analysis.* Richmond: Virginia Commonwealth University, Rehabilitation Research and Training Center on Supported Employment.

Wehman, P., & Melia, R. (1985). The job coach: Function in transitional and supported employment. *American Rehabilitation, 11*(2), 4–7.

Wehman, P., Sale, P., & Parent, W. (1992). *Supported employment: Strategies for integration of workers with disabilities.* Boston: Andover.

West, M., Kregel, J., & Banks, D. (1990). Fringe benefits available to supported employment participants. *Rehabilitation Counseling Bulletin, 34*(2), 126–138.

West, M., Revell, W. G., & Wehman, P. (1992). Achievements and challenges: I. A five-year report on consumer and system outcomes from the supported employment initiative. *Journal of the Association for Persons with Severe Handicaps, 17*(24), 227–235.

Supported Living and Collaborative Transition

Tom J. Clees

LEARNING GOALS

Upon completion of this chapter the reader will be able to

- enumerate the barriers to independent living;

- describe the continuum of residential services and settings typically available to persons with developmental disabilities;

- discuss the problems with the continuum of services approach to transition and community living;

- describe the supported living alternative to transition and community living;

- discuss the value of recreation and leisure skills training;

- discuss how transportation plays a major role in community integration;

- discuss the salient features of a collaborative approach to transition and community living;

- discuss the importance of advocacy in a supported living approach; and

- enumerate the service and political activities that can be conducted by advocates.

Persons with disabilities are not as likely to be assimilated into their communities as are individuals with no accompanying disability labels. Numerous databases have documented the cumulative failure of current publicly funded educational and vocational programs to consistently provide services that are predictive of postschool success in the areas of independent living (Edgar & Levine, 1987), employment (D'Amico, 1992; Frank, Sitlington, & Carson, 1991; Hasazi, Gordon, & Roe, 1985), and postschool education and training (Fairweather & Shaver, 1991; SRI International, 1989). This general lack of assimilation, however, cannot be directly attributed to (i.e., is not caused by) individuals' respective exceptionalities. This is clear simply by the fact that numerous individuals with disabilities do indeed succeed. Rather, inconsistencies in the quality, degree, and coordination of the services they receive during and after their school years are clearly the best predictors of poor adjustment to the community.

Perhaps the ultimate transition is that to the postschool world. During this period, individuals typically embark on their careers, take up their own residences, develop new relationships with individuals in their communities, and continue their education or training to advance their skills.

This period presents not only many new responsibilities but also an increasing demand to exhibit independence in meeting them. Many individuals with disabilities enter their communities with fewer skills and greater dependence on significant others than do the citizens in their communities who do not possess disabilities. For those with disabilities, the challenges to be met in their communities often become barriers to independence. The result is many poor postschool adjustments and, potentially, a loss of independent living status.

What skills, then, are needed to meet the challenges found in one's community? What are the barriers to successful transitions? What community living options do individuals with disabilities have, and how and what supports are needed to assist individuals in acquiring and maintaining their status as workers, players, and residents in their respective communities? These questions are the focus of this chapter and are all related to the concept of independence.

INDEPENDENCE

Independence, or more functionally stated, "independent living," is typically viewed as an outcome, but it has also been described as both an outcome and a process (Fisher, 1989). As an outcome, functioning independently within the community requires that an individual exhibit a wide range of skills across numerous settings and in the absence of supports not normally present, such as those provided by state or federal agencies (e.g., vocational rehabilitation). For many individuals, particularly those with disabilities, independent living is best described as a terminal goal that they are in the process of reaching. The ongoing process of providing a person with residential, financial, educational, career, and other supports to assist in the acquisition of functional skills across all relevant skill domains has, as its terminal goal, the maintenance of those adaptive responses once the supports have been faded to the minimum required to maintain the individ-

ual within the community. From this perspective, individuals utilize available supports to acquire skills and services that move them along a continuum of greater independence while maintaining their status as citizens within their own communities.

Many individuals require some degree of support to function within and outside of their residences. This assistance varies, depending on the needs of the individual served. Some examples include assistance in meal preparation or transportation to work, the use of augmentative communication devices, social skills training, and physical care.

Community living skills, or those competencies that individuals must utilize to function independently, are typically grouped into broad skill areas, or domains. Whereas conceptualizations differ both in the number of domains utilized to represent skills as well as in the number of competencies and subcompetencies falling within each domain, the domains generally include skills related to daily living (domestic and mobility skills), personal–social interactions (communication and interpersonal skills), and employment (job-seeking and work performance skills).

Thus, one's independence is a matter of degree and may be determined by

- the extent of one's community living skills;

- the resources and support services required by the individual to acquire and maintain those skills in relevant settings (i.e., to function as a working, playing resident of his or her community); and

- the extent, availability, and quality of the resources and support services in the individual's community.

This last factor is crucial. A deficit in either the scope, quality, or availability of supports, or in one's success at accessing needed supports, may adversely affect the acquisition of new skills and increase the likelihood that community living status will not be acquired and/or maintained. For example, consider the case of Laurie, a young woman with a physical disability that precluded her from traveling independently. Laurie lived alone in an apartment located in a rural setting. She required minimal assistance to maintain her independent living status (assistance with transportation to and from work and with shopping). Her employer described her as a superior worker who interacted well with her fellow employees. Her transportation had been provided or otherwise coordinated by a nondisabled neighbor with whom Laurie worked. However, the neighbor–coworker–advocate moved away, and Laurie was faced with the loss of consistent transportation. As a result, her job, income, and status as a resident in her community could no longer be maintained unless she moved to a group home in an area with more support services; a move that she unhappily made. Such unfortunate scenarios are not uncommon. There are many individuals to whom community-based career, residential, leisure, or mobility supports have never been available, either because of the limited number of existing services or because of the priorities, misconceptions, or prejudices of others.

For purposes here, the terms *independent living* and *independence* always imply *independence from* any setting more restrictive than the community. Such restrictive settings are considered to be those that segregate people with disabilities from the general population.

BARRIERS TO INDEPENDENT LIVING

Rusch, Mithaug, and Flexer (1986) identified six obstacles to competitive employment that, with minor addenda (/), apply equally well as barriers to independent living and integration. These obstacles include

1. specific employee/resident skill and behavior deficits,

2. deficient assessment and training procedures,

3. disregard for social validation of work/residential goals and (training) procedures,

4. lack of a systematic approach to service delivery,

5. inadequate personnel preparation, and

6. economic and policy considerations that deter efforts to promote competitive employment/independent living.

To this list of barriers may be added

7. public opinion and

8. the concept of "readiness" as a determinant of integration.

The first three items address what should be taught, how it should be taught, and the social validity, or functional significance, of each. These concerns are addressed in the Community Living Skills section of this chapter. The remaining items represent problems in the systems of service delivery and in the priorities and policies that determine levels and types of support. These problems are exemplified by fragmentation and duplication of services; a lack of communication and collaboration among schools, agencies, and community programs; and misconceptions regarding individuals' potentials.

The types of supports and the degree to which they are provided to individuals are affected by the availability of resources and are greatly determined by a set of guiding principles, or philosophy of operations (Pancsofar & Blackwell, 1986). The principles of normalization and least restrictive environment have greatly influenced the current range of school and postschool service delivery models. Pancsofar and Blackwell (1986) cited Wolfensberger, who described normalization (or as Wolfensberger preferred, *social valorization*) as "the use of means which are culturally normative to offer a person life conditions at least as good as the average citizen's and to as much as possible enhance or support personal behaviors, appearances, status and reputation to the greatest degree possible at any given time for each individual according to his or her developmental needs" (pp. 6–7).

The provision of services in the least restrictive environment (LRE), as originally engendered in the Education for All Handicapped Children Act of 1975 (P.L. 94–142), provides that

> to the maximum extent appropriate, handicapped children, including children in public or private institutions or other care facilities, are educated with children who are not handicapped, and that special classes, separate schooling, or other removal of handicapped children from the regular educational environment occurs only when the nature or severity of the handicap is such that education in regular classes with the use of supplementary aids and services cannot be achieved satisfactorily. (§ 612151B)

These principles have greatly affected the way in which persons with developmental disabilities are perceived and treated. Although individuals with disabilities have clearly benefitted from a growing philosophy of "community," there have been and remain difficulties not only with the implementation of practices related to the principles but also with their conceptualization as related to service models. The "deinstitutionalization" movement and the evolution of a "continuum of services" exemplify these problems. In the earlier phases of deinstitutionalization, many individuals were taken from state institutions and "dumped into the community without having the necessary skills to cope successfully in their new environment and without easy access to support and follow-up services that see that the transition was successful" (Heward & Orlansky, 1988, p. 586).

The difficulties faced by many deinstitutionalized individuals can be viewed either as a function of their lack of readiness to move into the community or as a function of an inadequate system of services with which to support them (regardless of their disabilities or skill levels). The former view, that of "readiness," is embodied in the concept of the least restrictive environment and implies a continuum-of-services approach to providing services. This implication is evidenced in the preceding citation regarding LRE, which has provisions for "public or private institutions . . . special classes, special schooling, or other removal." The harsh reality is that the least restrictive environment is actually the least restrictive environment *given* the current distribution of services.

Certainly there is a discrepancy between the number of people with disabilities who could, if provided supports, both hold jobs in integrated settings and live in their own apartments, homes, or small transitional group homes, and the number who do. This discrepancy is particularly troublesome in light of the long-standing evidence that individuals with even severe and profound disabilities can succeed in the least restrictive settings. In analyzing their data on community placements and outcomes, Seyelman, Bell, Schoenrock, Elear, and Danker-Brown (1978) concluded that clients of virtually any intellectual functioning level can succeed in the community, given the provision of adequate supports. Wehman's (1990) data refuted any notion that people with disabilities cannot be productive members of the workforce. If supports are the key to maintaining one's status within the community, then this conclusion can easily be expanded to include virtually all levels and types of disabilities. Unfortunately, people with disabling conditions are vastly underrepresented in integrated employment settings and residences. This is also the case for participation in active recreational activities (Hayden, Lakin, Hill, Bruininks, & Copher, 1992). According to Lakin and Bruininks (1985), a continuum of services approach, or one that ranges from highly integrated to highly segregated, clearly discriminates against those clients who have the most severe handicapping conditions. This argues for a redistribution of fiscal supports and support services so that they are tied to individuals in their residences and employment settings, and to supports (e.g., career education and training, transportation) that are made available within communities. The greater this redistribution is, the more commonplace it will become to see individuals with disabilities working, recreating, and residing in their communities.

LIVING ARRANGEMENTS AND EMPLOYMENT SETTINGS

Figure 18.1 depicts a continuum of services for each of three outcomes: educational, employment, and residential. The continuum runs from highly segregated services and settings that expect and perhaps foster extreme dependency to those that are integrated, or normalized, and that require either a high degree of independence or considerable support. Although this continuum is well entrenched across each of the categories, there has been some realization that severity of disability should not determine one's place on a waiting list for services, nor should it determine whether the setting in which the individual is served is integrated. Supported employment models have taken the lead in operationalizing this realization by providing citizens with severe

disabilities the opportunity to work in integrated settings with whatever supports they require. Much of this success may be owed to the priority of school–to–work transition that was established by the U.S. Department of Education (Will, 1984). This priority fostered collaboration within and between educational programs and service agencies. Since then, the meaning of the term *transition* has been expanded to include transitions to all aspects of community life.

Residential Settings

Numerous residential options are available to, or imposed upon, persons with disabilities. A full range of living arrangements has been identified in the literature (Baker, Seltzer, & Seltzer, 1977; Heal, Novak, Sigelman, & Switzky, 1980; Lensink, 1980; Thompson, 1977), and has been summarized by Pancsofar and Blackwell (1986). This

	Educational Settings	Employment Settings	Residential Settings
LEAST RESTRICTIVE	Regular Classroom	Competitive Employment	Independent Living
	Regular Classroom with Consultation	Supported, Integrated Competitive Employment	Supported Living in Own Apartment/Home
	Separate Class (self-contained)	Sheltered Employment in Integrated Setting (Enclave)	Supported Living in Group Home/Apartment:
	Separate School		small, transitional
		Sheltered Employment:	large, long-term
	Residential Facility or School	transitional employment	Nursing Home:
		extended employment	intermediate care facility (ICF)
	Homebound/ Hospital Environment	work activities	convalescent or county home
MOST RESTRICTIVE			State/Private Residential Facility

Figure 18.1. Continuum of educational, vocational, and residential outcomes associated with a "readiness" approach to service delivery.

range is presented in Table 18.1. Although clear differences exist between the degrees of independence required to function (with no support) within some of these options (e.g., institutions vs. nursing homes vs. group homes vs. independent living), in total they should be viewed as a list of residential classifications, not as a strict continuum related to the residential services generally afforded persons with disabilities.

Employment Settings

Following are brief descriptions of the settings in the employment continuum, from competitive to sheltered.

Independently, Competitively Employed

Competitive employment is work that produces valued goods or services at minimum wage or above, offers opportunities for advancements, and is in an integrated setting (Rusch, 1986). Integrated settings are those that include, primarily, persons without disabilities. Competitive employment settings, compared to others, are the most advantageous because they offer greater wages and benefits, integration with nondisabled persons, normalized settings, greater opportunity for advancement, and improved perceptions by family and friends (Wehman, Renzaglia, & Bates, 1985).

Persons who are independently and competitively employed have not or no longer receive assistance related to their jobs outside of that made available by the employer to all employees.

Supported, Integrated Competitive Employment

These settings offer the same advantages as those associated with nonsupported competitive employment but are for individuals who require some degree of short- or long-term assistance to

function within their job settings. The types of supports that individuals with disabilities might receive related to this option include job matching, modifications, and placement; on-the-job training; in-service training of supervisors and coworkers; advocacy by coworkers; transportation; ongoing evaluation; and follow-up.

Sheltered Employment in Integrated Settings: Enclaves

Short- or long-term employment of a small group of individuals with disabilities in local business or industry composes this category of employment. Employees in these positions are provided with intense training and supervision. Wages are usually based on production but generally fall below that of minimum wage standards. Enclaves may be well integrated with nondisabled individuals (i.e., workers with disabilities work, eat lunch, and take breaks alongside nondisabled workers), or they may occupy a segregated area within the setting, or some combination thereof. Depending upon the extent to which they are integrated, persons with disabilities in these settings benefit to varying degrees from appropriate work and social models.

Sheltered Employment in Segregated Settings

Transitional Employment. Individuals in transitional employment are placed on a temporary basis; the intent is to afford them the option of competitive employment following evaluation and subsequent training. In this and the extended employment option following, workers earn a percentage of minimum wage.

Extended Employment. This option may include either *sheltered employment* or *long-term work-adjustment* status (Wehman, Kregel, & Barkus, 1985). Sheltered employee status has, historically, often been considered terminal, although this is more likely a function of the numerous

Table 18.1.   Living Arrangements: Available Options and Residential Placements

1. INDEPENDENT LIVING: A site where an individual lives with a roommate, a spouse, or alone; usually an apartment or duplex, but occasionally a house.

    Single-Family Homes: A free standing single-family home in an average residential neighborhood.

    Shared Homes: Two or more persons with disabilities may prefer to share a single-family home and the cost of needed modification. Often the sharing is between those with disabilities and congenial, ablebodied persons.

    Individual or Shared Apartments: In large or small buildings, apartments occupied by a single person with disabilities, or shared by two or more, have been used successfully with or without services, depending on need.

    Groups of Individual Apartments: Groups of apartments—on one floor or scattered throughout the building or scattered among several buildings in an apartment complex.

    Dwellings in New Apartment Buildings: Some percentage of the living units in a large public or private apartment building can be designed for those with disabilities.

    Elderly Housing Project: Projects for older people that are designed with special facilities may have a percentage of the units set aside for persons with disabilities, with provision of the additional services needed.

    Congregate Housing: A residential environment—assisted independent living—that incorporates shelter and services for the functionally impaired and/or marginally socially adjusted older persons or persons with disabilities, enabling them to maintain or return to a semiindependent lifestyle and avoid institutionalization.

    Residential Hotels: Relatively large structures that provide private rooms and baths (not apartments) are adaptable for persons with disabilities, with housekeeping and meal service available at commercial rates.

2. NATURAL OR ADOPTIVE HOME: The home of one's parents, usually natural parents.

3. OTHER RELATIVE'S HOME: The home of a resident's sibling, grandparent, aunt, uncle, or offspring.

4. FRIEND'S HOME: The home of someone who has befriended the resident or the resident's family.

5. FOSTER FAMILY CARE: Serving five or fewer adults with mental retardation in a family's own home; families are not governed by board of directors, and they collect monthly payments for the care of residents.

6. DEVELOPMENTAL FOSTER HOME: Similar to natural homes, foster homes, and adoptive homes, these homes should offer a living situation to a child that encourages a sense of identity and security in a homelike setting for up to three children. Placements are often made with the expressed objective that a child will remain with his or her developmental foster family until he or she reaches adulthood. Developmental foster-home parents are trained to extend the services of the developmental center or public school program into the home environment.

7. GROUP HOMES: Homes that house as few as 2 or as many as 100 children or adults with developmental disabilities. Five or more such persons of both sexes may live in a relatively large home (purchased, rented, or constructed), assisted by house managers or counselors and providing access to any other services, internally and externally required.

    Small Group Home: Serving 10 or fewer adults with mental retardation.

    Medium Group Home: Serving 11 to 20 adults with mental retardation.

(continues)

Table 18.1. *Continued*

Large Group Home: Serving 21 to 40 adults with mental retardation.

Mini-institution: Serving 41 to 80 adults with mental retardation.

Mixed Group Home: Serving adults with mental retardation and people with previous mental illness and often nonretarded people as well in group homes or rest homes.

Group Home for Older Adults: Serving only older retarded people and often nonretarded people as well in group homes or rest homes.

8. NURSING HOMES: Include a variety of residential alternatives, all providing continuing medical care for anyone who needs it. The convalescent home and intermediate care facility are specially licensed nursing homes. Nursing homes are nearly always privately owned and are expected to make a profit for their owners.

Intermediate Care Facilities (ICF): Licensed as a nursing home, making it eligible for Federal Medicaid Support (Title XIX) of the Social Security Act and its Amendments. Two classes are distinguished according to size: 15 and under, and 16 and over. The larger homes must have a nurse (LPN) on duty at all times, whereas the smaller homes need only have one on call.

Convalescent Homes: A nursing home whose residents are expected to stay for a reasonably short period of time for rehabilitation before they return to the community.

The County Home: Type of nursing home whose residents are expected to stay for a reasonably short period of time for rehabilitation before they return to the community.

9. BOARDING HOMES: Homes where the resident is provided room and board for a fee, but no other services are contracted. These homes house individuals of varying abilities. They are usually not classified as group- or family-care homes.

10. HOSTEL: Similar to residential hotel but a hostel is usually supervised and is considered transitional or temporary.

11. SHELTERED VILLAGES: Provide a segregated, self-contained community for adults with mental retardation and live-in staff in a cluster of buildings usually located in a rural setting.

12. PUBLIC RESIDENTIAL FACILITY (PRF): State institutions. Until recently these were very large, typically having about 1,500 residents and occasionally having over 5,000, but today they average only about 500 residents each, and many have fewer than 50.

13. PRIVATE RESIDENTIAL FACILITY: A variety of privately owned and foundation-owned residential alternatives. Some of these are expensive, highly visible, multiple-treatment centers; some are largely custodial facilities; and some are communes that feature an idyllic life for residents with and without disabilities.

14. WORKSHOP-DORMITORIES: Living unit and a work-training program are associated administratively and sometimes physically.

15. MENTAL HOSPITAL: An institution for individuals with mental illness.

16. PRISONS: A building, usually with cells, where convicted criminals are confined or where accused persons are held while awaiting trial.

Note. Based on *A User's Guide to Community Entry for the Severely Handicapped* by E. Pancsofar and R. Blackwell, 1986, Albany: State University of New York Press.

barriers to competitive employment and independent living that are addressed later. Persons in long-term work-adjustment positions typically require great expenditures in occupational, behavioral, social, and other services to move into sheltered or extended employee status.

Work Activities Programs. Individuals considered (by the standards of those by whom they are served) to be unemployable or in need of prevocational skill training to advance along the continuum of employment options can earn a token wage for work completed. Activities programs also provide numerous services and activities such as recreational activities, daily living and social skills training, and work skills development.

Although sheltered employment settings provide daily maintenance for many individuals and additional opportunities for some, they provide few, if any, services that could not be delivered in less restrictive settings, given adequate supports within a community-based service delivery model.

Some of the disadvantages associated with sheltered settings include low wages and minimal benefits, limited opportunities for advancement due to a narrow scope of job training, limited exposure to appropriate social models, and perpetuation of public misconceptions regarding the capabilities of persons with disabilities.

Although there are numerous drawbacks to sheltered home and work settings, it is important to note that they are far more predominant than supported service settings and that, due to fiscal and philosophic factors, they will probably remain so for some time. Therefore, although the service delivery systems are moving toward a zero-reject policy of integration, it is imperative that those in less than integrated settings employ the best methods of habilitation available.

Housing Support and Supported Living

The categories of residential settings shown in Figure 18.1 represent the general continuum of

placements or options associated with serving individuals with developmental disabilities. Independent living arrangements include many types of residences. Individuals are considered to be living independently, however, only if they are receiving no supports other than those generally available to those who do not have disabilities. Supported living arrangements include assistance in maintaining community status in either a residence not owned, leased, or managed by an agency, or a residence owned, leased, or managed by an agency.

The second of these two options includes, primarily, supervised living in an apartment or group home that has been built or leased by the same agency that provides the support. The degree of supervision provided in group homes varies and depends on the type of residence it is. Today, group homes range from small (a few individuals) to large (10 or so, although group homes in which 20 or more people reside still exist), and from transitional in nature to long term. Transitional group homes are generally those in which people reside while they are either preparing to move to a more independent living arrangement (a readiness approach) or waiting for supports to be made available in less restrictive settings. Some individuals who reside in group homes do so on a long-term basis, primarily because of a lack of the available supports they require to live in more normalized residences. This situation occurs because agency costs are tied to facilities. Although group homes have greatly contributed to the integration of individuals with disabilities into the community as well as have kept people from living in more restrictive settings, such as nursing homes or institutions, the fact that the buildings themselves and the support services share the same budgets means that less is available to spend on supporting individuals in the mainstream. (Note: Many group homes are actually classified as Intermediate Care Facilities for the Mentally Retarded, or ICFs/MR, and fall under the heading of nursing facilities.)

Whereas a continuum-of-care model is intended to provide whatever level of assistance individuals need, perverse funding incentives, particularly at state and local levels (Copeland & Iverson, 1985), have unnecessarily made it less expensive to provide care in more restrictive settings.

Some individuals require assistance to function within their residences, whether they own, rent, or, in some cases, share them with their families. Just as the supported employment model has demonstrated that individuals can, if given proper support, hold real, paying jobs in integrated employment settings, there is a growing, although somewhat younger, movement to provide individuals with whatever supports they need to own, rent, or otherwise reside in non–agency-managed homes; regardless of disability. This is a consumer-centered model, which is generally referred to as an individualized, person-centered, or *housing–support* strategy to assist individuals to acquire normalized living options within their communities (Racino & Taylor, 1989). This approach is part of the conceptualization of supported living discussed previously. In a broader sense, it addresses not only living arrangements but also other aspects of community life, such as employment and recreation. A premise of the supported living model of community living is that living in one's community is a matter of individual rights, not of placement decisions made by significant others. This supported living approach rejects the continuum-of-services model and the principle of least restrictive environment as they pertain to current community living options. Despite ample demonstration that individuals with severe disabilities are, if given adequate supports, able to function within their respective communities (Hill, Bruininks, & Lakin, 1983), there is "still a pervasive tendency to believe that people have to acquire certain prerequisite skills before they're eligible or 'ready' to live where they choose" (Karan, Grantfield, & Suiter, 1990, p. 2).

Racino and Taylor (1989) have summarized the problems associated with the continuum concept:

1. People with severe disabilities are relegated to the most restrictive end of the continuum.

2. The most restrictive placements, such as institutions, are not necessary.

3. The continuum implies that people need to leave their homes every time they acquire new skills.

4. The most restrictive placements do not prepare people for the least restrictive placements.

5. The continuum concept confuses restrictions of people's rights with intensity of their support and service needs.

6. The continuum directs attention to physical settings rather than to the services and supports people need to be integrated in the community.

The major barrier to housing–support strategies is the generally accepted, facility-based funding approach to residential services. The development of facility-based residences, predominantly group homes or apartments, intermediate care facilities and other nursing homes, and residential facilities (i.e., institutions), is determined not by the community living support needs of individuals but by perceived group needs within a continuum-of-services model. This approach results in the construction, purchase, and rental by agencies of a variety of residences, thus precluding the utilization of funds for expanding community living support options.

In order to receive services within a facility-based model, which is typical in most communities, individuals must reside in licensed, agency-owned or agency-rented residences run by state; private; or private, nonprofit agencies. Leaving the agency-run facility means the loss of services, because the services are tied to the residence (i.e., the services do not generally follow the person). A partial solution to this problem is the Home and Community-Based Medicaid Waiver, which provides for services to be delivered in alternative settings such as the first option (i.e., supported living in a residence not owned, leased, or managed by an agency). Because it eliminates the cost associated with the agency facility, this option can provide a way to increase the level of supports to meet individuals' requirements for living in a preferred setting. Although many individuals with disabilities may be able to apply such benefits to community integration services, as is the case with Wisconsin's Medicaid Waiver Community Integration Program, few are even aware of such an option, nor are their parents, guardians, or advocates. Even when they are aware, few communities have developed programs that are comprehensive enough to allow persons to exercise such options (i.e., there are not ample support systems to allow individuals to contract out, or buy, the services they require to live independent of state-developed residences).

For persons to benefit from the supported living approach identified here, housing, support services, and funding options must all be available and coordinated. Racino and Taylor (1989) have identified some of these options in relation to one's place of residence. These and others are presented in Table 18.2.

The provision or coordination of support services is the responsibility of the agencies with whom the person with disabilities contracts. Such agencies may be state- or county-funded, or they may be private and paid through reimbursement for services. Grassroots organizations, or those consisting of families, friends, and advocates of individuals with disabilities, including service providers, influential members of the community, and professionals, can affect policy through advocacy as well as help to coordinate and supplement services (e.g., provide transportation or drop-in visits). One key element in a supported living model is that service providers do not also function as landlords. This allows the services provided by the agency and designated service personnel to follow a consumer to a new home or apartment, if the individual still wishes

---

Table 18.2. Living Arrangements, Support Strategies, and Funding Strategies Available to Consumers with Disabilities in a Housing–Support (i.e., Non–Facility-Based) Supported Living Model

Living Arrangements	Support Strategies (Examples of agency and other supports)	Funding Strategies
Own/rent own house, apartment, condominium, etc.	Live-in employee (physical/household care, meal, skill development)	Salary and wages
		Trusts for housing
Own and lease out part of residence	Drop-in/on-call employee development (maintenance, emergencies)	Subsidies
Jointly own/rent with roommate(s)	Volunteers (errands, shopping)	Medicaid waiver programs
Live alone, or with nonsupport roommate(s) in parent/guardian-owned or -rented residence (without owner)	Advocates (coordination, finances, friendship)	SSI
		HOW—income tax credits
	Paid companion (recreation, interaction)	Cooperatives
Live in cooperative	Adaptations/modifications (accessibility augmentative communication devices)	Purchases through housing associations
Foster home	Transportation (work, medical, education/training, recreation)	Private subsidies
	Family/friends	
	Acquisition of housing (finding housing, roommates, leasing/buying, furnishings)	

to employ them. In a facility-based approach, agencies must fill slots as they open. The slots are filled on the basis of the type and severity of a person's disability, not on his or her desire to move into it. In addition, individuals may become trapped in a facility-owned residence because the services they receive cannot be provided if they live elsewhere.

Restrictive settings are created by the belief that they are necessary. They are perceived to be necessary because resources are not sufficient to provide, on a consistent and comprehensive basis, the level of services required to assist individuals with disabilities of all levels of severity to live within their communities in the places of their choosing (or that, on their behalves, are advocated as normalized). Because most individuals with disabilities do not receive the support that would allow them to live in typical community residences, they do not live in them. This fact reinforces the misconception that individuals who are living in more restrictive settings do so because they are unable to live in less restrictive settings, and leads to the erroneous conclusion that a continuum of restrictive settings is necessary.

The skills, instructional methods, and service delivery approaches presented in the following sections are relevant to the integration of citizens with disabilities into their respective communities, regardless of their current living arrangements.

COMMUNITY LIVING SKILLS AND INSTRUCTION

Individuals are called upon to exhibit hundreds of skills each day, whether in their homes, on a bus, doing their jobs, talking with their coworkers, buying groceries, or playing softball in a city recreational league. Some of these skills are setting specific, whereas others are relevant across a variety of environments. Operating a machine in a plant, cleaning a particular office building, or using a particular type of microwave oven in one's own kitchen are examples of setting-specific skills. The area of social skills, such as introducing oneself to someone or asking for assistance, exemplifies the latter in that it is an integral component of interactions in virtually any setting in which people are found (e.g., work, home, school, shopping).

Recreation and Leisure Skills

Growing attention has been given to recreation and leisure skills in relationship to community integration. Hayden et al. (1992) reported that the community involvement of their sample of individuals with mental retardation, although greater than that of an earlier study (Hill & Bruininks, 1981), was still less than desirable. Individuals tended to be involved in passive leisure activities (e.g., watching TV) as opposed to active recreation (e.g., bowling). Although it has been documented that individuals with disabilities who live in community-based facilities are more likely to have friends and to socialize outside of their residences than are individuals living in state facilities (Anderson, Lakin, Bruininks, & Hill, 1987), mere community placement (if group homes can validly be called such) does not ensure recreational and social integration. Almost half the sample in the study by Hayden and colleagues (1992) reported having no friend. Moon and Bunker (1987) found that involvement in recreational activities may help prevent institutionalization and be related to improvements in other skills. Thus, the importance of individuals' involvement in recreation and leisure activities, particularly within their communities, is being increasingly recognized. Demchack (1994) has provided guidelines for selection of leisure activities. Foremost of these guidelines is integration with individuals without disabilities in a range of activities, such as social clubs, dances, shopping, and video arcades. Demchack (1994) also stressed age appropriateness, preference, adaptations to allow participation, partial participation, and feasibility of the activity. Concerns related to the latter are addressed within a supported living model by providing whatever supports are necessary (transportation, instruction, physical assistance) in order to facilitate integration into the full range of recreational activities offered within the community.

Best Practices in Instruction

The postschool results associated with special needs populations are perhaps best explained by the extent to which known effective teaching and transition strategies are *not* implemented. As Wehman (1990) stated, "Unfortunately, school systems either do not implement these practices or do not implement them well enough longitudinally, that is, over the duration of the students' tenure in school" (p. 17). There are, regardless of the skill being taught or the disability or age of the person learning, a set of best practices related to the instruction of independent living skills:

- teaching in integrated settings
- teaching functional skills
- teaching in target settings
- teaching early
- teaching for generalization

Teaching in Integrated Settings

Hasazi et al. (1985) found that students who had received special education services for mental retardation, learning disabilities, or behavioral disorders were more likely to be employed at 1 to 4 years postschool if they had received educational services through a resource program rather than through a self-contained classroom. Job retention has also been linked to integrated, chronologically age-appropriate schools (Wehman, Kregel, et al., 1985).

Segregated settings provide individuals with less exposure to appropriate models, often include models of inappropriate social behavior, and, by their very nature, do not afford the oppor-

tunity for reinforcement of prosocial skills in varied settings and with different people. Integrated settings, conversely, allow for imitation and reinforcement of appropriate interactional skills under natural conditions.

Integrated settings should be utilized in both school and community-based programs. For example, instruction in grocery shopping or bowling should not involve segregated activities with large groups of individuals with disabilities within otherwise integrated settings. The appropriate shopping, bowling, and social models offered by nondisabled peers are likely to go unnoticed in large, segregated groups. Segregated groups of individuals with disabilities within school and community settings are also likely to reinforce any stereotypes held by community members.

Teaching Functional Skills

Functional skills are those that directly define independent living. They are the skills that are integral to one's daily existence. Nonfunctional skills are those that do not, in and of themselves, relate to specific aspects of an individual's daily living. For example, sorting colored circles is a nonfunctional skill, whereas identifying colors on traffic lights while learning pedestrian skills is functional. Coloring coins on a worksheet is nonfunctional; selecting coins from one's pocket and buying a can of soda pop from a vending machine is functional.

The degree to which curricula are functional has been linked to success in the community. Participation in vocational education classes during high school and holding a part-time summer or high school job have both been linked to greater independence, as measured by employment status after exiting school (Hasazi et al., 1985; Hasazi, Johnson, Hasazi, Gordon, & Hull, 1989). Hasazi et al.'s (1985) data also indicated that there was no advantage to having participated in a work experience program over not having participated, at least with respect to postschool employment. One explanation for the apparent advantage of vocational education courses and actual employment over work experience programs in predicting future employment is that many work experience programs do not provide nearly the depth of training that vocational courses do; the latter utilize direct instruction to focus on mastery of a set of skills related to specific, community-referenced jobs (i.e., those which are available locally).

The preceding data indicate that persons with disabilities benefit from having taken vocational education courses; however, students with more severe disabilities are less likely to participate in vocational education courses and summer job programs, such as those associated with the Job Training Partnership Act. This finding is certainly not due to students' inability to benefit from such experiences. Limiting students' access to meaningful involvement in such curricula is a program decision made by significant others because of a real or perceived lack of supports; it does not necessarily reflect students' preferences or potentials.

These points reinforce the significance of providing students who have disabilities with the support services they require to be able to participate in school and postschool programs that emphasize the teaching of community-referenced competencies through functional curricula—not only those related to postschool employment but also those across all skill domains related to independent living.

Teaching in Target Settings

Generally speaking, the importance of providing instruction in the setting(s) in which a skill is to be performed, that is, the target setting(s), increases as the severity of a disability increases and as the similarity between a target setting and the instructional setting decreases (Snell, 1987). People with severe mental retardation, for example, are generally less likely to have dishwashing skills generalize from one home to another than are individuals with labels of mild retardation. The degree of transfer can be expected to decrease further as the differences in the stimuli associated with dishwashing in the different residences in-

crease. Some of these might include differences in the faucets (e.g., a single hot–cold lever vs. separate hot and cold handles), one sink compartment as opposed to two, different cupboard locations, or more or different distractors (e.g., more noise from the street or a roommate, different wallpaper). Even skills acquired by people with mild or moderate disabilities in one setting, however, cannot be expected to transfer to a different setting. Subtle differences in lighting, distance to objects, or the height of counters might affect the transfer of the practiced skills of individuals with mild or moderate visual or physical impairments.

To increase the likelihood that persons with disabilities will be able to perform functional skills in relevant settings, instruction in those settings, that is, community-based instruction, is extremely important. In addition, instruction using stimuli that vary but that are of the same class (e.g., different sink types, vending machines, lamps, fast-food restaurants), to whatever extent possible, can assist in the generalization of skills and maintenance of one's community living status. Additional benefits associated with community-based instruction are described by Wehman, Renzaglia, et al. (1985), including sampling of community reinforcers, increased awareness by nondisabled people of the presence and competence of people with disabilities, exposure to appropriate role models, elevated teacher/trainer expectations through observation of students' functional competencies, increased parental hope and interest through sons' or daughters' successful integrations, and improvements in curriculum selection and development through practice.

Teaching Early

Many individuals with disabilities enter school with substantial deficits in many skill areas. The general practice of delaying their instruction in functional, community-referenced skills until they are in secondary school may explain many of the poor postschool adjustments associated with having a disability. To improve on these outcomes, schools need to utilize age-appropriate, community-referenced curricula and community-based instruction in primary school and earlier.

Numerous curricula are available for teaching community living skills. One of the most comprehensive and functional is Brolin's (1993) *Life-Centered Career Education*, which consists of three broad skill domains, or curriculum areas, including daily living skills, personal–social skills, and occupational guidance and preparation skills. The three curriculum areas, along with their respective competencies and subcompetencies, are presented in Table 18.3. The curriculum is primarily competency based and includes a structure for rating students as they improve and demonstrate competencies within each domain. It consists of three phases: awareness, exploration, and preparation. All of the phases focus on the same competencies, but instruction varies according to the goals and general grade level of the particular student(s). In this way, younger students are exposed to community living skills at earlier ages than is typical. The curriculum focuses heavily on independent living skills and has great utility in that it allows for community-based instruction, is both comprehensive and structured, and can be adapted to address the individual characteristics of students' communities.

Teaching for Generalization

Although skill transfer is an instructional goal, it is also a challenge, particularly as the severity of disability increases. Although it is important to teach in the target setting, doing so may not always be possible. For example, traveling to the laundromat to teach the use of washers and dryers and the techniques for folding clothes may not be supported by a school's budget or administration. Many teachers rely on classroom simulations to teach relevant skills. Using washers and dryers in the school to simulate the stimulus conditions at the laundromat may help in generalizing loading and unloading clothes into and from the machines and in measuring and pouring detergent. Bring-

ing canned goods into the classroom may help in generalizing the skill of picking out those particular items in the classroom to finding them on the shelf in the grocery store. However, the degree of differences between the machine in the classroom and those in the laundromat (coin operated in the laundromat, differences in the dials and temperature settings), their relative positions (side by side in the classroom but separated in the laundromat), and other differences in the settings (people, noises, tables, lighting) might result in a failure to generalize skills across settings. Similarly, picking out one canned item from 10 on a table or simulated grocery store shelf in the classroom is very different than finding a particular aisle in the store and locating the particular item from among others that are numerous and similar. As a rule, the more similar the simulation is to the target setting, the greater is the likelihood that transfer will occur. Therefore, when classroom simulations are utilized in instruction, it is important for the teacher/trainer to program for maximum generalization (Stokes & Osnes, 1986) by

- using common physical stimuli (using real cans or packages rather than drawings or worksheets);

- using common social stimuli (inviting a local employer to come and conduct practice job interviews);

- using a sufficient number of examples of correct responses (teaching a student different greetings);

- using a sufficient number of examples of stimuli that precede the response (teaching a student to throw out different types of spoiled foods); and

- using natural reinforcers (selecting the correct vending change earns a can of pop).

These and additional concerns related to promoting generalizations are discussed in detail elsewhere (Stokes, 1992; Stokes & Baer, 1977; Stokes & Osnes, 1986).

Table 18.3.   Brolin's (1993) Life-Centered Career Education Curriculum Competencies and Subcompetencies

Curriculum Area	Competency	Subcompetencies	
Daily Living Skills	1. Managing family finances	1. Identify model and make correct change	2. Make wise expenditures
	2. Selecting, managing, and maintaining a home	6. Select adequate housing	7. Maintain a home
	3. Caring for personal needs	10. Dress appropriately	11. Exhibit proper grooming and hygiene
	4. Raising children, enriching family living	14. Prepare for adjustment to marriage	15. Prepare for raising children (physical care)
	5. Buying and preparing food	18. Demonstrate appropriate eating skills	19. Plan balanced meals
	6. Buying and caring for clothing	24. Wash clothing	25. Iron and store clothing
	7. Engaging in civic activities	28. Generally understand local laws and government	29. Generally understand federal government
	8. Utilizing recreation and leisure	34. Participate actively in group activities	35. Know activities and available community resources
	9. Getting around the community (mobility)	40. Demonstrate knowledge of traffic rules and safety practices	41. Demonstrate knowledge and use of various means of transportation
Personal–Social Skills	10. Achieving self-awareness	43. Attain a sense of body	44. Identify interests and abilities
	11. Acquiring self-confidence	48. Express feelings of worth	49. Tell how others see him/her
	12. Achieving socially responsible behavior	53. Know character traits needed for acceptance	54. Know proper behavior in public places
	13. Maintaining good interpersonal skills	58. Know how to listen and respond	59. Know how to make and maintain friendships
	14. Achieving independence	62. Understand impact of behaviors upon others	63. Understand self-organization
	15. Achieving problem-solving skills	66. Differentiate bipolar concepts	67. Understand the need for goals
	16. Communicating adequately with others	71. Recognize emergency situations	72. Read at level needed for future goals
Occupational Guidance and Preparation	17. Knowing and exploring occupational possibilities	76. Identify the personal values met through work	77. Identify the societal values met through work
	18. Selecting and planning occupational choices	82. Identify major occupational needs	83. Identify major occupational interests
	19. Exhibiting appropriate work habits and behaviors	87. Follow directions	88. Work with others
	20. Exhibiting sufficient physical-manual skills	94. Demonstrate satisfactory balance and coordination	95. Demonstrate satisfactory manual dexterity
	21. Obtaining a specific occupational skill		
	22. Seeking, securing, and maintaining employment	98. Search for a job	99. Apply for a job

(continues)

Table 18.3. *Continued*

Subcompetencies (continued)

3. Obtain and use bank and credit facilities	4. Keep basic financial records	5. Calculate and pay taxes	
8. Use basic appliances and tools	9. Maintain home exterior		
12. Demonstrate knowledge of physical fitness, nutrition, and weight control	13. Demonstrate knowledge of common illness prevention and treatment		
16. Prepare for raising children (psychological care)	17. Practice family safety in the home		
20. Purchase food	21. Prepare meals	22. Clean food preparation areas	23. Store food
26. Perform simple mending	27. Purchase clothing		
30. Understand citizenship rights and responsibilities	31. Understand registration and voting procedures	32. Understand Selective Service procedures	33. Understand civil rights and responsibilities when questioned by the law
36. Understand recreational values	37. Use recreational facilities in the community	38. Plan and choose activities wisely	39. Plan vacations
42. Drive a car			
45. Identify emotions	46. Identify needs	47. Understand the physical self	
50. Accept praise	51. Accept criticism	52. Develop confidence in self	
55. Develop respect for the rights and properties of others	56. Recognize authority and follow instructions	57. Recognize personal roles	
60. Establish appropriate heterosexual relationships	61. Know how to establish close relationships		
64. Develop goal-seeking behavior	65. Strive toward self-actualization		
68. Look at alternatives	69. Anticipate consequences	70. Know where to find good advice	
73. Write at the level needed for future goals	74. Speak adequately for understanding	75. Understand the subtleties of communication	
78. Identify the remunerative aspects of work	79. Understand classification of jobs into different occupational systems	80. Identify occupational opportunities available locally	81. Identify sources of occupational information
84. Identify occupational aptitudes	85. Identify requirements of appropriate and available jobs	86. Make realistic occupational choices	
89. Work at a satisfactory rate	90. Accept supervision	91. Recognize the importance of attendance and punctuality	92. Meet demands for quality work
96. Demonstrate satisfactory stamina and endurance	97. Demonstrate satisfactory sensory discrimination		
100. Interview for a job	101. Adjust to competitive standards	102. Maintain postschool occupational adjustment	

93. Demonstrate occupational safety

Note. From *Life-Centered Career Education* (4th ed.) by D. E. Brolin, 1993, Reston, VA: Council for Exceptional Children.

Domestic and Community Skills

Being able to function safely within and to maintain one's residence is an important aspect of independence. Individuals who lack basic home skills are put at risk for losing their community living status (Cuvo & Davis, 1981; Schalock & Lilley, 1986). It is therefore important for parents, teachers, group home and support service providers, advocates, and other individuals charged with providing or organizing community living instruction and supports for persons with disabilities to be able to design, implement, and evaluate instructional programs in the areas of domestic and other community living skills.

Domestic skills are those that individuals utilize to maintain themselves within their homes and to maintain their residences and respective grounds. These steps should be followed in designing and implementing instructional programs for domestic skills:

1. Assess present or potential (target) settings

2. Assess the learner's skills

3. Prioritize skills

4. Task analyze skills

5. Provide task analytic instruction

These steps are exemplified in the following case study.

•••

CASE EXAMPLE: TEACHING MICROWAVE COOKING TO AN ADOLESCENT WITH SEVERE MENTAL RETARDATION

Participant and Setting. Jenny is a 13-year-old adolescent with an educational label of severe mental retardation. Her expressive language skills are limited to some use of manual signing. Her self-care skills are good in the area of personal hygiene, partially because of the support she has received from her parents, with whom she lives. The training was conducted at their home before Jenny left for school.

Rationale. Microwave ovens are relatively common in today's households. They have an advantage over conventional ovens in that they are safer; they have no hot surfaces and "always" shut themselves off. The likelihood of starting fires or producing toxic fumes is virtually eliminated with their use. Although prepackaged microwave food products can be expensive, many are not. They are comparable in price to their conventional-oven counterparts. Learning how to cook simple, inexpensive meals in microwave ovens may assist individuals with severe disabilities to function more independently within their communities. Jenny's parents are excited to have her move into a supported living setting when she reaches adult age. They are aware that independent living skills should be established before that time to help facilitate the transition.

Task Analysis. The task analysis (Table 18.4) was developed in Jenny's kitchen by the trainer, with the help of Jenny's parents. The steps in the task analysis were specifically referenced to the microwave oven in Jenny's kitchen, a common brand with digital touch controls. The two frozen microwave breakfasts selected were those that Jenny commonly eats. Because scalding steam can be released when microwaved products are unsealed, a safety component was added to the task analysis: inserting a fork through the covering on the food tray (Steps 7 and 8) before putting the tray in the oven. In addition, the task analysis included the use of potholders whenever Jenny took food out of the oven or put food into it. Even though there was no danger associated with putting cold foods into the oven, her parents and the trainer believed that always using potholders would prevent any possible burns that might occur if Jenny made an error in discriminating putting in from taking out. Also, consistent use of potholders might transfer to other dangerous scenarios (e.g., picking up a hot casserole or microwaved tray at the request of someone who thought it was cold).

Table 18.4. Task Analysis of Safe Microwave Cooking of Frozen Breakfasts

---

1. Open freezer.
2. Select box from door:
   —pancakes with sausage
   —waffles
3. Close door.
4. Walk to counter by microwave oven.
5. Open box.
6. Take out tray and set on counter.
7. Get fork from drawer (close drawer).
8. Poke fork through tray covering twice (set fork down).
9. Get two potholders from drawer (close drawer).
10. Open oven door to at least 90°.
11. Using potholders, place tray in center of oven.
12. Place potholders on counter.
13. Close oven door.
14. Push "cook" on oven.
15. Find cooking time on back of box.
16. Push numbers on oven.
17. Push "start" on oven.
18. Set table (separate task analysis).
19. Open oven door when timer sounds (beeps).
20. Pick up potholders.
21. Using potholders, take out tray and set on counter.
22. While holding tray with left hand with potholder, pull off cover with right hand.
23. Discard cover and box in trash.
24. Using both potholders, place tray at kitchen table.
25. Put away potholders (close drawer).
26. Return to table and eat.

Teaching Procedure. Baseline probes on the entire task indicated that Jenny required assistance beginning with Step 3, closing the freezer door after picking out a breakfast box. To provide two trials per day, two meals had to be cooked. The first meal Jenny cooked was eaten by one of her parents. The trials were conducted each day with a constant time-delay procedure. The controlling prompt was a verbal prompt with physical guidance. Following 0-sec delay trials, for which all steps were prompted with no delay between steps, the delay time was set at 3 seconds. During these sessions, Jenny was provided with an initial task request, "Jenny, make your breakfast." Correct responses were praised. After a correct response or the delivery of a controlling prompt (e.g., trainer said, "Jenny, open the box" while providing the minimal physical guidance necessary to produce the response), the trainer would deliver the controlling prompt for the next response if Jenny did not initiate the response within 3 seconds. This procedure was repeated until all steps were performed or prompted. Probes were collected twice per week by Jenny's cooking a breakfast prior to the day's training session. Step 18, "Set table," was actually a separate task analysis of 13 steps. Setting the table while the food was cooking seemed an appropriate use of time that Jenny would otherwise have spent waiting. It also decreased the likelihood that she might leave the kitchen and not be able to hear the timer sound.

Results. Jenny was able to reach criterion (three consecutive correct sessions of two trials each) within 12 sessions on all steps except pushing the correct numbers on the touch control (Step 16). This step was trained separately by having Jenny match the numbers on enlarged copies of the instructions to those on the touch control. The size of the enlarged instructions was gradually reduced until Jenny was able to complete the step while using the actual packages.

Mobility Skills and Transportation

Orientation is the ability to establish one's position in relation to the environment. Mobility involves moving safely from one point to another (Lowenfeld, 1973). Orientation and mobility training was originally developed to assist individuals with visual impairments. Mobility specialists provide training in the use of aids such as electronic canes and in travel within the community. Over the last two decades there has been a growing realization that orientation and (particularly) mobility training is appropriate for members of other disability groups as well, including individuals with multiple or severe disabilities. As a result, a significant amount of research and training in the area of mobility training is available. Studies have demonstrated that individuals with severe disabilities can learn mobility skills such as street crossing (Matson, 1980) and riding buses (Sowers, Rusch, & Hudson, 1979).

One's mobility in the community includes movement within and between settings. Examples of mobility within a setting include movement from the bedroom to the bathroom, from a wheelchair to the toilet, from downstairs to the upstairs, from gymnasium to the locker room, or from one's work station or office to the cafeteria. Mobility between settings might include travel from home to school or work and vice versa, from the grocery store to home, from the park to a shopping mall, or from a restaurant to the theater.

Mobility can take the following forms:

1. *Ambulation within or between settings.* This category includes, primarily, walking or running. It also includes partial ambulation or movement within a setting, such as sliding or pulling oneself along, transferring oneself from a wheelchair to bed, or crawling. Ambulation can be accomplished either independently or with assistance. Forms of assistance include standard or electronic canes, crutches, prosthetic limbs or appendages, guide dogs, sighted guides, and physical adaptations (e.g., railings and bars) or people who give partial physical support.

2. *Conveyance within or between settings.* Conveyance is a means of transportation in which one is carried from one place to another (Wehman, Kregel, et al., 1985). This can be accomplished through the independent or assisted use of adapted or nonadapted automobiles, vans, motorcycles, scooters, bicycles and tricycles, manual and electric wheelchairs, or through being lifted or carried. Public transportation is another means of conveyance and includes buses, trains (including subways and elevated trains), planes, elevators, escalators, and taxis.

Barriers to Mobility

Physical and Social Barriers. Legislation such as the Architectural Barriers Act of 1968, § 504 of the Rehabilitation Act of 1973 (P.L. 93-112), and subsequent 1974 amendments (P.L. 93-516) has resulted in greater access to the community by individuals with disabilities. This legislation requires that federally funded programs "not discriminate against handicapped persons." As a result, public awareness regarding physical barriers has increased, and many improvements have been made. Many building owners in the private sector have installed ramps, widened bathroom stalls, lowered telephones and drinking fountains, and made other adaptations to assist individuals with physical disabilities. Television offers closed-captioned programming for persons with profound hearing losses or deafness. More recently, the Americans with Disabilities Act of 1990 (P.L. 101-336) has extended protection against discrimination specifically to individuals with disabilities. This legislation establishes the federal government as the central authority to ensure that protection against discrimination is provided by all states and increases the likelihood that individuals with disabilities will have access to all aspects of their communities.

Although such gains are encouraging, many physical barriers still remain in virtually any community. For example, steps, small bathrooms, and narrow aisles and doorways typify many restaurants and other businesses. There are, in addition to these physical barriers, attitudinal barriers such as the overprotectiveness and lowered expectations of some parents and professionals toward their children and clients who happen to have disabling conditions. Barriers to participation in normal activities are impositions on the rights of persons with disabilities to experience the same risks as do nondisabled individuals. Mobility within one's home and within and between different settings in the community (and between communities) is fundamental to the expression of this right to risk.

Lack of Transportation. The availability of transportation has been identified as one of the most important factors in transition planning (Bikson & Bikson, 1981; Clees, Stephens, Gwalla-Ogisi, & Jones, in press). Without it, employment, community-based training, generic services, and many other aspects of one's community become inaccessible. Liebert, Lutsky, and Gottlieb (1990) found the availability of transportation to be a key factor in the attainment and maintenance of employment by a sample of youth with physical disabilities.

As important as transportation is to those making the transition to living in the community, it is an equally crucial element in the preparation for community living of many school-aged people with disabilities. Such a simple service, though, is also one of the most difficult to obtain on a consistent basis—for both fiscal and philosophical reasons. Many administrators (and many teachers, parents, and professionals) are unlikely to support programs that they do not consider integral to their respective missions. Unfortunately, community-based instruction is not part of the perceived mission of enough school personnel. For example, it is not uncommon to hear that a public school administrator has denied a special education teacher use of the school van for community-based training in banking or laundry skills because "we just can't afford 'field trips' all the time." The importance of teaching skills to individuals in the community settings in which the skills will be used, such as teaching functional academics in restaurants or grocery stores (e.g., money skills), is sometimes lost in well-meant but misplaced overprotectiveness or in the shuffle of an "excellence in education" pro-

gram that stresses academics while overlooking individual needs. Unfortunately, although classroom-based academics allow many individuals with disabilities to be competitive and upwardly mobile once they reach the postschool world, they are not always in the best interests of all individuals with disabilities.

Keys to Community Mobility

Resources and Supports. For individuals to receive training in mobility skills, a system of adequate resources and supports needs to be in place. This is the case whether going to, coming from, or being at home, at school, at work, or in other community environments (e.g., stores, doctors' offices, recreation centers, or parks). Listed here are some of the resources and personnel supports that individuals may require to achieve mobility:

1. Adequate public and private or private nonprofit transportation services, including buses and vans equipped with lifts and seating adaptations.
2. State or local subsidies for transportation services and for conveyance and ambulation equipment (e.g., vans and buses for persons with disabilities, wheelchairs, guide dogs, prosthetics). Subsidies can be provided to individuals in the form of reimbursements for purchased services or equipment.
3. State or local equipment centers from which individuals with disabilities check out needed mobility aids and other equipment, such as wheelchairs, augmentative communication devices, and adapted furniture. These centers function much like a public library except that individuals keep the equipment for as long as it is needed. (There are very few of these centers at present; concerned individuals need to lobby for or organize them.)
4. Orientation or mobility instruction.
5. Mobility assistance as needed (e.g., paid or volunteer personnel who assist in transfers to and

from wheelchairs or who supervise travel in the community).

6. Support from parents, advocates, volunteers, organizations, and community groups (e.g., local chapters of the Association for Retarded Children, chamber of commerce, churches). Support may be in the form of organization of services, financial assistance, supervision, lobbying for improvements and expansion of supports, and companionship.

It is important to note that some individuals may always require some form of physical assistance in their mobility, whether within or between settings. This need should not affect their places in line to receive any of the services and supports just listed. They have, as much as anyone, the right to participate in their communities, even if they are only able to engage in partial participation (Brown et al., 1979). Partial participation can involve walking with support, touching the wheel of one's wheelchair even if not able to move it, or even laughter. Supports such as those associated with the supported living models discussed earlier should be provided to facilitate whatever level of participation an individual can accomplish.

Mobility Instruction. The development and implementation of instructional programs to assist individuals in acquiring specific mobility skills involve the same steps as those listed for domestic and community skills:

1. Assessing present or potential settings

2. Assessing learner skills

3. Prioritizing the skills

4. Task analyzing the skills

5. Providing task analytic instruction

These steps are exemplified in the following case study.

CASE EXAMPLE: TEACHING BUS-RIDING SKILLS TO A MAN WITH VISUAL IMPAIRMENTS AND CHALLENGING BEHAVIORS

Participant, Rationale, and Settings. Will is a 32-year-old man who is legally blind in his left eye, with a mild impairment in his right eye. He is able to ambulate independently although his visual impairment causes him to be somewhat uncoordinated in his gross motor movement; he has difficulty in judging distances. At the time of the implementation of the mobility program, Will displayed some challenging behaviors, including intermittent verbal and physical aggression that occurred primarily when Will was having difficulties in demonstrating required or requested skills. Because his parents were apprehensive about Will's potential for aggression in frustrating situations, he had not been given instruction on how to travel on the bus to work each day. Gaining competence in bus riding was viewed as crucial to his being able to maintain employment status over an extended period of time because the bus was the most stable means of transportation available to him. He had up until that point been totally dependent on his parents for transportation. His parents understood that they could not be expected to provide transportation indefinitely.

Will was employed doing benchwork tasks in a skills-training environment. He was earning a training (i.e., below minimum) wage at the time of the mobility training, which was conducted on his bus route to and from work.

Task Analysis. The task analysis was developed by Will's mobility specialist trainer by riding the bus to and from Will's work site. The task analysis is presented in Table 18.5. (Notice that it is specific to his route.) Different landmarks were used, and the order of the steps was reversed, for returning home. Other than the reverse order, the task analyses and training procedures were the same. Modifications were made to accommodate his visual impairment. These included the use of landmarks large enough for Will to see while riding, a request made to the bus driver to tell him if he had the correct bus (in case he could not see the destination sign on the bus), and a request to the driver to remind him of his stop if Will did not sound the stop bell on time.

Table 18.5.   Task Analysis: Riding and Transferring Buses from Work to Home Utilizing Landmarks

---

1. Select change for bus ride before leaving work.

2. Go to bus stop; stand 2 feet from curb at bus stop.

3. Motion to approaching bus.

4. When bus door opens, ask driver "Is this the Manona bus?"
   4a) If answer is "no," say "Thank you, this is not my bus" and wait for next bus (Step 3).
   4b) If answer is "yes," proceed to Step 5.

5. Holding rail, enter bus and pay fare.

6. Say to bus driver "I need a transfer please."

7. Wait for and take transfer.

8. Say to bus driver, "Would you please tell me when we get to the Buckeye bus?"

9. Thank driver.

10. Walking toward back of bus while grasping seat and/or overhead rail, sit in first front facing window seat in empty left row (left facing back of bus) (right row going to work).
    10a) If no empty row all the way back, sit in any aisle seat.

11. Watch for landmarks on right of bus (facing forward) (left going to work).
    a.   Walgreens
    b.   McDonalds
    c.   West Town Mall sign

12. When West Town Mall sign comes into view, ring bell to signal driver to stop by pushing signal button/pulling signal cord (depending on bus type).
    12a) If sitting in aisle seat while next to someone say, "Excuse me," and reach up/over to signal driver.
    12b) If driver says "Manona," prepare to leave.

13. Wait for bus to stop.

14. Exit bus by back door.
    14a) If sitting by window and next to someone, say, "Excuse me," before standing to exit bus.

15. Repeat Steps 3–10 except:
    4)   when bus door opens ask driver "Is this the Buckeye bus?"
    5)   holding rail, enter bus and hand driver the transfer pass.

16. Watch for landmarks on right of bus.

17. When Speedway sign comes into view, signal driver to stop.

18. Repeat steps 12a–14 (for 12, landmark is Speedway station and for 12b driver will say "Buckeye").

19. Turn right after exiting bus (toward Speedway service station).

20. Walk to corner.

21. Turn left.

22. Walk to next intersection.

23. Turn right and cross street (separate TA).

24. Walk home (4th house).

Teaching Procedure. Baseline analysis indicated that Will initially needed assistance on almost all of the steps in the sequence. The trainer met Will each day after work. Training began at the point when Will was leaving his work area to go home. A simultaneous instruction procedure with a progressive time delay was utilized during the training. After the initial zero-second time delay in which the trainer verbally prompted Will through each step in the task analysis, time delays progressed from 2 to 4 seconds across the training days. The controlling prompt was a combination of a verbal plus a modeling prompt. In this way the trainer would, after the specified delay period (e.g., if Will did not initiate the step within 2 seconds of the last step), model the step after verbally stating the step. On Step 5, for example, the trainer prompted Will by saying, "Will, get on the bus like this," while modeling how to enter the bus and put the money in the fare box. Will was then prompted to "Get on, Will," and was praised (e.g., "Nice job!") for completion of the target step. Will was then given the specified time-delay period to initiate the next response (e.g., 2 seconds) before the next step was prompted, and so on through all of the steps. The procedure required that the trainer ride the bus with Will (and take the next bus home). The trainer had informed the bus company driver who regularly drove Will's route of the basics of the training program and rationale. The driver expressed great willingness to cooperate (as is generally the case).

Results. The length of the time delay (up to 4 seconds in the latter days of training) did not seem to hinder the bus service; almost all of the delays occurred while the bus was moving. Will acquired the steps rapidly, reaching a criterion of three consecutive Monday–through–Wednesday trips (this permitted the trainer to evaluate maintenance of the skill over the weekend) with 100% accuracy on all steps (i.e., no prompts were delivered and all steps were self-initiated) in less than 3 weeks. The landmarks, although helping Will to locate his stops, also served to reduce inappropriate socialization (e.g., talking to people who did not want to talk, excessive greetings) because he needed to attend to the landmarks. The bus driver and confederates of the trainer (individuals who observed Will after the trainer had faded herself from the instruction, but of whom Will was unaware) socially validated the program, reporting that Will was riding the bus independently and with only minimal occurrences of behavior that might be construed as socially questionable (some incongruent conversation). Conversational skills (including when not to converse) were targeted for subsequent instruction across relevant settings (e.g., on the bus). Training on taking the bus to work was initiated after Will had reached the criterion on returning home. He reached this criterion by Wednesday of the second week of training (i.e., after 5 days of prompts being required during training).

COLLABORATION IN SUPPORTED LIVING AND TRANSITION

When a model for collaborative transition planning is paired with functional curricula, community-based training, and a system of supports to maintain a person's status as a community member (regardless of disability), postschool success rates will likely increase. The collaborative transition-supports model (Clees et al., in press) is designed to offer such a combination. The model is based on numerous best practices taken from the transition, supported living, and instructional literature, including Lombard's (1989) collaborative transition model, work in the area of supported living (Racino & Taylor, 1989), and the community-based instructional procedures initially framed by Brown and his colleagues (1979). The model is presented in Figure 18.2 and represents a structure within which to affect the supported living, transition and instructional approaches discussed above.

Key to the collaborative transition-supports model is the formation of the collaborative team. This group (a) is the guiding force behind the model; (b) must be carefully selected on the basis of a philosophy of support; and (c) consists of some combination of individuals with disabilities; their parents or guardians, teachers, and employers; private and state agency representatives and service providers; members of the business community; public officials; and advocates.

Leadership roles within the model are assumed by individuals with disabilities, their families, and committed advocates as soon as possible following the formulation of the collaborative team. Thus, the individuals who are the most affected by state policies and regulations regarding available supports (or their absence) function as the impetus in movement toward implementation of a comprehensive transition supports model. In order to facilitate this, the professional members of the team (teachers, agency representatives, etc.) function as consultants, liaisons,

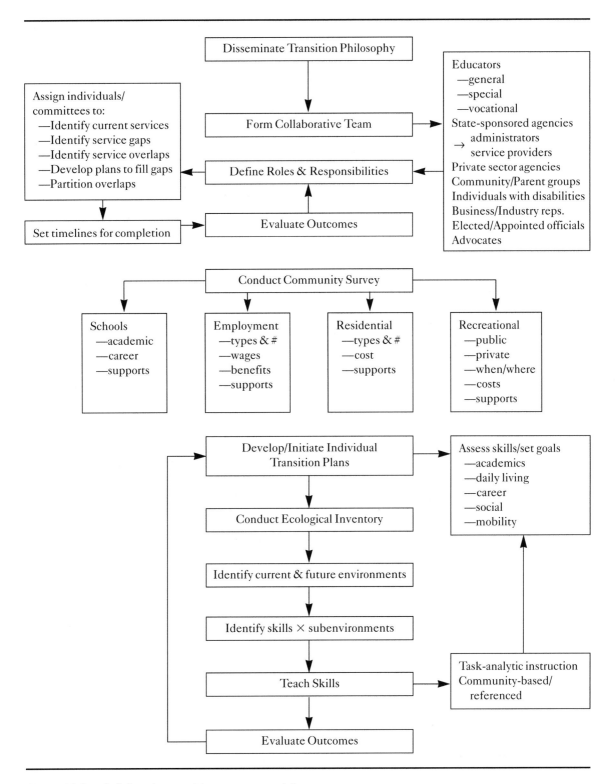

Figure 18.2.   Collaborative transition-supports model.

direct support providers, and advocates (Clees et al., in press). The rationale for this approach is that the collaborative team may be more likely to remain intact and to instruct new members if the leadership roles are filled by individuals with disabilities and their families and advocates, in other words, those who have the most at stake. Professionals, although likely very committed to the team's success, nonetheless may be more likely to leave the team for a variety of reasons (new job, moving, change of interests, etc.).

The individuals on the collaborative team assume numerous committee roles, depending on expertise, interests, and available time. The identification of services, service gaps, and service overlaps are initial steps. The community in which the individual to be served lives is the unit of consideration. A community survey of educational, employment, residential, and recreational resources, costs, and supports provides valuable information when it comes time to implement individuals' transition plans. Table 18.6 shows a community survey of some of the services available in Georgia.

The academic, daily living, career, social, and mobility skills of individuals are assessed and matched to available opportunities. Needed supports are identified and procured. Community-based instruction is provided as referenced to an ecological inventory specific to the individual's current and future environments. Finally, outcomes are evaluated and refinements are made.

ADVOCACY

Ongoing support is crucial to many individuals with disabilities being able to maintain their community living status. Advocates can play a vital role by acting on behalf of individuals with disabilities to maintain current levels of support in some areas while establishing or increasing the level of support in others. Advocates can be just about anyone, including parents and relatives, coworkers, organization representatives, friends, service delivery personnel and professionals, other per-

sons with disabilities, and the person with disabilities serving as self-advocate. Advocacy activities are equally varied. They can be on behalf of an individual with a disability or in the interests of persons with disabilities in general. Numerous types of advocacy activities are listed here:

- Service-related advocacy activities:

  - communicating goals to teachers, parents, employers, and coworkers

  - coordinating services such as education or training, benefits, medical care, transportation, and recreation

  - taking an active role in transition planning, beginning as early as possible during or after the school years

  - training the individual at home, work, or in the community

  - training parents and others such as group home and apartment supervisors in such skills as performing ecologic inventories and task analytic instruction

  - delivering instruction or services related to any or all settings

  - providing emergency support related to health, transportation, and interpersonal factors

- Politically related advocacy activities:

  - demonstrating publicly on behalf of a person or persons with disabilities

  - making demands

  - writing letters

  - developing newsletters and other communications

  - lobbying

  - boycotting businesses and organizations that are not accessible to or that support policies that discriminate against individuals with disabilities

Table 18.6. Community Survey[a]

Agency/Program	Responsibilities (as stated in interview)	Funding	Referred By/To	Eligibility Requirements
Adult Centered Education	1. Prepare for GED 2. Teach basic reading and math (illiteracy)	State	By self/advocate	16 years and older Dropouts, age-outs
Youth Detention Center (YDC)	1. Holding facility—Detention (waiting for court date) Hold up to 90 days 2. Short-term treatment a. academics b. socialization skills c. wilderness skills	State	By juvenile court system To youth services	Court assigned Juvenile
Youth Services	1. Treatment and Rehabilitation 2. Alternative Placement (16 years and younger) 3. 16 years and older a. Place in group home (Winder, Gainesville) b. Provides OJT c. 6–8 months average on job d. Probation until court sentence completed	State	By Courts, OTP, YDC To Kelly Diversified work programs (Warm Springs, etc.)	Committed by courts 16 years and younger Committed by courts 16 years and older dropouts
Troubled Children Committee	1. "Trouble Shooter" 2. Family Intervention	State	By Youth Services	Consistent problems in schools and/or with court system Juvenile
JTPA	1. Private company receives up to one half of wages for placement of client. 6-month requirement 2. Trainer—OJT 2 weeks (trainer salary tax credit)	State and Federal (Grant Program)	By schools to companies in community	14 years and older Economic needs Disabling condition Potential dropout or have dropped out
Jobs For Georgia	1. 6 schools in state 2. State Dept. employee works with St. (job specialist) –serves as middle man between student and employer 3. Job Specialist ID's 50 students –must place 80% –6 months to place –verbal contact every 2 weeks until placed	State Department of Labor	To companies in community	Graduating but not college bound

(continues)

Table 18.6. *Continued*

Agency/Program	Responsibilities (as stated in interview)	Funding	Referred By/To	Eligibility Requirements
Division of Vocational Rehabilitation Services (DVR)	1. Counselor works 1:1 –set up work experience in school setting (janitorial) –OJT (i.e., Florist, Nursing Home) 2. Work with family and school personnel 3. Teacher responsible for implementation within school setting	State and Federal	By school/agencies To Athens Tech., colleges, companies in the community	16 years and older Disabilities
Department of Mental Health	1. Referral Agency 2. Day Program—Adult work activity leading to supported or competitive employment 3. Teacher responsible for implementation within school setting	State	By schools, advocates To Hope Haven, Kelly, Voc. Rehab.	Handicapping condition
Department of Family/Child Services	1. Protective services 2. Day Care Services for young child Recreational services for older child 3. Home Intervention	State	By schools, MH, Day Care Services	
Kelly Diversified	1. Work adjustment 2. Voc. Evaluation 3. Provide transportation out of County 4. Half-day program for 16–19 year olds in school	Private, nonprofit	Contract with Voc. Rehab. By Voc. Rehab., private insurance agencies, MH, schools To companies in community	16–65 years 120-day limit; then placement or extension
Mental Health Residential Services	1. Assist with money management and apartment finding 2. Liaison between landlord and client 3. Daily living skills training 4. Assist with transportation	State—part of NE GA. MH Dept.	By MH (min. 3 months treatment) Hospital To Kelly, companies in community, group homes	18 years and older
Mental Retardation Residential Services	1. Assist with job placement 2. Provide group homes (5 homes in 10 counties) 3. Supportive living service	State	To Voc. Rehab., Kelly, Hope Haven	17 years and older
Parks & Recreation	No therapeutic recreational person employed locally 1. Summer—Project Reach –no transportation –serves 30–35 children	City, with federal assistance		Project Reach: County Resident Disabling condition
Handicap Life/Athens Transit	1. Transport physical/mental handicap as application from referring is received 2. $1.00 each way 3. Escorts free	1. Users 2. City of Athens General Funds 3. Urban Mass Trans. Adm.	By Voc. Rehab., Doctors, MH, Health Dept., Council on Aging, Council for Blind, UGA Student Services	Must live in city Physical/mental disability All ages

Note. The author wishes to acknowledge the work done on this survey by Lisa Griffin and Janet Carter.

aSome of the public and private agencies and programs serving disabled children, youth, and adults in Georgia.

- litigating and providing or procuring legal advocacy

- negotiating

- providing model program demonstrations (Biklen, 1979)

Advocates may, in addition, provide reinforcement to programs, politicians, teachers, and agencies for providing beneficial supports and for being advocates themselves. This reinforcement may take the form of public recognition, letters to their superiors, celebrations, and so forth.

Many advocates may lack the skills and the time to engage in all of the activities listed. The professions, interests, and other commitments of advocates will determine the type and extent of their advocacy activities. Advocates should, however, be willing to commit whatever strengths they have in a consistent manner over some period of time, particularly if that involves forming a personal relationship with a person who happens to have a disability. Even advocates who have no skills related to the disabilities of the persons for whom they advocate can provide valuable support, whether related to daily survival (e.g., grocery shopping, transportation) or given in the form of friendship.

FINAL THOUGHTS

Many individuals with disabilities require supports to attain and maintain their independence from environments that are less than integrated settings. This chapter has presented some of the barriers to community living and some solutions to overcoming those barriers. Supported living and employment models were identified as appropriate alternatives to a least restrictive environment conceptualization of community living because the latter discriminates against citizens with more severe disabilities by imposing a continuum-of-services approach on them. This continuum approach has come to require individuals to gain prerequisite skills, or be "ready," be-

fore they can enjoy, on any consistent basis, those advantages the community has to offer. The skills that are most crucial to maintaining one's status in the community were identified, as were methods for assessing relevant settings for respective skill requirements.

Task analytic assessment and instructional procedures were described and teaching examples provided. The importance of mobility to people's independence was emphasized, and instructional procedures and examples were described. Finally, the importance of developing a collaborative transition and postschool service delivery model was stressed.

Without cooperative efforts by all elements in the service planning and delivery process, service voids are likely to exist; such voids pose a threat to the community living status of individuals with disabilities.

Restrictive settings exist because our support resources have been historically tied to restrictive settings. To eliminate this propensity and to continue the positive evolution of services provided individuals with disabilities, four elements are considered here as necessary: (1) the redistribution of fiscal expenditures and formulas so that supports can be brought to individuals with disabilities as they work, reside, and recreate *within* their communities; (2) the formation of local collaborative transition and postschool service models, including those developed by the private sector; (3) the provision that leadership in collaborative models be primarily the function of individuals with disabilities and their families or guardians; and (4) organized and extensive advocacy.

REFERENCES

Anderson, D. J., Lakin, K. C., Bruininks, R. H., & Hill, B. K. (1987). *A national study of residential and support services for elderly persons with mental retardation.* Minneapolis: University of Minnesota, Center for Residential and Community Services.

Baker, B. L., Seltzer, G. B., & Seltzer, M. M. (1977). *As close as possible: Community residences for retarded adults.* Boston: Little, Brown.

Biklen, D. (1979). *Community imperative: A refutation of all arguments in support of deinstitutionalizing anybody because of mental retardation.* Syracuse, NY: Human Policy Press.

Bikson, T. A., & Bikson, T. K., (1981). *Functional problems of the visually impaired: A research approach.* Santa Monica, CA: Rowd.

Brolin, D. E. (Ed.). (1993). *Life-centered career education (4th ed.).* Reston, VA: Council for Exceptional Children.

Brown, L., Branston, M., Hamre-Nietupski, S., Pumpian, I., Certo, N., & Gruenwald, A. (1979). A strategy for developing chronological age appropriate and functional curricular content for severely handicapped and young adults. *Journal of Special Education, 13,* 81–90.

Clees, T. J., Stephens, J. T., Gwalla-Ogisi, N., & Jones, K. (in press). Collaborative transition supports model: Moving services to the disabled to their communities. *International Journal of Special Education.*

Copeland, W. C., & Iverson, I. A. (1985). Developing financial incentives for placement in the least restrictive alternative. In K. C. Lakin & R. H. Bruininks (Eds.), *Strategies for achieving community integration of developmentally disabled citizens* (pp. 291–312). Baltimore: Brookes.

Cuvo, A., & Davis, P. (1981). Home living for developmentally disabled persons: Instructional design and evaluation. *Exceptional Education Quarterly, 2,* 87–98.

D'Amico, R. (1992). The working world awaits: Employment experiences during and shortly after secondary school. In M. Wagner, L. Newman, R. D'Amico, E. D. Joy, P. Butler-Nalin, C. Marder, & R. Cox (Eds.), *Youth with disabilities: How are they doing* (pp. 8-1 to 8-55). Stanford, CA: SRI International.

Demchak, M. A. (1994). Helping individuals with severe disabilities find leisure activities. *Teaching Exceptional Children, 27*(1), 48–53.

Edgar, E., & Levine, P. (1987). *A longitudinal follow-along study of graduates of special education.* Unpublished manuscript. University of Washington, Seattle.

Fairweather, J. S., & Shaver, D. M. (1991). Making the transition to postsecondary education and training. *Exceptional Children, 57*(3), 264–269.

Fisher, A. T. (1989). Independent living. In D. L. Harnisch & A. T. Fisher (Eds.), *Transition literature review: Educational, employment, and independent living outcomes* (Vol. 3, pp. 93–117). Urbana-Champaign: University of Illinois.

Frank, A. R., Sitlington, P. L., & Carson, R. (1991). Transition of adolescents with behavioral disorders: Is it successful? *Behavioral Disorders, 16*(3), 180–191.

Hasazi, S. B., Gordon, L. R., & Roe, G. A. (1985). Factors associated with the employment status of handicapped youth exiting high school from 1979 to 1983. *Exceptional Children, 51,* 455–469.

Hasazi, S. B., Johnson, R. E., Hasazi, J. E., Gordon, L. R., & Hull, M. (1989). Employment of youth with and without handicaps following high school: Outcomes and correlates. *The Journal of Special Education, 23,* 243–255.

Hayden, M. F., Lakin, K. C., Hill, B. K., Bruininks, R. H., & Copher, J. I. (1992). Social and leisure integration of people with mental retardation in foster homes and small group homes. *Education and Training in Mental Retardation, 27*(3), 187–199.

Heal, L. W., Novak, A. R., Sigelman, C. K., & Switzky, H. N. (1980). Characteristics of community residential facilities. In A. R. Novak & L. W. Heal (Eds.), *Integration of developmentally disabled individuals into the community* (pp. 45–56). Baltimore: Brookes.

Heward, W. L., & Orlansky, M. O. (1988). *Exceptional children: An introductory survey of special education* (3rd ed.). Columbus, OH: Merrill.

Hill, B. K., & Bruininks, R. H. (1981). *Family, leisure, and social activities of mentally retarded people in residential facilities.* Minneapolis: University of Minnesota, Department of Educational Psychology.

Hill, B. K., Bruininks, R. H., & Lakin, K. C. (1983). Characteristics of mentally retarded people in residential facilities. *Health and Social Work, 2,* 85–95.

Karan, O., Grantfield, J., & Suiter, D. (1990). Supported living. *Kaleidoscope, 2*(1), 1–4.

Lakin, K. C., & Bruininks, R. H. (Eds.). (1985). *Strategies for achieving community integration of developmentally disabled citizens.* Baltimore: Brookes.

Lensink, B. R. (1980). Establishing programs and services in an accountable system. In P. Roos, B. M. McCann, & M. R. Addison (Eds.), *Shaping the future: Community-based residential services and facilities for mentally retarded people* (pp. 49–66). Baltimore: University Park Press.

Liebert, D., Lutsky, L., & Gottlieb, A. (1990). Postsecondary experiences of young adults with severe physical disabilities. *Exceptional Children, 57*(1), 56–64.

Lombard, R. (1989, April). *Collaborative community-based transition model: An implementation manual.* Paper presented at 67th annual convention of the Council on Exceptional Children, San Francisco.

Lowenfeld, B. (Ed.). (1973). *The visually handicapped child in school.* New York: John Day.

Matson, J. (1980). A controlled group study of pedestrian skill training for the mentally retarded. *Zehairis Modification, 4,* 397–410.

Moon, M. S., & Bunker, L. (1987). Recreation and motor skills programming. In M. E. Snell (Ed.), *Systematic instruction of persons with severe handicaps* (3rd ed., pp. 214–244). Columbus, OH: Merrill.

Pancsofar, E., & Blackwell, R. (1986). *A user's guide to community entry for the severely handicapped.* Albany: State University of New York Press.

Racino, J. A., & Taylor, S. J. (1989, November). New directions in community living. *Community Living for Adults* [Newsletter], pp. 7–15. Syracuse: Syracuse University, Research and Training Center on Community Integration, The Center on Human Policy.

Rusch, F. R. (1986). *Competitive employment issues and strategies.* Baltimore: Brookes.

Rusch, F. R., Mithaug, D. E., & Flexer, R. W. (1986). Obstacles to competitive employment and traditional program options for overcoming them. In F. R. Rusch (Ed.), *Competitive employment: Issues and strategies* (pp. 7–22). Baltimore: Brookes.

Schalock, R. L., & Lilley, M. A. (1986). Placement for community-based mental retardation programs: How well do clients do after 8 to 10 years? *American Journal of Mental Deficiency, 90*(6), 669–676.

Seyelman, C., Bell, N., Schoenrock, C., Elear, S., & Danker-Brown, P. (1978). *Alternative community placements and outcomes*. Paper presented at the Annual meeting of the American Association on Mental Deficiency, Denver, CO.

Snell, M. E. (1987). *Systematic instruction of persons with handicaps* (3rd ed.). Columbus, OH: Merrill.

Sowers, F., Rusch, F. R., & Hudson, C. (1979). Training a severely retarded young adult to ride the city bus to and from work. *AAESPH Review, 4*, 15–22.

SRI International. (1989). *The transition experience of youth with disabilities: A report from the national longitudinal transition study*. Menlo Park, CA: Authors.

Stokes, T. (1992). Discrimination and generalization. *Journal of Applied Behavior Analysis, 25*(2), 429–432.

Stokes, T. F., & Baer, D. M. (1977). An implicit technology of generalization. *Journal of Applied Behavior Analysis, 10*, 349–367.

Stokes, T. F., & Osnes, P. G. (1986). Programming the generalization of children's social behavior. In P. S. Strain, M. J. Guralnick, & H. M. Walker (Eds.), *Children's social behavior: Development and modification*. Orlando, FL: Academic Press.

Thompson, M. M. (1977). *Housing for the handicapped and disabled: A guide for local action*. Washington, DC: National Association of Housing and Redevelopment Officials.

Wehman, P. (1990). School-to-work: Elements of successful programs. *Teaching Exceptional Children, 23*(1), 40–43.

Wehman, P., Kregel, J., & Barkus, M. (1985). From school to work: A vocational transition model for handicapped students. *Exceptional Children, 52*, 25–37.

Wehman, P., Renzaglia, A., & Bates, P. (1985). *Functional living skills for moderately and severely handicapped persons*. Austin, TX: PRO-ED.

Will, M. C. (1984). *OSERS programming for the transition of youth with disabilities: Bridges from school to working life*. Washington, DC: Office of Special Education and Rehabilitative Services, U.S. Department of Education.

Social Security

Susan O'Mara and John Kregel

LEARNING GOALS

Upon completion of this chapter the reader will be able to

■ define what Social Security is, specifically the Supplemental Security Income (SSI) and Disability Insurance Programs;

■ discuss how an individual's social security payment can be affected by earnings from a job;

■ review two work incentives (i.e., PASS and IRWE) that can be used to help people with severe disabilities obtain or retain employment;

■ identify the barriers to employment inherent in the Social Security system; and

■ discuss current SSI disincentives to employment.

The Social Security Administration administers two separate income support programs for persons with disabilities: Supplemental Security Income (SSI, or Title IV) and the Social Security Disability Insurance Program (SSDI, or Title II). To be eligible for monthly cash payments under the SSI and SSDI programs, an individual must meet the Social Security Administration's statutory definition of *disability*, as well as other non–disability-specific requirements. Disability is defined as "the inability to engage in any substantial gainful activity (work) by reason of any medically determinable physical or mental impairment which can be expected to result in death or has lasted or can be expected to last for a continuous period of not less than 12 months" (*Federal Register*, April 6, 1989, p. 13981). Therefore, to meet the disability requirement for both programs it is necessary for a person to have a documented disability that precludes him or her

from engaging in *substantial gainful work* activity, or SGA. SGA is defined as the performance of significant mental or physical duties for profit and is usually determined to be gross earnings in excess of $500 a month.

The non–disability-related requirements for each program are outlined here.

SSI PROGRAM RULES

The SSI program is intended to provide a minimum level of monthly income for persons who are aged, blind, or disabled and demonstrate economic need. To qualify, a person must meet the disability requirements and have limited income and resources that fall below allowable limits established by statute.

Before July 1, 1987, the performance of SGA (monthly gross earnings over $500) after initial eligibility was established as a basis for ceasing SSI entitlement. Recognizing this severe disincentive to return to work, Congress enacted the Employment Opportunities for Disabled Americans Act of 1986 (P.L. 99-643). This law established two special provision statuses known as 1619A and 1619B. Section 1619A enables individuals who continue to be disabled to receive a special SSI cash benefit in place of their regular 1611 SSI benefit when earnings exceed the $500 SGA level. If an SSI recipient continues to meet all eligibility requirements, when earnings increase to greater than $500 a month but remain lower than the break-even point, he or she automatically moves into 1619A status.

Eligibility for a 1619A cash benefit continues until earnings fall below the SGA level, at which point the person automatically moves back into 1611 status and receives a regular 1611 check, or until gross earnings exceed the break-even point, at which time the SSI cash benefit ceases.

Section 1619B of the 1987 legislation provides for continued Medicaid eligibility when a person's income is too high to qualify for an SSI cash benefit, but is not high enough to offset the loss of Medicaid. An individual is eligible for the 1619B protected Medicaid status only if the sole cause for SSI benefit cessation is increased earnings over the break-even point. A second criterion for 1619B status is that an individual's gross earnings fall below certain limits called *threshold amounts*. Earnings at or above the threshold amount are considered to be sufficient to replace the cost of Medicaid coverage. A final criterion for 1619B requires that an individual must need Medicaid in order to work. Compliance with this criterion is established through the individual's statements to the Social Security Administration regarding his or her use of Medicaid in the last 12 months, expected use within the next 12 months, or need for Medicaid if he or she becomes injured or ill within the next 12 months.

Section 1619B is an extremely important provision of the Social Security Act because it protects not only an individual's Medicaid coverage but also maintains his or her eligibility for receiving an SSI cash benefit in any future month that countable income falls below the allowable limits (the break-even point for 1619A and $500 for 1611), provided that the individual continues to meet all other eligibility requirements for SSI. Because 1619B status maintains an active SSI case standing for an indefinite period, an individual may work for several years above the allowable levels for an SSI cash benefit then be reinstated automatically if loss of employment or reduction of earnings below the allowable levels occurs.

Because SSI is an economic need-based program, it is intended to supplement any income or resources an individual already possesses to ensure a minimum level of income. Therefore, the dollar amount of the SSI benefit received on a monthly basis varies from person to person. In January of each year, Congress establishes the Federal Benefit Rate (FBR), which is the maximum dollar amount that an individual or couple can receive in SSI cash benefit on a monthly basis.

The amount of an individual's SSI payment may be reduced below the FBR level, on the basis of the person's earned and unearned income. The more earned or unearned income received, the greater is the reduction in the SSI payment. Not all income a person receives, however, is considered in determining the amount of the benefit. The Social Security Administration allows a $20 general exclusion that is subtracted from a person's income regardless of its source. In addition to the general exclusion, a $65 earned-income disregard is subtracted from earned income. After the earned-income disregard is applied, one half of the remaining earned income is counted by the Social Security Administration in adjusting the benefit amount. The remaining amounts of earned and unearned income after exclusions are combined to determine the total countable income. This total is the dollar amount of an individual's SSI benefit reduction. The two examples shown in Figure 19.1 are simplified versions of the standardized formula used by the Social Security Administration in determining benefit reductions due to earned and unearned income.

EXAMPLE 1

Individual with earned income and unearned income (such as SSDI or Veterans' benefit). Example based on a person's earning $263 a month gross wages and receiving $225 SSDI.

Step 1 $225.00   Unearned income (SSDI)
        – 20.00   General exclusion
        $205.00   Countable unearned income

Step 2 $263.00   Earned income (monthly gross wages)
        – 65.00   Earned-income disregard
        $198.00
        ÷   2 $1 reduction for every $2 earned
        $ 99.00   Countable earned income

Step 3 $205.00   Countable unearned income
        + 99.00   Countable unearned income
        $304.00   Total countable income

Step 4 $458.00   Federal Benefit Rate (1995)
        –304.00   Total countable income
        $154.00   SSI check

EXAMPLE 2

Individual with earned income only. Example based on a person's earning $350 gross monthly earnings.

Step 1 $ 0.00   Unearned income
        $ 0.00   Countable unearned income

Step 2 $350.00   Earned income
        – 85.00   General exclusion and earned-
        $265.00   income disregard
        ÷   2 $1 reduction for every $2 earned
        $132.50   Countable earned income

Step 3 $ 0.00   Countable unearned income
        +132.50   Countable earned income
        $132.50   Total countable income

Step 4 $458.00   Federal Benefit Rate (1995)
        –132.50   Total countable income
        $325.50   SSI check

Figure 19.1. Examples of determining SSI benefit reductions due to earned and unearned income.

Persons receiving an SSI benefit are subject to two separate review processes to ensure continued compliance with eligibility criteria. Redeterminations are nonmedical reviews, which occur annually for persons in statuses 1611, 1619A, and 1619B. The purpose of redetermination reviews is to update nonmedical information that affects SSI eligibility and cash payment amounts. A second review process for SSI recipients is the Continuing Disability Review (CDR). The Social Security Administration is required by law to determine periodically whether a recipient continues to be disabled and is therefore eligible to continue receiving benefits.

SSDI PROGRAM RULES

The SSDI benefit program authorized under Title II of the Social Security Act enables former workers who become disabled and are unable to continue working to receive monthly cash benefits and Medicare insurance. To qualify for SSDI benefits as a former worker, an individual must have insured status (i.e., sufficient past work in Social Security–covered employment), be determined medically disabled, and must not be working or, if working, earning less than the SGA level. Eligibility for SSDI may also be established for a disabled adult child. A disabled adult child is an individual who is 18 years of age or older, who became totally and permanently disabled before age 22, and who is a dependent of an insured worker who is disabled, retired, or deceased.

Because the SSDI program is not based on economic need, there are no resource or unearned-income limitations for eligibility as there are for SSI. The dollar amount of income support received by SSDI beneficiaries on a monthly basis depends on the level of contributions made to the program and therefore varies significantly from person to person. There is no provision for a gradual reduction in SSDI cash benefits as earnings increase, as is the case with the SSI program. An SSDI beneficiary receives either the full amount of the SSDI benefit in a given month or no income support at all.

Unless medical recovery is an issue, SSDI beneficiaries are entitled to a 9-month trial work period, which provides an opportunity to test work skills while maintaining their benefit. An individual may attempt to work for a trial work period of 9 months while continuing to receive full benefit checks, regardless of the level of earned income. The trial work period begins automatically in the first month that earned income is equal to or exceeds $200. Any subsequent months that earned income is at or above $200 are counted toward the 9-month limit. These months do not have to be consecutive and may accumulate over a number of years. The trial work period is exhausted when an individual has 9 months of earnings over $200 within a rolling 60-month period. Only one trial work period is allowed per given determination of eligibility.

When an individual has accumulated 9 months of trial work, a continuing disability review is conducted by the local Social Security Administration office. The purpose of the review is to determine whether the individual is engaging in SGA. If an individual is determined to be engaging in SGA, he or she will receive the full benefit check for an additional 3 months and then the benefit will stop. If an individual is determined not to be engaging in SGA, he or she will continue to receive the full benefit check.

At the end of the 9-month trial work period, beneficiaries immediately enter into a 36-month extended period of eligibility, provided that medical recovery is not an issue. This 36-month period begins in the month following the trial work period regardless of whether a person is determined to be engaging in SGA during the continuing disability review. The extended period of eligibility is a minimum of 36 consecutive months during which an individual may work and have SSDI benefits reinstated for each month that earned income is below $500.

Social Security Administration Title XVIII Medicare provides medical services to SSDI beneficiaries. Persons with disabilities must complete a 5-month waiting period from the month of disability onset before SSDI benefits begin. An additional 24-month waiting period after disability benefits begin is required before an individual is entitled to receive Medicare coverage.

SSDI beneficiaries who lose benefit entitlement because of SGA but continue to be disabled are eligible for extended Medicare coverage. The extended coverage is for 24 months beginning at the end of the extended period of eligibility or the last month that SSDI benefits are payable, whichever is later. In addition, recent legislation makes it possible for persons with disabilities to buy into the Medicare program once the extended Medicare coverage is exhausted. Specifically, the Omnibus Budget Reconciliation Act of 1989 (P.L. 101–239), effective April 1, 1990, provides disabled beneficiaries who are not yet 65 years old and continue to be disabled, and who are no longer entitled to benefits solely because of having earnings in excess of the amount permitted, with the option of purchasing Medicare coverage after they have worked a full 48 months (9-month trial work period and 36-month extended period of eligibility) and have exhausted their extended period of Medicare eligibility.

ADDITIONAL WORK INCENTIVES

Plan for Achieving Self-Support

A plan for achieving self-support (PASS) is an SSI work incentive under which persons with disabilities can set aside income or resources to be used to achieve specific, individualized vocational goals. A PASS can be established for education, vocational training, starting a business, or purchasing job-coach and job-support services that enable a person to work. The purpose of a PASS is to increase the individual's income-producing capacity and thus to reduce reliance on government benefit support in the long run.

The income or resources used to pay for goods and services under a PASS are not counted in determining a person's eligibility for SSI or in calculating the amount of the SSI benefit that he or she will receive. By excluding this income or resources in a PASS, the individual is able to meet the income and resources test, thereby qualifying for SSI. Likewise, an individual who already receives SSI can maintain that SSI in the same amount or even receive a larger SSI benefit by setting aside his or her income or resources in a PASS. For a PASS to be approved by the SSA, the following criteria must be met:

1. The plan must be especially designed for the individual and have a designated and feasible occupational objective.

2. A specific time frame must be established for an objective to be achieved.

3. The plan must state the sources and the amounts of income or resources to be set aside to achieve the goal.

4. The plan must state how the money set aside will be spent to achieve the goal.

The PASS work incentive was part of the original Supplemental Security Income program enacted by Congress in 1972 (Social Security Act Amendments, 1972). The legislative history surrounding the Act clearly shows that Congress intended to provide "every opportunity and encouragement to the blind and disabled to return to employment" (U.S. Department of Health and Human Services, 1985, p. 293). To this end Congress directed that the PASS provisions "be liberally construed if necessary to accomplish these objectives of helping people work their way off of SSI without penalizing them for their efforts by reducing their benefits prematurely before they become self-supporting" (U.S. Department of Health and Human Services, 1985, p. 212).

In spite of the Congressional mandate, the Social Security Administration has not been successful in assisting beneficiaries in utilizing the PASS work incentive to help them realize their employment goals. Although there were 3,228,073 SSI recipients aged 18 to 64 in March 1994, only 8,700 PASSes were being utilized by individuals nationally, despite the fact that at that same time 266,740 SSI recipients were working and in a position to

take advantage of this incentive to help them reach their employment goal.

Although the number of PASS users remains small, the Social Security Administration reports that the proportion is increasing, particularly in recent years. "Between September 1991 and September 1992, the number of recipients with a PASS exclusion grew by 69 percent; the number of working recipients with a PASS exclusion grew by 79 percent" (Social Security Administration, 1993, p. 45).

Impairment-Related Work Expenses

An impairment-related work expense (IRWE) is an expense, directly related to enabling a person with a disability to work, that is incurred because of the individual's physical or mental impairments and that would not be incurred by unimpaired individuals in similar circumstances. The purpose of the IRWE work incentive is to enable individuals with disabilities to recover some of the costs of the expenses incurred to support their work as a result of their disability.

The Social Security Administration's list of allowable expenditures under IRWE is extensive and includes costs of adaptive equipment or specialized devices, attendant care, and special transportation costs, as well as the cost of job-coach services. This work incentive applies to both SSI recipients and SSDI beneficiaries and allows for certain costs or expenses to be excluded in calculating earnings and SGA. For an SSI recipient, deducting the cost of an IRWE from monthly gross wages increases the SSI cash payment he or she can receive. For an SSDI beneficiary, deducting an IRWE may keep monthly gross earnings below SGA and thus enable the individual to maintain SSDI eligibility. The cost of IRWEs can also be deducted from gross earnings during initial SSI and SSDI application processes, a deduction enabling an individual to meet the SGA requirement as well as the income test for SSI.

Subsidies

A subsidy exists when an employer pays a worker more in wages than the reasonable value of the actual services performed. To qualify as a subsidy recipient, an individual must have evidence of receiving a subsidy, such as extra support, supervision, or documentation of lower productivity when compared to unimpaired workers performing the same or similar work. In developing a subsidy, the employer is requested by the Social Security Administration to submit a statement documenting the actual value of the worker's services.

Subsidies apply to both SSI recipients and SSDI beneficiaries. The dollar amount of the subsidy is subtracted from gross monthly earnings during the initial eligibility process for both SSI and SSDI; this reduction potentially reduces gross earnings below $500 and enables an individual to meet the SGA requirement. Subsidies apply only to the SSI program during initial eligibility. For the SSDI program, however, subsidies are considered an ongoing SGA determination.

ISSUES, OBSTACLES, AND CHALLENGES

A growing concern of the federal government and the Social Security Administration itself lies in the steady growth of the social security programs over the past 10 years. The Social Security Administration has indicated that the number of young people enrolling for disability benefits has significantly increased during the last 5 years and anticipates that this trend will continue during the next 5 years. Specifically, between 1989 and 1993, the number of SSDI beneficiaries under the age of 30 increased 43%; an additional increase of 57% is projected by 1998. This program growth is significant in light of current statistics that show that less than one half of 1% of beneficiaries with disabilities leave the rolls to go to work (Social Security Administration, 1994).

Faced with the reality of extremely limited numbers of benefit-support recipients opting to return to work, the federal government and the Social Security Administration have responded over the past 15 years with legislative and regulatory changes in the SSI and SSDI programs. During this time, a majority of the work incentives outlined previously were added and liberalized under the Social Security Act Amendments of 1980 (P.L. 99–265), the Employment Opportunities for Disabled Americans Act (P.L. 99–643), and the Omnibus Budget Reconciliation Acts of 1987 and 1989. The program changes, return-to-work strategies, and demonstration projects implemented have been aimed at reducing the risks and costs associated with the reduction or loss of benefit support and medical services as a result of work activity. Despite these efforts to negotiate a system that encourages work, employment outcomes for beneficiaries with disabilities have remained largely unchanged.

Some of the significant barriers to employment inherent in the social security system were recently identified by the Social Security Administration (1994):

• The Social Security Administration does not have an effective infrastructure in place to steer beneficiaries toward employment. Currently, the only step taken is to refer some individuals (about 10%) to the state vocational rehabilitation agencies at the same time they are notified of their disability decision.
• The current Social Security Administration disability statute and claims process offer only the award or denial of benefits; they do not offer the option of rehabilitation or employment. They also do not recognize that people with disabilities can work with the right assistance and services.
• Only a small percentage of beneficiaries referred to the state vocational rehabilitation agencies are ever provided services. This is not expected to change unless the Social Security Administration develops a more effective and proactive relationship with the vocational reha-

bilitation agencies that results in more acceptances and individuals returning to work.

In addition, in their attempts to become independent and work, SSI recipients and SSDI beneficiaries are confronted with disincentives that are specific to each of the disability benefit programs.

CURRENT SSI DISINCENTIVES TO EMPLOYMENT

Legislative changes made under the Employment Opportunities for Disabled Americans Act of 1986 have virtually eliminated the disincentives to work for SSI recipients. Because work activity is no longer a consideration for cessation of SSI eligibility, a person receiving SSI is assured of an overall increase in net income as earnings increase. The ability to move freely between the 1611 and 1619A statuses as earned income fluctuates likewise provides a financial safety net in the event that employment stability is threatened. Section 1619B provides assurance that medical services under Medicaid will be protected despite the fact that cash benefits are suspended when earnings exceed the break-even point. Despite these significant improvements in the SSI program, several barriers to employment remain unaddressed.

The SGA consideration remains a key criterion in establishing initial eligibility for SSI benefits. An individual must first prove he or she is unable to work at the SGA level to qualify for benefits. This initial emphasis on limited work capacity forces individuals to limit any current work activity to qualify and may in fact provide an inaccurate message to recipients that future earnings at the SGA level will endanger their ability to maintain SSI support.

A second concern for SSI recipients returning to work relates to the requirement of additional medical reviews precipitated by increasing earnings. Although an increase in earnings will not result in termination of SSI due to SGA, it may indirectly result in the loss of benefits due to a determination of medical recovery. Because they recognize that movement into 1619 status due to increased earnings may precipitate a review of their medical files, individuals receiving SSI may choose to limit earnings to avoid further scrutiny of their disability status and a potential loss of eligibility.

Current Social Security Disability

Income Disincentives to Employment

Despite the issues just addressed, the incentives for SSI recipients to engage in work far outweigh those provided to SSDI beneficiaries. The risk of reduction in overall net income is a justified concern to these individuals because SGA continues to be a primary factor not only in establishing initial eligibility but also in maintaining eligibility after benefits are awarded.

The disincentives surrounding SGA determinations were somewhat diminished at the beginning of 1990 when the Social Security Administration implemented a change in program rules that increased the level of earnings that constitute SGA from $300 to $500 a month. This change becomes less of an accomplishment in improving the system when one considers that the $200 increase accounts for the growth in wages since 1980, when the SGA level was last adjusted. A second proposed rule change, which was not implemented, was a plan to index the SGA level to average wage growth in future years. The failure to implement such an index is particularly damaging in view of the subsequent increase in the federal minimum wage level.

The most effective resolution to the dilemma is clearly the removal of the SGA criteria altogether. A legislative change proposed in 1989 suggested the removal of the SGA disincentive by allowing SSDI beneficiaries who return to work and earn above the SGA level to be considered "disabled and working." Persons qualifying for this status, who would otherwise lose cash benefits due to SGA, would be eligible for cash and Medicaid benefits under § 1619 of the SSI program. The formula used to adjust monthly cash benefits as earnings increase for SSI recipients would apply to persons in the disabled and working status. This proposal, intended to be a parallel to the 1619 provisions of the SSI program, was not adopted by Congress. The Medicare buy-in, a second proposal of this legislation, was adopted and provides extended medical services for SSDI beneficiaries no longer qualifying for a cash benefit.

Concern regarding the disincentives is readily expressed by supported employees and their families, who must consider the risk factors involved when weighing the uncertainties of success in employment against the consistent support of benefit income.

Their willingness to utilize the work incentives and return to work depends in large part on their perceptions and understanding of the work incentives available to them. The system of Social Security regulations, policies, and procedures as they have evolved are complex and confusing.

For most supported employees and their families, mastery of the regulations and system is an unattainable goal. Many of these individuals are hesitant to return to work not only because they are unaware or unsure of the work incentive options but also because they lack confidence in their ability to advocate for resolution of potential benefit complications caused by increased earnings. Rehabilitation professionals are in a similar dilemma, finding it difficult to provide knowledgeable and effective advocacy on behalf of persons with disabilities entering the work force in growing numbers each year.

The Social Security Administration's awareness of and concern with the problems created by lack of understanding or misinformation about the benefit programs and work incentives is evidenced by its growing efforts to build effective working relations with service provider organizations. One step the Social Security Administration has taken to accomplish this goal is to position work incentive liaisons in each local SSA field office across the country. These individuals serve as a primary contact for rehabilitation professionals and agencies who work with people with disabilities and are a valuable source of information regarding the work incentives. Additionally, work incentive specialists are located in each of the Social Security Administration's regional offices to coordinate outreach and public affairs activities on the work incentives.

A principal strategy of this outreach endeavor focuses on effective use of resources by working through community organizations and agencies. This strategy requires action by the Social Security Administration to provide such organizations and agencies with the information and training they need to identify potentially eligible individuals, to inform them about program requirements and benefits, and to help them through the SSI application process. The Social Security Administration has established principles that form a foundation of what managers should be doing with regard to outreach efforts on a local level. These principles speak clearly to the need for local Social Security Administration offices to accomplish the following:

- Conduct periodic training sessions for service provider organizations.

- Improve access of provider organizations to local offices and work incentive liaisons to foster cooperation.

- Set up a mechanism for obtaining release forms to allow advocates access to records of individuals they are assisting.

- Encourage feedback from organizations about Social Security Administration service delivery.

In addition to these outreach activities, the Social Security Administration has most recently "launched an effort to develop a proactive strategy to increase the employment of current and potential disability beneficiaries" (1994, p. 1) and are utilizing focus groups and other methods to seek advice from people and organizations. This initiative coincides with a congressional study of the Social Security programs being conducted by the National Academy of Social Insurance.

Simultaneously with the federal government's efforts to improve and enhance the Social Security programs and services, developmental disabilities program leaders should be aggressive in their efforts to build a cohesive networking structure with the Social Security Administration to accomplish mutual goals. The local work incentive liaisons and public affairs specialists are good initial points of contact and are in a position to provide education about benefit programs, work incentives, and local outreach efforts. Educational and training efforts should be reciprocated by rehabilitation professionals to provide Social Security Administration personnel with a working knowledge of supported employment services and outcomes.

Although interagency collaboration and mutual understanding of benefit programs and employment services are critical elements, they unfortunately cannot ensure that persons with disabilities who go to work will experience smooth benefit transitions. Developmental disabilities program staff must continuously invest time and effort to advocate on behalf of the individuals they serve. Experience with benefit difficulties has demonstrated that the best results are achieved when a "preventive medicine" approach is applied as opposed to a "crisis intervention" strategy. Expending small amounts of energy to conduct periodic proactive monitoring activities will help circumvent major benefit problems.

Proactive Monitoring

The following proactive monitoring system comprises several stages that must be performed sequentially to minimize chances of experiencing major benefit complications. It is important for service providers to work cooperatively with the Social Security Administration when rendering such advice, to guard against misinformation and to ensure up-to-date information.

Investigate Current Benefit Status. In order to make accurate predictions of the impact of potential employment opportunities on benefit eligibility and payment amounts, it is essential that the individual and his or her advocates have a firm grasp of their current status. Research should be conducted to determine which benefits are received (SSI, SSDI), the dollar amounts of the benefits received, the dollar amounts of any other types of unearned income (Veterans Benefit, Civil Service Annuity), the number of trial work period and extended period of eligibility months used (for SSDI beneficiaries), and the individual's reporting history (i.e., has the individual been conscientious in reporting earnings from prior employment?). The object is to provide a complete and accurate picture of the individual's benefit status at that time. This knowledge cannot be obtained unless the entire benefit/earnings past has been thoroughly assessed. Failure to perform this research will likely result in some unpleasant surprises down the road.

Explore the Possible Effects of Future Earnings. When an employment opportunity becomes available, the individual and his or her advocate must carefully examine the job specifics that could affect SSA benefits. The pay rate, job hours, pay dates, and bonus or raise information are all necessary data. The service provider should contact the local SSA and present a "what if" scenario in which all possible outcomes are thoroughly explored and should ask for guidance in exploring the possible work incentive provisions that may affect the possible outcomes. The purpose is to obtain precise information about future benefit changes that can be expected to occur, based on the stated conditions. This prediction will be only as accurate as the research done on the past earnings history and present benefit status, so the service provider must be certain that this homework is done. (SSA representatives that can assist in this step include work incentive liaisons, SSI outreach coordinators, division supervisors, and claims representatives.)

Exchange Information with the Person and Family. Advocates providing assistance in this benefit-monitoring process will possess at this point complete information about how any given employment situation will affect a particular benefit recipient. This information must be shared openly with the individual and family members so that informed decisions can be made. Loss or changes in benefits must be discussed prior to the beginning of employment, not later when irreparable benefit damage might have been done. The service provider must never assume the individual and his or her family will have knowledge about the predicted course of benefit adjustment without checking with these persons. A benefit recipient or his or her family who is not informed about benefit reductions or terminations may lose faith in the advocate's ability and resign from employment or the family may act to sabotage the placement. All benefit facts must be brought out truthfully, in the open.

Report Earnings Correctly. Many substantial errors can be avoided if employment earnings are reported in the proper manner. First and foremost, the employment data must be communicated to and received by the appropriate person. Earnings must always be reported to the current claims representative or the division supervisor. Persons receiving both SSI and SSDI may have two claims representatives, in which case both divisions must be notified separately. For SSI recipients, any earnings over $85 a month must be reported. SSDI beneficiaries must report earnings over $200 as they qualify as trial work period months, even if they are sheltered workshop earnings. To facilitate the smoothest transitions, the advocate should be sure to relate information on start date, pay rate, pay dates, work schedule, address of employing company, and supervisor's name. A job loss must be reported immediately to hasten full benefit reinstatement. Be faithful and timely about notifying the Social Security Administration of changes in pay rate, hours worked, marital status, or residence. Procrastination will cause overpayment or underpayment.

Requests for continuing disability and other benefit reviews must be responded to promptly. Failure to comply may cause temporary benefit suspension. Discussions with the local SSA office can determine the most effective and efficient method of reporting information. Some local SSA offices have developed specific forms that can be used for this purpose.

Continue Monitoring of Benefit Statuses. Once initial earnings are reported, occasional checkup contacts with the claims representatives will be necessary. It is recommended that these checkups be conducted about every 3 months. For individuals receiving an SSI cash benefit, special attention must be supplied when an increase or decrease in earnings is experienced to ensure that the benefit is adjusted accordingly. SSI recipients will automatically receive a cash benefit under 1619A when earnings increase to $500 a month. Although it is not necessary to advocate for 1619A status, monitoring the adjustment in the SSI payment due to the increased earnings will safeguard against overpayment. For SSDI beneficiaries, contact should be made at the conclusion of the trial work period to ensure that a determination of SGA results in a timely cessation of benefits. Advocates assisting in this monitoring endeavor enlist the assistance of the employee and family. Usually they will receive the first indications of benefit trouble in the form of letters or in checks that fail to reflect the correct adjustment. Additionally, monitoring activities must include the person's employer. The SSA will send employment verification and wage information request forms to the employer. The employer may need assistance or encouragement in the completion process.

FINAL THOUGHTS

It is hoped that the information provided in this chapter will form a basic framework for understanding the internal workings of government benefit packages and avenues for gaining and sharing information on benefit outcomes for employees with disabilities. Successful utilization of work incentives and smooth benefit transitions ultimately depend on a cooperative effort between developmental disabilities staff, the Social Security Administration, workers with disabilities, and the workers' families. An excellent resource for additional information is the *Red Book on Work Incentives*. This 1991 publication is available from local Social Security offices.

REFERENCES

Employment Opportunities for Disabled Americans Act. (1986). Public Law 99–643, 42 U.S.C. 1382 *et seq.*, 100, 3575–3580.

Federal Register. (1989, April). Washington, DC: U.S. Government Printing Office.

Omnibus Budget Reconciliation Act. (1987). Public Law 100–203, 101 STAT. 1330 (December 22, 1987).

Omnibus Budget Reconciliation Act. (1989). Public Law 101–239, 42 U.S.C. 1396 *et seq.*, 103, 2253–2273.

Social Security Act Amendments. (1972). Public Law 92–603, 86 STAT. 1329 (October 30, 1972).

Social Security Act Amendments. (1980). Public Law 99–265, 94 STAT. 444 (June 9, 1980).

Social Security Administration. (1993, Spring). Shifting the cost of self-pay for SSI workers in supported employment. *Social Security Bulletin, 56*(1), 45.

Social Security Administration. (1994, September). *Developing a world-class employment strategy for people with disabilities.* Washington, DC: Author.

U.S. Department of Health and Human Services. (1985, May). *Program operations manual system.* Washington, DC: Author.

Author Index

Subject Index

Contributors

Rebecca Anderson Weissman, M.S., has enjoyed the roles of teacher, administrator, consultant, trainer, and adjunct professor in the field of special education. She is especially enjoying her newest role, that of mother to Joseph Charles. Her professional interest is in early childhood special education and all areas of severe disabilities. Rebecca worked with and learned from many families as the coordinator of the Niños Especiales Program at the Pediatric Research and Training Center, University of Connecticut, School of Medicine. She thanks these families for adding depth and character to the early intervention chapter. Her training and technical assistance emphasizes family-centered practices and the prevention of secondary disabilities.

William N. Bender, Ph.D., was a special education resource room teacher before obtaining his degree from the University of North Carolina. His research interests include social–emotional adjustment of students with learning disabilities, computer-assisted instruction, strategies for inclusive classroom instruction, and, more recently, classroom adjustment of students with attention deficit disorders. He has published over 50 articles and six books on these topics and hosted a television series on Georgia Public Television called *Education Today*. More recently he has served as a codirector of the *Interactive Teaching Network*, an internationally televised staff development series for educators.

Kathryn A. Blake, Ph.D., was Alumni Foundation Distinguished Professor of Special Education at the University of Georgia. She had extensive experience in programs for people with disabilities, both in the public schools and in higher education. Her teaching and research interests included mental retardation; physical and multiple disabilities; and research, development, and evaluation methodology. She published numerous books, monographs, chapters, and articles on topics within these specialty areas as well as on more general aspects of special education. Dr. Blake died in July of 1991.

Elaine Clark, Ph.D., is an associate professor and director of the school psychology program at the University of Utah. Dr. Clark's primary teaching and research interests are in psychopathology and neuropsychology. She is particularly interested in intervention-relevant assessments of a variety of disorders, including intellectual disabilities. She is actively involved with the Utah State Office of Education in providing statewide training to school personnel who are interested in developmental and acquired disabilities.

Tom J. Clees, Ph.D., is an associate professor of special education at the University of Georgia. He received his doctorate from the Department of Rehabilitation Psychology and Special Education at the University of Wisconsin–Madison. His teaching and research at the University of Georgia focus on habilitation methods and issues related to serving individuals with disabilities in their schools and communities. Dr. Clees's primary research areas are self-management, social skills, and transition, the latter with respect to collaborative models and supported employment and living.

Stacy Dymond is the Coordinator of the Severe Disabilities Technical Assistance Center at Virginia Commonwealth University and is currently pursuing a Ph.D. in the university's education and human services program. Previously she coordinated a community-based instruction and supported employment program for transition-aged youth with severe disabilities at the Rehabilitation Research and Training Center on Supported Employment. She has also served as a teacher of junior and senior high students with severe disabilities in Vermont.

Ronald C. Eaves, Ph.D., is a professor of special education, Auburn University. His career research interests have followed two main themes: emotional disturbance (particularly autism) and measurement issues in special education. He authored the *Pervasive Developmental Disorder Rating Scale* and coauthored the *Slosson Full-Range Intelligence Test* with Bob Algozzine, Lester Mann, and H. Robert Vance. Eaves served from 1980 to 1992 as editor-in-chief of *Diagnostique*, the official journal of the Council for Educational Diagnostic Services. He was named editor emeritus of *Diagnostique* in 1992.

Lisa M. Ehrhart received her Ph.D. in urban services leadership from Virginia Commonwealth University, where her academic focus was on business and marketing. As a rehabilitation counselor, her interests in job development and job placement led to her academic concentration in the marketing aspects of these rehabilitation processes. While in Virginia, she was employed at the Rehabilitation Research and Training Center on Supported Employment, where her research

interests evolved to include employer attitudes toward persons with disabilities. Dr. Ehrhart currently coordinates an international distance learning project based at the University of Georgia that provides in-service training to educators who work with students with disabilities.

Beth Bader Gilson, MSW, has spent years learning "what works" and "what doesn't work" in the provision of case management from hands-on experience as a case manager, supervisor, administrator, and consultant. Having a combined educational background of social work and physical therapy, she has had the opportunity for a continuously changing perspective in working with consumers who have developmental disabilities and their families. Ms. Gilson is currently a research associate at the Rehabilitation Research and Training Institute on Supported Employment at Virginia Commonwealth University.

Katherine J. Inge, Ph.D., OTR, is a training associate at the Rehabilitation Research and Training Center on Supported Employment at Virginia Commonwealth University. She has been the coordinator of several demonstration projects related to the employment of youth with severe disabilities and has coauthored two books as well as written numerous journal articles and book chapters. Her interests include staff development, systematic instruction, and community-based functional programming for students with severe disabilities.

John Kregel, Ed.D., is a professor of special education at Virginia Commonwealth University in Richmond. He also serves as the associate director and research director of the Rehabilitation Research and Training Center on Supported Employment. He has written extensively in the areas of supported employment and school-to-work transition. In 1993, he was awarded the NARF Research Award by the National Association of Community Rehabilitation Programs for his significant research contributions in the field of rehabilitation. His interests focus on identifying and eliminating barriers to employment for individuals with disabilities.

Nancy P. Kropf, Ph.D., is the assistant director of the Gerontology Center and an assistant professor in the School of Social Work at the University of Georgia. Her publications span both the developmental disabilities and gerontology literature, as her particular interest is in older people with lifelong disabilities and their families. She is coeditor of a text, *Developmental Disabilities: Handbook of Interdisciplinary Practice*, that is about to be published. In addition to her research in this area, she recently developed and taught a graduate-level course in social work to educate students about the aging process of people with a disability.

John Langone, Ph.D., is associate professor in the Department of Special Education at the University of Georgia, Athens. He teaches courses in both the undergraduate and graduate programs, specializing in the area of mental retardation. Dr. Langone was the project director for a federally funded teacher training program emphasizing special education technology and has been project codirector for a series of teacher training grants emphasizing secondary transitional programming. Currently, Dr. Langone is researching the effects of computer-based anchored instruction using videodisc and CD-ROM on the teaching skills of preservice special educators.

David Littman, Ph.D., is president of Advanced Intelligent Technologies, Ltd., a small high-tech company that pushes existing intelligent technologies one step further to solve today's problems. Littman has a doctorate from Cornell University, awarded in 1976, in psychology and a doctorate from Yale University in computer science, awarded in 1990. Littman's main interest concerns how people and machines think and learn, especially how they recast experience to satisfy current needs and goals. Currently his main areas of focus are human–machine systems (especially smart assistants), robotics, software engineering, planning, parallel programming, and evaluation of knowledge-based systems and empirically based policy. He has published or presented approximately 40 papers on theoretical and applied topics in computer science and psychology and has supervised several projects that have resulted in real software products.

D. Michael Malone, Ph.D., is the interdisciplinary training director of the Georgia University Affiliated Program (UAP) for Persons with Developmental Disabilities and adjunct assistant professor in the department of child and family development at the University of Georgia. His past work in the area of aging and developmental disabilities has included the coordination of the UAP master's and doctoral aging training initiatives, publications, professional presentations, and university lectures on the topics of the demographics of aging and developmental disabilities and family systems.

JoAnn Marchant, M.Ed., is the director of staff development for the Henrico County Schools in Richmond, Virginia. She has been administrator and teacher of students with disabilities in residential, center-based, and inclusive settings. Ms. Marchant's interests include community-based, functional programming and behavior-management techniques for students with severe or multiple disabilities.

Phillip J. McLaughlin, Ed.D., is associate professor of special education and director of the interactive teaching network at the University of Georgia. He has produced internationally acclaimed teleconferences on attention deficit disorders and inclusive schools. During 1995, over 18,000 educators and parents participated in his distance education programs. His scholarly focus is on least restrictive environment issues for students with mild mental retardation. Dr. McLaughlin has published two additional texts, *Recent Advances in Special Education and Rehabilitation* and *Vocational Curriculum for Developmentally Disabled Persons.*

Susan H. Neal, MSW, is currently the director of the Child and Adolescent Service System Project (CASSP) in the Virginia Department of Mental Health, Mental Retardation, and Substance Abuse Services. Ms. Neal has developed preservice and in-service case management curricula aimed at promoting best practice throughout the Commonwealth's developmental disabilities services system. Her experience in case management includes serving as the chair of a statewide case management task force that set policies and procedures for programs throughout Virginia; and direct service in local mental health and mental retardation community services boards.

Susan O'Mara, B.S., has extensive experience in developing and implementing supported employment programs for persons with severe developmental disabilities. She has been a consultant for the Virginia Office of Supported Employment, providing training and technical assistance to rehabilitation professionals. Ms. O'Mara is a specialist in the area of Social Security benefits.

Wendy Parent, Ph.D., is an assistant professor in the school of education and director of the Natural Supports Transition Project, Rehabilitation Research and Training Center at Virginia Commonwealth University. She has more than 10 years experience in direct service, project coordination, and research in the areas of transition and supported employment. Dr. Parent has presented nationally and has extensive experience in providing in-service and workshop training for employment specialists, rehabilitation counselors, special educators, family members, employers, transition coordinators, program

directors, and administrators. She is the coauthor of two books as well as the author or coauthor of more than 20 journal articles, book chapters, and monograph publications. Her particular areas of interest are consumer empowerment, vocational integration, job satisfaction, natural supports, and other consumer issues related to supported employment implementation.

David Pitonyak, Ph.D., is a private consultant interested in positive approaches to challenging behaviors. He believes that challenging behaviors are "messages" that can tell us important things about the individual and his or her surroundings. Understanding the "meaning" of an individual's challenging behaviors is the first step in supporting the person (and the person's supporters) to change. Pitonyak has consulted with families and professionals throughout the United States and in Canada. He has worked with people in a variety of settings, including home and professionally staffed residential settings, schools, supported competitive job sites, sheltered workshops, and day activity programs. He is currently the editor of *The Community Journal,* a disability rights newsletter that focuses on building community. Pitonyak lives in Blacksburg, Virginia.

Paul Sale, Ed.D. is an associate professor of education and chair of the special education program at the University of Colorado at Colorado Springs. He has contributed numerous articles and chapters related to issues associated with developmental disabilities. He is coauthor of a text entitled *Supported Employment: Strategies for Integration of Workers with Disabilities.* His current research interests include assisting the communication efforts of learners with severe disabilities and studying the effects of inclusion on students with disabilities and their educational programs.

William R. Sharpton, Ph.D., is an associate professor on the faculty of the department of special education and habilitative services at the University of New Orleans. Dr. Sharpton is the director of the Louisiana Institute on Developmental Disabilities and coordinates a graduate-level personnel preparation program focusing on the needs of individuals with severe disabilities. His research interests include the design of effective instructional programs that result in integrated opportunities for individuals with severe disabilities, including employment in community settings.

Elizabeth Perry-Varner has had epilepsy since the age of 3. She has a history of complex-partial seizures. At age 25, she underwent epilepsy surgery that resulted in a significant decline of seizure activity. She earned her B.S. in rehabilitation services and her M.S. in rehabilitation counseling, both from Virginia Commonwealth University. She is currently receiving clinical supervision to be a licensed professional counselor. Perry-Varner has worked in the rehabilitation field for approximately 8 years, with a specialization in consumer advocacy.

Paul Wehman, Ph.D., is professor at the department of physical medicine and rehabilitation, Medical College of Virginia, and director of the Rehabilitation Research and Training Center, Virginia Commonwealth University. Internationally recognized for his service and scholarly contributions in the fields of special education, psychology, and vocational rehabilitation, Dr. Wehman is the recipient of the 1990 Joseph P. Kennedy, Jr., Foundation Award in Mental Retardation and received the Distinguished Service Award from the President's Committee on Employment for Persons with Disabilities in October 1992. He is the author or editor of over 100 books, research monographs, journal articles, and chapters in the areas of traumatic brain injury, mental retardation, supported employment, and special education.

He also is editor of the *Journal of Vocational Rehabilitation,* an international journal published by Elsevier. Specific research interests include transition from school to work, supported employment, developmental disabilities, and brain injury.

Michael D. West, Ph.D., is a research associate with the Rehabilitation Research and Training Center on Supported Employment at Virginia Commonwealth University in Richmond. He holds an M.Ed. in special education and habilitative services and a doctorate in urban services leadership. While at the VCU-RRTC, he has primarily been involved in ongoing national surveys of the supported employment program, evaluations of state systems and demonstration projects, research on implementation issues, and the use of supported employment for persons with brain injuries. Along with Dr. Paul Wehman, he was principal coinvestigator for a project to develop an instrument and protocol to assess the self-determination of students with disabilities in secondary education and transition from school to work.

Pamela S. Wolfe, Ed.D., an assistant professor at the Pennsylvania State University, has conducted many facets of training and research involving persons with moderate and severe disabilities. Specifically, Dr. Wolfe has worked in both educational and postsecondary settings, where she has been involved in transition planning, systematic instruction, positive behavioral interventions, and community integration. She has published and presented in areas such as social validation of instructional techniques, outcome-based transition planning with an emphasis on planning for students from varying multicultural backgrounds, and implementation of the Americans with Disabilities Act. She has a strong interest in fostering self-advocacy for persons with disabilities in integrated community settings.